The Right to a Fair Trial

The International Library of Essays on Rights
Series Editor: Tom Campbell

Titles in the Series:

Disability Rights
Peter Blanck

The Right to a Fair Trial
Thom Brooks

Indigenous Rights
Anthony J. Connolly

Civil Rights and Security
David Dyzenhaus

Children's Rights, Volumes I and II
Michael D.A. Freeman

Language and Cultural Rights
Leslie Green

Group Rights
Peter Jones

Human Rights and Corporations
David Kinley

Genocide and Human Rights
Mark Lattimer

Animal Rights
Clare Palmer

Social Rights
Lord Raymond Plant and Selina Chen

Gender and Rights
Deborah L. Rhode and Carol Sanger

Health Rights
Michael Selgelid and Thomas Pogge

Theories of Rights
C.L. Ten

Bills of Rights
Mark Tushnet

The Right to a Fair Trial

Edited by

Thom Brooks

University of Newcastle, UK

Routledge
Taylor & Francis Group
LONDON AND NEW YORK

First published 2009 by Ashgate Publishing

2 Park Square, Milton Park, Abingdon, Oxfordshire OX14 4RN
711 Third Avenue, New York, NY 10017

Routledge is an imprint of the Taylor & Francis Group, an informa business

First issued in paperback 2018

British Library Cataloguing in Publication Data
The right to a fair trial. – (The international library of
essays on rights)
1. Due process of law 2. Justice, Administration of 3. Jury
I. Brooks, Thom
347'.07

Library of Congress Control Number: 2008939264

ISBN 978-0-7546-2808-8 (hbk)
ISBN 978-1-138-37852-0 (pbk)

Contents

PART V THE CIVIL TRIAL

PART VI TRIALS AND TERRORISM

Acknowledgements

The editor and publishers wish to thank the following for permission to use copyright material.

Copyright Clearance Center for the essay: Paul Mogin (1998), 'Why Judges, Not Juries, Should Set Punitive Damages', *University of Chicago Law Review*, **65**, pp. 179–224. Copyright © 1998 University of Chicago Press.

Christopher M. Evans (2002), 'Terrorism on Trial: The President's Constitutional Authority to Order the Prosecution of Suspected Terrorists by Military Commission', *Duke Law Journal*, **51**, pp. 1831–56. Copyright © 2002 Christopher M. Evans.

Michigan Law Review Association for the essays: Sherman J. Clark (1999), 'The Courage of Our Convictions', *Michigan Law Review*, **97**, pp. 2381–47. Copyright © Sherman J. Clark; Roselle L. Wissler, Allen J. Hart and Michael J. Saks (1999), 'Decisionmaking about General Damages: A Comparison of Jurors, Judges, and Lawyers', *Michigan Law Review*, **98**, pp. 751–826. Copyright © 1999 Roselle L. Wissler, Allen J. Hart and Michael J. Saks.

New York University of International Law and Politics for the essay: Yigal Mersel (2005–2006), 'Judicial Review of Counter-Terrorism Measures: The Israeli Model for the Role of the Judiciary during the Terror Era', *New York University of International Law and Politics*, **38**, pp. 67–120.

Northwestern University Law Review for the essay: Nancy S. Marder (1999), 'The Myth of the Nullifying Jury', *Northwestern University Law Review*, **93**, pp. 877–959. Copyright © 1999 Northwestern University Law Review.

Oxford University Press for the essay: Tatjana Hörnle (2006), 'Democratic Accountability and Lay Participation in Criminal Trials', in A. Duff, L. Farmer, S. Marshall and V. Tadros (eds), *The Trial on Trial, vol. II: Judgment and Calling to Account*, Oxford: Hart, pp. 135–53.

Springer for the essay: Thom Brooks (2004), 'A Defence of Jury Nullification', *Res Publica*, **10**, pp. 401–23. Copyright © 2004 Kluwer Academic Publishers.

Sweet & Maxwell Ltd for the essays: Penny Darbyshire (1991), 'The Lamp That Shows That Freedom Lives – Is It Worth the Candle?', *Criminal Law Review*, pp. 740–52. Copyright © 1991 Sweet & Maxwell Ltd; Sean Doran and John Jackson (1997), 'The Case for Jury Waiver', *Criminal Law Review*, pp. 155–72. Copyright © 1997 Sweet & Maxwell Ltd; John Jackson (2002), 'Modes of Trial: Shifting the Balance Towards the Professional Judge', *Criminal Law Review*, pp. 249–71. Copyright © 2002 Sweet & Maxwell Limited.

Wiley-Blackwell for the essays: Thom Brooks (2004), 'The Right to Trial by Jury', *Journal of Applied Philosophy*, **21**, pp. 197–212. Copyright © 2004 Society of Applied Philosophy; Sanja Kutnjak Ivković (1997), 'Lay Participation in Decision Making: A Croatian Perspective on Mixed Tribunals', *Howard Journal of Criminal Justice*, **36**, pp. 406–23. Copyright © 1997 Blackwell Publishing.

Every effort has been made to trace all the copyright holders, but if any have been inadvertently overlooked, the publishers will be pleased to make the necessary arrangement at the first opportunity.

Series Preface

Much of contemporary moral, political and legal discourse is conducted in terms of rights and increasingly in terms of human rights. Yet there is considerable disagreement about the nature of rights, their foundations and their practical implications and more concrete controversies as to the content, scope and force and particular rights. Consequently the discourse of rights calls for extensive analysis in its general meaning and significance, particularly in relation to the nature, location of content of the duties and responsibilities that correlate with rights. Equally important is the determination of the forms of argument that are appropriate to establish whether or not someone or some group has or has not a particular right, and what that might entail in practice.

This series brings together essays that exhibit careful analysis of the concept of rights and detailed knowledge of specific rights and the variety of systems of rights articulation, interpretation, protection and enforcement. Volumes deal with general philosophical and practical issues about different sorts of rights, taking account of international human rights, regional rights conventions and regimes, and domestic bills of rights, as well as the moral and political literature concerning the articulation and implementation of rights.

The volumes are intended to assist those engaged in scholarly research by making available the most important and enduring essays on particular topics. Essays are reproduced in full with the original pagination for ease of reference and citation.

The editors are selected for their eminence in the study of law, politics and philosophy. Each volume represents the editor's selection of the most seminal recent essays in English on an aspect of rights or on rights in a particular field. An introduction presents an overview of the issues in that particular area of rights together with comments on the background and significance of the selected essays.

TOM CAMPBELL
Series Editor
Professorial Fellow, The Centre for Applied Philosophy and Public Ethics (CAPPE), Charles Sturt University, Canberra

Introduction

The right to fair trial is often held as a central constitutional protection: an unfair trial is often held to be a grave injustice. Nevertheless, it remains very unclear what precisely should count as a 'fair trial' and who should decide verdicts. Indeed, this already difficult issue has become even more important given a number of proposed reforms of the trial, especially for defendants charged with terrorism offences. It is thus most important that we best grasp the concept of a fair trial to avoid potential future injustices.

This collection is the first to publish in one place the most influential work in a large field. Several central topics will be explored throughout, including the right to jury trial, lay participation in trials, jury nullification, trial reform, the civil jury trial, and the more recent phenomenon of contemporary trials for terrorism offences. The aim of the collection is to help better inform both scholars and students coming to the area for the first time of both the importance and the complexity of the right to fair trial, as well as to help shed light on how the trial might be further improved.

In my introduction to this volume, I cannot hope to adequately address the many contributions from all the work collected here. Instead, I will focus on some key themes that run throughout the following essays and their central topics. My hope is that this discussion will help forge a clearer coherence between the chapters and highlight some of the particularly key contributions found within.

Is There a 'Right' to a Fair Trial?

This volume, *The Right to Fair Trial*, centres on debates concerning the fairness of trials across several issues. For one thing, what 'fairness' requires is a matter of some controversy. Is justice fairness or is fairness something else?[1] Nevertheless, even if we could agree on a general view of what constitutes fairness, whether or not we may be said to have a *right* to a fair trial is a separate question.

The importance of a fair trial is easy to discern. A trial descends into farce if it makes no genuine effort to ensure that the innocence or guilt of defendants is properly recognized. A swift trial may bring temporary relief to the public, but this relief may become anguish where trials are conducted poorly. Not only should we make every effort to ensure that only the guilty are punished, but it is also important that justice is both done *and seen to be done*. Defendants and the public must have confidence in the trial. If they do not, then lawlessness may be a natural result.

Thus, fairness has at least two elements with trials. First, a fair trial is one that renders fair verdicts. If the trial arbitrarily reached verdicts, then its verdicts would be manifestly unfair even if all information feeding into the decision were known publicly. Of course, no trial will be error-free: as with all human institutions, mistakes will happen and it is important that there

---

1 See, for example, Rawls (2001).

are mechanisms to correct problems when they arise. Nonetheless, a fair trial will be one that will release the innocent and punish the guilty all things considered.

Secondly, a fair trial is a trial that is understood to be fair. However verdicts are reached, it is important that all parties to a trial – and, most especially, the general public – view the trial as a fair process. Fairness entails impartiality upon the part of judge and jury. Fairness further entails that trial procedural rules apply to all parties equally without clear disadvantage to one over the other.

When combined, these features help enable the public to gain confidence in the trial. We must be confident that all legal questions are answered for satisfactorily. We must also be confident in the relative safety of our trial verdicts. Fairness may consist in additional features than these, but these two features of fairness seem to reside at the core of any view of a fair trial all things considered.

While we may now recognize the *importance* of a trial's fairness, can we recognize a fair trial *as a right*? Surely, there have been numerous attempts to explain the nature of rights which I shall not replicate again here (see Wenar 2005). It is certainly true that various claims have been christened 'rights' to the point that some may now believe that rights talk has become somewhat meaningless. Nevertheless, there is reason to believe that we can speak of a right to fair trial – a view defended by much of the work in this collection (see Thom Brooks, Chapter 7 and, especially, Chapter 3).

Whatever else they may be, rights are claims of a special sort and we may view 'the right to fair trial' in a similar light. A right to fair trial may not be as equally important to me as a right not to be killed or a right to be free from sexual assault. However, it has a similar importance. Indeed, the very importance of a trial's fairness grounds its being a right. Much is at stake in a trial. A defendant may be imprisoned – even executed if it is a capital trial. He may become bankrupt, be forbidden from engaging in his occupation again or even gain an alias and go into hiding because of fear of public reprisal. Therefore, everything is in play – including a defendant's life in some cases. One's ability to live in a community, take up work, participate in one's community, freedom of movement, and even one's right to life may all be thwarted by a conviction. As a result, there truly is a right to a trial that fairly determines the equality between parties and safety of verdicts. Not only, then, do we have a right to fair trial broadly construed, but this is a right of significant importance.

Do We Have a Right to Trial by Jury?

If we have a right to a fair trial, then do we have a right to a jury trial? Often we find states with jury trials enshrining various 'rights to *jury* trial' on the grounds that the jury trial *is* a fair trial. Of course, most states do not have jury trials – are their trials unfair as a result? Furthermore, even in those states that have jury trials, juries are used infrequently at best. For example, the criminal trials in England and Wales are most often administered by unpaid magistrates normally sitting in panels of three: magistrates decide more than 90 per cent of all criminal trials. Almost none hold legal qualifications.[2] In the United States, plea bargaining accounts for more than 90 per cent of all cases: few of these ever see a full trial, let alone a jury trial.

2 A fantastic account of magistracy can be found in Grove (2002).

In Chapter 2, Sherman Clark sets out a clear case for this right (see Brooks Chapter 3). If we believe there is a right to a fair trial, then we demand fairness in verdicts. We may believe that trained judges are best suited for the task of determining verdicts. If so, then we would expect to find that, if asked, they would be likely to report that they often disagreed with the verdicts that juries awarded. While there have been far too few studies to examine, there is no evidence that judges disagree with juries. In fact, the reason for any disagreement was due to the fact that the judge had heard damning, yet inadmissible, evidence or that the judge was familiar with the defendant given previous court appearances and convictions for similar offences (Brooks, Chapter 3, pp. 86–8). Thus, the fact that jurors are shielded from any knowledge of inadmissible evidence and past court appearances may help ensure that it is more impartial than parties, including the judge, who have such knowledge. Therefore, what evidence we have suggests that juries arrive at safe verdicts even according to judges and that juries bring to the trial a special impartiality not replicated elsewhere.

In addition, only the jury trial can ensure full transparency of proceedings, an important second factor of fairness noted above:

> It is, of course, the state's responsibility to make its citizens familiar with its laws. But what mechanism ensures the state will do this? If all court proceedings were conducted in private, citizens might be educated to believe that the law says one thing when, in fact, the law is something quite different in actual practice. Yet, it is not inconceivable to imagine great confusion regarding the content of the law even if all proceedings were held in public. Every specialised profession – including law – develops its own terminology that may be indecipherable to those in different fields. Persons can be charged and convicted of crimes in a public hearing, but the legal arguments against them might sound as if the solicitors were speaking an unknown foreign language. It is easy to see the possibility of courtroom debate becoming the exclusive domain of legal professionals, whereby judicial transparency is not realised despite well publicised proceedings. (Brooks, Chapter 3, p. 90)

The mechanism that ensures fairness is the jury trial. Juries deliver safe verdicts that most often agree with the trial judge's views as we have seen. Moreover, juries ensure fairness in the process by which verdicts are determined. Without a jury, we have no guarantee that the defendant or the general public satisfactorily comprehend the charges brought before the court, the quality of the supporting evidence, and the grounds for any conviction. By placing the jury as the body that determines guilt or innocence (and, in some jurisdictions, the punishments or damages), legal professionals are required to convince the jury on all relevant matters. Thus, they must present legal arguments in a way that the public might understand: if a jury of twelve civilians cannot find a reason to convict, then we have good reason to believe that the defendant will understand the trial similarly. Likewise, if the jury convicts, then the defendant – even if she were to disagree – should be expected to comprehend the reasons for her conviction, all things considered.

For these reasons, one manifestation of 'the fair trial' is as 'the jury trial'. A well-administered jury trial is a fair trial. If we have a right to a fair trial, then this right includes a right to a trial by jury. This is not then to claim that fair trials are jury trials and nothing else. Instead, fair trials may take other forms and many states without formal juries do have civilian magistrates untrained in law sit with professional judges in hearing trials.

Is Jury Nullification Defensible?

We may accept all the above, but have a lingering doubt about the jury trial in particular. Perhaps I have a right to fair trial. Perhaps it is the case that juries may often guarantee the fairness of a trial. Juries do nullify law on occasion and this available option renders fragile their ability to act fairly. Jury nullification occurs when a defendant clearly breaks the law, but found innocent by the jury. The problem is that if the trial is supposed to be a fair proceeding then it appears highly unfair to change the rules of the game – that laws must be enforced except a blind eye will be turned in a particular case – during a trial.

Juries lack any *right* to nullify in any constitutional sense. Instead, juries only hold a *power* to nullify. This power derives from their right to exercise judgment without fear of consequence. For example, if a jury might be imprisoned for rendering a verdict that disagrees with the view of judges or politicians, then the conscience of the jury is undermined: why have a jury present at all? A jury can only be expected to offer its genuinely supported verdicts where these have not been predetermined for them in advance and they have the independence (and protection against imprisonment) for rendering potentially unpopular verdicts.

Jury nullification very rarely happens. However, when it does, it has contributed to much legal progress more often than not. For example, juries were once imprisoned if their views disagreed with the trial judge. This has long since changed. In the past, jurors were denied access to food, water and toilets until they decided upon a verdict. This has also long since changed and for the better. Furthermore, much trial reform – including the bifurcation of capital trials – is a result of jury nullification, suggesting that those rare moments where juries surprise the judge does help shine light on how the trial may be improved (and without curtailing future attempts to nullify laws).

In addition, nullification is defensible. When a jury (or even a judge) 'nullifies' the law, it is not at all the case that it is making new law in violation to its remit. Instead, when law is nullified, it is simply judged not to apply in a particular case and nothing more. These decisions are determined on a case-by-case basis. Not least, given the rarity of nullification, like cases are largely treated alike. However, cases should receive verdicts most appropriate to the relevant particulars. A case can be made that jury nullification in trial *x* does not represent a lack of fairness with regards to similar trial *y* given certain relevant differences between them. What is more, if we demand judicial independence where judges may sit on our courts without fear of imprisonment, then the same should exist for jurors when they are in court. We will only discuss what a body truly believes to the best of its conscience when it has the opportunity to exercise its conscience.

In his *A Theory of Justice* (1971, p. 517) John Rawls calls the 'judicial virtues' of impartiality and considerateness 'the excellences of intellect and sensibility'. If he is right, then we should try to curtail or eliminate the power of juries to nullify the law. Provided that juries continue to be instructed on matters of law by judges, 'intellect' and common 'sensibility' may be best brought together by allowing the flourishing of judicial virtue.

Terrorism Trials

Criminal trials for persons accused of engaging in terrorist activities are not a new phenomenon. What is new is the increased attention such trials have received post 11 September 2001 and the greater discussion of possible changes to such trials amongst academic legal scholars and politicians to an unprecedented degree.

Much of this discussion has focused on debates held in the United States. One such debate concerns President George W. Bush's promulgation of a Military Order ordering the trial of non-citizens accused of complicity in the 9/11 attack before military commissions lacking further judicial review. The implication is that civilians would be tried in military courts.

In Chapter 13, Christopher Evans argues that while this Order was not unconstitutional, it is unlawful as it is inconsistent with international law. Evans argues that there are precedents for such military tribunals from at least the American Civil War (pp. 438–40). Persons engaged in war crimes against the United States may be punished by military commissions for violations of the law of war. Evans argues that the 9/11 attack represented a 'quasi-war' between the United States and terrorist organizations, such as al-Qaeda, given the motivations and scale of the attack's devastation and its being the single largest attack ever on American civilians (p. 448). Thus, those complicity in the 9/11 attack may be tried by military commissions and this does not appear to be unconstitutional.

The problem is that these commissions are inconsistent with international law. International law recognizes state actors and not non-state actors. Thus, persons acting on behalf of an organization but not of a state fall outside international laws of war (p. 454). This, in turn, is problem for the United States as these customary laws are incorporated within federal common law. The proposed military commissions fall outside these customary laws and represent a marked unilateral break, as other states have not followed suit. Therefore, military commissions violate international law and, if retained, would exist as *ex post facto* law thus rendered unconstitutional.

Cases like this have required the courts to decide on the fair treatment of defendants in terrorism cases. Yet, even where we may agree that certain persons may be tried on terrorism charges, it may appear that different rules should apply in terrorism trials. With any trial, prosecutors may compromise sources of information in bringing evidence against a defendant. This is justified because defendants should know the full evidence against them and the identity of their accusers as otherwise defendants would be at a great disadvantage in answering charges against them. Terrorism trials may seem a different category of trial as the compromised sources may interfere with a state's ability to combat terrorism. How closely should our courts scrutinize counter-terrorism efforts and do different rules apply?

These questions are taken up by Yigal Mersel in Chapter 14. Mersel holds the Israeli Supreme Court as a model to be followed, not least given its greater experience than many other courts in terrorist trials. What we find is that the Israeli Supreme Court has played an active role in the judicial review of terrorism trials. One benefit is that the state's executive branch is continually challenged to defend their strategies. A second benefit is that the Court has aided in redefining key elements of counter-terrorism efforts, such as ensuring that the scope of 'state security' balances security with a respect for human dignity which, in turn, has led to important changes for the better in Israel in its fight against terrorism (p. 466). No doubt the view that the Israeli Supreme Court is a model for others to follow will strike some readers as a controversial view.[3] Nevertheless, Mersel's argument covers numerous case studies that challenge us to rethink how the trial may fairly deal with some difficult situations.

---

[3] I believe that the United States Supreme Court is a superior model.

This collection contains the most important work in the area of terrorism and fair trials, although this literature is growing exponentially as new cases come to light. Indeed, the ability to ensure that trials of terrorists are satisfactorily fair is perhaps the new frontier in contemporary work on the trial.

Conclusion

We now have a clearer view of the importance of fairness in our trials and how it may be manifested as a right, such as a right to jury trial. We have also seen the complexity of a right to fair trial regarding issues such as jury nullification and the continuing problem of terrorism, and how best to ensure trials remain fair. These are just a small handful of foundational debates and issues concerning the right to fair trial.

This collection brings together the top work in the field across all major areas with contributions from criminology, law, philosophy, and political science that are international in scope while bringing together both empirical and normative considerations. It is my great hope that this collection will inspire readers onward to plunge even deeper into an understanding of how best to realize the fair trial and protect it from increasing efforts by governments to undermine long-fought freedoms. The debate is far from over on how we might protect, promote and realize the right to fair trial. Indeed, the work has now only just begun.

Acknowledgements

I owe a major debt of gratitude to the many friends and colleagues with whom I have discussed work in this area over several years. I remain ever grateful to Brenda Almond, Reza Banakar, Chris Bennett, Stephan Blatti, Roger Cotterrell, Andrew Howatt, David Liggins, Matt Matravers, Joe Morrison, James Penner, Jenny Szende and, most especially, Penny Darbyshire, Antony Duff, Fabian Freyenhagen and Peter Jones. None may agree with the positions I have defended from our conversations although I have benefited enormously from their encouragement and even disagreement. In addition, I must also offer my sincere thanks to my friend Tom Campbell, as well as to John Irwin and Valerie Saunders at Ashgate, for the strong support of this project from its beginnings.

References

Grove, T. (2002), *The Magistrate's Tale: A Frontline Report from a New JP*, London: Bloomsbury.

Rawls, J. (1971), *A Theory of Justice*, Cambridge: Harvard University Press.

Rawls, J. (2001), *Justice as Fairness: A Restatement*, Erin Kelly (ed.), Cambridge: Belknap/Harvard University Press.

Wenar, L. (2005), 'The Nature of Rights', *Philosophy and Public Affairs* **33**, pp. 223–52.

Part I
The Right to Trial by Jury

[1]

THE SACRED COW OF TRIAL BY JURY

R.J. O'HANLON

I. INTRODUCTION

I propose to commence this lecture by outlining what is meant by the constitutional right to trial by jury and to follow up by giving the historical background to these provisions in the Irish Constitution. Finally I intend to invite you to look at these provisions critically and consider whether it is in our best interests to retain them as part of the Constitution and as a fundamental part of the law of the land.

Article 38 of the Constitution of 1937 is headed, 'Trial of Offences'. It is fairly short and simple. It provides that what we called 'minor offences' may be tried summarily – this refers to the right of a District Justice, sitting without a jury, to try in a summary or fairly informal manner, criminal charges which relate to petty or minor offences. These are offences which do not call for the imposition of a sentence of imprisonment of more than 12 months, or the imposition of a fine of a very large sum of money, say in excess of £1,000.[1]

The same Article provides that military tribunals may be set up to deal with a state of war or armed rebellion, and such emergency courts would be composed of army officers, sitting without a jury. Such courts can also be set up to deal with offences against military law committed by members of the Defence Forces while subject to military law – the conventional court-martial with which we are all familiar.

Another provision in Article 38 permits the setting up of Special Criminal Courts when it is determined in accordance with law that the ordinary courts are unable to deal adequately with certain categories of offences and the Act under which such courts are set up will determine the mode of trial – who may sit as judges in the courts and what procedure is to be followed.

With these exceptions – trial of petty offences in the District Court, trial of members of the Defence Forces by army courts, the use of military courts in time of war or armed rebellion, and the use of Special Criminal Courts when the ordinary courts are considered inadequate to secure the effective administration of justice and the preservation of public peace and order – all other serious criminal charges must be tried before a judge and jury sitting in the Circuit Criminal Court, or in the Central Criminal Court (which is the High Court dealing with murder charges and a few other of the most serious criminal charges).[2]

1. See *Melling* v. *O Mathghamhna* [1962] I.R. 1; Criminal Justice Act, 1951, s.4, amended by the Criminal Procedure Act 1967, s.3, sch.; J.M. Kelly, *The Irish Constitution*, 2nd ed., p. 393 et seq., and *1987 Supplement*, p.124 et seq. and cases therein cited.
2. Courts of Justice Act, 1924, ss. 10, 24; Courts (Supplemental Provisions) Act 1961, ss. 8, 11; Criminal Law (Rape) Amendment) Act, 1990, s. 10.

Because these provisions are written into the Constitution, it means that we are committed to trial by jury in almost all serious criminal charges, unless and until the Constitution is amended to provide otherwise – and this would now involve going to the people by referendum and obtaining a majority vote in favour of a change by those who vote in such referendum.

It was not necessary to include these provisions in the Constitution. England, the birth-place of trial by jury, has no written constitution and could change over to trial by judge alone by simple Act of Parliament. The Constitution of the United States, however, contains a similar guarantee to that found in our own Constitution that the trial of serious offences will be trial by jury.[3] Some other countries make no mention of criminal procedure in their constitutions and deal with the matter in their penal code, that is to say, by ordinary legislation.

Why are these special provisions found in our own Constitution and in the American Constitution? The answer to the question involves some examination of the historical background to this method of trial.

II. HISTORICAL BACKGROUND

The Normans brought the concept of the juror with them to England, but in those early days the expression merely referred to a person who was required by the king to take an oath about something. For example, in the compilation of the Domesday Book, recording the title to land all over England, people were required to swear up to their right of ownership. The oath was at that time a fairly sure guarantee of the truth of what was being stated.[4]

The primitive methods of trial of offences generally involved trial by combat, or trial by ordeal. In the first case, the victor in combat was taken to have proved his case – he was regarded as having God on his side. In the second case – the ducking of suspected witches, for example – if the body floated to the surface it was considered that the water was rejecting the person, and he or she was regarded as guilty, whereas the person who sank to the bottom was regarded as having been accepted by the water and innocent, so they went free if it was possible to fish them out in time for this verdict to be of benefit to them.[5]

As trial by ordeal derived much of its efficacy from the apparent approval of the Church, it lost its appeal when Pope Innocent III in November 1215 proscribed trial by ordeal by forbidding clerics to take part in it.[6] The science of law and legal procedure were much further advanced on the Continent than in England and new methods of trial were quickly devised, but the filling of the vacuum in England was a slow and laborious procedure.

3. Art. III, s.2; 6th Amendment.
4. Jolliffe, *Constitutional History of Medieval England*, 4th ed. publ. A. & C. Black, p. 209; see, however, Taswell-Langmead, *Constitutional History*, Sweet & Maxwell, 11th ed., p. 101 et seq., for alternative theory as to origin of jury.
5. *Wharton's Law Lexicon*, 4th ed., p. 201.
6. Taswell-Langmead, op. cit., p. 107.

The first appearance of the juror in criminal procedure was in the 'jury of presentment' – not unlike the grand jury which operated here and in England down to early in the present century and is still alive and well in the United States. The king's judges were sent out all over England to do justice, and a jury of presentment in each area they visited reported on oath as to the persons suspected of committing certain crimes.[7]

This happened in the reign of Henry II, and by a gradual process a jury of 12 jurors evolved which took a more active part in the criminal trial. If 12 jurors could be assembled who would swear to the guilt of the party charged, this was sufficient to convict him – so at that stage the jurors, or 'compurgatores', were swearing as to their own knowledge as to the offence committed and the person responsible. Very unlike our modern juror, who would be immediately disqualified from service if it emerged that he had any personal knowledge of, or contact with, the subject-matter of the charge.[8]

The king's travelling judges appear to have devised the new form of trial on their own initiative – was the prisoner willing to 'put himself upon his country' and be tried by his peers? If so, let him plead not guilty and take their verdict.

The prisoner could not be tried unless he agreed to this course, and many held out against trial because a guilty verdict could carry with it the forfeiture of all their lands. Many were willing to endure anything rather than leave their families destitute. Every effort was made to persuade them to change their minds – including the procedure of *peine forte et dure*, which involved the piling up of sacks of earth on the recumbent body of the accused person until he either submitted to trial or was crushed to death slowly and painfully.[9]

In 1352 it was enacted that no member of the jury of presentment (who swore up to the charges) should be included in the jury of inquest, yet the old formula of charging the jury, which read as follows, was still in use in England up to the year 1948:

> If anyone can inform my Lords the King's Justice or the King's Attorney General, on this Inquest to be taken between our Sovereign Lord the King and the Prisoner at the Bar, of any Treasons, Murders, Felonies or Misdemeanours, done or committed by the Prisoner at the Bar, let him come forth and he shall be heard, for the Prisoner now stands at the Bar upon his Deliverance.[10]

By slow degrees the jury changed from a body that acted on its own inherent knowledge to one that received information from outside. And having heard all the evidence and received directions from the judge about the rules of law applicable to the case, the jury of 12 retired to the privacy of the jury-room and worked out their verdict. This was announced to the judge by

7. Assize of Clarendon (1166).
8. Taswell-Langmead, op.cit., p. 107.
9. 3 Bl.Comm. 337; Taswell-Langmead, op. cit., p. 107.
10. Devlin, *Trial by Jury* (Hamlyn Lectures, 8th series), Stevens 1956.

the foreman of the jury and the judge had to enter judgment finding the defendant guilty or not guilty in accordance with the jury's verdict, regardless of whether he agreed with it or not. The jury could not be asked to explain their verdict or how they arrived at it or give an account of their deliberations, and this is still the position in modern times.

Lord Devlin in his Hamlyn Lectures entitled *Trial by Jury*, published in 1956, and to which I am indebted for much historical information on the origins of jury trial, said:

> Judges give their reasons, to satisfy the parties or because they themselves want to justify their judgments. Even arbitrators detail their findings of fact. The jury just says Yes, or No. Indeed it is not allowed to expand on that and its reasons may not be inquired into. This is still an essential characteristic of the system.[11]

III. WHO MAY SERVE ON THE JURY?

The object is to gather together 12 ordinary, reasonable men and women who will apply their collective common-sense to the task of weighing up the evidence, determining what witnesses are telling the truth and what witnesses are not, and reach a conclusion based on what they have heard in court (but not otherwise), as to whether the defendant is guilty or not guilty.

For most of its history, spanning several centuries in England, and in this country to which it was introduced as part of the Common Law of England, the jury was drawn from a very small and confined class of people – the owners of property. It was felt that men of property were more trustworthy as a class than the rest of humanity. The test laid down in England from 1825 onwards required that the juror own property of a certain yearly valuation, or should live in a house containing not less than 15 windows.[12] (It must be remembered that people were taxed for many years both in England and Ireland on the number of windows in their houses – which probably explains the terrible squalor of the windowless cottages in which people in Ireland were still living in the 19th century.)

Women were regarded as unfitted for jury service until 1919 in England,[13] and were effectively excluded from jury service in this country until much later (Juries Act, 1976). Lord (then Sir Patrick) Devlin said in 1956:

> The jury is not really representative of the nation as a whole. It is predominantly male, middle-aged, middle-minded and middle-class – due mainly to property qualification and the character of exemptions . . . The need for unanimity must be helped to some extent by the fact that the jury is drawn from the central bloc of the population . . . Safe judgment is most likely to repose in the middle of the community.[14]

11. Devlin, op. cit.
12. Devlin, op. cit.
13. Sex Disqualification (Removal) Act, 1919.
14. Devlin, op. cit.

The pendulum has now swung very far from the previous position and today everyone on the voters' register may serve, unless included in certain classes described as ineligible or disqualified – people involved in the legal and security systems, army personnel, gardai, prison officers, persons who have been convicted of fairly serious criminal offences, persons who are illiterate or mentally incapable and so forth.[15]

When the jury is being sworn, both the prosecution and the defence may challenge up to seven jurors without showing cause for doing so, and are entitled to have them excluded from the jury. However, if cause can be shown why any person should not serve on the jury, he or she will be excluded and there is no limit to the number of challenges for cause shown.[16]

For most of its history the verdict of the jury had to be the unanimous verdict of all 12 jurors, but in modern times both here and in England, a majority verdict can be taken if supported by not less than 10 jurors, and provided the jury have spent not less than two hours endeavouring to reach a unanimous verdict.[17]

If agreement cannot be reached on a verdict supported by not less than 10 jurors, the jury records a disagreement, and the trial comes to an end and must commence again before a new jury at a later date.

The former practice was to keep the jury confined together until they produced a unanimous verdict, and as an incentive to them to do so they were kept 'without meat and drink, fire and candle' up to 1870, and this rule was strictly enforced.

Lord Devlin refers to an incident occurring during the reign of Elizabeth I:

> The jury being withdrawn after evidence and remaining a long time without concluding their verdict, the Officers who attended them seeing their delay, searched them and found that some had figs and others had Pippins; which, being moved to the Court, they were examined on oath and two of them confessed that they had eaten figs before they were agreed on their verdict, and three confessed that they had Pippins, but had not eat any of them, and that this was unknown to the parties. Those who had eaten were each of them fined £5 and those who had not eaten the Pippins were each of them fined forty shillings, but the verdict was upon great consideration and conference with the other judges, held to be good.[18]

By the Jurors Act, 1870, jurors were permitted to have fire and refreshment at their own expense.

Lord Devlin adds:

> About the same time, John Mucklow was fined 20 shillings for being found with 'sugar-candy and liquorish' . . . It is very difficult for a

15. Juries Act 1976. *De Burca* v. *A.G.* [1976] I.R. 38.
16. Juries Act 1976, ss. 20, 21.
17. Criminal Justice Act 1984, s.25.
18. Devlin, op. cit. (from *The Complete Juryman*, 1752).

> minority to hold out in such conditions and without pippins or liquorish. Many verdicts so obtained must in fact have been majority verdicts – perhaps even determined minority verdicts. All that is very reminiscent of the verdict's origin – what was sought was not a rational conclusion but a sign, akin to the result of the ordeal or triumph in battle – once obtained the methods of obtaining it were thought less important than the fact that it was there. As recently as 1908 a jury who told the judge that they could not agree were told by the judge that they would be locked up for two hours – they found the prisoner guilty and the verdict was upheld by the Court of Criminal Appeal.[19]

Juries are no longer starved into submission, nor are they imprisoned to compel them to arrive at an agreed verdict. They are no longer drawn exclusively from the ranks of the property-owners, but can be drawn from every class of society – the underprivileged as well as the privileged; the employed and the unemployed; the well-educated and the badly-educated – and their age can vary from 18 up to 70. Women are just as numerous as men in the modern jury-box. The jury has, so to speak, 'come of age'.

IV. OTHER CRIMINAL LAW SYSTEMS

The United States have clung fast to the institution of the trial jury which they inherited from the Common Law, and in fact have retained some archaic features which have long since been discarded on this side of the Atlantic. The grand jury of presentment can still be assembled to decide if a criminal prosecution should be commenced against some person.[20] And the swearing in of the trial jury is a much more elaborate and long-drawn-out process than obtains in England or Ireland. It will be recalled that before a jury could be sworn to try the case of Colonel Oliver North, an inquisition went on for weeks in the attempt to find a jury consisting of persons who had not read about him in their newspapers or watched television programmes which told them about his alleged activities.

The American legal system gives scope for examining everyone called as a prospective juror as to his or her knowledge of the matters in issue and as to prejudices of any kind which might affect them in trying the case. Vast amounts of time can be lost in the process. In our jurisdiction, as in England, a juror can only be questioned when it is first alleged that there are grounds for believing that he or she is not a suitable person to serve on the jury, and this form of challenge for cause takes place very rarely in England or Ireland. We thereby save ourselves much time and trouble, but presumably we also leave ourselves open to a greater danger than exists under the United States system of persons finding their way onto the jury whose minds are already strongly conditioned in favour of one side or the other.

19. Devlin, op. cit.
20. U.S. Constitution, 5th Amendment. *The Constitution of the United States of America, Analysis and Interpretation,* Congressional Research Service.

With the exception of these features, jury trial in the United States, as in other countries which formerly were or still are part of the British Commonwealth, corresponds by and large with the form of trial as found in operation here and in England to the present day.

We cannot claim, however, to have a monopoly of enlightenment in the manner in which we deal with the problems of crime and criminals, and some of the European countries have expended much greater effort and resources in research on all aspects of the penal system. Two such countries which, I think, would be recognised as being among the most liberal in their approach to criminal law, while seeking to protect society as a whole as well as the person accused of crime, are Sweden and the Netherlands, and I think it is instructive to look at the approach they have adopted to the criminal trial.

In the Netherlands no use is made of the jury system. A court – generally composed of three judges – deals with prosecutions for the graver criminal charges, while a court of a single judge deals with lesser offences. The judiciary is independent of the executive (as in this country) and judges are appointed for life – retiring at age 70. There are about 800 judges for a population of 14 million inhabitants.

Considerable efforts are made to deal with persons against whom criminal charges are brought otherwise than by the imposition of custodial sentences. Attempts are being made to get away from the closed aspect of prison life to prevent prisoners from becoming alienated from the community outside. Prisoners are brought into contact with the outside world wherever possible and are allowed a lifestyle in prison approximating to that outside. No one can be prosecuted for an offence committed before he has reached the age of 12. Young persons between 12 and 18 are not subject to adult criminal law. The age of criminal responsibility is 18.[21]

I mention these features of the penal system as illustrating the efforts made to deal with every aspect of the criminal law in a humane and enlightened way. In their efforts to achieve this goal the Netherlands have not found it necessary to resort to trial by jury in determining the guilt or innocence of the accused.

A further contrast can be found in the Swedish Code of Judicial Procedure. Here the jury does exist, but in a rather different guise to that found in our own jurisdiction and in England. Criminal trials take place in the District Courts, of which about 100 in number serve the whole country.

To assist in the work of these courts, panels of lay assessors are elected in each district for three-year terms by local representative councils from a roster of eligible local citizens. Most are re-elected for consecutive terms. Each lay assessor is on duty for around ten days in any one year. The panels develop considerable experience over a period of time. They serve mainly on more serious criminal and family cases. In such cases the bench consists of a legally-trained judge and three lay assessors, for the less serious, and a judge with five assessors for the more serious criminal charges. For a case of exceptional length, the number of legally-trained judges may be increased to two.

21. See Swart, 'The Netherlands', in Van Den Wyngaert *et al*, eds., *Criminal Procedure Systems in the European Community* (London, 1993).

Persons eligible to serve as lay judges must be Swedish citizens registered in the district and not more than 70 years of age. The decision is reached after the legally-trained judge(s) and the lay judges deliberate together and the decision of the majority prevails. In the case of a tie the opinion that is the most lenient shall prevail. Each member shall state the grounds upon which he rests his opinion. In deciding on sentence, if a tie exists the half containing the chairman shall prevail. If there are more than two opinions, the votes most unfavourable to the defendant shall be counted with those next most unfavourable.

So it will be seen that a court comprised in part of judges and in part of carefully-selected lay assessors sits together in judgment and the basis for the conclusions of each member is announced openly before the final decision is reached.[22]

In Belgium trial by jury exists, and the verdict of the majority prevails. The jury then participate with the judge in deciding what punishment should be imposed on the person convicted.[23]

In Spain, the Constitution permits trial by jury, but it has not been utilised in practice.[24]

These are some of the examples I have taken to illustrate the fact that the mode of trial can vary considerably from one country to another and that countries which might be regarded as enlightened and forward-looking in the manner in which they deal with the problems of crime and criminals have not always seen fit to follow the English Common Law in their mode of trial.

V. SHOULD TRIAL BY JURY BE RETAINED?

We now come to the critical question – should trial by jury be retained or should we be willing to consider a change in the provisions of the Constitution to allow for a different form of criminal trial for all serious offences?

At one time not only criminal cases but also the preponderance of civil claims were dealt with in the courts in Ireland and England by means of jury trial. However, a constant process of erosion of the use of juries for civil claims took place beginning in England and gradually expanding to this country as well, so that at the present time they are retained only for a very limited class of cases, of which libel, slander, assault and false imprisonment are examples. In England there was still trial by jury in the majority of civil cases up to 1913; by 1918 the figure was down to 36% and in 1919 to 16½%. It revived temporarily after the War years, but by 1956 the proportion of jury trials had declined to two or three per cent of the whole.

Ireland clung on to the system of trial by jury for claims for damages for personal injuries up to 1988 – about 40 years after England, the home of jury trial, had effectively turned her back on it.

22. The Swedish Institute, *Law and Justice in Sweden* (London, 1990).
23. See Van Den Wyngaert, 'Belgium', in Van Den Wyngaert *et al*, eds., op. cit.
24. See Ruiz Vadillo, 'Spain', ibid.

What are the arguments in favour of retaining trial by jury for criminal cases, and what can be said in favour of a move to a system more akin to that in use in some other European countries?

Trial by jury has always been regarded in Great Britain and in some other countries as a great bulwark of the freedom of the citizen. Lord Devlin, while conceding that a case could be made for abolishing trial by jury in civil cases, waxed lyrical in defence of the jury in serious criminal charges. He said:

> Each jury is a little parliament. The jury sense is the parliamentary sense. I cannot see the one dying and the other surviving. The first object of any tyrant in Whitehall would be to make Parliament utterly subservient to his will; and the next to overthrow or diminish trial by jury, for no tyrant could afford to leave a subject's freedom in the hands of twelve of his countrymen. So that trial by jury is more than an instrument of justice and more than one wheel of the constitution; it is the lamp that shows that freedom lives.[25]

This eloquent passage, however, ignores the fact that freedom lives and thrives in other countries which have abandoned, or have never enjoyed, the great bulwark of freedom of which Lord Devlin speaks. When the oppressive regime of the Colonels was ruling in Greece, the infringement of fundamental freedoms and human rights was challenged before the European Court of Human Rights by a combination of the Scandinavian countries and the Netherlands.

The applicability of Lord Devlin's deeply-felt beliefs is also less clear in a country such as our own where fundamental freedoms are protected by the provisions of a written constitution, and most of all by the constitutional guarantee of free elections at intervals of not longer than five years, whereas in the United Kingdom all laws, no matter how fundamental, may be changed at any time at the whim of Parliament.

It can be seen from the brief outline of its history, that trial by jury grew up in a piecemeal and haphazard fashion, and it still carries with it some of the faults and failings which have arisen in the process.

The jury verdict is given in the form of a simple statement, 'guilty' or 'not guilty'. The deliberations of the jury have taken place in secret. There is no means of ascertaining the basis on which they reached their verdict – whether they were motivated by prejudice or bias or whether they understood the rules of law they were told to apply in their deliberations. The 'packed jury' was a well-known feature in former times, when the Crown used its powers to ensure that the jury was made up of persons who would comply with its wishes – yet this is the institution which is put forward as the bulwark of freedom.

Lawyers who practise in the criminal courts quickly become aware of the idionsyncrasies and unpredictability of the jury system. Lord Devlin, while championing the cause of the jury, gives many examples of the weaknesses inherent in the system. He quotes Lord Justice Scrutton, who said:

25. Devlin, op. cit.

> When first I was called to the Bar it was very difficult for an insurance company to get a verdict in their favour from a jury. Better counsel prevailed and the time came with a more extended insurance practice when one could rely *fairly confidently* on a fair hearing from a jury . . . Then came the introduction of the motor policy with third party claims and for part of my experience it was almost impossible to get a jury to find in favour of motorists when there were very few motors. As time went on and as probably half the jurors owned motors themselves the view of the jurors changed and they *might* be relied on to decide fairly, between plaintiff and defendant even though the defendant was a motorist. In fact it was very difficult, and I believe it is still very difficult, to get any criminal conviction against a motorist from a jury.

Lord Devlin adds, from his own experience:

> Thirty years later, those words are still true. The Lord Chief Justice said last year that the number of cases in which motorists were charged with reckless driving and the evidence was enough to shock decent people and yet juries would not convict, was remarkable.[26]

We are all creatures of bias and prejudice to some extent, and conditioned by our family circumstances and other factors. The difference between the judge sitting alone and the jury is that the judge, in the first place, has to explain how he arrived at his decision and justify it in the light of the evidence that he has heard and the rules of law he is called upon to apply. The jury operates under none of these constraints. An appeal may be taken to the Court of Criminal Appeal, which could scrutinise closely a judgment delivered by the judge, but has much less scope for overturning a jury verdict unless no reasonable jury could have reached the same conclusion.

In the second place, the judge has been trained throughout his legal career to stand back from every case and try to look at it objectively and impartially, without letting his judgment be clouded by his own instinctive reaction or personal inclinations.

The barrister taking on a case may find himself totally out of sympathy with the individual he is called upon to represent, but his task is to make the best case he can for his client, and when he has done this, year in year out, for a long time, he has been given a good training for the work of a judge. He has also acquired a respect for the law and has learned the truth of the maxim that 'hard cases make bad law' – which means that decisions based on sympathy without regard for correct legal principles simply reduce the law into a state of confusion and uncertainty and ultimately produce more harm than good.

The reason why so much time and trouble is taken in the United States over the composition of the jury, is partly in an effort to exclude persons clearly prejudiced against one side or the other, but also to try to muster a jury who will, in fact be sympathetic, not to say prejudiced, in favour of one side or the other. To quote again from Lord Devlin:

26. Devlin, op. cit.

> Through the careful use of peremptories [challenges] and skilful use of the power of questioning and personal contact with the jurors, the advocate will seek to secure a jury favourably disposed towards himself and his case. Textbooks in the United States make this quite clear. The selection of the jury is considered a 'fine art' which the advocate must carefully study . . . [It] offers an opportunity to 'create a favourable atmosphere' or 'condition the jury to the desired viewpoint'. It is part of the art that an advocate should be alert to detect jurors who seem unsympathetic and get rid of them if he can.

He refers, by way of contrast, to cases in the United Kingdom where no preliminary examination of the jurors takes place. In a case in Wales, two jurors made an affidavit after the case had ended saying they understood no English. In another case from Monmouthshire the solicitor for an accused noticed one juror huddled in a corner and after his client had been convicted was told by another juror that the man in question appeared very sleepy and had drink taken. In the case which followed it was found impossible to proceed, the juror in question having fallen fast asleep and only being roused by repeated shakings. The Court of Criminal Appeal refused to set aside the conviction in the first case, by reason of the delay in doing anything about it so long as the solicitor thought there was a chance of his client being acquitted.

The perverse verdict is well-known in this country and in the United Kingdom. And while there is scope for appealing against a guilty verdict and having it set aside, the only scope for appealing against a perverse finding of not guilty in favour of an accused person, is to apply to have some principle of law determined – regardless of the outcome of the appeal the accused cannot be again put on trial on the same charge.

For all these reasons, it appears to me that there is a strong case to be made in favour of what I will call the Continental system of criminal trial, whereby a court of three judges, sitting without a jury, would try all serious criminal cases, and give a reasoned verdict at the end of the case.

They would have the advantage of knowing and understanding the law which has to be applied. They could read and understand the documentary evidence put before the court. In the course of trial by jury, it is not the practice for jurors to keep notes of the evidence as the trial proceeds, although there is no objection to their doing so. The trial may continue for days, weeks or even months – as happened in some of the serious fraud cases in the United Kingdom – and the jury at the end of the day is expected to keep the evidence before their minds, jogged as far as possible by the judge's final charge before they retire to consider their verdict.

It can take a very long time to explain legal principles to a jury – take for example questions of self-defence and provocation which often arise in murder trials. A student in a law school would be hard-put to reproduce these principles having listened to a single lecture on the topic, but a jury of ordinary laymen some or all of whom may have had very limited education, is expected to carry their legal lore with them into the jury room and apply it while mulling over the facts of the case at the same time. It is all very unrealistic.

The other argument most frequently put forward in favour of retaining trial by jury is that the combined wisdom of 12 jurors selected at random is better calculated to get to the truth of the matter and detect which side is to be relied on and which to be rejected.

I do not know what evidence there is to support this conclusion. It is quite possible that a jury of 12 may be dictated to by one or more dominant personalities among their number, who impose their will on their companions and the theory of collective wisdom may be a myth in many cases. The judge of trial has spent his legal career listening to evidence, much of it conflicting, being given by witnesses and parties in the court-room situation, and doing his best to assess the truth and falsity of what is being said.

Another factor which may be of greater significance now than in former times is the danger of intimidation which may be practised against jurymen. We have all heard of notorious cases in England, and of cases involving criminal gangs, such as the Mafia and the Red Brigade in different parts of the Continent, but to come much nearer home, the scope for intimidating members of our own juries is considerable. The names and addresses of persons on the jury panel are made available to the prosecution and the accused so that they may exercise their right of challenge. We have in our midst well-organised and vicious criminals who would not hesitate to use any methods of terror available to them to secure verdicts of acquittal.

Finally, it is often put forward as one of the merits of the jury system that a jury can bring about changes in the law of the land by refusing to enforce laws which appear to them to be unjust or oppressive in some way. We have seen an example of this happening in England in relation to the Official Secrets Act. What this means in reality is that the jury, having taken an oath that they will 'true verdicts give according to the evidence' have broken their oath by refusing to give effect to the law of the land. They have usurped the role of parliament which is entrusted by the people with the task of making laws which are in conformity with the will of the people. However pardonable such action on the part of a jury may be in defiance of an oppressive and autocratic regime, it is indefensible in a modern democracy where fundamental rights and freedoms are protected by the country's constitution.

The many weaknesses inherent in the present system of jury trial have led to its gradual abandonment as a means of dealing with civil claims. There is a strong case for saying that its retention in the criminal courts is in anachronism in the modern constitutional democracy.

I hesitate to suggest that my dear friend, John Kelly, would have approved of this as a contribution to his memorial issue of the *Irish Jurist*. I remember him recoiling in horror when I proclaimed my support for the proposal that there should be a Central Fingerprint Register on which the fingerprints of all members of the population should be retained, to assist in the war against crime. However, I offer it as my humble tribute to his memory — 'a poor thing, lord, but mine own'.

The Hon. Mr. Justice O'Hanlon is a Judge of the High Court. This essay is the text of a lecture delivered in Carraigburn University Centre, Dublin, winter 1992.

[2]

THE COURAGE OF OUR CONVICTIONS

*Sherman J. Clark**

TABLE OF CONTENTS

I. INTRODUCTION

This article argues that criminal trial juries perform an important but inadequately appreciated social function. I suggest that jury trials serve as a means through which we as a community take responsibility for — own up to — inherently problematic judgments regarding the blameworthiness or culpability of our fellow citizens. This is distinct from saying that jury trials are a method of *making* judgments about culpability. They are that; but they are also a means through which we confront our own agency in those judg-

* Assistant Professor of Law, University of Michigan. B.S. 1989, Towson State; J.D. 1992, Harvard. — Ed. I would like to thank Phoebe Ellsworth, Thomas Green, Samuel Gross, Daniel Halberstam, and William Miller

ments. The jury is an institution through which we as individuals take a turn acknowledging and coming to terms with the difficult things we as a community find it necessary to do.

I suggest that the jury's responsibility-taking role is important primarily because of what it may be understood to say about who we are as a community. My aim, therefore, is to examine one of the ways in which the criminal trial jury may function as an expression of community identity. I argue that the way in which we go about performing certain difficult societal tasks says something about what we stand for, what kind of people we are, and what sort of community we want to be. I suggest that the passing of judgment on our fellow citizens is just such a task. How we do it may be as important to us as what we do. In particular, we may want to face this difficult and defining task in a way that allows us to describe ourselves as a forthright and courageous community — a community willing to confront and acknowledge responsibility for its judgments.

Conceptually, the argument operates at several levels of generality. Most broadly, I suggest that meaning does matter. I argue that the social meanings and expressive content of legal rules and practices ought to be understood as primary goods. Alongside consequentialist arguments keyed to concerns such as efficiency and deterrence — and alongside normative arguments rooted in principles such as fairness, justice, and rights — lawyers need to find ways of arguing about meaning. Because arguments about social meaning and expressive content are inevitably contextual and contingent, the subject lends itself less to abstract theorizing than to concrete illustration. Accordingly, although one of my claims is that lawyers ought to be more willing to argue about social meaning as a primary good in a wide range of contexts, the bulk of this article is addressed more specifically to the criminal trial jury. I hope to demonstrate that expressive content can be argued about coherently, and that the criminal trial jury is an institution well suited to this form of argument.

More specifically still, I focus on just one of the myriad of potentially meaningful aspects of the criminal jury trial and on just one of the many potential meanings which might be ascribed to that aspect. The critical variable for purposes of this argument is the extent to which the procedures governing the criminal jury trial tend to engender in jurors a sense of personal responsibility for the fate of the accused. The meaning I attempt to ascribe to that variable is courage, or rather a particular quality of forthrightness and integrity for which courage is as good a label as any. I suggest that we might admire those individuals and communities who are willing to stand behind what they do. We might want to count ourselves among those who confront, rather than evade responsibility for, the difficult things which we as a society find it necessary to do. In particular, we might consider it cowardly and base to construct a system through which we could hold others responsible for their actions — for that is what we do though the criminal justice system — without any of us ever having to take responsibility for those assignments of responsibility.

The structure of the argument is as follows: Part II describes and defends my approach. I argue that the meaning of a criminal trial jury may be as important as its consequences. I also defend the claim that the social meaning of legal institutions, such as the jury, is worth arguing about.[1]

Part III briefly describes the jury's responsibility-taking role and attempts to flesh out my claim regarding its potential expressive significance. I defer until Parts IV and V a discussion of precisely how that role is manifested and how it is or might be enforced. Instead, Part III addresses the more fundamental, and more difficult, question of why it might be seen as important to express, through the device of jury responsibility, the form of courage I describe.

Part IV argues that recognizing the jury's responsibility-taking function has explanatory power. Several otherwise puzzling facets of the procedural and evidentiary structure governing the criminal trial jury can be partially explained or illuminated by ascribing this function to the jury. Specifically, I point to four aspects of jury trial practice and procedure: the uncertain status of jury nullification, persistent concerns that certain forms of evidence will "usurp the role of the jury," the doctrine of *Caldwell v. Mississippi*,[2] and the invocation of "conscience" in prosecutorial argument. Each of these contentious areas makes more sense if viewed through the lens of jury responsibility, rather than solely through the lens of jury decisionmaking.

---

1. Considerations of this sort, when acknowledged at all, are sometimes referred to as the "expressive" or "symbolic" functions of law. *See, e.g.*, F. Patrick Hubbard, *The Physicians' Point of View Concerning Medical Malpractice: A Sociological Perspective on the Symbolic Importance of Tort Reform*, 23 GA. L. REV. 295 (1989); Richard H. Pildes & Richard G. Niemi, *Expressive Harms, "Bizarre Districts," and Voting Rights: Evaluating Election-District Appearances After* Shaw v. Reno, 92 MICH. L. REV. 483 (1993). These terms, however, seem to me inadequate, insofar as they suggest a merely tertiary status for what I believe is a critical, if often-ignored, aspect of law.

2. 472 U.S. 320 (1985).

In Part V, I ground my argument in concrete recommendations. In sum, jury decisionmaking in criminal cases ought to be structured in such a way as to ensure that each juror understands, acknowledges, and confronts his or her agency in that jury's decision. Several concrete measures appear capable of achieving this end without unduly compromising the jury's ability to perform its more generally recognized decision*making* function. First, if juries are to be the place where we take turns confronting and accepting individual responsibility for what we have collectively decided to do, we ought actually to take turns — all of us. We ought not be able to put that obligation on the shoulders of some identifiable subset of the community. Second, consistent with overwhelming current practice, unanimous verdicts ought to be required in criminal cases. Third, contrary to current practice, juries ought to be informed as to what punishment will be imposed in the event of a conviction.

My fourth and final recommendation is more tentative. Jurors should be instructed in such a way as to encourage them to feel a sense of agency in bringing about the consequences of their decisions. While this recommendation may appear on its face uncontroversial, its implications are serious, and its application uncertain. It amounts to a suggestion that juries should be made aware, albeit indirectly, of their power to nullify, but without being encouraged to use that power. I use the term "power" rather than "right" because I do not advocate nullification. On the contrary, I argue that jurors have a duty to bring in a conviction when the evidence so warrants; and a refusal to do so represents a breach of that duty. Nullification, on my view, is not a right that jurors ought to exercise, but rather a risk that we ought to bear.

II. Why Argue About the Meaning of the Jury?

A. *The Meaning of the Criminal Trial Jury*

The jury has been described and justified from a wide range of perspectives. So why muddy the theoretical waters with yet another justification? In particular, why seek to articulate an additional role rooted in difficult-to-articulate and highly subjective notions of courage or cowardice? Four reasons:

First, and most obvious, juries perform a range of roles which need not be mutually exclusive. Debate over the evidentiary and procedural rules and practices governing jury trials ought to be informed by the fullest possible understanding of the societal role played by those trials. Analysis of the jury should not, for the sake of simplicity or theoretical elegance, ignore significant functions merely because they may be difficult to quantify. Imagine, for example, a family lawyer studying potential reform in child custody law. He or she would recognize that families provide children with food, shelter, and education — three good justifications for the family as an institution. However, only the most narrow of Gradgrind's intellectual descendants would ignore things like love, companionship, and personal identity formation, merely because they are hard to define with precision.

Second, recognizing the jury's responsibility-taking function does not require setting aside more traditional explanations for the jury. Nothing in this article is intended to deny that the jury's central and primary function, both doctrinally and in fact, is and ought to be the fair and accurate resolution of disputed questions of fact. It would be a mistake, however, to allow the regulation of the jury trial, let alone its continued existence in various contexts, to turn entirely on its efficacy as a factfinding device.

Among the many other functions assigned or attributed to the jury are those keyed to political, rather than strictly judicial, concerns. At least since De Tocqueville pointed out the way in which the jury in nineteenth-century America served as both a locus for popular participation and a device for civic education,[3] scholars have debated the propriety and efficacy of the jury as a civic or educational institution. These political or civic roles may be loosely referred to as the communitarian function of the jury. For example, it has been suggested that juries may help secure public acceptability of otherwise controversial outcomes,[4] or provide a needed sense of public catharsis.[5] By one account, the criminal trial jury in par-

3. De Tocqueville opens his discussion of the jury by observing that "[i]t would be a very narrow view to look upon the jury as a mere judicial institution; for however great its influence may be upon the decisions of the courts, it is still greater on the destinies of society at large." ALEXIS DE TOCQUEVILLE, DEMOCRACY IN AMERICA 282 (Phillips Bradley ed. & Henry Reeve & Francis Bowen trans., Alfred A. Knopf 8th ed. 1960) (1835).

4. *See, e.g.*, HARRY KALVEN, JR. & HANS ZEISEL, THE AMERICAN JURY 7 (1966); Charles Nesson, *The Evidence or the Event? On Judicial Proof and the Acceptability of Verdicts*, 98 HARV. L. REV. 1357, 1368 (1985) ("Many of the procedures of our legal system are best understood as ways to promote public acceptance of verdicts.").

5. *See, e.g.*, George C. Harris, *The Communitarian Function of the Criminal Jury Trial and the Rights of the Accused*, 74 NEB. L. REV. 804, 809 (1994) (acknowledging that "the communitarian value of trial by jury results from its ability to induce a societal catharsis"); Charles R. Nesson & Michael J. Leotta, *The Fifth Amendment Privilege Against Cross-Examination*, 85 GEO. L.J. 1627, 1688 (1997) ("The essence of this catharsis is a public airing of grievances of charges and rebuttals from all parties."). Chief Justice Berger has referred to the "therapeutic value of open justice," and has maintained that public jury trials provide "an outlet for community concern, hostility, and emotion." Richmond Newspapers Inc. v. Virginia, 448 U.S. 555, 569-571 (1980). *But see* Peter L. Arenella, *Televising High Profile Trials: Are We Better Off Pulling the Plug?*, 37 SANTA CLARA L. REV. 879, 886 (1997) (argu-

ticular is described as performing three sorts of communitarian roles: "1) a vehicle for direct community participation in the criminal justice system; 2) a means by which the community is educated regarding the criminal justice system; and 3) a ritual by which the faith of the community in the administration of justice is maintained."[6]

The communitarian perspective on the jury is illuminating in that it focuses attention upon the jury's role in the expression of community identity.[7] In general, however, these analyses have emphasized the way in which the criminal law expresses community identity or community mores through the substantive content of rules and punishments.[8] I suggest further that the very decision to use juries to make decisions may itself be a significant expressive act.

Third, the jury is an institution which seems to call for, and be particularly suited to, the sort of social-meaning analysis I suggest

ing that there is "no empirical evidence supporting his contention that open trials actually served this cleansing/purging function. Moreover, it is highly unlikely that a trial's public nature will encourage appropriate community catharsis when the public disagrees with the jury's verdict.").

6. Harris, *supra* note 5, at 807-08 (acknowledging the importance of the communitarian function of the criminal trial jury but arguing that this function should give way to the jury's function of protecting the rights of the accused in those rare circumstances where the two functions come into conflict).

7. Indeed, two commentators have gone so far as to assert that "[i]t is now commonplace to assert that the jury performs an important ideological or symbolic role." Peter Duff & Mark Findlay, *Jury Reform: Of Myths and Moral Panics,* 25 INTL. J. SOC. LAW 363, 363 (1997); *see also* MARGARET JANE RADIN, CONTESTED COMMODITIES 173 (1996) ("Legal institutions can express culture, or they can help shape it. Where legal institutions help shape culture, they do so in part by instantiating and reinforcing particular conceptions of the nature of persons and their good."); Steven I. Friedland, *The Competency and Responsibility of Jurors in Deciding Cases,* 85 NW. U. L. REV. 190, 192 (1990) (describing "a theory of jury responsibility, in which the jury is conceptualized as a democratic representative of the community through its verdicts" and thus a body that should "convey the moral condemnation of the community in a criminal case and the range of viewpoints of the community in a civil case"); Phoebe A. Haddon, *Rethinking the Jury,* 3 WM. & MARY BILL RTS. J. 29, 60-61 (1994) ("The significance of adjudication also lies in defining public values.").

8. *See, e.g.,* A.C. EWING, THE MORALITY OF PUNISHMENT WITH SOME SUGGESTIONS FOR A GENERAL THEORY OF ETHICS (1970) (describing punishment as "a form of language"); R.A. Duff, *Penal Communications: Recent Work in the Philosophy of Punishment,* 20 CRIME & JUST. 1, 33 (1996) (describing punishment as "communication"); Joel Feinberg, *The Expressive Function of Punishment, in* 4 PHILOSOPHY OF LAW: CRIMES AND PUNISHMENTS (Jules L. Coleman ed., 1994); Jean Hampton, *An Expressive Theory of Retribution, in* RETRIBUTIVISM AND ITS CRITICS 1, 11-15 (Wesley Cragg ed., 1992); Herbert Morris, *A Paternalistic Theory of Punishment,* 18 AM. PHIL. Q. 263, 264-65 (1981). For a concise overview of this literature, see Carol S. Steiker, *Punishment and Procedure: Punishment Theory and the Criminal-Civil Procedural Divide,* 85 GEO. L.J. 775, 800-08 (1997). It is also arguable that some work which does not use the language of expression might best be understood as hinging on the social meaning of certain punishments. *See, e.g.,* James Q. Whitman, *What is Wrong with Inflicting Shame Sanctions?,* 107 YALE L.J. 1055, 1059 (1998) (arguing that shame sanctions amount to a form of "official lynch justice" involving "an ugly, and politically dangerous, complicity between the state and the crowd").

in this article. The jury as an institution has a long and complex history, and one which is closely tied to Anglo-American history generally.[9] It was not created by an Advisory Committee as a focused response to some clearly identifiable set of consequentialist concerns. Rather, it has evolved slowly, over time, and in ways intimately connected to the collective self-understandings of the communities it has served.[10] Moreover, the jury has become a distinctively if not yet uniquely American institution.[11] Even England, the historical source of our own heavy reliance on jury decisionmaking, has reduced dramatically its use of the institution.[12] Yet we persevere. Despite persistent uncertainty over accu-

9. *See* John P. Dawson, A History of Lay Judges (1960) (describing the evolution of legal decisionmaking and dispute resolution by those other than full-time professional judges); William Forsyth, History of Trial by Jury (London, John W. Parker & Son 1852) (seminal study of the early English jury trial); Thomas Green, Verdict According to Conscience: Perspectives on the English Criminal Trial Jury, 1200-1800 (1985) (describing the evolution of the criminal trial jury in England from the demise of the trial by ordeal in 1215 to the beginning of the nineteenth century).

10. *See* Dawson, *supra* note 9, at 1 (arguing that the structure of court systems throughout history, including "the alternative or competing means by which group decisions could be made . . . are a product and a reflection of many forces in society at every stage in their growth [and] also react on the societies that created them").

11. As both comparative law scholars and critics of the jury are quick to point out, the jury is far from universal. Continental systems following the inquisitorial model of criminal procedure make little or no use of juries. In France, for example, juries are used only in the cour d'assisses, the jurisdiction of which is limited to crimes for which the sentence is five years or more and which requires just a 2/3 majority verdict. *See* Criminal Procedure Systems in the European Community 113-14 (Christine Van Den Wyngaert ed., 1993); *see also* Comparative Criminal Procedure 73-74 (John Hatchard et al. eds., 1996). Germany does not use juries as we understand them but does employ lay decisionmakers in the form of mixed courts consisting of citizens and judges. *See* Criminal Procedure Systems in the European Community, *supra*, at 141-42; *see also* Comparative Criminal Procedure, *supra*, at 143; Markus Dirk Dubber, *The German Jury and the Metaphysical Volk: From Romantic Idealism to Nazi Ideology,* 43 Am. J. Comp. L. 227 (1995). *See generally* Criminal Justice in Europe: A Comparative Study (Phil Fennell et al. eds., 1995). The Netherlands does not use juries; nor does Luxembourg. Italy makes use of juries only at the appellate level; and Portugal only in cases involving crimes punishable by more than eight years imprisonment. *See* EC Legal Systems: An Introductory Guide (Maurice Sheridan & James Cameron eds., 1992) (France-33; Germany-41; Netherlands-25; Luxembourg-28; Italy-36; Portugal-26). It is worth noting, however, that both Spain and Russia have recently reintroduced trial by jury in criminal cases. *See* Gennady M. Danilenko & William Burnham, Law and Legal System of the Russian Federation 530-39 (1999); Stephen C. Thaman, *Spain Returns to Trial by Jury,* 21 Hastings Intl. & Comp. L. Rev. 241 (1998). Japan does not use juries. *See* Glenn Theodore Melchinger, *For the Collective Benefit: Why Japan's New Strict Product Liability Law Is "Strictly Business,"* 19 U. Haw. L. Rev. 879, 913 n.207 (1997) ("Japan had a quick prewar 1923 experiment with jury trials for serious criminal cases with the Baishinhou [Jury Act], which went into effect in 1928 and was suspended permanently in 1943 . . . ."); Nobutoshi Yamanouchi & Samuel J. Cohen, *Understanding the Incidence of Litigation in Japan: A Structural Analysis,* 25 Intl. Law. 443, 450 (1991). Israel has never used juries, and India not since 1961. *See* Steven J. Adler, The Jury: Trial and Error in the American Courtroom xv (1994).

12. Except in rare situations, such as libel cases, juries are not used at all in civil proceedings in England, having been almost completely eliminated by the Supreme Court Act, 1981, § 69 (Eng.). *See generally* Julius Levine, Discovery: A Comparison Between English

racy and fairness of particular verdicts, Americans continue to hold the jury dear.[13] Criminal jury trials continue to be an object of widespread public interest. Why? What role does the jury play in our collective self-understanding? Plausible answers to these questions, including the partial response I offer here, will need to be contingent, socially situated, and subjective.

Fourth, criminal jury trials are relatively rare as a percentage of total adjudications. Nationwide, a substantial if not overwhelming majority of criminal convictions are a result of plea bargains rather than trials.[14] In addition, a growing percentage of criminal cases that do go to trial are, at the election of the defendant, tried before judges rather than juries.[15] These realities have led some commentators to conclude that the criminal jury trial no longer plays a significant role in American life. Albert Alschuler and Andrew Deiss, for example, maintain that "[o]nly a shadow of this communitarian institution has survived into the urbanized America of the late twentieth century."[16] This view overstates the demise of the criminal jury trial. There are, after all, still thousands of criminal jury trials conducted each year. In addition, trials, however rare, do provide a bargaining baseline for the vast majority of cases which result in plea bargains. More to the point, it is a mistake to conflate frequency with importance.

AND AMERICAN CIVIL DISCOVERY LAW WITH REFORM PROPOSALS 95-111 (1982). Even in criminal cases, where jury trials remain available in England, they have become quite rare. *See* Joseph C. Wilkinson, Jr. et al., *A Bicentennial Transition: Modern Alternatives to Seventh Amendment Jury Trial in Complex Cases,* 37 U. KAN. L. REV. 61, 71 (1988) ("[T]he British system continues to evolve toward further reduction of the availability of jury trials, even in criminal cases."); *see also* Laura Mansnerus, *Under Fire, Jury System Faces Overhaul,* N.Y. TIMES, Nov. 4, 1995, § 1 (National Report), at 9 ("[In Britain,] only 1 percent of civil trials and 5 percent of criminal trials are heard by juries.").

13. *See, e.g.,* Robert J. MacCoun & Tom R. Tyler, *The Basis of Citizens' Perceptions of the Criminal Trial Jury,* 12 LAW & HUM. BEHAV. 333, 337 (1988) (showing 97% of respondents to survey viewed the jury as "somewhat or "very" important as a national institution).

14. *See* ADMINISTRATIVE OFFICE OF THE U.S. COURTS, ANNUAL REPORT 12 (1990) (showing that 86.5% of convictions in federal courts were through guilty pleas or pleas of nolo contendere); NATIONAL CENTER FOR STATE COURTS, STATE COURT CASELOAD STATISTICS 57 (1988) (showing percentages of all criminal cases disposed of through guilty pleas, ranging from 46.7% in Pennsylvania to 87.2% in California); RICHARD SOLARI, U.S. DEPT. OF JUSTICE, NATIONAL JUDICIAL REPORTING PROGRAM, 1988, at 47 tbl. 4.2a (1992) (determining that guilty pleas account for 93% of state court criminal convictions); *see also* Neil Vidmar et al., *Should We Rush to Reform the Criminal Jury? Consider Conviction Rate Data,* 80 JUDICATURE 286 (1997) (collecting conviction rate data from federal courts and from the state courts of North Carolina, Florida, California, New York, and Texas).

15. *See* Albert W. Alschuler & Andrew G. Deiss, *A Brief History of the Criminal Jury in the United States,* 61 U. CHI. L. REV. 867, 922 (1994) ("[N]early half of the convictions in the cases that go to trial are the products of trials before judges sitting without juries.") (citing PATRICK A. LANGAN & JOHN M. DAWSON, U.S. DEPT. OF JUSTICE, FELONY SENTENCES IN STATE COURTS, 1988, at 1 (1990)).

16. Alschuler & Deiss, *supra* note 15, at 927.

Rare things can matter; and, in particular, they can matter because of what they mean. The actual infliction of the death penalty is rare, but people care about it a great deal. Flag burning may be even more rare, yet it has been the subject of heated public and political debate. The relative infrequency of criminal jury trials need not mean that they are insignificant. That rarity does suggest, however, that the importance of the criminal trial jury may lie as much in its symbolic or expressive value than in its narrowly instrumental use as a method for determining disputed questions of fact.

B. *Why Argue About Meaning?*

Underlying this entire argument is a claim that the social meaning of a legal institution is worth arguing about. It is difficult to know how much need be said in defense of this general point. On the one hand, I certainly do not claim to have discovered the importance of social meaning in law. Legal Realists, Law and Society scholars of various stripes, Crits, Feminist Legal theorists, and Critical Race theorists, just to name a few, have from various perspectives highlighted the ways in which law can serve to embody, express, or legitimate underlying social values. In this sense, my focus on social meaning is nothing new. On the other hand, at least two concerns prompt me to say something in defense of my particular approach.

First, even though it might be common knowledge that social meaning matters, it is knowledge often ignored. Lawyers and legal academics seem willing to confront the meanings or expressive content of rules and practices only when there is nothing else more manageable to argue about. In this sense we are too often like the economist in the old joke who is searching under a street light for a contact lens. A passerby offers to help, and asks the economist, "Where did you lose it?" Pointing to a dark spot down the street, the economist says "Over there." "So why are you looking here?" the passerby asks. "Because the light is better," responds the economist.

My second reason for taking space to defend the importance of social meaning is that, unlike most others who have addressed the issue, I emphasize meaning as a primary good, rather than as a means to consequentialist ends. My point is not that we must understand the social meaning of rules so that we might better predict, understand, or evaluate the substantive impact of those rules. In this sense, my claim differs from prior work, and in particular from ideas advanced by Dan Kahan, Tracey Meares, Eric Posner, and others who have recently called attention to the role played by the social meaning of law in securing obedience or achieving deterrence.[17] I argue that we, as a community, might prefer to act nobly and bravely not only because doing so may accomplish more effective deterrence, but also because we want to be able to understand and describe ourselves as noble and brave.

What do I mean by "we"? Do I suggest that "we" at some level do or would agree on who we are as a community, if only a sufficiently appealing vision could be articulated with sufficient force and clarity? I do not. Despite my liberal use of the first person plural, I do not claim that there is some static and potentially definable "community identity" just out there waiting to be identified and elucidated. On the contrary, legal institutions play a role in community identity formation primarily because the question of who "we" are is perpetually in dispute and because there are few other places where we might be said to speak *as* a community. If the United States were a nation unified by religion, culture, or even by a powerful common enemy, it might not be necessary for our legal and political institutions to play a substantial role in the construction or maintenance of collective meaning. We are not so unified. We are a diverse and chaotic nation of millions, tied together by neither common faith nor by common fear but, if at all, by how we have agreed to describe ourselves.[18] If we are to be a community, rather than a mere assemblage, we need for our public institutions (and those who argue about and argue within those institutions) to provide fora through which we can go about the business of community self-definition.

By distinguishing a community from a "mere assemblage" and by positing the importance of community identity formation, I do not mean for my argument to hinge on any mysterious notions of collective consciousness. It is possible to argue that a community is more than just the sum of its individual members — that the well-being of the community need not be understood as merely the aggregate well-being of its members. While sympathetic to this per-

17. *See* Dan M. Kahan, *Social Influence, Social Meaning, and Deterrence,* 83 VA. L. REV. 349 (1997); Tracey L. Meares, *Social Organization and Drug Law Enforcement,* 35 AM. CRIM. L. REV. 191 (1998). For a an overview of this emerging approach to the study of social norms and deterrence, see Lawrence Lessig, *The New Chicago School,* 27 J. LEGAL STUD. 661 (1998); *see also* TOM R. TYLER, WHY PEOPLE OBEY THE LAW (1990).

18. Consider Abraham Lincoln's description, in the Gettysburg Address, of Americans as "dedicated to a *proposition*" rather than to an institution, faith, or set of substantive goals. Granted, Lincoln's assertion was an act of construction rather than a historically accurate description, and one which was not immediately or universally embraced. But the point remains. What are we dedicated to?

spective, I recognize that it is inordinately difficult to articulate clearly or persuasively.[19] Accordingly, I do not rely on such a claim; or, to be precise, I rely only upon a weak version of the communitarian perspective on the individual vis-à-vis society. For purposes of my argument, it is enough to posit that individuals might want to understand themselves as belonging to a community defined by certain traits or qualities.[20] From there, it is but a small step to recognize that those traits or qualities might find expression through the structure and operation of public institutions, including but not limited to the jury. Put differently, substantive legal disputes often serve as proxies for underlying arguments about who we are as a community.

Granted that the social meaning of the institutions like the jury may in fact matter to people, what business does a law professor have arguing about it? Perhaps lawyers and legal academics should leave it to the sociologists and anthropologists to describe and debate what the jury "means" to people in various contexts. Unfortunately, we cannot afford to do so. Social scientists, despite De Tocqueville's precedent, so far have surprisingly little to tell us about the role played by the jury in modern America.[21] Next to the virtual cataract of social-scientific work on public and institutional

19. In particular, I am sympathetic to the claim, articulated most effectively by Michael Sandel, that individuals are as much a product of communities as vice versa, and that to envision people as isolated choosers — unconstrained self-actualizers using communities as methods of getting what they want or becoming who they want to be — is to miss much of what makes people who and what they are. *See* MICHAEL SANDEL, LIBERALISM AND THE LIMITS OF JUSTICE (1982).

20. Accordingly, those uncomfortable with the anthropomorphism implicit in phrases like "community self-definition" should feel free to substitute them with "individual self-definition through association with a larger group defined by particular traits or qualities," or any such equivalent formulation. What I do insist upon, however, is that community identity, however labeled, matters. It would simply be missing what makes us who we are to deny that communities can be constructed, maintained, and unified by more than their ability effectively to aggregate individual materialistic preferences. People define themselves not only by what they want, but also by what they stand for and who they stand with.

21. A substantial amount of social-psychological work has examined juror decision-making processes. Significant empirical studies include: Phoebe Ellsworth, *Are Twelve Heads Better than One?*, LAW & CONTEMP. PROBS., Autumn 1989, at 205; Geoffrey P. Kramer & Dorean M. Koenig, *Do Jurors Understand Criminal Jury Instructions? Analyzing the Results of the Michigan Juror Comprehension Project*, 23 U. MICH. J.L. REFORM 401 (1990); Alan Reifman et al., *Real Jurors' Understanding of the Law in Real Cases*, 16 LAW & HUM. BEHAV. 539 (1992); and David U. Strawn & Raymond W. Buchanan, *Jury Confusion: A Threat to Justice*, 59 JUDICATURE 478 (1976). For an overview of research on juror decisionmaking in light of recently proposed reforms, see Phoebe Ellsworth & Alan Reifman, *Juror Comprehension and Public Policy: Perceived Problems and Proposed Solutions*, *in* PSYCHOLOGY, PUBLIC POLICY, & LAW (forthcoming). Regarding proposed reforms, see JURY TRIAL INNOVATIONS (G. Thomas Munsterman et al. eds., 1997). What remain largely unstudied, however, are the attitudes and understandings of the community as a whole toward the use of juries to decide criminal cases.

attitudes toward related matters such as crime control and criminal sentencing, the social meaning of the jury remains largely unexamined.[22]

Social scientific research into public perceptions and understandings of the criminal trial jury would be particularly useful given the extent to which public discourse is so heavily dominated by discussions of particular high-profile verdicts. Trials like those of O.J. Simpson and the Menendez brothers are exceptional, and it is at least likely that they are understood as such by the public. The little available evidence suggests that while many people are dissatisfied with particular verdicts and particular features of the criminal justice system, most Americans continue to view the criminal trial jury as an important and even defining institution.[23] How members of the public would defend that view, if they chose to, remains an unanswered question.

In the end, however, the lawyer's work is distinct from, though hopefully informed by, that of the social scientist. Lawyers need not only to describe social meaning, but also to argue about it. If and when social scientists are able to offer thorough accounts of what the jury means, lawyers will still need to find ways of talking about what it ought to mean.

There are two closely related reasons why lawyers should learn to argue about, rather than merely describe, the social meanings or expressive content of legal rules and practices. Both of the reasons depend, of course, upon the assumption that many people do in fact care about those meanings — that substantive rules and policies do sometimes serve in part as proxies in arguments grounded in competing conceptions of community identity. First, a lawyer cannot represent his or her clients or constituents effectively unless he or she can find ways of giving voice to the things that really matter to those clients or constituents. Second, a lawyer cannot argue effectively or persuasively unless he or she is able to speak to the things that really concern those whom he or she is called upon to persuade or come to terms with. If one's audience — be they judges, jurors, legislators, members of the public at large, or academic colleagues — really care, at some deep if not fully articulated level, about the social meaning of a rule or practice, the best efficiency or deterrence or other consequentialist arguments are unlikely to move that audience.

22. A noteworthy exception is MacCoun & Tyler, *supra* note 13.

23. *See id.*

It is tempting to think that legal academics, as opposed to practicing lawyers or lawyer-politicians, can afford to ignore these sorts of "irrational" concerns. We cannot. At least we cannot if we desire our work to have relevance within the real world in which the rules and regimes we critique must operate. We cannot afford to disregard the meaning of rules and practices because to disregard is to discount. To conclude that a rule or policy is desirable or undesirable, wise or unwise, based on an evaluation of consequentialist concerns such as efficiency or deterrence is to argue about the effect that rule or policy will have on people. And to make that calculation without accounting for what the rule or policy means to those people (because meanings are too difficult to evaluate or quantify) would in some cases be akin to arguing that one's bank account is more important than one's spouse (because the value of the latter is so hard to quantify).

In popular media, a lawyer is sometimes described as a "mouthpiece." Although probably not intended as a compliment, this description need not be understood as entirely pejorative. Setting aside the questionable implication that lawyers lack moral agency in the work they do for their clients, society needs mouthpieces. In a complex world, someone must strive to give voice to the concerns of their fellow citizens. If, as seems certain, people care about things like bravery and nobility, those who purport to speak for the people need ways of talking about those things. If lawyers are to speak — in courtrooms, in state houses, and through our writings — to the concerns of our fellow citizens, we cannot simply disregard salient concerns because they may be difficult to articulate or impossible to quantify precisely.

Lawyers, and legal academics in particular, seem to have lost track of a tremendous amount of territory between first principles and the bottom line. In some contexts, the importance of social meaning is evident. For example, in the debate over a potential constitutional amendment prohibiting the burning of the American Flag, it is impossible to ignore the expressive and symbolic components. The issue is, in a sense, all about expression; and the flag is the very archetype of a socially significant symbol. In other contexts, however, it is tempting to continue to look at claims about the expressive or symbolic value of legal rules as arguments of last resort — to be called upon only when nothing else is available.

The resulting lacuna — the argumentative gap caused by an unwillingness or inability to argue about social meaning as a primary good — might be called the problem of the last grizzly bear, because it is well illustrated by the discourse of environmental law. Why would it bother us to cause the extinction of a species? Why care about the last grizzly bear, or the last bald eagle, let alone the last snail darter or spotted owl? Environmental lawyers and activist have of course assembled a repertoire of consequentialist arguments for preservation, many of which are quite persuasive.[24] These arguments are not wrong, but they appear incomplete.[25] I suggest that at least some of our reasons for not wanting to wipe out the grizzly bear have to do with what it would say about us as a community if we were willing to do so. Specific environmental issues serve to some extent as proxies for deeper concerns about who we are and how we understand our relationship with nature.

Nor is environmental law the only intellectual domain that suffers from an inability to argue effectively about social meaning as a primary good. Why do many people object to chain gangs as a method of criminal punishment? Are chain gangs likely to have dangerous social consequences? Perhaps, but the point would be difficult to demonstrate. Is it the humiliation people object to? Perhaps, but being forced to dig ditches on the roadside hardly seems the most humiliating thing many prisoners are required to endure. Are chain gangs unconstitutionally cruel and unusual?[26] The United States Supreme Court has refused to so hold.[27] I sub-

24. For example, perhaps a patch of rain forest holds a bug that will provide a cure for AIDS or cancer. We will never know if we continue to clear cut. Similarly, environmental lawyers are masters of the one-way-door argument: if we save it today, we can always decide to wipe it out tomorrow, but if we wipe it out today, we can never get it back. Economic arguments are available as well, such as the argument that it is only a market failure (in particular the failure to account for future generations' utility) which causes us to undervalue wilderness.

25. *See, e.g.,* David A. Westbrook, *Liberal Environmental Jurisprudence,* 27 U.C. DAVIS L. REV. 619, 693-95 (1994) (arguing that traditional environmental jurisprudence is inadequate because "[i]t is difficult to include harmony or environmental damage as goods within the intellectual framework of liberalism").

26. On the constitutionality of chain gangs, see Tessa M. Gorman, *Back on the Chain Gang: Why the Eighth Amendment and the History of Slavery Proscribe the Resurgence of Chain Gangs,* 85 CAL. L. REV. 441 (1997); Sander Jacobowitz, *Rattling Chains and Smashing Rocks: Testing the Boundaries of the Eighth Amendment,* 28 RUTGERS L.J. 519 (1997); Nancy A. Ozimek, *Reinstitution of the Chain Gang: A Historical and Constitutional Analysis,* 6 B.U. PUB. INT. L.J. 753 (1997); Wendy Imatani Peloso, Note, *Les Miserables: Chain Gangs and the Cruel and Unusual Punishments Clause,* 70 S. CAL. L. REV. 1459 (1997) (claiming chain gangs are unconstitutional); and Emily S. Sanford, Note and Comment, *The Propriety and Constitutionality of Chain Gangs,* 13 GA. ST. U. L. REV. 1155 (1997) (conceding that "chain gangs would likely survive constitutional attack today").

27. *See* McLamore v. South Carolina, 409 U.S. 934, 936 (1972) (Douglas, J., dissenting) ("Does the chain gang fit into our current concept of penology? If not, does it violate the Eighth Amendment? This is an important question never decided by the Court."). A ruling that chain gangs are unconstitutional would represent an exception to the longstanding background rule that requiring prisoners to work is not constitutionally problematic. *See* United States v. Reynolds, 235 U.S. 133, 149 (1914) ("There can be no doubt that the State has

mit that many people object to chain gangs because of what they say about us as a community. Forget the consequences, and set aside concerns about cruelty; we as a community, given our history, still might care about what it means to have a line of black men in chains paraded down the highway under the supervision of a white man with a shotgun.

Some scholars have recently demonstrated a willingness to confront the messy fact that meaning matters. In addition to moral philosophers and criminal law theorists who have highlighted the social meaning of punishment, others have come to appreciate the significance of expressive concerns as a motivating force in the law. Richard Pildes, for example, has argued persuasively that the doctrine of *Shaw v. Reno*[28] cannot be otherwise understood.[29] Bizarrely shaped voting districts are troubling because of what they say about us as a political and social community. If we are to argue persuasively about voting districts, Pildes argues, we will need to find ways of appreciating and articulating those expressive concerns, however difficult they are to nail down.[30]

Nor will it suffice to say that arguments about important legal policy issues should be severed from the underlying questions of social meaning with which they are bound — that the formulation of community identity should take place elsewhere, and not pollute substantive debates. First of all, there is no elsewhere. There are no fora through which we speak *as a legal and political community* other than through our legal and political institutions. We have modes of expression as individuals and as subgroups within the community as a whole, but if we are to express what it means to be a member of the community as whole, we can only do so through actions taken by that community as a whole. It is of course possible to imagine hortatory pronouncements by legislatures or a plebiscite wherein we announce that we would like to be understood, and would like to understand ourselves, as a brave or honorable people. But, as the saying goes, actions speak louder than words, and in this

authority to impose involuntary servitude as a punishment for crime."); United States v. Pridgeon, 153 U.S. 48 (1894) ("There is no question but that federal prisoners may be required to work in accordance with institution rules.").

28. 509 U.S. 630 (1993).

29. Pildes & Niemi, *supra* note 1, at 537 ("*Shaw* thus sets into motion constitutional doctrine ultimately concerned with social perceptions and collective understanding[ ] . . . .").

30. *See id.* at 484 ("That most people, judges included, recoil instinctively from willfully misshapen districts is understandable enough. Yet defining values and purposes that might translate this impulse into an articulate justifiable set of legal principles is no easy task.").

case infinitely so. If we consider it important to describe ourselves as brave, we have to find ways of acting bravely.

The second reason why we cannot hope to sever substantive policy debates from the underlying questions of meaning for which those debates often serve as proxies is that we cannot exert complete control over the meanings of our actions. Imagine, for example, that a legislature were to try and argue the propriety of legislation providing for the use of chain gangs without getting muddled in the difficult business of what that practice might symbolize. Perhaps the sponsors of the chain gang bill could affix a prologue to the proposed legislation: "The chain gangs provided for herein should not be interpreted as reminiscent of slavery." Meanings do not work like that. You cannot spit on a man and tell him not to take it as an insult. And you cannot behave as a coward and expect people to take your word for it that you are brave.

Arguments of this sort will prove difficult for lawyers to learn to make. They will prove difficult not because they are necessarily analytically complex, or conceptually subtle, but rather because they call for a mode of argument, a form of rhetoric, somewhat alien to legal academic discourse. The social scientist seeking to describe "attitudes" towards this or that institution may try to describe or report empirically what the institution "means" to a given group. The law-and-society scholar can then use that data to argue about what a given rule or practice will or will not accomplish. The moral theorist seeking to argue the rightness or lack thereof of an institution or practice may attempt to demonstrate its consistency or inconsistency with some set of principles. The lawyer, however, who seeks to *argue* about social meaning — who seeks to argue about what a practice *ought* to mean — faces a task different from any of these. Arguments about social meaning, if successful, lead not to conclusive proof, but to conditional, partial, and temporary assent. The question is not whether a given social meaning follows necessarily from a given rule or practice. Instead, the question is whether it resonates as consistent with an evolving and multifaceted sense of community identity. Moreover, arguments about social meaning inevitably seek to create, as well as to identify, that meaning. The required mode of argument is therefore neither purely descriptive nor purely prescriptive. Instead, the operative rhetorical mode might best be described as ascriptive — an attempt to ascribe certain meanings to certain practices. The stance is as much one of invitation as that of argument, and the conclusion, therefore, is less the logician's "QED" than the preacher's "Can I get a witness?"

Finally, it would be unwarranted hubris to presume that those who would attach importance to meaning are behaving foolishly or irrationally — to view it as unfortunate that people might place expressive content on a par with, or even above, "real" concerns such as material benefits, deterrence, or efficiency. While it is beyond the scope of this paper to examine, or even fully to elucidate, the position, it certainly cannot be dismissed as presumptively irrational for a person to believe that meaning contributes as much or more to well-being than does material comfort, physical safety, or wealth. That person might point out that history, psychology, and social science, not to mention theology and philosophy, all provide arguments for the proposition that well-being — happiness, if you will — is only weakly related to material prosperity. This is of course a difficult and contestable proposition, and one over which social-psychologists in particular have become increasingly engaged. My point here is that it is not obviously foolish for a person to come to believe that our mothers were right: more stuff does not make one more happy.

Beyond this, it would be equally reasonable for a person to conclude that what does conduce to real well-being, what does make people happy, is meaning. A person might well come to the conclusion that those people are happiest who have found something worth sacrificing some material well-being for; and that being a member of a community which stands for something is more important — more conducive to well-being — than being one of an assemblage of people who are marginally more wealthy or more safe. According to such a view, the capacity of an institution to express or provide a forum for the formation of community identity might well be as important as the capacity of that institution to achieve particular consequentialist ends. Again, this paper is hardly the place to address this fundamental question, but there is no need for me to do so. It is sufficient to acknowledge that when people — our clients, constituents, and fellow citizens — behave as though the meaning of a practice matters as much as the material consequences, we cannot safely or fairly dismiss them as foolish.

III. The Meaning of Jury Responsibility

In this Part, I offer my reasons for believing that the responsibility-taking function of the criminal trial jury may be worth recognizing and preserving. I do not, in this Part, delineate in detail the ways in which this function is manifested and enforced — a discussion I put off until Parts IV and V. Instead, and at some risk of putting the cart before the horse, I focus in this Part on the more basic question of why responsibility taking might matter.

That said, I can and should perhaps outline briefly the function I hope to describe and defend. Reduced to its bare bones, my claim has four elements. First, there are certain difficult and inherently problematic actions and decisions required of our society. By inherently problematic I mean actions and decisions which, however necessary or justified, can and should be troubling to us. Examples might include the allocation of scarce medical resources and the decision to go to war. Guido Calabresi famously termed these inherently problematic decisions "tragic choices."[31] While I have no quarrel with Calabresi's label, my argument regarding how we as a community might desire to respond to those choices is fundamentally at odds with his.

The second element of my claim, and the one least provable, is that we as a community might consider it important to confront rather than hide from those actions and decisions. Specifically, I suggest that we might consider it nobler and braver to acknowledge the necessity for those decisions and actions, and to acknowledge our role in them, rather than to consign them to some procedural black box. This is distinct from the related claim that we should confront rather than hide from troubling decisions because doing so will encourage us to make those decisions more fairly and wisely. While I do make those sorts of consequentialist arguments on behalf of my specific claim, I do not rely upon them. Instead, I hope to explore the more difficult-to-articulate possibility that we might want to behave bravely primarily because we want to be able to understand and describe ourselves as brave.

Third, I suggest that judging our fellow citizens, which we do through the criminal justice system, is just such a difficult and troubling task. We have, as a community, no complete, shared understanding of when an individual's actions are fairly described as his or her own "fault." Thus it should not surprise us that judgment is troubling, for a thorough theory of criminal responsibility would require nothing less than the resolution of the difficult philosophical problem of free will. For this reason, the act of judgment is and will remain inherently problematic. I do not mean that it is unjustified. We have good and sufficient reasons for assigning criminal responsibility. Judging our fellow citizens is an unavoidable necessity — justified, necessary, and troubling. And if one assents to my

31. Guido Calabresi & Philip Bobbitt, Tragic Choices (1978).

suggestion that such inherently problematic acts ought when possible to be confronted and acknowledged, rather than disguised and denied, then perhaps we ought to devise or maintain practices or institutions through which we as a community, to the extent practicable, own up to and accept responsibility for what we find it necessary to do.

Finally, my claim is that the criminal trial jury serves as just such an institution. It would be neither possible nor perhaps desirable for each member of the community to take personal responsibility for each act of judgment. But we can take turns.

Two important distinctions are in order. First, I am not arguing that jurors should be *accountable* for their verdicts, whether to the public at large, to defendants, or to anyone else. In fact, as argued below, there is a sense in which a certain absence of accountability — in the sense of a freedom from any obligation to explain or justify verdicts — might be understood as a necessary condition for the sort of responsibility I would have jurors assume. I am arguing that jurors ought to feel a sense of responsibility for judgments of culpability, not that they ought to be *held* responsible for those judgments.[32]

A second distinction is between those rules and practices that might preserve or engender a sense of responsibility, on the one hand, and, on the other hand, those rules and practices that might increase the sense in which the jury is understood to be a responsibility-taking institution by the community at large. The distinction here is between psychological reality and public meaning. Stated differently, it might be profitable to sever the question of the jury's role in the courtroom (the jury's relationship with defendants and the court), from the question of the jury's role in the community (the public's perception of that role and the meanings attached to that perception). Nonetheless, I largely conflate these two ideas. For the most part, I assume that what increases jurors' sense of responsibility will also tend to increase the ability of the jury to be perceived as a responsibility-taking institution.

I make this assumption not because I believe it is necessarily correct in every case. On the contrary, I readily acknowledge the

32. A related distinction is between the jury as "they" and the jury as "we." The claim is not that jurors, as some identifiable subset of the population, are for some reason the right people to take responsibility for troubling judgments of culpability. Rather, the claim is that the jury is the institution through which each of us — all of us — takes turns taking responsibility. When, therefore, I say "jurors" should do this or that, or when for convenience I speak of jurors as "they," I should be understood as saying "each of us, in our occasional capacity as jurors."

possibility that some procedures which actually increase juror responsibility might for various reasons *not* serve to further the expressive purposes I have described, either because the actual effect of those procedures will be misunderstood or because those procedures have other expressive content. I assume a congruence between reality and perception merely because it seems the wisest default option, in the absence of evidence to the contrary. I am fully prepared to listen to, and indeed invite, analysis of the extent to which the rules and practices described below — rules and practices which I argue serve to preserve the jury's responsibility-taking function — might fail to enhance the jury's meaning as a responsibility-taking institution.

The debate over the use of anonymous juries can help us understand these distinctions. In recent years, an increasing number of courts and legislatures have been willing to protect the identity of jurors in criminal trials when necessary for reasons of safety or privacy.[33] It has been further suggested that anonymity be routine, in order to alleviate juror fears, protect juror privacy, and facilitate better decisionmaking.[34] Opponents argue, among other things, that anonymity will compromise juror accountability.

At first blush it might appear that the claim set out in this article — we should "look each defendant in the eye," and "stand behind what we find it necessary to do" — would argue strongly against juror anonymity. In fact, I am unprepared to take a position on the issue, for reasons that track and help illustrate the distinctions described above. First, my concern is with responsibility rather than accountability. It seems to me unnecessary, and arguably inappropriate, to hold jurors accountable to the public for their judgments. As one commentator has argued, "we do not give jurors the robes, the tenure, the professional training, and the prerequisites to make it either fair or appropriate to ask them to play so public a role."[35] My emphasis is rather on how jurors perceive their own roles and on the public meaning of that perception.

A second difficulty inherent in the question of juror anonymity tracks the distinction between psychological reality and social meaning. On one hand, it is at least plausible that jurors free from any fear of reprisal or harassment will be better able to focus on the

33. *See* Nancy J. King, *Nameless Justice: The Case for the Routine Use of Anonymous Juries in Criminal Trials*, 49 VAND. L. REV. 123 (1996).

34. *See id.*

35. Abraham S. Goldstein, *Jury Secrecy and the Media: The Problem of Postverdict Interviews*, 1993 U. ILL. L. REV. 295, 314, *quoted in* King, *supra* note 33, at 141.

responsibility they bear in passing judgment. If so, anonymity might actually facilitate the jury's responsibility-taking role. Nonetheless, the language used by opponents of anonymity — language like "noxious" and "star chambers" — suggests that courage would not be the primary social meaning attached to the routine use of anonymous juries. One judge remarked that "[n]ext we'll be putting all the judges under hoods."[36] Juror responsibility may in general serve as an expression of courage, but practices designed to facilitate that responsibility will not further the expressive purpose if they themselves at the same time express or symbolize, rightly or wrongly, a form of cowardice.

In Parts IV and V, below, where I describe the ways in which the jury's responsibility-taking function is fulfilled and might be protected, I focus on doctrinal elements, which, unlike the question of juror anonymity, do not appear to present a potential disconnect between reality and perception. I describe aspects of the criminal jury trial that may promote an actual sense of responsibility on the part of jurors, aspects it seems safe to assume do or might also contribute to our ability to understand the jury as a responsibility-taking institution expressing or symbolizing the quality I have chosen to label "courage." In this Part, however, my aim is to tackle two logically prior questions. Why might courage be considered worth expressing? And why might the jury be understood as a means of expressing it?

A. *The Problem of Judgment*

The criminal justice system brings us face to face with a deep tension in our collective understanding of human behavior. On one hand, we live in an age of cause and effect. Developments in social and behavioral sciences have taught us to look for social, environmental, genetic, chemical, psychological, or other explanations for behavior. On the other hand, we recognize the necessity of living and acting as though notions of individual responsibility are meaningful.[37] We refuse, and rightly so, to abandon the idea of desert.

36. King, *supra* note 33, at 123.

37. *See, e.g.*, Thomas A. Green, *Freedom and Criminal Responsibility in the Age of Pound: An Essay on Criminal Justice*, 93 MICH. L. REV. 1915, 1916-17 (1995) (analyzing the responses of Roscoe Pound and others to the tension between social ideas of cause and effect and legal/moral notions of free will and personal responsibility); Rachel J. Littman, *Adequate Provocation, Individual Responsibility, and the Deconstruction of Free Will*, 60 ALB. L. REV. 1127, 1130 (1997) (defending free will as a descriptive concept and claiming that "the human ability to reason and act rationally can never be totally overborne by external influences" (footnote omitted)); John L. Hill, Note, *Freedom, Determinism, and the Externalization of Responsibility in the Law: A Philosophical Analysis*, 76 GEO. L.J. 2045, 2046 (1988)

As a consequence, the criminal law struggles mightily with the question of when it is appropriate to hold an individual responsible for his or her actions.[38]

I make no attempt to canvass the millennia-old moral, religious, and philosophical debate over free will.[39] I simply submit that the

("[W]hile the notion of responsibility traditionally has been viewed as descriptive in nature, it is in fact an evolving prescriptive concept which serves to delineate the boundaries between those consequences for which the individual will be held accountable and those for which society will be so held.").

38. The resulting tension manifests itself in the criminal law not only through ongoing theoretical uncertainty over the appropriate definition of *mens rea,* but also through continuing debates regarding specific doctrinal issues such as the insanity defense, the doctrine of duress, and criminal sentencing.

39. Early sources include the following: Aristotle, *Nicomachean Ethics, in* THE BASIC WORKS OF ARISTOTLE 935-1112 (W.D. Ross trans. & Richard McKeon ed., Random House 1941) and Plato, *Timaeus, in* THE COLLECTED DIALOGUES OF PLATO 1151-211 (B. Jowett trans. & Edith Hamilton & Huntington Cairns eds., Princeton Univ. Press 1994). Central philosophical works on free will would include: BENEDICT DE SPINOZA, ETHIC (W. Hale White & Amelia Hutchinson Stirling trans., Oxford Univ. Press 1923) (containing De Spinoza's philosophy of determinism); THOMAS HOBBES, BODY, MAN, AND CITIZEN (Richard S. Peters ed., Collier Books 1962) (collecting selections from Hobbes representing his attempt to reconcile free will and determinism); DAVID HUME, AN INQUIRY CONCERNING HUMAN UNDERSTANDING 90-111 (Charles W. Hendel ed., Library of Liberal Arts 1955) (containing Hume's attempt to reconcile free will and determinism); IMMANUEL KANT, GROUNDING FOR THE METAPHYSICS OF MORALS (James W. Ellington trans., Hackett Publishing Co. 1981); and JOHN LOCKE, AN ESSAY CONCERNING HUMAN UNDERSTANDING (Peter H. Nidditch ed., Clarendon Press 1975). Among modern book-length treatments, see EDWARD D'ANGELO, THE PROBLEM OF FREEDOM AND DETERMINISM (1968) (maintaining that human behavior, though caused, is and will remain fundamentally unpredictable); DANIEL C. DENNET, ELBOW ROOM: THE VARIETIES OF FREE WILL WORTH WANTING (1985); J. FEINBERG, DOING AND DESERVING: ESSAYS IN THE THEORY OF RESPONSIBILITY 95-118 (1970) (addressing "expressive" value of the notion of responsibility, in that it allows the community to react to and express attitudes towards given forms of behavior); HANS JONAS, THE IMPERATIVE OF RESPONSIBILITY 79-135 (1984) (delineating contexts in which the idea of responsibility is useful or indispensable); MARION SMILEY, MORAL RESPONSIBILITY AND THE BOUNDARIES OF COMMUNITY: POWER AND ACCOUNTABILITY FROM A PRAGMATIC POINT OF VIEW (1992) (arguing that the philosophical approaches to the question of free will slight the pragmatic significance of community recognition of individual moral responsibility); GALEN STRAWSON, FREEDOM AND BELIEF (1986) (describing possible alternative philosophical approaches to the question of free will); and DETERMINISM AND FREEDOM IN THE AGE OF MODERN SCIENCE (Sidney Hook ed., 1958) (collecting articles on determinism and free will). Among book-length treatments of free will and the law, see FRANZ ALEXANDER & HUGO STAUB, THE CRIMINAL, THE JUDGE, AND THE PUBLIC 211-12 (1956) (lamenting the fact that attempts to make the criminal justice system more progressive and responsive to the causes of criminal behavior must confront an enduring popular desire for retribution); HERBERT FINGARETTE & ANN FINGARETTE HASSE, MENTAL DISABILITIES AND CRIMINAL RESPONSIBILITY 117-33 (1979) (addressing the relationship between traditional understandings of free will and the relevance of mental state to criminal responsibility); H.L.A. HART, PUNISHMENT AND RESPONSIBILITY: ESSAYS IN THE PHILOSOPHY OF LAW 90-112 (1968) (describing and critiquing traditional legal/moral understandings of individual responsibility); and JAMES Q. WILSON & RICHARD J. HERRNSTEIN, CRIME AND HUMAN NATURE (1985) (describing behavioral causes and explanations for crime). Shorter works are far too numerous to list, but among the most relevant are Paul Campos, *The Paradox of Punishment,* 1992 WIS. L. REV. 1931 (1992) (arguing that "contemporary societies still lack a coherent deontological justification for the social practices that go by the name of punishment"); Richard Delgado, *"Rotten Social Background": Should the Criminal Law Recognize a Defense of Severe Environmental Deprivation?,* 3 LAW & INEQ. J. 9, 24-37 (1985) (describing the way in

problem remains, and is likely to remain for the foreseeable future, unresolved.[40] Nor do I weigh in on any of the myriad disputes, within substantive criminal law, that implicate the consequent tension and uncertainty. Instead, my aim is to consider whether, and to what extent, we as a community are willing to confront and acknowledge our *own* personal responsibility for the difficult and perplexing decisions that an ongoing commitment to the *idea* of personal responsibility requires us to make. My concern here is not so much with how well we resolve the problem of free will as with how nobly we confront it.

Consider the terrible act of convicting a man of a crime and sentencing him to prison. We know that there are facts about that man's life — his background, childhood, or genetic makeup — which, if we could understand them fully, would explain his actions. But to explain is not to excuse; and so we convict. As we should. We have good and sufficient justifications for holding people responsible for their actions, justifications which need not hinge on any naive or oversimplified view of free will. We recognize, among other things, the need for deterrence and the need to protect ourselves from predation, however explainable. When I describe the act of convicting a fellow human being as terrible, I do not mean that it is necessarily wrong. Even if it is right in a given case, fully justified under the best moral reasoning, it remains disturbing. We

---

which a poor environment contributes to the development of criminal behavior); Deborah W. Denno, *Human Biology and Criminal Responsibility: Free Will or Free Ride?*, 137 U. PA. L. REV. 615 (1988) (exploring the tension between individual freedom and social protection or responsibility in assessing culpability based on biological defenses); Patricia J. Falk, *Novel Theories of Criminal Defense Based upon the Toxicity of the Social Environment: Urban Psychosis, Television Intoxication, and Black Rage*, 74 N.C. L. REV. 731, 733-74 (1996) (arguing that, unlike short-term causal explanations for criminal behavior, novel extensions provide otherwise unavailable insight into criminal behavior); Carl Goldberg, *The Reality of Human Will: A Concept Worth Reviving*, 7 PSYCHIATRIC ANNALS 566 (1977) (reviewing the history of the idea of will in modern thought); Lenn E. Goodman, *Determinism and Freedom in Spinoza, Maimonides, and Aristotle: A Retrospective Study*, *in* RESPONSIBILITY, CHARACTER, AND THE EMOTIONS: NEW ARTICLES IN MORAL PSYCHOLOGY 107 (Ferdinand Schoeman ed., 1987); Stephen J. Morse, *Failed Explanations and Criminal Responsibility: Experts and the Unconscious*, 68 VA. L. REV. 971 (1982); and Ronald J. Rychlak & Joseph F. Rychlak, *Mental Health Experts on Trial: Free Will and Determinism in the Courtroom*, 100 W. VA. L. REV. 193, 195 (1997) (arguing that courts must "demand that psychological and psychiatric expert witnesses function within the [free will based] assumptions of the legal system").

40. This should not be understood as a claim that the problem of free will is unamenable to moral, religious, or philosophical discourse. Much less do I suggest that attempts to address the problem are futile. On the contrary, as I discuss below, one of the reasons I consider it important for us as a community to confront and come to terms with our agency in perplexing decisions — meaning here those decisions which implicate our uncertainty over the idea of free will — is that doing so will keep the pressure on us to work for better and fairer ways of resolving or dealing with that tension, in general and in its specific substantive manifestations.

say to a fellow human being, in effect: "We know that each of us, if born as you were born and faced with what you have faced, may well have done as you have done. And yet we will judge you. We will imprison you for ten years, or for twenty, because it is *you,* and not us, who has come to be the person you are and to do the thing you have done."

Liberalism, or, more specifically, a combination of democracy and the rule of law, offers a partial response to the problem of judgment. By seeking to ground our laws in popular consent, and by working toward a regime in which all citizens have equal input into the content of those laws, we increase the extent to which any given individual judged under those laws may be said to have judged himself or herself. In addition, we strive to couch our laws in general terms — applicable equally to all citizens — with the aim being that the law itself, rather than individual men and women, will sit in judgment.

I embrace the attempt to reduce the extent to which people are required, or permitted, to sit in judgment on one another. But the project is and will remain incomplete. However full and equal the political input, only unanimity would allow us to say that to be judged under the law is merely to judge oneself. And the idea of general laws is a legitimating principle, not a literal description. Laws equally applicable on their face impact some people and not others. Moreover, unless laws are generated from behind a Rawlsian veil of ignorance, those who make or approve laws will be aware of those differential impacts.[41] In addition, however successful we may be at reducing opportunities for arbitrariness, no regime can eliminate entirely the exercise of discretion in the enforcement phase of the criminal justice system.

The upshot is that we as a community must judge and, on occasion, condemn our fellow citizens. If we are thoughtful people, aware that there but for the grace of God go we, the obligation to play God in this way should disturb and discomfit us, however justified we are in doing so. Granted, then, that we should judge as fairly, legitimately, and uniformly as possible, one question remains. Do we do so bravely and honestly — by designing and maintaining structures and processes which force us to acknowledge as fully as possible our agency in the act of condemnation? Or, do we hide behind a regime of facially neutral procedures in an effort to wash our hands of responsibility for the fate of those we condemn?

41. *See* John Rawls, A Theory of Justice 12, 19 (1971).

Thomas Green has suggested that the jury might play an ongoing role in moderating the tension generated by our uncertainty regarding free will and criminal responsibility.[42] In this article I follow up on that suggestion. I argue, however, not that the jury serves as a means of moderating this tension, in the sense of avoiding it, or of rendering the troubling act of judgment less difficult or more palatable. On the contrary, I suggest that the jury serves as a means of confronting this tension — of ensuring that it remains difficult and does not become more palatable.

Here it is important to distinguish between what makes judgment troubling and what makes it difficult. I do not argue that the act of judgment is difficult primarily *because* it is morally problematic. As described below, jurors often do find it difficult to bring in a conviction. And no doubt in some of those cases at least part of the difficulty may stem from the jurors' underlying uncertainty regarding the idea of personal responsibility. However, it appears that jurors find it difficult to convict *even when they are fully convinced that a conviction is justified.* My claim is that the morally troubling nature of judgment makes it important for us to confront our responsibility for the judgments we make, *despite* the fact that it may be difficult to do so.

If the polity were small (or if the criminal justice system had access to unlimited resources), and if all that mattered about the system were the extent to which we as a community confront our agency in it, we might aim to design a system in which all or a substantial portion of the community were involved in each act of condemnation — in which each of us had to look into the eyes of each of those we judged. But resources are far from unlimited. And I readily acknowledge that the conscience-implicating function I describe is far from all we care about. We need a criminal justice system that is workable. We need a system that will, with limited resources, achieve its substantive ends as well and fairly as possible, whether those aims be deterrence, debilitation, rehabilitation, or even retribution. I acknowledge as well that these ends might often best be served through the *reduction* of individual agency in the system.

If, therefore, we want to avoid the ignobility of anonymous condemnation, we might design a system in which at least some of us were forced to acknowledge what we do. We might take turns. We might seek structures though which some number of us, drawn, per-

42. *See* GREEN, *supra* note 37.

haps, from as wide as possible cross-section of the community, were forced to look each defendant in the eyes. How many of us? Twelve might be as good a number as any. The jury is one of the places — one of the few places — where each of us is asked to take a turn facing up to what it is that we as a community are required to do. Jurors stand in for the community not only as decisionmakers, but also as responsibility takers.

Contrast my argument with that made two decades ago by Guido Calabresi.[43] Calabresi focused on the civil jury and argued that it is just the sort of institution that ought to be employed in making choices of the sort which I have described as perplexities, and which he terms tragic choices — decisions as to which one of the available alternatives appear morally unproblematic. As an example, Calabresi cites the allocation of limited medical resources, such as kidney dialysis machines, "[which] compels a tragic choice because the assignment of the machine to one patient necessarily implies the otherwise unacceptable decision to allow other patients to die from renal failure."[44] According to Calabresi,

> The jury's representativeness and lack of responsibility [which] have at times been identified as the reason why certain decisions are committed to it . . . [are] the source of the characteristic and powerful way in which the jury operates. Juries apply societal standards without ever telling us what those standards are, or even that they exist. This is especially important in those situations in which the statement of standards would be terribly destructive.[45]

Initially, Calabresi's primary example seems a poor fit with the actual work done by civil juries. As George Priest has noted, the allocation of limited medical resources is not in fact entrusted to civil juries, which adjudicate relatively few matters that could be described as tragic choices.[46] One might, however, apply Calabresi's claim with more effect to the criminal jury, which, as I have suggested, faces a "tragic choice" each time it brings in a conviction. In the criminal context, Calabresi's argument, or one quite similar, has a distinguished pedigree. Montesquieu couched it as follows:

> The power of judging should not be given to a permanent senate but should be exercised by persons drawn from the body of the people . . . In this fashion the power of judging, so terrible among men, being

43. *See* CALABRESI & BOBBITT, *supra* note 31.

44. George L. Priest, *The Role of the Civil Jury in a System of Private Litigation,* 1990 U. CHI. LEGAL F. 161, 168 (citing CALABRESI & BOBBITT, *supra* note 31, at 186-89).

45. CALABRESI & BOBBITT, *supra* note 31, at 57 (citations omitted).

46. *See* Priest, *supra* note 44, at 168-69.

> attached neither to a certain state nor to a certain profession, becomes, so to speak, invisible and null. Judges are not continually in view; one fears the magistracy, not the magistrates.[47]

Juries, on this reading, take the sting out of difficult judgments by preventing the people from fixing responsibility for those judgments on any specific agent or institution of government.[48] I suggest, to the contrary, that juries help keep the sting *in* difficult judgments by ensuring that at least some of us will be unable to avoid fixing responsibility on ourselves.

The judging of our fellow citizens is of course only one of many perplexing decisions a community must make. As Calabresi suggests, the allocation of limited resources can also give rise to situations in which none of the available options seems unambiguously correct.[49] Along lines more closely related to those traced in this article, Markus Dubber has described the American system of capital punishment as "a complex system of denying and dispersing responsibility for the infliction of pain."[50] In Dubber's view, a collective inability to justify or come to terms with the infliction, as opposed to the threat, of death as a criminal sanction manifests itself in a "mad and futile scramble to deny personal responsibility for the necessarily violent aspect of law."[51] The process represents a modern and sophisticated version of allowing one member of the firing squad to fire a blank. Dubber objects to these evasions and argues that each participant in the capital punishment process, from legislator to judge to jury to governor to prison official, should be encouraged to feel a greater sense of agency in making substantive choices about the infliction of death.[52] His implication appears to be that a greater willingness to confront the reality of capital punishment would render us as a community less willing to impose it.

47. MONTESQUIEU, THE SPIRIT OF THE LAWS 158 (Anne M. Cohler et al. eds. & trans., Cambridge Texts in the History of Political Thought 1989) (1748).

48. Charles Clark, speaking of civil juries, and of the governmental agents most likely to bear the brunt of that responsibility, observed that jury decisionmaking "relieves the judges of the burden and the odium of deciding close questions of fact in cases, such as personal injury actions, where the feelings of the litigants are apt to run high." Charles E. Clark, Comment, *Union of Law and Equity and Trial by Jury Under the Codes,* 32 YALE L.J. 707, 711 (1923). Harry Kalven and Hans Zeisel similarly listed, among the "collateral advantages" of the jury system, that juries serve as a "lightning rod for animosity and suspicion which otherwise might center on the more permanent judge . . . ." *See* KALVEN & ZEISEL, *supra* note 4, at 7.

49. *See* CALABRESI & BOBBITT, *supra* note 31, at 18-19.

50. Markus Dirk Dubber, *The Pain of Punishment,* 44 BUFF. L. REV. 545, 545 (1996).

51. *Id.* at 605-06.

52. *See id.* at 608-11.

I am unconvinced by Dubber's implication that an unwillingness to confront the reality of a practice reveals a belief that that practice is unjustifiable. As I argue below, it can be hard to face what one must do even when one is truly convinced that it ought to be done. Moreover, his prescription — that everyone in the process be encouraged to feel agency — is doomed to failure. Responsibility, I argue, requires a fixed locus; and for the reasons I suggest, the jury would appear to be the best candidate. Dubber is on the mark, however, when he describes the way in which our current system facilitates the denial and shifting of personal responsibility for the actual infliction of the death penalty. In this light, one might argue that a truly courageous community would confront and acknowledge agency in all of its tragic choices and troubling actions. I focus on the perplexity inherent in assigning criminal responsibility; but why stop there? Perhaps we should require some individual or group of individuals to sign their names to decisions allocating organ transplants. Perhaps we should not allow any executioner to fire a blank. In a sense, however, the *assignment* of criminal responsibility is unique. Unlike allocation decisions, and unlike even the infliction of pain or death — both of which may be under some circumstances more troubling than the fixing of blame — the act of judgment itself presupposes a commitment to the idea of personal responsibility. It would seem particularly ignoble, not to mention hypocritical, to assign personal responsibility while at the same time denying any personal responsibility for that assignment. It may be too much to ask that we confront, and judge ourselves, for every difficult thing we do, but we should at least be willing to judge ourselves for our judgements.

B. *The Expression of Courage*

Insofar as it may be helpful to put a name to the quality we might hope to express through a willingness to confront the perplexity of judgment, the term courage seems to me apt. It will be objected that courage means different things to different people and that labelling something or someone as courageous or cowardly represents a conclusion rather than an argument. Describing a practice as brave, one might object, simply does not prove anything about whether that practice is a good idea. I agree. I use "courage" to refer narrowly to a particular trait which seems to me admirable — the willingness to confront and acknowledge agency in what one finds necessary to do. Accordingly, my argument does not hinge on whether or not "courage" is the appropriate label for that trait, though it seems to me fitting. Instead, my argument hinges on the question of whether that trait, that willingness, is in fact admirable.

This sort of argument, I readily acknowledge, admits of no proof. I can no more prove a quality admirable than I can prove a symphony beautiful or a landscape sublime.[53] The question, in the end, is what kind of people we want to be. And this question, while an appropriate subject of argument, cannot be an object of proof. All I can do is describe the sort of courage I suggest we might care about, and contrast it with the sort of cowardice we might want to eschew.

In the spirit, therefore, of illustration rather than demonstration, permit me an imperfect analogy. Parents sometimes find it necessary to punish or discipline their children. Some might use "time outs," or the denial of certain privileges, or grounding, or even spanking; but some form of discipline seems an inescapable if unfortunate aspect of rearing responsible children. Now, imagine if it were possible to delegate that responsibility entirely, not just partially as we do when we send our children to school. Imagine a new service, whereby parents could distance themselves entirely from the act of discipline by paying the service to monitor their children's behavior and administer appropriate punishment. Parents could choose what sort of behavior to punish, how to punish it, and how severely, but the service would do the rest. Imagine further that the service, by virtue of the expert training and emotional detachment of its employees, would do a better job than parents. It would never be fooled, never make a mistake, and, unlike parents, never punish too mildly out of weakness or too severely out of frustration or anger.

I suggest that many of us would choose not to employ such a service were it available. Many of us would consider it important to discipline our own children, even if we are unable to do so as efficiently (or even as fairly) as might be possible through some sort

53. The analogy to aesthetics is imperfect but potentially illustrative, given the way in which arguments about the social meaning or expressive content of public practices can be dismissed as irreducibly subjective — "just a matter of taste." It is a matter of taste, but it need not be "just" that. An inability to agree upon a definition of beauty has not prevented people from talking and arguing about it. Moreover, it is at least possible that an aesthetic approach may provide a way of addressing or grounding discussion of troubling normative issues. By learning to talk about bravery and beauty, we may better learn how to talk about right or wrong. Kant's final work is an attempt in the direction of just such a moral aesthetic. *See* DIETER HENRICH, AESTHETIC JUDGMENT AND THE MORAL IMAGE OF THE WORLD: STUDIES IN KANT 29-56 (1992); IMMANUEL KANT, THE CRITIQUE OF JUDGMENT (James Creed Meredith trans., Clarendon Press 1952) (1790).

of delegation. Punishing our children, however necessary, *ought* to hurt us more than it hurts them.

The analogy to the family is imperfect for a number of reasons, not the least of which is that the sense of personal attachment and obligation one feels to one's own children is qualitatively different from that which one is likely to feel toward fellow citizens of the polity. Again, analogies of this sort illustrate rather than prove. In this case, the analogy at least suggests, or so I hope, that there are some actions which we would not be willing to pay someone else to do for us. I further suggest, and this is the unprovable part, we have a term for someone who would hide from the unpleasant necessity of disciplining his or her own children by delegating that responsibility. The term is "coward."

To reiterate, my goal here in this subpart is merely to illustrate what I mean by courage. If, through examples of this sort, I can capture or give a sense of the quality I suggest may be expressed through a willingness to use juries in criminal trials, I will have done all I can. It is not for me ultimately to say whether this quality, once described, is in fact worth having or expressing. That depends on what kind of people we want to be. What I do maintain, however, here and throughout the remainder of this article, is that *if* we consider this form of courage and forthrightness worth cultivating and expressing, the criminal trial jury is an institution well suited to that expression.

Before returning, however, to the question of how and why the jury might be understood to symbolize this form of courage, consider an alternative analogy designed to flesh out further the nature of the quality itself. This analogy is drawn from the world of business, where the personal bond, which makes the family example of limited application, cannot be presumed. Suppose you run a business, employing sales representatives, and that you have established certain bare minimum performance standards for your employees. In line with those standards, you have determined conditions under which an employee should be fired — that a certain combination of performance failures or misbehavior should lead to termination. If, for example, an employee is late for work more than ten times in one quarter, and fails to meet sales quotas for six straight months, and has unsatisfactory performance evaluations from his or her supervisor for four consecutive quarters, then, according to your policy, that employee is to be fired. In order to be completely fair, you make sure all employees are fully familiar with the standards — the policy is described in the employee handbook as the "firing line."

In addition, you provide training, counseling, and other assistance to employees who seem to be in danger. All in all, you have no doubt that you do in fact want to let go any employee who fails to meet these minimal requirements and that you are fully justified in doing so.

Now, suppose your software vender describes to you a new and inexpensive program. The program will collect data from accounting, personnel, and sales, and will determine if and when any employee has crossed the "firing line." In addition, the program can be designed actually to do the deed. Firing a person, as anyone who has had to do it knows, is an unpleasant experience. The program could take you off the hook. Once an employee meets the conditions for termination, the computer would issue and mail a severance check, freeze the employee's access to company records, and cancel his or her corporate credit card. The computer would also generate a polite email message informing the employee that he or she has been terminated and instructing the employee to clean out his or her desk. Would you make use of that program? Or would you feel an obligation to look the employee in the eye and deliver the news yourself? More to the point, what would it say about you and your operation to make use of that program to avoid having to confront the person you have decided to fire? Is this the kind of operation you would want to work for, let alone design?

Although I do not mean for my argument to turn on whether or not courage is the best label for the characteristic or trait potentially expressed by a decision to put the act of judgment into the hands of juries, the term does offer a way of distinguishing between several related and overlapping qualities which might go under that name, only some of which I believe are plausibly symbolized by the use of criminal trial juries. One sort of courage would be a willingness to act, in specific cases, in a way consistent with principles we as a community purport to define ourselves by. For example, if we stand for, or purport to stand for, a certain vision of free speech, perhaps we should have the courage to stand by that commitment even in cases where the speech in question is of a form we dislike or would prefer to live without. Although this is the form of courage which might be initially suggested by the title of this article, it is not my focus here. I do not argue that using juries symbolizes a willingness to apply general principles to specific cases. On the contrary, and as I acknowledge below, the use of juries may come at some cost to this type of consistency with principles.

Instead, my claim is that the use of juries may be understood to express a willingness to do two things: first, to *confront* the specific consequences of whatever we decide to do; and second, to *acknowledge* our own agency in and responsibility for bringing about those consequences. The form of courage I refer to is not a willingness to act in this way or that, but rather a willingness to stand behind whatever actions we take. Perhaps one might choose another label for this quality: forthrightness, honor, frankness, or nobility come to mind as possibilities. In any event, the focus here is less on acting rightly than on taking responsibility for actions. The opposite of courage, as I am using the term, is not hypocrisy but cowardice.

In the end, if one believes that taking responsibility for one's difficult decisions is unimportant — that this form of courage is not worth having or displaying — then this part of my argument will fall on deaf ears. By arguing that a willingness to acknowledge agency in judgments is admirable and by using the language of courage to flesh out that claim, I do not appeal to or assume the presence of an unambiguous preexisting shared understanding of courage or cowardice. Rather, this article represents an effort to contribute to and participate in the ongoing effort to construct such an understanding.

C. *Consequentialist Arguments*

Although I have insisted that social meaning matters for its own sake, and that we as a community might prefer to behave bravely simply because we prefer to understand ourselves as brave, I am not a purist on the point. Given the extent to which objections to my concrete recommendations are likely to be of a consequentialist nature, it is worth noting that there are instrumental arguments for my position. I hesitate in making these arguments, however, out of fear that my overall claim will be understood to hinge upon them. It does not. Making instrumental arguments against cowardice is like arguing that one should not spit on one's mother because it spreads germs. It may do that, but to highlight that fact risks missing the point. With that caveat, however, I am willing to offer three consequentialist arguments for confronting the perplexity of judgment — for implicating the conscience of as many of us as possible when judging our fellow citizens.

First, and most concretely, we might make fairer laws to the extent that we know that we, or at least some of us, will have to acknowledge responsibility for the particular human consequences of those laws. In a sense, this is a variation of the argument traditionally made on behalf of jury nullification. The traditional claim is that juries protect citizens from the State and mitigate the harsh and potentially unfair particular consequences of general laws by occasionally exercising their power to nullify.[54] My claim, however, is somewhat different. I suggest that our awareness that we will have to confront the human consequences of our laws might cause us to make those laws more fair in the first place.

To the extent that lawmakers, and those who vote for lawmakers, understand themselves as potential jurors, this ex ante deterrence function (deterring, in this case, lawmakers rather than lawbreakers), might function directly: "Do not support a law imposing a given criminal sanction unless you are willing to look a man in the eye and impose that sanction." Given, however, that most of those who support or vote for a given law will not anticipate having to enforce that particular law themselves, the effect is likely to be more indirect: "Do not support a law imposing a given sanction unless you believe that twelve of your fellow citizens will be able to look a man in the eye and impose it."

A second instrumental argument, albeit one closely related to the first, might go under the heading of moral or political cost-internalization. Assume we make our laws as fair as possible; they will still give rise to troubling consequences. Social and economic realities, coupled with human frailty, will continue to give rise to criminal behavior. That behavior, in turn, will continue to need to be punished, deterred, and protected against through criminal sanctions. To the extent that we force ourselves to be troubled and discomforted by the necessity of imposing those sanctions, we may be motivated to work towards eliminating or abating the conditions which contribute to criminal behavior. Dysfunctional families, drug addiction, ravaged neighborhoods, poor schools, racism, and poverty (moral and economic) should trouble us primarily because of what they do to our fellow citizens. Perhaps we should also be troubled, and motivated, by what they make *us* do to our fellow citizens.

It might appear that fear of crime itself ought to motivate a community to mitigate the social and economic circumstances giving rise to that crime. Why should one expect that the discomfort inherent in imposing punishment will serve any additional motivating function? If people will not work for social change in order to prevent crime, why would they work for social change in order to avoid having to punish criminals? Two reasons: For one, the

54. *See infra* sections III.D & IV.D (outlining the arguments surrounding the question of jury nullification and situating my overall thesis within those arguments).

classes of potential jurors and potential crime victims are not necessarily congruent. Not only do criminals emerge primarily from and inhabit the low end of the socioeconomic spectrum, so too do crime victims.[55] Granted, the rich fear crime, and see themselves as potential victims, but they are also able to devise ways of protecting themselves. Those who are most free from deprivation are also able to shield themselves from much of the criminal behavior generated by that deprivation.[56] Build a high enough wall, and it may be possible to avoid confronting either crime or the underlying social conditions which contribute to it. For some, jury service may provide a rare opportunity, albeit an unwanted one, to look closely at what lies on the other side of the gate.

More to the point, juries are forced to look at particular criminals rather than at crime in general.[57] Knowing about and fearing crime, even being a victim of crime, however painful and disturbing that may be, can allow one to retain a sense of righteousness. Having to decide that a man or woman will spend the next twenty years in prison is different — it implicates one in the system. It dirties one in a way that being a victim or potential victim does not.

In addition, jurors must confront the individual who has come to be a criminal. They see at close quarters the man or woman whose life need not have taken this course. Assume they are fully justified in bringing in a conviction and that they do so. Assume that they have no doubts about the necessity of judging as they have. They may still come to wish for a world in which the thing they have done is less often necessary. The strength of this argument depends upon

55. For example, people in families with annual incomes less than $7500 experience a crime victimization rate of 89.5 per 1000. By contrast, those with annual incomes over $75,000 experience a crime victimization rate of 38.2 per 1000. *See* URIE BRONFENBRENNER ET AL., THE STATE OF AMERICANS: THE DISTURBING FACTS AND FIGURES ON CHANGING VALUES, CRIME, THE ECONOMY, POVERTY, FAMILY, EDUCATION, THE AGING POPULATION AND WHAT THEY MEAN FOR OUR FUTURE 22 fig. 1-17 (1996), *cited in* Peter M. Cicchino, *The Problem Child: An Empirical Survey and Rhetorical Analysis of Child Poverty in the United States,* 5 J.L. & POLY. 5, 28 (1996); *see also* Violent Crime Control and Law Enforcement Act of 1994, H.R. REP. NO. 103-324 (1994), *reprinted in* 1994 U.S.C.C.A.N. 1803, 1804 ("The impact [of violent crime] is particularly harsh in poorer communities, many of which are literally being destroyed by violence . . . ."); CHARLES MURRAY, LOSING GROUND: AMERICAN SOCIAL POLICY, 1950-1980, at 119-20 (1984).

56. *See* EDWARD J. BLAKELY & MARY GAIL SNYDER, FORTRESS AMERICA (1997) (describing the ways in which the well-off seek to protect themselves from crime methods, including hiring private security, living in closed or walled-off neighborhoods, installing alarms or other security devices, and insuring valuables).

57. As the United States Supreme Court has observed in the context of capital sentencing, the jury is required to focus on the defendant as a "uniquely individual human being." *See* Woodson v. North Carolina, 428 U.S. 280, 304 (1976).

the extent to which juries are truly representative and provides an argument for ensuring that jurors are drawn from a true cross-section of the community.

Finally, and most long term, is an argument situated at the place where consequentialist concerns meet claims of social meaning. If we allow ourselves to become a cowardly people — if we begin to deal with perplexities by hiding from them — what will we allow ourselves to do next? Granted that judging and punishing criminals as we do is pragmatically necessary and morally justified, there is no guarantee that our future public acts will be equally laudable. History has shown what can be done by people who do not feel agency in their actions — who understand themselves as merely playing a role in a larger system, or just following orders. If we get into the habit of ducking responsibility for our tragic choices, or get used to delegating them to people who know not what they do, it becomes increasingly likely that we will allow ourselves to take that small but terrible step from cowardice to cruelty.

D. *Meanings and Consequences*

Having offered a set of consequentialist arguments for asking the jury to play a responsibility-taking role, I readily acknowledge that there may be attendant risks. The most obvious risk may be that of nullification. By nullification I refer, here and throughout this article, to a decision on the part of a jury to acquit a defendant despite believing that the defendant is guilty of the crime charged.[58] One possible risk attendant on asking that each of us take a turn looking defendants in the eye is that occasionally we will blink. Those of us called upon to embody the community and to acknowledge our agency in judgments of culpability will sometimes shrink from the task. In section IV.D below, I return to the issue of jury nullification, and to the question of whether recognizing the jury's responsibility-taking function might shed light on the uncertain legal status of nullification. Here, however, let me make the preliminary and simplifying assumption that nullification is simply un-

58. I recognize that one might use the term nullification more broadly to refer to any decision by a jury to disregard the law. In the criminal context, for example, a jury might convict despite believing a defendant to be innocent of the crime charged. It is this sort of "nullification" against which rules excluding prejudicial evidence are intended to guard. *See, e.g.*, FED. R. EVID. 404(a) (excluding evidence of "character or a trait of character . . . for the purpose of proving action in conformity therewith"). I focus on the question of nullification acquittal not because I believe that nullification convictions are unproblematic. On the contrary, I assume that it is always a bad thing to convict an innocent defendant. The question that generates impassioned debate is whether we should tolerate, or even encourage, the occasional acquittal of an guilty defendant.

desirable. I make this assumption not because I believe that it is necessarily correct, but rather because my goal here is to acknowledge the risks potentially attendant upon making jurors aware of their responsibility for and agency in criminal convictions. Nullification is a risk only to those who believe it to be a bad thing. The question, therefore, is how we might think about the intersection between that clearly identifiable (if difficult to quantify) risk, on the one hand, and the inchoate social meaning potentially expressed by encouraging juror responsibility, on the other.

In framing this question, it seems safe to make a further assumption that, however important we consider the expression of courage, we would not desire to increase juror's sense of responsibility beyond the point of reason. So, in outlining below the ways in which that sense of responsibility might be enforced or engendered, I do not recommend extreme or bizarre measures. For example, I do not suggest that jurors be required to pay daily visits to the families of those they have convicted. I do not suggest that jurors be required to visit or correspond regularly with those they have sent to prison. I do not suggest that capital juries be required to attend or preside at executions. While steps such as these would certainly engender a sense of responsibility and would certainly fix the consciences (in the retrospective sense) of jurors, such measures would with equal certainty inhibit the ability of jurors to bring in convictions when warranted.

The question, therefore, is how to evaluate the risks which might attend the more modest measures described below. And that only experience can tell. The risks may not, however, be as great as might first appear. As an initial matter, cases of actual nullification are arguably quite rare. Opponents of nullification, particularly in the popular press, often argue anecdotally, pointing to certain high profile verdicts such as the O.J. Simpson criminal verdict as evidence that "jury nullification is undermining our system of justice."[59] One academic has gone so far as to describe the United States as "in an age of radical and frequent acts of criminal jury nullification."[60] I have located no evidence in support of these dire descriptions. In fact, it is difficult to imagine how one might measure the rate of nullification. As Judge Weinstein has pointed out,

59. Daniel Levine, *Race Over Reason in the Jury Box,* READERS DIGEST, June 1996, at 123.

60. Victor Williams, *A Constitutional Charge and a Comparative Vision to Substantially Expand and Subject Matter Specialize the Federal Judiciary: A Preliminary Blueprint for Remodeling Our National Houses of Justice and Establishing a Separate System of Federal Criminal Courts,* 37 WM. & MARY L. REV. 535, 609-10 (1996).

distinguishing "between a 'right' outcome — a verdict following the letter of the law — and a 'wrong' one — a 'nullification' verdict — can be dangerous, and this endeavor depends largely upon personal bias."[61] In addition, not every "wrong" verdict represents a case of nullification. One must distinguish, for example, cases in which juries doubt the credibility of state witnesses whose testimony on its face appears to support a conviction. Mistrust of the police may be troubling, but it is not the same thing as disrespect for the law. Similarly, one must distinguish cases in which juries are simply mistaken, or confused, rather than defiant.

Moreover, it is not at all clear that making juries aware of their role in embodying community conscience would increase the likelihood of an acquittal. As described below, prosecutors know how to exhort juries to their duty. Recognizing the possibility of nullification, prosecutors have developed a repertoire of arguments designed to achieve just that end.[62] We cannot know whether we, in our capacity as jurors, will be courageous unless and until we give ourselves the opportunity to display courage.

Assume for the sake of argument, however, that we will not always be up to the task — that jurors will on occasion be unwilling to convict if forced to acknowledge agency in the conviction. Assume that convictions would decrease by 1%, or even 10%, which seems highly unlikely. And assume further that all of those additional acquittals would be unwarranted. What we as a community then need to decide is if that cost is worth paying. It is often described as better to let ten guilty men go free than to convict even one innocent. We might similarly decide that it is better to convict 65% of defendants bravely than to convict 70% by behaving as cowards.

In deciding whether to accept some increase in unwarranted acquittals, it is important to keep in mind that unwarranted acquittals themselves represent just a fraction of unpunished crimes. Before a defendant can be acquitted, he must become a defendant. The crime must be solved, the police must choose to make an arrest, and

61. The Honorable Jack B. Weinstein, *Considering Jury "Nullification": When May and Should a Jury Reject the Law to Do Justice?*, 30 AM. CRIM. L. REV. 239 (1993).

62. One of my personal favorites is the "summer soldier" argument, in which the prosecutor quotes Thomas Paine to the effect that no one needs "summer soldiers" who will only turn out in support of the community when the going is easy. Instead, the argument goes, we all need to take our turn doing the difficult and unpleasant work of citizenship. Interestingly, a version of this argument is described in a journal published by the National Association of Criminal Defense Lawyers, in which defense lawyers are advised to exhort jurors not to be "summer soldiers and sunshine patriots in following the law of reasonable doubt." Ray Moses, *The Last Word*, CHAMPION, Jan.-Feb. 1997, at 51.

the State must elect to prosecute. As Albert Alschuler has noted, "[W]hen the discretion of prosecutors and other officials not to enforce the law is not only tolerated but applauded, it is difficult to argue (as prosecutors, of all people, often do) that affording a dispensing power to jurors would bring the rule of law to an end."[63] Add to this the fact that the vast majority of defendants plead guilty or no contest, and that most of those who do go to trial are convicted, and the question of nullification comes into perspective. To the extent that jury nullification is a problem, it is arguably not because the already substantial number of unpunished crimes may thereby increase by some small increment. Rather nullification is potentially troubling because of what it means.

Contrary to those who appear to believe that nullification, however rare, must be interpreted as disrespect for the law, I am unwilling to draw any oversimplified conclusions as to the social meaning of nullification. It seems inescapable that juries that nullify do so for a variety of reasons. Some juries may simply be merciful. Others may believe that the defendant's actions should not be considered criminal at all. Other juries may nullify because they believe the attendant punishment (or what they are able to guess about the punishment) is out of proportion with the crime. As Thomas Green has detailed, nullification has a long, rich social history.[64] A refusal to convict need not mean anarchy.

To this I add that a willingness to risk such a refusal may itself be meaningful. It may mean not that we lack respect for the law, but that we have respect for ourselves — that we are willing to trust ourselves to have the courage to look into the eyes of those we are forced to judge.

What this further suggests is that the question is not simply one of balancing material costs against inchoate meanings. The matter is more complicated. Perhaps, for example, some material costs are necessary for an action to be meaningful. Perhaps an effective expression of courage, honor, or other aspect of community identity requires that we demonstrate, rather than merely announce, our commitment to that self-description. It is hard for an act that costs one nothing to stand for much more.

63. Albert W. Alschuler, *A Teetering Palladium?*, 79 JUDICATURE 200, 201 (1996) (reviewing STEVEN ADLER, THE JURY: TRIAL AND ERROR IN THE AMERICAN COURTROOM (1994) and JEFFREY ABRAMSON, WE THE JURY: THE JURY SYSTEM AND THE IDEAL OF DEMOCRACY (1994)).

64. *See* Green, *supra* note 9.

Accordingly, in thinking about the manifestations of juror responsibility described in Part IV below, and the recommendations for engendering juror responsibility in Part V, it should not only be asked whether the risks imposed by these measures are too great a cost to pay for the expression of courage. It should be asked as well whether the costs imposed by these measures are *large enough* to allow them to carry that expressive content.

IV. Manifestations of Jury Responsibility

If the jury does in fact perform the role I ascribe to it, one would expect to find that role reflected in the practices and procedures governing the criminal jury trial. I do not maintain that this function has been explicitly delineated through the case law and rules surrounding the jury trial. On the contrary, the jury's responsibility-taking function has not been expressly described or defended, and for that reason has gone unappreciated. I do maintain, however, that aspects of the procedural and evidentiary structure surrounding the jury, as well as aspects of the language employed by courts in maintaining that structure, make more sense if understood as informed by an awareness that the jury does and should perform this function.

I use the phrase "informed by an awareness" rather than "motivated by an intention" because I am not making a strong claim about the conscious intent or motivation of the many judges, lawyers, and litigants who have contributed to the evolution of the criminal justice system. As Charles Nesson has observed:

> Rules that evolved without conscious design may now serve important objectives that are not consciously appreciated. The evolving pattern of the system may thus shed light on its underlying values; inversely, the positing of such values may help to explain the existing structure of the system.[65]

Imagine a person who prides himself or herself on a neatly manicured lawn and a perfectly washed and waxed car. He or she might come to recognize that these tastes are in part manifestations of an underlying but not consciously appreciated desire for order. This realization might help that person better understand not only his or her attention to the lawn and car but also other seemingly unconnected aspects of his or her life. I suggest that aspects of the criminal jury trial are in part manifestations of an underlying but not consciously appreciated desire to preserve the jury's responsibility-taking function.

65. Nesson, *supra* note 4, at 1369.

In particular, four aspects of criminal jury trial practice can be illuminated in this way: the invocation of "conscience" in arguments to and about juries, judicial concern that certain forms of evidence or testimony will "usurp the role of the jury," the doctrine of *Caldwell v. Mississippi,* and the continuing uncertainty over the legal and conceptual status of jury nullification.

A. *The Invocation of Conscience*

The jury is frequently referred to as the "conscience of the community," or variations on that theme. In many cases, this usage can be explained by reference to the jury's primary role as factfinder. I suggest, however, that the language of conscience is not fully explicable by reference to the jury's traditionally recognized decision-making function. In at least some cases it points to and reveals an implicit awareness of the responsibility-taking function ascribed to the jury in this article. The jury serves as the "conscience of the community" in that the jury is the institution through which we acknowledge and accept responsibility for our judgments — the institution through which our individual consciences are implicated in those judgments.

The term "conscience" has a long history in connection with the institution of the criminal trial jury. In one early formulation of the reasonable doubt standard, for example, jurors were instructed to convict only "if the evidence is sufficient to satisfy your conscience."[66] As Barbara Shapiro has demonstrated, the "satisfied conscience" language was common in seventeenth- and eighteenth-century criminal jury instructions.[67] Shapiro has argued that, historically, this language should be understood as epistemological, expressing merely a belief that, with absolute certainty always out of reach, "[j]ury verdicts must be based on the very highest knowledge available to humans in matters of fact."[68] Although I am unprepared to challenge Shapiro's extensively documented historical claim, it does seem to me that something is lost by understanding references to conscience as nothing more than epistemological.

66. Barbara J. Shapiro, "Beyond Reasonable Doubt" and "Probable Cause": Historical Perspectives on the Anglo-American Law of Evidence 14 (1991) (citation omitted).

67. *See id.* at 38.

68. *Id.* at 27. Shapiro attributes this understanding in part to Locke's *Essay Concerning Human Understanding, see* Locke, *supra* note 40, and its incorporation into legal doctrine in part, to early treatise writers such as Geoffrey Gilbert and John Morgan. Her overall claim is that the reasonable doubt standard and its precursors should be understood as a response to developments in epistemology that highlighted the pervasiveness of uncertainty in human knowledge.

And one need only glance at the OED to see the rich and varied etymology of the term. It is not my goal to trace that etymology, nor even to trace the history of the term in connection with the jury. Instead, the question is this: What does it mean, in the context of the modern jury trial, to say that juries function as the "conscience of the community"?

In some cases, conscience appears to mean nothing more than common sense or sound judgment.[69] References to the jury as the conscience of the community in such contexts do not ascribe any additional role to the jury beyond its traditional one as factfinder and judge of witness credibility. Similarly, substantive law under some circumstances incorporates a community standard. The most familiar example might be the negligence standard in tort, at least one understanding of which refers to the reasonableness of the defendant's behavior in the eyes of the community. In this sense, when the jury is asked to "represent the feeling of the community,"[70] it is being asked for something like expert testimony. Jurors are deemed the best authority on the behavior of "the ideal average prudent man, whose equivalent the jury is taken to be."[71] In such contexts, the term "conscience" might mean merely a "sense of what is considered appropriate or acceptable." This appears to be the manner in which the language of conscience is used

69. *See, e.g.*, Jacobson v. United States, 503 U.S. 540, 560-61 (1992) (In a child pornography case in which defendant claimed entrapment, "[i]t was, however, the jury's task, as the conscience of the community, to decide whether Mr. Jacobson was a willing participant in the criminal activity here or an innocent dupe."); Middleton v. Reynolds Metals Co., 963 F.2d 881, 884 (6th Cir. 1992) ("The role of the jury in interpreting the evidence and finding the ultimate facts is an American tradition so fundamental as to merit constitutional recognition. The conscience of the community speaks through the verdict of the jury." (quoting Horton v. Union Light, Heat & Power Co., 690 S.W.2d 382, 385 (Ky. 1985))); United States v. Dwyer, 843 F.2d 60, 63 (1st Cir. 1988) ("Confidence in our jury system leads us to leave credibility solely to the jury which, as the conscience of the community, is expected to act with sound judgment." (quoting United States v. Gleason, 616 F.2d 2, 24 (2d Cir. 1979))).

70. O.W. Holmes, Jr., The Common Law 111 (1881), *reprinted in* 3 The Collected Works of Justice Holmes 109, 171 (Sheldon M. Novick ed., 1995).

71. *Id.*; *see also, e.g.*, Kentucky Fried Chicken of California, Inc. v. Superior Court *ex rel.* Brown, 927 P.2d 1260, 1278 (Cal. 1997) (Kennedy, J., dissenting) ("As the conscience of the community, the jury plays an essential role in the application of the reasonable person standard of care."); Tweedley v. Tweedley, 649 A.2d 630, 633 (N.J. Super. Ct. Ch. Div. 1994) ("The jury is the conscience of the community in tort cases, articulating and imposing minimum standards of civilized behavior." (quoting Hutchings v. Hutchings, No. 05449S, 1993 WL 57741, at *9 (Conn. Super. Ct. Feb. 22, 1993))). Consider, for example, the instruction approved four decades ago by the United States Supreme Court in a case upholding an obscenity statute against a challenge that the statute was impermissibly vague:

> In this case, ladies and gentlemen of the jury, you and you alone are the exclusive judges of what the common conscience of the community is, and in determining that conscience you are to consider the community as a whole, young and old, educated and uneducated, the religious and the irreligious — men, women and children.

Roth v. United States, 354 U.S. 476, 490 (1957).

in the death penalty context, where juries play a role (either final or advisory, depending upon the jurisdiction) in sentencing.[72]

Where substantive law does not expressly incorporate a community standard, descriptions of the jury as the conscience of the community are more difficult to interpret. What role is the jury being asked to play? One such role is that of "defense against arbitrary law enforcement."[73] Asking criminal trial juries to act as the conscience of the community might be a way of asking them to nullify — to refuse to convict — if a particular application of the criminal law would offend community standards. In the words of the United States Supreme Court, "The availability of trial by jury allows an accused to protect himself against possible oppression by what is in essence an appeal to the community conscience, as embodied in the jury that hears his case."[74] This seems also to be the implication of Judge Bazelon's oft-quoted assertion that "the very essence of the jury's function is its role as a spokesman for the community conscience in determining whether or not blame can be imposed."[75]

I return in section IV.D below, to the uncertain status of jury nullification, but for now it is sufficient to note that if usage is any guide, references to the jury as conscience cannot always be understood to refer to nullification, or even lenity, given that the phrase is most often employed not by judges or by defense lawyers, but by prosecutors.[76] Prosecutors regularly attempt, and are frequently permitted, to argue that the jury must serve as the "conscience of

---

72. In the sentencing phase of the trial of Oklahoma City bomber Timothy McVeigh, the district court instructed the jury in part,

> Your role in this process is to be the conscience of the community in making a moral judgment about the worth of a specific life balanced against the societal value of what the government contends to be — or is the deserved punishment for these particular crimes. Your decision must be a reasoned one free from the influence of passion, prejudice or any other arbitrary factor.

United States v. McVeigh, 153 F.3d 1166, 1222 n.50 (10th Cir. 1998), *cert. denied,* 119 S. Ct. 1148 (1999); *see also* Witherspoon v. Illinois, 391 U.S. 510 (1968) (stating that the function of the sentencing jury is to "express the conscience of the community on the ultimate question of life or death").

73. Duncan v. Louisiana, 391 U.S. 145, 156 (1968).

74. McKeiver v. Pennsylvania, 403 U.S. 528, 554-55 (1971) (Brennan, J., concurring in part and dissenting in part) (holding that trial by jury in adjudicative stage of state juvenile court delinquency proceeding is not constitutionally required).

75. United States v. Dougherty, 473 F.2d 1113, 1142 (D.C. Cir. 1972) (Bazelon, C.J., concurring in part and dissenting in part).

76. I have not examined the use of the language of conscience by defense lawyers in criminal cases. While such an investigation might well be interesting or illuminating, my goal here is merely to shed light on one potentially problematic use of the term conscience — that by prosecutors — rather than to catalogue or comment upon the full range of usage of the term.

the community."[77] The courts attempt to distinguish between exhorting and inflaming. If the prosecutor's argument appears intended to inflame the jury or to encourage the jury to convict in response to outside factors such as community expectations or deterrence unrelated to the particular defendant's guilt or innocence, the court will hold community conscience arguments improper.[78] If, on the other hand, the prosecutor appears only to be exhorting the jury to its duty, closing arguments using "conscience of the community" are generally permitted.[79]

77. *See, e.g.,* United States v. Alloway, 397 F.2d 105, 113 (6th Cir. 1968) (permitting prosecutor to argue to jury that "[y]ou the jurors, are called upon in this case to be the world conscience of the community. And I'm calling on this jury to speak out for the community and let the John Alloways know that this type of conduct will not be tolerated, that we're not going to tolerate"); Wilson v. State, 697 N.E.2d 466, 477 (Ind. 1998) (approving jury instruction, tendered by prosecutor and given by the trial court in a noncapital murder case, that "[y]ou are further instructed that in determining the criminal responsibility of the Defendant, if any, that you are the moral conscience of our society"); State v. Patterson, 966 S.W.2d 435, 446 (Tenn. Crim. App. 1997) (holding that prosecutor's reference to jury as "conscience of the community" was not improper).

78. *See, e.g.,* United States v. Ghazaleh, 58 F.3d 240, 246 (6th Cir. 1995) ("[T]he type of appeal we have considered improper is one where the prosecutor urges the jury to send a message to all drug dealers in the community by convicting the defendant."); United States v. Johnson, 968 F.2d 768, 770 (8th Cir. 1992) (holding that prosecutor's closing argument exhorting jurors to act as a "bulwark" against drug dealing was improper and inflammatory); United States v. Solivan, 937 F.2d 1146, 1148 (6th Cir. 1991) (finding it improperly inflammatory to exhort the jury "to tell her and all of the other drug dealers like her — (defense counsel's objection and Court's response omitted) — [t]hat we don't want that stuff in Northern Kentucky and that anybody who brings that stuff in Northern Kentucky and . . ."); Coreas v. United States, 565 A.2d 594, 604 (D.C. 1989) ("Argument which encourages the jury to 'send a message' has been found improper . . . ."); Powell v. United States, 455 A.2d 405, 410 (D.C. 1982) (holding that the question "isn't it time that this jury, acting as the conscience of this community, stood up and sent a message loud and clear to [the defendant?]" was "irrelevant and inappropriate"). In civil cases also, an appeal to jurors to be the conscience of the community will be found objectionable where it appears calculated to focus the jury's attention on community expectations rather than on the fair resolution of the case at hand. *See, e.g.,* Westbrook v. General Tire & Rubber Co., 754 F.2d 1233, 1238 (5th Cir. 1985) (per curiam).

79. *See, e.g.,* United States v. Durbin, No. 96-30223, 1997 WL 464626, at *3 (9th Cir. Aug. 7, 1997) ("A prosecutor's appeal to the jury to act as a 'conscience of the community' is acceptable unless it is 'specifically designed to inflame the jury.'" (quoting United States v. Lester, 749 F.2d 1288, 1301 (9th Cir. 1984))); United States v. Williams, 989 F.2d 1061, 1072 (9th Cir. 1993); United States v. Smith, 918 F.2d 1551, 1562-63 (11th Cir. 1990) (holding that prosecutorial appeals to the jury to act as the community conscience are permissible "when they are not intended to inflame"); United States v. Lewis, 547 F.2d 1030, 1037 (8th Cir. 1976) ("Unless calculated to inflame, an appeal to the jury to act as the conscience of the community is not impermissible."); State v. Campbell, 460 S.E.2d 144, 156 (N.C. 1995) (holding it proper to urge the jury to act as the voice and conscience of the community). Some courts, those in Massachusetts, for example, have been less tolerant of prosecutorial "conscience of the community" arguments. *See, e.g.,* Commonwealth v. Matthews, 581 N.E.2d 1304, 1310 (Mass. App. Ct. 1991) ("It was also inappropriate for the prosecutor to tell the jurors that they were 'the conscience of the community.' They bear no such burden; their role in a trial is limited to finding the facts on the basis of the evidence, dispassionately and impartially."). Even there, however, the comments must be inflammatory in order to be objectionable. *See, e.g.,* Commonwealth v. Smith, 444 N.E.2d 374 (Mass. 1983) (barring prosecutor's words, which, in effect, connoted that defendant "should not be let loose on soci-

What do prosecutors mean when they ask jurors to act as the conscience of the community, given that they are certainly not asking for nullification? One explanation might be that they are asking for just the opposite. Just as defendants would, if permitted, ask juries to acquit "according to conscience" despite evidence supporting a conviction under the law, perhaps prosecutors are implicitly asking juries to convict according to community conscience — in response to community expectations, for example — notwithstanding any uncertainty regarding the guilt or innocence of the particular defendant. If so, such arguments would be improper not only under the case law described above, but also as a matter of basic fairness. If defendants are barred from asking for lenity outside of the law, surely prosecutors should be precluded from asking for vengeance (or even deterrence) outside of the law.[80] It is possible, however, to interpret prosecutorial, conscience-of-the-community arguments in a way that does not attribute improper motives to every prosecutor who makes such arguments and that may help explain why so many courts have found such arguments acceptable.

Prosecutors appear to have learned through experience that, in the eyes of at least some jurors, judgment is indeed a terrible thing. Those whose job it is to ask juries for convictions have learned that turning in a conviction can be a difficult thing to do, even for jurors convinced that a conviction is warranted and fully justified. It is for this reason that prosecutors often augment talk of conscience with that of courage. In a marijuana distribution case, for example, the prosecutor asked the jury in closing argument to "please have the courage to go out there and find these Defendants guilty and come back and return guilty verdicts, because we need juries like yourselves that have the courage to do that."[81] It takes guts to look a man in the eye and convict, even if one is certain that a conviction is deserved.

---

ety"); *see also* Commonwealth v. Sanchez, 540 N.E.2d 1316, 1321 (Mass. 1989) (stating that a verdict of guilt would end victims' nightmares); Commonwealth v. Ward, 550 N.E.2d 398, 406 (Mass. App. Ct. 1990) (criticizing prosecutor's rousing summons that "sounded a persistent theme that the jury had a duty to confront crime in the streets bravely and to avenge the wrong done the victim").

80. *See, e.g.,* James Joseph Duane, *What Message Are We Sending to Criminal Jurors When We Ask Them to "Send a Message" With Their Verdict?,* 22 Am. J. Crim. L. 565, 581-82 (1995) (categorizing "conscience of the community" arguments with "send a message" arguments, and arguing that such arguments represent improper attempts to shift the jury's attention away from guilt or innocence and toward community expectations or deterrence unrelated to the particular defendant's guilt or innocence).

81. *See* United States v. Caballero, 712 F.2d 126, 131-32 (5th Cir. 1983) ("A fair reading of the closing argument confirms the accuracy of the district judge's ruling that the prosecutor made a vigorous, but permissible, plea for law enforcement.").

In the recent Florida trial of an arms dealer, the prosecutor's closing arguments included the following:

> I leave you with one last thought to help you with th[e] difficulties [of deciding this case]. It's a quote John Kennedy gave just shortly before he was inaugurated president, quoting Luke 12:24. And he said: For those to whom much is given, much is required. And when at some future date the high court of history sits in judgment of each of us, determining whether in our brief span of service we have fulfilled our obligations to the state, the answers to those questions will be determined by the responses to four questions: Are we truly men of dedication? Are we truly men of judgment? Are we truly men of integrity? And were we truly men of courage? Back in that jury room you have a difficult job to do. Walk back there and be men and women of dedication, judgment, integrity, and, most important, courage. Do what you have to do and then get on with the business of living.[82]

In a North Carolina murder case, for which the death penalty was not being sought, the prosecutor put it this way:

> Ladies, Gentlemen, when you hear of such acts, you say, gee, somebody ought to do something about that. I want you to look around. You're that somebody that everybody else talks about. . . . So, folks, you might as well look around. There is no mythical somebody hiding in this Courtroom. You are the somebody. You, the buck, as bad as you hate it, stops right here with you twelve people.
>
> Today you are the moral conscious [sic] of that community. It's up to you to see that justice is done.[83]

Though ungrammatical, "as bad as you hate it" seems apt. But why hate it?

In some cases, judgment will be difficult — will weigh on the conscience — in the sense that it is hard to be certain whether one is doing the right thing. But anecdotal evidence suggests that at least some jurors find it difficult to convict even when they are persuaded a conviction is justified. Anyone who has spent time in a criminal courtroom will recall scenes of jurors in tears as they bring in a conviction. In addition, postverdict interviews tend to confirm that jurors struggle mightily with the burden of judgment.[84] In what

82. United States v. Bailey, 123 F.3d 1381, 1401 (11th Cir. 1997) (alteration in original) ("These comments merely reiterated and exhorted to the jurors their duty to obey their oaths and to decide the case with dedication, judgment, integrity, and courage. The remarks by the prosecutor were as likely to lead to an acquittal as a conviction.").

83. State v. Larrimore, 456 S.E.2d 789, 812 (N.C. 1995) (alteration in original).

84. Nancy Marder has examined reports of postverdict interviewers with jurors and, under the heading "The Difficulty of Judging," reports the following:

> Occasionally jurors in post-verdict interviews comment on the difficulty inherent in the act of judging. Eight percent of the jurors' total comments included some reference to the process of decisionmaking as difficult, painful, or upsetting. Comments varied among jurors but the sentiment remained the same. For example, one juror in the

way is one's conscience implicated by turning in a fully justified conviction? I suggest that jurors' consciences are implicated because they are being asked to play the role I have described. They are being asked to look at, and confront their agency in, the act of judgment. Not only does it implicate the conscience to make a tough decision — to figure out what one must do: it also may weigh upon the conscience — and thus require courage — to confront what one must do.

The term "conscience" thus has both an outward or forward-looking aspect *and* an inward or retrospective aspect. In the first sense, conscience is a guide to behavior. We hope that our conscience will steer us toward right action. There is also, however, an inward or reflective sense of the term, as when a person is described as having a "clear conscience" or a "guilty conscience." That usage refers to conscience not as a guide to action but rather as a mental state — a state of awareness of responsibility for actions taken. Shakespeare's Hamlet illustrates both senses of the word "conscience." When Hamlet says that "conscience does make cowards of us all," he is talking about the difficulty inherent in figuring out what to do. When he schemes that "[t]he play's the thing/ Wherein I'll catch the conscience of the King," he is, however, talking about something else entirely. He is talking about bringing the King face to face with what he has done.[85]

I suggest that the jury may serve as the conscience of the community in both senses. Not only might we hope that a community-based sense of right and wrong will guide juror decisionmaking in appropriate cases, we might recognize as well, and thereby better comprehend the various uses of the term "conscience," that the jury

> Oliver North trial described the process as "the most difficult decision of [her] life," while another in that case described herself as "mentally and physically exhausted." A juror in the Tyson trial described decisionmaking as "a difficult thing to do." In the Rodney King civil suit, one juror recounted "br[eaking] down in tears on several occasions," "be[coming] sick to her stomach from watching the taped beating," and being "haunted" by King's screams, while another described how "some nights he tossed and turned in a fitful slumber with the day's debate playing over and over in his head." A juror in the Gotti trial described decisionmaking as "tough," whereas a juror in the trial of Colin Ferguson, who was convicted of several counts of murder and attempted murder in the shooting of several passengers on the Long Island Railroad, described the process as "a once in a lifetime experience that was very, very draining." The foreman in the Crown Heights trial, speaking for the entire jury, described the jury's task as "not easy" and "very nerve-racking," and the mother of a young juror in the Reginald Denny beating explained that her daughter "had never before been forced to make difficult decisions like this."

Nancy S. Marder, *Deliberations and Disclosures, A Study of Post-Verdict Interviews of Jurors*, 82 IOWA L. REV. 465, 484-85 (1997) (footnotes omitted) (alteration in original).

85. *See* WILLIAM SHAKESPEARE, HAMLET, PRINCE OF DENMARK act 3, sc. 1, l. 82, act 2, sc. 2, ll. 604-05 (G. Blakemore Evans ed., 2 Riverside Shakespeare 1974).

is the institution through which some of us are forced to an awareness of our responsibility for what we do.

B. *The* Caldwell *Doctrine*

George Priest has described the jury as "aresponsible," in light of the fact that jury verdicts are largely immune to review.[86] In a sense, however, this characterization gets it exactly wrong. If, as I have suggested, being "responsible" is understood to mean, at least in part, "taking responsibility" — acknowledging agency — then perhaps only the unreviewable are capable of performing the role. Perhaps only those who know they have the last word will feel truly responsible for their actions. To be specific, if jurors are to act as the conscience of the community in the way I have described, they need to understand two things. First they should know that they do in fact have the last word — that no one will go behind them and fix what they have done. Second, they should understand that the last word is in fact theirs — that no one can or will tell them what to do.

If jurors' consciences are to be fully implicated, they must understand themselves to be acting, rather than merely deciding. For this to be the case, they must understand that no one — no higher authority — stands between them and the fate of the defendant. This concern may be best illustrated by *Caldwell v. Mississippi.*[87] There, the United States Supreme Court reversed a death sentence imposed after the prosecutor had emphasized to the jury that any decision they reached would be subject to appeal.

In closing argument, defense counsel asked the jury to "confront both the gravity and the responsibility of calling for another's death."[88] In response, "the prosecutor forcefully argued that the defense had done something wholly illegitimate in trying to force the jury to feel a sense of responsibility for its decision."[89] The prosecutor argued:

> Now, they would have you believe that you're going to kill this man and they know — they know that your decision is not the final decision. My God, how unfair can you be? Your job is reviewable. They know it. Yet they . . . [are] insinuating that your decision is the final

86. *See* Priest, *supra* note 44, at 168.

87. 472 U.S. 320 (1985).

88. *Caldwell,* 472 U.S. at 324 (quoting the defense counsel's argument to the jury as: "I implore you to think deeply about this matter. It is his life or death — the decision you're going to have to make . . . . You can give him life or you can give him death. It's going to be your decision. . . . You are the judges and you will have to decide his fate. It is an awesome responsibility, I know — an awesome responsibility.").

89. 472 U.S. at 324.

> decision and that they're gonna take Bobby Caldwell out in front of this Courthouse in moments and string him up and that is terribly, terribly unfair. For they know, as I know, and as Judge Baker has told you, that the decision you render is automatically reviewable by the Supreme Court.[90]

In vacating the sentence, the Court concluded that "it is constitutionally impermissible to rest a death sentence on a determination made by a sentencer who has been led to believe that the responsibility for determining the appropriateness of the defendant's death rests elsewhere."[91] The Court further observed that "the uncorrected suggestion that the responsibility for any ultimate determination of death will rest with others presents an intolerable danger that the jury will in fact choose to minimize the importance of its role."[92]

Similar concerns were expressed by the Eleventh Circuit in reviewing a capital sentence imposed in Florida.[93] Under Florida's capital-sentencing scheme, the jury's recommendation was merely advisory. Nonetheless, it violated the Eighth Amendment to allow the prosecutor to minimize the jury's responsibility by repeatedly emphasizing that: "You understand you do not impose the death penalty; that is not on your shoulders. . . . You will have the opportunity after you have heard everything there is to hear to make a recommendation . . . . But it is not legally on your shoulders, though. It is not your ultimate decision."[94] The court held that "[u]nder such circumstances, a real danger exists that a resulting death sentence will be based at least in part on the determination of a decisionmaker that has been misled as to the nature of its responsibility."[95]

The *Caldwell* doctrine offers an example of a situation in which the jury's awareness of its responsibility has been considered central. In this light, it seems plausible to look for other circumstances

90. 472 U.S. at 325-26.

91. 472 U.S. at 328-29.

92. 472 U.S. at 333; *see also* Wheat v. Thigpen, 793 F.2d 621 (5th Cir. 1986) (vacating death sentence). In *Wheat,* the prosecutor first described the appellate procedure in detail and then argued as follows:

> Again, I say to you, and then I'll leave it to you, just remember this, if your verdict is that of the death penalty, that's not final. There's so many more people who will look at this case after you have made your decision in this case. Others will look at it, and look at your work, and see if you've made the right decision. And I can assure you, Ladies and Gentlemen, that if one finds that you have not, that they will send him back, and tell us to try it over, because someone made a mistake.

793 F.2d at 527-28 n.7.

93. *See* Mann v. Dugger, 844 F.2d 1446 (11th Cir. 1988) (en banc).

94. 844 F.2d at 1455.

95. 844 F.2d at 1455.

under which the failure on the part of the jury to acknowledge responsibility for a verdict may be, if not unconstitutional, at least troubling. It would be a mistake, however, to make too much of *Caldwell* and its progeny. First of all, the doctrine applies only to capital cases.[96] Second, *Caldwell* has been interpreted narrowly to apply not to all statements that might diminish the jury's sense of responsibility, but only to false and misleading statements likely to have that effect.[97] Finally, *Caldwell* was about fairness rather than courage. The improper attempt to diminish the jury's sense of responsibility violated the Eighth Amendment because of the possibility that the jury might not otherwise have imposed the death penalty.

Accordingly, *Caldwell* offers only indirect support for my claim that the responsibility-taking role of the jury should be valued in its own right. I argue, however, that *Caldwell*-like concerns transcend the narrow boundaries of the doctrine itself. As the Court in *Caldwell* observed, death penalty jurisprudence is informed by the assumption that "jurors confronted with the truly awesome responsibility of decreeing death for a fellow human will act with due regard for the consequences of their decision."[98] Capital sentencing need not be understood as unique in this regard. Sentencing a person to prison may lack the finality of death, but that hardly makes it a less than "awesome responsibility"; and one might hope that criminal juries would in general have "due regard for the consequences of their decision[s]."

96. The court's decision was grounded in a belief that "the qualitative difference of death from all other punishments requires a correspondingly greater degree of scrutiny of the capital sentencing determination." *See Caldwell,* 472 U.S. at 329 (quoting California v. Ramos, 463 U.S. 992, 998-99 (1983)).

97. *See* Romano v. Oklahoma, 512 U.S. 1 (1994) ("As Justice O'Connor supplied the fifth vote in *Caldwell* and concurred on grounds narrower than those put forth by the plurality, her position is controlling. Accordingly, we have since read *Caldwell* as 'relevant only to certain types of comment — those that mislead the jury as to its role in the sentencing process in a way that allows the jury to feel less responsible than it should for the sentencing decision.' Thus, '[t]o establish a *Caldwell* violation, a defendant necessarily must show that the remarks to the jury improperly described the role assigned to the jury by local law.'" (citations omitted)). In addition, the doctrine has not been applied retroactively. *See* Sawyer v. Smith, 497 U.S. 227 (1990) (stating that the *Caldwell* rule is not a watershed rule of criminal procedure fundamental to integrity of criminal proceeding and, thus, a prisoner whose murder conviction became final before rule was announced could not use rule to challenge his capital sentence in federal *habeas corpus* action).

98. *Caldwell,* 472 U.S. at 329-30 (quoting McGautha v. California, 402 U.S. 183, 208 (1971)).

C. *Usurpation and Abdication*

In addition to understanding that they have the last word, juries should understand as well that there is no one to whom they can or should defer in determining what that last word should be. Recognizing the responsibility-taking role of the jury may thus help explain judicial resistance to certain forms of expert testimony and scientific evidence. If expert testimony or scientific evidence appears sufficiently authoritative, jurors may be tempted to ease their sense of responsibility for a verdict. I do not mean that jurors will abdicate their decisionmaking function; they still have to decide whose experts to believe. Rather, jurors may evade their responsibility-taking role; they may understand themselves as merely deciding whose experts to believe.

Courts have repeatedly greeted new forms of evidence with concerns that such evidence will usurp the role of the jury. Traditionally, this concern manifested itself in the form of testimonial limitations. Lay witnesses were precluded from offering opinions;[99] and expert witnesses were precluded from testifying to "ultimate issues."[100] While the opinion rule and the ultimate issue rule have been largely abandoned,[101] judicial uneasiness over certain forms of expert testimony persists. For example, courts continue to resist expert testimony on witness credibility, including testimony regarding polygraph results. Contrary to one commentator's assertion that "[t]he objection that an eyewitness expert usurps the jury's role by giving an expert opinion of witness credibility has largely been

99. The opinion rule was a nineteenth-century common law offshoot of the rule requiring witnesses to have personal knowledge. The personal knowledge rule, in turn, traces its history to at least the fifteenth century, with Coke's assertion that it "is not satisfactory for the witness to say that he thinks or persuadeth himself." Rolfe v. Hampden, 73 Eng. Rep. 117, 118 n.15 (K.B. 1622); *see also* Mason Ladd, *Expert Testimony,* 5 VAND. L. REV. 414, 415 (1952); Maury R. Olicker, *The Admissibility of Expert Witness Testimony: Time to Take the Final Leap?,* 42 U. MIAMI L. REV. 831, 835 (1988). For a discussion of the opinion rule, see CHARLES ALAN WRIGHT & VICTOR JAMES GOLD, FEDERAL PRACTICE AND PROCEDURE, FEDERAL RULES OF EVIDENCE § 6252 (1997).

100. The leading case stating the ultimate issue rule was *United States v. Spaulding,* 239 U.S. 498, 506 (1935) (ruling that medical expert testimony that plaintiff was "totally and permanently disabled" was inadmissible because "[t]he experts ought not to have been asked or allowed to state their conclusions on the whole case").

101. For example, Federal Rule of Evidence 701 permits lay witnesses to offer opinions that are "rationally based on the perception of the witness and . . . helpful to a clear understanding of the witness' testimony or the determination of a fact in issue." *See* FED. R. EVID. 701. Federal Rule of Evidence 704 provides that expert testimony "is not objectionable because it embraces an ultimate issue to be decided by the trier of fact." *See* FED. R. EVID. 704(a). An exception to Rule 704 retains the ultimate issue bar as to expert testimony on "whether the defendant [in a criminal case] did or did not have the mental state or condition constituting an element of the crime charged or of a defense thereto." *See* FED. R. EVID. 704(b).

abandoned,"[102] many courts continue to exclude expert testimony about credibility, and on just that basis.[103] Similar concerns have been expressed in the debate over polygraph evidence.[104]

So long as one understands the function of the jury as being solely that of factfinder, however, this concern appears to reduce to nothing more than a mistrust of the jury's ability to evaluate evi-

---

102. Michael R. Leippe, *The Case for Expert Testimony About Eyewitness Memory,* 1 PSYCHOL. PUB. POL'Y. & L. 909, 922 (1995).

103. *See, e.g.,* United States v. Cecil, 836 F.2d 1431, 1439 (4th Cir. 1988) (en banc) ("[A]n opinion on the credibility of a witness by a psychiatrist is not allowable."); United States v. Scop, 846 F.2d 135, 142 (2d Cir. 1988) ("[W]itnesses may not opine as to the credibility of the testimony of other witnesses at the trial."); United States v. Addison, 498 F.2d 741, 744 (D.C. Cir. 1974) (stating that expert scientific evidence "may in some circumstances assume a posture of mystic infallibility in the eyes of a jury of laymen"); United States v. Wertis, 505 F.2d 683, 685 (5th Cir. 1974) (per curiam) (finding opinion of psychiatrist as to whether a witness could distinguish truth from nontruth was "beyond the competence of any witness"); United States v. Barnard, 490 F.2d 907, 912 (9th Cir. 1973) (finding that expert testimony on credibility "may cause juries to surrender their own common sense in weighting testimony"); Washington v. United States, 390 F.2d 444, 451 (D.C. Cir. 1967) ("It has often been argued that in the guise of an expert, the psychiatrist became the thirteenth juror, and unfortunately the most important one."); Commonwealth v. O'Searo, 352 A.2d 30, 32 (Pa. 1976) ("To permit psychological testimony . . . would be an invitation for the trier of fact to abdicate its responsibility to ascertain the facts relying upon the questionable premise that the expert is in a better position to make such a judgment."); Steven I. Friedland, *On Common Sense and The Evaluation of Witness Credibility,* 40 CASE W. RES. L. REV. 165, 195 & n.165 (1990) ("Courts have also excluded expert testimony about credibility as unfairly prejudicial on the ground that the jury will accord it exaggerated importance. The expert would usurp the role of the jury by substituting the conclusions of the expert for the independent conclusions drawn by the lay jurors." (citing United States v. Azure, 801 F.2d 336, 340 (8th Cir. 1986), where the court stated that "putting an impressively qualified expert's stamp of truthfulness on a witness's story goes too far")). Some courts have been more lenient and have held that the admission of such testimony is within the discretion of the trial judge. *See, e.g.,* Bastow v. General Motors Corp., 844 F.2d 506, 510-11 (8th Cir. 1988); *Azure,* 801 F.2d at 339-40; State v. Kim, 645 P.2d 1330, 1339 n.14 (Haw. 1982) ("Essentially, the difference between an opinion as to character for truthfulness and an opinion as to the believability of a witness' [sic] statements is the difference between 'I think X is believable' and 'X's statement is believable.' We feel the admissibility of either statement should not turn on niceties of phraseology but on the probative value of the testimony."); United States v. Pacelli, 521 F.2d 135, 140 (2d Cir. 1975) ("[W]hether or not psychiatric testimony is admissible to impeach the credibility of a witness is within the discretion of the trial judge."). *See generally* 28 WRIGHT & GOLD, FEDERAL PRACTICE AND PROCEDURE, EVIDENCE *supra* note 99, § 6114 (1993).

104. *See, e.g.,* Brown v. Darcy, 783 F.2d 1389, 1396-97 (9th Cir. 1984) (arguing that polygraph evidence "interferes with . . . the deliberative process"); United States v. Alexander, 526 F.2d 161, 168 (8th Cir. 1975) (arguing that polygraph evidence is "likely to be shrouded with an aura of near infallibility"); *Alexander,* 526 F.2d at 168-69, *quoted in* U.S. DEP'T. OF DEFENSE, MANUAL FOR COURTS-MARTIAL 48 (1995) ("To the extent that the polygraph results are accepted as unimpeachable or conclusive by jurors, despite cautionary instructions by the trial judge, the jurors' traditional responsibility to collectively ascertain the facts and adjudge guilt or innocence is preempted."); Dowd v. Calabrese, 585 F. Supp. 430, 434-35 (D.D.C. 1984) (arguing that juries would likely give undue deference to polygraph evidence); State v. Dean, 307 N.W.2d 628, 651-53 (Wis. 1981); Kenneth A. Wittenberg & Kenneth L. Simmons, *Truth or Consequences: The Changing Dynamics of Polygraph Tests,* 58 OR. ST. B. BULL. 23, 24 (1997) ("Those that oppose the use of polygraph exams . . . believe that science usurps the jury's role when it purports to claim which witness is telling the truth."); *see also* David Gallai, *Polygraph Evidence in Federal Courts: Should It Be Admissible?,* 36 AM. CRIM. L. REV. 87, 103 (1999).

dence.[105] Seen in this light, the language of usurpation seems misplaced. Wigmore, for example, maintained that such talk was "a mere bit of empty rhetoric."[106] He argued that no witness can usurp the jury's role because "the jury may still reject his opinion and accept some other view, and no legal power, not even the judge's order, can compel them to accept the witness's opinion against their own."[107] Perhaps the real concern is that juries will be bamboozled — will be overawed by scientific-sounding expert testimony. This fear, however, appears largely unwarranted. For example, research does not support the claim that juries give inordinate weight to expert testimony on credibility.[108] Similarly, evidence suggests that juries would not in fact overestimate the reliability of polygraph evidence.[109]

105. *See* Maury R. Olicker, *The Admissibility of Expert Witness Testimony: Time to Take the Final Leap?*, 42 U. Miami L. Rev. 831, 849 (1988) ("[A]t the heart of the matter, underlying the ultimate issue rule was an assumption that jurors would abdicate their factfinding role to the witness. Judges apparently felt that . . . jurors could easily be led to whatever ultimate conclusion was desired by the proponent of the expert testimony."); Teri Breuer, Note, *The End of* Frye *is the Beginning of Successful Sexual Assault Prosecution,* 2 S. Cal. Rev. L. & Women's Stud. 333, 338 (1992) ("The courts are also concerned with the possibility that the expert would usurp the role of the jury. Courts fear that the jury would substitute the conclusions of the expert for its own independent conclusions, especially as the expert's testimony approached ultimate issues.").

106. 7 John Henry Wigmore, Evidence § 1920, at 18 (James H. Chadbourn ed., rev. ed. 1978).

107. *Id.* § 1920, at 19.

108. *See, e.g.*, Margaret A. Berger, United States v. Scop: *The Common-Law Approach to an Expert's Opinion About a Witness's Credibility Still Does Not Work,* 55 Brook. L. Rev. 559, 604-16 (1989); Charles Robert Honts, *Assessing Children's Credibility: Scientific and Legal Issues in 1994,* 70 N.D. L. Rev. 879, 896 (1994) ("There does not seem to be any reason to suspect that direct expert testimony on child witness credibility will have the magical powers to overwhelm juries that other scientific evidence lacks."). *See generally* Michael W. Mullane, *The Truthsayer and the Court: Expert Testimony on Credibility,* 43 Me. L. Rev. 53 (1991).

109. *See, e.g.*, Ann Cavoukian & Ronald J. Heslegrave, *The Admissibility of Polygraph Evidence in Court: Some Empirical Findings,* 4 Law & Hum. Behav. 117 (1980); Charles R. Honts & Mary V. Perry, *Polygraph Admissibility: Changes and Challenges,* 16 Law & Hum. Behav. 357, 366 (1992) ("Studies tend to show that juries are more inclined not to give extraordinary weight to polygraph evidence."); James R. McCall, *Misconceptions and Reevaluation — Polygraph Admissibility After* Rock *and* Daubert, 1996 U. Ill. L. Rev. 363, 375-77 (1996) ("[R]ecent studies suggest that jurors do not give polygraph results disproportionate weight."); *see also* United States v. Piccinonna, 885 F.2d 1529, 1533 & n.14 (11th Cir. 1989) (en banc) (citing Stephen C. Carlson et al., *The Effect of Lie Detector Evidence on Jury Deliberations: An Empirical Study,* 5 J. Police Sci. & Admin. 148 (1977) for the proposition that many studies refute contention that jurors give disproportionate weight to polygraph evidence); Alan Markwart & Brian E. Lynch, *The Effect of Polygraph Evidence on Mock Jury Decision-Making,* 7 J. Police Sci. & Admin. 324 (1979); Robert A. Peters, *A Survey of Polygraph Evidence in Criminal Trials,* 68 A.B.A. J. 162 (1982)). *See generally* 1 Paul C. Giannelli & Edward J. Imwinkelried, Scientific Evidence 520 (2d ed. 1993) (arguing that "the clear weight of the available hard data calls into question the assumption . . . that scientific evidence overwhelms the typical lay juror").

Yet one need not dismiss concerns about expert testimony as mere judicial mistrust of the jury. Assume that jurors are in no way overwhelmed or bamboozled by expert testimony — that they still decide the case themselves. The jurors then may come to understand themselves as doing that and no more. If jurors understand the question before them to be merely "whose experts do you believe," they may be less likely to confront — to feel truly responsible for — the act of judgment that follows from choosing to believe the State's witnesses.[110] If juries are to feel responsible for verdicts, they must see themselves as participants rather than commentators. Doing, not deciding, implicates the conscience. Even if expert testimony cannot usurp the jury's decisionmaking role, it may put at risk the jury's responsibility-taking function by allowing jurors to understand themselves as merely deferring to authority. "Abdication" might be a more accurate term than "usurpation," for the risk is not in what the experts will take, but in what the jurors might too willingly let go — the sense of personal responsibility for judgments.

I am not prepared to argue that expert testimony should be excluded in order to make sure juries feel responsible for verdicts. My particular claim regarding expert testimony is more modest, and is explanatory rather than prescriptive. I merely suggest that recognizing the jury's responsibility-taking role may shed light on judicial discomfort with the ever-increasing role of expert witnesses in the courtroom.

D. *The Uncertain Status of Jury Nullification*

Few matters related to the criminal trial jury have received as much attention lately as the question of jury nullification.[111] When,

110. Charles Nesson offers a related explanation for judicial resistance to statistical evidence. Nesson argues that effective deterrence depends upon verdicts that the public will view "as statements about what [actually] happened," rather than as statements about the evidence presented at trial. *See* Nesson, *supra* note 4, at 1367. Similarly, the jury's responsibility-taking function demands that they not understand themselves as merely deciding which expert to believe.

111. A sample of recent law review literature focusing entirely or in part on nullification would include: Darryl K. Brown, *Nullification Within the Rule of Law,* 81 MINN. L. REV. 1149 (1997) (arguing that "in contrast with prevailing assumptions about nullification by both its supporters and detractors, . . . nullification can, and in many contexts does, occur within the rule of law rather than subvert it."); Paul Butler, *Racially Based Jury Nullification: Black Power in the Criminal Justice System,* 105 YALE L.J. 677 (1995); David N. Dorfman & Chris K. Iijima, *Fictions, Fault, and Forgiveness: Jury Nullification in a New Context,* 28 U. MICH. J.L. REF. 861 (1995); James Joseph Duane, *Jury Nullification: The Top Secret Constitutional Right,* LITIGATION, Summer 1996, at 6; David Farnham, *Jury Nullification: History Proves It's Not a New Idea,* CRIM. JUST., Winter 1997, at 4; Robert E. Korroch & Michael J. Davidson, *Jury Nullification: A Call for Justice or an Invitation to Anarchy?,* 139 MIL. L. REV. 133 n.16 (1993); Andrew D. Leipold, *The Dangers of Race-Based Jury Nullification: A Response to Professor Butler,* 44 U.C. LOS ANGELES L. REV. 109 (1996) (arguing, among other things,

if ever, can or should juries refuse to convict despite the fact that the law appears to warrant a conviction? The arguments on this issue are contentious and energetic, and often conflate issues which might helpfully be distinguished. As noted above, there is substantial uncertainty regarding the empirical question of how rare or frequent nullification actually is.[112] Beyond that, there are debates regarding the legal status of nullification. Is it a right?[113] An extra-legal power?[114] An unlawful practice?[115] These arguments are often tied to underlying disputes over the desirability or normative status of nullification. Do we call to mind the brave Massachusetts jurors of a century and a half ago who refused to convict under the fugitive slave laws? Or do we envision white Southern juries refusing to convict those guilty of lynching blacks?

Without intending to slight the complexity of these debates, my aim here is neither to catalogue nor to adjudicate between them. Instead, I focus on a particular puzzle which appears to underlie arguments about the legal and normative status of nullification. The puzzle is this. On one hand, courts work very hard to prevent jurors from nullifying. At the same time, however, courts are equally energetic in preserving an array of procedural rules and practices which seem calculated to preserve the jury's power to nullify. Recognizing the jury's responsibility-taking role helps reconcile the apparent contradiction.

The key is that responsibility depends upon an awareness of choice. If jurors did not have the power to acquit, they could not and would feel a sense of responsibility for or agency in convictions. The power to nullify thus plays a role which does not depend on an argument that that power should ever be utilized. We hope that juries will convict when convictions are warranted. The criminal justice system depends upon their doing so. We hope that juries will follow instructions, but we do not want for them to understand themselves as "just following orders." If the jury is to perform the

that race-based jury nullification subverts the rule of law and will ultimately rebound to the detriment of the very minority groups which appear to be short term beneficiaries); Andrew D. Leipold, *Rethinking Jury Nullification,* 82 VA. L. REV. 253 (1996); Alan W. Scheflin & Jon M. Van Dyke, *Merciful Juries: The Resilience of Jury Nullification,* 48 WASH. & LEE L. REV. 165, 175 (1991) (describing grass roots support for nullification and claiming that "[t]he jury nullification movement is more active now than at any previous period"); Weinstein, *supra* note 61, at 240 ("When juries refuse to convict on the basis of what they think are unjust laws, they are performing their duty as jurors.").

112. *See supra* notes 59-61, and accompanying text.

113. *See* Duane, *supra* note 111, at 6.

114. *See* Butler, *supra* note 111; Dorfman & Iijima, *supra* note 111.

115. *See* Korroch & Davidson, *supra* note 111, at 133 n.16; Leipold, *supra* note 111.

responsibility-taking role described above, jurors need to know that they are being asked, rather than forced, to convict when the law so warrants.

In order to highlight the potential incongruity, I again make the simplifying assumption that nullification is generally undesirable. I do not suggest that the issue is simply a binary question of "desirable" v. "undesirable." Much less do I intend to dismiss arguments in favor of nullification.[116] Rather, the assumption is warranted as a matter of argument simply because courts continue to behave as if nullification were a thing to be avoided. The courts have come down firmly against efforts to describe nullification as a right rather than a power.[117] Similarly, courts have rejected efforts by defendants to have juries instructed as to their nullification power.[118] The

116. In particular, I readily recognize that nullification is not without its supporters. On the popular front, an energetic group based in rural Montana (but operating nationwide), known as the Fully Informed Jury Association, goes so far as to hand out pamphlets to potential jurors outside of courtrooms. The pamphlets advocate nullification and "inform" jurors they "cannot be forced to obey a 'jurors oath.'" *See* Frederic B. Rogers, *The Jury in Revolt? A "Heads Up" on the Fully Informed Jury Association Coming Soon to a Courthouse in Your Area,* JUDGES J., Summer 1996, at 10, 11. Although the Fully Informed Jury Association appears to be a fringe group, nullification has found support within the mainstream. *See* Rogers, *supra,* at 10 ("[T]he Fully Informed Jury Association is led by its national coordinator, Don Doig, of Helmville [Montana], population 26. Its antecedents are in the radical anti-Semitic right and the writings of militia activist M.J. "Red" Beckman."); *see also* Erick J. Haynie, Comment, *Populism, Free Speech, and the Rule of Law: The "Fully Informed" Jury Movement and Its Implications,* 88 J. CRIM. L. & CRIMINOLOGY 343 (1997). For example, former federal prosecutor and current law professor Paul Butler has argued that, in light of the discriminatory and utterly ineffective manner in which drug laws are drafted and enforced, black jurors would be justified in refusing to convict blacks accused of nonviolent drug crimes. *See* Butler, *supra* note 111.

Less notorious, but no less thought provoking, are the arguments mounted by James Duane. *See* Duane, *supra* note 111, at 6. Duane has argued that the Sixth Amendment, the Double Jeopardy Clause, and a history of judicial deference to jury verdicts all suggest that juries should be informed not only of their *power* to nullify, but also of their right to do so. Duane is careful to disavow the straw man claim that juries should be encouraged to disregard the courts' instruction for whatever reason they choose. Instead, his claim is that juries have a well-established and long-recognized right to acquit for the specific purpose of lenity — to inject "a slack into the enforcement of the law, tempering its rigor by the mollifying influence of current ethical conventions." *Id.* at 9 (quoting United States *ex rel.* McCann v. Adams, 126 F.2d 774, 775-76 (2d Cir. 1942)); *see also* Brown, *supra* note 111; Farnham, *supra* note 111.

117. *See, e.g.,* Strickland v. Washington, 466 U.S. 668, 695, (1984) (describing nullification as a "lawless decision"); United States v. Perez, 86 F.3d 735, 736 (7th Cir. 1996) (describing jury nullification as "lawless"); United States v. Sepulveda, 15 F.3d 1161, 1190 (1st Cir. 1993) (describing nullification as moments when juries "choose to flex their muscles, ignoring both law and evidence"); United States v. Dellinger, 472 F.2d 340, 408 (7th Cir. 1972) (citing Sparf v. U.S., 156 U.S. 51, 106 (1895), which held that "[t]he principle . . . that it is the duty of the jury to apply the law as declared by the court (notwithstanding the finality of an acquittal inconsistent with the law, and the resulting 'pardoning power' of the jury) was firmly established by the Supreme Court").

118. *See, e.g., Sepulveda,* 15 F.3d at 1190 (holding that courts are to "instruct the jury on the dimensions of their duty to the exclusion of jury nullification"); United States v. Krzyske, 836 F.2d 1013, 1021 (6th Cir. 1988) (approving trial court's refusal to give nullification in-

courts may be wrong, but for the time being they refuse to encourage or applaud jury nullification.

This seems all well and good until one reflects upon the wide array of ways in which the courts have made sure juries retain this power (which they have no right to use and which they should not be told about). For example, directed verdicts are prohibited in criminal cases, regardless of the weight of the evidence.[119] As a consequence, appellate courts are not permitted to take judicial notice of facts, however undisputed, that are necessary to a conviction.[120] Special verdicts as well are disfavored in criminal cases, out of a concern that requiring juries to explain their verdicts will limit their ability simply to acquit.[121]

---

struction and statement to jury that "valid jury nullification" does not exist); United States v. Trujillo, 714 F.2d 102, 105-06 (11th Cir. 1983) (stating that jury instructions on nullification would invite juries to disregard the law).

119. *See* Sandstrom v. Montana, 442 U.S. 510, 516 n.5 (1979) (holding that the Constitution bars directed verdicts against defendants in criminal cases regardless of strength of State's evidence); *see also* Gregg v. Georgia, 428 U.S. 153, 200 n.5 (1976) (finding directed verdict to be "totally alien to our notions of criminal justice [because] the discretionary act of jury nullification would not be permitted").

120. *See, e.g.,* FED. R. EVID. 201(g); United States v. Jones, 580 F.2d 219 (6th Cir. 1978) (holding appellate court was not permitted to take judicial notice of undisputed fact that South Central Bell Telephone Company was "a common carrier . . . providing or operating . . . facilities for the transmission of interstate or foreign communications" (citations omitted)). This rule has been roundly and justifiably criticized on the grounds that it amounts to the following claim: appellate courts should not take notice of any fact necessary to a conviction, however undisputed, because of the possibility that the jury, which decided *not* to acquit, might have acquitted if presented with the possibility of using a patently false finding — e.g., that the telephone company is not a common carrier — as a hook for that acquittal, despite the fact that, if the jury had decided to acquit, no explanation for nullification could or would have been required. *See* 10 JAMES WM. MOORE ET AL., MOORE'S FEDERAL PRACTICE § 201.70 (2d ed. 1996).

121. *See, e.g.,* United States v. Ellis, 168 F.3d 558, 562 (1st Cir. 1999); United States v. Shelton, 588 F.2d 1242, 1251 (9th Cir. 1978), *cert. denied,* 442 U.S. 909 (1979); *see also* WAYNE R. LAFAVE & JEROLD H. ISRAEL, CRIMINAL PROCEDURE § 24.7a, at 1050 (2d ed. 1992) (noting that special verdicts in criminal cases are "not favored"); 3 CHARLES ALAN WRIGHT, FEDERAL PRACTICE AND PROCEDURE: FEDERAL RULES OF CRIMINAL PROCEDURE § 512 n.5 (2d ed. 1982) ("The rule against special verdicts in criminal cases is nothing more nor less than a recognition of the principle that 'the jury, as conscience of the community, must be permitted to look at more than logic.'" (citing United States v. Spock, 416 F.2d 165, 182 (1st Cir. 1969))); Eric L. Muller, *The Hobgoblin of Little Minds? Our Foolish Law of Inconsistent Verdicts,* 111 HARV. L. REV. 771, 835 (1998) ("Courts have resisted special verdicts in criminal cases precisely because such verdicts would endanger the jury's capacity to be merciful." (citing United States v. Ruggiero, 726 F.2d 913, 927 (2d Cir. 1984) (Newman, J., concurring in part and dissenting in part)). For cases dealing with concerns regarding special verdicts, see United States v. Desmond, 670 F.2d 414, 416-18 (3d Cir. 1982); United States v. Wilson, 629 F.2d 439, 443 (6th Cir. 1980); and *Spock,* 416 F.2d at 182. There are, however, cases in which special verdicts in criminal cases are considered appropriate. *See* United States v. Melvin, 27 F.3d 710, 716 (1st Cir. 1994) (holding that trial court may use a special verdict in certain entrapment cases). There are even cases in which such verdicts are required. *See* FED. R. CRIM. PROC. 31(e) for an example of requiring special verdicts in certain criminal forfeiture cases.

Why work so hard to protect a power if we do not want it to be used? If jurors are obligated and expected to follow instructions, why is their power to do otherwise considered so important? One answer may lie in jury's responsibility-taking role. Without the possibility of nullification, juror agency would be vitiated. Unless they could refuse to convict, jurors will not feel responsible for convictions. On this reading, it is the possibility, rather than the event, of nullification that matters. Nullification is a risk we must bear if we want jurors to feel agency. When, therefore, courts protect the jury's nullification power while at the same time refusing to endorse nullification, it is not necessary to accuse them of hypocrisy or confusion. Nor is it necessary to accuse (or credit) the courts with encouraging nullification. Recognizing the jury's responsibility-taking function offers an explanation for why we might well desire to protect a power even if we hope it is never used.

V. Engendering Jury Responsibility

What follows? If courage of the sort I have described is worth having, and the jury is in fact one institution through which this form of courage might be displayed, what concrete aspects of jury decisionmaking can contribute to the jury's ability to perform this role? In this Part, I make four recommendations. Two will be relatively uncontroversial: first, juries ought to be as representative as possible; second, criminal juries ought to be required to turn in unanimous verdicts. My third recommendation will be less readily embraced: juries ought to know what punishment will follow a conviction. My final recommendation is more tentative and might be difficult to apply without unduly risking the jury's decisionmaking function: juries ought to be instructed in such a way as to impress upon them their agency in bringing about the consequences of a conviction.

A. *Jury Representativeness*

The most straightforward implication of my claim is that juries ought to be drawn from a true cross-section of the community. Granted, one need not reimagine the jury in order to generate arguments on behalf of representativeness. For example, it has been argued that making juries more representative will reduce bias, facilitate deliberation, enhance the public acceptability of verdicts, and inject differing viewpoints into the criminal justice system.[122] The United States Supreme Court has systematically invalidated practices of exclusionary jury selection.[123] In general, the history of the criminal jury in America reveals an inexorable, if yet unfinished, march towards inclusiveness.[124] Recognizing the jury's responsibility-taking function, however, does put an interesting twist on the matter. While many arguments for jury representativeness hinge on a desire to ensure that those at the margins of society are not excluded, my concern here is that those in the mainstream not be permitted to exclude themselves.

Throughout this article I refer to juries and jurors in the third person, as I argue that "they" ought to feel responsibility for and acknowledge agency in judgments made on behalf of the community. I should emphasize, however, that they are us. I am not advocating that jurors as some separate and identifiable subset of the population are the appropriate people to take responsibility for troubling judgments. Rather, my claim is that ideally all of us would acknowledge that agency. This being impractical, we should take turns. The jury is the institution through which we, as jurors, acknowledge responsibility for what we, as members of the community, find it necessary or appropriate to do. Accordingly, my claim both depends upon and provides an argument for jury representativeness.

If the jury is to function as an institution through which we take turns acknowledging agency, rather than as a method of asking some subset of the population to do so on our behalf, all those who would seek to influence the content of the law ought to be willing as well to accept responsibility for the consequences of the law. For this reason, it seems appropriate that all registered voters should be required to serve on criminal juries from time to time. I do not

---

122. *See, e.g.*, Edward S. Adams & Christian J. Lane, *Constructing a Jury That Is Both Impartial and Representative: Utilizing Cumulative Voting in Jury Selection*, 73 N.Y.U. L. REV. 703 (1998); Andrew G. Deiss, *Negotiating Justice: The Criminal Trial Jury in a Pluralist America*, 3 U. CHI. L. SCH. ROUNDTABLE 323 (1996); Nancy J. King, *The Effects of Race-Conscious Jury Selection on Public Confidence in the Fairness of Jury Proceedings: An Empirical Puzzle*, 31 AM. CRIM. L. REV. 1177 (1994); Kenneth S. Klein, *Unpacking the Jury Box*, 47 HASTINGS L.J. 1325 (1996); Anne Bowen Poulin, *The Jury: The Criminal Justice System's Different Voice*, 62 U. CIN. L. REV. 1377 (1994).

123. *See, e.g.*, J.E.B. v. Alabama *ex rel.* T.B., 511 U.S. 127 (1994) (invalidating preemptory challenges based on gender); Vasquez v. Hillery, 474 U.S. 254 (1986) (holding exclusionary practices in grand jury selection not remedied by subsequent fair trial untainted by racial discrimination); Batson v. Kentucky, 476 U.S. 79 (1986) (invalidating racially discriminatory jury selection practices); *see also* James H. Coleman, *The Evolution of Race in the Jury Selection Process*, 48 RUTGERS L. REV. 1105 (1996).

124. *See* Alschuler & Deiss, *supra* note 15.

mean that jury service should be limited to registered voters. On the contrary, all should serve. My claim is that those who would fancy themselves lawmakers ought as well to take a turn as responsibility takers.

It will perhaps be objected that laws are most often made not by the people directly, but by legislatures. As a result, one might argue that those laws may or may not reflect the actual desires of the people themselves. Perhaps it is unfair to ask us to take responsibility for what they have decided. Perhaps the people should be asked to take direct responsibility for only those laws which they have directly endorsed through referenda or initiatives.

To this I have two responses. First of all, it may be unwarranted to claim that legislative decisions are less representative of popular will than are direct democratic outcomes. As I have argued elsewhere, neither direct democracy nor representation is capable of producing results unambiguously describable as the will of the people.[125] More to the point, it should not matter what processes we as a people have decided to employ in the construction of our criminal law. It remains our law. The democratic project depends upon the premise that rules generated through certain agreed-upon processes are fairly attributable to the whole. We have agreed to call our own those laws made by processes into which we are each given fair and equal input. Each of us is required to follow laws we did not vote for. Beyond that, each of us as jurors is asked to enforce laws we did not vote for. It seems equally fair, and equally a consequence of democratic politics, that we each be asked to accept responsibility for those laws.

I embrace, however, the connection between democratic politics and the jury's responsibility-taking role. On one view of the jury, the institution is understood as protecting against the illegitimate exercise of state force. Juries, on this reading, must serve as the conscience of the community in order to protect defendants against arbitrary and unwarranted prosecution. On my terms, however, the jury's role as the passive, responsibility-taking conscience of the community is equally important, and perhaps more fairly imposed upon jurors, to the extent that the power being exercised is legitimate. The clearer it is that a law has the support of the people, the fairer it is to ask the people to take responsibility for that law's consequences.

125. *See* Sherman J. Clark, *A Populist Critique of Direct Democracy,* 112 HARV. L. REV. 434 (1998).

This does not mean that the jury's responsibility-taking function should be modulated according to the perceived legitimacy of each law. As I have argued, it is our law, like it or not. Rather, the connection between legitimacy and responsibility suggests that each should be maximized independently. Both our lawmaking and our responsibility-taking institutions should be as broadly representative as possible.

B. *The Unanimity Requirement*

A juror is unlikely to feel truly responsible for a conviction unless he or she understands that the verdict depends upon his or her agreement. Put more strongly, no juror will feel truly responsible for a criminal conviction if that juror feels that the defendant would have been convicted with or without his or her concurrence. For this reason, the jury's responsibility-taking function is best facilitated by requiring that criminal trial juries return unanimous verdicts.

American courts for the most part require unanimous verdicts for criminal convictions. In 1972, the United States Supreme Court held that unanimous verdicts are not constitutionally required and that 10-2 or 9-3 verdicts would suffice to perform the essential function of the criminal jury; but unanimity remains the overwhelming norm.[126] The unanimity requirement has been explained or defended on several grounds. Traditionally, it has been argued that only by requiring unanimous verdicts can criminal trials adequately protect defendants from the power of the state.[127] Recently, theorists have emphasized the deliberative and representative functions of the jury and argued that the requirement of unanimity forces jurors to talk to one another and to take into consideration the opinions and perspectives of the other jurors.[128]

Justice Kennedy, concurring in *McKoy v. North Carolina,* expressed a combination of these concerns and connected them to the idea of community conscience, when he noted that the unanimity requirement "is an accepted, vital mechanism to ensure that real

126. *See* Johnson v. Louisiana, 406 U.S. 356 (1972). To date, only Louisiana and Oregon permit criminal convictions by less than unanimous verdicts.

127. *See, e.g.,* Thompson v. Utah, 170 U.S. 343, 353 (1898) ("The wise men who framed the Constitution of the United States were of [the] opinion that life and liberty, when involved in criminal prosecutions, would not be adequately secured except through the unanimous verdict of twelve jurors."), *quoted in* JEFFREY ABRAMSON, WE THE JURY 179 (1994).

128. *See, e.g.,* ABRAMSON, *supra* note 127, at 191-96; REID HASTIE ET AL., INSIDE THE JURY 173-74 (1983).

and full deliberation occurs in the jury room, and that the jury's ultimate decision will reflect the conscience of the community."[129]

The *McKoy* case involved the requirement of unanimity on the part of juries making capital sentencing recommendations. In the same context, the North Carolina Supreme Court has recognized the role played by the unanimity requirement in preventing jurors from avoiding their responsibility to make difficult decisions: "[T]he jury unanimity requirement prevents the jury from evading its duty to make a sentence recommendation. If jury unanimity is not required, then a jury that was uncomfortable in deciding life and death issues simply could 'agree to disagree' and escape its duty to render a decision."[130] In addition to forcing juries to make difficult decisions in the context of sentencing recommendations, where avoiding the decision entirely might seem possible, I suggest that unanimity also plays a role in ensuring that each juror confronts his or her own "but-for" agency in that decision.

Take the easy case first. Imagine a scenario in which 10-2 would suffice for a conviction, but the verdict is in fact unanimous or 11-1. In such a case, each convicting juror would reasonably believe that his or her vote was not in fact necessary for the conviction. Each juror might believe that the defendant would have been convicted with or without that juror's vote. Granted, some jurors might be mistaken in this belief. For example, an influential juror's willingness to convict might sway others, in which case that juror might well have been a but-for cause of the conviction. Nonetheless, it is easy to see how jurors on a jury with "extra" votes for conviction might be able to ease their own sense of agency in the verdict.

But what about verdicts that come in "on the number," with precisely the ten votes needed for conviction? In those cases, it might seem that at least the convicting jurors would feel agency — would know that the verdict did in fact depend upon their concurrence. Maybe. It is entirely possible, however, that even the juror casting the critical tenth vote would be able to escape acknowledging agency in the verdict. For a convicting juror to feel full responsibility for the conviction, he or she would need to be convinced that neither of the two holdouts could have ever been persuaded to vote for a conviction. The tenth juror, indeed each convicting juror, might well believe that one of the holdouts would have given in eventually. If so, he or she would understand his concurrence not

129. 494 U.S. 433, 452 (1990).

130. State v. McCarver, 462 S.E.2d 25, 39 (N.C. 1995).

as a but-for cause of the conviction, but merely as a concession to the inevitable.

Indeed, that tenth juror would probably be right. Research suggests that nine out of ten verdicts, even where unanimity is required, eventually go the way of the initial poll.[131] Holdouts eventually go along with the majority. It is not clear whether this is a consequence of reasoned deliberation, as one might hope, or a result of pure exhaustion or pressure. It remains the case, however, that a juror casting the tenth and deciding vote in a 10-2 regime would have every reason to expect that if he or she did not give in, someone else would. Accordingly, only unanimity can ensure a sense of agency.

Agency is an individual, rather than a group, experience. The Supreme Court of California called attention to this reality in the context of reviewing jury instructions which, like those described above, asked the jury to serve as the conscience of the community. The court noted that "[t]o the extent that the proposed instructions intimate that the jury must reach such decision in accordance with the community conscience, they are incorrect. The verdict must express the individual conscience of each juror."[132]

Conscience is like that. While it reflects and emerges from collective identity, it works only upon the individual — the mob having, as the saying goes, none at all. For juries to take responsibility on the community's behalf, jurors, as individuals, must do so. And for any juror to feel truly responsible for a verdict, he or she needs to understand that he or she could have hung the thing.

C. *Punishment*

Juries cannot take responsibility, on the community's behalf, for what we as a community are required to do, unless they know what we are doing. If the jury is to be the forum in which each of us takes a turn confronting and acknowledging agency in troubling judgments, jurors must understand what those judgments are. I have argued above that for juries to serve their responsibility-taking function, they must understand themselves as participants rather

131. *See* KALVEN & ZEISEL, *supra* note 4, at 488 ("[W]here there is an initial majority either for conviction or for acquittal, the jury in roughly nine out of ten cases decides in the direction of the initial majority."); *see also* JEFFREY T. FREDERICK, THE PSYCHOLOGY OF THE AMERICAN JURY 286-87 (1987); MICHAEL J. SAKS, JURY VERDICTS: THE ROLE OF GROUP SIZE AND SOCIAL DECISION RULE 94 (1977); *cf.* HASTIE ET AL., *supra* note 128, at 99-106 & 103 tbl. 6.2.

132. People v. Harrison, 381 P.2d 665, 671 (Cal. 1963) (noting further that "[y]our verdict must express the individual opinion of each juror" (quoting trial court's jury instructions)).

than as commentators. While the jury's primary role is to figure out what happened, jurors cannot, if they are to feel agency in the judgment, understand themselves as doing that and nothing more. They must recognize as well that they are determining what will happen next. Juries should know what will happen to a defendant if they convict. Juries should be instructed as to what punishment, or what possible range of punishments, will be imposed in the event of a conviction.

This argument, I recognize, runs counter to current doctrine. In cases in which juries play no role in sentencing, jurors are generally not informed as to what punishment will likely attend a conviction.[133] The rationale for this practice was neatly captured by the United States Supreme Court, in *Shannon v. United States*, in which the Court observed that "providing jurors sentencing information invites them to ponder matters not within their province, distracts them from their factfinding responsibilities, and creates a strong possibility of confusion."[134] As the Court recognized, "[t]he principle that juries are not to consider the consequences of their verdicts is a reflection of the basic division of labor in our legal system between judge and jury."[135] In most categories of noncapital cases, juries convict and judges sentence. The Court elaborated as follows:

> The jury's function is to find the facts and to decide whether, on those facts, the defendant is guilty of the crime charged. The judge, by contrast, imposes sentence on the defendant after the jury has arrived at a guilty verdict. Information regarding the consequences of a verdict is therefore irrelevant to the jury's task.[136]

The operating assumption here is that factfinding is the jury's sole function. In this light, information regarding sentencing does

133. *See, e.g.*, Shannon v. United States, 512 U.S. 573, 579 (1994); *see also* United States v. Richardson, 130 F.3d 765, 778 (7th Cir. 1997) ("Curry contends that, given his culpability and the severity of the sentence he was facing, he should have been allowed to tell the jury of his possible punishment during closing argument. Unfortunately for him, arguing punishment to a jury is taboo . . . ."), *revd. on other grounds*, 119 S. Ct. 1707 (1999); United States v. Lewis, 110 F.3d 417, 422 (7th Cir.) ("In [defendant's] trial, the jury had no sentencing function, and no statute required that the jury be informed of the consequences of the verdict. The district court correctly refused to allow [the defendant] to argue about his potential punishment."), *cert. denied*, 522 U.S. 854 (1997). Juries are, of course permitted to consider punishment when, as in capital cases, sentencing is part of the jury's doctrinal function. *See, e.g.*, Mahaffey v. Page, 151 F.3d 671, 684 (7th Cir. 1997) (rejecting a claim of ineffective assistance of counsel and noting that "Mahaffey's counsel presented a coherent closing argument to the jury . . . . [He] discussed the nature of punishment and argued that the jury should act mercifully and not be responsible for an individual's death"), *revd. in part on other grounds*, 162 F.3d 481 (1998), *cert. denied*, 119 S. Ct. 1786 (1999).

134. *Shannon*, 512 U.S. at 579.

135. *Shannon*, 512 U.S. at 579.

136. *Shannon*, 512 U.S. at 579.

appear "irrelevant to the jury's task."[137] If, however, the jury is not merely making decisions but is also being asked to take responsibility for those decisions, sentencing information emerges as not only relevant but essential. Juries cannot take responsibility for what they do if they do not know what they are doing.

Given that a refusal to provide juries with sentencing information is a consequence or manifestation of the judicial division of labor, through which juries convict and judges sentence, it is worth looking more closely at that division. It appears that the bifurcation of criminal trials in this way is itself partially explainable as a response to the very perplexity of judgment that I am arguing we as a community ought to confront. As Thomas Green has observed, this "phenomenon of bifurcation is a central feature of the approach we take to the criminal law, one of those developments that tell us a great deal about who we are, or what we seek to be."[138] On Green's reading, this long-standing split between conviction and sentencing was deepened and entrenched during the Progressive Era in response to our deep uncertainty regarding free will. At trial, the jury would determine guilt or innocence according to traditional, generally accepted notions of personal responsibility. At the sentencing phase, however, judges were to consider more individualized, explanatory, or mitigating factors such as the "defendant's background, upbringing, associates, and so on — matters rarely formally admissible during the trial . . . ."[139]

In this way the bifurcation of the trial process allows us, so long as we do not examine the matter too closely, to understand ourselves as both a community that believes in holding people responsible for their actions *and* a progressive community that recognizes and appreciates the influences of upbringing, environment, and similar individualized considerations, on human behavior. Unfortunately, this same bifurcation, depending upon how it is implemented, might say something else about us as well — something substantially less flattering "about who we are, or what we seek to be."[140] Ironically, a method developed in part to help us deal fairly with the problem of judgment is now employed to help us avoid confronting that problem.

Consider the concrete circumstances under which defendants might most want juries to have sentencing information. The dif-

137. *Shannon,* 512 U.S. at 579.

138. Green, *supra* note 37, at 1923.

139. *See id.* at 1923-25.

140. *Id.* at 1923.

ficulty arises when the punishment a defendant will receive if convicted is substantially more harsh than the jury might reasonably expect. The paradigmatic cases arise under "three strikes" statutes, which mandate dramatically increased sentences for defendants with prior felony convictions. In such cases, it is feared that juries will refuse to convict if informed of the extended sentence that will accompany conviction for what may seem to the jury a relatively minor offense.[141]

In these contexts, talk about juries being "confused" appears somewhat misleading, if not disingenuous. Jurors asked to sentence a person to life in prison for holding an ounce of marijuana would not be confused — they would be unwilling. They would be understandably hesitant to look a man or woman in the eye and take responsibility for imposing what appears to be a disproportionate punishment. Seen in its best light, concealing from jurors the consequences of their decisions might be described as a precommitment strategy — a way of protecting against the possibility that people will shrink from a difficult task. But what a cowardly strategy it is. In order to ensure that we do not blink when called upon to do a difficult task, we contrive to do the job with our eyes closed entirely.

The problem is not juror confusion but community cowardice. Administering a troubling three-strikes statute through the medium of blinkered juries represents an ignoble, if cleverly designed, method of assigning responsibility without anyone ever having to take responsibility for that assignment.[142] If we as a community truly feel it is appropriate to sentence a person to life in prison for any third felony conviction, we should be willing to look that person in the eye and say so. What we should not do is assign this difficult and perplexing task to those who know not what they do.

141. An interesting variation on this theme occurs when the punishment a defendant will receive is less than what the jury might expect. In *State v. Short,* 618 A.2d 316, 321-23 (N.J. 1993), a murder case, the Supreme Court of New Jersey held that the jury should not have been informed that if the jury found defendant guilty of the lesser-included offense of manslaughter, he would be acquitted because the statute of limitations had run as to that offense. The court reasoned that, given that information, the jury might bring in a murder conviction even if they felt that only manslaughter was warranted.

142. Paul Robinson has argued that three-strikes statutes, as well as other similar sentencing policies, are not really about assigning responsibility, but in fact methods of achieving incapacitation — responses not to individual desert but to perceived future dangerousness. Paul H. Robinson, Punishing Dangerousness: Cloaking Preventive Detention as Criminal Justice (unpublished manuscript). Assuming Robinson is correct, my argument remains. Whatever we hope to accomplish through the imposition of criminal sentences, we ought to be able to acknowledge our own agency in imposing those sentences.

D. *A "Responsibility Instruction"*

As I have argued above in attempting to look at the ongoing debate over jury nullification through the lens provided by the notions of responsibility-taking and decisionmaking, coercion subverts agency. If juries are to stand in for the community in taking responsibility for convictions, they should not feel that they are being coerced. Juries ought to understand that they are being asked, rather than required, to perform a difficult and important task. We as a community want juries to convict when the evidence warrants; we need for them to do so. But if juries are to feel responsible for convictions, they need to understand that they have the power not to convict. We need for juries to follow instructions, but we ought to hope as well that they do not understand themselves as "just following orders."

This does not mean that jury instructions should advocate or even suggest nullification. Nor do I argue that juries have a right to nullify. I am not talking about rights, but about obligations and agency. Consider the following possible jury instruction:

> Ladies and gentlemen, you are called upon to perform a difficult and important job. First of all, you are being asked to decide whether the State has proven beyond a reasonable doubt that the defendant did in fact commit the crime for which he is charged. If you determine that the State has not met this burden, you are to acquit the defendant and set him free. If you decide that the State has in fact proven beyond a reasonable doubt that the defendant committed this crime, your responsibility is to convict.
>
> In performing this difficult and important job, each of you should understand that the responsibility for this decision is entirely yours and that you will not be required to explain or justify your verdict except to your own conscience. If you acquit this defendant, he will go free today. If you convict, I will sentence him to _____ [as required by federal law] or _____ [depending upon my analysis of mitigating factors]. I am aware that this is a terrible burden that you are asked to bear on behalf of your community. But our system depends upon each of us taking a turn, serving on juries, and bearing that burden as honestly, fairly, and bravely as we can.

It seems to me that such an instruction might fix responsibility without unduly encouraging nullification.

As I have acknowledged, measures that serve to increase jurors' sense of responsibility present the risk that we might put too much weight on the shoulders of the jury. By continuing to require unanimity from criminal trial juries, by making juries aware of the punishment that will accompany a conviction, and by making sure they understand that no one will question them if they acquit, we increase the chance that juries will simply refuse to convict — that they will nullify. Perhaps a responsibility instruction would increase this risk unacceptably. Jurors made too vividly aware of their own agency and responsibility might lack the courage to convict. In the end, we cannot hope to express more courage than we have — to describe ourselves as braver than we are.

VI. Conclusion

Plato argued that responsibility for the conviction of criminals, and for the resolution of at least some civil suits, ought to rest with laymen rather than with professional judges:

> In the judgment of offences against the state, the people ought to participate, for when any one wrongs the state all are wronged, and may reasonably complain if they are not allowed to share in the decision. . . . And in private suits, too, as far as is possible, all should have a share; for he who has no share in the administration of justice, is apt to imagine that he has no share in the state at all.[143]

To this I would add that when the State judges a wrongdoer, all judge and might reasonably be asked to acknowledge responsibility for that judgment, for he who feels no responsibility for the administration of justice is apt to feel that he has no responsibility for the State at all.

I cannot prove that if we allow ourselves to become a cowardly society we will slip into cruelty. Much less do I claim that accepting agency in assignments of blame is the best or only way to display courage. I simply suggest that we might want to be the kind of people who do not always hide from our tragic choices and that juries, conceived of as institutions through which we each take turns confronting the perplexity of judgment, offer one way of owning up to what we find necessary to do.

143. Plato, *Laws IV* 768, *in* 2 The Dialogues of Plato 529 (B. Jowett trans., Random House rev. ed. 1937).

[3]

The Right to Trial by Jury

THOM BROOKS

ABSTRACT *Recently, the right to trial by jury has attracted a number of vociferous critics with deep reservations about the use of juries, most of whom are in favour of greatly restricting the use of juries with a minority desiring complete abolition. This article offers a justification for the continued use of jury trials. I shall critically examine the ability of juries to render just verdicts, judicial impartiality, and judicial transparency. My contention is that the judicial system that best satisfies these values is most preferable. Of course, these three values are not the only factors relevant for consideration. Empirical evidence demonstrates that juries foster both democratic participation and public legitimation of legal decisions regarding the most serious cases. Nevertheless, juries are costly and, therefore, economically less efficient than competing modes of trial. I do not argue that all human beings possess an inalienable legal right to be tried by a jury. However, it is my hope that this analysis will make clear what we might gain or lose when we propose jury reforms.*

We abhor the idea of losing the transcendent privilege of trial by jury, with the loss of which, it is remarked by [Blackstone], that in Sweden, the liberties of the commons were extinguished by an aristocratic senate: and that trial by jury and the liberty of the people went out together [1].

Introduction

It has been said that 'England owes more of her freedom, her grandeur, and her prosperity to [the jury trial], than to all other causes put together' [2]. In Britain, as well as in many other countries, trial by jury has been seen traditionally as their citizens' great bulwark of freedom: 'the lamp that shows that freedom lives' [3]. Yet, despite these strong demonstrations of support, the use of jury trials was nearly abolished recently in all but the most serious of criminal cases in England and Wales [4]. The right to trial by jury has attracted a number of vociferous critics who hold deep reservations about the use of juries [5]. While only a minority desire complete abolition, critics are in wide-scale agreement on the need to restrict their use. For example, they are quick to point out that the emergence of the jury trial is more of an historical accident than a conscious decision by any single legal body, evolving in 'a piecemeal and haphazard fashion' [6]. Indeed, there does not seem to be any clearly perceptible nor rational justification for the jury's historical use in criminal trials [7].

Unsurprisingly, critics like Penny Darbyshire argue that the jury trial 'seems to attract the most praise and least theoretical analysis' [8]. She says:

> The symbolic function of the jury far outweighs its practical significance . . . this sentimental attachment to the symbol of the jury is dangerous. Adulation of the jury is based on no justification or spurious justification [9].

Indeed, some dispute that there is any 'right' at all to a trial by jury, arguing that most countries which use jury trials lack legal guarantees and that defendants lack a choice to opt for a trial by judge without a jury [10]. In addition, there does not appear to be any right to lay justice under the *European Convention on Human Rights* [11]. Moreover, most countries do not have jury trials, opting instead for mixed tribunals where judges sit and decide cases with jurors [12]. In countries with jury trials, this mode of trial is used infrequently, at best. For example, in England and Wales, only about two percent of all cases are tried by juries. In Australia and Scotland, the figure is less than one percent.

This article offers a theoretical justification for the continued use of jury trials. It is *not* my contention that all human beings possess an inalienable right to be tried by a jury. However, I do believe the judiciary is obliged to decide cases correctly. That is, a judicial system is best when it attributes guilt or innocence to deserving persons as well as possible. In addition, it is often thought that a judiciary should be both impartial and transparent to ensure, as well as safeguard, that the judiciary adjudicates correctly. Consequently, I shall critically examine the following three issues: our ability to decide just verdicts, judicial impartiality, and judicial transparency. My contention is that the judicial system that best satisfies these values is *most* preferable — and that juries satisfy these values, all things considered.

Of course, these three values are not the only factors relevant for consideration. Empirical evidence demonstrates that juries foster both democratic participation and public legitimation of legal decisions regarding the most serious cases, typically serious criminal cases. However, juries are costly and, therefore, economically less efficient than competing modes of trial. It is my hope that this analysis will make clear what we might *gain* or *lose* when we propose jury reforms.

1. Deciding just verdicts

The most fundamental argument of the jury trial's critics is that jurors are less capable than judges at deciding legal cases correctly: juries are more vulnerable to render mistaken verdicts. This criticism revolves around two key issues: the role of the judiciary in a modern, liberal democracy and an epistemic claim about the best manner of ascertaining just verdicts in trials.

1.A. The role of the judiciary

One major problem for critics of jury trials is the fact that juries render different verdicts on occasion from those professional judges would have given. Critics argue that when this happens, juries are effectively rewriting the law, something neither juries nor judges should do [13]. For example, Judge R. J. O'Hanlon says:

> it is often put forward as one of the merits of the jury system that a jury can bring about changes in the law of the land by refusing to enforce laws which

> appear to them to be unjust or oppressive in some way . . . What this means in reality is that the jury, having taken an oath that they will 'true verdicts give according to the evidence' have broken their oath by refusing to give effect to the law of the land. They have usurped the role of parliament which is entrusted by the people with the task of making laws which are in conformity with the will of the people. However pardonable such action on the part of the jury may be in defiance of an oppressive and autocratic regime, it is indefensible in a modern democracy where fundamental rights and freedoms are protected by the country's constitution [14].

O'Hanlon should not suggest that — *contra* juries — judges never adjudicate in a similar manner. In fact, as Darbyshire notes, lay justices and judges 'are frequently criticised for their irrational and inconsistent sentencing patterns and gratuitous remarks' [15]. Indeed, in jurisdictions where the judiciary offers reasoned judgements for its decisions — such as the United States' Supreme Court — it has been observed that politics is 'inherent in the judicial process' [16]. As a result, this 'problem' of judicial decisions failing to apply relevant laws does not lie solely with activist juries.

Nevertheless, the idea that the court's function is to apply, not create, the law is popular in both civil and common law jurisdictions [17]. In France and Germany, there is not a strict doctrine of precedent: the law can be applied with some variation in identical cases by the courts [18]. Their claim is that the creation of judicial precedent effectively creates new laws. There is something substantive to this claim. For example, abortion was not made legal in all fifty American states by legislative mandate, but by the high court decision *Roe v Wade* [19]. Thus, the use of judicial precedent may in effect 'make new laws', although it is important to note the fact that the decisions of juries do not hold any precedent.

What justifies the right of juries to refuse to adjudicate according to laws that might appear unjustified to them? Critics charge that both judges and juries should always apply the relevant case law without reservation. This is a gross misunderstanding of the judiciary's role, which is to determine the *applicability* of law [20]. For example, consider the relationship between a national legislature and a local government. We might attempt to plot this relationship on a linear scale: on one side is the national legislature whose laws have universal scope; on the other side is the local government which can only legislate for a particular locality at the discretion of the national government. Both legislative bodies have the ability to legislate. The difference is that the scope of one is far wider than that of the other.

Courts might be thought of similarly. On one end of the scale might lie the constitutional courts; on the other courts of first instance with a jury. Both of these judicial bodies have the ability to adjudicate. For instance, constitutional courts do not have the power to 'make' new laws or even to enforce laws. On the contrary, they only have the power to declare whether or not certain legislation ought to be recognised — that is, whether or not it is constitutional. In this manner, the judiciary acts as a check on the executive and legislative branches by prescribing their scope of power [21]. Constitutional courts have the ability to nullify or uphold universally any law. Jury courts have similar powers with much less scope. As a judicial body, juries have the right to adjudicate. In a way not dissimilar to the role of local government in the legislative branch, the jury's power extends to its particular jurisdiction only. For juries, this jurisdiction is the particular trial which confronts them.

If we were to argue that juries lack a right to determine the applicability of laws limited to their particular cases, this bottom tier of the judiciary would lack the ability to function as a part of the judiciary. Indeed, we have no similar expectations with other branches: we accept the right of local government to make laws limited in scope and local police to enforce law and order in their communities. Thus, juries in no instance can be said to usurp power from the legislature. Juries can only do what all judicial bodies are entitled to perform: determine the applicability of the law. The difference between the constitutional court and the jury is that the former determines the law's applicability in *all* cases and the jury determines applicability in the *particular* case they have been selected for [22]. It therefore makes a great deal of sense to see that the decisions of juries carry no precedent — as their powers to adjudicate are limited to a single case — whereas higher court decisions carry greater precedent — as their powers have wider scope [23].

1.B. Does the combined wisdom of twelve randomly selected jurors surpass the professional judge's ability to decide a case?

It is difficult to ascertain how often a jury or judge render a 'correct' verdict, owing to the general fallibility of human knowledge in determining responsibility. Critics tend to determine how often juries decide cases correctly by comparing how often judges would have decided the same case likewise, implying that these judges, in turn, always decide cases correctly — which is not entirely justified. Nevertheless, it is striking how often juries and judges agree. In their classic study, Harry Kalven and Hans Zeisel found that judges and jurors agreed at least seventy-eight percent of the time [24]. This is not to say that juries made mistakes in twenty-two percent of cases (nor were correct in all other cases), but only that judges would have decided differently if given the chance. These findings are similar to studies of mixed tribunals in civil law jurisdictions [25]. In general, civil law mixed tribunals return unanimous decisions up to ninety-five percent in some jurisdictions [26].

All things considered, it is amazing how well juries have been able to perform their function at all. In most instances, the jury is forbidden from taking down notes during the trial. Jurors lack transcripts of the case when deciding on a verdict and, instead, rely primarily on oral evidence. Unsurprisingly, former jurors have suggested that their job would be much improved if the judge outlined the jury's role and essential laws pertaining to the case at the trial's onset and they were permitted to take notes during the trial and refer to them in jury deliberations [27]. Indeed, there is every reason to believe these amendments would further improve jury decision-making.

A further possible reason for disagreement between judges and juries on verdicts may stem from the influence of inadmissible evidence on the judge's decision. In jury trials, the judge endeavours to shield the jury from as much inadmissible evidence as possible. Thus, while the jury decides a case with n facts, a judge decides a case with n+1 facts whenever he has been exposed to inadmissible evidence [28]. Perhaps in a majority of cases judges can separate acceptable versus inadmissible evidence during the course of a trial when coming to their verdicts. However, it might be rather difficult for any judge in a case involving scant circumstantial evidence to be unpersuaded by damning, yet inadmissible, DNA evidence linking the accused with his alleged crime.

Critics argue that a judiciary administered by professionals, instead of a jury, would ensure verdicts of greater uniformity and consistency with precedent. At present, most trials in common law jurisdictions *are* juryless: about ninety percent of all cases are presided over by a judge or magistrate sitting without a jury [29]. Of course, not all judges agree with each other. For example, in *Bush v Gore* [30] judges could not agree on the relevant facts of the case nor applicable legislation and precedents. Judges and magistrates have been criticised frequently for 'their irrational and inconsistent sentencing patterns and gratuitous remarks' [31]. In addition, even ardent defenders of juryless trials admit 'the quality of ratiocination by Diplock Court judges has not always been uniformly high' [32]. Although one might *prima facie* be tempted to argue that judges would provide more uniform verdicts than juries, it would appear that this has not been the case in practice.

Even if juries performed adequately in a majority of cases, critics argue that juries are much less capable of deciding complex cases (especially fraud) than a professional judge. This claim is largely theoretical, based on the following considerations: (*i*) since well-educated persons are better at understanding complex cases than less educated persons and (*ii*) as professional judges are generally better educated than most members of a jury, then (*iii*) professional judges would better adjudicate complex cases than a jury. On these grounds, all complex cases ought to be decided by a judge sitting without a jury. There are several problems with this argument [33]. A British law reform committee found no evidence for a higher rate of acquittals in fraud cases versus other criminal cases [34]. In fact, the complexity and vagueness of fraud trials was blamed for causing problems for juries, leading the committee to argue for simplification of the legal code [35]. This committee found that lawyers deliberately appeared to confuse jurors in fraud trials [36]. A minority opinion of the committee said: 'Most judges and lawyers who made submissions to us thought that juries mostly reached the right result, or at least an understandable result' [37]. Indeed, past studies strongly suggest that practising judges do *not* find juries particularly gullible [38]. Thus, if there is evidence of jury confusion, then something else may well be to blame for it. As a result, arguments alleging that juries are inferior to judges at adjudicating complex fraud cases are unsubstantiated.

In most jurisdictions, jury decisions are possible only by a unanimous decision. If the jury cannot decide with unanimity whether to acquit or convict, then the jury is 'hung' and the trial must be conducted a second time with a new set of jurors. Most studies demonstrate crucial differences between juries where a majority prevails and juries where only unanimity prevails [39]. Majority decision juries tend to be 'verdict-driven', where the goal of jurors centres on arriving at a verdict category and fashioning a story to justify the decision afterwards. On the other hand, juries requiring a unanimous verdict are 'evidence-driven' as dissenting jurors may hang a jury [40]. It is thought that because only one or two dissenting jurors can hang the jury, jurors engage in a more thorough analysis of the evidence in order to persuade others into unanimity. Unsurprisingly, jurisdictions are increasingly coming to favour majority verdicts as they make it easier to prosecute defendants successfully. One problem with this approach is that it discourages jurors from more thoroughly investigating the evidence in their deliberations. A second problem is that majority verdicts give greater weight to convicting the guilty at the expense of acquitting the innocent [41]. If distributing just deserts is a judicial virtue we should promote, then we may be more justified in preferring unanimous verdicts over majority decisions.

Of course, juries, as well as judges, make mistakes [42]. For example, some research suggests that juries convict defendants on occasion due to the charisma and performance of barristers rather than on the basis of the evidence [43]. In addition, juries may not be solely to blame for their decisions, as studies have revealed that judges possess great influence on jury decision-making [44]. Nevertheless, virtually all studies have demonstrated a greater tendency for caution when choosing verdicts with juries, as they are more lenient than judges in about nineteen percent of cases: in only three percent of cases were juries less lenient than judges [45]. One consequence is that it is generally more difficult to convict a person in a jury trial than in trials by a judge sitting without a jury [46]. While juries have convicted innocent persons, they may be less likely to do so than a judge, owing to widespread agreement on most cases and a greater tendency to opt for acquittal. It is often overlooked by critics of jury trials that *if* juries decide incorrectly, there is a legal right of appeal to a professional appellate court in certain circumstances — although this is exceptionally rare. Thus, if critics believe that ultimately judges are better decision-makers than juries, this is not necessarily a conclusive reason to end jury trials, all things considered, as *only judges* are entitled to make final legal decisions.

2. Impartiality

One of the hallmarks of a just judiciary is its impartiality in adjudicating cases [47]. Judicial impartiality is thought to stem from an independence from the disputing parties, as well as from an ability to treat each side with similar consideration. Critics charge that juries are less impartial because they are more likely to acquit than judges [48]. Of course, the converse is equally true: judges may be less impartial because they are more likely to convict than juries. In fact, the acquittal rate of juries is twenty-seven percent, just barely more than magistrates' [49]. While a slightly greater tendency towards acquittal is not proof that juries are less impartial than judges or magistrates, there is a notably 'high rate of correspondence between the views of prosecutors and magistrates' decisions' [50]. Indeed, critics such as Jackson and Doran concede that judges are not independent of the environment within which they work and 'any pressure to increase quantitative output at the expense of qualitative output could work to the disadvantage of defendants' [51]. If British magistrates must 'bring qualities of impartiality and fairness' to bear on cases, we may have more reason to question their ability to adjudicate impartially rather than juries' [52].

A second more serious criticism of jury impartiality involves suggestions of jury 'nobbling' (i.e., jury intimidation) in cases involving gang-related or politically-motivated offences [53]. To counter these suggestions, some critics believe we should either abolish jury trial or curtail access to jury trial even further [54]. While the fear of jury intimidation persuaded the United Kingdom Parliament to introduce juryless trials in Northern Ireland in alleged terrorism cases, there is *no* hard evidence — nor any successful prosecution — of 'nobblers' to support these allegations [55]. Indeed, there is no suggestion that nobbling occurs in the vast majority of criminal trials. This raises the question: why should we think that juries — which decide verdicts by super majority vote in England and Wales — are *more* likely to be affected by intimidation than a single judge or a lay magistrate? If juries are more vulnerable to intimidation, it seems reasonable to provide to them the effective police protection afforded to judges and magistrates. One solution would be to redesign court-rooms by putting the jury-box under the public gallery and out of public view in order to protect the jury [56]. Moreover, if a party wanted to influence the jury, they would have to successfully intimidate three or more jurors to acquit: there would only be a single judge to target if the trial were juryless [57].

A third criticism regards the process of choosing jurors for a trial. Ideally, jurors are chosen to reflect the views of the greater community [58]. It is thought that jurors should be randomly selected from the electoral roll, making the juries impartial. In the words of Lord Denning: 'We believe that 12 persons selected at random are likely to be a cross-section of the people as a whole and thus represent the view of the common man' [59]. Critics are right to claim 'randomness is treated as a synonym for representativeness' as juries often fail to represent a cross-section of the population [60]. This problem is easy to fix: there should be some form of stratified sampling to ensure a better cross-section of society. Thus, the current failure of juries to be as representative *as they could be* is not a good reason to abolish trial by jury.

However, neither randomness nor representativeness should be equated with impartiality. Either method may yield jurors harbouring prejudices that unfairly influence how they weigh evidence. Jury impartiality can be better ensured by removing persons suspected to harbour prejudices. The most extensive use of jury vetting takes place in the United States through *voir dire* [61]. For example, in capital trials, approximately twenty percent of potential jurors are disqualified owing to their reservations against the death penalty. As a result, the final composition of capital juries contrasts greatly with that of the general American populace [62]. The main problem with *voir dire* is not that it produces an *unrepresentative* jury, but rather that it is not used in order to create an *impartial* jury. Instead, lawyers on both sides endeavour to select jurors that are more favourably predisposed to their particular cause. While *voir dire* may be performed for these unsatisfactory reasons, juries are selected through compromise, as both sides must come to some agreement on a jury's composition. Thus, a jury is seen to be impartial insofar as both parties are satisfied relatively equally with the jury's composition. On the other hand, in England and Wales, only the prosecution can, without cause, remove potential jurors from participating in a case thus making a jury's impartiality less likely, at least in the eyes of the accused [63].

It is often taken for granted by critics that judges are impartial. Judges are almost always appointed by politicians or popular election, either method presenting numerous difficulties. Judges who are political appointments are generally chosen owing to their prejudices for certain doctrines or ideological positions, rather than on the basis of their commitment to impartiality. The practice of direct popular election of judges has had a number of bad consequences, and it is still a common manner of selecting judges in a number of American states. In *Ring v Arizona* [64], the US Supreme Court ruled that only juries could impose a death sentence on persons convicted of a capital crime. A contributing reason for the decision is the common practice of judges' running for office to campaign on how many murderers had been sentenced to death in jurisdictions where there was popular support for the death penalty. If anything, popular elections of judges in the United States will almost ensure a lack of judicial impartiality [65].

I would argue that juries may well be both more impartial and representative than judges. Of course, neither judges nor lay justices are representative of the community at large [66]. Yet, more importantly, *only* juries may be better predisposed to render verdicts from a standpoint of greater impartiality — as prejudiced jurors are more easily removed prior to trial, they are chosen at random instead of as a result of political activism or popular election, and shielded from inadmissible evidence — while being more representative of the larger society.

3. Transparency

Crucial to judicial transparency is the law's publicity. For example, suppose the state kept its laws secret to all except government officers. Upon arrest, citizens would continue to be unaware of what law they had violated nor would they be told the reason for detention. In such instances, legal punishment is an arbitrary injustice. Judicial transparency requires publicity of the law so that most, if not all, persons have knowledge of what the legal code is. Additionally, transparency requires that anyone charged with violating a law be told which law she may have broken.

It is, of course, the state's responsibility to make its citizens familiar with its laws. But what mechanism ensures the state will do this? If all court proceedings were conducted in private, citizens might be educated to believe that the law says one thing when, in fact, the law is something quite different in actual practice. Yet, it is not inconceivable to imagine great confusion regarding the content of the law even if all proceedings were held in public. Every specialised profession — including law — develops its own terminology that may be indecipherable to those in different fields. Persons can be charged and convicted of crimes in a public hearing, but the legal arguments against them might sound as if the solicitors were speaking an unknown foreign language. It is easy to see the possibility of courtroom debate becoming the exclusive domain of legal professionals, whereby judicial transparency is not realised despite well publicised proceedings [67].

By involving citizens without a legal background in the judicial process, legal professionals must endeavour to persuade without recourse to their specialised terminology. In his *Philosophy of Right*, G. W. F. Hegel notes that professional courts without juries may adjudicate perfectly well. However, there is a danger: 'knowledge of right and of the course of court proceedings, as well as the ability to pursue one's rights, may become the *property* of a class which makes itself exclusive . . . by the terminology it uses' [68]. Indeed, the more important nonprofessionals are in deciding a verdict, the greater chance transparency has to take root. If two citizens had to decide the guilt or innocence of an accused alongside ten professional judges and only ten votes were sufficient to acquit or convict, the influence of the citizens might be entirely negligible. However, if only nonprofessionals had a say in the verdict, their influence would be central to the administration of justice. Even if nonprofessional juries adjudicated less well, they would be preferable on grounds that they would best safeguard the transparency of judicial decision-making.

Some claim that the best safeguard against unfair convictions is the deliverance of a judgement, rather than a verdict. Justice O'Hanlon of the Irish High Court argues:

> The difference between the judge sitting alone and the jury is that the judge . . . has to explain how he arrived at his decision and justify it in the light of the evidence that he has heard and rules of law he is called upon to apply. The jury operates under none of these constraints [69].

Critics point to the fact that only judges are required to give an explanation for their verdict: juries can elect to acquit or convict for any reason they wish. Furthermore, all jury deliberations are conducted under a veil of secrecy. Transparency would be better facilitated if the jury gave reasoned judgements. The critics' position has been reinforced by the decision *Van De Hurk v The Netherlands* [70], where the European Court of Human Rights ruled that the courts of member countries are obliged to provide reasons for their decisions.

Jury deliberations once took place in the court-room in full view of the public. Juries were later allowed to deliberate in private because it was thought that holding their discussions in public was hampering 'frank discussion and expression of views' [71]. In a sense, the privilege granted to juries is akin to those of diplomatic negotiators. Jurors might not vote their conscience if transcripts were made public of every sentence uttered in jury-room deliberations. This is not an argument against delivering a reasoned judgement, but rather for private consultation in coming to a judgement. The decision by the European Court of Human Rights need not demand that juries create elaborate explanations for their verdicts. The Court might be satisfied with a system whereby the presiding judge draws up a list of questions the jury must provide answers to. The accused would then see the points his case rested upon and how these points affected the final verdict. One major problem we ought not to overlook is that the workload of most judiciaries would increase substantially [72]. However, this process would ensure greater transparency in jury decision-making.

We would be mistaken to think that judges offer well-reasoned judgements in every instance. For example, judges need not provide judgements in cases involving plea bargaining, a practice prevalent in all contemporary common law jurisdictions. It is well-known that the vast majority of persons accused of criminal activity plead guilty in court [73]. A guilty plea is usually enough to secure conviction. In plea bargaining, solicitors strike a deal. The defendant is charged with a crime punishable by sentence x if found guilty. If the accused is willing to plead guilty before trial, they will be punished by a lesser sentence. In *United States v Ruiz* [74], the US Supreme Court ruled that a defendant who refuses a 'fast track' plea bargain, but pleads guilty prior to trial, forfeits her chance of receiving a reduced sentence and/or reduced charges. Undoubtedly, plea bargaining punishes those who exercise their right to trial, either by judge or jury.

In addition, plea bargaining runs contrary to the judicial virtue of distributing just deserts, as it rewards people who are genuinely guilty with less severe penalties and denies defendants a presumption of innocence. When defendants simply plead guilty, guilt is *not* demonstrated beyond a reasonable doubt. Some studies have found that as many as eighteen percent of defendants who had pleaded guilty believed themselves innocent on at least one charge [75]. Perhaps worringly, the most common reason given for pleading guilty was their own lawyer's advice while under great pressure [76].

This is not entirely due to a lawyer's laziness: British legal advisors are under a legal obligation to warn clients of the risk of losing credit by delaying a guilty plea. Contrary to *Turner* [77], judges seem to indicate the likely sentence upon a plea of guilty [78]. This may strongly influence persons accused of wrongdoing. Indeed, there are many incentives for innocent persons to enter a guilty plea. Sanders and Young argue:

> These incentives include less time spent inside the system (as more time is needed to prepare a contested case than a guilty plea), less time spent in court (it takes longer to fight a case than to concede it), lower court costs, the chance to mitigate on the basis of remorse, sparing any defence witnesses (such as friends or family) the ordeal of testifying, [and] sparing oneself the ordeal of cross-examination [79].

If the problem with juries is that they do not give reasoned arguments for their decisions, this is not cause to abandon juries, since judges rarely give reasoned arguments at this judicial level. Moreover, plea bargaining often takes place behind closed doors. Indeed, some argue that the only thing wrong about the way plea bargaining is performed is 'the secrecy and Old Boys' manner in which it is conducted' [80]. Thus, the practice does not promote either transparency or distributing just deserts. There is no reason for this to be the case, as most civil law jurisdictions do not recognise formal pleas of guilt.

Conclusion

The modern legal right to trial by jury is not rationally justified in history, its roots in the Norman compilation of the Domesday Book. Consequently, critics make the mistake of thinking the use of juries is unjustifiable. This article provides a theoretical justification for the continued legal right to trial by jury. There is widespread agreement on verdicts amongst judges and juries. When they disagree with judges, juries may be said to err on the side of caution. Juries may also be more impartial than judges, as jurors are not political appointees nor elected to office and they are more easily vetted for prejudice. In addition, only the use of jurors in judicial decision-making may ensure transparency. All things being equal, if juries are as competent as judges — if our main concern is rendering just verdicts — and juries better ensure impartiality and transparency as I claim, then a judicial system using jurors is superior to a judiciary run exclusively by professional judges [81].

This system is certainly expensive, and maximising systemic efficiency is an important consideration. For example, if we had to choose between two criminal justice systems that were equal in every regard other than cost, it might make more sense to choose the less expensive option. However, if one system better administers justice than the other and is only marginally more expensive, we may compromise justice in cutting costs. By 'compromise justice' I do not refer to an overly abstract conception, but claim instead that impartiality and transparency are compromised, as well as increasing the likelihood of guilty verdicts for innocent persons [82]. It can be argued that attacks on jury trials are attempts to sacrifice these values and that the jury has been made into a scapegoat for defects elsewhere in the criminal justice system [83]. It seems clear that cost, efficiency, and 'a more acceptable conviction rate' underlie most reforms of the modern jury trial [84]. Indeed, the Runciman Commission endeavoured to balance convicting more persons with greater 'value for money' [85]. Reforms made in order to streamline the criminal process fail to take account of the fact that cases come to trial more quickly in Crown Court than in the magistrates' court [86] and the Crown Court is not overburdened by its case load [87]. In fact, one critic even admits that if the practice of plea bargaining is banned, the Crown Court 'will not collapse under the strain' [88]. Rather than improve the criminal justice system, perhaps the British government's principal aim in reforming jury trials is to save the Treasury more than £120 million [89]. The ability to secure convictions more efficiently appears to outweigh other concerns.

Finally, all concede that the jury helps legitimate trial outcomes in the eyes of the public [90]. Studies have demonstrated that jury participation increases civic awareness and participation [91]. Indeed, the legal right to jury trial is viewed by most citizens as 'something of irreplaceable value' [92]. Jurors *and* judges rate trial by jury as either a good or very good system [93]. Any attempts to restrict or abolish this legal entitlement ought to be subjected to the highest scrutiny, and they are not.

Blackstone argued: 'let it be again remembered, that delays and little inconveniences in the forms of justice, are the price that all free nations must pay for their liberty in more substantial matters' [94]. I hope we see can jury trials as an institution justifiable and worthy of retention [95].

Thom Brooks, Department of Politics, University of Newcastle, Newcastle upon Tyne NE1 7RU, UK. tbrooks@web.de

NOTES

[1] The Address and Reasons of Dissent of the Minority of the Convention of Pennsylvania to their Constituents in RALPH KETCHUM (ed.) (1986) *The Anti-Federalist Papers and the Constitutional Convention Debates* (Harmondsworth, Penguin), p. 250.

[2] *Ex parte Milligan*, 71 U.S. 2 at 65 (1865) (Montesquieu). Statement of advocate, not the Court.

[3] See LORD DEVLIN (1956) *Trial by Jury* (London, Methuen), p. 164.

[4] See CLARE DYER (9 October 2001) Criminal Justice Review urges removal of right to trial by jury, *The Guardian*, p. 15. More recently, the current Labour government has tried (and failed) for the third time in three years to curb rights to jury trial. (See my (2003) The future of the right to trial by jury, *Philosophy Today*, 17, pp. 2–4 and MICHAEL WHITE (16 July 2003) Peers snub Blunkett on jury trials, *The Guardian*, p. 1.)

[5] Perhaps the best representation is from JUDGE JEROME FRANK: 'While the jury can contribute nothing of value so far as the law is concerned, it has infinite capacity for mischief, for twelve men can easily misunderstand more law in a minute than the judge can explain in an hour'. (*Skidmore v Baltimore and Ohio Railroad*, 167 F. 2d. 54 (1948).) See ANDREW ASHWORTH (1998, 2nd Edition) *The Criminal Process: An Evaluative Study* (Oxford, Oxford University Press); LOUIS BLOM-COOPER (2001) Article 6 and modes of criminal trial, *European Human Rights Law Review*, 1, pp. 1–14; PENNY DARBYSHIRE (1991) The lamp that shows that freedom lives — is it worth the candle? *Criminal Law Review*, pp. 740–52; and R. J. O'HANLON (1990/1992) The sacred cow of trial by jury, *Irish Jurist*, 25/27, pp. 57–68.

[6] O'HANLON op. cit., p. 65. Regarding England and Wales, DARBYSHIRE says: 'There is little legal logic or design . . . They have simply evolved through the last 10 centuries or more. (op. cit., p. 741.) Interestingly, Scotland developed quite differently than England, Wales, or Ireland, despite being a close cousin of their common law tradition. (See PETER DUFF (2000) The defendant's right to trial by jury: a neighbour's view, *Criminal Law Review*, pp. 86, 89.)

[7] For a general history, see J. H. BAKER (1990, 3rd Edition) *An Introduction to English Legal History* (London, Butterworths), pp. 84–111; Sir WILLIAM BLACKSTONE (1825, 16th Edition), *Commentaries on*

the Laws of England (Vol 4) (London, Butterworths); and THOMAS GREEN (1985) *Verdict According to Conscience: Perspectives on the English Criminal Trial Jury, 1200–1800* (Chicago: University of Chicago Press).

[8] DARBYSHIRE op. cit., p. 740.

[9] DARBYSHIRE op. cit., p. 741. Baldwin and McConville suggest that 'the very conception of a jury might be thought absurd' (JOHN BALDWIN and MICHAEL MCCONVILLE (1979) *Jury Trials* (Oxford, Clarendon), p. 1.)

[10] On lack of constitutional right, see DARBYSHIRE op. cit., p. 743; JOHN JACKSON (2002) Modes of trial: shifting the balance towards the professional judge, *Criminal Law Review*, pp. 253–54; and O'HANLON op. cit., p. 58. It is argued that Britain could simply abolish jury trials by an Act of Parliament. Most states in Australia, Canada, the Republic of Ireland, and the United Sates, amongst other countries have constitutional rights to trial by jury. On lack of right due to a lack of choice, see DARBYSHIRE op. cit., pp. 743–44; BLOM-COOPER op. cit., p.13; and SEAN DORAN and JOHN JACKSON (1997) The case for jury waiver, *Criminal Law Review*, pp. 155–72. Many argue that only defendants in places with right of jury waiver have a right to trial by jury as they have the option to be tried by judge without a jury.

[11] See JACKSON op. cit., p. 254. The *European Convention for the Protection of Human Rights and Fundamental Freedoms* (1950) states in Article 6, section 1: 'In the determination of his civil rights and obligations or of any criminal charge against him, everyone is entitled to a fair and public hearing within a reasonable time by an independent and impartial tribunal established by law'.

[12] The following countries permit trial by jury for serious criminal offences: Australia, Belgium, Canada, England, New Zealand (*Bill of Rights Act* [1990], s. 25(e); *Crimes Act* [1961], ss. 361b–c), Northern Ireland, the Republic of Ireland (*Bunreacht na hÉireann*, Art. 38 (1937)), Scotland, the United States of America (*U.S. Constitution*, Sixth Amendment (1789)), and Wales. Spain's constitution permits trial by jury, but it has not been utilised. Sweden uses elected lay assessors. On Canada, see GRAHAM PARKER (1987) Trial by jury in Canada, *Journal of Legal History*, 8, pp. 178–89. On the Republic of Ireland, see J. M. KELLY (1967, 3rd Edition) *Fundamental Rights in the Irish Law and Constitution* (Dublin, Allen Figgis), pp. 293–94. On the United States, see WILLIAM B. LOCKHART, YALE KAMISAR, and JESSE H. CHOPER (1970, 3rd Edition) *Cases and Materials on Constitutional Rights and Liberties* (St Paul, West Publishing), pp. 314–22 and UNITED STATES (2001, 5th Edition) *Federal Jury Practice and Instructions*, §1.01–3 (2001).

[13] DARBYSHIRE argues: 'What business have the jury to be rewriting the law? . . . The jury is an anti-democratic, irrational and haphazard legislator, whose erratic and secret decisions run counter to the rule of law'. (DARBYSHIRE op. cit., p. 750.)

[14] O'HANLON op. cit., p. 68. See BLOM-COOPER op. cit., p. 6: 'There can be no room for what the jury perceives to be an oppressive law, and to decline to apply it'.

[15] DARBYSHIRE op. cit., p. 751.

[16] See EDWARD LAZARUS (1999) *Closed Chambers: The Rise, Fall, and Future of the Modern Supreme Court* (Harmondsworth, Penguin) and KAREN O'CONNOR (2001) The Supreme Court and the South, *Journal of Politics*, 63, p. 702.

[17] German philosophers such as FICHTE and HEGEL even questioned whether the judiciary could ever be independently separate from other governmental branches of power: if the executive's duty is to apply universal laws approved by the legislature in particular cases, then the judiciary is best seen as part of the executive. (See J. G. FICHTE (2000) *Foundations of Natural Right: According to the Principles of the Wissenschaftslehre*, F. NEUHOUSER (ed.), M. BAUER (trans.) (Cambridge, Cambridge University Press), pp. 142–43 [§16:161–62]; and G. W. F. HEGEL (1991) *Elements of the Philosophy of Right*, A. W. WOOD (ed.), H. B. NISBET (trans.) (Cambridge, Cambridge, Cambridge University Press), pp. 308 [§273], 328 [§287], and 330 [§290 Addition].)

[18] This is not to say that the system suffers from irrationality, as lower courts do tend to follow decisions of higher courts. Nor would it be true to say that detailed judgements with full statements of statutory and judicial authority for decision are not given. (See RAYMOND YOUNGS (1998) *English, French and German Comparative Law* (London, Cavendish), pp. 51–53.)

[19] 410 U.S. 113 (1973).

[20] See my A defence of jury nullification, *Res Publica*, forthcoming.

[21] One consequence is that juries serve as a popular check on the legislative and executive branches. Of course, democratic citizens have the ability to exert accountability to politicians, but the citizenry may only do so generally, either for or against a candidate. Citizens largely lack a means to have an influence on particular legislation (especially if not high profile). Juries are best suited for democratic citizens to

have a say on particular laws normally beyond their grasp. In this sense, juries expand democratic checks and balances.

[22] It may be said a problem with my analogy is that constitutional courts appeal to a constitution, but juries may not have anything to appeal to. When constitutional courts render a verdict in a particular appeal this verdict is decided upon as the best available option in keeping with the rule of law and becomes precedent, as well as part of constitutional law. I would argue juries likewise appeal to the rule of law but their verdicts apply only to one trial alone.

[23] For an elaborate defence of jury nullification, see my op. cit. and *United States v Moylan*, 417 F. 2d 1002 (4th Cir. 1969) at p. 1006.

[24] HARRY KALVEN, Jr, and HANS ZEISEL (1966) *The American Jury* (Boston, Little, Brown, & Co.), p. 63.

[25] As an example, the French use a mixed tribunal — the *Cour d'assises* — in criminal cases where the maximum punishment is six months or greater. The tribunal is composed of three judges sitting with nine jurors chosen from the electoral register. The presiding judge questions the accused prior to the introduction of witnesses. Jurors are entitled to ask questions of the accused and any witnesses at the discretion of the presiding judge. At the conclusion of the trial, the judges and jurors retire together to deliberate and choose a verdict. A majority of at least eight are required to issue a guilty verdict.

[26] SANJA KUTNJAK IVKOVI (1997) Lay participation in decision making: A Croatian perspective on mixed tribunals, *Howard Journal of Criminal Justice*, 36, p. 407.

[27] See TREVOR GROVE (2000) *The Juryman's Tale* (London, Bloomsbury). In *R v James Edward Jeffs and Others* [unreported, 28 April 1978] decided by the New Zealand Court of Appeals, the Court said: 'As a court of three judges we have enjoyed many advantages that were not shared by members of the jury who tried the case'. (MICHAEL LEVI (1988) The role of the jury in complex cases in M. FINDLAY and P. DUFF (eds.) *The Jury Under Attack* (London, Butterworths), p. 98.) See *Mechanical and General Inventions Co. v Austin* [1935] A.C. 346, at 356.)

[28] See KALVEN and ZEISEL op. cit., pp. 121–32.

[29] Not all judges enjoy their isolation in decision-making, preferring a means — such as jury trial — where adjudicators have an opportunity to deliberate options before coming to a final verdict. (See JUDGE CHARLES W. JOINER (1975) From the Bench in R. SIMON (ed.) *The Jury System in America: A Critical Overview* (London, Sage), p. 146.)

[30] 531 U.S. 98 (2000).

[31] DARBYSHIRE op. cit., p. 751; PENNY DARBYSHIRE (2000) The mischief of plea bargaining and sentencing awards, *Criminal Law Review*, pp. 906–7; and ENRIGHT and MORTON op. cit., p. 91.

[32] BLOM-COOPER op. cit., p. 8.

[33] Even if we were to grant that premises (*i*) and (*ii*) are correct, we need not accept the conclusion (*iii*) that judges should sit without a jury. Instead, this could be grounds for greater investment in public education enabling improved citizen performance. Or one might suggest we ought to be more selective of who sits on the jury, as one British commission has done. (LORD JUSTICE AULD (2001) *Review of the Criminal Courts of England and Wales* (London, HMSO), para. 191 and CORKER op. cit., p. 291.)

[34] ROSKILL COMMITTEE (1986) *Fraud Trials Committee Report* (London, HMSO), para. 8.35. Unfortunately, the committee appears to have accepted mistakenly the *a prior* argument against the use of juries in fraud trials: 'Nevertheless, we do not find trial by a random jury a satisfactory way of achieving justice in cases as long and complex as we have described. We believe that many jurors are out of their depth'.

[35] There are eight separate offences of deception, but no one offence of fraud in the criminal code: 'The result is that the wrong offence may be charged, leading to unjustified acquittals. Several different offences may need to be charged in one indictment to cover all the fraudulent conduct, leading to long and confusing trials'. (CLARE DYER (30 July 2002) Fraud laws need to be simplified, says Commission, *The Guardian*, p. 9.)

[36] ROSKILL COMMITTEE op. cit., para. 8.28. See RICHARD W. HARDING (1988) Jury performance in complex cases in M. FINDLAY and P. DUFF (eds.) *The Jury Under Attack* (London, Butterworths), pp. 74–94.

[37] ROSKILL COMMITTEE op. cit., p. 195.

[38] KALVEN and ZEISEL op. cit., p. 168. Nor are expert witnesses to blame for potential jury misunderstandings. As DAVID CORKER says: 'in my experience only a small minority of fraud prosecutions are mounted with the assistance of experts'. (CORKER op. cit., p. 289.) One study found that not a single expert witness is called in seventy-two percent of all jury trials (KALVEN and ZEISEL op. cit., p. 139.)

[39] In a controversial study, it was found that the probability of convicting an innocent defendant might increase with the size of the jury where the jury must arrive at a unanimous verdict. The problem is that

study did not look at what actual juries did: used strategic voting schemas. (See TIMOTHY FEDDERSEN and WOLFGANG PESENDORFER (1998) Convicting the innocent: the inferiority of unanimous jury verdicts under strategic voting, *American Political Science Review*, 92, p. 23.) In addition, they found that juries make fewer mistakes together than any individual juror as they aggregate information.

[40] PENNY DARBYSHIRE (2001) What can we learn from published jury research? Findings from the Criminal Court Review, *Criminal Law Review*, p. 974.

[41] See SANDERS and YOUNG op. cit., p. 568.

[42] As JUDGE JEROME FRANK argues: 'You can outlaw fraud, but not mistakes — in voting or any other endeavour. Laws exist because, as James Madison reminded us, men are not angels'. (JEROME FRANK (1930) *Law and the Modern Mind* (New York, Brentano), p. 358.)

[43] DARBYSHIRE, (1991, op. cit.), p. 749. Critics of the common law tradition question whether or not the adversarial method is the best method of legal decision-making. ZWEIGERT and KÖTZ argue that: 'It will be obvious that "adversary procedure" encourages attorneys to go to the very limits of what is morally and professionally acceptable, perhaps sometimes even to overstep them, by "preparing" their witnesses rather intensively for examination and cross-examination, and by dressing up as unalloyed truth what the attorney well knows to be a pack of lies'. (KONRAD ZWEIGERT and HEIN KÖTZ (1998, 3rd Edition) *Introduction to Comparative Law* T. WEIR (trans.) (Oxford, Clarendon), p. 275.)

[44] See ROBERT W. SHUY (1995) How a judge's voir dire can teach a jury what to say *Discourse and Society*, 6, pp. 207–22.

[45] KALVEN and ZEISEL op. cit., p. 59. Critics — such as Baldwin and McConville — are troubled particularly by evidence of perverse jury decisions, which they claim is as high as five percent. They do not demonstrate that a juryless system will do better. (BALDWIN and MCCONVILLE op. cit., pp. 86–7.)

[46] ANDREW SANDERS and RICHARD YOUNG claim: 'It is no exaggeration to say that magistrates' courts are crime control courts overlaid with a thin layer of due process icing'. (ANDREW SANDERS and RICHARD YOUNG (2000, 2nd Edition) *Criminal Justice* (London, Butterworths), p. 548.

[47] See JOHN RAWLS (1972) *A Theory of Justice* (Cambridge, Harvard University Press), p. 517.

[48] See ASHWORTH op. cit., p. 257.

[49] ENRIGHT and MORTON op. cit., pp. 132–35.

[50] DORAN and JACKSON op. cit., p. 166.

[51] JOHN JACKSON and SEAN DORAN (1995) *Judge Without Jury: Diplock Trials in the Adversary System* (Oxford, Clarendon), p. 292.

[52] *R v Birmingham City Justices, ex parte Chris Foreign Foods (Wholesalers) Ltd* [1970] 3 All ER 945 (Lord Parker CJ).

[53] CORKER op. cit., p. 285. It is probably true to say most intimidation in trials affects victims and witnesses rather than jurors. (See SANDERS and YOUNG op. cit., p. 558n14.)

[54] See O'HANLON op. cit., p. 68.

[55] See NICHOLAS BLAKE (1988) The Case for the Jury in M. FINDLAY and P. DUFF (eds.) *The Jury Under Attack* (London, Butterworths), pp. 143–44; STEVEN GREER and ANTHONY WHITE (1988) Restoring Jury Trial to Terrorist Offences in Northern Ireland in M. FINDLAY and P. DUFF (eds.) *The Jury Under Attack* (London, Butterworths), p. 186; and STEVEN GREER and ANTHONY WHITE (1986) *Abolishing the Diplock Courts: The Case for Restoring Jury Trial to Scheduled Offences in Northern Ireland* (London, The Cobden Trust), esp. p. 78.

[56] See ENRIGHT and MORTON op. cit., p. 153.

[57] A related worry is general tampering of the jury. In some common law jurisdictions jury tampering may be facilitated by legality of behaviour designed to influence members of the jury *after* a verdict has been rendered. The worry is that this may threaten the jury's impartiality if any juror thought it would be possible to gain a benefit from one of the parties after the trial. (See ERICA SUMMER (2001) Post-trial jury payoffs: a jury tampering loophole, *St. John's Journal of Legal Commentary*, pp. 353–72.)

[58] 'The law is the expression of the general will. All citizens have a right to take part (*concourir*), personally or by their representatives, in its formation'. (Article VI of *The Declaration of the Rights of Man* (26 August 1789). See SHERMAN J. CLARK (1999) The courage of our convictions, *Michigan Law Review*, 97, pp. 2381–2447.) The International Criminal Court poses an interesting question about jury representativeness. While it might be best always to employ juries, the great scope of the International Criminal Court — as it also has an appellate function — may make the choosing of a representative, impartial jury of the international community practically impossible. (See WILLIAM A. SCHABAS (2001) International Criminal Court: the secret of its success, *Criminal Law Forum*, 12, pp. 415–28.)

[59] *Crown Court at Sheffield, ex p Brownlow* [1980] QB 530 at 541.

[60] DARBYSHIRE op. cit., pp. 744–45. Of course, once potential jurors *are* selected randomly, lawyers on both sides may remove persons under certain conditions. I will defend briefly the use of *voir dire* below as an acceptable alternative.

[61] See R. MAY (1998) Jury selection in the United States: are there lessons to be learned? *Criminal Law Review*, p. 270.

[62] See WILLIAM E. CONNOLLY (1999) The Will, capital punishment, and cultural war, in A. SARAT (ed.) *The Killing State: Capital Punishment in Law, Politics, and Culture* (Oxford, Oxford University Press), p. 196; V. P. HANS (1995) Death by jury in N. FINKEL (ed.) *Commonsense Justice: Juror's Notions of the Law* (Cambridge, Harvard University Press), p. 184; BARRY LATZER (1998) *Death Penalty Cases: Leading U.S. Supreme Court Cases on Capital Punishment* (London, Butterworths–Heinemann), p. 155; and *Turner v. Murray*, 476 U.S. 28, 106 S. Ct. 1683, 90 L. Ed. 2d. 27 (1986). *Ham v. South Carolina* established the right to question prospective jurors about potential biases they might harbour when the facts of the case suggested that bias might be a problem (409 U.S. 524 (1973)).

[63] The defence can only remove potential jurors for cause.

[64] 122 S. Ct. 2428, 2002 WL 1357257 (2002). See my A Matter of Life and Death: The Use of Judge or Jury in Capital Sentencing, unpub. TS.

[65] Problems with judge selection are not specific to the United States alone. Indeed, a recent commission led by Sir Colin Campbell found 'no clear "audit trail" in the Queen's Counsel selection system to show the reasoning and judgement when candidates are chosen or rejected'. (DYER op. cit., p. 9.)

[66] In Britain, the vast majority of judges are white males from a more affluent background. (See CLARE DYER (8 October 2002) Judge selection found to lack transparency: system 'helps perpetuate a white, male judiciary', *The Guardian*, p. 9.)

[67] Indeed, transparency is particularly lacking in the vast majority of court cases which do not employ jury verdicts. It is also worth noting that one good example of professional manipulation of the legal system to the detriment of the general public might be Ireland under British rule. (See DAVID JOHNSON (1996) Trial by jury in Ireland 1860–1914, *Journal of Legal History*, 17, pp. 270–93.) In addition, JACKSON and DORAN argue '[t]he gradual waning of the jury's influence has led in many common law jurisdictions including England and Wales to substantial numbers of cases being concluded on the basis of professional advice and negotiation which is not subject to any open scrutiny'. (JACKSON and DORAN op. cit., p. 298.)

[68] HEGEL op. cit., p. 258 [§228 Remark]. Emphasis is given. See G. W. F. HEGEL (1995) *Lectures on Natural Right and Political Science: The First Philosophy of Right, Heidelberg 1817–1818 with Additions from the Lectures of 1818–1819* J. STEWART and P. HODGSON (trans.) (Berkeley, University of California Press), pp. 203–5 [§116].

[69] O'HANLON op. cit., p. 66.

[70] [1994] 18 E.H.R.R. 481. In *Condron v United Kingdom* [(2000) *Criminal Law Review* 679] the European Court of Human Rights indicated that trial by jury was not necessarily incompatible with Article 6 of the *European Convention on Human Rights.*

[71] Suggestion of the Discussion Paper of the New South Wales Law Reform Commission on 'The Jury in a Criminal Trial' (1985). Cited in The Hon Mr Justice MCHUGH (1988) Jurors' deliberations, jury secrecy, public policy, and the law of contempt in M. FINDLAY and P. DUFF (eds.) op. cit., p. 62.

[72] CORKER op. cit., p. 293.

[73] In the United States, ninety-two percent plead guilty, ninety-three percent in British magistrates' courts, and seventy-three percent in the Britain's Crown Court. (DARBYSHIRE, (2000, op. cit.), p. 898).

[74] 122 S.Ct. 2450, 2002 WL 1357244.

[75] DARBYSHIRE (2000), op. cit., p. 903n69.

[76] DARBYSHIRE (2000), op. cit., p. 903.

[77] *R v Turner* [1970] 2 Q.B. 321.

[78] DARBYSHIRE (2000), pp. 899–900.

[79] SANDERS and YOUNG op. cit., p. 478.

[80] MORTON op. cit., p. 1843. In addition, defence counsels are under an obligation to inform the judge of an accused's admission of guilt. There is no obligation to profess admissions of innocence, even when entering a guilty plea. Thus, the system 'appears to be prepared to tolerate some frauds more than others'. (SANDERS and YOUNG op. cit., p. 475.)

[81] In essence, my argument defends the use of lay participation in judicial decision-making and, thus, there are implications for the mixed tribunal system in civil law jurisdictions. Interestingly, lay judges tend to

agree with professional judges on verdicts as much as 95 percent of the time. (IVKOVI op. cit., p. 407.) My claim that impartiality and transparency is best facilitated by lay participation in judicial decision-making would apply to common law juries as well as civil law mixed tribunals: mixed tribunals would sacrifice these judicial values in limiting the use of lay judges. However, I accept many of Sanders and Young's criticisms of the inquisitorial method. (See SANDERS and YOUNG op. cit., pp. 13–7.)

[82] JOHN BRAITHWAITE and PHILIP PETTIT argue that the jury trial's high cost is a good thing as it would justify 'fewer prosecutions, fewer trials', commensurate with their Republican theory of parsimony where less intervention is favoured to more. (J. BRAITHWAITE and P. PETTIT (1990) *Not Just Deserts: A Republican Theory of Criminal Justice* (Oxford, Clarendon), pp. 120, 203.) There are several difficulties with their analysis, including the fact they simply assume all criminal trials should be tried by a jury without giving any indication of how exactly *justice* is compromised without jury trials.

[83] JAMES GOBERT says: 'the jury has become a convenient scapegoat which allows more permanent participants in the criminal justice system — police, lawyers, and judges — to deflect criticism from themselves. The jury not only relieves the judge of the burden of having to make the difficult decision, but also provides the judge with a convenient skirt behind which to hide when a verdict which may have been virtually dictated by the jury's directions fails to meet with public approval'. (J. GOBERT (1997) *Justice, Democracy and the Jury* (Aldershot, Ashgate), p. 62.)

[84] See ENRIGHT and MORTON op. cit., p. 155.

[85] See ROYAL COMMISSION ON CRIMINAL JUSTICE (1993) Report (Cm 2263) (London, HMSO), pp. 4–5 and SANDERS and YOUNG op. cit., p. 481.

[86] DAVID WOLCHOVER and ANTHONY HEATON-ARMSTRONG (2000) The Right to Trial by Jury, *New Law Journal*, p. 158.

[87] DARBYSHIRE (2000, op. cit.), p. 908.

[88] DARBYSHIRE (2000, op. cit.), p. 908. Cf. ASHWORTH op. cit., p. 262.

[89] *The Economist* op. cit., p. 22.

[90] For example, see DARBYSHIRE, (1991, op. cit.), pp. 740, 744–6.

[91] See JOHN GASTIL, E. PIERRE DEESS, and PHIL WEISER (2002) Civic awakening in the jury room: a test of the connection between jury deliberation and political participation, *Journal of Politics*, 64, pp. 585–95.

[92] BRUCE HOULDER (1997) The importance of preserving the jury system and the right of election for trial, *Criminal Law Review*, p. 881.

[93] See SANDERS and YOUNG op. cit. pp. 598–9.

[94] BLACKSTONE op. cit., pp. 349–50.

[95] Earlier versions of this paper were presented at the Association for Legal and Social Philosophy at the University of Newcastle; at the European Ethics Summit at the European Parliament, Brussels; at the Ockham Society at the University of Oxford; and at both the Philosophy Society and the Senior Postgraduate Seminar at the University of Sheffield. I am most grateful to Brenda Almond, Reza Banakar, Chris Bennett, Stephan Blatti, Meagan Brooks, Roger Cotterrell, Matt Matravers, Joe Morrison, James Penner, Jenny Szende, and, especially, Penny Darbyshire, Antony Duff, Fabian Freyenhagen, Peter Jones, Suzanne Uniacke, and an anonymous referee for their very helpful comments on earlier drafts.

Part II
Lay Participation

[4]

Lay Participation in Decision Making: A Croatian Perspective on Mixed Tribunals

SANJA KUTNJAK IVKOVIĆ
Senior Research Associate, University of Delaware, USA

Abstract: This paper studies mixed tribunals, a form of lay participation in which professional and lay judges decide cases jointly. The focus of the analysis is the interaction of professional judges and lay judges in tribunals that decide criminal cases in two regions of Croatia. The respondents in this study were professional judges and lay judges, as well as 'the observers' of the trials by mixed tribunals, that is, state attorneys and attorneys. A theoretical framework for the study of interaction of the members of mixed tribunals is developed by applying status characteristics theory. Lay judges ask questions during trials only infrequently; lawyers (professional judges, state attorneys, and attorneys) perceive that those questions are not very important. Lay judges are only sometimes given an opportunity to ask questions during trials. Deliberation typically starts with the summation of evidence by the professional judge. Consistent with the findings about the trials, the comments offered by lay judges during deliberations are perceived by professional judges to be minor, both in regard to frequency and importance. Disagreements between professional and lay judges occur rarely. Lay judges very rarely outvote professional judges. All of the findings are consistent with status characteristics theory.

Previous Research on Mixed Tribunals

Mixed tribunals are a form of lay participation in legal decision making in criminal cases in which professional and lay judges hear and decide legal cases jointly. The most important difference between professional and lay judges is that professional judges have graduated from law school, whereas lay judges do not have legal education. Although some of the members do not have any legal education, mixed tribunals need to decide criminal cases according to the legal rules; they do not have the right to bend the law.

Although mixed tribunals are a form of lay participation frequently used in Europe (especially in the countries whose legal systems are based on the Roman law), there are very few studies about mixed tribunals: in the last 20 years, only six studies about mixed tribunals have been conducted in Poland, Germany, the former Czechoslovakia, Bosnia and Herzegovina, Hungary, Finland, and Sweden, and several journal articles or books have been published in English which describe the results of these studies (Kubicki and Zawadzki 1970; Kulcsár 1972; Casper and Zeisel 1972; Pomorski 1975; Borucka-Arctowa 1976; Krystufek 1976; Kulcsár 1982; Klami and Hämäläinen 1992). The study about mixed tribunals in Bosnia and

Herzegovina conducted by Kamhi and Čalija (1974) was published only in Croatian.

The researchers tried to determine the lay judges' contribution to and influence on the tribunal. The lay judges' contribution was measured variously: as the frequency of questions and comments during trial and deliberation and frequency of disagreements (Kubicki and Zawadzki 1970), as the frequency of disagreements with professional judges (Casper and Zeisel 1972), or as the frequency of majority verdicts (Kahmi and Čalija 1974). The conclusions about the lay judges' impact in the tribunal differ, since the understanding of the lay judges' contribution is measured and interpreted differently.

Based on a set of informal interviews conducted in Czechoslovakia, Krystufek (1976) concluded that lay judges in criminal cases generally formed and expressed their opinion, that is, they participated actively. Contrary to these findings, the results reported by other researchers suggested that the majority of lay judges did not contribute actively to the work of the tribunals during trials. Only one out of eleven lay judges (9%) read the case file in the Polish study (Kubicki and Zawadzki 1970, p. 104) and two-thirds of lay judges did not ask questions at all during trials (66% in the Polish study, Kubicki and Zawadzki 1970, p. 104; 68% in the Hungarian study, Kulcsár 1982, p. 103).

The lay judges' contribution to the final outcome in the case was also measured; Kamhi and Čalija (1974, p. 5) concluded that lay judges contributed actively in only 25% of the cases and that only one out of four professional judges thought that the presence of lay judges was beneficial for reaching the verdict. Kubicki and Zawadzki (1970, p. 106) reported that lay judges actively contributed in a higher percentage of the cases (40%) by expressing their personal views and evaluations concerning the case. Similarly, Kulcsár (1982, p. 105) wrote that approximately one-half of the lay judges in Budapest and one-third of lay judges in other areas in Hungary made comments of merit in connection with facts, legal qualification, determination of guilt, or sentencing. It is important to note that this is only an *explicit* influence, while Pomorski (1975) and Borucka-Arctowa (1976) argue that there is also an *implicit* influence of lay judges – their presence in the tribunal itself.

Lay judges' influence and contribution can be measured through the frequency of disagreements too; Casper and Zeisel (1972, p. 189) examined the frequency of disagreements and reported that lay judges affected the verdict in a mere 1.4% of the cases. Some of the researchers wrote that lay judges contributed more actively when the tribunal made a decision about the sentence than when the tribunal made a decision about guilt (Kamhi and Čalija 1974; Kulcsár 1972, 1982), while others tried to determine the issues that were frequent causes of the lay judges' disagreement. Although researchers generally reported that the frequency of unanimous verdicts was relatively high, in some studies up to 95% (Klami and Hämäläinen 1992), they tried to determine the issues which were more likely to trigger the lay judges' disagreement. Casper and Zeisel (1972) and Kubicki and Zawadzki (1970) reported that the lay judges' disagreements were more likely to be centered on sentencing issues than on the issue of guilt.[1]

Finally, it is interesting to examine how disagreements were resolved. In the German study (Casper and Zeisel 1972), lay judges affected the verdict in one out of five cases with disagreements. Since disagreements were not very frequent, the conclusion provided by Casper and Zeisel (1972, p. 189) was that when all the cases were examined, including those with a full confession, lay judges affected the verdict in 1.4% of the cases.

In summary, the results of the existing studies differ; the measured influence of lay judges ranges from 40% (Kubicki and Zawadzki 1970) to 1.4% (Casper and Zeisel 1972) of all cases. This study examines opinions about mixed tribunals in Croatia in the early 1990s, 20 years after the other studies on mixed tribunals were conducted[2] and after the abolition of the socialist regime in Croatia. Furthermore, a theoretical framework is given to the study of mixed tribunals; the results of the study were interpreted by applying status characteristics theory. This study reports the opinions expressed by both professional and lay members of the tribunals, and, in addition, the opinions expressed by the 'observers' of the trials by mixed tribunals – state attorneys (prosecutors) and attorneys. The study focuses on the lay judges' activity during trials and deliberations and the importance of their contribution.

Theoretical Framework: Status Characteristics Theory

Status characteristics theory is a theoretical explanation of the interaction among the members of small task-oriented informal groups (Berger *et al.* 1977; Balkwell 1994) that will be applied to explain the interaction in mixed tribunals. Members of the groups develop expectations about the potential task-oriented contributions and the power of other members in their group (Berger *et al.* 1980; Berger *et al.* 1986) based on status characteristics.

Status characteristics can be viewed as attributes possessed by group members whose culturally specified meaning makes such characteristics potentially relevant to performance of the group's task (Balkwell 1994). Each specific status characteristic can be divided in at least two categories, one of which carries a more positive judgment, the other one a more negative one. The common feature of specific status characteristics is that they are linked to the task directly, whereas diffuse status characteristics, such as gender, age, race, are more general in nature, and they have indirect connotations for performance of the group's task.

In terms of status characteristics theory, professional judges[3] and lay judges differ with respect to specific status characteristics directly relevant to the *legal* decision making. Professional judges have legal education and training in deciding legal cases, that is, specific status characteristics that suggest a high status compared to lay judges, who lack such specific skills important for legal decision making.

However, it could be argued that professional judges and lay judges do not necessarily perform the same role in the tribunal. The majority of lay judges in the Polish study (72%, Borucka-Arctowa 1976) reported that lay judges served a function in counteracting the tendency of statutory law to ignore the realities of life. The 'social' role of lay judges and the 'professional' role of professional judges may be perceived as mutually complementary, as reported by Borucka-Arctowa (1976). The majority of professional judges, on the other hand, may have a different view about the lay judges' role and their capacity to make quality legal decisions – only the educated and trained members of a profession are qualified to make high-quality legal decisions. Or, according to Dow (1981), to be a real judge requires 'no less than a law degree, a license to practice, and trial experience' (p. 196). Therefore, it is reasonable to expect that professional judges will emphasise the 'professional' role as more important than the 'social' role, both for themselves and for lay judges.

Within the context of status characteristics theory, the aggregation hypothesis (Balkwell 1994) implies that the expectation and power of each group member will include all status characteristics, but different weights will be attached to them. The expectation is that specific status characteristics directly relevant to the task will be more important for the aggregate expectation than diffuse status characteristics which are only indirectly related to the task. In terms of mixed tribunals, legal education and experience in deciding legal cases will have a stronger impact and weigh more heavily on the overall expectation about professional judges' or lay judges' ability to decide legal cases than their gender or age, since the former is directly related to the task while the latter is not. Therefore, the primary and dominant bases of professional judges' high status or lay judges' low status are specific status characteristics, whereas diffuse status characteristics, such as gender, age, or nationality, are expected to play a very marginal role, if any.

In forming aggregate expectations, diffuse status characteristics will be more important in situations in which members of the group are strangers than in situations in which members of the group have some information that may be used for the judgment about other members' competency (Carli 1991). The situation is, then, specific for mixed tribunals which are formal groups: although professional and lay judges may be strangers, they will still have enough information about specific status characteristics to form expectations simply based on the fact that they know that some of them are *professional* judges (lawyers) and some of them are *lay* judges (they do not have any legal education). Although lay judges and professional judges are formally equals during trials and deliberations and their votes have the same power according to the Croatian Regular Courts Law (1977), only professional judges may preside over the tribunals. However, if professional or lay judges have decided other cases in the same tribunal, then their knowledge about the other members' abilities will partially, or even completely, overshadow the stereotype.

Specific propositions are developed to predict the interaction in mixed tribunals. Lay judges, who have lower status, because of their lack of legal knowledge and experience, are expected to be evaluated as less competent than professional judges. Furthermore, lay judges are expected to be given less 'floor time' (Balkwell 1994) – to participate less frequently and to have fewer opportunities to make contributions; once they make contributions, their contributions are more likely to receive less favourable reactions from others (Berger *et al.* 1980). Studies show similar results even in the situations when high- and low-status individuals behave in similar ways – higher status individuals are evaluated more positively (Humphrey 1985). In addition, professional judges, high-status members, are supposed to be *more influential* than lay judges, low-status members (Carli 1991). Berger *et al.* (1977) proposed that in the cases in which disagreements occur, high-status members will wield more influence, and disagreements will be usually resolved in their favour. The theory argues that the power of the argument is not of primary importance; rather, the most important factor is the power of the source.

A unique opportunity for social scientists to study the work of social security appeal tribunals and to compare the dynamics in the tribunals in which the chairmen were lay persons to the dynamics in the tribunals in which the chairmen were lawyers existed in the United Kingdom between 1984 and 1989. Based on research results known as 'The Bell Report' (Bell *et al.* 1974; Bell *et al.* 1975; Bell 1982), the legislature passed a new law which introduced the requirement that all chairmen of the social security appeal tribunals should be legally qualified. The transition was gradual, and between 1984 and 1989 the tribunals were presided over by either legally qualified chairmen or lay chairmen. The results of research studies (Jackson *et al.* 1987; Wikeley and Young 1992) suggested that professionalisation and judicialisation, in addition to greater reliance on rules and regulations, resulted in the marginalisation of lay members. Lay chairmen were more likely to invite contributions from other members than were legal chairmen (85% *v.* 67% in Jackson *et al.* 1987, pp. 249–50); lay members were more likely to ask questions of appellants and the representatives in the tribunals with lay chairmen than they were in the tribunals with legal chairmen (Jackson *et al.* 1987, p. 250).

Wikeley and Young (1992) found additional evidence of the marginalisation of lay members by comparing the results of their study, in which they reported that approximately one-half of all lay members were entirely silent throughout the appeal hearing, to the results of the study by Jackson *et al.* (1987), in which the researchers reported that lay members made no contribution in approximately one-fifth of hearings. Furthermore, Wikeley and Young (1992, p. 138) reported that lay members were not very active in the work of tribunals: they 'often fail to participate actively in the deliberations', the majority of deliberations took five minutes or less, and that in 98% of the cases the decision was unanimous. Wikeley and Young (1992, p. 139) explained the lay judges' marginalisation through the advantages legal chairmen have over lay members. These advantages are very similar to specific status characteristics professional judges in mixed tribunals have and lay judges in mixed tribunals lack: 'a legal background, superior training and an expertise built up through their more frequent attendance at hearings' (Wikeley and Young 1992, p. 139).

Data Collection

Mixed tribunals are employed for trials in Croatia in which offenders are charged with offences punishable by five or more years of imprisonment

(Article 21, Item 2, Criminal Procedure Law, 1993). The composition of mixed tribunals changes depending on the offence. For offences punishable with imprisonment of between five and 15 years, the tribunal is composed of one professional and two lay judges ('small tribunal'). For offences exceeding 15 years of imprisonment, the tribunal is composed of two professional and three lay judges ('large tribunal'). Small tribunals meet at the district and regional courts, while large tribunals meet only at the regional courts.

The data were collected at eight district courts, six regional courts, at twelve state attorneys' offices and at attorneys' offices in the Zagreb and Bjelovar regions.

The Locations

The data were primarily collected in two regions in Croatia – the Zagreb Region and the Bjelovar Region. These two regions differ in terms of *demographic and socio-economic characteristics* and in terms of the organisation of their respective courts. Zagreb, the centre of the Zagreb Region, is the political, administrative, business, cultural, and educational centre of Croatia. The city population was 953,607 in 1991 (*1992 Statistical Yearbook*, Republički zavod 1993, p. 464). Bjelovar, the 17th largest city in Croatia (66,039 inhabitants in 1991, *1992 Statistical Yearbook*, p. 464), is the centre of the Bjelovar Region, which is dominated by agriculture and the food-preparation industry. A number of smaller cities (between 20,000 and 60,000 inhabitants) in the Bjelovar Region were also included in the study. Those two regions differ with respect to the educational levels of the active population: in the cities from the Bjelovar Region which were included in the study, approximately one-half or more of the active population did not finish elementary school, whereas this can be said about only 18% of Zagreb's population (*1981 Census of Population, Households, and Residences*, Republički zavod 1983).

Two regions, the Zagreb Region and the Bjelovar Region, differ not only in terms of their demographic and socio-economic characteristics, but also in terms of the *organisation of their respective courts.* The Regional Court of Zagreb, as a Court of Second Instance (Appellate Court), has jurisdiction over the District Court of Zagreb, the biggest district court in the country with 24 professional judges in the Criminal Division alone (June 1993). The jurisdiction of the Regional Court of Bjelovar in Second Instance extends over a number of smaller district courts, ranging from two to six professional judges who, among other types of cases, decide criminal cases as well.

The Respondents

The respondents in the study were professional judges, lay judges, state attorneys, and attorneys. Ninety professional judges, 229 lay judges, 58 state attorneys, and 102 attorneys were included in the study, with the response rates from 70% for attorneys to 92% for professional judges.

The majority (60%) of professional judges are experienced judges, since they have been judges for over ten years. Furthermore, the majority of them (75%) are also considered to be experienced in trials with mixed tribunals, since they decided more than 200 cases in mixed tribunals, although the majority of professional judges are below 40 years of age (62%). Slightly more than one-half of all professional judges are women (54%), and 64% are married.

The majority (54%) of lay judges have been lay judges for three or more years, which means that they are experienced lay judges since they are at the end of their first term or even their second term as lay judges. Only 14% of lay judges have been lay judges for less than a year. One-quarter of lay judges do not have a high-school diploma, 41% reported that the highest level of their education is graduation from high school, and one-third reported that they have graduated from college or community college. Only one-third of all lay judges are women, 76% are married, and 12% are below 40 years of age.

The majority of state attorneys and attorneys are experienced, since they have been employed as state attorneys or attorneys for five years or longer (65% of attorneys and 71% of state attorneys). For the majority of the respondents, experience with mixed tribunals comes exclusively from being on the observers' bench, since they have never tried criminal cases (80% of attorneys and 84% of state attorneys). Three out of four state attorneys and attorneys are married (70% and 75%, respectively). Differences with respect to gender exist: while the majority of state attorneys in the study are women (55%), only one out of five attorneys is a woman (18%). Less than one-half of state attorneys and attorneys are below 40 years of age (47% and 43%, respectively).

The Questionnaires

One of the appropriate methods to study group interaction is observation. Unfortunately, since the observation of the deliberations by mixed tribunals is illegal, according to Article 118, Criminal Procedure Law, 1993, this method could not have been used. Furthermore, it is illegal to examine the records of deliberations, so it was impossible to use this method in the study of mixed tribunals too. The data for this study were collected by means of detailed questionnaires which examined the respondents' perceptions of their own activity during trials and deliberations (for lay judges) or lay judges' activity (for professional judges, state attorneys, and attorneys). Asking respondents to report about their own behaviour is not the same as observing their actual behaviour. Consequently, the methodology selected somewhat limits the conclusions of this study. The results of this study are based on *perceptions* of lay judges' and professional judges' behaviour. Although the results in this study were collected mainly as survey data,[4] the opinions expressed by various groups of respondents (lay judges, professional judges, state attorneys, and attorneys) form a very uniform picture which enhances the validity of the study.

The questionnaires were distributed to the respondents, professional judges and lay judges in the courts, to state attorneys in their offices, and to attorneys either in their offices or left in their mailbox in the court building in spring and summer months of 1993.

Each questionnaire contained approximately 60 items and had several sections. The first section explored how members of the tribunal evaluated their own behaviour and *behaviour* of other members *during trials*. The second section dealt with perceptions of *the lay judges' ability to understand and evaluate evidence and legal issues*. The third section focused on *behaviour during deliberation*. The fourth section examined *disagreements during deliberation*. Finally, the fifth section dealt with *general opinions about mixed tribunals*. In addition, there was a number of questions about the respondents' demographic characteristics.

Results and Discussion

The results of this study are presented in an order that follows the natural flow of the criminal process. Therefore, the interaction that occurs in mixed tribunals during trials, with a special emphasis on the lay judges' activity, is analysed first, followed by an analysis of the deliberation of mixed tribunals.

Mixed Tribunals During Trials

The presiding judge, who may be only a professional judge (Article 13, Regular Courts Law, 1977), examines the defendant, witnesses, and expert witnesses first, before all other persons. Members of the tribunal are allowed to question the defendant, witnesses, and expert witnesses directly *after* the presiding professional judge has completed his/her examination (Articles 318 and 327, Criminal Procedure Law, 1993). But the presiding professional judge has no procedural duty to invite members of the tribunals to ask questions, so it depends on a particular professional judge and his or her style and preference whether or not other members of the tribunal will be invited to ask questions, and if so, how frequently.

One of the items in the questionnaire inquired about the frequency with which professional judges asked lay judges whether they had any questions. The results suggest that the responses differ with respect to the type of the court/office; professional judges, lay judges, and state attorneys from regional courts/offices seemed more likely to say that professional judges asked lay judges for questions frequently, while the respondents from district courts/offices seemed more likely to say that professional judges invited lay judges to ask questions infrequently (χ^2 = 43.28, 6df $p < 0.001$). The majority of the attorneys also reported that professional judges invited lay judges to ask questions infrequently.

Why do these differences by type of court arise? The seriousness of criminal cases may be the answer: professional judges at regional courts, who preside over trials for more serious cases (rape, murder), may want to initiate a more thorough examination of witnesses, expert witnesses and defendants by appealing to the different perspectives provided by the heterogeneity of the tribunal.

The second group of possible explanations assumes that professional judges at regional courts apply the same routine that they use when conducting trials in large tribunals to trials in small tribunals, and that this routine is different from the routine professional judges at district courts use to conduct trials. Why would professional judges in large tribunals at regional courts conduct the trials differently from professional judges who conduct the trials in small tribunals at district courts? There are several reasons. Ignoring lay judges in a large tribunal is much more difficult than in a small tribunal. The key reason for this does not seem to be only the increased number of lay judges but the presence of another professional judge as well. Among important factors that may explain these differences, such as, for example, a professional judge's general opinion about mixed tribunals and lay judges, is the fact that in the large tribunals the presiding professional judge asks other members of the tribunal (lay judges and *another professional judge*) for questions. By contrast, in small tribunals all members, except for the presiding professional judge, are lay judges. Thus, it is likely that presiding professional judges in large tribunals provide more opportunities for a colleague, that is another professional judge and an associate at work of equal rank, to clarify remaining unclear issues. Therefore, wording the question as: 'Do you have any questions?' would give more opportunities to ask questions *both* to another professional judge and three lay judges in the large tribunal.

When developing expectations about the frequency of lay judges' questions during trials, it is important to note that the basic examination, performed by the presiding professional judge, is chronologically first, and supplementary examinations, performed by other members of the tribunal, may or may not follow.[5] In cases in which professional judges tend to provide as thorough and careful examination of the case as the state would expect and ask all questions that they consider to be relevant to the examination of the case from various perspectives, assuming that the important pieces of testimony and important factors in their decisions are the same for professional and lay judges, there is little room left for lay judges' questions.

On the other hand, it could be argued that the pieces of the testimony that are important for evaluation and the factors used while making a decision only partially overlap for professional and lay judges. Furthermore, lay judges may bring to the case some additional issues, such as knowledge of the values in a particular community or a focus on a particular defendant and his/her situation. Based on the results of the study of mixed tribunals in Poland, Borucka-Arctowa (1976) concludes that lay judges perceived the different roles that they and professional judges had as 'mutually complementary' and that they corrected each other; 72% of lay judges felt that lay judges in general serve to counteract the tendency of statutory law to ignore the realities of life (Borucka-Arctowa 1976, p. 289).

About 30% of the lay judges in the same study (Borucka-Arctowa 1976) asked questions during trial, and therefore actively intervened in the course of the trial. An interesting question is when lay judges asked questions. As Borucka-Arctowa (1976) explains:

> A lay judge will intervene actively only when the professional judge does not take due account of circumstances which the lay judge feels are essential to the case, or when the questions the lay judge poses may help to elucidate the case. (p. 290)

Lay judges reported that they asked questions infrequently in the last ten trials; they most frequently reported that they asked questions 'in only a few' of the last ten trials or 'in none of the last 10 trials'. It is also interesting to point out that, on the average, one of ten lay judges in each group reported that he or she did not ask questions in any of the last ten trials.[6] Further analysis of the lay judges' answers with respect to their gender,[7] age, educational level, occupational prestige, or the length of mandate did not produce statistically significant differences: none of the demographic categories of lay judges turned out to report asking questions more frequently than any other demographic category.

When the results of this study are compared to the results of the study by Kubicki and Zawadzki (1970), where court apprentices observed trials, it seems that the majority of lay judges in the Croatian sample reported asking questions somewhat more frequently than was recorded, based on observations, for lay judges in the Polish study.[8] The majority of lay judges in the Polish study did not ask questions at all (66%), 28% asked questions sporadically, and 5.4% asked questions systematically (Kubicki and Zawadzki 1970, p. 104).

Did lay judges underestimate or overestimate the frequency of their participation? Professional judges, state attorneys, and defence attorneys are regularly present during the trials as a part of their occupation and are able to observe the behaviour of lay judges. The question asked of professional judges, state attorneys, and attorneys did not inquire about their experience of the last ten deliberations, but rather about the perceived frequency of lay judges' question-asking based on the respondents' overall experience.[9] Professional judges, state attorneys, and attorneys, had similar opinions ($\chi^2 = 3.78$, 2df, $p > 0.05$, n.s.); they suggested that lay judges asked questions during trials infrequently. Furthermore, more than 85% of the respondents within *each* group of professional lawyers reported that lay judges either only sometimes asked questions or that they did not ask questions at all.

The lay judges' contribution to the work of the tribunal may be significant even if they do not ask questions frequently as long as those infrequent questions are perceived to be important. We did not ask lay judges about the importance of their questions. The reasons are twofold: since they ask questions only infrequently, once they ask a question, it is probably very important for them; further, even if they assumed that their own questions were not very important, nobody would characterise his/her own statements as insignificant. Instead, professional judges, state attorneys, and attorneys were asked to evaluate the importance of questions that lay judges raised.

The expectation was that not many professional judges would classify the questions that lay judges asked as very important. This could be interpreted negatively for professional judges – they did not cover all important issues with their basic examination, assuming that the definition of important issues is the same for lay and professional judges. Furthermore, based on status characteristics theory, professional judges (members with higher status in the tribunals which is established through their legal education and experience in deciding legal cases), will typically perceive lay judges (members with lower status) and their contributions, as less important. In the Kamhi and Čalija's study (1974), only 28% of professional judges reported that the presence of lay judges was beneficial for reaching the verdict. One of the respondents from this study, an attorney, vividly depicted his opinion and the general stereotype about lay judges in the following anecdote:

Mladen Kerstner, a Croatian writer, wrote:

Drašek: Tetec, what are lay judges?
Tetec: They are two heads of cabbage behind which is hidden the professional judge.

The results are striking: only 5% of all 240 professional judges, state attorneys, and attorneys thought that the lay judges' questions were 'important' or 'very important',[10] while the majority of lawyers (professional judges, state attorneys, and attorneys) perceived those infrequent questions asked by lay judges to be 'somewhat important' or even 'not important' ($\chi^2 = 2.56$, 2df $p > 0.05$, n.s.). So, even when lay judges try to contribute to the work of the tribunal, their contribution during trial is perceived at best as 'somewhat important'.

Mixed Tribunals During Deliberations

After the defendants, witnesses, and expert witnesses are examined and the hearing of the evidence is finished, the prosecution and the defence give their closing statements. If, after the closing statements, the tribunal does not conclude that it is necessary to examine additional evidence, the presiding professional judge will declare that the trial is concluded (Article 344, Item 1, Criminal Procedure Law, 1993). The tribunal will start with deliberation (Article 344, Item 2, Criminal Procedure Law, 1993). The presiding judge votes last, after all other members of the tribunal (Article 116, Item 2, Criminal Procedure Law, 1993). Since deliberations are secret and only members of the tribunals may be present (Article 118, Criminal Procedure Law, 1993), the questions about deliberations were asked only of the members of tribunals themselves.

The Criminal Procedure Law, 1993, does not regulate the order in which the discussion during deliberation proceeds. From experience as a court apprentice at the District Court of Zagreb and the Regional Court of Zagreb, and from informal discussions with several professional judges, the researcher learned that professional judges frequently started deliberation by summarising the evidence, although they are not obligated to do so by law. Similarly, Casper and Zeisel (1972) show that overall three-quarters of the German mixed tribunals they studied began with such a summary.[11]

In the present study professional and lay judges were asked about the frequency with which professional judges summarised evidence.[12] As expected, the majority of professional judges stated that they have always summarised the evidence at the beginning of deliberation. In general, the majority of lay judges in three out of four groups agree with professional judges that it is indeed unusual behaviour when professional judges do not summarise evidence.[13]

If professional judges are not required by law to start the deliberation with the summation of evidence, why do they perform it so consistently? The purpose of this summation, according to the respondents, is either to 'familiarise lay judges with evidence', or to 'present complex evidence'.[14] Professional and lay judges from the district courts most frequently said that the purpose of summation was to 'familiarise lay judges with the evidence in the case', while professional and lay judges from the regional courts most frequently said that the purpose of summation was to 'present complex evidence in a way that is more understandable for lay judges' ($\chi^2 = 9.57$, 3df, $p < 0.05$).

Cases tried at the regional courts were more likely to include complex evidence and involve more serious offences. However, it is not only the complexity of evidence and seriousness of the cases that may be important, but also the lay judges' familiarity with the evidence in the case. Lay judges at both types of courts, district and regional, hear the evidence, but, as the results show, they did not read the case file, and therefore did not familiarise themselves with other evidence in the file, equally often. While 7.5% of lay judges from regional courts reported that they never[15] read the case file, 28% of lay judges from district courts reported the same ($\chi^2 = 9.15$, 1df, $p < 0.01$). The professional judges' opinion about the frequency with which lay judges read the case file follows the same pattern but is less positive: 29.2% of professional judges from regional courts said that lay judges never read the case file, while 48.2% of professional judges from district courts said the same. Therefore, it is not surprising that professional and lay judges at the district courts, where the evidence in the case is less likely to be complex and lay judges less likely to read the case file, report the need to familiarise lay judges with the evidence in the case as the most frequent reason for the summation. By the same token, it is not surprising that professional and lay judges at the regional courts, where the evidence in the case is more likely to be complex, the cases more serious, and the lay judges more likely to read the case file, report most frequently that the purpose of summation is to 'present complex evidence in a way that is more understandable for lay judges'.

What happens between the summation by a presiding professional judge at the beginning of deliberation and the moment when a decision is reached by the tribunal and the task is completed? Since the decision is reached by a group, the expectation is that the tribunal will spend sometime discussing important issues in the case before reaching the final decision. The questionnaire asked respondents about the frequency and importance of lay judges' contributions during deliberation, and in particular, about the lay judges' comments.

Professional and lay judges were asked about the perceived lay judges' frequency of comments during deliberations.[16] Professional judges from district courts perceived lay judges to make comments less frequently than any other category of respondents ($\chi^2 = 19.09$, 3df, $p < 0.001$). However, the pattern is more obvious when the opinions of the respondents from regional courts (both professional judges and lay judges) are contrasted with the opinions of the respondents from district courts; respondents from regional courts were significantly more likely to say that lay judges participated actively during deliberations than respondents from district courts ($\chi^2 = 8.54$, 1df, $p < 0.01$).

How can such differences in opinion expressed by the respondents from two different types of courts (district, regional) be explained? Three issues seem to be important. First, cases discussed at regional courts are more serious and lay judges at these courts are more likely to read the case file. Lay judges may be more interested in the cases tried and therefore participate more actively. Second, the number of lay judges in small tribunals and in large tribunals may be important. Assuming that the frequency of comments is the same for lay judges from district and regional courts, the presence of two or three lay judges who frequently made comments has a different impact on the professional judges' opinion about the frequency of lay judges' comments in general. Finally, professional judges at the regional courts are more likely to solicit contributions from other members during trials than professional judges from the district courts, and this as well may extend into deliberation. Furthermore, by inviting other members of the tribunal to ask questions, professional judges may be creating an environment in which contributions by other members are welcome even when they are not explicitly solicited.

We inquired not only about the frequency of lay judges' comments during deliberations but also about their importance.[17] The results suggest that professional judges may evaluate lay judges' comments as of lesser importance than do lay judges themselves; the chi-square test suggested that lay judges were significantly more likely to evaluate their own comments as more important than were professional judges ($\chi^2 = 42.24$, 1df, $p < 0.001$). It also seems that respondents from the regional courts were more likely to evaluate lay judges' comments as important than were respondents from the district courts ($\chi^2 = 11.27$, 1df, $p < 0.001$).

One of the objectives of the study was to determine the perceptions about the frequency of lay judges' disagreements with professional judges' opinion.[18] Disagreement between lay judges and professional judges was not very frequent; the majority of the respondents, both professional judges and lay judges, said that lay judges disagreed with professional judges in only 'a few cases' or 'never'.[19] Lay judges were more likely than were professional judges to say that they experienced disagreements between professional and lay judges ($\chi^2 = 12.82$, 1df, $p < 0.001$).

Disagreements that existed at the beginning of deliberation may or may not be resolved during the discussion; not all disagreements will result in a *votum separatum*. Research studies show that the frequency with which lay judges outvote professional judges is low. Kubicki and Zawadzki (1970) reported such instances in 6.3% of all cases. Casper and Zeisel (1972) reported that in all instances in which lay judges disagreed about guilt, they did not outvote the professional judge, while for sentencing issues lay judges won in 22.0% of the cases with disagreement.

The respondents in this study were asked to report the frequency with which they had been outvoted by lay judges (the wording of the question asked of professional judges) or the frequency with which they outvoted the professional judges (the wording of the question asked of lay judges).[20] Although, it was possible for lay judges to outvote professional judges in both 'large tribunals' and 'small tribunals' since they outnumber professional judges, the results show that outvoting by lay judges, as was predicted, did not happen very often. To be more precise, the majority of professional and lay judges from the district courts reported that lay judges had never outvoted professional judges, while the majority of professional and lay judges from the regional courts reported that instances when lay judges outvoted professional judges happened, but they were not very frequent; they occurred 'in a few cases' ($\chi^2 = 6.49$, 1df, $p < 0.05$).

Conclusion

Several aspects of the interaction between professional and lay judges in the tribunals were examined in this study: the frequency and importance of lay judges' participation, both during trials and deliberations, and the opportunities given to lay judges to participate. The arguments raised by status characteristics theory were used to explain this interaction. Members of the tribunals differ, based on a number of characteristics, some of which are task-oriented and specific (legal education and experience in deciding legal cases), while others are more general in nature and diffuse (age, gender, education, occupation).

The results of this study in general support the arguments maintained by status characteristics theory. Presiding professional judges were in a leadership position in both trial and deliberation. This position was assigned to them by law (for example, their examination of the witnesses is a basic one; they are assigned to co-ordinate deliberations). Consequently, they had more opportunities to participate, and they are perceived as more influential members of tribunals. Lay judges are not perceived as being very active either during trial (by asking questions of the defendants, witnesses, or expert witnesses), or during deliberation (by making comments), nor were their contributions evaluated by professional judges as very important for the work of the tribunals. Furthermore, it seems that lay judges disagreed with professional judges rarely, and, according to the respondents from the district courts, they would never outvote the professional judge.

There are some indications that regional courts in comparison with district courts can provide an environment which is more conducive to the lay judges' active participation: professional judges are more likely to invite lay judges to ask questions during trials, lay judges are more likely to make comments during trials, their comments are more likely to be perceived as important, and lay judges are more likely to outvote professional judges. These differences may be explained by some of the following arguments. Lay judges may be more interested in participating in trials and deliberations held at the regional courts. Professional judges at the regional courts may be more interested in hearing different opinions, since the cases are more serious. In addition, they may behave in the same manner when they conduct trials in 'small tribunals' and 'large tribunals' (and ask for questions more frequently in 'small tribunals' because they are used to doing so in 'large tribunals' where they ask another professional judge for his or her questions), and thus base their general opinion about lay judges and mixed tribunals on their experience in tribunals of both sizes.

The results of this study and other studies on mixed tribunals (Lucas, in Kalven and Zeisel 1966; Kubicki and Zawadzki 1970; Pomorski 1975; Borucka-Arctowa 1976; Casper and Zeisel 1972; Kamhi and Čalija 1974; Krystufek 1976) reveal that lay judges in mixed tribunals are not perceived as very prominent contributors to the legal decisions reached by the mixed tribunals, nor are they viewed as very competent. These findings are very similar to the results of the studies on administrative tribunals conducted in the United Kingdom (Jackson *et al.* 1987; Wikeley and Young 1992). It seems that the internal dynamics of decision making in mixed tribunals and in administrative tribunals with legal chairmen exhibit many common characteristics. Professional judges – lawyers in the tribunals – are in a more powerful position, although, in most of the tribunals in various countries, they are in the minority in terms of numbers. The professional judges' dominant position in the tribunal is based on legal knowledge and experience in deciding legal cases, as predicted by status characteristics theory and is further strengthened by the law itself. Therefore, the existence of the professional judges' powerful position strengthens the lay judges' passivity. However, the importance of the lay judges' participation is affected not only by the expected frequency of activity, but also by the way this participation is facilitated. Lay judges who are familiar with their rights and duties in the proceedings, who are well-informed about the circumstances of the case, and who have time and opportunities to read the case file, participate more actively and, as a result, contribute toward emphasising positive functions of lay participation.

Notes

1 In the Polish study, lay and professional judges were virtually unanimous on the issue of guilt (they disagreed in only 4% of the cases [Kubicki and Zawadzki 1970, p. 106]), while they disagreed more often on sentencing issues (they disagreed in 54% of the cases [Kubicki and Zawadzki 1970, p. 106]).

2 The only study on mixed tribunals conducted after the 1970s is the study by Klami and Hämäläinen (1992), but the authors did not try to determine the lay judges' contribution or behaviour during trials and deliberations; rather, they focused primarily on the opinions about the positive and negative features of lay participation and the hypothetical verdicts given in several cases constructed by the researchers.

3 The term 'professional judges' in this paper refers to the presiding professional judges in the tribunals.

4 The author was a law clerk in these same courtrooms for a period of two years and observed numerous trials and deliberations by mixed tribunals, but at that point in time the author was not interested in a study of mixed tribunals as such, but rather in a preparation for the bar exam. During the distribution of the questionnaires the author tried to discuss the topic of this paper with the respondents, but professional judges gave informal comments and refuse to be formally interviewed.

5 The order of the examination suggests that it is not reasonable to expect that lay judges would ask as many questions as presiding professional judges would. Thus, the comparison of the frequency of lay judges' questions to the frequency of the questions of the presiding professional judge would not be appropriate.

6 It can be argued that the number of lay judges who do not ask questions at all may be higher, since these results are based on the self-reports. However, the general result (lay judges ask questions very infrequently) is presented by the majority of lay judges and the majority of other categories of respondents (professional judges, state attorneys, and attorneys), and, therefore, the picture seems to be very uniform.

7 For a detailed discussion of this topic, see Kutnjak Ivković 1995.

8 The differences may also be due to the different methodology used in these studies.

9 Since the questions are worded differently for lay judges and other groups of respondents, a direct comparison by chi-square test cannot be performed. The question for professional judges, state attorneys, and attorneys was worded as follows: 'According to your experience, how frequently do lay judges ask questions during trial?' The answers ranged from 'never' to 'always' (five-point scale).

10 Professional judges, state attorneys, and attorneys were asked: 'How would you evaluate the importance of the questions asked by lay judges during the trial?' Possible answers were 'very important', 'important', 'somewhat important', and 'not important'.

11 In 'Schoeffengericht' cases (misdemeanors), the summation was given in 68% of the cases, in 'Gross Strafkammer' (felonies, less serious crimes, minor political offences) in 100%, and in 'Schwurgericht' (serious felonies and serious political offences) in 86% of the cases (Casper and Zeisel 1972, p. 152, *Table 21*).

12 The wording of the question for professional judges was: 'Do you usually summarise the evidence at the beginning of deliberation?'. A similar question was asked of lay judges. The answers were 'yes, always', 'no, never', and 'sometimes'. Two reasons for summations are given if it is not given always – it may depend on the case or on the lay judges (answer for professional judges) and professional judges (answer for lay judges). In addition, the respondents were offered the opportunity to specify some other reasons.

13 Only 1 out of 309 respondents (both professional and lay judges) said that professional judges never summarise evidence.

14 The question was worded as follows: 'In your opinion, the purpose of summation is to (Put '1' next to the most important feature, '2' next to the next most important, etc., down to the least important feature)'.

15 The question was worded: 'How often do you read the case file?'. Answers ranged on a five-point scale from 'always' to 'never'.

16 The question was worded as follows: 'In how many of the last 10 deliberations in which you participated did lay judges make comments other than just stating their vote?'. Six answers were offered, on a scale from 'in all 10 deliberations' to 'in none of the deliberations'.

17 The wording of the question was as follows: 'The comments made by lay judges during deliberation are'. The answers offered ranged from 'very important' to 'not important'.

18 Professional judges were asked about the frequency of disagreements in the following way: 'According to your experience, how frequently do lay judges disagree with you during deliberation?'. The answers offered ranged from 'in almost all cases' to 'never – we always agree'. The question asked of lay judges was similar.

19 Although the majority of respondents within each group reported that lay judges disagree very infrequently, the differences were statistically significant ($\chi^2 = 13.12$, 3df, $p < 0.01$).

20 Six offered answers were on a sale from 'very frequently' through 'never'.

References

Balkwell, J.W. (1994) 'Status', in: M. Foschi and E.J. Lawler (Eds.), *Group Processes: Sociological Analyses*, Chicago, IL: Nelson-Hall Publishers.

Bell, K. (1982) 'Social Security tribunals: a general perspective', *Northern Ireland Legal Quarterly*, *33*, 132–47.

Bell, K., Collison, P., Turner, S. and Webber, S. (1974) 'National Insurance local tribunals: a research study – Part I', *Journal of Social Policy*, *3*, 289–315.

Bell, K., Collison, P., Turner, S. and Webber, S. (1975) 'National Insurance local tribunals: a research study – Part II, *Journal of Social Policy*, *4*, 1–24.

Berger, J., Fisek, M.H., Norman, R.Z. and Zelditch, M., Jr. (1977) *Status Characteristics and Social Interaction: An Expectation-States Approach*, New York, NY: Elsevier.

Berger, J., Rosenholtz, S.J. and Zelditch, M., Jr. (1980) 'Status organizing process', in: A. Inkeles, N.J. Smelser and R.H. Turner (Eds.), *Annual Review of Sociology*, *6*, Palo Alto, CA: Annual Reviews.

Berger, J., Webster, M., Jr., Ridgeway, C. and Rosenholtz, S. (1986) 'Status cues, expectations, and behavior', in: E.J. Lawler (Ed.), *Advances in Group Processes*, *3*, Greenwich, CT: Jai Press, Inc.

Borucka-Arctowa, M. (1976) 'Citizen participation in the administration of justice: research and policy in Poland', in: L. Friedman and M. Rehbinder (Eds.), *Zur Soziologie des Gerichtsver-fahrens*, Jahrbuch fur Rechtssoziologie und Rechtstheorie, 4. Opladen: Westdeutscher Verlag.

Carli, L.L. (1991) 'Gender, status and influence', in: E.J. Lawler, B. Markovsky, C. Ridgeway and M.A. Walker (Eds.), *Advances in Group Processes*, *8*, Greenwich, CT: Jai Press, Inc.

Casper, G. and Zeisel, H. (1972) 'Lay judges in the German criminal courts', *The Journal of Legal Studies*, *1*, 135–91.

Criminal Procedure Law. Zakon o krivičnom postupku (pročišćeni tekst) (1993) Narodne novine, XLIX (CLV), Br. 34.

Dow, P.E. (1981) *Discretionary Justice: A Critical Inquiry*, Cambridge, MA: Ballinger.

Humphrey, R. (1985) 'How work roles influence perception: structural-cognitive processes and organizational behavior', *American Sociological Review*, *50*, 242–52.

Jackson, M., Stewart, H. and Bland, R. (1987) 'Tribunals hearing supplementary benefit appeals: the members' role', *Policy and Politics*, *15*, 245–51.

Kalven, H., Jr. and Zeisel, H. (1966) *The American Jury*, Chicago, IL: The University of Chicago Press.

Kamhi, S. and Čalija, B. (1974) *Sistem porote u našoj zemlji i problemi vezani za učešće gradjana u vršenju pravosudja*, Sarajevo: Svjetlost.

Klami, H.T. and Hämäläinen, M. (1992) *Lawyers and Laymen on the Bench*, Helsinki: Suomalainen Tiedeakatemia.

Krystufek, Z. (1976) 'The function of the lay judge in Czechoslovakia', in: L. Friedman and M. Rehbinder (Eds.), *Zur Soziologie des Gerichtsverfahrens*, Jahrbuch für Rechtssoziologie und Rechtstheorie, 4. Opladen: Westdeutscher Verlag.

Kubicki, L. and Zawadzki, S. (1970) 'Lay assessor judges in penal proceedings in the light of empirical research', in: S. Zawadzki and L. Kubicki (Eds.), *Udzial Lawników W Postepowaniu Karnym*, Warszawa: Wydawnictwo Prawnicze.

Kulcsár, K. (1972) 'Lay participation in organizational decision making', in: P. Halmos (Ed.), *Hungarian Sociological Studies. The Sociological Review, Monograph*, *17*, Keele: University of Keele.

Kulcsár, K. (1982) *People's Assessors in the Courts*, Budapest: Akadémiai Kiadó.

Kutnjak Ivković, S. (1995) 'Does gender matter: the role of gender in legal decision-making by Croatian mixed tribunals', *International Journal of the Sociology of Law*, *23*, 131–55.

Pomorski, S. (1975) 'Lay judges in the Polish criminal courts: a legal and empirical description', *Case Western Reserve Journal of International Law, 7,* 198-209.

Regular Courts Law. Zakon o redovnim sudovima (1977) Zagreb: Narodne novine, XXXIII (CXXXIX), Br. 5., and the subsequent changes: *Zakon o izmjenama i dopuni Zakona o redovitim sudovima* (1986) Narodne novine, XLII (CXLVIII), Br. 17; (1990), XLVI (CLII), Br. 16; (1990), XLVI (CLII), Br. 41; (1991), XLVII (CLIII), Br. 66

Republički zavod za statistiku Republike Hrvatske (1983) *1981 Census of Population, Households, and Residences: Active Population and Employed Workers.* Document 526, Popis stanovništva, domaćinstava i stanova 1981, Aktivno stanovništvo i zaposleni radnici. Dokumentacija 526, God. 1983. Zagreb.

Republički zavod za statistiku Republike Hrvatske (1993) *1992 Statistical Yearbook,* Statistički ljetopis Republike Hrvatske, Zagreb: Republički zavod za statistiku Republike Hrvatske.

Wikeley, N. and Young, R. (1992) 'The marginalization of lay members in Social Security appeal tribunals', *Journal of Social Welfare and Family Law, 2,* 127–42.

Date submitted: July 95
Date accepted: April 96

[5]

Democratic Accountability and Lay Participation in Criminal Trials

TATJANA HÖRNLE*

1. INTRODUCTION: JURIES AND LAY JUDGES IN ENGLAND AND IN GERMANY

WHICH CONDITIONS MUST a court fulfil to rule legitimately about the defendant and his or her offence? To what degree are the topics 'democratic accountability' and 'just and fair trials' related? Specifically, is lay participation an essential or at least an important element—or is it merely a matter of historic developments and conventions? Lay participation is a central element in the organisation of criminal trials in the United Kingdom—both in jury trials and in the magistrates' courts. Although jury trials are rare events and the vast majority of sentences are not based on juries' decisions,[1] the *existence* of juries plays a crucial role in the theoretical framework for criminal trials. The introductory summary of our workshop bears witness to that by stating that one of the three conditions thought crucial to ensure legitimacy (besides separation of powers and publicity of the trial) is the involvement of laypeople.[2] The words 'involvement' and 'participation' point to a modus in which professional judges and lay persons co-operate. One could take the concept of democratic accountability further and argue that a truly democratic model should rely on lay judges *only*. Magistrates' courts could be seen as a model of democratic jurisdiction. However, I will not pursue this line of thought. The status quo in England is not generally praised for the outstanding quality of the magistrates' work. Rather, criminal lawyers criticise their lack of professional training.[3] One would hardly recommend putting all

* I am grateful to Dudley Knowles and Victor Tadros, whose comments on this paper encouraged me to rewrite substantial parts of a previous version of this chapter.

[1] See, eg, Auld LJ, *Review of the Criminal Courts in England and Wales* (hereafter Auld Report) (London, TSO, 2001) 135.

[2] But see also P Darbyshire, 'The Lamp that Shows that Freedom Lives: Is it Worth the Candle?' [1991] *Crim L Rev* 740; for a more cautious evaluation of a 'right to jury trial' see also AJ Ashworth, *The Criminal Process* (2nd edn, Oxford, Oxford University Press, 1998) 257.

[3] Ashworth, n 2, 262; P Darbyshire, 'For the New Lord Chancellor: Some Causes for Concern about Magistrates' [1997] *Crim L Rev* 861.

criminal trials (the most serious cases and those with difficult evidence procedure) in the hands of lay judges without the guidance of a professional judge. Therefore, a *mixed system including lay persons and professional judges* could be recommendable or even necessary.

Before I analyse the 'democratic accountability'—approach, a brief description of the German court system is useful.[4] Lay participation is not mentioned in the German Constitution (the *Grundgesetz*). The Supreme Court permits the involvement of lay judges in different court branches; however, it does not demand such inclusion.[5] On the level of *court organisation*, the German legal system is still strongly influenced by the idea of lay participation. Juries were abolished in 1924, but criminal courts today include lay judges presiding at the trial together with the professional judges (they are called *Schöffen*). Only minor offences before the lower courts (*Amtsgerichte*) are heard by a single professional judge.[6] For any other offence, the lower courts sit with two lay judges and one professional judge.[7] In the higher courts which deal with serious crimes (*Landgerichte*) two lay judges and two or three professional judges decide.[8] Lay judges have similar rights and duties to the professional judges. Usually they remain passive in the courtroom, but they can and sometimes do ask questions. Lay judges participate in the adjudication of guilt and in sentencing decisions, and their vote is crucial: any decision to the defendant's disadvantage requires a two-thirds majority.[9] Thus the lay judges can outvote their professional colleagues. One has to add: they could in theory—in practice, the professional judge will most likely use his or her authority to suppress any such idea through the course of the deliberative process after the judges have retreated to their room. Many professional judges perceive the need to co-operate with the *Schöffen* as tiresome, and they have been successful in restricting their influence. For example, lay judges are denied the opportunity to read the court files, while for the professional judges a thorough examination of the files is essential when preparing for a trial. Also, lay judges do not participate in the drafting of the written verdict or sign it.[10] But despite such discrimination between professional and lay judges in the day-to-day work of the courts, German law allows lay judges an influential role.

[4] See also M Dubber, 'American Plea Bargains, German Lay Judges, and the Crisis of Criminal Procedure' [1997] 49 *Stanford L Rev* 547, 556 ff.

[5] Entscheidungen des Bundesverfassungsgerichts, 27, 312, 319 f.; 42, 206, 208 f.; 48, 300, 317.

[6] S 25 Gerichtsverfassungsgesetz.

[7] S 28, 29 Gerichtsverfassungsgesetz.

[8] S 76 Gerichtsverfassungsgesetz.

[9] S 263 Strafprozessordnung.

[10] See H-L Schreiber, 'Akteneinsicht für Laienrichter' in G Stratenwerth et al (eds), *Festschrift für Hans Welzel* (Berlin and New York, de Gruyter, 1974) 941; T Hillenkamp, 'Zur Teilhabe des Laienrichters' in H-J Albrecht *et al* (eds), *Festschrift für Günther Kaiser* (Mainz, von Zabern, 1998) 1443; D Spona, *Laienbeteiligung im Strafverfahren* (Frankfurt am Main, Peter Lang Publishing Group, 2000) 101 ff; Dubber, n 4 above, 580 ff.

There is little support for lay participation among *German criminal theorists*, however. There are voices relating the work of lay judges to democracy. But these are mainly to be found in brochures produced for the benefit of lay judges[11] and occasionally in political speeches praising the merits of our judicial system. Within serious theoretical work, enthusiasm for lay participation is rare. A colleague from Munich University concludes that the only reason for retaining the institution of lay judges is the fact that we already have them.[12] Hardly anybody sees lay participation as an important feature of democracy or as an essential element for the justification of criminal trials. For many decades writers have either half-heartedly defended lay participation or have proposed its abolition.[13]

2. THE STRONG CLAIM: LAY PARTICIPATION IS A NECESSARY CONDITION FOR LEGITIMATE VERDICTS

If one examines lay participation in criminal trials, it is helpful to differentiate between two claims: first, one could defend the *strong claim* that lay participation is a *necessary condition* for a *legitimate conviction* (or a legitimate acquittal) in any democratic state. According to this view, lay participation is crucial as the 'democratic backbone' of court proceedings in that it *supports and authorises the outcome*. This would be to suggest that a trial without lay participation would pose a serious problem because the final decision would lack a proper democratic foundation.[14] Or a *weaker claim* could be made, according to which lay participation is *useful or valuable*—but not a necessary condition for the legitimacy of the verdict. Let me start with the strong claim.

[11] See J Limbach, 'Ehrenamtliche Richter—Demokratie oder Dekoration am Richtertisch?' [1999] *Zeitschrift des Bundesverbandes ehrenamtlicher Richterinnen und Richter* 55; C Hohmann-Dennhardt, 'Der verfassungsrechtliche Rahmen der Beteiligung ehrenamtlicher Richterinnen und Richter an der Rechtsprechung' [2002] *Zeitschrift des Bundesverbandes ehrenamtlicher Richterinnen und Richter* 42–3.

[12] K Volk, 'Der Laie als Strafrichter' in E-W Hanack, P Rieß and G Wendisch (eds), *Festschrift für Hanns Dünnebier* (Berlin and New York, de Gruyter, 1982) 389.

[13] Proposals for abolition: F Baur, 'Laienrichter—heute' in Rechtswissenschaftliche Abteilung der Rechts- und Wirtschaftswissenschaftlichen Fakultät der Universität Tübingen (ed), *Tübinger Festschrift für Eduard Kern* (Tübingen, JBC Mohr, 1968) 54; Spona, n 10 above, 131; P Windel, 'Soll am Laienrichterwesen festgehalten werden?' [1999] 112 *Zeitschrift für Zivilprozess* 293; H Lilie, 'Blinde Kontrollinstanz? Zur Zukunft des Schöffenamtes' in E-W Hanack *et al* (eds), *Festschrift für Peter Rieß* (Berlin and New York, de Gruyter, 2002) 303.

[14] The strong claim does not have many advocates in Germany; it is mostly rejected: Volk, n 12 above, 373–4; Windel, n 13 above, at 295; P Rieß in P Rieß (ed), *Die Strafprozeßordnung und das Gerichtsverfassungsgesetz: Großkommentar, Band 1* (25th edn, Berlin and New York, de Gruyter, 1999), Einl. I Rn. 30; U Benz, *Zur Rolle der Laienrichter im Strafprozess* (Lübeck, Schmidt-Römhild, 1982) 208–9.

(i) Democratic Accountability—Why Only in Some Trials?

One could argue that lay participation must be guaranteed as an indispensable requirement for legitimate verdicts in a truly democratic state. To make this argument, however, it would have to be explained why for example in the English system lay participation is not mandatory.[15] Why should the individual defendant be able to decide whether to demand or to refuse a trial before a jury? If a trial before a professional judge without lay participation is incompatible with the principle of democracy, how could procedures without a jury be reconciled with the strong claim? In Germany, the participation of lay judges is not a matter of the defendants' choice. Lay participation is necessary in trials dealing with more serious accusations, minor cases are heard by one professional judge. This kind of dividing line between trials with and trials without lay participation is not necessarily an argument against the strong claim that democracy requires lay persons to decide in criminal trials. If the strong claim were supported in principle, one might nevertheless limit lay participation to serious cases, eg to decisions of great consequences in terms of sentence severity. If, however, the defendant has a choice *even when confronted with serious indictments*, this suggests a different explanation. The idea is that one can involve 'one's peers' or choose not to do so. Behind this option stands the defendant's personal interest in enhancing her chances of acquittal; lay participation serves as a *protective mechanism*. From this perspective, a 'democratic backbone' would be needed for convictions; acquittals without lay participation would not pose difficulties. The demand for lay participation as a device to protect the rights and interests of the defendant has historical roots to which I will turn next.

(ii) The Historical Background

The historical support for the claim that 'lay participation is necessary to protect defendants' is impressive. For someone living in Germany in the *nineteenth century*, the combination of 'democracy' and 'lay participation in criminal trials' was immediately convincing (at least for the nineteenth-century liberal). It was part of the fight for a democratic society to demand lay participation in the criminal justice system which did not exist at that time. The draft of a German constitution proposed by the assembly in the *Paulskirche* in Frankfurt, dating from 1848, included this demand. The introduction of lay participation into the

[15] If the defendant pleads guilty, there is no jury trial (see J Sprack, *Emmins on Criminal Procedure,* 9th edn, Oxford, Oxford University Press, 2002, 246). For offences 'triable either way' he can opt to be tried by a jury or accept a summary trial at the magistrates' court (ibid 110). For the difference in Scottish Law, see P Duff, 'The Defendant's Right to Trial by Jury: A Neighbour's View' [2000] *Crim L Rev* 85.

Organisation of the Courts Act (*Gerichtsverfassungsgesetz*) in 1877 was seen as a victory of the democratic movement.[16]

But what does the fact that historically a relationship was drawn between 'lay participation' and 'democracy' tell us? Does this prove a necessary link between the two? This is not the case if one takes a closer look at the matter. The goals assembled under the heading 'democracy' were aimed at overcoming deficiencies in the organisation of state authority. The demand for lay participation can be traced back to obvious problems with the judiciary. Judges in the nineteenth century were dependent servants of the ruling sovereign. They did not closely resemble the modern image of a judge, nor did their position resemble that of a modern civil servant. Their position depended entirely on the monarchs' administration and on their goodwill. If a verdict did not please the monarch or influential persons in his environment, they could remove the judge from office and income or inflict criminal punishment on him.[17] Under such conditions, it is not surprising that judges were attentive to the wishes of the royal court. The demand for lay participation forcefully proposed in the nineteenth century must be seen against this background. It was a direct response to the unjust and unfair treatment that defendants had to expect from professional judges. Lay participation was a means of protection against *arbitrariness* and *despotism* exercised by sovereigns through judges who were dependent on them.[18]

A crucial conclusion that was drawn from the nineteenth-century abuses was that the judiciary had to be organised as a third power distinct from other branches of state authority. The ending of the unity of monarchs' administration and the judiciary and the implementation of a separation of powers are of central importance for an enlightened state. *Independence of the judiciary* is firmly entrenched in every modern constitution. The historical movement for lay participation fought for a state organised according to the principles of a *Rechtsstaat*. This goal has been reached in Western European countries. Independence of judges from direct interference and personal, financial independence have been achieved. Consequently, general distrust of professional judges, based on deficiencies of the state organisation, is no longer warranted. Thus, the need to control and restrict professional judges, which historically was the motivation behind the campaign for lay participation, no longer exists.[19]

The view that defendants have to be protected against *arbitrary* decisions by professional judges has lost credibility. Of course, judges remain fallible, that is, prone to *individual biases and prejudices* like any human being making decisions. But such weaknesses can hardly be eliminated by shifting responsibility to jurors and lay judges. It is unlikely that they will be less susceptible to biases and

[16] For the historical development, see H Rüping, 'Funktionen der Laienrichter im Strafverfahren' [1976] *Juristische Rundschau* 269–70; Benz, n 14 above, 44 ff.; Spona, n 10 above, 4 ff.

[17] For the position of judges in 19th-century Germany see Spona, n 10 above, 14 ff.; Benz, n 13 above, 44.

[18] Spona, n 10 above, 17; Benz, n 14 above, 208.

[19] Rieß, n 14 above.

prejudices. On the contrary, experience can foster a more critical stance, whereas lack of experience and education are not conclusive to self reflection. Lay people are in some instances more competent to evaluate factual circumstances—if they are closer to the social background of offenders (and victims) than many judges are.[20] But a gain in terms of social experience is not necessarily a gain in terms of unbiased judgement. It may be in the interest of the defendant to let peers with 'friendly biases' decide. But this cannot be a normative criterion as long as the search for truth remains a central objective of criminal trials. It must be sufficient that professional judges are insulated as much as possible against external pressure. Remaining imperfections on the level of individual psychology deserve attention when decisions about training and recruitment of judges are made. Rather than trying to compensate for the individual biases of professional judges with lay persons' biases, improvements should be sought with respect to the composition of the judiciary. This has to begin with adequate scholarships and funding to attract a wide spectrum of law students. Furthermore, access to judicial positions has to be organised in a way to admit a diversity of social backgrounds and experiences. Insofar as this is not achieved, it is understandable that criminal lawyers favour lay participation as a short-term remedy. Within a judicial system dominated by professional judges with somewhat homogenous personal backgrounds, lay participation might be seen as a counterbalance. However, if one thinks about the organisation of criminal trials from a theoretical perspective, it is doubtful whether this is the best solution in order to minimize biases and prejudices.[21]

(iii) The Meaning of Democracy Today

The question remains whether—*independent of the historical background*—the moral significance of lay participation could be derived from the principle of democracy. As I have just argued, that is not the case if one uses the term 'democratic movement' as a general term for the nineteenth-century efforts to fight the evils resulting from the absolute power of monarchs. In this general sense, the democratic movement encompasses claims which belong to the notion of *Rechtsstaat*, like the separation of powers. But perhaps the necessity of lay

[20] For this point, see B Schäfer and O Wiegand, 'It's Good to Talk—Speaking Rights and the Jury', this volume; M Redmayne, 'Principled Jury Reform', this volume.

[21] If one thinks about the necessity to control state power which goes astray it would not be the judiciary that immediately springs to mind in modern times. Abuse happens, but mainly in the *administrative branch* of state power. In Germany, corruption has been a topic for discussions about implementing better systems of control. Whether lay participation (eg in decision-making bodies composed of civil servants and lay persons) would be a remedy cannot be discussed in detail here. It seems doubtful. The 19th-century notion that decent citizens control professional judges assumed diverse interests. With respect to corruption, it would not be likely that control could be achieved through lay participation. The inducement to obtain some money "on the side" works for lay persons as well as for civil servants.

participation in criminal trials could be derived from the principle of democracy in a more *contemporary sense*? One could argue that in a truly democratic state decisions (or at least *important decisions*) need democratic authorisation. It would not matter if the trial's outcome were a conviction or an acquittal. Lay persons would not participate in the defendant's interest but be necessary in *the public interest*—to guarantee the democratic foundation for criminal punishment, because criminal punishment is a central exercise of state power.

This thesis leads to two questions. First, can democratic authorisation be achieved through lay participation? Secondly, does every important question require immediate democratic legitimation? I will not dwell extensively on the second point as I hope to show that the 'strong claim' can be refuted because lay participation is not sufficient to make the decision a 'democratic decision'. It would be too simplistic to equate lay participation with a 'democratic' trial. It is not obvious that the mere involvement of a few persons without legal training makes the outcome more democratic. If 'democracy' is to be more than a nice catchword, one needs to pay closer attention to the requirements stemming from this principle. Unfortunately, it is not possible to start with a clear definition of 'democracy'. The word is used in an ambiguous way. As in the nineteenth-century discourses, in contemporary political debates it is sometimes introduced as a general heading which circumscribes a widely shared picture of a 'good state' in contrast to totalitarian states. Democracy in this extensive sense encompasses values essential for a satisfyingly organised society (liberty, equality, fairness, etc).[22] However, such a rich picture of the ideal 'democratic state' is not very useful for analytical purposes. At least some of the ambiguity can be reduced if the term 'democracy' is used to describe certain organisational structures and not a bunch of values that distinguish legitimate from totalitarian states.

The starting point for analysis is the common translation of the Greek words *demos* and *kratos*, that is 'the rule of the people'. However, this yields a rather vague starting point because it remains open what kind of 'rule of the people' is required to call a state 'democratic'. 'The rule of the people' might result in either plebiscitarian or representative democracy. At first glance, lay participation could be a way to implement *plebiscitarian democracy* into the criminal trial. One might argue that both in a jury system and in the German system of lay judges 'the people' themselves participate directly and are responsible at least for finding the defendant guilty and perhaps for the sentence as well (as is the case in Germany). It is, however, doubtful whether laypeople in the deciding body can secure plebiscitarian democracy. Can the term 'the people' really be used to describe the two lay judges sitting on the judges' bench or 12 (or 15) jurors? The answer must be no. It is only a small number of individuals who

[22] M Hättich, in Görres-Gesellschaft zur Pflege der Wissenschaft (ed), *Staatslexikon*, Vol. 1 (Freiburg, Herder, 1985) 1182–1183.

decide, not an assembly which could plausibly constitute 'the people'. It can be left open who 'the people' are (all citizens in the country? members of the 'local community', whatever that is?). In any case, a plebiscitarian mode of democracy requires more than the inclusion of a few lay persons. One would need a majority opinion based on a *voting procedure* open to any member of the relevant group.

Consequently, if the participation of a very limited number of lay persons is an instrument of democracy it can only be as an instance of *representative* democracy. This leads to the question what makes lay judges or jurors representative? To answer this, one might suggest *similarity*. Those sitting in court represent, one could argue, all citizens if their opinions and their social backgrounds resemble a cross-section of society as a whole. The assumption is that those constituting 'the public' have to accept decisions as 'rule by the people' provided that the actual decision-makers are 'like themselves'. Problems result if similarity cannot be achieved. The available data for Germany suggest that the social characteristics of lay judges are comparable to those of professional judges, but are not representative of the population as a whole.[23] But even if this difficulty could be overcome, a second problem remains: the problem of numbers. Even if all lay judges assembled for example on the court lists for the state of Bavaria provide a representative sample of the Bavarian population as a whole, the two persons sitting in an individual case do not. If Mr Hinterhuber and Ms Niedermair decide, one cannot claim that they actually represent the community as a whole. They may have found their way onto the list of lay judges because of their profession, age, race and gender, after it has been determined that in these characteristics the list mirrors the 'Bavarian people'. In making their decisions, however, Mr Hinterhuber and Ms Niedermair will rely on their personal, idiosyncratic view of the criminal justice system and the world in general. Democratic legitimitation through similarity presumes that those deciding (not always, of course, but with a certain degree of reliability) take the 'typical stance' which those they represent expect them to take. Two lay persons sitting on the judges' bench do not reliably represent 'the sovereignty of the people'. The similarity model provides a rather weak foundation for the claim that lay participation is necessary, and that would be the case even if great efforts were made when selecting the pool of jurors or lay judges. A representative decision would require a much larger number of decision-makers for each individual case. With 12 or 15 jurors, the situation is somewhat better than with two lay judges. But even then, the opinions of 12 or 15 women and men cannot yield a truly representative picture of what 'the people' would opt for in any particular case.

[23] Spona, n 10 above, 92 ff; Volk, n 12 above, 375. It would be hard to achieve a more careful selection of lay judges: the mode in which they are chosen in Germany is complicated and not suited to establishing a pool of lay judges closely mirroring society: see Windel, n 13 above, 301 ff.

The deficiencies of the 'representation through similarity'—model may invite the conclusion that a stronger democratic foundation is necessary. The classical picture of representative democracy looks like this: those who are represented have the right to elect those representing them. Even if voters are surprised by acts of their representatives, they have made a choice and they may express disapproval in future elections. 'Representation through vote' could be applied not just to Parliament, but also to the judicial branch, as it is, for example, in the United States.[24] From this point of view, combining professional and lay judges only disguises the lack of genuine representative democracy as long as *both* groups and most importantly, professional judges are not elected by the people. To implement a 'representation through vote' approach could also have another substantial advantage. It could provide democratic legitimation without the drawback of having people exercising judicial powers who lack legal training and sufficient experience. Voters could choose from qualified lawyers.

However, this would inevitably create conflicts between two important goals: 'democracy' on one hand, *Rechtsstaat* on the other hand. For every gain in terms of democratic legitimacy, a toll in form of *judicial dependence* would need to be paid. Elected judges are not independent. They have to take into account what the public thinks about specific sentences if they wish to have a stable and lasting career. A prudential judge needs to anticipate public reactions and to act accordingly. One might argue that adapting outcomes to the perceived wishes of the public is the essence of democracy. However, this is problematic in criminal trials, especially given the dominant 'get tough on crime' mood displayed by the population or at least by the media. As a judge would not be in a position to determine actual opinions in the population, he or she would need to rely on the popular media to obtain an approximation of 'the public's needs'. At least occasionally a judge who depends on her prospects for re-election would be tempted to modify a sentence against her professional judgement. The danger this poses is substantial. Judicial independence as part of the *Rechtsstaat* is too important to sacrifice for a model of representative judges. This point leads back to a question which I asked at the beginning of this paragraph: does every important decision in a democratic state require direct democratic legitimation? With respect to the tension between the goal of democracy and the goal of *Rechtsstaat*, there are reasons for limiting democratic involvement to questions concerning the content of abstract laws and rules. Decisions concerning individual cases, especially criminal cases which stir the emotions, are better left to professional judges who are emotionally detached and independent from public pressure.

To conclude this section: lay participation in criminal trials is not a version of decision-making according to the rules of either representative or plebiscitarian

[24] In Germany, the Socialist parties at the beginning of the 20th century opted for elected judges in order to get the proletarian perspective into the courts which were markedly anti-socialist: Rüping, n 16 above, 270.

democracy. This refutes the strong claim that the outcome of a criminal trial is only legitimate if there is a 'democratic backbone'. Convictions or acquittals do not lack legitimacy if they are imposed by professional judges without lay participation.

3. THE WEAK CLAIM: LAY PARTICIPATION IS VALUABLE

Lay participation is not a necessary requirement for legitimate verdicts because democracy cannot be achieved in the criminal trial; it is not possible to justify the *outcome* by the significance of democracy. However, *weaker claims* about appropriate *procedures* remain to be examined. One could argue that lay participation has merits, and therefore that it should be part of a decent criminal justice system, albeit that the principle of democracy does not demand it for legitimate outcomes. Involvement of lay persons either may be useful for the criminal justice system in a functional way or it might promote or express normative values. Lay participation may serve ends which are valuable and which may justify its retention. Democracy reappears—not to support the trial's outcome but as an argument why certain modes of organising trials may be more in accordance with a normative framework than others.

(i) Increased Public Trust

German criminal lawyers who argue in favour of lay participation typically point to beneficial effects, not for individual actors, but for the legal system. The inclusion of lay judges is said to enhance the *public's trust* in the criminal justice system.[25] At first sight, this may sound convincing. But, like many arguments pointing to social psychology, it is hard to substantiate. How are we to substantiate the alleged increase in public trust? One possibility would be to count on the positive experiences of lay judges, which they communicate to their families, friends and neighbours, etc. However, there are objections to the hypothesis that personal participation and increased public trust are linked. Serving as a juror or lay judge will sometimes be frustrating, which will influence the individual's perception of the criminal justice system and consequently the narrative which the juror or lay judge communicates. Furthermore, it does not seem likely that public perceptions of the criminal trial are simply products of such personal accounts. Stories lay judges may spread at family celebrations or in their local pubs are less influential than the picture of criminal trials portrayed in the media. Public trust in the legal system depends to a large extent both on the media coverage of real trials and on fictional crime stories. In Germany, the majority of people do not even know about the existence of lay

[25] Schreiber, n 10 above, 952. See Rieß, n 14 above, for a more sceptical view.

judges.[26] Other than the jury as the background for dramatic court scenes in English or American movies, the lay judge is not attractive for entertainment purposes. Due to his passive role, popular court programmes do not pay him much attention.

But even if many of those constituting 'the public' knew about the existence of lay judges in Germany, the thesis that such knowledge is important to generate trust in criminal courts barely survives critical examination. The argument would presuppose a certain level of distrust of professional judges. If the public trusted professional judges both to examine the facts competently and to apply the law in a proper way, it would not perceive a need for lay persons' assistance. In Germany, there are no data to support the hypothesis that the work of professional judges is regarded as inadequate. On the contrary, compared with other institutions representing the state, courts enjoy a remarkably high degree of trust.[27] It is unlikely that the esteem expressed for the courts is due to, or depends on, the integration of lay judges. The situation may be different in the United Kingdom and the United States. Juries have a more visible role in the criminal justice system and are popularly portrayed in numerous books and films. If juries are perceived as essential for the legal culture, and I presume this is the case, it is plausible that they become an important indication of a 'good legal system' for the citizens. Consequently, abolishing lay participation may cause discontent, and it makes sense to claim that the existence of the jury is useful to secure public trust in the criminal justice system. However, one must bear in mind that this is an argument based on social psychology, not on normative reasoning. It may be useful to have juries because their popularity helps to strengthen public support for the legal system as a whole. This does not establish that normative principles require lay participation.

(ii) Active Citizens

There is a further argument that might be used to support lay participation in criminal trials. I will call this the 'active citizenship' argument. It relates the lay participation to democracy along the following lines: having citizens engaged in the administration of state power is important in a democratic system; democracy needs citizens who are active participants rather than passive subordinates; therefore one should organise state institutions in a way that allows opportunities for lay participation.[28] This could be formulated as a functional claim (the system runs more smoothly with competent and responsible citizens), but also as

[26] S Machura and M Asimov, 'Das Ansehen von Anwälten bei Jurastudenten' [2004] *Zeitschrift für Rechtssoziologie* 3 at 23.

[27] See T Raiser, *Das lebende Recht. Rechtssoziologie in Deutschland* (3rd edn, Baden-Baden, Nomos, 1999) 355.

[28] See, eg, Limbach, n 11 above, 55.

a normative reason (participation is valuable as such, as it expresses commitment to the ideal of the citizen in a democratic state). In contrast with the argument discussed above, the 'active citizenship' argument does not authorise final decisions in criminal trials, but rather makes *procedures* more appropriate or more in accordance with fundamental values.

The 'active citizenship' argument seems convincing at first glance, especially if one considers the normative side. On a closer look, however, some doubts remain. If citizens' commitment and active participation are to be promoted, such participation ought to be primarily voluntary. Putting citizens under an obligation to fulfil functions of the state does not come as close to the ideal of active citizens. This would mean that lay participation in criminal trials ought best to be *voluntary*. However, this would also have its drawbacks. The question is whether lay judges and jurors who are chosen on the basis of voluntary applications compromise other important normative values.[29] In contrast with the rhetoric of active citizenship, in real life not everybody can afford to spend time in court. Only rather small subgroups of the population with sufficient spare time could realistically be expected to take the role of juror or lay judge on a voluntary basis. They would hardly be representative of 'the people'; they might be far removed from the social background of the offender and thus heighten his perception of alienation. In the worst case they might not even be well suited to the truth-finding task of the trial. Therefore, although voluntary activities in general should be encouraged, it would need further examination whether this applies to lay participation in criminal trials. If lay participation is *not voluntary*, other difficulties arise. Extending the notion of 'active citizenship' to participation in criminal trials, which is mandatory and time-consuming, conflicts with individual interests citizens have. The interest in deciding for oneself how to balance personal pursuits and commitment to tasks fulfilled for the community is a legitimate interest. Respect for autonomy requires the right not to be bothered with assignments for the sake of the public and the right to have tasks delegated to specialised professionals paid by the state. Therefore, the notion of 'active citizenship' is not a strong foundation for lay participation in criminal trials.

(iii) Influence on the Development of Law

In his comment to this paper, Victor Tadros made a further suggestion as to how lay participation may be connected to democracy. Lay participation allows different people to affect how the criminal law develops and is applied to cases. This is not just a claim about 'public trust', but a normative claim relating lay participation to democracy. Rule of the people, so the line of reasoning goes,

[29] In Germany, lay judges are chosen from lists handed in by political representatives on the local level (see for details Windel, n 13 above, 302–3). The persons on these lists consent to be included.

should not be restricted to parliamentary proceedings creating statutes but also be extended to the judicial development of legal norms. Although true representation of 'the people' cannot be achieved with a limited number of jurors or lay judges, Tadros argues that it is still preferable in a democratic state to have at least some lay persons involved. In contrast with the argument I have discussed as the 'strong claim', Tadros's argument does not require lay participation to legitimate the outcome of any particular trial as democratic. He connects the *creation of law as a process* (with all of its consequences beyond the individual conviction) with the principle of democracy.

This is an important argument, especially for *common law systems*. If the content of legal norms is not decided by elected members of parliament but through individual court decisions, these norms lack immediate democratic authorisation. The plea to have at least a few people take responsibility alongside professional judges (even if democratic decision making, strictly speaking is not possible) is understandable. In a *civil law system*, on the other hand, laws are passed by parliament. The development of law is the task of those elected by the people. However, one has to take into consideration the fact that, even in civil law systems, law is not identical with statutes. There are gaps in the statutes (for example, many important elements of the general part of criminal law are not defined in the Penal Code) and vague or broad legal terms within statutes need to be defined. Thus, law is also partly shaped by judicial work even if a bulk of statutes exists.

Does this mean that in the common law system as well as in civil law jurisdictions the principle of democracy calls for lay participation? There are indeed reasons supporting Tadros' line of argument. The development of law should be based on a careful, balanced evaluation of conflicting standards and values. Leaving these considerations to professional judges can exclude voices which could express differing, but legitimate, interests and bring in other normative perspectives completing the picture. One could opt for lay participation in criminal trials, so that the process of law-making allows the inclusion of diverse views. However, there are objections to the thesis that lay participation is valuable on these grounds. The advantages of including different people have to be weighed against disadvantages. Laypeople will not only bring in different views about questions of normative relevance, but it is also likely that they will add stronger emotional components. These may be emotions favouring the particular defendant or emotions operating to her disadvantage. Either way, this would be an unwanted input. To develop legal norms requires the setting aside of strong emotions, the evaluation of the law's significance as far as possible with rationality and detachment, and the estimation of the effects of legal change. It seems plausible that professional judges are better at controlling emotions than lay people. Of course, like every human being they are not immune to emotional reactions, but education and experience help judges to recognise those reactions and to achieve a somewhat more detached stance over time. Lay judges' opinions, especially the punitive views they sometimes express, can become an obstacle in the effort to reach sensible agreement.[30] Also, law-making requires skill and knowledge, for example to foresee the consequences that a particular decision can have for the interpretation of other legal norms and for future cases. Consequently, although lay participation may introduce more diversity into the development of legal norms, it bears risks for the quality and the consistency of the legal system which results from this process.

(iv) Local Values

Another argument in favour of juries (or lay judges) emphasises *specific local practices* and *local legal customs* which have not been fully appreciated by a national or federal law-maker (or which are even incompatible with the evaluation by a national parliament).[31] The 'local value' argument has its strongest persuasive force in very large states with populations not united by a shared national identity or a shared cultural background. If historical or political contingencies have thrown together heterogeneous groups in one state (as it was the case in the former Soviet Union) which are governed by uniform statutes, the resulting conflicts between local cultures and the federal or national legal system can be ameliorated by allowing some compromises when controversial norms are applied. Under such circumstances, juries or lay judges may give voice to local values which have been neglected by the central parliament. If the state's population is too diverse to achieve consent about legal norms, but uniform statutes exist, it may be a compromise in practice to allow 'diluted' application. However, one has to bear in mind that these are awkward solutions for coping with an imperfect mode of state organisation in order to help groups which are powerless on the national or federal level. A central state which is too large should be reorganised according to the principle of federalism and delegate law-making to local parliaments in areas of diverging cultural backgrounds. If one thinks about the criminal trial on a theoretical level, its role should not be to compensate shortcomings in the law-making process. Furthermore, it is not even compelling to introduce lay participation to give weight to local values: if the professional judges were appointed on a local level, they could seek compromises when federal or national law clashed with the local culture.

The 'local values' argument could also be applied to smaller and traditionally more homogenous states like most Western European states—it retains some plausibility as cultural differences have grown with processes of immigration. 'Local values' do not, in that context, refer in a strict sense to geographic distri-

[30] I remember (in my legal training) deliberations in the judges' chamber where one of the lay judges expressed the view that all drug dealers should get life imprisonment. The lay judge tried to apply his view to the case in question (where a pound of cocaine had been sold) and he had almost convinced his fellow lay judge before the professional judge managed to control the situation.

[31] For this argument, see M Matravers, '"More than Just Illogical": Truth and Jury Nullification' in RA Duff, *et al* (eds), *The Trial on Trial, Vol. 1* (Oxford, Hart Publishing, 2004), 71, at 80.

butions of larger groups in parts of the country, but mainly to values shared by minorities in terms of ethnic origin (and possibly also to values characteristic of social classes). But the argument that minority values can be introduced into the criminal trial by lay persons does not only raise questions about their capability for law-making, which I discussed in the preceding section. More importantly, the argument leads to difficulties if such so-called 'local values' run contrary to acknowledged normative values. It is not possible to discuss such conflicts extensively here. In most cases where there are manifest differences, it would not be warranted to let 'local values' override an established normative framework, especially if the latter is written down in a constitution. Central principles like gender equality, equal treatment of different religions (and of religious beliefs versus atheism or indifference), autonomy and personal responsibility, etc. should not be challenged with reference to 'local values'. Also, even if fundamental normative values do not stand in the way, deviation from the terms of a statute is problematic. For such deviation would violate the principle of equal application of the law. One could only seriously consider letting local values affect a trial's outcome if a legal norm is sufficiently flexible and if there are no conflicts with fundamental normative principles. And, even if one makes this concession, it does not substantiate an urgent need to let lay persons decide. If relevant 'local values' are unknown to the judge, it is for the interested party to describe them and demand that they are taken into account.

(v) Defendants' Autonomy

In 'The Criminal Trial and the Legitimation of Punishment'[32] Markus Dubber outlines another argument that might be used to defend the participation of lay persons in criminal trials, in the context of the use of the jury in the US. This argument is based not on the principle of democracy but rather on that of *autonomy*. The legitimacy of the trial's outcome presupposes, so Dubber claims, that the proceedings reflect the defendant's autonomy. Despite the (in most cases) obvious lack of actual consent, the defendant must be able to see the act of criminal punishment as an act of self-government. This requires that the persons who are responsible for convictions must *represent* her, and this role of representative is to be taken by the jury.[33] Other than the widespread notion discussed above, from this perspective the jury's role is not to be a representative of the public, but of the defendant. Dubber argues that 'the diminuition of lay participation in the United States, Germany, and elsewhere reflects the gradual but continuous disappearance of concern for the legitimacy of state punishment'.[34]

[32] In RA Duff et al, n 31 above, 85.

[33] M Dubber, n 32, at 96–7; Dubber, n 4 above, 591–2.

[34] N 4 above, 602.

The notion of 'representation through similarity' cannot be applied in the context of this argument. If one consciously chose lay persons who in their social background, opinions and attitudes were as similar as possible to those of the defendant, conflict both with the truth-finding goal of the criminal trial and the equal application of the law could arise. Dubber refers to empathy as the factor linking the representative to the represented and as the foundation of self-government.[35] However, too much empathy with the defendant obviously blurs the assessment of facts as well as running counter to fair legal evaluation. Thus, the concept of 'representative' must be taken to a more abstract level, which Dubber describes as being a member of a 'community of justice'. He assumes that a hypothetical or idealistic 'community of justice' exists between the jury and the defendant despite a factual non-similarity between the actual persons. However, if one does *not* see representation as a matter of *actual* social and psychological similarities, it remains unclear why the defendant should see jurors or lay judges as members of 'his community'. Why should a verdict by professional judges without lay participation be perceived as a heteronymous decision, while the decision of a jury could be labelled 'self-government' or autonomous? If lay participants are not 'peers with a friendly bias' or at least 'similar peers', it remains unclear how a merely hypothetical 'community of justice' could make the sentence an act of self-government. If the *only* basis of the 'community of justice' is the lay status of the jury members, this implies a rather suspicious, even hostile, attitude towards state organs.[36] It may be true that in reality many offenders distrust state officials more than the lay persons acting in court. However, as a normative claim, it is not obvious that a mere fiction of 'self-government' should make convictions more legitimate than conviction by professional judges—provided, the judiciary is organised according to the principles of a *Rechtsstaat*.[37] As important as autonomy and self-government are for the creation of penal norms, it might be more honest to admit that the actual infliction of criminal punishment cannot be derived from these values. Conviction and sentencing are judgments by others. Seeing them as crucial parts of the communication with the defendant or, more specifically, of the process of blaming the defendant, requires that proper standards of communication are met. These standards of communication (amongst other criteria) also have to be compatible with the (adult) offender's status as an autonomous being. But it seems artificial to stretch the notion of autonomy further and to see actual blame itself as an autonomous act of the defendant.

[35] Supra n 32, at 97.

[36] Dubber does not draw this conclusion. He leaves open the question whether juries are indispensable: see Dubber, n 32 above, 100.

[37] I have argued above that election of judges is problematic and not in accordance with the principle of '*Rechtsstaat*'. Therefore, the idea of establishing a 'community of justice' besides the professional judge is understandable in the US-system.

(vi) Lay Participation to Counterbalance Habits of Professional Judges

In the German literature, one finds another line of reasoning. It runs like this: a court consisting solely of professional judges tends to develop negative professional habits, specifically a *technical or esoteric use of language*. Lay judges could be a *counterweight*: the arguments of professional judges have to pass two tests: they must be both plausible and capable of being understood by persons without legal training.[38] This argument has persuasive power if one considers how judicial careers are made in Germany. Judges choose their profession at a relatively young age; the decision to become a judge has to be taken shortly after passing the law exams. At a later stage in life, even with excellent grades and rich experience as a practising lawyer, one is considered too old to become a judge. Early entry into the judicial rank fosters developments I have just described. To rely in legal discourse on language rather far removed from ordinary language is characteristic for legal teaching. In contact with clients, legal counsel are forced to express themselves in a more understandable way. Such efforts are also recommended for professional judges.[39]

It could thus be useful to integrate lay persons into the system because the necessity to communicate properly is more urgent if the professional judge has to convince lay colleagues.[40] (I am not sure how far this argument is applicable to the judiciary in countries where the habit of esoteric legal language and the sense of judges as a 'separate class' among lawyers is less pronounced.[41]) This argument could be formulated as a normative one—appropriate communication not only affects the contentment of defendants and others appearing in court, but communication aiming at mutual understanding is an essential normative function of the trial.[42] Thus the role of lay persons could be defended as a means to promote language understandable by non-lawyers. This argument does not point to the immediate consequences of the participation of lay persons, but rather to the consequential effects that they may have. Of all the arguments discussed, this seems to be the most convincing. Whether the ideal of improved communication through lay participation can be realised in practice is another question. This would rest on lay participants not merely passively accepting what happens around them—as it is often the case in practice.

38 See Schreiber, n 10 above, 951; Benz, n 14 above, 210–11.

39 Of course, it would be unfair to German judges to state that they all resort to incomprehensible language. Many are well aware of the fact that communication is essential for their performance. However, one has to distinguish between individual persons' efforts and the idea that lay participation might counteract some structural deficiencies produced by the way the German judiciary works.

40 Windel, n 13 above, 300, more sceptically points to the fact that lay judges are not involved when the reasons given for a certain sentence outcome are written; see also Volk, n 12 above, 387.

41 But see for a similar argument Redmayne, n 20 above.

42 See, eg, TRA Duff, *Trials and Punishments* (Cambridge, Cambridge University Press, 1986) 114 ff; RA Duff, *Punishment, Communication and Community* (New York, Oxford University Press, 2000).

4. CONCLUSION

In a German text, it has been commented that lay judges 'look good' in a democratic system.[43] That suggests that there are no reasons beyond a pleasant façade to have lay persons in the courts. This rather critical remark expresses reservations about the necessity of lay participation, reservations which are widespread in Germany. Indeed, a sceptical stance towards enthusiastic appraisals of lay participation in criminal trials is justified. One cannot corroborate the *strong claim* that the legitimacy of a criminal trial's outcome requires democratic underpinning in the form of lay participation. Lay judges and juries do not introduce plebiscitarian elements into the trial, nor do they convince as a feature of representative democracy. Very small numbers of lay persons can not represent 'the people'. They may claim to present 'the view of the community', but in fact they express their personal views—which may or may not be identical to the decision one would obtain through a general vote on the matter in question.

Before rejecting the concept of lay participation, however, one has to pay attention to arguments which support *weaker claims* defending the *desirability* of lay participation. These go back to the premise that a criminal trial ought to be organised in a way which gives weight to central normative principles like democracy or autonomy. The problem with most of these arguments is that there are also important counter-arguments. One reason given for lay participation is to encourage active citizenship (rather than passive subordinates)—but difficulties arise: it is questionable whether lay judges and jurors who participate eagerly, that is voluntarily, are well suited to their task. Arguing for lay participation because lay persons bring different values and attitudes into the process of law-making also invites objections. One can raise doubts about lay persons' ability to take on the difficult task of creating legal norms (which requires knowledge and lack of emotional commitment). The idea that lay persons voice 'local values' leads to the question whether 'local values' ought to override the conflicting normative framework (in most cases, this would not be an appropriate result). To stress the defendants' autonomy and capacity for self-government and the need to have a jury as their representative utilises a highly abstract concept of self-government and implies distrust of the state which weakens the position of the judiciary. In the end, one argument in favour of lay participation remains: having to co-operate with lay colleagues compels professional judges to use language which is understandable by everybody. Here, the difficulty is in realising this idea in practice. In a society in which lay judges have low esteem, such as Germany, they play only a marginal role in the day-to-day work of the courts and despite all idealistic rhetoric, the professional judges will not strive to communicate effectively with them, but rather ignore their presence

[43] Volk, n 12 above, 373.

as much as possible. Only with strong cultural support for the idea of lay participation will the legal system grant them influence.

This highlights an important point: lay persons in courts have *symbolic* meaning. The degree of support for this institution expresses, more or less explicitly, *distrust of the state and professional judges as state officials*. The desire to control state organs through lay persons is a cultural phenomenon. Differences between German writers and those from English-speaking countries concerning the significance of lay participation stem from different ways of seeing the relationship between the state and its citizens. Germans are more inclined to let professional judges do their job. Distrust is more frequently expressed about the work of lay judges.[44] From this perspective, it is easier to feel comfortable with decisions made by people who are professionally trained. Trust in the work of the judiciary is trust in education and professional standards. The contrasting Anglo-American point of view is a symptom of a more profound underlying distrust both of lawyers and of power exercised by the state. The role of juries and lay judges from this perspective is predominantly of symbolic significance: their existence signifies that 'state officials are not allowed to make important decisions on their own'. In the end, the prevailing attitudes towards the state and the degree of trust professional judges enjoy will determine both the continuing existence of lay participation and the actual influence lay persons have in criminal trials.

[44] See for example Schreiber, n 10 above, 952.

Part III
Jury Nullification

[6]

THE MYTH OF THE NULLIFYING JURY

*Nancy S. Marder**

I. INTRODUCTION

The jury is an institution under threat, and the form that the threat has taken most recently is an attack on jury nullification. Members of the press, judiciary, and academia have criticized jurors for not following the law as it has been given to them by the judge. Recent high-profile cases, such as the criminal trial of O.J. Simpson for the murders of Nicole Brown Simpson and Ron Goldman[1] and the criminal trial of police officers Stacey Koon and Laurence Powell for the beating of motorist Rodney King[2] have brought the subject of jury nullification onto the front pages of newspapers.[3] In these

* Associate Professor of Law, University of Southern California Law School. B.A. 1980, Yale University; M. Phil. 1982, Cambridge University; J.D. 1987, Yale Law School. I am particularly grateful for suggestions and comments from Scott Altman, Jennifer Arlen, Scott Bice, Howard Chang, Erwin Chemerinsky, David Cruz, Mary Dudziak, Jeremy Eden, Catherine Fisk, Ron Garet, Thomas Green, Tom Griffith, Ariela Gross, James Hackney, Deborah Hensler, Tom Lyon, Ed McCaffery, Tom Rowe, Elyn Saks, Larry Simon, Nomi Stolzenberg, Chuck Weisselberg, and Jamison Wilcox, for the opportunity to present my work to faculty workshops at American, Boston University, Chicago-Kent, Minnesota, Quinnipiac, Rutgers-Camden, UC-Davis, and USC, the USC Faculty Women's Writing Group, the Southern California Law Review, a conference entitled "Jury Reform: Making Juries Work" at the University of Michigan Law School, and at the 1998 Law & Society Annual Meeting, and for valuable research assistance by Quesiyah Ali-Chavez, Deja Hemingway, Kim Leone, and Jennifer Zolezzi. My research was generously supported by the USC Faculty Research Fund.

[1] *See* People v. Simpson, No. BA097211 (Cal. Super. Ct. 1995).

[2] *See* People v. Powell, No. BA035498 (Cal. Super. Ct. 1991); *see also* Richard A. Serrano, *All 4 Acquitted in King Beating; Verdict Stirs Outrage*, L.A. TIMES, Apr. 30, 1992, at A1.

[3] As one columnist remarked, prior to the verdict in the Simpson trial, "'jury nullification' was just another obscure little doctrine that hardly anyone but lawyers cared about. No more. Barber shops and beauty parlors everywhere are all abuzz with talk of 'jury nullification,' whether they call it by its proper name or not." Clarence Page, *O.J. Verdict Rekindles an Old Jury Debate*, CINCINNATI POST, Nov. 16, 1995, at 21A. Other journalists also focused on nullification. *See, e.g.*, *All Things Considered: Simpson Case Focuses Attention on Jury Nullification* (NPR radio broadcast, Oct. 16, 1995), *available in* 1995 WL 9892228 [hereinafter *All Things Considered: Simpson Case*] ("The acquittal of O.J. Simpson has renewed interest in the legal concept of jury nullification."); Editorial, *Jury in the Simpson Case Sent Resounding Message*, STATE J.-REG. (Springfield, Ill.), Oct. 5, 1995, at 6 ("In his closing argument, Simpson lead attorney Johnnie Cochran made a thinly veiled appeal for jury nullification—that is, for jurors to look beyond the evidence of the case and to send a message .... And that is precisely what the jury did."); Editorial, *The Simpson Case: Black and White Justice*, S.F. CHRON., Oct. 4, 1995, at A18 ("Although Cochran denies it, many observers concluded that the skill and legal dexterity of the well-financed defense team led to a case of 'jury nullification,' in which jurors were able to dismiss overwhelming evidence of guilt."); Robert Marquand & Daniel B. Wood, *Lessons Drawn From Simpson in*

instances, the press used the term so loosely that it came to mean any verdict with which the press and public disagree. With such a misunderstanding of nullification, it is not surprising that the jury is increasingly viewed as an institution gone awry.

At the same time as the press has decried jury nullification, the judiciary and legislature have attempted to rein in the jury's power, including its power to nullify. The U.S. Court of Appeals for the Second Circuit recently ruled that judges have an obligation to inquire further of jurors if during deliberations they give any indication that they are considering nullification.[4] Any juror intending to nullify is to be removed from the jury by the judge.[5] Thus, the Second Circuit puts judges in the position of second-guessing jurors in some circumstances, and in doing so, limits a jury's nullification power. The judiciary is not alone in its concerns about the jury; the legislature has also engaged in efforts to constrain the jury's power.[6]

Black, White, CHRISTIAN SCI. MONITOR, Oct. 5, 1995, at 1 ("'Jury nullification' is the legal buzzword of the hour."); Mark Whitaker, *Whites v. Blacks*, NEWSWEEK, Oct. 16, 1995, at 28, *available in* 1995 WL 14646939 ("When the acquittal came back so swiftly, many commentators assumed that the largely black jury had engaged in what legal experts call 'jury nullification'—ignoring the evidence to send a broader message, in this case to the police."); Michael Paul Williams, *Jury Nullification Question is Fallout of Simpson Trial*, RICHMOND TIMES-DISPATCH, June 3, 1996, at B1 ("Jury nullification became part of our national vocabulary after the verdict in the O.J. Simpson trial.").

Jury nullification was also one explanation offered to help the public make sense of the acquittals of Stacey Koon and Laurence Powell. *See, e.g.*, Gail Appleson, *King Verdict Shakes Faith in Jury System*, REUTERS, May 3, 1992 ("Legal experts said the King verdict spotlights one of the most difficult problems to overcome with jurors—a problem they call 'nullification.'"); Jason Berry, *Crime Punishment: Why Do Some Juries Condone Criminal Behavior?*, DALLAS MORNING NEWS, Feb. 27, 1994, at 1J ("The nullification factor in these cases [including Simi Valley] stemmed from a parochial protectiveness layered in denial."); Alan W. Bock, *Criminal Justice: King Beating Started a Cycle of Violence*, ORANGE COUNTY REG. (Cal.), May 1, 1992, *available in* 1992 WL 6349907 ("[W]hat we saw in Simi Valley . . . was a case of surreptitious jury nullification. The jury simply decided, in this case, to ignore the law, although it's unlikely any of them would admit it."); Alan Dershowitz, *Once Again, Jury Errs on Defendants' Side*, BUFFALO NEWS, May 5, 1992, at B2 ("[T]he most common manifestation of what has come to be called 'jury nullification' has always been in cases where policemen were charged with the use of excessive force, especially when that force was directed against so-called 'undesirable elements.'"); Richard Lacayo, *Anatomy of an Acquittal*, TIME, May 11, 1992, at 30 ("In the eyes of many people, both white and black, it appears that the jury simply chose to nullify the evidence—to put it aside in making their decision—which American law allows."); Michael W. Rosen, *Juries Should Have To Follow the Law*, COLO. SPRINGS GAZETTE TELEGRAPH, May 17, 1992, at G2 ("If you liked the Rodney King verdict, you'll love jury nullification."); Jerome H. Skolnick, *The Jury Was Never Meant To Be Rational*, L.A. TIMES, May 1, 1992, at B7 ("The independence of juries is so valued that they are allowed to nullify the evidence and fail to convict, when it is perfectly clear, as in the King trial, that the defendants are guilty.").

[4] *See* United States v. Thomas, 116 F.3d 606 (2d Cir. 1997).

[5] *See id.* at 608, 617.

[6] After the Koon/Powell and Simpson verdicts, among others, there were legislative efforts to constrain juries and to make convictions easier to obtain. *See* Jan Crawford Greenburg & Ginger Orr, *Simpson Trial Yields a Verdict Against the System*, NEWS TRIB. (Tacoma, Wash.), Oct. 8, 1995, at F1 ("State legislators in California have responded to the [Simpson] trial by introducing legislation to change the jury system. . . . [One change] would do away with the requirement that juries be unanimous in their

The first step toward countering the press's mislabeling of verdicts as jury nullification and slowing the judicial and legislative efforts to weaken the jury and to limit the jury's nullification power is to examine precisely what is meant by jury nullification. In Part II, I develop a working definition of jury nullification. In Part III, I identify three situations in which jury nullification is likely to occur. First, a jury may nullify to avoid applying a law to a particular defendant. Second, a jury may nullify to avoid applying a law that it regards as bad. Third, a jury may nullify as a response to social conditions. Although an instance of nullification may fit into more than one of these categories, the categories are a useful heuristic device for understanding what is meant by nullification and for assessing whether jury nullification is harmful or beneficial to the judicial system.

Before analyzing the harms and benefits of jury nullification, however, I consider two different conceptions of the jury. In Part IV, I describe one view, which I label the conventional view, in which the jury is supposed to find facts and apply the law. In some cases, this might be a mechanical operation; in others, the jury might have to work harder to decipher ambiguous terms. However, in both cases, the jury is supposed to apply the law consistent with the legislature's words and the judge's instructions. To the extent the jury does more than this, it is intruding upon the legislature's or judge's respective roles. This conception of the jury exists more in theory than in practice, but the theory has proven compelling to both judges and some academics, and it is this theory of the jury that judges convey to jurors throughout the trial.

---

decisions."); Editorial, *The O.J. Simpson Case: A Legal Aberration*, S.F. CHRON., Oct. 7, 1995, at A18 ("The Simpson trial and verdict ha[ve] given rise to a host of quick-fix proposals to reform the courts, including one particularly misguided notion to replace unanimous jury verdicts with 10-to-2 decisions."); Whitaker, *supra* note 3, *available in* 1995 WL 14646939 ("[D]isgust over the Simpson outcome might simply leave whites determined to make it more difficult for black juries to acquit black defendants. Prospects suddenly brightened for a California amendment that would allow 'non-majority' verdicts of 10-2 . . . .").

One proposal debated in California called for abandoning the unanimity required in criminal trials and switching to an 11-1 or 10-2 decision rule. *See, e.g., California Blue Ribbon Panel Urges Wide Range of Jury Reforms*, WEST'S LEGAL NEWS, May 3, 1996, *available in* 1996 WL 260677 (announcing the Judicial Council's Blue Ribbon Commission's proposals for jury reform, which included a recommendation for nonunanimous verdicts); Greg Krikorian, *Committee Hearing a Trial by Fire for the Jury System*, L.A. TIMES, July 28, 1995, at B3 (describing a proposal by State Senator Charles Calderon (D-Whittier), Chair of the Senate Judiciary Committee, which "would allow 11-1 verdicts in all but capital cases"); Jason L. Riley, *Rule of Law: Should a Jury Verdict Be Unanimous?*, WALL ST. J., Nov. 22, 1995, at A11 (recounting California District Attorneys Association's proposal to amend the state's constitution to allow for nonunanimous juries); *Wilson Touts Jury Reform*, L.A. DAILY NEWS, July 18, 1995, at N4 ("[Gov. Pete] Wilson told a group of prosecuting attorneys . . . that he supports a bill . . . that would allow criminal convictions on a 10-2 vote of jurors in all but death penalty cases."). The purpose behind these efforts was to make it easier for juries to convict and more difficult for one or two jurors, who may be advocating nullification or some other outsider position, to create a hung jury, which adds costs and delays.

In Part V, I propose another conception of the jury, which describes a broader role for the jury. I label this understanding of the jury a process view. This view recognizes that the jury does more than find facts or apply the law; inherent in all of the jury's activities is an interpretive role. The jury engages in interpretation whenever it is asked to find facts or apply a legal standard that is vague or ambiguous. In addition to its interpretive role, the jury also plays a political role; it provides feedback to other branches of government about when they are overstepping their own roles.

These competing views of the jury lead to different conclusions about whether jury nullification is helpful or harmful to the judicial system. Under a conventional view of the jury, the three situations in which nullification can occur are all causes for concern. In each, the jury is usurping the responsibilities of another branch. The conventional account of the jury means that any time the jury does more than find facts or apply law, such as nullify, it is doing something harmful. The myth of the nullifying jury, as told by proponents of the conventional view, is that nullification is always harmful.

Under a process view, however, the jury does more than just find facts and apply law; it also plays interpretive and political roles. Under this broader conception of the jury's roles, the three situations when nullification occurs provide more benefits than harms. In all three, though perhaps to a lesser extent in the third, nullification is consistent with the jury's broad role, and nullification enables the jury to provide valuable feedback to the legislature, executive, or judiciary.

Just as the conventional and process views of the jury lead to different conclusions about the efficacy of nullification, they also lead to different proposals about how best to respond to nullification, as I explore in Part VI. Those who hold a conventional view seek to limit opportunities for jury nullification. The Second Circuit has suggested that this can be done through judicial intervention. For academics and activists who go beyond a process view of the jury, and see the jury mainly as a vehicle to bring about social change, they seek to increase nullification in cases that promote their respective causes. However, I believe there is a middle ground, in which nullification is neither forbidden nor advocated, but is permitted in those rare instances when justice so requires.

II. DEFINING NULLIFICATION

A. What Constitutes Nullification?

At the most general level, jury nullification occurs when jurors[7] choose[8] not to follow the law as it is given to them by the judge. Theoretically, this could occur in a civil or criminal case.

In a civil case, however, the judge can decide either at the close of evidence or even after the jury has rendered its verdict that, based on the evidence, there is only one way that the case can reasonably be decided, and if the jury has decided otherwise, the trial judge in federal court and in many state courts can grant a motion for judgment as a matter of law.[9] The trial judge then has the power to review the civil jury's verdict immediately and to reverse it.

The trial judge also may reverse certain jury results in criminal cases. At the close of evidence, or even after a jury has returned a verdict of guilty

---

[7] When some, but not all, of the jurors choose to nullify and vote accordingly, this results in a hung jury technically, rather than a nullifying jury. *See infra* text following note 36 (discussing why a hung jury should be considered a nullifying jury).

[8] I use "choose" intentionally because I will discuss later why I do not think the jury nullifies if it mistakenly fails to follow the law. *See infra* text accompanying notes 16-17, 20-26.

[9] Federal Rule of Civil Procedure 50 permits federal judges to grant motions for judgment as a matter of law. *See* FED. R. CIV. P. 50 ("Judgment as a Matter of Law in Actions Tried by Jury"). Many states have similar provisions. *See, e.g.*, CAL. CIV. PROC. CODE § 663 (West Supp. 1998) ("A judgment or decree, when based upon . . . *a decision* by the court, or the special verdict of a jury, may, upon motion of the party aggrieved, be set aside and vacated by the same court, and another and different judgment entered, for either of the following causes, materially affecting the substantial rights of . . . *the* party and entitling . . . *the party* to a different judgment . . . ."); 735 ILL. COMP. STAT. 5/2-1202 (West 1992) ("If at the close of the evidence, and before the case is submitted to the jury, any party moves for a directed verdict the court may (1) grant the motion . . . . Relief after trial may include the entry of judgment if under the evidence in the case it would have been the duty of the court to direct a verdict without submitting the case to the jury . . . ."); LA. CODE CIV. PROC. ANN. art. 1810 (West 1990) ("The order of the court granting a motion for a directed verdict is effective without any assent.of the jury."); MO. ANN. STAT. § 510.290 (West Supp. 1998) ("[A] party who has moved for a directed verdict may move to have the verdict and any judgment entered thereon set aside and to have judgment entered in accordance with his motion for a directed verdict; or if a verdict was not retumed, such party . . . may move for judgment in accordance with his motion for a direeted verdict."); NEB. REV. STAT. § 25-1315.02 (1995) ("Motion for directed verdict at close of evidence; effect; motion to set aside verdict or judgment; power of court"); N.Y. C.P.L.R. C4404:2 (McKinney 1992) ("If . . . the court finds the verdict unsupportable and finds that the faets are clear and the other side is entitled to judgment as a matter of law, the court can grant that side judgment . . . ."); OKLA. STAT. ANN. tit. 12, § 698 (West Supp. 1999) ("When a motion for a directed verdict made at the close of all of the evidence should have been granted, the court shall, at the request of the moving party, grant judgment in the moving party's favor, although a verdict has been found against the moving party, but the court may order a new trial where it appears that the other party was prevented from proving a claim or defense by mistake, accident or surprise."); S.D. CODIFIED LAWS § 15-6-50(b) (Michie 1984 & Supp. 1998) (Motion for judgment notwithstanding the verdict); VA. CODE ANN. § 8.01-430 (Michie 1992) ("When final judgment to be entered after verdict set aside"); MONT. CODE ANN. Rule 50(a) ("[T]he court may grant a motion for judgment as a matter of law . . . .").

or no verdict at all, the trial judge in federal court may grant a motion for judgment of acquittal[10] if he or she believes that the evidence is insufficient to support a conviction for the offense charged.[11]

The only instance in which the trial judge does not have such power is in a criminal case in which the jury acquits. In a case of acquittal, there is no review by any judge; the jury's decision stands. The constitutional provision of double jeopardy precludes review.[12] Because a criminal defendant need defend himself only once on a given charge brought by a given sovereign,[13] if an acquittal ensues then that is the end of the matter; no further review can be sought.

It is in this context alone that I wish to consider jury nullification. Although jury nullification can occur in the other contexts,[14] the judge can[15] immediately review and alter what the jury has done, thus mitigating the effect of jury nullification. Only when the jury nullifies and acquits in a criminal trial does the jury's act of nullification have serious consequences: the judge cannot review the jury's verdict and the defendant is set free. My focus will be on this narrow instance of jury nullification—when the jury acquits a defendant in a criminal case even though it believes the defendant is guilty under the stated legal standard.

Jury nullification requires a subjective intent by the jurors to nullify, even if they do not use that exact word.[16] Mere mistake is not nullification.

---

[10] *See* FED. R. CRIM. P. 29 ("Motion for Judgment of Acquittal").

[11] *See* FED. R. CRIM. P. 29(a) ("The court . . . shall order the entry of judgment of acquittal . . . after the evidence on either side is closed if the evidence is insufficient to sustain a conviction of such offense or offenses.").

[12] *See* U.S. CONST. amend. V ("nor shall any person be subject for the same offence to be twice put in jeopardy of life or limb").

[13] *See, e.g.*, Barry Gewen, *The Second Time Around*, N.Y. TIMES BOOK REV., June 14, 1998, at 12 (reviewing DANIEL PETROCELLI WITH PETER KNOBLER, TRIUMPH OF JUSTICE: THE FINAL JUDGMENT ON THE SIMPSON SAGA (1998)) ("Like the trials of Lemrick Nelson Jr. in the Crown Heights killing and the police officers in the Rodney King affair, the Simpson case may not have been in any legal sense an example of double jeopardy, yet it does seem in some other sense to violate the spirit of the double jeopardy ban. In all three instanees, prosecutors, or prosecutor surrogates, essentially got to retry cases that had been lost the first time around, and to learn from the mistakes of their predecessors.").

[14] I leave consideration of jury nullification in these other contexts (civil cases and criminal convictions) to future articles.

[15] I say "can" because I recognize that as a practical matter, a judge may be reluctant to grant a motion for judgment of acquittal after a jury has returned a verdict of guilty, even though the judge has the power to do so. *See, e.g.*, Richard St. John, Note, *License to Nullify: The Democratic and Constitutional Deficiencies of Authorized Jury Lawmaking*, 106 YALE L.J. 2563 (1997) (claiming that judges may have the power to grant a motion for judgment of acquittal but are reluctant to exercise that power as a practical matter); Eleanor Tavris, *The Law of an Unwritten Law: A Common Sense View of Jury Nullification*, 11 W. ST. U. L. REV. 97, 112 (1983) (questioning whether judges would overturn nullification convictions as a practical matter).

[16] Jurors are unlikely to use the word nullification because they are never informed about it by the judge. *See infra* note 127 (referring to federal circuits and state cases explaining that courts do not instruct on nullification). They may, however, become familiar with it through the grassroots educational efforts of the Fully Informed Jury Association (FIJA). *See infra* text accompanying notes 285-89. But

Thus, if a jury misunderstood the law, misjudged the eredibility of a witness, or overlooked some critical piece of evidence, such a mistake,[17] even if unreasonable, is not the same as nullification.

Intent matters in this context, just as it matters in other areas of the law. For example, if a person breaks into a building and destroys property, that person has committed a criminal act. If a person engages in the same misconduct to protest a government policy, that person has committed the same criminal act, but also can describe his or her act as one of civil disobedience.[18] Although the law will treat the two the same, the protester may be seen in a different light than the mere criminal wrongdoer. Society understands the protester to be acting out of conscience. Intent is what distinguishes the act of civil disobedience from simply a violation of the law.[19] Intent works in a similar way with nullification; it is what distinguishes nullification from mere mistake even if the result, an acquittal, is the same in both instances.

One reason this distinction between mistake and nullification is important is that each is remedied in a different way. There is no dispute that jury mistakes are to be avoided. To this end, courts have experimented with

---

even if they do not know the word, they may be familiar with the concept, and express their intent to nullify as an effort "to do justice" or "to act according to their conscience." *See Frontline: Inside the Jury Room* (WGBH broadcast, Apr. 8, 1986) (transcript at 15) [hereinafter *Inside the Jury Room* transcript] ("I'm trying to decide in my own mind—has justice been done here?") (quoting Juror Lester Sauvage, who was part of a nullifying jury); *infra* notes 203-19 and accompanying text (describing the jury's deliberations in *Inside the Jury Room*); *CBS Reports: Enter the Jury Room* (CBS broadcast, Apr. 16, 1997) (transcript at 43) [hereinafter *Enter the Jury Room* transcript] ("And [our verdict] has to have nothing to do with justice?") (quoting juror named "Joe" who was urging nullification); *id.* at 49 ("I was not going to do something that was against my beliefs and conscience . . . .") (quoting Joe).

[17] Juries are less likely, however, to make mistakes when they are of sufficient size, representative in composition, and fairly selected. *See, e.g.*, Ballew v. Georgia, 435 U.S. 223, 232-38 (1978) (concluding that reducing the jury in a state criminal trial to five members would reduce the amount of evidence accurately recalled by and available to the jurors, hinder effective jury deliberations, increase the likelihood of erroneous decisions, weaken the minority's ability to defend its view, and decrease the representation of minorities on the jury).

[18] *See, e.g.*, United States v. Dougherty, 473 F.2d 1113, 1117 (D.C. Cir. 1972) (describing the case of Vietnam war protesters who broke into the Dow Chemical Company offices and vandalized furniture and smeared a blood-like substance areund the office in protest of Dow's manufacture of napalm).

[19] I do not mean to equate nullification with civil disobedience because nullification is within the scope of the jury's role and does not require breaking the law in any way. Others, however, have described nullification as a form of civil disobedience. *See, e.g.*, *Dougherty*, 473 F.2d at 1130 (Leventhal, J.); *see also* David Farnham, *Jury Nullification: History Proves It's Not a New Idea*, CRIM. JUST., Winter 1997, at 4, 6 (describing the jurors who had nullified in the 1554 trial of Sir Nicholas Throckmorton, charged with treason, and who stood by their verdiet even though it meant imprisonment and fines for them because they had "exercised a power to which they had no right, and, much like practitioners of civil disobedience in later centuries, they had to pay the price"). I simply wish to make the point that intent matters when it comes to nullification. Even the Second Circuit recognized the importance of intent when it described the nullifying juror as one who exhibited a "*purposeful refusal* to apply the law" and who could be dismissed for "*purposeful* disobedience." United States v. Thomas, 116 F.3d 606, 617, 618 (2d Cir. 1997) (emphasis added).

a variety of changes in procedure, such as allowing jurors to take notes,[20] to submit written questions to the judge, to receive preliminary instructions, to take written instructions into the jury room,[21] and to be instructed in plain language that laypersons can understand.[22] All of these procedural changes, many drawn from empirical studies,[23] are directed toward helping juries avoid mistakes. However, these same responses will not help juries avoid nullification. Other responses, such as not instructing the jury on its power to nullify[24] and instructing the jury on the need to follow the law[25] are intended to reduce instances of jury nullification. Though the goal of reducing or increasing instances of jury nullification is one that is open to debate,[26] it is clear that the methods used to help juries avoid mistake are different than those used to deter juries from engaging in nullification.

---

[20] *See, e.g.*, ABA/BROOKINGS INST., CHARTING A FUTURE FOR THE CIVIL JURY SYSTEM 18-19 (1992) (recommending notetaking); SAUL M. KASSIN & LAWRENCE S. WRIGHTSMAN, THE AMERICAN JURY ON TRIAL 128-29 (1988) (considering why there is so much resistance to allowing jurors to take notes); David Margolick, *A Call for the Jurors to Take Bigger Roles in Trials*, N.Y. TIMES, Jan. 1, 1993, at A19 (reporting on notetaking recommendation).

[21] *See, e.g.*, ABA/BROOKINGS INST., *supra* note 20, at 24-25; THE ARIZ. SUPREME COURT COMM. ON MORE EFFECTIVE USE OF JURIES, JURORS: THE POWER OF 12 (1994) [hereinafter THE POWER OF 12] (including a list of recommendations and a proposed bill of rights); Harold J. Bursztajn et al., *Keeping a Jury Involved During a Long Trial*, CRIM. JUST., Winter 1997, at 8 (recommending that jurors be permitted to ask questions because it keeps them actively engaged in the trial, which will in turn lead to more well-reasoned, rather than emotional, decisionmaking); B. Michael Dann & George Logan III, *Jury Reform: The Arizona Experience*, 79 JUDICATURE 280 (1994) (describing some of Arizona's more controversial reforms to its jury system, including giving jurors preliminary jury instructions, allowing them to ask questions in writing, telling jurors that they can discuss the evidence before the close of trial in a civil case, giving judges discretion about the timing of instructions, and having the judge and jury engage in a dialogue if the jury has reached an impasse); *see also* William H. Carlile, *Arizona Jury Reforms Buck Legal Traditions*, CHRISTIAN SCI. MONITOR, Feb. 22, 1996, at 1 (reporting that Arizona has adopted 18 of the jury reform panel's 55 recommendations); Junda Woo, *Arizona Panel Suggests Jury Reforms*, WALL ST. J., Oct. 25, 1994, at B12 (describing the proposals of a reform panel, headed by Judge B. Michael Dann).

[22] *See, e.g.*, AMIRAM ELWORK ET AL., MAKING JURY INSTRUCTIONS UNDERSTANDABLE 6-24 (1982); Fred H. Cate & Newton N. Minow, *Communicating with Juries*, 68 IND. L.J. 1101, 1101-02, 1105-12, 1117-18 (1993); Robert F. Forston, *Sense and Non-Sense: Jury Trial Communication*, 1975 BYU L. REV. 601, 601-06, 616-23; *see also* Theodore Eisenberg & Martin T. Wells, *Deadly Confusion: Juror Instructions in Capital Cases*, 79 CORNELL L. REV. 1 (1993) (describing confusion experienced by jurors trying to understand instructions in capital cases); Arthur S. Hayes, *Jurors' Grasp of Instructions May Stir Appeal*, WALL ST. J., July 16, 1992, at B1.

[23] *See, e.g.*, AMERICAN JUDICATURE SOC'Y, TOWARD MORE ACTIVE JURIES: TAKING NOTES AND ASKING QUESTIONS (1991); KASSIN & WRIGHTSMAN, *supra* note 20, at 128-31 (describing studies); Leonard B. Sand & Steven Alan Reiss, *A Report on Seven Experiments Conducted by District Court Judges in the Second Circuit*, 60 N.Y.U. L. REV. 423, 437-59 (1985) (describing experiments with pre-instruction, juror questions, juror notetaking, and furnishing jurors with a copy of the charge); Arthur D. Austin, *Why Jurors Don't Heed the Trial: A Set of Proposals*, NAT'L L.J., Aug. 12, 1985, at 15 (offering proposals based on a study of two antitrust juries).

[24] *See infra* note 127.

[25] *See infra* text accompanying note 131 (quoting sample instruction).

[26] *See infra* subparts VI.A-C.

What underlies these different responses is a difference as to what causes each: With mistake, the fault lies perhaps in the way material is presented to or understood by the jurors; with nullification, the fault, to the extent it can be considered one, is with the jurors' understanding of their role as jurors.

B. Knowing When Nullification Occurs

An intent requirement for nullification means that the most reliable way to determine whether a jury has nullified is to ask the jurors.[27] This requirement poses several potential difficulties, which those who believe that nullification can be objectively determined without having to rely on jurors' intent do not face. However, the problem with objective nullification is that it assumes an omniscient observer who judges from "an ideal post of observation."[28] Because no observer occupies such an ideal post from which to have "full perspective," at best observers can offer "partial perspectives."[29] Even the judge, who at least is present in the courtroom, cannot escape his or her own position, which offers only a limited point of view.[30] For those of us who believe that there is no ideal post from which to reach a judgment, but that all decisionmaking is limited by one's perspective, then the determination about nullification seems appropriate to leave to the jurors, who at least have informed partial perspectives to contribute. Although they offer perspectives that are not free from bias and even self-interest, at the very least, jurors are present not only in the courtroom but also in the jury room. They occupy a "post of observation" to which no other observers have access.[31]

One difficulty in relying on intent to determine when a jury has nullified is that jurors could lie about their motivations. They could nullify, but then say that their decision was based on reasonable doubt. There are several reasons why jurors might lie about their motivations. Jurors who nullify may feel bad or guilty about acting contrary to the judge's instruction or their oath, and so they may try to mask their true reasons. Or jurors may worry about public criticism if it were revealed that they nullified, and thus, they may say that they acted based on reasonable doubt. Finally, they might want others to think that the defendant is innocent, and so they might

---

[27] The jurors must be asked because otherwise all that is known is the jury's verdict. *See* Nancy S. Marder, *Deliberations and Disclosures: A Study of Post-Verdict Interviews of Jurors*, 82 IOWA L. REV. 465, 472-73 (1997) (describing the power and limits of a jury verdict).

[28] Catharine Pierce Wells, *Tort Law as Corrective Justice: A Pragmatic Justification for Jury Adjudication*, 88 MICH. L. REV. 2348, 2402 (1990).

[29] *Id.*

[30] *See* Catharine Wells, *Situated Decisionmaking*, 63 S. CAL. L. REV. 1727, 1745-46 (1990) ("[Judges'] judgments are relative to a perspective; they are situated in prior experience and affected by normative attitudes.").

[31] Wells, *supra* note 28, at 2402.

not want to admit that they acquitted him even though they actually thought he was guilty.

Although all of these motivations are plausible, there are countervailing reasons why jurors are unlikely to lie about whether they nullified. The most compelling reason is that jurors suffer no legal consequences if they nullify. Whether they acquit based on nullification or reasonable doubt, they cannot be penalized in any way; indeed, the court cannot even inquire into their motives.[32] Moreover, they may be proud of their act of nullification. The history of juries includes accounts of juries that nullified based on a strong sense of moral purpose.[33] These instances have been regarded "as historic and seminal assertions, like the Magna Carta and the Bill of Rights, of man's right to be free of unjust laws."[34] Unfortunately, there is no empirical evidence on whether jurors are prone to lie about whether they have nullified.[35] Even if jurors are not completely trustworthy in their post-

[32] There are very few circumstances in which judges can question jurors about their verdict. At most in federal court, in cases where juror misconduct has been alleged, jurors can be asked whether "cxtraneous prejudicial information was improperly brought to the jury's attention or whether any outside influence was improperly brought to bear upon any juror." FED. R. EVID. 606(b). Under Fed. R. Evid. 606(b), if a juror misunderstands the judge's instructions, or even feels personally coerced by a fellow juror, such circumstances would be insufficient to justify inquiry into the verdict. *See, e.g.*, Scogin v. Century Fitness, Inc., 780 F.2d 1316, 1320 (8th Cir. 1985); Jacobson v. Henderson, 765 F.2d 12, 14-15 (2d Cir. 1985) (holding that "screaming, hysterical crying, fist banging, name calling, and . . . obscene language" alleged in the jury room is incompetent evidence); United States v. Gerardi, 586 F.2d 896, 898 (1st Cir. 1978) (noting that juror felt "persuaded"). Matters of conscience or mental processes of a juror are supposed to remain inviolate and beyond court scrutiny. However, if a juror were approached by an interested third party, such a situation would fall within the exception for external influences and would be admissible to impeach the verdict. *See* FED. R. EVID. 606(b).

[33] Two of the most famous examples of jury nulliflcation are *Bushel's Case* and the case of Peter Zenger. John Peter Zenger, an American who published critical, but thoughtful articles about the governor, was charged with seditious libel, to which the truth was not a defense. Sce JEFFREY ABRAMSON, WE, THE JURY: THE JURY SYSTEM AND THE IDEAL OF DEMOCRACY 73-74 (1994). Andrew Hamilton represented Zenger and urged the jurors to disobey the instructions and question the law. The jury returned a verdict of not guilty. *See id.* at 74-75. For a description *of Bushel's Case*, see *infra* note 336. In both, the jury believed it was taking the moral high ground. For other more recent examples of juries guided by their moral principles, see *infra* text accompanying notes 88-107 (discussing juries that nullified based on strongly felt disagroement with the law they were asked to apply).

[34] MORTIMER R. KADISH & SANFORD H. KADISH, DISCRETION TO DISOBEY 54 (1973).

[35] There have been only two empirical studies to date specifically on nullifying juries, and they do not examine how truthful jurors are about the motivations for their verdicts. *See* Irwin A. Horowitz, *Jury Nullification: The Impact of Judicial Instructions, Arguments, and Challenges on Jury Decision Making*, 12 LAW & HUM. BEHAV. 439 (1988) [hereinafter Horowitz, *The Impact of Judicial Instructions*] (testing the effects on the jury of a judge's instruction or a lawyer's argument on nullification); Irwin A. Horowitz, *The Effect of Jury Nullification Instruction on Verdicts and Jury Functioning in Criminal Trials*, 9 LAW & HUM. BEHAV. 25 (1985) (testing the effeets of nullification information on jury verdicts).

verdict interviews, particularly immediately after the verdict,[36] it seems unlikely that large numbers of jurors are lying about nullification.

Another difficulty with relying on the jury's intent is that individual jurors may differ as to reasons for their votes. Even if most jurors voted to acquit based on reasonable doubt, some may have voted to acquit based on nullification. Thus, it may be difficult to decide how to classify a jury that acquits. How many jurors does it take for an acquitting jury to be considered a nullifying jury? It seems fair to say that where some, even if not all, jurors voted to acquit based on nullification, the jury can be described as a nullifying jury. Of course, the problem can grow murkier. For example, what if one or two jurors voted to acquit based on nullification, but might have voted to acquit based on reasonable doubt if they had been pushed on the issue? The line between nullification and reasonable doubt can be difficult to draw, and jurors' reasons may not always be clear even to themselves, and can be in flux depending on the course that the deliberations take.

Another type of classification difficulty is when almost all of the jurors vote to convict, but one or two vote to acquit based on nullification. Even though the resulting jury is technically a hung jury, rather than a nullifying jury, there are reasons for viewing it as a nullifying jury. A hung jury, like a nullifying jury, can result in the defendant going free if the prosecutor decides not to retry the defendant. Thus, the results of a hung jury can potentially be the same as a nullifying jury. In addition, the nullifying holdouts voted to acquit even though they believed the defendant met the standards for conviction as stated by the judge. Thus, it seems that to some limited extent the intent requirement would be satisfied, even though all of the jurors did not vote to nullify.

III. Situations Giving Rise to Jury Nullification

Nullification has been widely perceived as a negative act undertaken by the jury.[37] Not all nullification, however, is harmful, and some types might even be beneficial. In this Part, I discuss three situations in which nullification is likely to occur. In Parts IV and V, I describe two different conceptions of the jury, a conventional view and a process view, and I evaluate the harms and benefits of these three types of nullification based on these two different conceptions of the jury.

---

[36] *See* Alan W. Scheflin, *Jury Nullification: The Right To Say No*, 45 S. CAL. L. REV. 168, 199 (1972) ("Revelations by jurors after the rendition of the verdict, although somewhat self-serving at that time, furnish some help.").

[37] *See supra* note 3 (providing instances in which the press and public criticized the verdicts of O.J. Simpson and Stacey Koon and Laurence Powell as nullification).

A. *Not Applying the Law to the Defendant*

A jury might nullify because it does not think the law should be applied to the defendant before it. With this type of nullification, a jury does not object to the law per se, but rather, a jury objects to the law as it is applied to this particular defendant. The jury's decision to engage in this form of nullification may stem from bad or good motives.

1. *Bad Motives.*—A jury might decide not to apply the law to the particular defendant out of racial motivations. The jury might feel racial animus toward the defendant if he or she is of a different race than the jurors or may feel racial sympathy for the defendant if he or she is of the same race as the jurors. One example of such racial motivations, according to some in the mainstream press, was that the jury acquitted O.J. Simpson because of the largely African-American jury[38] that chose not to apply the law to this particular defendant, a popular African-American hero.[39] Another example, according to African-American journalists writing about the Stacey Koon and Laurence Powell verdicts, was that the largely white jury[40] chose not to apply the law to the white defendants out of racial sympathy for them and out of racial animus toward the African-American defendant.[41]

The most ignominious examples of juries refusing to convict defendants based on racial affinity for the defendants and animosity for the victims were the Southern all-white,[42] and initially all-male juries.[43] In the

[38] The jury in the criminal trial of O.J. Simpson consisted of eight African-American women, one African-American man, two white women, and one Latino man. *See* Jeffrey Rosen, *The Bloods and the Crits: O.J. Simpson, Critical Race Theory, the Law, and the Triumph of Color in America*, NEW REPUBLIC, Dec. 9, 1996, at 27, *available in* 1996 WL 9233825 (describing the jury composition); Charles E. Williams, *George Will and the Incompetent O.J. Simpson Jury*, WASH. AFRO-AM., Dec. 9, 1995, at A5.

[39] *See* Nancy S. Marder, *The Interplay of Race and False Claims of Jury Nullification*, 32 U. MICH. J.L. REFORM (forthcoming Winter 1999) (describing some mainstream press accounts of the O.J. Simpson verdict as nullification based on racial sympathy).

[40] The jury in the state criminal trial of Stacey Koon and Laurence Powell included ten white jurors, one Latina, and one Asian-American. *See* Richard A. Serrano & Tracy Wilkinson, *All 4 in King Beating Acquitted*, L.A. TIMES, Apr. 30, 1992, at A1. Six of the jurors were men and six were women. *See id.*

[41] *See* Marder, *supra* note 39.

[42] States were not allowed to exclude African-American men from jury service by virtue of their race after the Supreme Court declared, in *Strauder v. West Virginia*, 100 U.S. 303 (1879), that such statutes were unconstitutional. However, even when African-American men were officially allowed to serve on the jury, they were often not permitted to serve. *See* Ware v. State, 225 S.W. 626, 627-28, 631 (Ark. 1920) (holding that the trial court erred in denying appellants' motion to quash the indictment and in refusing to hear evidence on motions to set aside the regular panel of the petit jury because the grand jury by which appellants were indicted "was composed of white men selected by the jury commissioners, who were also white men, negroes being excluded therefrom on account of their color; that the jury commissioners . . . excluded all colored men therefrom solely on account of their color . . . . [and that] the jury commissioners [discriminated] against the colored race in the selection of the petit jury, by which negroes were excluded from that jury solely on account of their color . . . ."); Montgomery v. State, 45 So. 879, 882 (Fla. 1908) (reversing denial of defendant's writ of error, challenging the array,

debate over the Ku Klux Act of 1871,[44] Senator Sherman recounted the testimony of a Southern white judge who said: "'In nine cases out of ten the [white] men who commit the crimes [against African-American victims] constitute or sit on the grand jury, either they themselves or their near relatives or friends, sympathizers, aiders, or abettors; and if a bill is found it is next to impossible to secure a conviction.'"[45] In 1955, an all-white, all-

because there was "uncontroverted testimony that the people of one race and color are numerically in the majority in Duval county . . . that about two-thirds of the men of that race are of fair character, sound judgment and intelligence, and fully qualified for jury duty, but that in the list of several hundred names drawn for jury duty not more than half dozen, if any, names of men of that race are found . . . [and] it has been a long time since men of that race have served on the jury in the court."); Miller v. Commonwealth, 127 Ky. 387 (1907) (finding that there was no discrimination by the jury commissioners when the defendant, a Negro, was indicted by an all-white jury because there were no Negroes on the list of persons qualified for jury service); Cooper v. State, 64 Md. 40, 45 (1885) (concluding that because jurors could be drawn either from the list of those who paid taxes or those who were registered to vote, it was not discriminatory that the tax list consisted of "'the white male taxable inhabitants of the county'"); Farrow v. State, 91 Miss. 509, 511 (1908) (reversing judgment to deny motion to quash the indictment because the board of supervisors of Tate County "failed and refused to select and list the names of any negroes whatever, although there were then, and are now, on the registration books of voters in said Tate county negroes of good intelligence, sound judgment, and fair character, competent and qualified for jury service under the laws of the state."); State v. Peoples, 131 N.C. 784, 788 (1902) (finding error and unlawful discrimination that the defendant, a Negro, was indicted by a grand jury in which Negroes could not serve even though they met the qualifications for jury service of having paid taxes the previous year and of being of "good moral character and sufficient intelligence"); Smith v. State, 42 Tex. Crim. 220, 222 (1900) (holding that the motion to quash the indictment should have been sustained because "[t]he record . . . shows that for 20 years negroes had been excluded from service upon the juries" and the Texas courts must follow the U.S. Supreme Court's decisions). *See generally* Batson v. Kentucky, 476 U.S. 79, 103-04 (1986) (providing statistics from several states demonstrating how infrequently African Americans were actually permitted to serve on juries) (Marshall, J., concurring).

[43] States varied as to when they allowed women to serve as jurors. The California Supreme Court believed the decision was best left to the legislature, and the legislature's decision to allow women to serve was certainly consistent with the California constitution prohibiting discrimination against women "entering upon or pursuing any lawful business, vocation or profession," *see* CAL. CONST. art. 20, § 18, *amended by* CAL. CONST. art. 1, § 8 (Nov. 5, 1974), and with an amendment giving women the right to vote and hold office, *see* CAL. CONST. art. 2, § 1 (Oct. 10, 1911). *See Ex Parte* Mana, 172 P. 986 (Cal. 1918). The Supreme Court of Illinois granted a petition for the issuance of a writ of mandamus requiring jury commissioners to revise the jury lists to include eligible women, as provided for by the Jury Commissioners' Act, 78 Ill. Rev. Stat. § 25 (1937), making women eligible for jury duty. *See* Denny v. Traeger, 22 N.E.2d 679 (Ill. 1939). For some states, the Nineteenth Amendment, which enfranchised women, served as a catalyst for allowing women to serve as jurors. *See, e.g.*, State v. Chase, 211 P. 920, 920, 923 (Or. 1922) (noting that "[i]n 1921 it was deemed expedient so to amend the laws providing for the selection of jurors that women otherwise qualified should be eligible to jury duty . . . . Women are now the peers of men politically, and there is no reason to question their eligibility upon constitutional grounds."); *In re* Opinion of the Justices, 130 N.E. 685, 688 (Mass. 1921) (concluding that "a change by an amendment to the Constitution in the qualifications of the electorate, such as that wrought by the Nineteenth Amendment, by its own force authorizes the General Court to make a corresponding change in the qualifications of jurors").

[44] *See* Act of Feb. 28, 1871, ch. 99, 16 Stat. 433, *repealed by* 2 U.S.C. § 9 (1997); Act of Apr. 20, 1871, ch. 22, 17 Stat. 13, *repealed by* 10 U.S.C. § 333 (1983).

[45] Andrew G. Deiss, *Negotiating Justice: The Criminal Trial Jury in a Pluralist America*, 3 U. CHI. L. SCH. ROUNDTABLE 323, 344-45 & n.109 (1996).

male Mississippi jury acquitted the white defendants charged with the murder of Emmett Till, a fourteen-year old African American who had spoken to a white woman in a manner viewed as inappropriate.[46] The jury took less than an hour to reach its acquittal even in the face of strong evidence against the defendant.[47] In the 1960s, white defendants charged with the murders of African-American civil rights workers Medgar Evers, Lemuel Penn, Viola Liuzzo, and Herbert Lee were set free when all-white, all-male juries either acquitted or deadlocked in spite of strong evidence against the defendants.[48] On September 25, 1961, Herbert Lee was murdered soon after registering to vote.[49] There was no question that E.H. Hurst was the killer because the murder took place before witnesses, and Hurst bragged about it in public; nevertheless, he was quickly acquitted.[50] The defendant in the Medgar Evers case, Byron de la Beckwith, was finally convicted by a racially mixed jury of men and women[51] in 1994 after two earlier trials in the 1960s had ended in hung juries.[52]

2. *Good Motives*.—A jury also may decide not to apply the law to a defendant out of more appropriate motives. A jury may decide to acquit even if it believes the defendant is guilty if there are extenuating circumstances that the law does not take into account, but that provide an explanation for the defendant's crime. For example, Leroy Reed,[53] who was charged with illegally possessing a handgun, had limited intelligence and a second-grade reading level.[54] He wanted a job and thought that he could become a private investigator through a mail-order course that he had seen advertised in a magazine.[55] In spite of his past felony conviction, he bought a handgun, as described in the course, and stood by the courthouse door,

---

[46] *See* ABRAMSON, *supra* note 33, at 111-12; Albert W. Alschuler, *A Teetering Palladium?*, 79 JUDICATURE 200, 203 (1996) (book review).

[47] *See* Alschuler, *supra* note 46, at 203 ("One juror explained, 'If we hadn't stopped to drink pop, it wouldn't have taken that long.'").

[48] *See, e.g.*, W. William Hodes, *Lord Brougham, the Dream Team, and Jury Nullification of the Third Kind*, 67 U. COLO. L. REV. 1075, 1090 & n.39 (1996).

[49] *See id.* at 1096-97 & n.57.

[50] *See id.*

[51] *See* Ed Timms, *Jury Convicts Beckwith of Evers' Murder*, DALLAS MORNING NEWS, Feb. 6, 1994, at 1A ("The jury that convicted Mr. Beckwith . . . was made up of three black men, five black women, two white women and two white men.").

[52] *See* Hodes, *supra* note 48, at 1090 n.39; Robert P. Burns, *The History and Theory of the American Jury*, 83 CAL. L. REV. 1477, 1485 n.22 (1995) (review essay); Ellen Goodman, *Changing Venues, Changing Values in the Jury Room*, BOSTON GLOBE, Feb. 20, 1994, at 83 ("In 1964, the man accused of killing Medgar Evers was let off by two hung juries of white men. It took 30 years and a racially mixed jury before Byron De La Beckwith was found guilty this month. Justice may emerge over time.").

[53] *See generally Inside the Jury Room* transcript, *supra* note 16.

[54] *See id.* at 6 (describing Reed as reading "at the second grade level" and having "borderline intelligence").

[55] *See id.* at 5.

waiting for business.[56] When a sheriff asked him what he was doing, he explained, and when he was asked to bring in his handgun, he went home to retrieve it and deposited it with the Sheriff's office.[57] The jury found Reed's limited mental capacity, his effort to be gainfully employed, and his cooperation with the sheriff to be extenuating circumstances that led it to nullify.[58]

Another reason a jury might believe the law should not be applied to a particular defendant is that the case seems too trivial to warrant involvement by the criminal justice system.[59] At least one juror who advocated nullification in Reed's case suggested that the jury needed to send a message to the prosecutor that the State was wasting the jury's time.[60] In this juror's view, there were more serious offenses to which the prosecution should have been devoting its limited resources. As this juror explained to his fellow jurors during deliberations: "I don't want to send a message over to the D.A.'s office, sort of, patting them on top of the head and say, 'Bring me some jaywalkers next time. We'll really get them.'"[61]

A jury also might decide not to apply the law to a particular defendant because it believes that the sanction that follows will be too harsh given the facts of the defendant's case. Of course, a jury is only supposed to decide guilt or innocence and is not supposed to concern itself with punishment.[62]

---

[56] *See id.* at 4.

[57] *See id.*

[58] *See, e.g., id.* at 21 (quoting juror Dr. Lester Sauvage: "[Reed] didn't understand so many things. But when somebody told him, 'This is wrong. Please bring this [gun] in,' he did it right away . . . . I, deep inside, believe there's an exception in this case."). By the end of the deliberations, all but one of the jurors were persuaded to nullify; the remaining juror, Karl Buetow, agreed to vote with the others, but was skeptical whether nullification was appropriate in this case. *See infra* text accompanying notes 203-19 (detailing the dynamics of the deliberations).

[59] *See* HARRY KALVEN, JR. & HANS ZEISEL, THE AMERICAN JURY 258-85 (1966) (finding that instances of judge and jury disagreement as to the verdict often involved cases where the stakes were trivial); Michael R. Smythers, *Equitable Acquittals: Prediction and Preparation Prevent Post-Panel Predicaments*, ARMY LAW., Apr. 1986, at 3 (observing that "equitable aequittals" occur most often in the military setting at special courts-martial involving minor offenses in which the consequences of conviction, such as ruining the career of an otherwise good soldier, appear unjust).

[60] *See Inside the Jury Room* transcript, *supra* note 16, at 22 ("I'm sort of sitting to myself thinking, this is 'Mickey Mouse'. . . . I really don't feel that this is a justified expenditure of my time and attention as a juror.") (quoting Juror John Boly, English Professor).

[61] *Id.* (quoting Juror John Boly).

[62] The exception is in a capital case, where in many states, the jury decides (sometimes in conjunction with the judge) whether to impose a life or death sentence. *See, e.g.*, ARK. CODE. ANN. § 5-4-602(3) (Michie 1997) ("If the defendant is found guilty of capital murder, the same jury shall sit again in order to hear additional evidence . . . and to determine sentence . . . ".); FLA. STAT. ANN. § 921.141(2) (West 1998) ("Advisory sentenee by the jury."); MISS. CODE ANN. § 99-19-101 (1998) ("Jury to determine punishment in eapital cases in separate sentencing proceeding; aggravating and mitigating circumstanccs to be considered."); N.M. STAT. ANN. § 31-20A-1(B) (Michie 1998) ("In a jury trial, the scntencing proceding shall be conducted . . . by the original trial judge before the original trial jury [after a verdict of capital felony]."); OKLA. STAT. ANN. tit. 21, § 701.10A (West 1998) ("Upon conviction . . . the court shall conduct a separate sentencing proceeding . . . before the same trial jury . . . ."); OR. REV.

Indeed, the jury is not given any information about the sentence, and if it asks, it is told that that is a matter for the judge, and not the jury, to decide.[63] And yet, a jury can sometimes glean information about the sentence, and respond with an acquittal if it has decided that the sentence is too harsh and will do more harm than good in the particular case. This reasoning was behind one juror's vote for acquittal in a mandatory drug sentence case,[64] producing a hung jury,[65] and has motivated other juries to nullify in three strikes cases in California.[66]

One caveat is that a jury can decide not to apply the law to a particular defendant for any of these reasons, or some combination of them. The jury may find the defendant to be attractive, his or her circumstances to be extenuating, the application of the law to this particular defendant to be ludicrous, and the penalties to be too harsh given the circumstances. While it is useful to tease out some of the reasons that a jury might decide not to apply the law to a defendant, it is also important to keep in mind that a juror may be motivated by some combination of these reasons, some of greater and some of lesser force.[67]

B. Not Applying a Bad Law

Another situation in which jury nullification is likely to arise is when the jury disagrees with the law it is being asked to apply. In such a case, the jury regards the law as a "bad law," and even though it believes the defendant meets the legal standard for the crime as explained by the judge, it does not vote to convict.

1. Examples From the Past.—Perhaps the most famous example in the United States is the Fugitive Slave Act of 1793,[68] which provided for en-

---

STAT. § 163.150(1)(a) (1998) ("Upon a finding that the defendant is guilty of aggravated murder, the trial court . . . shall conduct a separate sentencing hearing . . . before the trial jury . . . .").

63 *See, e.g., Enter the Jury Room* transcript, *supra* note 16, at 48 (showing the jury sending a question to the judge about the sentence, and the judge responding that that is a matter for the court to decide).

64 *See id.* (providing the basis for Juror Joe's vote).

65 *See id.* at 49. The case was then retried and resulted in a conviction. *See id.* at 57.

66 *See infra* text accompanying notes 88-101.

67 In Kalven and Zeisel's study, they identified five reasons to explain judge-jury disagreement: sentiments on the law, sentiments on the defendant, issues of evidence, facts only the judge knew, and disparity of counsel. *See* KALVEN & ZEISEL, *supra* note 59, at 111. They discovered that "[e]ach of the reason categories appears more frequently in combination with other reasons than it does alone." *Id.* at 113. They further noted: "The sharing of reasons is particularly interesting with respect to disparity of counsel and jury sentiments about the defendant, both of which combine with other reasons over 90 per cent of the time they operate." *Id.* at 114.

68 Act of February 12, 1793, ch. 7, 1 Stat. 302 (1793). The Act provided in relevant part:

> [T]he person to whom such labour or service may be due . . . is hereby empowered to seize or arrest such fugitive from labour, and to take him or her before any judge of the circuit or district courts of the United States . . . and upon proof to the satisfaction of such judge or magistrate . . .

forcement of the Fugitive Slave Clause of the U.S. Constitution.[69] The 1793 Act required the return of an escaped slave upon proof of title before a magistrate.[70] The Fugitive Slave Act of 1850[71] authorized fugitive-slave proceedings before special federal commissioners who would issue certificates of removal without hearing testimony from the fugitive and from whose decisions there was no right of appeal,[72] thus allowing agents of slaveholders to seize fugitives without judicial oversight.[73] One response by some Northern states to the 1793 Act was to pass personal liberty laws giving alleged runaway slaves the right to trial by jury.[74] Another response by abolitionists was to assist fugitives to escape.[75] One of the abolitionists' legal arguments, which was eventually accepted in several state cases[76] after the Act of 1850,[77] was that a person who assisted another to escape had a right to a trial by jury.[78] For the aiders and abettors, who were the subject of criminal and civil proceedings, this right had a very practical effect: the opportunity to appear before decisionmakers who could potentially be sympathetic. In several jurisdictions, it became difficult, if not impossible, for prosecutors to obtain convictions from jurors who opposed the slavery

> that the person so seized or arrested doth, under the laws of the state or territory from which he or she fled, owe service or labor to the person claiming him or her, it shall be the duty of such judge or magistrate to give a certificate thereof to such claimant. . . .

Id.

69 The Fugitive Slave Clause provided:

> No person held to service or labor in one state, under the laws thereof, escaping into another, shall, in consequence of any law or Regulation therein, be discharged from such service or labor, but shall be delivered up on claim of the party to whom such service or labor may be due.

U.S. CONST. art. IV, § 2.

70 *See* ch. 7, 1 Stat. 302 (1793).

71 *See* Act to amend and supplementary to the Act entitled, "An Act respecting Fugitives from Justice, and Persons escaping from the Service of their Masters," ch. 60, 9 Stat. 462 (Sept. 18, 1850) (repealed 1862).

72 *See* ROBERT M. COVER, JUSTICE ACCUSED 175, 185 (1975).

73 *See* ch. 60, 9 Stat. 463, § 6 (1850).

74 *See* THOMAS D. MORRIS, FREE MEN ALL: THE PERSONAL LIBERTY LAWS OF THE NORTH, 1780-1861, at 42-58 (1974). The Supreme Court eventually held Pennsylvania's personal liberty law unconstitutional. *See* Prigg v. Pennsylvania, 41 U.S. 536, 624-25 (1842). Some states responded with other remedies, such as the writ of habeas corpus and the writ *de homine replegiando* (allowing a jury trial). *See* Albert W. Alschuler & Andrew G. Deiss, *A Brief History of the Criminal Jury in the United States*, 61 U. CHI. L. REV. 867, 890 n.119 (1994). However, in *Ableman v. Booth*, 62 U.S. 506, 523-26 (1859), the Supreme Court held that state courts lacked the power to interfere with federal orders enforcing the Fugitive Slave Act, thus ending such procedures.

75 *See, e.g.*, Alschuler & Deiss, *supra* note 74, at 928 n.119; Clay S. Conrad, *Jury Nullification as a Defense Strategy*, 2 TEX. F. CIV. LIBERTY & CIV. RTS. 1, 9 n.50 (1995). For a fictional account, see LORENE CAREY, THE PRICE OF A CHILD (1996) (describing the escape of a slave woman and her two children and the assistance provided by abolitionists).

76 *See* COVER, *supra* note 72, at 191 (providing examples).

77 *See* ch. 60, 9 Stat. 462 (1850).

78 The Act of 1850 did not provide for a right to jury trial. *See* ch. 60, 9 Stat. 462 (1850); Alschuler & Deiss, *supra* note 74, at 890-91 n.119.

laws.[79] Jurors might have felt more inclined to vote their consciences at that time because the judge's instructions to the jury typically included an instruction that told jurors they should do what they thought was right.[80] Such admonitions, however vaguely worded, are no longer a part of today's jury instructions in any federal courts or in almost any state courts.[81]

Another law that inspired juries to nullify was the National Prohibition Act.[82] Kalven and Zeisel, writing in *The American Jury* in 1966, in what proved to be a landmark study of the jury,[83] described the Prohibition era as "the most intense example of jury revolt in recent history."[84] Prohibition was, in their view, a "crime category in which the jury [was] totally at war with the law."[85] According to their statistics, in 1929 and 1930, twenty-six

---

[79] *See, e.g.*, Alschuler & Deiss, *supra* note 74, at 890-91 n.119; Conrad, *supra* note 75, at 8 (citing one source that reported that "violence against slave-catchers and the refusal of juries to convict persons who aided escaping slaves effectively nullified the federal fugitive slave law in several free states") (quoting Harold M. Hyman & Catherine M. Tarrant, *Aspects of American Trial Jury History*, *in* THE JURY SYSTEM IN AMERICA: A CRITICAL OVERVIEW 23, 37 (Rita James Simon ed., 1975)); John T. Reed, Comment, *Penn, Zenger and O.J.: Jury Nullification—Justice or the "Wacko Fringe's" Attempt to Further its Anti-Government Agenda?*, 34 DUQ. L. REV. 1125, 1133 (1996) ("Many people were opposed to the [Fugitive Slave] law on moral grounds, which made most prosecutions under the law unsuccessful."); Steven M. Warshawsky, Note, *Opposing Jury Nullification: Law, Policy and Prosecutorial Strategy*, 85 GEO. L.J. 191, 201 n.71 (1996) ("Due to widespread opposition to the [1850] law among abolitionists and nonabolitionists alike . . . the law 'became virtually unenforceable.'") (quoting JOHN A. GARRATY, A SHORT HISTORY OF THE AMERICAN NATION 235 (6th ed. 1993)); Lisa Kern Griffen, *"The Image We See Is Our Own": Defending the Jury's Territory at the Heart of the Democratic Process*, 75 NEB. L. REV. 332, 362 (1996) (book review). In *Justice Accused*, Robert Cover recounted instances of jury trials of aiders and abettors in Massachusetts and Pennsylvania who were freed because of hung juries or acquittals. *See* COVER, *supra* note 72, at 191.

[80] *See infra* text accompanying notes 154-66 (describing instructions to juries at the time of the nation's founding and early in our history).

[81] *See infra* note 155 (describing instructions).

[82] *See* National Prohibition Act of Oct. 28, 1919, ch. 85, 41 Stat. 305, *amended by* Supplement to National Prohibition Act, Nov. 23, 1921, ch. 134, 42 Stat. 222, *amended by* Jan. 15, 1931, ch. 29, 46 Stat. 1036, *repealed by* U.S. CONST. amend. XXI, § 1. The National Prohibition Act prohibited the production, sale, and transportation of alcoholic beverages; however, it did not criminalize their use, purchase, or possession. The Act was based on the Eighteenth Amendment to the U.S. Constitution, which provided in relevant part: "Section 1. After one year from the ratification of this article the manufacture, sale, or transportation of intoxicating liquors within, the importation thereof into, or the exportation thereof from the United States and all territory subject to the jurisdiction thereof for beverage purposes is hereby prohibited." U.S. CONST. amend. XVIII, § 1.

[83] *See supra* note 59. As significant as this study was, it suffered from several methodological problems, one of which was the authors' decision to assess the accuracy of jury verdicts by comparing them to judges' assessments of the same cases. This meant using judges' views as the benchmark for the correct answer when it was not at all clear that their views should be taken as correct. Some academics have discussed whether the Kalven and Zeisel study should be updated, and if so, how some of their methodological shortcomings could be avoided. *See, e.g.*, Is It Time to Replicate *The American Jury*?, Association of American Law Schools, Panel Discussion, Jan. 9, 1998 (author's notes on file with the Northwestern University Law Review).

[84] KALVEN & ZEISEL, *supra* note 59, at 291.

[85] *Id.* at 76.

percent of prosecutions for alleged violations of this law resulted in acquittals in federal courts.[86] The high acquittal rate in these cases, particularly during the 1920s and early 1930s, made it difficult to enforce the Prohibition laws, and eventually, they were repealed.[87]

2. Modern-Day Examples.—A recent example of juries engaging in nullification because of their opposition to a law involves the so-called "three strikes" law in California.[88] The legislative statute[89] provides that any person who is convicted of a serious felony and has two prior felony convictions defined as "violent" or "serious,"[90] is to receive a sentence of life imprisonment.[91] The law has led to some harsh results,[92] such as the person who was sentenced to life in prison after stealing a slice of pizza,[93] and another who was similarly sentenced after the theft of cookies;[94] there

---

[86] *See id.* at 292 n.10.

[87] *See* Alan Scheflin & Jon Van Dyke, *Jury Nullification: The Contours of a Controversy*, 43 LAW & CONTEMP. PROBS., Autumn 1980, at 51, 71.

[88] *See* CAL. PENAL CODE § 667 (West Supp. 1998).

[89] *See id.* The statute took effect on March 7, 1994, which was the date on which the Governor signed Bill No. 971. The statute had been passed by both the Senate and Assembly on March 3, 1994. There was also a ballot initiative (Proposition 184), which was approved by voters on November 8, 1994, and took effect the next day, codified as CAL. PENAL CODE § 1170.12 (West Supp. 1998). The two statutes differ only in minor ways.

[90] CAL. PENAL CODE § 667(b) (West Supp. 1998) ("It is the intent of the Legislature . . . to ensure longer prison sentences and greater punishment for those who commit a felony and have been previously convicted of serious and/or violent felony offenses.").

[91] The statute provides that such a defendant is to receive a sentence of "an indeterminate term of life imprisonment." CAL. PENAL CODE § 667(e)(2)(A) (West Supp. 1998). The law has been interpreted by the California Supreme Court to allow judges, as well as prosecutors, to decide whether to disregard prior convictions and not treat a case as a "three strikes" case in the furtherance of justice. *See* People v. Superior Court (Romero), 53 Cal. Rptr. 2d 789, 808 (1996) (holding that the court can strike allegations of prior felony convictions in furtherance of justice on the court's own motion in a case brought under the three strikes law).

[92] *See, e.g.*, Ken Ellingwood, *Three-Time Loser Gets Life in Cookie Theft*, L.A. TIMES, Oct. 28, 1995, at B1 ("Orange County Superior Court Judge Jean Rheinheimer acknowledged the three-strikes law was 'a harsh one' but left her no alternative" in the case of a man she sentenced to life imprisonment after he was found guilty of breaking into a restaurant and stealing four cookies.).

[93] *See* Frank J. Murray, *Is a Pizza Worth 25 Years to Life?*, WASH. TIMES, Apr. 29, 1995, at A6 ("Opponents of California's 'three strikes and you're out' law . . . said it was excessive and absurd to invoke it against Jerry Dwayne Williams for taking a slice of pepperoni pizza from a group of children."); Eric Slater, *Pizza Thief Gets 25 Years to Life*, L.A. TIMES, Mar. 3, 1995, at B3 ("Jerry Dewayne Williams was sentenced to prison for 25 years to life Thursday under the state's 'three strikes' law for stealing a slice of pepperoni pizza."); *see also* Carey Goldberg, *California Judges Ease 3-Strike Law*, N.Y. TIMES, June 21, 1996, at A1 ("'If you ask [the public] about a guy who steals pizza, 80 percent will want judicial discretion.'") (quoting Franklin Zimring, director of the Earl Warren Legal Institute at the University of California at Berkeley).

[94] *See* Ellingwood, *supra* note 92, at B1 ("A homeless parolee convicted for breaking into a Santa Ana restaurant and stealing four cookies was sentenced to life in prison . . . after the judge said she had no choice under the state's 'three strikes' law."); *see also* Jane Gross, *In the New Ball Game, These Two Would Have Struck Out*, N.Y. TIMES, Mar. 20, 1994, at 7 ("Among those already charged as a three-

is much debate about whether it has led to the results intended by the legislators and voters.[95] Of course, juries are not given any information about sentencing because such considerations are not supposed to enter into their decision about the defendant's guilt or innocence. Yet, juries are sometimes able to surmise[96] which cases are three strikes cases.[97] One pattern that has emerged so far is that juries in San Francisco are likely to nullify when they believe the case is a three strikes case—one that is likely to send a person to jail for the rest of his life for the commission of a seemingly mi-

---

strikes offender is a Los Angeles man with a 52-page rap sheet whose latest crime was rolling an elderly Skid Row transient for 50 cents."); Murray, *supra* note 93, at A6 ("Carping questions also were heard when Keith Egly took a 12-pack of beer from a Sacramento convenience store, and Roosevelt Carlton McCowan stole 18 bottles of cologne in Ventura. Egly, 26, managed to get the beer at knifepoint, which is armed robbery .... McCowan, 52, also was cited as another example of too-tough sentencing despite his seven prior convictions for robbery, burglary and attempted murder."); Tony Perry & Maura Dolan, *Two Counties at Opposite Poles of '3 Strikes' Debate Crime: San Francisco is Restrictive in Applying Law, San Diego Takes Hard Line, Approaches Reflect Will of Electorate*, L.A. TIMES, June 24, 1996, at A1 ("There have been cases of convictions in which the 'third strike' was the theft of bluejeans, a six-pack of beer or, in the case of one 60-year-old defendant, a pint of whiskey."); Slater, *supra* note 93, at B3 (describing the cases of Duane Silva, who has an IQ of 70 and suffers from manic depression, and who was "sentenced to 30 years to life for stealing a video recorder and a coin collection from his neighbors" and Michael Garcia, "whose 'strikes' are a nonviolent robbery and theft ... [and who] could receive 25 years to life for stealing a $5.62 package of meat").

95 *See, e.g.*, Linda S. Beres & Thomas D. Griffith, *Do Three Strikes Laws Make Sense? Habitual Offender Statutes and Criminal Incapacitation*, 87 GEO. L.J. 103 (1998) (explaining that three strikes laws, even if they are effective at sentencing high-rate offenders to long prison terms, will have a limited effect on the crime rate because even without such laws most high-rate offenders will spend most of their criminal careers in prison); Fox Butterfield, *'3 Strikes' Law in California Is Clogging Courts and Jails*, N.Y. TIMES, Mar. 23, 1995, at A1 (describing unintended consequences of California's three strikes law, including defendants in felony cases refusing to accept plea bargains, clogged courts, overcrowded prisons, early release of nonviolent inmates, and fewer civil trials as civil judges are needed to serve as criminal judges).

96 Another instance in which a jury became aware of the mandatory sentence that was likely to follow a conviction was a drug case in Arizona state court, in which the jury deliberations were filmed by CBS as part of its two-hour special on the jury system. In that case, jurors were able to infer that the defendant before them was likely to receive a very lengthy prison sentence if convicted of drug charges because the defense was able to introduce a chart showing various sentence ranges in order to explain the sentence received by the defendant's co-conspirator. The co-conspirator, who had cooperated with the government, had received in exchange a very light sentence. During deliberations, the lengthy prison sentence figured heavily in one juror's mind. *See Enter the Jury Room* transcript, *supra* note 16, at 40, 48. He and another juror voted to acquit; as a result, there was a hung jury of six to two. *See id.* at 49.

97 *See* Perry & Dolan, *supra* note 94, at A1 ("In a case of a man convicted of robbing a security guard and trying to steal his car, a juror became agitated and started to cry when she realized it was a 'three strikes' case. She and other jurors objected to the proceeding, and the judge was forced to declare a mistrial."). Edward Nino, a Silicon Valley Public Defender, described the case of Joe Louis Lugo, who was stopped by San Jose Police for driving with bald tires. *See All Things Considered: Simpson Case*, *supra* note 3, *available in* 1995 WL 9892228. The police found a small amount of crack cocaine under Lugo's cap, and Lugo later confessed to drug possession. Lugo, who had two prior felony convictions, would, if convicted in this case, receive a 25-year prison sentence. However, the jury acquitted, "in part, on reasonable doubt, because the police never produced Lugo's cap, and because they didn't agree with the 'three strikes and you're out' law." *Id.* (quoting Edward Nino).

nor third crime—because they are opposed to the three strikes law.[98] In response, prosecutors in San Francisco say they have been very careful about which cases they bring as three strikes cases, knowing that they are likely to obtain convictions only in the most egregious cases.[99] In contrast, in San Diego, juries appear less likely to nullify in three strikes cases,[100] and as a result, prosecutors appear less exacting in the cases they choose to bring as three strikes cases.[101] What is interesting about this law is that even though it applies statewide, it is being enforced differently on the local level because of local juries' respective views of the law.

When a jury nullifies and chooses not to apply a bad law, the law may be a controversial one in its time. Although there is nearly universal agreement today that slavery is wrong,[102] and that the Fugitive Slave Law was a bad law, it certainly did not command such uniformity of opinion in its day. One example of a law today that arouses strongly held views on both sides is the law regulating blockades of abortion clinics. A federal statute, the Freedom of Access to Clinic Entrances Act (FACE),[103] prohibits abortion protesters from preventing access to abortion clinics. With this legislation, Congress hoped to strike a balance between protecting a woman's constitutional right to have an abortion, as articulated in *Roe v.*

---

[98] *See* Butterfield, *supra* note 95, at A1 ("[J]uries in San Francisco have refused to convict people when they learn it will make the defendants third-time felons."); Perry & Dolan, *supra* note 94, at A1.

[99] *See* Butterfield, *supra* note 95, at A1 ("In San Francisco, District Attorney Arlo Smith has brought only eight third-strike cases to trial. 'We are using a commonsense approach,' Mr. Smith said . . . ."); Perry & Dolan, *supra* note 94, at A1 ("'We pretty much use 'three strikes' [only] for vicious people.'") (quoting Terence Hallinan, San Francisco District Attorney).

[100] *See* Perry & Dolan, *supra* note 94, at A1 ("San Diego County prosecutors have sent more 'three strikes' defendants to prison per capita than any urban or suburban county in the state.").

[101] *See id.*

[102] Slavery endures in both Mauritania and Sudan, even though both countries claim to have abolished it officially. *See* Elinor Burkett, *'God Created Me To Be a Slave,'* N.Y. TIMES, Oct. 12, 1997, (Magazine), at 56 ("The Government claims to have abolished human bondage, making Mauritania the last nation on the planet to have done so. But in the endless expanses of wind-swept nothingness between Senegal and Morocco, an estimated 90,000 slaves labor as they have for more than 500 years . . . ."); Jack McKinney, *The Slave Trade Is Alive and Well in the African Sudan*, BUFFALO NEWS, May 14, 1995, at F9 ("The latest account of how the Arab militants of the North Sudan have been reviving slavery in the twilight of the 20th century was reported recently by respected Muslim journalist Shyam Bhatia . . . .").

[103] *See* 18 U.S.C.A. § 248 (West Supp. 1998). The Act provides in relevant part:

> (a) Whoever—
>
> (1) by force or threat of force or by physical obstruction, intentionally injures, intimidates or interferes with or attempts to injure, intimidate or interfere with any person because that person is or has been, or in order to intimidate such person or any other person or any class of persons from, obtaining or providing reproductive health services . . . ;
>
> [or] . . .
>
> (3) intentionally damages or destroys the property of a facility, or attempts to do so, because such facility provides reproductive health services . . . , shall be subject to the penalties provided in subsection (b) and the civil remedies provided in subsection (c) . . . .

Id.

Wade,[104] with a protester's First Amendment right to express disagreement with that right.[105] Courts have tried to maintain this balance by creating buffer zones between protesters and abortion clinics.[106] Jurors opposed to abortion have sometimes nullified when it came time to apply this law or applicable state laws barring trespass in cases of abortion clinic protesters.[107]

3. *Observations*.—One observation drawn from the above examples is that nullification as a response to an unpopular law becomes clearer when it happens on a systemic basis. In any one case, it is difficult to know why or even whether a jury has actually engaged in nullification. It is only after a series of cases involving the same law that a pattern emerges and one is able to say that juries seem to be refusing to apply a particular law.[108]

Another observation is that this form of nullification may result in national or state laws being tailored according to more regional or local views. The Fugitive Slave Laws were federal laws and yet were unpopular in Northern states. Although it is assumed that federal laws will be enforced uniformly throughout the country, the effect of nullifying juries in Northern states meant that these laws could not be enforced as strictly in that region. Similarly, the three strikes law is intended to apply to the entire State of California, yet nullifying juries in San Francisco have made enforcement of

---

[104] 410 U.S. 113 (1973).

[105] *See* SENATE COMM. ON LABOR & HUMAN RESOURCES, FREEDOM OF ACCESS TO CLINIC ENTRANCES ACT OF 1993, S. REP. NO. 103-117, at 28 (1993) ("The Act is carefully drafted so as not to prohibit expressive activities that are constitutionally protected . . . ."); HOUSE COMM. ON JUDICIARY, FREEDOM OF ACCESS TO CLINIC ENTRANCES ACT OF 1994, H.R. CONF. REP. No. 103-488, at 12 (1994).

[106] *See, e.g.*, United States v. Dinwiddie, 76 F.3d 913 (8th Cir. 1996) (holding that an injunction barring protesters from protesting within 500 feet of an abortion clinic did not violate their rights under the First Amendment); United States v. McMillan, 946 F. Supp. 1254 (S.D. Miss. 1995) (providing for 25-foot buffer zone between abortion protesters and abortion clinic to permit protesters to exercise their right to free speech while clinic employees and patients might feel more secure that any threats of force or damage to property would be more difficult to carry out).

[107] *See* John Harris & Elaine Shelly, *Jury Acquits 3 of 4 Abortion Protesters*, AUSTIN AM.-STATESMAN, Apr. 14, 1989, at B1 (reporting that a jury acquitted three of four men charged with misdemeanor trespassing for blocking an abortion clinic in Austin, Tex.); Lillie-Beth Sanger, *Anti-Abortion Activist Convicted of Assault, Battery in Norman*, DAILY OKLAHOMAN, June 16, 1993, *available in* 1993 WL 7985464 (describing jury's acquittal of anti-abortion activist Joe Wilbanks for trespassing at the Abortion Surgery Center in Norman, Okla.); *16 People Acquitted In Abortion Protest*, OMAHA WORLD-HERALD, May 10, 1989, at 1989 WL 3027263 (describing the jury's acquittal of 16 anti-abortion protesters of criminal trespass during a protest at the University of Iowa's abortion clinic). *But see* Michael Granberry, *Abortion Protest Juries Told to Ignore Nullification Ad*, L.A. TIMES (San Diego County Edition), Jan. 27, 1990, at B1 (noting case in which an advertisement in a local newspaper informing jurors of their right to nullify failed to persuade a jury in one trial in which seven anti-abortion protesters were convicted of resisting arrest and trespassing, and three others were convicted of trespassing); Sanger, *supra*, *available in* 1993 WL 7985464 (describing jury's conviction of Aaron Joe Baker for assault and battery outside the Abortion Surgery Center in Norman, Okla.).

[108] *See infra* text accompanying notes 112-21 (questioning whether Bronx jury acquittals indicate nullification).

the three strikes law there much less prevalent than in San Diego. The National Prohibition Act initially enjoyed widespread public support. In 1919, Prohibition was passed by Congress and two-thirds of the states,[109] and yet, when it came time to apply the law, many juries throughout the country refused. The rejection was not limited to a particular locale; rather, it "was almost universally condemned and disregarded by the public."[110] Fourteen years later, the law was repealed.[111]

C. Responding to Factors Other Than Law

Juries also might nullify to register disapproval of social conditions or general features of the justice system. Unlike the previous case, in which jurors are refusing to apply a particular law, with this type of nullification, they are responding to conditions outside of the particular law. Nor are they moved to nullify because of unique characteristics of the defendant before them, as in the first case; rather, they are moved by conditions that are not limited to the defendant's particular situation, though the defendant's situation may highlight the conditions in a particularly sympathetic light.

One recent example of juries that may[112] be nullifying in response to social conditions is the so-called "Bronx jury."[113] This term has been used by some to describe the high acquittal rate among largely minority juries in

---

109 *See* Sidney J. Spaeth, *The Twenty-First Amendment and State Control Over Intoxicating Liquor: Accommodating the Federal Interest*, 79 CAL. L. REV. 161, 175 (1991).

110 Joseph L. Sax, *Conscience and Anarchy: The Prosecution of War Resisters*, 57 YALE REV. 481, 490 (1968).

111 In 1933, the Twenty-first Amendment, *see* U.S. CONST. amend. XXI, § 1 ("The eighteenth article of amendment to the Constitution of the United States is hereby repealed."), ended Prohibition.

112 I use "may" beeause this type of nullification is the most difficult to identify. Indeed, this is one of the drawbacks of this type of nullifieation, namely that it is particularly difficult to know that nullification has taken place. *See infra* text accompanying notes 113-21 (describing why this is the least effective form of nullification).

113 There is debate about the acquittal rates of Bronx juries. According to one writer, Bronx juries are not acquitting at unusually high rates, but are merely at the high end of the norm. *See* Roger Parloff, *Race and Juries: If It Ain't Broke*, A.B.A. J., June 1997, at 5, 6 (concluding that the acquittal rate for jury trials in the Bronx of hlack defendants charged with felonies was 43.6 % in 1995 and 39.1 % in 1996). *But see* Benjamin A. Holden et al., *Racism on Trial*, MONTREAL GAZETTE, Oct. 7, 1995, (Weekly Review), at B1 [hereinafter Holden et al., *Racism on Trial*] (claiming that in the Bronx, "black defendants are acquitted in felony cases 47.6 per cent of the time—nearly three times the national acquittal rate of 17 per cent for all races") (originally reported in Benjamin A. Holden et al., *Color Blinded? Race Seems to Play An Increasing Role in Many Jury Verdicts*, WALL ST. J., Oct. 4, 1995, at A1 [hereinafter Holden et al., *Race Seems*]). Parloff, while challenging others' figures of Bronx acquittal rates as "nearly triple" those of the national average, acknowledged that the figures he offered indicate that the rates of acquittals in the Bronx "*are* high for state courts in New York, and probably for state courts nationwide." Parloff, *supra*, at 6. From the interviews he conducted with Bronx judges, prosecutors, and defense attorneys, however, he concluded that nullification is not viewed as a problem, but rather, that there might be greater juror skepticism of police testimony. *See id.* at 7. In his view, there is no crisis of nullification, much less racially-based nullifieation. *See id.* at 72.

the Bronx, a borough of New York.[114] Many of these juries appear to be refusing to convict, particularly in drug cases.[115] Several explanations have been offered for the high acquittal rate, including nullification explanations ranging from jurors who want to focus attention on racism, a criminal justice system that targets minorities, and police misconduct.[116]

---

[114] The increase in acquittal rates is not limited to juries in the Bronx, according to some observers. In areas with large minority populations, such as Washington, D.C. and Wayne County, Michigan, similar increases in acquittal rates have been noted. *See, e.g.*, Holden et al., *Racism on Trial*, *supra* note 113, at B1 ("In Washington, D.C., where more than 95 per cent of defendants and 70 per cent of jurors are black, 28.7 per cent of all felony trials ended in acquittals last year, significantly above the national average."); *id.* ("In Wayne County, Mich., which includes mostly black Detroit, 30 per cent of felony defendants were acquitted in 1993, the last year for which statistics were available."); *see also All Things Considered: Simpson Case*, *supra* note 3, *available in* 1995 WL 9892228 ("[C]ases in Baltimore, New York, and Los Angeles have been cited as anecdotal evidence that African-American juries are engaging in jury nullification. Furthermore, there is evidence of a gradual increase in acquittal rates in some predominantly black cities and regions.") (quoting correspondent Richard Gonzales); Tony Knight, *Debating Simpson Verdict Opinion Split on Whether Acquittal Was Really Condemnation of the System*, L.A. DAILY NEWS, Oct. 16, 1995, at N1 ("[S]ome court watchers said there is growing evidence that African-American jurors are acquitting defendants of all races more often largely because of their skepticism of the criminal justice system."); Jerome H. Skolnick, *Racial Grievances Won O.J. Acquittal*, NEWSDAY, Oct. 4, 1995, at A33, *available in* 1995 WL 5123199 ("Lately, predominantly black juries in Washington, D.C., have been reluctant to convict obviously guilty young African-American men . . . . But these are mostly drug cases, and perhaps jury nullification here is more understandable."); Michael E. Young & Margorie Lambert, *Trial Seeped into Every Part of Life Series: The Simpson Verdict*, SUN-SENTINEL (Ft. Lauderdale), Oct. 3, 1995, at 4A ("[L]egal scholars believe [race-based nullification] is on the rise in the United States, particularly in cases involving non-violent crimes in minority communities."). *But see All Things Considered: Simpson Case*, *supra* ("[W]e should be very skeptical of anyone who purports to be identifying a trend around the country or among certain groups because there's just so much that we don't know . . . .") (quoting Jeff White, Associate General Counsel, American Trial Lawyers of America); Richard Goldstein, *O.J. Con You See It?*, VILLAGE VOICE, Oct. 17, 1995, at 18 ("[D]espite their plausible mistrust of the police, black juries vote to convict most black defendants. That should have been the [*Wall Street Journal's*] headline . . . ."); Page, *supra* note 3, at 21A ("It is important to note that black leniency toward black defendants has been vastly overrated by frustrated prosecutors. If black jurors were that lenient, we would not have seen black incarceration rates grow as swiftly as they have in the past three decades . . . .").

[115] *See, e.g.*, Goldstein, *supra* note 114, at 18 ("The [Wall Street] Journal might have considered the charges against most of these acquitted defendants. (The war on drugs, as AP reports, has targeted blacks.).").

[116] *See, e.g.*, Holden et al., *Race Seems*, *supra* note 113, at A1 (offering explanations that include keeping black men in the community, protesting racial injustice, and rejecting a justice system skewed against blacks); Holden et al., *Racism on Trial*, *supra* note 113, at B1 ("Some jury-nullification advocates now say blacks are justified in using their jury-room vote to fight what they perceive as a national crisis: a justice system that is skewed against them by courts, prosecutors and racist police like former Los Angeles Detective Mark Fuhrman."); John Kifner, *Bronx Juries: A Defense Dream, a Prosecution Nightmare*, N.Y. TIMES, Dec. 5, 1988, at B1 ("[I]n the Bronx, . . . the juries in criminal cases—overwhelmingly black and Hispanic—have established a reputation for skepticism of the testimony of police officers, mostly white."); *id.* ("In the Bronx, [jurors] do not necessarily look at [police] as a friendly force. . . . They are not going to automatically believe a police officer. They will look on him with suspicion.") (quoting attorney William M. Kunstler); Dan Morrison, *Odds on Rumble in the Bronx*, NEWSDAY, Mar. 22, 1996, at A26 ("The late Mario Merola, the legendary Bronx district attorney, used

Bronx juries have become a source of controversy for those on both sides of the political spectrum. Those on the right contend that Bronx juries exist, and are not limited to the Bronx but extend to other inner cities with large minority populations,[117] and that this pattern of nullification by minority jurors makes the job of law enforcement extremely difficult.[118] Those on the left question whether Bronx juries exist, and contend that to the extent they exist, they are not instances of nullification but rather of minority jurors' reasonable doubt, drawn from their experiences with police misconduct and police willingness to lie on the stand.[119]

Some commentators viewed the O.J. Simpson case as nullification in response to social conditions. In their view, the largely African-American jury[120] had nullified to send a variety of messages of protest to white America. These messages included telling white America that they were tired of being singled out for prosecution, for having a disproportionate number of African-American men sent to prison, for allowing police officers to engage in misconduct and racism, and for maintaining a system of justice that had a long history of discriminating against African Americans.[121]

---

to bemoan the Bronx juries and once told Newsday that his office's low trial conviction rate was due in part to what he believed was the distrust minority communities had of police.").

[117] *See, e.g.*, Holden et al., *Race Seems*, *supra* note 113, at A1 (describing a pattern that includes Washington, D.C., the Bronx, Wayne County, Michigan, and other "heavily black urban areas").

[118] *See* Morrison, *supra* note 116, at A26.

[119] *See* Goldstein, *supra* note 114, at 21 ("[T]he papers have been full of harrowing tales of false arrest perpetrated against blacks in Philadelphia by a police force so corrupt that hundreds of convictions may be thrown out."); Holden et al., *Race Seems*, *supra* note 113, at A1 ("'It's not just race. It's life experiences. Blacks are more likely to have been jacked by the police, and less likely to view police testimony with quite the same pristine validity as a white male from the suburbs.'") (quoting Robert E. Kalunian, Assistant Public Defender for Los Angeles County); *see also* HENRY LOUIS GATES, JR., THIRTEEN WAYS OF LOOKING AT A BLACK MAN 109 (1997) ("Blacks—in particular, black men—swap their experiences of police encounters like war stories, and there are few who don't have more than one story to tell.").

[120] Simpson was acquitted by a jury consisting of eight African-American women, one African-American man, two white women, and one Latino man. *See* Rosen, *supra* note 38, *available in* 1996 WL 9233825 (describing jury composition).

[121] *See, e.g.*, B.G. Gregg, *Simpson: The Civil Verdict: Racial Issues Subdued This Time; Some Hope Trial Promotes Dialogue*, CINCINNATI ENQUIRER, Feb. 6, 1997, at A12 ("'Th[e] first jury verdict was not so much an exoneration of O.J. Simpson as it was finding the criminal justice system guilty. Most individual blacks interpreted that as a victory over what was a racist criminal justice system.'") (quoting Rodney D. Coates, director of Black World Studies and associate professor of sociology at Miami University); Marquand & Wood, *supra* note 3, at 1 ("[S]cholars disagree whether Johnnie Cochran's final argument asking the jury to 'send a message' to the Los Angeles Police Department was nullification. Abbe Smith, deputy director of the Criminal Justice Institute of Harvard University, says it probably was."); Editorial, *Race Isn't the Issue*, PORTLAND OREGONIAN, Feb. 6, 1997, at C8 ("The Simpson acquittal in the criminal trial had to do in large part with the jurors' lack of faith in the criminal justice system to treat black defend[a]nts fairly. That skepticism was borne out by tainted evidence and testimony that echoed a history of official misconduct in the treatment of people of color."); Whitaker, *supra* note 3, at 28 ("When the acquittal came back so swiftly, many commentators assumed that the largely

D. Hybrids

One caveat about these three situations in which nullification is likely to occur is that a particular case might fall into more than one category. One could imagine a scenario in which a jury was not applying a particular law but also found the defendant to be very sympathetic, so that the jury might nullify because it thought the law to be a bad one and also because the law should not be applied to this particular defendant. Another caveat is that while it is useful to tease out the different forms that nullification can take, the categories are not meant to be fixed and immutable. They can overlap or blur, which is the way that jurors also may perceive them. One example of nullification that might belong to more than one category is the acquittal of anti-war protesters or draft resisters during the time of the Vietnam War. Juries nullified[122] to protest the social condition of the war, but they also might have nullified to protest particular laws, such as the Selective Service Act,[123] that contributed to that social condition. In addition, in some cases, they may have found the defendants to be particularly sympathetic. In the protest cases, the government would typically prosecute one or more anti-war demonstrators who had broken laws in the course of their protests. These acts ranged from the destruction of government property,[124]

black jury had engaged in what legal experts call 'jury nullification'—ignoring the evidence to send a broader message, in this case to the police.").

[122] Indeed, it was the Vietnam war that sparked a debate among legal scholars about whether courts should instruct juries on their power to nullify. Up until that time, there had been sparse interest in the subject. *See* Alan W. Scheflin & Jon M. Van Dyke, *Merciful Juries: The Resilience of Jury Nullification*, 48 WASH. & LEE L. REV. 165, 175 (1991) ("The controversy over the propriety of a jury nullification instruction lay dormant for most of this century until resurrected in the 1960s as part of the defense strategy in anti-Vietnam War demonstration trials."); Chaya Weinberg-Brodt, Note, *Jury Nullification and Jury-Control Procedures*, 65 N.Y.U. L. REV. 825, 836 (1990) ("After Sparf and Hansen [v. United States, 156 U.S. 51 (1895)], the issue of jury nullification did not arise again in the federal courts until the 1960s, when conscientious objectors and protesters against government policy began to demand that their juries be informed about the power to nullify."). For those who advocated such an instruction, see Sax, *supra* note 112, at 481; Scheflin, *supra* note 36, at 168; Jon M. Van Dyke, *The Jury as a Political Institution*, 16 CATH. LAW. 224, 225 (1970) ("My thesis is that justice would be better served if jurors were told that they have the power to act mercifully if they decide that applying the law to the defendant's act would lead to an unjust result."); for those who opposed such an instruction, see Gary J. Simson, *Jury Nullification in the American System: A Skeptical View*, 54 TEX. L. REV. 488, 490 (1977) ("I argue that jury nullification has no place, historically or functionally, in the federal jurisprudence. I then suggest that jury nullification in the federal courts may be not only unprecedented and unwise but unconstitutional as well.").

[123] *See* Selective Service Act of 1948, ch. 625, Title I, 62 Stat. 604 (codified as amended at 50 App. U.S.C.A. § 451).

[124] *See, e.g.*, United States v. Simpson, 460 F.2d 515 (9th Cir. 1972); United States v. Moylan, 417 F.2d 1002 (4th Cir. 1969) (involving nine members of the Catholic clergy who entered a Local Board of the Selective Service System in Catonsville, Maryland, removed draft files and destroyed them with homemade napalm; they sought and were denied a nullification instruction and were convicted); United States v. Anderson, Crim. No. 602-71 (D.N.J. 1973), *cited in* Scheflin & Van Dyke, *supra* note 87, at 52 & n.1 (recounting the acquittals of 28 defendants who were charged with destroying records of their lo-

violations of the Selective Service Act,[125] conspiracy to aid in draft evasion,[126] and malicious destruction and unlawful entry.[127] Some of these cases resulted in acquittals[128] because jurors sympathized with the protesters who were voicing their opposition to an unpopular war.[129] In the draft resister cases, in which defendants were typically charged with a single violation of the Selective Service Act, juries began to acquit as popular support for the war waned.[130]

Although cases of jury nullification can sometimes fit into more than one category, the categories are nevertheless a useful heuristic device for evaluating the benefits and harms of jury nullification. But before embarking on that analysis, it is useful to describe two competing visions of the jury because the particular vision one holds will provide the lens through which one looks at these three types of nullification and assesses whether they are beneficial or harmful.

---

cal selective service office, but who were allowed to make statements about their feelings on the Vietnam War and whose jury was instructed on nullification).

[125] *See, e.g.*, United States v. Boardman, 419 F.2d 110 (1st Cir. 1969).

[126] *See, e.g.*, United States v. Spock, 416 F.2d 165 (1st Cir. 1969).

[127] *See, e.g.*, United States v. Dougherty, 473 F.2d 1113 (D.C. Cir. 1972) (describing the case of the "D.C. Nine," who broke into the Dow Chemical Company offices and vandalized them in protest of Dow's manufacture of napalm). In *Dougherty*, the defendants were convicted of the violations with which they had been charged: On appeal, they claimed that they should have been permitted to inform the jury about nullification or that the court should have instructed the jury about nullification. In a 2-1 decision, Judge Leventhal, writing for the court, held that there is no right to instruct the jury about the jury's power to nullify; rather, the jury will reach that knowledge if the jurors are so moved by their sense of justice. To tell juries of this power, according to Judge Leventhal, would run the risk that they would exercise it far too freely. In a powerful dissent, Chief Judge Bazelon explained why juries should be educated as to their power. The exchange between Judge Leventhal and Chief Judge Bazelon offers one of the more interesting and comprehensive debates between judges on the question whether juries should be told about their power to nullify. Federal Circuits remain unanimous in their view that juries should not be so instructed. *See* Marder, *supra* note 39, at n.116 (reviewing case law).

[128] *See, e.g.*, STEVEN E. BARKAN, PROTESTERS ON TRIAL: CRIMINAL JUSTICE IN THE SOUTHERN CIVIL RIGHTS AND VIETNAM ANTIWAR MOVEMENTS 143 (1985) (describing the acquittal of ten protesters who had been charged with blocking a munitions train carrying bombs for Vietnam); Scheflin, *supra* note 36, at 199 (describing the acquittal of "the Oakland Seven," who had been indicted for conspiracy (a felony) to commit the misdemeanors of trespass, creating a public nuisance, and resisting arrest, when demonstrators attempted to interfere with the activities of the Oakland Armed Forces Induction Center in October, 1967). Although Scheflin acknowledged that this might have been a case of reasonable doubt rather than nullification, he relied on post-verdict interviews conducted by Elinor Langer for *The Atlantic* to support the view that it was the latter rather than the former. *See* Scheflin, *supra*, at 200.

[129] *See* Horowitz, *The Impact of Judicial Instructions*, *supra* note 35, at 441 ("The evidence reveals that juries convicted at a higher rate in draft evasion cases when a war was popular than when the war (Vietnam and Korea) lost public support.") (summarizing the results of James Levine).

[130] *See* James P. Levine, *The Legislative Role of Juries*, 1984 AM. B. FOUND. RES. J. 605, 606, 615-18 (comparing public opinion polls on the Vietnam War with conviction rates among draft resisters and finding that as the war became more unpopular, conviction rates in selective service cases decreased).

IV. NULLIFICATION AND THE CONVENTIONAL VIEW OF THE MODERN JURY

A. Two Variations of the Conventional View

Under the conventional view of the jury, the jury's primary role is to find facts. Although few academics espouse such a view, this is the view that judges, both state and federal, communicate everyday in their courtrooms and their opinions. Judges tell jurors, sometimes many times throughout the trial, that their job is to find the facts. As one typical instruction provides: "Your purpose as jurors is to find and determine the facts. Under our system of criminal procedure you are the sole judge of the facts."[131] Judges instruct jurors that their role is to find facts and to take the law as the judge gives it to them: "I instruct you that the law as given by the court in these and other instructions constitute the only law for your guidance. It is your duty to accept and to follow the law as I give it to you even though you may disagree with the law."[132] Judges make clear that the jury's role is quite distinct from the judge's role: "Your job is to decide all of the factual questions in this case . . . . I will decide all of the legal questions in this case . . . ."[133] Although judges, if pressed in private on the subject of the jury's role, might agree that juries actually do more than find facts, their public description of the jury's central role is as fact finder.[134]

Although judges might emphasize to jurors that they find facts, they also instruct them that jurors apply the law, as the judge explains it to them, to the facts. What do they mean when they say that today's jury "applies the law to the facts"? The first, and probably the more prevalent meaning is that the jury performs a mechanical operation: the judge gives the jury the law and the jury simply applies that law to the facts it has found. The typical instruction conveys this mechanical operation: "You will then apply the law, as I give it to you, to those facts. You must follow my instructions on the law, even if you thought the law was different or should be different."[135] A second meaning is that the act involves some jury discretion. There may be cases where the law is unclear, the facts are uncertain, or the standards are ill-defined. These grey areas give the jury room to bring their sense of community norms into the process of applying the law to the facts. While this second meaning of applying the law is accepted perhaps as unavoidable, it is not acknowledged by courts, and certainly not encouraged. With both the first and second meanings, however, the jury is still understood to

---

[131] 2 FEDERAL JURY PRACTICE AND INSTRUCTIONS § 10.01, at 256 (1987).

[132] *Id.*

[133] *Id.* at 259.

[134] *See, e.g.*, *id.* at 263 ("You, and you alone, are the judge of facts.") (quoting Fifth Circuit instruction); *id.* at 275 ("By your verdict(s) you will decide the disputed issues of fact.") (quoting Eleventh Circuit instruction); *id.* at 329 ("It is your duty to find the facts from all the evidence in the case.") (quoting Ninth Circuit instruction).

[135] *Id.* at 329, § 12.01 (quoting Eighth Circuit instruction).

be bound by the law as it was written by the legislature and given to the jury by the judge. Thus, applying the law, even when it may entail some jury discretion, does not give the jury authority to make law but only to try to apply the law the legislature has passed, as explained by the judge.

Either version of the conventional view of the jury envisions a jury that performs fairly limited functions. Under the conventional view, the jury has a role to perform that is distinct from those of the other branches of government. The jury, filled with laymen, needs to be constrained so that it does not intrude on the functions of the other branches. The judge, a professional, provides the jury with the law as he or she understands it. The legislature, elected by the majority, passes laws that represent the views of the majority. The executive, also elected, crafts policies that are consistent with views favored by the majority. The other branches, filled by professionals who are elected (with the exception of federal and some state judges), have functions that are non-overlapping with that of the jury and need to be protected from jury encroachment. The jury's role is narrowly envisioned by the conventional view, and to the extent juries perform more than fact finding or application of law in a narrow sense, they are seen as overstepping their bounds in the political schema and threatening the other branches' roles.

B. *Nullification Assessed from the Conventional View*

Under the conventional view, nullification is always harmful because it threatens boundaries between the jury and the other branches of government and enables the jury to perform functions that have ostensibly been assigned to other branches. When the jury nullifies by choosing not to apply the law to a particular defendant, the jury harms the legislature, and by implication the electorate that it represents. The nullifying jury does so by failing to apply the law uniformly as the legislature intended and by carving out an exception for the particular defendant that the legislature may not have intended. The legislature, in passing laws, assumes that the laws will be applied to everyone. If the legislature intends to create any exceptions, it will specify what they are in the statute, or at least refer to them in the legislative history.[136] Under the conventional view, the jury that nullifies in this situation harms the legislature by encroaching upon its proper function.

---

[136] Of course there are some who believe that legislative history should not be used as an aid in construing a statute or attempting to understand the intent of Congress. Justice Scalia, for example, has renounced the use of legislative history. Among his many objections are the following: it tends to be used selectively simply to support one's construction of the statute, *see* Conroy v. Aniskoff, 507 U.S. 511, 519 (1993) (Scalia, J., concurring) ("Judge Harold Leventhal used to describe the use of legislative history as the equivalent of entering a crowded cocktail party and looking over the heads of the guests for one's friends."); the statute is the law, not the legislative history, *see id.* at 519 ("We are governed by laws, not by the intentions of legislators."); Wisconsin Pub. Intervenor v. Mortier, 501 U.S. 597, 616, 621 (1991) (Scalia, J., concurring) ("[W]e are a Government of laws, not of committee reports."); and if words of the statute are not clear then Congress, and not the Court, should rewrite them. *See* Conroy v.

Under the conventional view, a jury that nullifies what it regards as a bad law, plays a legislative role, and again harms the legislature and those whom the legislature represents. It is the role of the legislature to pass laws and if the legislature passes bad laws, then it is the role of the legislature to repeal them. The nullifying jury, consisting of only twelve jurors, rejects the view of the majority of the legislature, which in turn, represents the will of the people. The nullifying jury does this by declining to apply the law in a particular case. The jury, which may not be representative of the populace, is substituting its judgment for that of democratically elected legislators. Moreover, according to this view, if jurors find a law repugnant, then they have other avenues to register their disapproval. After their jury service is completed, they can write to their legislator, engage in lobbying, draw up petitions, march in protests, write letters to the editor, or any number of activities. Also under this view, if jurors nullify to militate against the effects of a bad law, they reduce the legislature's incentive to act, thus increasing the chances that a bad law will remain on the books. A nullifying jury only masks the defective law by attempting to fix it on an ad hoc basis when what is required is a uniform correction. When a jury nullifies by not applying what it regards as a bad law, it is most clearly stepping into the legislative role and posing a challenge to the legislative function. Commentators who have objected to jury nullification have typically objected on this ground.[137]

In addition, under the conventional view, the nullifying jury is a threat to the judge because the law is the proper domain of the judge, not the jury. The jury is supposed to find facts and to follow the law as instructed on it

---

Aniskoff, 507 U.S. at 528 ("The language of the statute is entirely clear, and if that is not what Congress meant then Congress has made a mistake and Congress will have to correct it."). *See generally* ANTONIN SCALIA, A MATTER OF INTERPRETATION: FEDERAL COURTS AND THE LAW 29-37 (1997). *But see* Stephen Breyer, *The 1991 Justice Lester W. Roth Lecture: On the Uses of Legislative History in Interpreting Statutes*, 65 S. CAL. L. REV. 845 (1992) (defending the use of legislative history as an aid to statutory construction).

[137] *See, e.g.*, George C. Christie, *Lawful Departures From Legal Rules: "Jury Nullification" and Legitimated Disobedience*, 62 CAL. L. REV. 1289, 1300 (1974) (reviewing KADISH & KADISH, *supra* note 34) ("[W]hy should the articulation and ordering of these ends be the function of private citizens who are randomly selected and largely unable to assess the importance of consistency in applying the law in question? Should not this function be left to a popularly elected legislature?"); Simson, *supra* note 122, at 507 ("The recently proposed right to nullify . . . is not a right for jurors to act like judges but, rather, one for them to take on the role of legislators. Like a legislature, a jury with a right to nullify defines blameworthy conduct according to its own notions of justice."); *id.* at 508 ("The need for protection against unjust laws is primarily a function of the lawmaker's responsiveness to the people's will."); *id.* at 513 n.111 ("[J]ury nullification denies the legislative process in a democracy."); *see also* KADISH & KADISH, *supra* note 34, at 49 (describing, but not subscribing to, the conventional view as "the-rule-of-law model" which views nullification with disfavor because it "would invite any jury to abrogate a law duly enacted by the legislature on the basis of its own views. Protection against bad laws should not come through the nullification of democratically enacted legislation by any dozen jurors, but through the established democratic processes for changing the law.").

by the judge.[138] The judge is trained in the law, whereas the jurors are not. To the judge, then, jury nullification is a form of insurrection, and not surprisingly, judges often write or speak about nullification as leading to "chaos" or "anarchy."[139] Jury nullification is a threat not only to the judge's task, but also to the premise of the judicial system, which is that laws should be applied uniformly.

Under the conventional view, juries that nullify in response to social conditions may interfere with their own fact-finding function and harm the legislature and executive as well by appropriating tasks that are best left to these other branches. Under this view, jurors are supposed to decide only the facts of a case; to the extent they stray from this task they are no longer performing the function for which they have special competence. Moreover, the executive and legislative branches are supposed to respond to social conditions through policies and laws respectively. They are the appropriate branches to perform these tasks because they are elected and presumably will reflect the majority of the citizens' views about which are the pressing social issues of the day and how best to respond to them. To the extent that nullifying juries attempt to respond to social conditions, they perform other branches' functions, and these functions are not ones that the jury is particularly well suited to perform.

V. NULLIFICATION AND A PROCESS VIEW OF THE MODERN JURY

A. A Description of the Process View

I offer a different conception of the jury, which I will call a process view. I choose this name because I want to focus on jury processes on at least two different levels. The first is the interpretive process that goes on

---

[138] *See* KADISH & KADISH, *supra* note 34, at 56-57. These authors describe the conventional view, to which they do not subscribe, as follows:

> According to this way of understanding the situation, official formulations fully state the jury's proper role, which is strictly that of a fact-finding agency. A jury reaches its general verdict by deciding the facts of the case and applying the law as given by the judge. Of no consequence are its own sentiments concerning the law's justness . . . . When juries reach verdicts that run counter to the judge's instructions, they usurp a discretion not theirs to exercise. That jury nullification has sometimes produced good results does not show that nullification is within the jury's legal role.

Id.

[139] *See, e.g.*, *Dougherty*, 473 F.2d at 1133 ("This so-called right of jury nullification is put forward in the name of liberty and democracy, but its explicit avowal risks the ultimate logic of anarchy. . . ."); Stephen J. Adler, *Courtroom Putsch? Jurors Should Reject Laws They Don't Like, Activist Group Argues*, WALL ST. J., Jan. 4, 1991, at A1 (quoting former Federal Judge and Director of the Federal Judicial Center, William Schwarzer, who described nullification as producing "chaos and lawlessness"); Bruce Fein, *Judge, Jury . . . and the Sixth*, WASH. TIMES, Nov. 8, 1990, at G3 ("The jury is not a minidemocracy or a minilegislature. They are not to go back and do right as they see fit. That's anarchy. They are supposed to follow the law." (quoting Judge Thomas Penfield Jackson commenting on the jury verdict in the trial of Mayor Marion Barry, in which he was acquitted of the most serious charges)).

within the jury room as the jury deliberates and attempts to reach a verdict. The second is the process that the jury uses to communicate with other branches of government. In both cases, a process view starts with the jury as the jury functions in practice, and it provides a theory of the jury's role that is more consistent with that practice than the conventional view, which gainsays or minimizes these other functions of the jury. Whereas the conventional view sees the jury as finding facts or applying law, the process view sees the jury as also providing an interpretive function. Whereas the conventional view sees the jury as intruding on the legislature if it does anything more than find facts or apply law, the process view sees the jury as providing feedback to other branches about when they are overstepping their bounds. Under the process view, the roles of each branch are less compartmentalized; rather, each branch's functions must be seen in relation to the others.

Although conventional and process views of the jury may have some overlap, they are separated by a fundamental difference. At the core of the conventional view is a skepticism about the jury and a need to limit its reach, whereas at the core of the process view is a fundamental faith in the jury, and a belief that the jury does and should play important roles because of its unique institutional features. Thus, the role of nullification is more complicated under a process view of the jury. Unlike the conventional view, where nullification is always harmful, under the process view, nullification can, in some instances, be beneficial.

1. The Jury's Interpretive Role.—

a. Judge and Jury Share in Legal Interpretation.—Under a process view of the jury, judge and jury share in the process of interpreting the law, and this is recognized, rather than hidden. Although the judge instructs the jury on the law, the jury takes the legal standard that the judge has provided and applies it to the facts of the particular case. In doing so, the jury continues the process of interpretation.

The description of a judge's interpretive task offered by Justice Cardozo in *The Nature of the Judicial Process*[140] is similar in some ways to the jury's interpretive task. In one of his Storrs Lectures, Cardozo described the judge as having to fill in the gaps in a statute as part of the act of construing it. Cardozo described the process as follows:

> [Both judge and legislator are] legislating within the limits of [their] competence. No doubt the limits for the judge are narrower. He legislates only between gaps. He fills the open spaces in the law. How far he may go without

[140] *See* BENJAMIN N. CARDOZO, THE NATURE OF THE JUDICIAL PROCESS (1921).

> traveling beyond the walls of the interstices cannot be staked out for him upon a chart. . . . . [W]ithin the confines of these open spaces and those of precedent and tradition, choice moves with a freedom which stamps its action as creative. The law which is the resulting product is not found, but made. The process, being legislative, demands the legislator's wisdom.[141]

Although the judge must fill in gaps or resolve ambiguities, the judge is not free to create his or her own statute: "He is not a knight-errant roaming at will in pursuit of his own ideal of beauty or of goodness."[142]

The juror, like Cardozo's judge, is engaged in a similar interpretive activity. The juror, like Cardozo's judge, fills in the gaps left by the statute and instructions by drawing from his or her own experiences.[143] This becomes most apparent when the jury is given a legal standard, and the standard is vague and requires interpretation. Although the jurors do not have the vehicle of a judicial opinion in which to explain their interpretation, it is through a verdict that the jury gives shape to the law, albeit incrementally. The jury, in saying that the law applies in this kind of case, or that it does not apply in another kind of case, moves the law over time.

Cases involving mixed questions of fact and law,[144] such as negligence cases,[145] provide the most clear-cut example that juries perform an interpretive function.[146] In negligence cases, it is left to juries to decide what

[141] *Id.* at 113-15.

[142] *Id.* at 141.

[143] *See id.* at 113 ("If you ask how [the judge] is to know when one interest outweighs another, I can only answer that he must get his knowledge just as the legislator gets it, from experience and study and reflection; in brief, from life itself.").

[144] Another area involving mixed questions of fact and law is the determination of "voluntariness" in the context of a federal habeas petition. *See, e.g.*, Miller v. Fenton, 474 U.S. 104 (1985). In *Miller*, the Court had to decide whether the voluntariness of a confession made by petitioner was a factual determination, entitled to a presumption of correctness under 28 U.S.C. § 2254(d), or whether it was a legal question requiring independent federal review. The Court decided to adhere to its longstanding view that it was "a legal inquiry requiring plenary federal review," *id.* at 115, but not before acknowledging that "[i]n the § 2254(d) context, as elsewhere, the appropriate methodology for distinguishing questions of fact from questions of law has been, to say the least, elusive" and that "the Court has yet to arrive at 'a rule or principle that will unerringly distinguish a factual finding from a legal conclusion.'" *Id.* at 112-13.

[145] *See* Wells, *supra* note 28, at 2388 ("It is frequently acknowledged that the jury has broad discretion in deciding negligence cases. Negligence cases are 'mixed' in the sense that factual and legal questions are so intertwined that the roles of judge and jury cannot be separated cleanly."); Stephen C. Yeazell, *The New Jury and the Ancient Jury Conflict*, 1990 U. CHI. LEGAL F. 87, 113-17.

[146] Of course, even factfinding, which is the narrowest conception of the jury's role, involves interpretation. To arrive at "the facts," jurors must weigh evidence and credibility of witnesses, which involves interpretation of what they are seeing and hearing. From this pastiche, jurors must construct a version of the facts that makes sense to them. Some have suggested that jurors begin the trial process with a framework or story into which they place information that is presented at trial. *See, e.g.*, Nancy Pennington & Reid Hastie, *A Cognitive Theory of Juror Decision Making: The Story Model*, 13 CARDOZO L. REV. 519, 521 (1991) ("[O]ne central claim of the model is that the story the juror constructs determines the juror's decision."); *id.* at 525 ("Because all jurors hear the same evidence and

behavior constitutes negligence. Although juries are instructed that the law requires "duty, "breach," "cause in fact," and "proximate cause," it is the jury's task to give content to these terms. Juries bring to these terms their sense of prevailing norms. With these standards in mind, they must decide whether to hold a defendant liable for the consequences of his conduct. In deciding whether there has been a breach, they must decide whether the defendant took reasonable care. The jury shapes the law in small, incremental ways each time it decides that someone did or did not take reasonable care in a particular case. Over time, a picture emerges as to what is meant by reasonable care.

For Professor Stephen Yeazell, not only are juries involved in interpretation of legal standards, but also they are involved in lawmaking in limited areas of the law. He explained that juries, by declining to find contributory negligence, essentially created a regime of comparative negligence long before the legislature and judges had eliminated contributory negligence as a defense.[147] He noted a similar, albeit more complicated, development in the area of products liability. Once judges let the issue of product safety go to the jury, then juries, through their awards and verdicts to plaintiffs, created "a new legal regime."[148] In other areas as well, from the law of wrongful discharge, in which jury verdicts slowly created a form of job security that the common-law doctrine of employment-at-will denied, to the award of punitive damages,[149] in which juries are essentially "fashioning an ad hoc criminal statute,"[150] juries are engaged in the process of lawmaking.

Similarly in criminal cases, the jury is told that the prosecution must establish its case "beyond a reasonable doubt." But the meaning of this

have the same general knowledge about the expected structure of stories, differences in story construction must arise from differences in world knowledge; that is, differences in experiences and beliefs about the social world."); Nancy Pennington & Reid Hastie, *Evidence Evaluation in Complex Decision Making*, 51 J. PERSONALITY & SOC. PSYCHOL. 242 (1986) (finding that jurors organize trial evidence into a story framework); Nancy Pennington & Reid Hastie, *Explaining the Evidence: Tests of the Story Model for Juror Decision Making*, 62 J. PERSONALITY & SOC. PSYCHOL. 189, 189 (1992) ("The Story Model is based on the hypothesis that jurors impose a narrative story organization on trial information . . . ."); Daniel Goleman, *Jurors Hear Evidence and Turn It into Stories*, N.Y. TIMES, May 12, 1992, at C1 (explaining that people "process [evidence] as they go along, composing a continuing story throughout the trial that makes sense of what they're hearing").

147 *See* Yeazell, *supra* note 145, at 113.

148 *Id.* at 114.

149 Judge Kozinski lamented this process in which juries award punitive damages even though the defendant's activity is authorized by legislation. He decried the jury's role as that of a "minilegislature," which is "at odds with the central democratic principle that policy questions are decided by the people's elected representatives." Alex Kozinski, *The Case of Punitive Damages v. Democracy*, WALL ST. J., Jan. 19, 1995, at A18. According to Judge Kozinski, "juries imposing punitive damages may be usurping the role of the legislature, thereby benefiting a few plaintiffs and their lawyers, but denying the large majority of the people goods and services that make life safer, easier and more enjoyable." *Id.*

150 Yeazell, *supra* note 145, at 114.

phrase is vague and difficult to define, as courts have acknowledged,[151] and it is left to juries to decide what meaning to give the standard. When courts tried to say more about reasonable doubt, such as that it requires that jurors know something to a '"moral certainty,"' the Supreme Court rejected that language, holding that courts had gone too far and had "suggested a higher degree of doubt than is required for acquittal under the reasonable doubt standard."[152] At best, judges can tell jurors that there is no formula for deciding what constitutes "beyond a reasonable doubt," and that jurors are to draw from their commonsense and everyday experiences as to what it means.[153] Even though jurors fill in the gaps left by the ambiguous phrase "beyond a reasonable doubt," they have some authorization by the judge, who has instructed them to do so. Their determination as to whether reasonable doubt has been met is based on more than finding of facts or applying the law. They must engage in a weighing of the evidence presented by the State, and it is likely that this amorphous process of weighing and judging will be shaped by attitudes they hold on a wide range of issues, from whether they distrust the State and worry about it abusing its power to how vulnerable they feel to crime and whether they believe it is the State's responsibility to protect law-abiding citizens. Thus, under this view of the jury, the jury plays a role in interpreting the law.

This view of the jury as participating with the judge in the interpretive process, whether through interpreting legal standards or developing legal regimes, may seem more radical than it is; in fact, its antecedent can be found in the way judges and juries interacted at the time of the founding of this country. At that time, the functions of judge and jury were shared, with the judge performing the more perfunctory role of the two.[154] Jurors were not told by judges, as they are today,[155] that they were limited to factfinding

---

[151] *See, e.g.*, Victor v. Nebraska, 511 U.S. 1, 25 (1994) (Ginsburg, J., concurring) ("This Court, too, has suggested on occasion that prevailing definitions of 'reasonable doubt' afford no real aid."); United States v. Adkins, 937 F.2d 947, 950 (4th Cir. 1991) ("This circuit has repeatedly warned against giving the jury definitions of reasonable doubt, because definitions tend to impermissibly lessen the burden of proof."); United States v. Hall, 854 F.2d 1036, 1039 (7th Cir. 1988) ("An attempt to define reasonable doubt presents a risk without any real benefit.").

[152] Cage v. Louisiana, 498 U.S. 39, 41 (1990) (*per curiam*).

[153] The Federal Judicial Center's pattern instruction informs jurors: "Proof beyond a reasonable doubt is proof that leaves you firmly convinced of the defendant's guilt. There are very few things in this world that we know with absolute certainty, and in criminal cases the law does not require proof that overcomes every possible doubt." FEDERAL JUDICIAL CTR., PATTERN CRIMINAL JURY INSTRUCTIONS 28 (1988) (instruction 21).

[154] *See, e.g.*, Mark DeWolfe Howe, *Juries as Judges of Criminal Law*, 52 HARV. L. REV. 582, 591 (1939) ("The judges in Rhode Island held office not for the purpose of deciding cases, for the jury decided all questions of law and fact; but merely to preserve order, and see that the parties had a fair chance with the jury.") (quotation omitted).

[155] For example, in California, a judge typically instructs jurors that they have "a duty to apply the law as I give it to you to the facts as you determine them." CALIFORNIA JURY INSTRUCTIONS, CRIMINAL (CALJIC), no. 1.00 (1989). In some federal courts, jurors are instructed as follows:

and that judges were the sole purveyors of the law.[156] Rather, judges typically instructed jurors that they were free to decide the facts and the law.[157] Furthermore, the decision they reached was one that should be consistent with their sense of what was right.[158] William Nelson, in his study of the

---

> It will be your duty to decide from the evidence what the facts are. You, and you alone, are the judge of facts. You will hear the evidence, decide what the facts are, and then apply those facts to the law which I will give to you. That is how you will reach your verdict. In doing so you must follow that law whether you agree with it or not.

MANUAL OF MODERN CRIMINAL JURY INSTRUCTIONS FOR THE NINTH CIRCUIT, nos. 1.01 and 3.01 (1992). Today, only two states, Indiana and Maryland, still instruct jurors that they have the right to determine the law as well as the facts. These two states' respective constitutions provide for this right. *See* IND. CONST. art. 1, § 19 ("In all criminal cases whatsoever, the jury shall have the right to determine the law and the facts."); MD. CONST. DECLARATION OF RIGHTS art. 23 ("In the trial of all criminal cases, the Jury shall be the Judges of Law, as well as of fact, except that the Court may pass upon the sufficiency of the evidence to sustain a conviction."). However, in both states, the judiciary has narrowed this right through case law. *See, e.g.*, Beavers v. State, 141 N.E.2d 118, 125 (Ind. 1957) ("Although the constitution gives the jury the right to determine the law in criminal cases, it does not follow . . . that it is an 'exclusive' right . . . . Neither does it follow . . . that the jury is the judge of the law at every step in the proceedings."); Montgomery v. State, 437 A.2d 654, 656 (Md. 1981) ("[T]he jury's role in judging the law under Article 23 is confined 'to resolv[ing] conflicting interpretations of the law . . . and to decid[ing] whether th[at] law should be applied in dubious factual situations,' and nothing more.").

[156] Judges today help to perpetuate the myth of the jury acting solely as a factfinder. However, the distinction that judges make between their role and that of the jury is overstated. Commentators have long noted that the jury does more than find facts—that it performs both factfinding and lawmaking functions. *See, e.g.*, ABRAMSON, *supra* note 33, at 64 ("The fact/law distinction, so starkly posed in judges' instructions to juries today, is, however, a fiction that seldom corrals the behavior of actual jurors."); Drew L. Kershen, *Vicinage*, 30 OKLA. L. REV. 3, 83 (1977); Scheflin & Van Dyke, *supra* note 87, at 68. Yeazell further explains:

> For the jury is not now and never has been a simple, functional piece of the judicial machine, to be judged on how well it finds facts. Instead it plays a complicated role, simultaneously functional and symbolic, checking judicial power and strengthening judicial institutions, reshaping law as it gives a remarkable efficacy to the legal regime.

Yeazell, *supra* note 145, at 88.

> [B]oth those who attack and those who defend the modern jury ought to be clear about the political character of the institution under discussion. . . . [O]ne cannot simply discuss the jury as if it were an entirely utilitarian institution to be judged by how well it performed a factfinding function. . . . The debate is about the shape of government as much as it is about the reconstruction of facts.

Id. at 117.

[157] *See* Howe, *supra* note 154, at 589 ("[I]n the federal courts until 1835, lower court judges and Justices of the Supreme Court, sitting on circuit, had time and again specifically instructed juries that they were 'the judges both of the law and the fact in a criminal case, and are not bound by the opinion of the court . . . .'") (quoting United States v. Wilson, Fed. Cas. No. 16,730 (C.C.E.D. Pa. 1830) (Baldwin, J.)); *id.* at 595 ("[T]he usual practice in Pennsylvania was for judges to inform the jurors 'what in the opinion of the court, was the law, but that the jury were the judges of the law and the fact.'") (quoting Edward Tilghman's testimony at the impeachment of Samuel Chase in REPORT OF THE TRIAL OF THE HON. SAMUEL CHASE 27 (Evans ed., 1805)); *see also* Adler, *supra* note 139, at A1 ("After the Revolution, many U.S. judges continued to show deference to juries by routinely telling them that they could determine for themselves what the law should provide.").

[158] John Adams described the juror's right to decide a case according to his conscience: "It is not only his right but his duty, in that case to find the verdict according to his own best understanding, judgment, and conscience, though in direct opposition to the direction of the court." Howe, *supra* note 154, at 605 (quoting 2 LIFE AND WORKS OF JOHN ADAMS 253-55 (C.F. Adams ed., 1856)).

legal system in Massachusetts before the Revolutionary War, noted that even if judges tried to instruct jurors on the law, their instructions could be confusing because they were delivered seriatim by at least three judges; they could easily be disregarded because the lawyers also presented competing versions of the law; and the judge had few means available to compel the jury to follow his instructions.[159] Jeffrey Abramson noted that in most state jurisdictions and in many federal cases, criminal juries retained their power to decide the law after the Revolution and well into the nineteenth century.[160] Abramson pointed to the Georgia Constitution of 1777,[161] the Pennsylvania Constitution of 1790,[162] a Vermont Supreme Court decision of 1849,[163] and a Pennsylvania Supreme Court decision of 1879,[164] among others, that took the position that the jury was to judge the law as

---

[159] *See* WILLIAM E. NELSON, AMERICANIZATION OF THE COMMON LAW: THE IMPACT OF LEGAL CHANGE ON MASSACHUSETTS SOCIETY, 1760-1830, at 26-27 (1975) (providing explanations for why the jury did not follow the law as given by the judge).

[160] *See* ABRAMSON, *supra* note 33, at 75. At the very least, according to Scheflin, "[t]here is agreement among many commentators that the right of the jury to decide questions of law and fact prevailed in this country until the middle 1800's." Scheflin, *supra* note 36, at 177. Howe described how a number of States, including Pennsylvania, New York, Vermont, Virginia, Louisiana, Georgia, Tennessee, Connecticut, Massachusetts, and Illinois maintained that juries could decide questions of both fact and law, at least until the 1850s. *See* Howe, *supra* note 154, at 590 n.2, 592, 594-96, 596 n.57, 597 n.58, 603, 605-09, 611.

According to Howe, judges acted "arrogant[ly]," *id.* at 616, in gradually wresting this power from juries, even when legislatures in some states had passed statutes that explicitly provided that juries were to be the finders of fact and law. *See id.* at 597 n.58 ("In early years the juries, by statute [in Louisiana], were made judges of law in both civil and criminal cases.... Modification began, however, in State v. Tally, 23 La. Ann. 677 (1871)."); *id.* at 602-03 (describing Connecticut's statutes concerning judge and jury roles and court decisions that held that jurors still could not disregard the law); *id.* at 609-10 ("In 1855 the [Massachusetts] legislature passed a statute which ... provided that 'in all trials for criminal offenses, it shall be the duty of the jury ... to decide at [its] discretion, by a general verdict, both the fact and the law involved in the issue ....'" but in that same year, the Massachusetts Supreme Court held that such a statute "'would be repugnant to the Constitution of the Commonwealth.'"); *id.* at 611 (describing a transformation in Illinois, where there was a statute providing that "'juries in all [criminal] cases shall be judges of the law and fact,'" but courts eventually instructed juries that although they were to judge the law, they could only do so if they knew the law better than the court). In Georgia:

> [The] constitution of 1777 in article 41 provided that 'the jury shall be judges of law, as well as of fact' and forbade the finding of special verdicts.... Until 1870 the jury's right to make independent decisions on questions of criminal law was acknowledged.... In 1870, however, Brown v. State, 40 Ga. 689, held that the jury must accept the law from the court.

Id. at 597 n. 58.

[161] *See* ABRAMSON, *supra* note 33, at 76 (providing that "the jury shall be judges of law, as well as fact.").

[162] *See id.*

[163] *See id.* (citing State v. Croteau, 23 Vt. 14 (1849) (stressing that the "opinion of the legal profession in this state, from the earliest organization of the government ... has been almost if not quite uniform in favor of the ... right of the jury" to decide questions of law), *overruled by* State v. Burpee, 65 Vt. 125 (1892)).

[164] *See id.* ("[T]he power of the jury to judge of the law in criminal cases is one of the most valuable securities guaranteed by the Bill of Rights." (quoting Howe, *supra* note 154, at 595)).

well as the facts. Abramson attributed the transformation in judge/jury roles not only to a Supreme Court case,[165] but also to the growing transparency of the law and a growing faith in judges, rather than juries, to protect the rights of the criminal defendant.[166]

In an article tracing the development of the modern-day jury,[167] Stephen Yeazell explained that judges and juries used to share in the factfinding and lawmaking functions, and only when judges began to view themselves as professionals[168] was there a shift toward seeing the functions as separate, with judges attempting to limit jurors to the factfinding function only.[169]

Although the jury has only the verdict through which to interpret the facts and law, it is significant that the verdict is general rather than specific. In all criminal cases, the jury returns a general verdict in which it says only whether the defendant is guilty or not guilty, and provides no reasons for its decision. If the jury acquits, then the acquittal is final and binding. Attempts to restrict the general verdict in the criminal context have been rebuffed and regarded as an intrusion into the jury's domain.[170] Underlying this protection of the general verdict may be an understanding that the jury, or at least the criminal jury, does something more than factfinding or mechanical application of the law. One court concluded that any restrictions on the general verdict "would partly restrict [the jury's] historic function, that of tempering rules of law by common sense brought to bear upon the facts of the case."[171] Through the general verdict, then, the jury not only decides whether the defendant is guilty or not guilty, but also interprets the judge's instructions and decides whether and how to follow them. The gen-

[165] *See* Sparf and Hansen v. United States, 156 U.S. 1 (1895).

[166] *See* ABRAMSON, *supra* note 33, at 88-90.

[167] *See* Yeazell, *supra* note 145, at 87.

[168] *See id.* at 103 ("The conflict that emerged at the birth of the jury has proved durable—that between juries as mirrors of popular (or at least lay) values and judges as representatives of a professional elite."); *see also* NELSON, *supra* note 159, at 33 ("The key to becoming a [colonial] judge was not that one was a lawyer, for nearly all Massachusetts judges were not, but that one was a man of substance who commanded the respect of his community."); Howe, *supra* note 154, at 591 (noting that after Independence, colonial judges exercised limited powers, in large part because "judges were laymen"); Simson, *supra* note 122, at 504 ("The subsequent death of the practice [of the "colonial jury's right to redetermine issues of law decided by the judge"] in federal courts . . . can be understood in light of the widening disparity between judge and jury in professional qualifications and the gradual disappearance of the people's intense distrust of the judiciary . . . .") (footnote omitted).

[169] *See* Yeazell, *supra* note 145, at 93-96. Schefiin explained the transformation as the result of "a power struggle in which professional judges sought tighter controls over the legal apparatus of the trial." Scheflin, *supra* note 36, at 207 & n.134.

[170] *See, e.g.*, United States v. Spock, 416 F.2d 165 (1st Cir. 1969) (reversing a conviction of conspiracy to counsel evasion of the draft because the trial court had put to the jury ten special questions in addition to a general verdict).

[171] United States v. Ogull, 149 F. Supp. 272, 276 (S.D.N.Y. 1957) (quoted in *Spock*, 416 F.2d at 181).

eral verdict gives the jury flexibility to do this, and if the jury renders a verdict of not guilty, its decision cannot be further examined.

The civil jury does not always have as much leeway as the criminal jury to interpret the law because the judge in a civil trial has several procedural devices to control the jury that are unavailable in a criminal trial. In a civil case in federal court, the judge can instruct the jury to return a special verdict, in which the court submits a form to the jury that requires it to make written findings of fact.[172] The court then enters judgment based on the jury's findings of fact. Another procedural device available to a judge in a civil case in federal court is to ask the jury to answer written interrogatories as well as to reach a general verdict.[173] In this way, the court helps to structure the reasoning process that leads the jury to its verdict. Each of these methods is a means for the judge to limit the jury's opportunity to reach a verdict contrary to what the judge views as correct. However, judges tend to be fairly circumspect about using special verdicts and interrogatories, perhaps because they are worried about invading the province of the jury.[174] Thus, even in the civil context, juries usually return general verdicts. In addition, in a civil case, juries are often asked to assess damages, and general damages, as well as punitive damages, are another means through which juries can give expression to their interpretation of a case.[175] In assessing damages, juries are called upon to do something more than find facts.[176]

Although the jury's role in interpreting the law might have been more explicit in the past than it is today, the jury still performs this role. Today, judges may instruct juries to the contrary, insisting that their task is only to find facts and to apply the law as the judge explains it to them, but in prac-

[172] *See* FED. R. CIV. P. 49(a) (Special Verdicts).

[173] *See* FED. R. CIV. P. 49(b) (General Verdict Accompanied by Answer to Interrogatories).

[174] *See, e.g.*, James A. Henderson Jr. et al., *Optimal Issue Separation in Modern Products Liability Litigation*, 73 TEX. L. REV. 1653, 1674 (1995) ("The special verdict arguably separates the issues to a greater degree than is justified. Consequently, many commentators, including judges, have criticized the practice as an interference with the traditional role of the jury."). Justices Hugo L. Black and William O. Douglas viewed Rule 49 as "another means utilized by courts to weaken the constitutional power of juries" and called for its repeal. 31 F.R.D. 617, 619 (1963) (statement of Mr. Justice Black and Mr. Justice Douglas on the Rules of Civil Procedure and the Proposed Amendments). Other judges have also been wary. *See, e.g.*, Morris v. Pennsylvania R.R., 187 F.2d 837, 840-41 (2d Cir. 1951) (noting that special verdicts and answers to interrogatories can lead to inconsistencies, which courts should attempt to reconcile with "discrimination and foresight"); Melancon v. McKeithen, 345 F. Supp. 1025, 1046 (E.D. La. 1972) ("[S]pecial verdicts . . . and general verdicts accompanied by answers to interrogatories . . . involve inroads by the judge into the jury function.").

[175] *See, e.g.*, STEPHEN J. CARROLL, THE INSTITUTE FOR CIVIL JUSTICE (RAND), JURY AWARDS AND PREJUDGMENT INTEREST IN TORT CASES 14, 16 (1983) (describing Cook County juries' tendency to include prejudgment interest implicitly in their awards of general damages in tort cases, thus appearing to compensate plaintiffs who had to wait a long time for their award).

[176] *See id.* at 16 (noting that Cook County juries included prejudgment interest in general damages in torts cases and questioning whether, as a matter of policy, it is best for juries or legislatures to determine these rates).

tice juries perform more than factfinding and more than application of law in a narrow sense. The jury is called upon to interpret legal standards that are vague and to give meaning to these, and the jury is given a general verdict through which to deliver its decision, thus ensuring that it has room to interpret and that its interpretation cannot in certain circumstances be reviewed by the judge.

b. Judge and Jury Are Uniquely Situated to Interpret Law.— Judges and jurors are uniquely situated to engage in their shared interpretive functions because they are present in the courtroom and learn the facts of the case. This gives them special competence to judge the parties' case, and in doing so, to interpret the law as it applies to those individuals.

The judge and jury are also uniquely situated to interpret the law because they are supposed to have no personal stake in the outcome, unlike the legislator, who is beholden to his constituents and perhaps to special interest groups if he or she wants to be re-elected.[177] Jurors serve in only one case, and they can serve only if they have no personal connection to the case.[178] Ideally, the process of voir dire is supposed to enable attorneys and judges to remove those prospective jurors who cannot be impartial.[179] Judges, too, can serve only if they have no personal connection to the case; otherwise, they must recuse themselves.[180] The prerequisite for both judges' and jurors' service is impartiality.[181] Impartiality helps judges and

---

[177] The exception would be those state court judges who are elected rather than appointed. *See, e.g.*,. FLA. ADMIN. CODE ANN. r.1S-2.0001 (1998) (providing for the election of judges).

[178] When juries were first used in England, the opposite was true. Jurors were chosen because they had knowledge of the parties or the dispute. *See* THOMAS ANDREW GREEN, VERDICT ACCORDING TO CONSCIENCE: PERSPECTIVES ON THE ENGLISH CRIMINAL TRIAL JURY 1200-1800, at 52 (1985) ("The trial jurors, drawn from the hundred where the homicide was committed, but not necessarily from the immediate vicinage, probably reflected already settled attitudes of the countryside toward individual defendants."); *id.* at 98 ("Moreover, juries were forced to make decisions about individuals partially on the basis of the reputation of those individuals in the community."); Farnham, *supra* note 19, at 5 ("Contrary to the modern concept of a jury ignorant except as enlightened by the facts presented at trial, medieval jurors took an oath to tell what they knew to be true."); Yeazell, *supra* note 145, at 91 ("The jurors were to be selected for their knowledge of the underlying events; if they were ignorant, the solution was not to present evidence, but to select more jurors until one found those who knew.").

[179] *See* KASSIN & WRIGHTSMAN, *supra* note 20, at 50 (describing the legitimate purposes of voir dire, including the search for impartial jurors); Barbara A. Babcock, *Voir Dire: Preserving 'Its Wonderful Power,'* 27 STAN. L. REV. 545 (1975) (defending voir dire and urging that it become more extensive). *But see* Nancy S. Marder, *Beyond Gender: Peremptory Challenges and the Roles of the Jury*, 73 TEX. L. REV. 1041, 1086-90 (1995) (describing the aspirations of voir dire, but also the ways in which the practice falls short of the ideal).

[180] *See* 28 U.S.C. §§ 144, 455 (1988). Attorneys can move to recuse a judge who fails to do so on his or her own; however, these motions are difficult to win. *See, e.g.*, Pennsylvania v. Local Union 542 Int'l Union of Operating Eng'rs, 388 F. Supp. 155, 181-82 (E.D. Pa. 1974) (denying a motion to recuse filed pursuant to 28 U.S.C. § 144 because Judge Higginbotham did not believe that a black judge should have to recuse himself simply because he is black and the case involved race).

[181] This is a constitutional prerequisite in the case of a jury. The Sixth Amendment requires that the defendant in a criminal case receive a trial by an "impartial jury." U.S. CONST. amend. VI. Although

jurors to perform their tasks in that they are supposed to decide the case based only on the information that is presented to them at trial. The legislator does not have the luxury of such a disinterested stance from which to pass the laws.

c. Jury's Institutional Features Assist in Interpretive Role.—The jury has several institutional features that, while not unique to its interpretive role, make it particularly well suited to perform that role. Foremost, the jury is a collective body that reaches its decisions through a deliberative process. As a group, it can draw upon the recollections, assessments, and analyses of twelve individuals,[182] each of whom will have his or her own strengths, viewpoints, backgrounds, and life experiences.[183] The jurors might not start out at the same point in their initial view of the case, but through group discussions, they try to reach a common understanding. Through this process, they can correct each other's mistaken notions,[184] broaden each other's perspectives, and suggest different ways of looking at

---

the Seventh Amendment does not explicitly provide for an impartial jury, the requirement is understood to apply to the civil jury trial as well. *See, e.g.*, Thiel v. Southern Pac. Co., 328 U.S. 217, 220 (1946) ("The American tradition of trial by jury, considered in connection with either criminal or civil proceedings, necessarily contemplates an impartial jury drawn from a cross-section of the community.") (citations omitted).

For federal judges, Article III helps to structure the role so that judges remain independent and are less likely to succumb to outside influences. *See* U.S. CONST. art. III, § 1 ("The Judges, both of the supreme and inferior Courts, shall hold their Offices during good Behaviour, and shall, at stated Times, receive for their Services a Compensation, which shall not be diminished during their Continuance in Office."). In addition, impartiality is both a statutory and ethical requirement. *See* 28 U.S.C. § 455(a) (1998) ("Any justice, judge, or magistrate of the United States shall disqualify himself in any proceeding in which his impartiality might reasonably be questioned."); MODEL CODE OF JUDICIAL CONDUCT Canon 2(A) (1990) ("A judge shall respect and comply with the law and shall act at all times in a manner that promotes public confidence in the integrity and impartiality of the judiciary.").

182 *See* REID HASTIE ET AL., INSIDE THE JURY 236 (1983) ("The group memory advantage over the typical or even the exceptional individual is one of the major determinants of the superiority of the jury as a legal decision mechanism."); *id.* at 81 (describing the impressive collective memory of a jury and noting that jurors remember 90% of the evidence and 80% of the judge's instructions); JAMES P. LEVINE, JURIES AND POLITICS 182 (1992) ("Remembering what was said is no small part of competent fact finding, and the collective memory of twelve jurors (over even six) is likely to be better than that of one individual."); Harry Kalven, *The Dignity of the Civil Jury*, 50 VA. L. REV. 1055, 1067 (1964) ("Different jurors remember, and make available to all, different items of the trial so that the jury as a group remembers far more than most of its members could as individuals."); Goleman, *supra* note 146, at C1 ("In a study of more than 700 jurors . . . the average rate at which individual jurors remembered evidence from a trial was 60 percent; for judge's instructions the average was 44 percent. But for the jury as a whole, the memory rates were far better: 93 percent for facts and 82 percent for instructions.").

183 *See* VALERIE P. HANS & NEIL VIDMAR, JUDGING THE JURY 50 (1986) ("[A] jury composed of individuals with a wide range of experiences, backgrounds, and knowledge is more likely to perceive the facts from different perspectives and thus engage in a vigorous and thorough debate.").

184 *See* Ballew v. Georgia, 435 U.S. 223, 233 (1978) ("When individual and group decisionmaking were compared, it was seen that groups performed better because prejudices of individuals were frequently counterbalanced . . . ."); HANS & VIDMAR, *supra* note 183, at 50 ("The jury's heterogeneous makeup may also lessen the power of prejudice.").

the evidence. Their interpretation of the case benefits from this collaborative method—a method that is unavailable to the trial judge, who works alone.[185]

Another important feature of the jury is that it is made up of ordinary citizens. This is significant because it means their contribution to the deliberative and interpretative process is not any specialized knowledge, but common sense. They may approach their decisionmaking as they would approach decisionmaking in other aspects of their lives. The jury is able to decide, as it did in the Leroy Reed case,[186] that the law should be interpreted in a way that did not send Leroy Reed to prison. Thus, the jury is a check on professionals, who may have grown too removed from the experiences and common sense reasoning of ordinary citizens.[187]

Relatedly, jurors are nonrepeat players. They hear only one case, which means they bring to their interpretation of the law a freshness that a judge who has heard many cases may no longer have. Their status as one-time decisionmakers also makes it more likely that the verdict they reach will be accepted by the rest of the citizeury. They are likely to be viewed as fair arbiters not only because they have no personal stake in the outcome, but also because they shed their official role of juror as soon as they render a verdict.

A key feature of the process view of the jury is that the jury should be as diverse as possible, and this feature also assists the jury in performing an interpretive role. The Sixth Amendment requires that the venire for a criminal jury be drawn from a fair cross section of the community.[188] However, there is no requirement that the petit jury be similarly representative,[189] which means that occasionally a jury may not be diverse. A diverse jury is key to interpretation because it makes available for group considera-

[185] Although appellate judges do work in panels of three and have the benefit of each other's ideas, they typically do not engage in deliberations until after oral argument, by which time they have already read the briefs and done independent research on the issues, and have usually formed tentative views of the case.

[186] *See Inside the Jury Room* transcript, *supra* note 16, at 31-58.

[187] When Abe Fortas was a justice, he described this tendency of judges as follows: "[J]udges do become case-hardened. Judges do sometimes tend, after many years, to take a somewhat jaundiced view of defendants. Many trial judges tend to become a bit prosecution-minded. That's the basic justification for a jury." Scheflin, *supra* note 36, at 213.

[188] *See, e.g.*, Taylor v. Louisiana, 419 U.S. 522 (1975) (holding that women cannot be automatically exempted from the venire because a defendant has a Sixth Amendment right to a venire drawn from a fair cross section of the community). Although the Sixth Amendment does not apply to a civil jury, in practice, venires for civil and criminal juries are drawn in the same way. Even Congress has adopted a unified approach to the jury; the procedures it sets forth for jury service are applicable to both civil and criminal juries. *See* 28 U.S.C. §§ 1861-1878 (1988).

[189] *See* Holland v. Illinois, 493 U.S. 474 (1990) (holding that the Sixth Amendment's fair cross section requirement of the venire need not be applied to the petit jury); Batson v. Kentucky, 476 U.S. 79, 85 n.6 (1986) ("[I]t would be impossible to apply a concept of proportional representation to the petit jury in view of the heterogeneous nature of our society.").

tion a wide range of experiences and perspectives. It also means that different jurors may be able to shed light on different witnesses' credibility, from the police to the criminal defendant, and this becomes particularly important in deciding how to interpret a legal standard such as "beyond a reasonable doubt." Although in practice it would be unworkable and divisive to mandate representative juries,[190] and therefore, any one jury may not be diverse, diverse juries are certainly the ideal. Toward that end, courts are trying to make jury venires more representative than they currently are[191] to increase the chances that petit juries will be representative as well. Moreover, juries as an institution are far more diverse than the judiciary, particularly the federal judiciary.[192]

---

[190] *See* JON M. VAN DYKE, JURY SELECTION PROCEDURES 18 (1977) ("[A] juror selected under this [quota] system might feel that he or she is filling some predetermined 'slot' and might attempt to give the view generally associated with those demographic characteristics rather than the juror's personal feelings about the case."); Marder, *supra* note 179, at 1104-07 (describing the harms of a quota system, including how to agree on which groups are distinctive; how to categorize people who belong in several groups; and whether the state should be involved in such categorization). *But see* Nancy J. King, *Racial Jurymandering: Cancer or Cure? A Contemporary Review of Affirmative Action in Jury Selection*, 68 N.Y.U. L. REV. 707, 768 (1993) (suggesting that "courts analyze which race-conscious reforms are reasonably necessary to maintain public confidence in the impartiality of jury proceedings by considering [six circumstances]").

[191] *See, e.g.*, Dennis Bilecki, *Program Improves Minority Group Representation on Federal Juries*, 77 JUDICATURE 221 (1994) (describing a pilot program in Northern California that used lists of licensed drivers and California identification card holders in addition to voter registration lists to improve minority representation on the venire); David Kairys et al., *Jury Representativeness: A Mandate for Multiple Source Lists*, 65 CAL. L. REV. 776 (1977) (urging the use of multiple source lists for the venire, rather than simply relying on voter registration lists); Rocco Cammarere, *$5 Jury Pay 'an Outrage'; Recommendations Made*, N.J. LAW., Dec. 13, 1993, at 1 (describing recommendations in New Jersey to use multiple lists for venire, including lists of state income taxpayers and people who file for a homestead rebate claim). Some states have gone further, and have made sure that jurors are drawn for the venire in proportion to their group's numbers in the community. For example, Georgia requires that in death penalty cases, the composition of the venire must resemble the racial and gender composition of the counties from which the jurors are drawn. *See* David Margolick, *Question for the '90s: Just What Is a Jury of One's Peers?*, CHI. DAILY L. BULL., Feb. 18, 1992, at 2. A similar effort was made in Michigan. *See* Nancy J. King & G. Thomas Munsterman, *Stratefied Juror Selection: Cross-Section by Design*, 79 JUDICATURE 273, 275 (1996) ("[In the Eastern District of Michigan, t]he court . . . randomly strikes from the list of persons qualified the specific number of 'white and other' potential jurors needed to obtain a qualified list with racial demographics identical to that of the population."). *But see* United States v. Ovalle, 136 F.3d 1022 (6th Cir. 1988) (holding the practice violative of 28 U.S.C. § 1862 and the equal protection component of the Fifth Amendment).

[192] The vast number of federal judges are men. *See, e.g.*, NINTH CIRCUIT GENDER BIAS TASK FORCE, THE EFFECTS OF GENDER IN THE FEDERAL COURTS 10 (1993), *reprinted in* 67 S. CAL. L. REV. 745, 772 (1994) (concluding that "the world of the federal courts is still predominantly male"). Only seven percent of federal appellate judges and six percent of federal district court judges are women. *See id.* at 12. Whereas federal judges tend to fit a certain profile (white men over the age of 50), *see id.* at 13, the jury potentially reflects a much more diverse group. This profile of the federal judge mirrors that of many state judges as well. *See, e.g.*, John K.C. Mah, *Diversity of Bench Takes the Stand in Simpson Case*, L.A. TIMES, Aug. 8, 1994, at B5 (discussing statistics showing that, in California, "most judges are white"). According to the Commission on the Future of the California Courts, 5% of the state's

Jurors also play a unique role as observers during the trial. Their sole task is to observe the witnesses, the evidence, and the proceedings. Unlike the judge, they do not have to make rulings on the evidence or ensure that the trial proceeds in an orderly fashion. Rather, they can focus on the witnesses' demeanor and note nuances that might later assist them in assessing the witnesses' credibility. The fact that there are twelve jurors,[193] and that they can all focus on subtleties revealed throughout the trial, should assist them during the deliberations when they must interpret the evidence and testimony and decide whether the legal standards, as they understand them, have been met.

d. A Judge Is Not a Substitute for a Jury.—Not only is the jury well suited to perform its interpretive role, but also the judge is ill-equipped to perform this role alone, which would be the alternative if there were no jury or if the judge were supposed to patrol the jury's deliberations to eliminate this function. All of the institutional features that the jury brings to the process—that jurors are ordinary citizens drawn from a cross section of the population, that they engage in a process of group deliberation, and that they are nonprofessionals who hear only one case—are critical features that the trial judge cannot offer. The trial judge has many other institutional advantages that he or she brings to the interpretive task, such as professional training, a perspective developed from hearing many cases over time, the vehicle of the judicial opinion in which to express his or her reasoning, and resources such as prior cases to consult for guidance, but these are not substitutes for the institutional features of a jury. To insist that the jury not engage in interpretation would be to require the elimination of the jury and the use of the judge in its place. Although the trial judge brings to the process of interpretation important institutional features, they are different from, and not intended to substitute for, those of the jury. In fact, jury deliberations are carefully protected from judicial oversight or interference, suggesting that the judge is not intended to take the place of or patrol the jury and limit its activities in any way.[194]

1,554 judges are African American, 5% are Hispanic, 3% are Asian or Pacific Islanders, and 0.1% (a single judge) is Native American. *See id.*

193 There are typically 12 jurors on a criminal jury in federal court. *See* FED. R. CRIM. P. 23 ("Juries shall be of 12 but . . . the parties may stipulate in writing with the approval of the court that the jury shall consist of any number less than 12 or that a valid verdict may be returned by a jury of less than 12 should the court find it necessary to excuse one or more jurors for any just cause after trial commences."). The number of jurors on a criminal jury in state court varies, but cannot go below six jurors. *See* Ballew v. Georgia, 435 U.S. 223, 232-38 (1978) (holding that a jury in a state criminal trial cannot go below six jurors). A civil jury in federal court may have from 6 to 12 jurors. *See* FED. R. CIV. P. 48 ("The court shall seat a jury of not fewer than six members and not more than twelve members . . . .").

194 *See* FED. R. EVID. 606(b) (limiting judicial inquiries into jury deliberations to "the question whether extraneous prejudicial information was improperly brought to the jury's attention or whether any outside influence was improperly brought to bear upon any juror").

e. Jury Interpretation and Nullification.—Nullification is connected to the jury's interpretive function in at least three ways. In a general way, jury nullification is consistent with the process view's broad notion of the jury's roles. The process view, unlike the conventional view, recognizes that juries do more than factfinding and narrow application of law; juries also interpret facts and law, and in the process of interpretation, jurors' values come into play. The conventional view offers a more limited conception of the jury. In its most narrow form, it focuses mainly on factfinding, and some who take this view would even deny that jurors bring values to the process of factfinding. The conventional view denies that there is any role for nullification; it is a threat to the neatly compartmentalized and limited view of the jury's role.

The process view embraces a more expansive role for the jury, including a jury that performs an interpretive function, and nullification is consistent with an expansive view of the jury. However, I do not mean to suggest that one who holds a process view of the jury must necessarily accept nullification. One could believe that the jury performs an interpretive role, consistent with the process view, but stop short of acceding to nullification. My point is simply that nullification is consistent with, though it does not necessarily follow from, a broad view of the jury's functions.

There is another connection between interpretation and nullification. In the act of interpreting, one is trying to make sense of a text, or in the case of a trial, a pastiche of texts, including statutes, instructions, testimony, and evidence. Some jury scholars have described the task of juror decisionmaking as proceeding in accordance with a "story model."[195] The juror has to sort through the vast amount of material that has been presented at trial and mold it into a coherent whole, into a story that makes sense. Jurors have been described as having frameworks into which they place the material from the trial.[196] Such a framework would aid in the process of story construction and explain how jurors who sit through the same trial may emerge with very different interpretations of the same evidence and the same instructions.[197] Just as interpretation involves trying to make sense of the material presented at trial, nullification can be seen as an extension of that process in that the jurors are trying to make sense of the verdict in the case. They want to arrive at a verdict that seems appropriate for the case, just as they try to arrive at an interpretation of the facts and law that give the case coherence. Although all jurors might not enter into this process, particularly because they are admonished by the judge throughout the trial about the limited task before them[198] and those who take seriously the instructions might believe that their hands are effectively tied and they are

[195] *See supra* note 146 (describing story model of juror decisionmaking).

[196] *See id.*

[197] *See id.*

[198] *See supra* notes 131-35, 155 and accompanying text (describing judge's instructions).

constrained to follow the law as the judge has given it to them,[199] others struggle to arrive at a verdict that accords with their sense of what is right.[200]

Jury nullification is related to the act of interpretation in a more process-oriented way as well. The conventional view of how juries decide to nullify is that the jury simply chooses to "disregard" the facts or law. What conventionalists seem to mean by this is that jurors enter the jury room with fixed notions about the defendant or the law, and so they simply decide to follow those notions and go immediately to the outcome they want, without consideration of the facts or law. The portrayal of the acquittal of O.J. Simpson as jury nullification fits this model of decisionmaking. Members of the mainstream press labeled the verdict as nullification and described a process in which the jury simply "disregard[ed] the facts."[201] The speed with which the jury returned a verdict reinforced the view that this was how the jury had proceeded.[202]

The process view, however, offers another view of how a jury might reach a decision to nullify through a deliberative and interpretive process that is law-regarding. According to this view, the nullifying jury does not fail to consider the facts and the law. On the contrary, this jury conscientiously considers the law, both in the narrow sense of the law to be applied to the particular case, and in the broader sense of interpreting norms and principles that animate the law and the legal system, and perhaps even considers the institutional role of the jury. From this law-regarding process, the jury may arrive at an outcome to "disregard the law" in the end. However, it reaches this outcome through a process in which it gave full and careful consideration to the facts and the law. It disregarded the law only in the

---

[199] *See, e.g.*, Farnham, *supra* note 19, at 13 (describing three jurors in the trial of Dr. Spock who convicted him and three of his four codefendants on charges of counseling draft evasion during the Vietnam War because of the judge's instructions; they felt they had no choice but to accept the law as given to them by the judge). Farnham regretted that these jurors, "believing themselves able to nullify, but not entitled to, . . . followed legal instructions that led to a result that they did not agree with." *Id.*

[200] *Compare Enter the Jury Room* transcript, *supra* note 16, at 37 (Juror #1 explaining that the jurors were not permitted to consider what sentence Modesta Solano might receive if convicted) *with id.* at 43 (Juror Joe who believed the jury had "to find two things. Guilt or innocence is one, and justice is two.").

[201] Knight, *supra* note 114, at N1.

[202] *See, e.g.*, *'Nullification' Becomes Factor in Simpson Case*, ARIZ. REPUBLIC, Oct. 2, 1995, at A2 ("In jury nullification verdicts, the panel rarely takes time to examine the evidence."); Whitaker, *supra* note 3, at 28 ("When the acquittal came back so swiftly, many commentators assumed that the largely black jury had engaged in what legal experts call 'jury nullification'—ignoring the evidence to send a broader message, in this case to the police."). Interestingly, there were few claims of nullification or bad faith in the time period after the jury had come to a verdict, but before it was announced. At that point, many in the mainstream press believed there would be a verdict of guilty, and gave the best possible gloss to the speed with which the jury had reached a verdict. *See, e.g.*, Henry Weinstein & Tim Rutten, *Jury's Quick Decision Stuns Trial Analysts*, FRESNO BEE, Oct. 3, 1995, at A12 ("'Based on that readback [of Allen Park's testimony], the defense should be very worried.'") (quoting former Los Angeles County District Attorney Robert Philibosian).

sense that after full discussion of the law and how it could be interpreted, it chose not to follow the law, but not in the sense that it ignored the law. Although the two juries described above would reach the same result, the processes would be quite different. Nullification reached through a process that is law-regarding should not arouse the same fears as nullification reached through a process that is law-disregarding. With the law-regarding process, jurors may end up deciding not to follow the law, but they do so in a constrained fashion; they regard the law and try to interpret the law and move to nullification only after efforts to interpret the law seem to lead to a verdict that would, in the jury's view, be unjust. With the law-disregarding process, jurors reach their verdict with a complete disregard for the law.

An example of an actual jury that engaged in a law-regarding process and yet still decided to nullify was the jury considering the case of Leroy Reed.[203] Reed, a man of limited intelligence, had been charged with possessing a handgun in violation of a state statute that prohibited convicted felons from possessing handguns. The jurors began their deliberations by going around the table and describing their tentative views and the points that seemed most significant to them.[204] Individual jurors then looked to the language of the statute to see what precisely was required and whether Leroy Reed's limitations were taken into account by the legislature. In particular, they focused on what it meant for Leroy Reed to "know" he possessed a handgun.[205] As one juror asked: "I wonder if we could find room in the law . . . that perhaps [Reed] didn't, in [the] full sense of the word, 'know' he was a felon, and didn't, in the full sense of the word, 'know' that he possessed a firearm."[206] The jurors debated whether they should focus on what Reed might have known or whether they should not delve so deeply into the meaning of the words of the statute. Some jurors argued for

---

[203] *See generally Inside the Jury Room*, *supra* note 16.

[204] Thus, the jury engaged in an evidence-driven deliberation, in which public balloting occurred late in the process and the individual jurors offered evidence without reference to a particular verdict, as they tried to recreate the events at the time of the alleged crime. *See* HASTIE ET AL., *supra* note 182, at 163-65 (describing an evidence-driven deliberation, and contrasting it with a verdict-driven deliberation, which begins with a public ballot and is dominated by statements of verdict preference); *see also* EDGAR H. SCHEIN, PROCESS CONSULTATION: ITS ROLE IN ORGANIZATIONAL DEVELOPMENT 55-56 (1969) (using the terms "Decision by Majority Rule: Voting and/or Polling" and "Decision by Consensus"); Charles Hawkins, Interaction and Coalition Realignments in Consensus-Seeking Groups: A Study of Experimental Jury Deliberations 106-09 (Aug. 17, 1960) (unpublished doctoral dissertation, University of Chicago) (identifying two styles of jury deliberation: "deliberating in unity" and "deliberating in factions").

[205] *See Inside the Jury Room* transcript, *supra* note 16, at 14 (describing what jurors thought Reed "knew"). The Assistant District Attorney, Douglas Simpson, had explained to the jury that "[a] person who has possessed a firearm, with knowledge that they [sic] possessed a firearm while being convicted of a felony, has violated the statute." *Id.* at 7.

[206] *Id.* (quoting Juror Barbara Bornstein). Although other jurors pointed out to her that the statute did not require Reed to "know" he was a convicted felon, it did require him to "know" that he possessed a handgun. Therefore, other jurors focused their comments on whether Reed knew he possessed a handgun.

the plain meaning of the word "know," and for a cut-and-dried application of the statute. In response, one juror explained that he thought the role of juror demanded more than that; it demanded that they ask the following: "Has justice been done? And in my mind, I'm still trying to decide that. And that's my basic point. That's what we're here to do. It's not to just say, 'The law says this.' The judge says that, but I don't think that's what he means."[207]

After one hour and four minutes of deliberations, the jury took its first vote.[208] Nine jurors voted not guilty, and three voted guilty. Immediately after the vote, one juror who had voted guilty capitulated.[209] At this point, the discussion turned to issues of justice, as those who had voted not guilty tried to help those who had voted guilty to see the case in a larger framework. As one juror explained: "I'm having a lot of trouble with that larger frame, too. I'm starting to ask some of these bigger questions about: where is justice; who is being served; even, why was this case brought?"[210] The jurors also returned to a more detailed discussion of the facts, including what Reed knew when he purchased the gun. One interpretation of the facts was that Reed was purchasing a gun, not as a weapon, but merely as one of the accoutrements, like the badge, that was needed to assume the role of detective as delineated in the magazine advertisement.[211]

After two hours of deliberation, and a second ballot, there was one juror, Karl Buetow, who voted guilty. He worried that the others were trying to delve too deeply into Reed's psychology—into what Reed knew or did not know. Although Buetow acknowledged that there could be exceptions to the law,[212] he thought that the jury seemed to pick and choose what Reed knew or did not know. Buetow was able to agree with the others that even though the law is "a good law,"[213] the case should not have been brought by the prosecutor[214] and the prosecution of such a case seemed "grotesque and unreasonable."[215] However, Buetow thought the statute should be applied, in another juror's words, on "a very concrete level."[216] Ultimately, Buetow agreed that he would not "hold out to hold up 11 people that are very strong in their feelings."[217] The other jurors wanted to make him feel more com-

[207] *Id.* at 15 (quoting Juror Lester Sauvage).

[208] *See id.* at 16 (describing initial ballot).

[209] *See id.* (same).

[210] *Id.* (quoting Juror John Boly).

[211] *See id.* at 16-17, 18-19.

[212] *See id.* at 21 (acquiescing that there are exceptions to the law).

[213] *Id.* at 22 (quoting Juror John Boly).

[214] *See id.* (showing agreement of Juror Karl Buetow with Juror John Boly's point that the prosecutor had been overzealous in bringing this case).

[215] *Id.* at 24 (quoting Juror Barbara Bornstein).

[216] *Id.* (quoting Juror Barbara Bornstein).

[217] *Id.* (quoting Juror Karl Buetow).

fortable with his decision and spoke in terms of justice and the role of the jury. As one juror explained her vote to Buetow:

> I was aware of the weight that's on each one of us as a juror, and I thought, hey, this guy's guilty. . . . Could I live with my writing 'guilty' for this particular person. Boy, I mashed around with that for a while and I said, 'If there's any justice, really, it's in drawing attention to this man's personal situation or limitations.' . . . But judging him 'not guilty', then I can believe in 'jury'.[218]

Thus, this jury moved from consideration of the statute and trying to interpret its meaning, particularly its ambiguous terms, to a consideration of what justice required in this case and what the proper role of the jury was, particularly in relation to other branches of government. Although the jury reached a decision to nullify, it reached that decision only after a full and careful consideration of the law and facts. It reached a result that conventionalists would label as law-disregarding insofar as it did not engage in a literal application of the statute, but it reached its result through a process that was law-regarding insofar as it tried to interpret the statute's ambiguous terms and reconcile them with the larger purposes of the law and the jury.[219]

2. *The Jury's Role in the Political Structure.*—Under a process view, the jury not only participates with the judge in the process of interpreting the law, but also is engaged in a "dialogue"[220] with the legislative and executive branches through which it informs them when they have overstepped their bounds, and it does this through nullification. Under this view, when the jury nullifies it provides feedback to the other branches, rather than usurping their functions.

---

[218] *Id.* at 25 (quoting Juror Roberta Bass).

[219] Consider the jury deliberations in the case of Modesta Solano, tried for drug possession and transportation. *See Enter the Jury Room* transcript, *supra* note 16, at 31-58. The first jury, which deliberated for 12 hours, ended up technically as a hung jury because 2 jurors, rather than all 12, nullified. In contrast, when Solano was retried, the second jury convicted in 45 minutes. *See id.* at 57. The first jury engaged in a law-regarding process, even though its result would be viewed as law-disregarding insofar as it was a hung jury because of nullifying jurors. The second jury, which was law-regarding insofar as it did not nullify, engaged in a deliberation process that was law-disregarding in that it took a mere 45 minutes to decide to convict, and as a result of 45 minutes of deliberation, the defendant will spend 25 years in jail.

[220] I use "dialogue" even though in some cases the jury might "speak" to the other branches, but they might not listen, or they might not listen until juries have spoken over time in the same way. Moreover, the other branches might or might not respond. Nevertheless, in some instances, the dialogue might be more immediate. For example, when a jury nullifies because it does not believe the law should be applied to a particular defendant, the jury sends that message through its verdict of not guilty, and the prosecutor, who is in the courtroom, understands that message immediately. The message can be made even clearer, if need be, by the prosecutor's post-verdict interviews with jurors.

Under a process view, nullification is a means for juries to signal overstepping by another branch of government, as will be described more fully in the sections that follow. At this point, I simply want to suggest the contours: When juries acquit because they do not believe the law should be applied to a particular defendant, they provide valuable feedback to the executive branch. In such a case, the jury is telling the prosecution that it needs to be more careful in deciding which cases to prosecute. When a jury acquits in the case of a bad law, it also provides valuable feedback to the legislature. Such a jury indicates to the legislature that there is a problem with the law. The legislature may have created a law that resonated with the populace in the abstract, but not when it came time for the law's application.[221] Whereas a jury that acquits so as not to apply the law to a particular defendant provides feedback to the executive and a jury that acquits so as not to apply a bad law provides feedback to the legislature, it is less clear that a jury that acquits in response to social conditions provides feedback to any other branch of government. This type of message becomes increasingly difficult to convey as the jury moves farther afield from the case before it and the message is susceptible to multiple interpretations. Although this type of nullification may be the least effective as a feedback mechanism, it cannot be eliminated if the first two types are to exist.

B. *Nullification Assessed from the Process View*

1. *Benefits.*

a. Not Applying the Law to the Defendant.—Under a process view, when a jury nullifies because it does not believe the law should be applied to a particular defendant, the jury provides a benefit by giving feedback to the prosecution (the executive) that it needs to be more careful about which cases to prosecute. The prosecution has discretion about which cases to pursue, and indeed, it does not pursue all cases.[222] Were it to

---

[221] James Levine has observed:

> Capital punishment . . . is a good example: whereas Americans overwhelmingly support the death penalty, juries faced with imposing the death sentence do so infrequently; they reserve this dire punishment for the most grievous of crimes and the very worst offenders. What this suggests is that the prevailing view on this grave matter is much more complex than frequency tabulations generated by Gallup polls would indicate. On this issue and so many others, jurors like the ordinary people from which they are drawn prefer fine-grained judgements to gross generalizations.

James P. Levine, *Commonsense Justice: Jurors' Notions of the Law*, 16 CRIM. JUST. ETHICS 49 (1997), *available in* 1997 WL 14380413 (book review); *see also Some Jurors Are Rebelling Against '3 Strikes' Law*, ORANGE COUNTY REG. (Cal.), Sept. 25, 1996, at B6 ("'It's easier for people to vote for the 'three strikes' law when they're faced with the chaos around them . . . . But it's much more difficult when you're in the courtroom dealing with a real human being.'") (quoting jury consultant Karen Jo Koonan).

[222] *See* KADISH & KADISH, *supra* note 34, at 81 ("[T]he prosecutor's self-determined power not to prosecute, if legally not as broad as the policeman's power not to arrest, is nonetheless substantially uncontrolled."); *id.* at 82 ("Indeed, it is widely accepted that a vital part of the prosecutor's official role is

do so, the prosecution would be overwhelmed by its docket; it would lose a greater number of cases; it would be prosecuting cases that could be better dealt with through some other means; and it would be perceived by the citizenry as overzealous. Not all violations of the law are or should be prosecuted, and thus, police and prosecutors have discretion in their respective roles to decide which violations to pursue and which to overlook. Interestingly, when prosecutors and police decide not to pursue a violation, it is not called prosecutorial or police nullification; it is simply recognized as consistent with the discretion their roles confer. Even with such discretion, however, these officials can sometimes be overzealous, and invoke the criminal justice system in inappropriate cases. The nullifying jnry is able to stand as a buffer between the overzealous police officer or prosecutor and the defendant[223] and prevent inappropriate uses of the criminal justice system. The jury, like prosecutors, police, and judges, also has discretion and can decide that the case was too trivial or the circumstances too extenuating such that the case should not result in a conviction even though the defendant met the legal standard for conviction. Under this view, the jury acts as a safety valve so that justice can be done in the individual case.

Under a process view, the nullifying jury that refuses to apply the law to a particular defendant can also be viewed as assisting the legislature rather than intruding upon its function. Legislatures create general laws both because they cannot foresee every variation that may arise and also because legislators may have competing views about what should be included in legislation and must settle for broad language if any laws are to be passed. If the legislature had anticipated the particular type of case that the jury has to consider, it might have agreed with the jury that it had not intended the law to apply. For example, if the Wisconsin legislature had considered the case of those with limited mental capacity, like Leroy Reed, it might not have intended them to be embraced by a statute that punishes convicted felons who knowingly purchase a firearm,[224] and it might have

to 'determine what offenses, and whom, to prosecute,' even among provably guilty offenders, and that in so doing the prosecutor must 'consider the public impact of criminal proceedings [and] balance the admonitory value of invariable and inflexible punishment against the greater impulse of the quality of mercy.'") (citation omitted); Kent Greenawalt, *Conflicts of Law and Morality—Institutions of Amelioration*, 67 VA. L. REV. 177, 211 (1981) ("As to many laws, it is doubtful if there is any heavy presumption in favor of enforcement. For these laws at least, one may speak of police and prosecutors as possessing an implicit delegated discretion to decide whether to go forward."); Van Dyke, *supra* note 122, at 240 ("If an arrest is made, the prosecutor has discretion to bring the matter to court or not.").

[223] The Supreme Court described the role of the jury in this way, *see* Duncan v. Louisiana, 391 U.S. 145, 156 (1968) ("Providing an aecused with the right to be tried by a jury of his peers gave him an inestimable safeguard against the corrupt or overzealous prosecutor and against the compliant, biased, or eccentric judge."); however, I think it is also an apt description of the role of a nullifying jury.

[224] *See Inside the Jury Room* transcript, *supra* note 16, at 7. As described earlier, *see supra* text accompanying notes 203-219, the trial and jury deliberations in the case of Leroy Reed wcre filmed and aired on television. The case involved Reed, a convieted felon, who was found to be carrying a firearm, and was charged with violating a Wisconsin statute that prohibited convicted felons from knowingly carrying firearms. *See supra* notes 205-06 and accompanying text. Reed was acquitted by the jury beeause

carved out an exception for them. In effect, that is what the jury did, though it created an exception only for Leroy Reed, and not for those who are similarly situated. Of course, there is also the chance that the legislature might have intended the law to apply in Leroy Reed's case, and thus, the jury should not be second-guessing the legislature; rather, it should wait until the legislature has addressed the particular situation. But because the legislature cannot consider all possible variations that could arise, the jury's action should be viewed as complementary to, rather than intruding upon, the legislature. The jury can consider details and variations that the legislature, with many laws to pass and many constituents to satisfy, cannot possibly consider. Under this view, the jury is assisting the legislature, and is thus, providing a benefit rather than a harm.

When the jury nullifies in this kind of situation it is uniquely situated to assist the legislature and to signal to the prosecutor's office that it has been overzealous. The jury can assist the legislature because it is present in the courtroom and knows facts about the defendant's case that the legislature cannot possibly know. The jury is also a neutral body; it does not have professional ambitions, like the prosecutor or the legislator. The jury can signal to the prosecutor's office that it has overreached because as a group of laypersons, it can draw upon the everyday common sense of its members, who have ideally been drawn from a representative sampling of the population, to reach consensus and to say whether the prosecutor has gone too far in trying to apply the law to this particular defendant. Sometimes these jurors will be persuaded by factors that are useful to take into account; other times they will be persuaded by factors that they should have ignored. Some considerations, such as whether there are extenuating circumstances, seem more appropriate than others, such as whether the defendant is sympathetic. But the point is that jurors are asked to evaluate the evidence presented at trial and to arrive at a judgment, not with the assistance of any professional training or experience, but simply based on what they know from their everyday experiences.[225] This is one of the contributions that jurors make to the judicial system. Whereas those who hold conventional views of the jury worry because jurors are untrained and may allow their decisions to be guided by improper considerations, those who hold a process view of the jury recognize that jurors do draw from their everyday expe-

---

the jury chose to nullify. The jurors recognized that Reed met the criteria of the statute and should have been convicted, but they chose not to convict for a variety of reasons, including the following: there were extenuating circumstances (Reed's limited intelligence and cooperation with the police); the crime seemed trivial; and the prosecution should direct its efforts to more serious crimes.

[225] *See* John Marshall Mitnick, *From Neighbor-Witness to Judge of Proofs: The Transformation of the English Civil Juror*, 32 AM. J. LEGAL HIST. 201, 235 (1988) (citing an empirical study from which "no valid generalizations may be drawn" but merely noting that "verdicts are still often influenced by jurors' personal knowledge of local customs, attitudes, and even people and places") (citing Dale W. Broeder, *The Impact of the Vicinage Requirement: An Empirical Look*, 45 NEB. L. REV. 99, 100, 117-18 (1966)).

riences in interpreting what they have seen at trial, and that this should not only be acknowledged, but also encouraged.

b. Not Applying a Bad Law.—Under a process view, when a jury nullifies and decides not to apply a bad law, it provides feedback to the legislature that the law is in need of re-examination, and possibly of repeal. The Fugitive Slave Act was one such law; another was the National Prohibition Act.[226] More contemporary examples might be the sodomy laws or the law punishing crack cocaine more severely than cocaine. The jury that nullifies a bad law can be seen as performing a useful function vis-à-vis the legislature by indicating to it that there is a serious problem with the law.

The nullifying jury in this situation can also provide a moderating effect. It cannot repeal the law; only the legislature can do that. But it can apply the law so that it fits more closely with local views. This occurred with the Fugitive Slave Act, in which Northern juries often refused to give effect to the law. It is also occurring today, to some extent, with California's three strikes law, in which residents of San Francisco and San Diego disagree on the law.[227] Nullifying juries have helped to tailor application of the law, at least in San Francisco, so that the law is being applied in a way that meets local standards.[228] The advantage to the justice system of such an approach is that there is likely to be greater support for verdicts in particular and for the laws in general if they are consistent with local views.

The importance of local views was not lost on the founders when they required that "[i]n all criminal prosecutions, the accused shall enjoy the right to a speedy and public trial, by an impartial jury *of the State and district wherein the crime shall have been committed.*"[229] The jury system allows for the local citizenry to decide whether to convict or acquit, and by voting to acquit because jurors regard the law as a bad one, they have some say, albeit limited to the case before them, about the laws by which they are governed.

A process view also recognizes that a jury which nullifies a law that it regards as bad acts consistent with a tradition that accords great respect to the strongly held view of the individual juror. Jurors bring their values into the jury room, whether they are determining facts[230] or interpreting law,[231]

[226] *See supra* notes 68-87 and accompanying text.

[227] *See supra* notes 88-101 and accompanying text.

[228] *See supra* notes 98-99 and accompanying text.

[229] U.S. CONST. amend. VI. (emphasis added).

[230] Jurors' values infuse the factfinding process. Jurors, in deciding whether they find the testimony of a police officer to be credible, which is often part of factfinding in criminal cases, necessarily draw upon their own views about the reliability of police officers. These views are informed by their past experiences, such as whether the police are people to whom they turn for protection or from whom they are likely to receive harassment.

[231] According to one theory of jury decisionmaking, jurors bring to their task a framework, based on their own experiences, perspectives, and world views, in which they place the evidence that they hear at trial and the instructions given to them by the judge. *See, e.g.*, Richard Lempert, *Telling Tales in Court:*

and they are typically encouraged to adhere to their views, which shape their way of seeing the case, and not to abandon either their values or their views simply to go along with the other jurors.[232] Although jurors are expected to keep an open mind throughout the trial,[233] and to listen to other views during deliberations in an effort to reach a consensus, they are not supposed to vote contrary to their own views simply because others see the case differently.[234] If, after listening to all the arguments and engaging in deliberations, a juror still cannot be persuaded to see the case differently, then the result is a hung jury. The hung jury has been described by Professor Hans Zeisel as a "treasured paradoxical phenomenon."[235] He explained that the hung jury is "treasured because it represents the legal system's respect for the minority viewpoint that is held strongly enough to thwart the will of the majority," and it is paradoxical because the hung jury can only be tolerated in "moderation"—"too many hung juries would impede the effectiveness of the courts."[236]

What undergirds the hung jury is the judicial system's respect for the strongly held view of the individual juror, whatever that view is after careful thought and deliberation, and even if that view fails to persuade any

---

Trial Procedure and the Story Model, 13 CARDOZO L. REV. 559, 570-71 (1991) ("Pennington and Hastie note that jurors construct different stories and that jury deliberations often consist of a contest over which story is to prevail. . . . A major cause of different juror stories is the different background information that jurors bring to their deliberations."); *supra* note 146 and text accompanying notes 195-97.

[232] A typical instruction to the jury on this point is as follows:

> Each of you must decide the case for yourself, but should do so only after a discussion of the evidence and instructions with the other jurors.
>
> You should not hesitate to change an opinion if you are convinced it is erroneous. However, you should not be influenced to decide any question in a particular way because a majority of the jurors or any of them favor such a decision.

3 Reporter's Transcript of Proceedings, at 733, People v. Tillman (Cal. Super. Ct.) (No. A-623621).

[233] For example, Judge Lance Ito admonished jurors throughout the trial of O.J. Simpson as follows: "Please remember all my admonitions to you; do not discuss the case amongst yourselves, form any opinions about the case . . . ." 231 Reporter's Transcript of Proceedings, Wed., Sept. 27, 1995, at 47,792, People v. Simpson (Cal. Super. Ct. 1995) (No. BA097211).

At the close of the trial, jurors are instructed to continue to keep an open mind during deliberations:

> It is rarely productive o[r] good for a juror at the outset to make an emphatic expression of his opinion on the case or to state how he intends to vote.
>
> When one does that at the beginning, his sense of pride may be aroused, and he may hesitate to change his position, even if shown that it is wrong.

3 Reporter's Transcript of Proceedings, at 734, People v. Tillman (Cal. Super. Ct.) (No.A-623621).

[234] *See* KASSIN & WRIGHTSMAN, *supra* note 20, at 185 ("[T]he ideal deliberation [i]s one in which the informational influences are strong and the normative influences are weak. Some degree of social pressure is inevitable and perhaps even desirable. . . . The question is, how much pressure is too much?").

[235] Hans Zeisel, . . . *And Then There Were None: The Diminution of the Federal Jury*, 38 U. CHI. L. REV. 710, 719 (1971).

[236] *Id.* at 719 n.42.

other juror.[237] The holdout juror is never questioned by the court to explain his or her views.[238] In fact, if the jury reaches an impasse and indicates this in a note to the judge, the jury is not even supposed to reveal the distribution of interim votes.[239] At most, the judge can deliver an *Allen* charge, in which the judge instructs the jurors to deliberate further to see if they can reach agreement.[240] If a jury is unable to reach agreement, even after hearing an *Allen* charge,[241] then the trial judge has no recourse but to accept that the jury is a hung jury. If one juror can adhere to his or her views, whatever they are (including nullifying views), resulting in a hung jury, then twelve jurors should be able to do this as well, resulting in an acquittal rather than a hung jury. Similarly, the respect that the judicial system has for the views of the individual juror, which is at the heart of the hung jury, should also be accorded to the twelve jurors, who, though they happen to be in agreement with each other about the need to nullify, are voting consistent with their strongly held views and values.

Another benefit that the judicial system derives from jurors when they vote in accordance with their consciences is that jurors are fulfilling a gov-

---

237 Unfortunately, the hung jury is under attack and is not held in high esteem by everyone. There are some critics who question the integrity and worth of the views of holdout jurors. *See, e.g.*, Jeffrey Rosen, *One Angry Woman*, NEW YORKER, Feb. 24 & Mar. 3, 1997, at 54. Others criticize the hung jury because of the expense and delay it creates for the judicial system. California state legislators, for example, were considering moving from a unanimity requirement in criminal cases to a 10-2 or 11-1 decision rule, in part to save money and in part to "lessen the number of hung juries" in criminal cases. Riley, *supra* note 6, at A11.

238 Of course, this might change under the Second Circuit's decision in *United States v. Thomas*, 116 F.3d 606 (2d Cir. 1997). *See infra* Part VI.A.1. (discussing the harmful effects that might ensue from this opinion, including the threat to the holdout juror).

239 *See* United States v. Amaya, 509 F.2d 8, 11 (5th Cir. 1975) (citing with approval an earlier case that held that disclosure of the numerical division of a jury that has reached an impasse is a per se error); 1 EDWARD J. DEVITT ET AL., FEDERAL JURY PRACTICE & INSTRUCTIONS, § 5.23, at 163-64 (4th ed. 1992) ("[I]t is a cardinal rule that the court should not ask the jury to report [its] numerical division. This is ground for reversal.").

240 In such a charge, approved in *Allen v. United States*, 164 U.S. 492 (1896), the judge usually "remind[s the jurors] of the nature of their duty and the time and expense of a trial, and urg[es] them to try again to reach a verdict." United States v. Anderton, 679 F.2d 1199, 1203 (5th Cir. 1982) (citations omitted). Judges in Arizona are now experimenting with an alternative to the *Allen* charge; they are speaking to juries that have reached an impasse and trying to see how they can help. *See* THE POWER OF 12, *supra* note 21, at 120-22; Dann & Logan, *supra* note 21, at 280 (describing some of Arizona's more controversial jury reforms, including having the judge and jury engage in a dialogue if the jury has reached an impasse to see if the judge or attorneys can provide the jury with additional information).

241 However, there are those who disagree with an *Allen* charge because it encourages holdouts to succumb to the views of the other jurors or because it fails to serve any useful purpose. According to Judge Brown:

> In the final analysis the Allen charge itself does not make sense. All it may rightfully say is that there is a duty to consider the views of others but that a conscientious person has finally the right and duty to stand by conscience. If it says that and nothing more it is a superfluous lecture in citizenship. If it says more to declare that there is a duty to *decide*, it is legally incorrect as an interference with that rightful independence.

Huffman v. United States, 297 F.2d 754, 759 (5th Cir. 1962) (Brown, J., concurring and dissenting).

ernmental function as jurors and should take responsibility for the votes they cast. As the trials at Nuremberg taught, it is not enough for government actors to claim that they are merely following the law; they have a moral duty to challenge the law if they believe it is an unjust law.[242] If jurors find a law, such as the Fugitive Slave Act, repugnant, then they should vote to acquit; to do otherwise, is to vote against their sense of what is right. At the heart of the jury system, though certainly unspoken at least by courts,[243] is a belief that jurors will bring to the task of judging their sense of justice. They are ordinary citizens who are called to serve in only one case and are not inured to the criminal justice system as judges may be. Thus, the jury often has been described as representing the "conscience of the community."[244] Lester Sauvage, a juror in the Leroy Reed case explained the juror's task in this way:

> I am not a computer, and I will not accept everything that[] I'm told for—just because I am told that—that it is true. I can't do that as a thinking, breathing, human being.
>
> . . . .
>
> I'm trying to decide in my own mind—has justice been done here? . . . . That's what we're here to do. It's not to just say, 'The law says this.' The judge says that, but I don't think that's what he means."[245]

When the juror votes as his or her conscience dictates, this action also benefits the juror, in addition to the justice system. Jury service is not voluntary. A juror is summoned by the court to appear for jury duty.[246] Al-

---

[242] *See* TRIAL OF THE MAJOR WAR CRIMINALS BEFORE THE INTERNATIONAL MILITARY TRIBUNAL, NUREMBERG, GERMANY (1947); *see also* CHARTER OF THE INTERNATIONAL MILITARY TRIBUNAL arts. 6(b), 7, 8, 59 Stat. 1546, 1547-48 (Aug. 8, 1945).

[243] Judge Ryan, who presided over the case of Modesta Solano, the woman charged with possession and transportation of drugs, commented on the nullifying juror's decision to vote consistent with his conscience in that case. Judge Ryan said of that juror: "He just didn't feel comfortable with what went on here, and so he's interjecting his personal and moral beliefs into it, his—his conscience. And maybe . . . it was legally and rationally the wrong thing to do, but morally he is probably right." *Enter the Jury Room* transcript, *supra* note 16, at 49. Although judges do not usually have an opportunity to witness jury deliberations, the judge in this case did because the deliberations had been filmed, and afterward, he acknowledged that there might possibly be a benefit to the nullifying juror who votes consistent with his conscience.

[244] United States v. Dougherty, 473 F.2d 1113, 1140 & n.5 (D.C. Cir. 1972) (Bazelon, J., dissenting); United States v. Spock, 416 F.2d 165, 182 (1st Cir. 1969); *see also* Dunean v. Louisiana, 391 U.S. 145, 156 (1968) (describing "the common-sense judgment of a jury" and comparing it to "the more tutored but perhaps less sympathetic reaction of a single judge").

[245] *Inside the Jury Room* transcript, *supra* note 16, at 11, 15.

[246] *See* 28 U.S.C. § 1866 (g) ("Any person summoned for jury serviee who fails to appear as directed shall be ordered by the district court to appear forthwith and show cause for his failure to comply with the summons. Any person who fails to show good cause for noncompliance with a summons may be fined not more than $100 or imprisoned not more than three days, or both."). States have similar provisions. For example, Califomia recently increased its penalties for noncompliance. *See, e.g.*, Nora

though a juror can be excused from service because of extreme hardship[247] or for failure to meet the statutory requirements for service,[248] jury service is otherwise obligatory. To require that a juror perform this obligatory service, and then to put the juror in the quandary of personally having to cast a vote that will convict the defendant for having violated a law that the juror comes to view[249] as repugnant is to put the juror in an untenable position.[250] Other governmental actors who cannot support a policy are able to resign their positions. Jurors are not given this option.[251] Yet, jurors have to be able to live with their votes for the rest of their lives. The holdout juror in the drug case broadcast by CBS could not find it within himself to cast a vote of guilty for the defendant, who would then be subject to what the juror regarded as an unduly long and harsh mandatory sentence.[252] He explained: "I was not going to do something that was against my beliefs and conscience and logic that would make me regret what I had done for the rest of my life."[253] Accordingly, he voted to acquit. To ask him to vote

---

Zamichow, *County Gets Tough With Jury Duty* Scofflaws, L.A. TIMES, June 26, 1996, at B1 (describing a new fine of $1,500 for those who fail to respond to a jury summons).

[247] *See* 28 U.S.C. § 1866(c) ("[A]ny person summoned for jury service may be (1) excused by the court . . . upon a showing of undue hardship or extreme inconvenience, for such period as the court deems necessary, at the conclusion of which such person . . . shall be summoned again for jury service . . . .").

[248] *See* 28 U.S.C. § 1865.

[249] If jurors start out with this view of the law, then they should not serve on that particular jury. During voir dire, jurors are asked if they can be impartial, which at the very least means that they do not have a fixed view of the case and could vote either way. If they know they cannot be impartial, then they should say so. Such jurors will be excused from that jury panel and placed on another. I part company with Professor Butler and the Fully Informed Jury Association (FIJA), both of whom believe, though for very different reasons, that jurors should lie during voir dire so that they can serve on that particular jury and vote to nullify. *See infra* text accompanying notes 259-91.

[250] It could be argued that when men are drafted into the army, they are required to serve and to do things that their conscience might oppose. While this is certainly true, there are ways in which military service is unlike jury service. For example, jurors are asked to think on their own and to reach what they believe to be the right answer; those in the army are seldom given such instructions. Admittedly, jurors are also told to follow the law, but they are left to their own devices in the jury room with no supervision from the judge, which is quite unlike the military that operates with a strict sense of hierarchy. Finally, one of the lessons of My Lai during the Vietnam War was that even in the military, officers at least, are required to take responsibility for exercising judgment, including the judgment to challenge orders that are morally repugnant.

[251] If a juror announced to the judge in the middle of the trial that he or she could no longer be impartial, then the judge would have to dismiss the juror. However, this would be an extraordinary occurrence. Jurors are not told of this possibility, and all of the pressures on them are in the direction of continued jury service.

[252] *See Enter the Jury Room* transcript, *supra* note 16, at 48-49.

[253] *Id.* at 49 (quoting Juror "Joe"). Similarly, the jury in *Inside the Jury Room,* when trying to convince the holdout juror to agree to nullify and to vote to acquit Leroy Reed, also recognized the need for that juror to vote in a way that was consistent with his sense of what was right. It was less clear that the holdout juror managed to do that. He explained: "I will change and vote along with you to make a unanimous vote. But I will never feel right about it." *Inside the Jury Room* transcript, *supra* note 16, at

contrary to his conscience would make jury duty into a more burdensome task than it already is.[254] Also, to ask citizens to serve as jurors because they introduce a community sense into the decisionmaking, and then to say that they are to act "like a computer" and simply follow the law and not bring their own notions of justice to the process, is to undercut one of the reasons for calling upon ordinary citizens rather than professional judges to make these decisions.

c. *A Response to Social Conditions.*—Under a process view, juries that nullify in response to social conditions or conditions pertaining to the criminal justice system may bring about fewer benefits than in the other two cases. This is so because the message that such juries are trying to convey is sometimes difficult to discern, in part because there may be several messages and in part because the message may not always be closely related to the case at hand.

One benefit of a jury that nullifies in response to social conditions is that it gives voice to citizens who might otherwise not be heard. Such jurors may hold views that are not represented by those in the legislature or the executive, so the jury might be the only forum for their expression. In that sense, then, such juries are not encroaching upon the legislature or executive because there are no representatives expressing these jurors' views in those branches. Such jurors may be disempowered and believe that the jury is their last hope for expressing their disapproval of the way society in general or the criminal justice system in particular is structured. One benefit of using the jury to convey such messages is that it allows jurors to voice their concerns through some official mechanism. If they cannot speak through the jury, then their views might not be heard at all. Or, if their views are heard, it might be because they have found more destructive ways to express them, such as through riots or other acts of violence.

Another benefit of a jury nullifying in this situation is that its messages may be related to the criminal justice system and so the jury might be the best vehicle for conveying such messages. Juries that nullify because they see disparate treatment of blacks and whites as criminal defendants or because they discern racist attitudes among testifying police officers might be in the best position to voice these messages and the jury might be the best platform from which to draw attention to such conditions.

24. The other jurors continued to try to help him feel better about his decision to join them. *See id.* at 25.

[254] Several states formed commissions to examine jury service and to recommend reforms that would ease some of the burdens currently placed on jurors. *See, e.g.*, POWER OF 12, *supra* note 21 (Arizona); The Jury Project, Report to the Chief Judge of the State of New York (Mar. 31, 1994).

2. Potential Harms.

a. Not Applying the Law to the Defendant.—When juries nullify by not applying the law to a particular defendant, there is the potential for abuse. Jurors may reach their decision in response to bias, in which case, they cause harm to defendants and threaten the integrity of the jury system. The all-white, all-male Southern juries that refused to apply the law to white men charged with crimes against African Americans certainly epitomized jurors led astray by their prejudices. Their practice of judging and acquitting according to race was exacerbated by the homogeneity of those juries. The use of race by Southern white jurors went unchallenged because the jurors were among the powerful in their society whereas those who were the victims of unpunished crimes were among the marginalized. This meant that the white jurors were in a position to maintain their control and the marginalized had few available routes to challenge it. When Southern white juries acquitted defendants based on race, they tarnished the integrity of the jury system for those who were victims, as well as for those who witnessed the debasement of the institution.

b. Not Applying a Bad Law.—If it became commonplace for juries to nullify and not apply bad laws, at that point, the harms of this type of nullification would begin to outweigh the benefits. Even at current levels, however, one could worry that *any* variation in enforcement of the laws is detrimental.[255] One response, as described earlier,[256] is that variation provides a "safety valve" of sorts, so that a law can be tailored to be more acceptable to diverse communities. Another response is that variation already exists because there are differences in the way that local police, prosecutors, judges, and other participants in the legal system exercise discretion and apply the law.[257]

Another potential harm created by jurors who nullify in this type of situation is that they put themselves in the role of legislators, and they need not do so because they have alternate routes, such as writing their legislator or marching in protest, to express their disapproval of a law. Jurors could wait until they have completed their jury service before they challenge the law. However, while these avenues are certainly open to any citizen dis-

255 As the frieze at the entrance to the U.S. Supreme Court reads: "Equal Justice Under Law." *See* FRED J. MAROON, THE SUPREME COURT OF THE UNITED STATES 40, 42, 44-45 (1996). This is supposed to mean that those who are similarly situated receive equal treatment.

256 *See supra* text accompanying notes 68-81, 88-101, 108-11, 227-29.

257 *See* KADISH & KADISH, *supra* note 34, at 73-76, 81-83, 85-91 (describing the ways in which those in official positions have discretion and can decide whether to pursue a case or not); *see also* Van Dyke, *supra* note 122, at 240 ("Whenever a criminal act occurs, the policeman investigating the matter has discretion whether to make an arrest. If an arrest is made, the prosecutor has discretion to bring the matter to court or not. The trial judge then has discretion to allow the matter to be brought into his court or not.").

pleased with a law, the role of juror entails additional responsibilities, and concomitantly, should provide an additional means of response. The juror is asked to apply the law in a direct and personal way; the juror's vote of guilty results in the defendant's loss of liberty or even life. While these other methods of protest can affect the law in the future, jurors are faced with the immediate consequences that their votes will have on the person before them. In addition, the jurors' verdict will typically affect only the defendant. The jurors are not changing the law; only the legislature can do that. The jury's decision is not binding on future cases; only a judge's opinion has precedential effect. Admittedly, if juries systematically nullify the same bad law, then prosecutors may alter their decisions about which cases to prosecute,[258] so in this somewhat indirect sense, nullifying juries can have an effect beyond the case before them. However, the impact of a lone nullifying jury remains limited to the case before it.

Another potential harm posed by a nullifying jury deciding not to apply a bad law is that the populace may not agree on what constitutes a "bad" law. While juries signaled and the legislature eventually agreed that the National Prohibition Act was a bad law, there is no such societal agreement today, for example, on the blockade of abortion clinics. Those who oppose abortion continue to disobey the laws that govern where abortion protesters may stand in relation to an abortion clinic. If those who oppose abortion find themselves on a jury in an abortion blockade case in spite of a voir dire designed to eliminate those jurors who have fixed views and cannot consider the evidence impartially, they may vote to acquit out of a sense of conscience. Thus, in suggesting that there are benefits to the judicial system from this type of nullification, I also recognize that the law a jury chooses to nullify as bad may be one that I and others will regard as good. This problem is similar to the one raised by offensive speech under the First Amendment. One might not agree with a particular jury's view of a bad law, just as one might not agree with an individual speaker's point of view, but one still might believe in protecting a process that allows a jury or a speaker to make their views known. Through this type of nullification, jurors make their views about particular laws known. Even if one does not agree with their views about which laws are bad, one may still believe that nullification is an important vehicle for expression that ought to be maintained.

c. *A Response to Social Conditions.*—One of the difficulties of using the jury to convey a message of discontent about social conditions is that the message may not be easy to discern. If a jury nullifies to protest a number of conditions, then the messages may be far from clear. If Bronx juries are engaging in nullification in response to social conditions, are they

[258] *See supra* notes 98-99 and accompanying text (describing the effect of nullifying juries on prosecutorial decisions in three strikes cases in San Franciseo).

responding to police harassment, the targeting of minorities for arrests and imprisonment, or lack of economic opportunities? Also, the farther removed the jury's message is from the particular case, the harder it may be for others to discern the message. A jury that nullifies to protest bad police behavior in general, even though the case before it actually involved good police behavior, will have a hard time conveying its message.

In addition, the jury has institutional limitations as a policymaking body. Jurors are not repeat players. They hear only one case, and thus, they are not in the best position to see the big picture and to determine which issues should receive attention at the expense of others. Also, jurors are called to serve because they are laymen; they do not necessarily have any expertise as policymakers. The farther the jury ventures from the particular case before it, and the closer it moves into the policymaking arena, the less it can lay claim to any special competence.

Perhaps the gravest danger, however, is that the jury that nullifies in response to social conditions may appear to be driven by an agenda rather than by impartial decisionmaking. One African-American law professor, Paul Butler, has explicitly advocated an agenda for African-American jurors as a way of expressing their discontent with the criminal justice system and its treatment of African-American men.[259] In an article in *The Yale Law Journal*,[260] which received coverage in *The Wall Street Journal*[261] and numerous other influential publications[262] and broadcasts,[263] Butler argued that African-American jurors should use the jury as a forum for their protests about the criminal justice system's treatment of African Americans and should vote to acquit African-American defendants so that more African-

---

[259] *See* Paul Butler, *Racially Based Jury Nullification: Black Power in the Criminal Justice System*, 105 YALE L.J. 677, 691 (1995) (describing the criminal justice system as racist).

[260] *See id.* at 677.

[261] *See* Linda Chavez & Robert Lerner, *Is the Justice System Rigged Against Blacks?*, WALL ST. J., Dec. 4, 1996, at A19 (describing Paul Butler's proposal that black jurors should engage in "widespread jury nullification"); Holden et al., *Race Seems*, *supra* note 113, at A1 ("In a forthcoming law-review article, Mr. Butler even argues that in nonviolent crimes, black jurors should 'presume in favor of nullification.'").

[262] *See* Paul Butler, *Black Jurors: Right to Acquit? (Jury Nullification)*, HARPER'S MAG., Dec. 1, 1995, at 11 (carrying an abridged version of Butler's article); *Crime and Punishment? Jury Nullification Is a Clear Signal That Blacks Are Losing Confidence in the Criminal Justice System*, CHI. TRIB., Nov. 15, 1995, at 21 ("Paul Butler . . . writes in the December issue of The Yale Law Journal (excerpted in the December issue of Harper's) that it often is entirely appropriate for black jurors to take race into account."); Jeffrey Rosen, *Journey to Justice*, NEW REPUBLIC, Dec. 9, 1996, at 27 (book reviews) ("Accepting the idea of legal instrumentalism—that blacks should use power, when they have it, to serve the interests of the black community—Butler called on African American jurors to use their power to free guilty black defendants accused of nonviolent drug crimes."); David Van Biema, *Marching to Farrakhan's Tune*, TIME, Oct. 16, 1995, at 74 ("A forthcoming article in the *Yale Law Review* by Paul Butler, a law professor at George Washington University, reports that inner-city juries are increasingly acquitting black men they know to be guilty.").

[263] *See ABC Nightline: America in Black and White (Part I)* (ABC television broadcast, Aug. 26, 1997) (providing an interview with Butler and examining his views on jury nullification).

American men will remain in the community rather than in prison.[264] Butler would limit his proposal to African-American defendants who have been charged with nonviolent, victimless crimes.[265] In his view, the criminal justice system is stacked against African Americans, and unless they use the jury to acquit African-American men even though they have clearly met the standards for conviction, they will continue to be arrested in disproportionate numbers, sentenced for lengthier terms, and separated from their communities, where their involvement is sorely needed.[266] Butler has focused on the jury because he believes that African Americans as a minority group do not have the political power to insist that legislators address the plight of African Americans caught in the criminal justice system,[267] and policymakers, judges, and others in positions of power are ignoring the issue.[268] Thus, in his view, if African Americans want to voice their views, then they need to do so by using the one venue that is available to them—the jury.[269]

One problem with Butler's proposal is that he urges those of one race to vote to acquit those of the same race. In this sense, his proposal for nullification recalls the practice followed by white Southern juries, except that his is directed at acquitting African Americans rather than whites, and his is limited to property crimes rather than including crimes of violence. Butler believes that his proposal does not fall into the same category as that of the white Southern juries because African Americans are an oppressed group being ensnared by a criminal justice system that has been designed by the oppressors.[270] Butler also tries to distinguish his proposal from the nullification of Southern white juries by viewing his form of protest as a message about race and crime, and arguing that it will highlight a message that white Americans are otherwise apt to ignore, which is that African Americans are oppressed by the criminal justice system.[271]

---

[264] *See* Butler, *supra* note 259, at 679.

[265] *See id.* at 715 ("Finally, in cases involving nonviolent, *malum prohibitum* offenses, including 'victimless' crimes like narcotics offenses, there should be a presumption in favor of nullification. . . . If my model is faithfully executed, the result would be that fewer black people would go to prison . . . .").

[266] *See id.* at 695-97 (providing examples of disparate treatment of African Americans by the criminal justice system).

[267] *See id.* at 709-11; *id.* at 712 ("African-Americans should embrace the antidemocratic nature of jury nullification because it provides them with the power to determine justice in a way that majority rule does not.").

[268] *See id.* at 681-88 (describing two cases in which judges failed to acknowledge the difference that race might make in criminal cases).

[269] *See id.* at 709-12 (describing how other avenues for democratic change are closed to African Americans, leaving the jury as the only available vehicle).

[270] *See id.* at 694 ("[W]hen many African-Americans are locked up, it is because of a situation that white supremacy created.").

[271] *See id.* at 689-90 ("[R]ace matters when a black person violates American criminal law and when a black juror decides how she should exercise her power to put another black man in prison.") (footnote omitted).

Butler's proposal of urging African-American jurors to protest the criminal justice system's treatment of African Americans by acquitting nonviolent African-American defendants charged with victimless crimes will politicize the jury. Jurors are supposed to decide the case before them on the evidence presented at trial. To urge jurors to vote a certain way because of their race and the race of the defendant, is not only reminiscent of Southern white juries, but also has jurors deciding the case before they have heard it. One of the reasons that juries are respected is because they are made up of ordinary people who have no stake in the outcome. Jurors are supposed to enter the jury room without having formed a fixed view of the case so that they can enter freely into deliberations with other jurors. Butler's proposal seeks to subvert this ideal of the jury and replace it with a jury in which jurors vote in racial blocs to send a message about social conditions.

Under Butler's proposal, the jury would become a mini-legislature in which jurors represent constituencies based on race and try to change social policy through their vote of not guilty. According to Butler, African-American jurors should vote in accordance with the interests of African-American defendants.[272] Their vote of not guilty is set even before they hear the evidence. In fact, they could ignore the trial and deliberations because they already know how they will vote.[273] Not only does Butler's plan for the jury compromise a basic tenet of due process—the need for an impartial decisionmaker—but it does so in a particularly cynical and divisive way. Butler's proposal is cynical because it seeks to replicate in the jury the politics of the legislature, in which politicians vote according to the interests of their constituents and because it reduces all African-American jurors to one view based upon their race.[274] Butler's plan is divisive because it pits African-American jurors against jurors of all other races and backgrounds. The extent of the harm can be gauged when one juxtaposes Butler's plan for the jury of racial bloc voting with the ideal of the jury as a diverse and deliberative body in which all jurors feel free to express their individual views during deliberations knowing they will be listened to and

---

[272] *See id.* at 690-700 (offering moral and legal reasons why African Americans should support Butler's proposal).

[273] However, African-American jurors would need to participate in deliberations if they wanted to try to convince others to vote their way (otherwise the jury would be a hung jury rather than a nullifying one).

[274] African-American feminists have urged white feminists not to see all women as if they have only one race, and it is white. *See* ELIZABETH V. SPELMAN, INESSENTIAL WOMAN: PROBLEMS OF EXCLUSION IN FEMINIST THOUGHT 122-23 (1988); Kimberle Crenshaw, ***Demarginalizing the Intersection of Race and Sex: A Black Feminist Critique of Antidiscrimination Doctrine, Feminist Theory and Antiracist Politics***, 1989 U. CHI. LEGAL F. 139, 155, 156. Butler makes a similar mistake when he sees all African Americans as having only one point of view. *See, e.g.*, GLORIA NAYLOR, THE WOMEN OF BREWSTER PLACE (1980) (depicting the lives of a fictional community of African-American women living on Brewster Place and exploring their different attitudes, perspectives, and life experiences as well as the points at whicb they come into confiict with other members of Brewster Place).

that each juror's unique background contributes to the diversity of ideas available for group consideration. Even if juries in practice fall short of this ideal, the ideal inspires respect for the jury and the verdict.

Butler's proposal would also exacerbate racial tensions in several ways. Butler's plan, of having African-American jurors vote to acquit African-American defendants in nonviolent, victimless cases would undoubtedly cause resentment among white jurors who would see African-American jurors as assuming their role as jurors under false pretenses. Indeed, Butler acknowledged that African Americans may well have to lie about their views during voir dire.[275] Under Butler's proposal, African-American jurors who claim during voir dire that they can be impartial and do not have a fixed view of the case, would not necessarily be telling the truth. Moreover, why create this racial divide? If the laws are being enforced unfairly against African-American criminal defendants[276] or if there is injustice in the criminal justice system that needs to be rectified, then why limit the protest to African-American jurors? All jurors, of every race, should respond through votes for acquittal. In addition, Butler concedes that African Americans are likely to be the victims of crime.[277] If they are, why should they be asked not to convict the defendants who are victimizing

[275] *See* Butler, *supra* note 259, at 724 n.236 ("The African-American juror facing this situation [of being asked her views during voir dire] would be placed in the difficult position of having to choose between revealing her racial sympathy, and thus surrendering her power, or denying her racial sympathy, and thus committing perjury. Yet the legal and moral case for jury nullification might lead the juror to believe that her perjury would be morally justifiable.").

[276] Leaving aside drug crimes, there is little evidence that racially discriminatory law enforcement accounts for a large part of the incarceration rate of African Americans. Michael Tonry explains:

> [P]erhaps surprisingly, for nearly a decade there has been a near consensus among scholars and policy analysts that most of the black punishment disproportions result not from racial bias or discrimination within the system but from patterns of black offending and of blaeks' criminal records. Drug law enforcement is the conspicuous exception. Blacks are arrested and confined in numbers grossly out of line with their use or sale of drugs.

MICHAEL TONRY, MALIGN NEGLECT—RACE, CRIME, AND PUNISHMENT IN AMERICA 49 (1995). However, with respect to drug crimes, Butler has a stronger claim as to enforcement that discriminates against African Americans. *See, e.g.*, Bob Herbert, *The Quality of Mercy*, N.Y. TIMES, Nov. 27, 1997, at A39 ("A research fellow at Harvard Medical School, William Brownsberger, reported this week that nearly half the inmates serving long mandatory drug sentences in Massachusetts had 'no record of violenee' and—not surprisingly—most were African-Americans and Latinos from poor neighborhoods."). But if this is the case, then Butler should ask all jurors to respond to this more limited claim of discriminatory enforeement in drug cases, rather than enlarge his claim to include all nonviolent crimes, and he should not limit his appeal to jurors of one race, but should make his appeal to jurors of all races and urge them to vote consistent with their sense that discriminatory enforcement of drug crimes is unjust.

[277] *See* Butler, *supra* noto 259, at 697 n.110 ("There is no doubt that African-Americans are disproportionately the victims of crime. For example, in 1992, blacks aceounted for approximately 49% of all murder victims."); *id.* at 699 (noting that "blacks are more likely to be the victims of crimes"); *id.* at 699 n.117 ("The victimization rate of blacks is higher than that of any other racial group for almost all crimes, including murder, rape, robbery, aggravated assault, and larceny.").

other African Americans? Under Butler's plan, African Americans would be victimized twice: once by the criminal justice system that unfairly enforces laws against African-American criminal defendants, and again by African-American jurors who would vote to acquit and send these same defendants back into the community to victimize African Americans again. Finally, Butler sees jurors as only white or African American, but juries are more heterogeneous and Butler's proposal reduces jurors to one race or the other.[278]

Finally, Butler's plan contains the seeds of its own undoing. If African-American jurors take Butler's advice seriously and vote to acquit in all cases of nonviolent African-American defendants as a way of protesting social conditions, then African-American jurors will no longer be seated on juries. Judges could excuse such jurors with for cause challenges on the theory that these jurors could not be impartial.[279] Prosecutors could also use their peremptory challenges to remove these jurors, and even if they could not remove them on the basis of race,[280] they could probably offer various seemingly unrelated reasons, as they are already able to do,[281] such as lack of eye contact or poor rapport.[282] Ironically, as the different barriers to jury service for African Americans have been lifted, from exclusionary venire lists[283] to the use of racially discriminatory peremptories,[284] Butler would

[278] *See, e.g., id.* at 722 ("What if White People Start Nullifying Too?"); *id.* at 706 n.158 (explaining that his focus is on African Americans and their unique history which provides justification for nullification that is inapplicable to whites; however, Butler docs not mention other groups, many of which might have a similar history).

[279] One of the main reasons for a for-cause challenge is to remove those jurors who cannot be impartial. *See* Hopt v. Utah, 120 U.S. 430, 433 (1887) (explaining that a for-cause challenge is appropriate if the prospective juror has "formed or expressed an unqualified opinion or belief that the prisoner is guilty or not guilty of the offense charged").

[280] *See* Batson v. Kentucky, 476 U.S. 79 (1986) (prohibiting the prosecutor's use of peremptory challenges based on race).

[281] *See* Purkett v. Elem, 514 U.S. 765 (1995) (*per curiam*) (allowing reasons for the exercise of the peremptory challenge to be unrelated to the facts of the case as long as they are nondiscriminatory).

[282] *See* Jean Montoya, *The Future of the Post-*Batson *Peremptory Challenge: Voir Dire by Questionnaire and the "Blind" Peremptory*, 29 U. MICH. J.L. REFORM 981, 998-1009 (1996) (describing an empirical study showing the ineffectiveness of *Batson*). The Supreme Court has permitted lawyers to give unrelated reasons, no matter how fanciful, by holding in *Purkett*, 514 U.S. at 765, that the reasons need not be related to the facts of the case.

[283] *See supra* note 191 (describing efforts to broaden the lists from which names for the venire are selected).

[284] *See* J.E.B. v. Alabama *ex rel.* T.B., 511 U.S. 127 (1994) (extending *Batson* to gender-based peremptory challenges); Georgia v. McCollum, 505 U.S. 42 (1992) (holding that defendants are bound by the same rules as prosecutors with respect to race-based peremptory challenges); Edmonson v. Leesville Concrete Co., 500 U.S. 614 (1991) (holding that private litigants in a civil suit cannot use peremptory challenges to exclude jurors on account of their race); Powers v. Ohio, 499 U.S. 400 (1991) (establishing that white defendants can challenge a prosecutor's use of a race-based peremptory challenge); Batson v. Kentucky, 476 U.S. 79 (1986) (holding that the Equal Protection Clause of the Fourteenth Amendment prohibits a prosecutor from using peremptory challenges to strike prospective jurors on the basis of race).

lay the groundwork for a new barrier to service. Butler is right to be concerned about the criminal justice system's treatment of African Americans, but he is wrong to think that the jury is the appropriate means to challenge that social policy in the manner that he suggests. Butler's proposal puts the jury and the continued service of African-American jurors at risk.

Butler is not the only one who advocates that jurors nullify based on an agenda. Another proponent of such action is the Fully Informed Jury Association (FIJA), a Montana-based group that publishes a newspaper[285] and catalogue,[286] among other writings.[287] FIJA tries to reach prospective jurors through grassroots organizing, including distribution of leaflets at the door to the courthouse, in an effort to educate them about their power to nullify so that they will use that power to advance various agendas, from the right to bear arms to the right to grow marijuana. FIJA represents a variety of agendas, and so in that sense, it is a less focused effort than Butler's. On the other hand, FIJA reaches people on the steps to the courthouse, whereas Butler tries to reach them through law journals, so FIJA's efforts may prove more of a threat to the jury. FIJA has persuaded state legislators in a number of states to introduce bills that would inform jurors about nullification;[288] it has also circulated petitions for ballot initiatives in other states.[289]

One problem presented by both Butler's and FIJA's approach to nullification is that they explicitly urge jurors to use their jury experience to advance an agenda, thus compromising the impartiality of the jurors and the integrity of the jury system. For both Butler and FIJA, jurors need not pay attention to the case before them because they already know how they will vote. Thus, such jurors enter the courtroom not only with a closed mind but also under false pretenses. They may be dishonest during voir dire[290] and

---

[285] *See generally* FIJA ACTIVIST.

[286] *See* Activists Supply Shop (visited Mar. 24, 1998) <http://www.FIJA.org>.

[287] *See* Web Page (visited Mar. 23, 1998) <http://www.FIJA.org>.

[288] As of 1991, FIJA had persuaded legislators in Alaska, Arizona, Georgia, Louisiana, Massachusetts, New York, Oklahoma, Tennessee, and Wyoming to introduce bills that would inform jurors of their power to nullify. *See* Scheflin & Van Dyke, *supra* note 122, at 177. FIJA's proposal to inform jurors about nullification was contained in a bill that reached the Iowa House floor in 1994, *see* Santiago Frank, *A Red-Hot Subject for Judges, Lawyers*, DES MOINES REG., Dec. 17, 1995, at 1, and "[s]imilar bills have appeared in 25 state legislatures since 1991." Joe Lambe, *Bill Would Let Juries Decide Law in Cases; Legal Establishment Reacts to Measure with Shock, Dread*, KANSAS CITY STAR, Apr. 8, 1996, at A1. The bills, after making some legislative progress, were, in the end, unsuccessful: "One failed this year in Kansas. One passed the Oklahoma House last year but died in the Senate. Others have passed the Arizona Senate and Legislative committees in Utah, Montana and Iowa before failing in those states." *Id.* In 1996, Assemblyman Steve Baldwin introduced "a bill to amend the Code of Civil Procedure [in California] to include a jury nullification clause in juror instructions for misdemeanor cases." Mike Lewis, *Will the State Codify Jury Nullification?*, L.A. DAILY J., Apr. 3, 1996, at 1.

[289] FIJA has circulated petitions for ballot initiatives in Arkansas, California, Colorado, Florida, Idaho, Montana, Utah, and Washington. *See* Scheflin & Van Dyke, *supra* note 122, at 178.

[290] Before the trial of Shelley Shannon, charged with the shooting of George Tiller, a doctor who performed abortions, anti-abortionists distributed FIJA leaflets at the courthouse which said: "'Do not admit knowledge of this material. . . . Agree (in jury selection) to uphold the law. . . . When you go into

perjure themselves in taking the oath because they are intent upon serving on the jury.[291] Once on the jury, they may be recalcitrant in the jury room because they already know their vote and are unwilling to consider others' points of view. Butler's or FIJA's ideal juror should be seen in stark contrast to the ideal process view juror who enters the courtroom and the jury room with an open mind, and who, only through the course of considered and thorough deliberations, reaches a just verdict, which may, on rare occasion, require nullification.

3. *Institutional Constraints on Potential Abuses.*—There are institutional features of the jury that constrain the jury and make it unlikely that nullification will be exercised in any but the most compelling cases. One of these institutional constraints is voir dire, the process of questioning prospective jurors prior to selection. During voir dire, prospective jurors are questioned in public and on the record as to their beliefs and attitudes.[292] Although the questioning, at least by judges, tends to be somewhat cursory[293] and although prospective jurors may be reticent about admitting to certain views in public,[294] the process does give prospective jurors the opportunity to declare their views, and those with extreme views will be removed from the panel either through for cause or peremptory challenges.[295] In addition, voir dire can present an opportunity for educating jurors, including educating them on the need to put aside prejudices.[296] Jurors are also instructed by the judge during voir dire and throughout the trial that they need to keep an open mind until they have heard all of the evidence.[297]

---

deliberations, do not admit knowledge of FIJA or this material to other jurors.'" Lambe, *supra* note 288, at A1.

[291] For a fictional account of an anti-smoking juror who sought to serve on the jury and influence the verdict in a case involving tobacco companies, see JOHN GRISHAM, THE RUNAWAY JURY (1996).

[292] *See, e.g.*, Press-Enterprise Co. v. Superior Court, 464 U.S. 501, 505, 513 (1984) (noting that "since the development of trial by jury, the process of selection of jurors has presumptively been a public process with exceptions only for good cause shown" and holding that the district court erred in excluding the public from six weeks of voir dire); United States v. Brooklier, 685 F.2d 1162, 1167 (9th Cir. 1982) (observing that "[u]nder current practice, *voir dire* is normally conducted in open court" and concluding that the district judge should not have done otherwise without satisfying the procedural prerequisites for closure to the press and public).

[293] *See, e.g.*, Babcock, *supra* note 179, at 549 ("[T]he limited questions put by the judge to the panel as a group greatly reduce the information produced by the voir dire.").

[294] *See* Kimba M. Wood, *The 1995 Justice Lester W. Roth Lecture: Reexamining the Access Doctrine*, 69 S. CAL. L. REV. 1105, 1118-20 (1996) (noting that during voir dire jurors are more forthcoming in private than in public); *see also* Babcock, *supra* note 179, at 547 ("[A]nother method of restricting the information-gathering function of voir dire is to address all questions to the jury panel at once, rather than as individuals.").

[295] *See* FED. R. CIV. P. 47(b); FED. R. CRIM. P. 24(b).

[296] *See, e.g.*, KASSIN & WRIGHTSMAN, *supra* note 20, at 50 (describing the process of using voir dire to educate jurors, though that is not the main purpose of voir dire).

[297] For an example of a typical admonition to the jury, see Judge Lance Ito's admonition at the close of each trial session: "Please remember all my admonitions to you; do not discuss the case amongst

Jurors are questioned during voir dire as to whether they can be impartial. Those who say they cannot be impartial, though it is a rare admission, will be removed from the jury. Of course, prospective jurors intent upon advancing an agenda may lie during voir dire in order to be selected for the jury,[298] but if the deception is later uncovered, such jurors can be charged with perjury.[299] Through voir dire, jurors with extreme views are removed from the jury, and those who remain are admonished on the need to be fair and impartial.

Another constraint on jurors is that they first take an oath in which they swear to follow the law.[300] They take this oath as soon as all of the jurors have been selected. They are asked to stand and the oath is administered by the bailiff in the presence of the public, parties, and judge. The significance of the oath is reinforced throughout the trial by the judge's instruction to the jurors that they are to follow the law as the judge instructs them on it.[301] Because the judge is a figure of authority, and the jurors are laypersons, there is a tendency for jurors to defer to the judge's expertise and instructions, including the judge's instruction to follow the law.[302] The judge instructs the jurors to follow the law,[303] but does not instruct them on their power to nullify.[304] Jurors, who may have little knowledge of the history of the jury, may have no familiarity with the jury's power to nullify.[305]

---

yourselves, form any opinions about the case, conduct any deliberations until the matter has been submitted to you, do not allow anybody to communicate with you with regard to the case." 231 Reporter's Transcript of Proceedings, Wed., Sept. 27, 1995, at 47,792, People v. Simpson (Cal. Super. Ct. 1995) (No. BA097211). Some judges, however, are experimenting with allowing jurors to engage in some discussion even before the trial has ended. *See* Dann & Logan, *supra* note 21, at 281, 283.

[298] *See* GRISHAM, *supra* note 291.

[299] *See infra* note 335 (describing the perjury charge brought against Laura Kriho, a juror who had served in a drug case).

[300] In California Superior Court, for example, jurors in criminal trials take the following oath: "You and each of you, do solemnly swear that you will well and truly try the cause now pending before this Court, and a true verdict render therein, according to the evidence and the instructions of the Court, so help you God?" CALIFORNIA SUPERIOR COURT CRIMINAL TRIAL JUDGES' DESKBOOK 356 (Ronald M. George ed., 1988 ed.).

[301] *See supra* notes 132-35, 155 and accompanying text (describing judge's instructions to jurors on the need to follow the law as given to them by the judge).

[302] *See* Note, *Judges' Nonverbal Behavior in Jury Trials: A Threat to Judicial Impartiality*, 61 VA. L. REV. 1266, 1278 (1975) (noting jurors' tendency to look to the judge for guidance because they are uncertain how to perform their new role); *see also* Note, *The Appearance of Justice: Judges' Verbal and Nonverbal Behavior in Criminal Jury Trials*, 38 STAN. L. REV. 89 (1985) (describing the ways in which judges may convey their expectations for trial outcomes to jurors through subtle, nonverbal cues, such as facial expressions or tone of voice); Robert J. Hirsh et al., *Attorney Voir Dire and Arizona's Jury Reform Package*, ARIZ. ATT'Y, Apr. 1996, at 24, 32 ("Jurors very quickly pick up on judges' expectations and mannerisms .... While it is seldom the intention of judges to reveal these, expectations of the court for the jurors in courtrooms are usually quite evident, especially to those anxious jurors.").

[303] *See supra* note 301.

[304] *See supra* notes 127, 155 (noting that federal and almost all state courts do not provide an instruction on nullification).

[305] *See infra* note 336 (describing *Bushel's Case*).

Once inside the jury room, any juror urging nullification must convince eleven other members of the jury to vote that way.[306] This is a difficult task because there is pressure to conform and to follow the other jurors, rather than to take a contrary position.[307] Even the juror motivated by an agenda would have to persuade the other jurors by means of argument and reason.[308] It is a rare juror who can, like Henry Fonda in *12 Angry Men*,[309] convince those in the majority to switch their position.[310] Studies have shown that one or two espousing a minority point of view are unlikely to persuade those in the majority.[311] Of course, a holdout juror need not con-

---

[306] In criminal cases in federal court, the jury usually consists of 12 jurors. *See* FED. R. CRIM. P. 23(b) ("Juries shall be of 12 but . . . a valid verdict may be returned by a jury of less than 12 should the court find it necessary . . . ."). Juries in civil cases typically consist of fewer jurors. Juries in civil cases in federal court must consist of at least six jurors. *See* FED. R. CIV. P. 48 ("The court shall seat a jury of not fewer than six members and not more than twelve members . . . .").

[307] *See, e.g.*, KASSIN & WRIGHTSMAN, *supra* note 20, at 182 ("The majority almost always wins."). For studies in other disciplines that show how people begin to doubt their own views and eventually conform to others' views, see Solomon E. Asch, *Opinions and Social Pressure*, SCI. AM., Nov. 1955, at 31; see also Robert Buckhout, *Eyewitness Testimony*, SCI. AM., Dec. 1974, at 23, 28-29 (describing experiments in which subjects have acquiesced with others in making judgments, even when they are right and the others are wrong).

[308] In criminal cases in federal court, unanimity is required for conviction. *See* FED. R. CRIM. P. 31(a) ("The verdict shall be unanimous."). Many states also require unanimous verdicts in criminal trials. *See, e.g.*, ARIZ. CONST. OF 1910, art. II, § 23 (1982) ("In all criminal cases the unanimous consent of the jurors shall be necessary to render a verdict."); OKLA. CONST. OF 1907, art. II, § 19 (1981) ("In all other cases [other than civil and criminal cases less than felonies] the entire number of jurors must concur to render a verdict."); COLO. REV. STAT. § 16-10-108 (1997) ("The verdict of the jury shall be unanimous."); HAW. REV. STAT. ANN. § 83 (Michie 1997) ("No person shall be convicted in any criminal case except by unanimous verdict of the jury."); 725 ILL. COMP. STAT. 5/115-4(o) (West 1996) ("A defendant tried by the court and jury shall only be found guilty . . . upon the unanimous verdict of the jury."); KY. REV. STAT. ANN. § 29A.280 (Michie 1992) ("A unanimous verdict is required in all criminal trials by jury."); MINN. STAT. ANN. § 480.059 (West 1990) ("The supreme court shall not have the power to adopt or promulgate any rule requiring less than unanimous verdicts in criminal cases."); MONT. CODE ANN. § 46-16-603 (1997) ("The verdict must be unanimous in all criminal actions."); N.C. GEN. STAT. § 15A-1201 (Supp. 1997) ("In all criminal cases the defendant has the right to be tried by a jury of 12 whose verdict must be unanimous."); OR. REV. STAT. § 221.349(1) (1997) ("The verdict of the jury shall be unanimous."); W. VA. CODE § 50-5-8 (1994) ("Any defendant in any criminal action shall be entitled to a trial by jury, and any such verdict must be unanimous."); WYO. STAT. ANN. § 7-11-501 (Michie 1997) ("In all criminal cases the verdict shall be unanimous."); N.M. R. CRIM. P. 5-611(A) (Michie 1998) ("The verdict shall be unanimous . . . ."). Of course, in those states in which unanimity is not required of criminal juries, all of the jurors do not need to be persuaded, and thus, the deliberation operates as less of a constraint than in states in which unanimity is required.

[309] *See* 12 ANGRY MEN (Metro-Goldwyn-Mayer/United Artists 1957) (depicting Henry Fonda's success in convincing 11 other jurors to vote for acquittal after they had voted initially for a guilty verdict).

[310] Outcomes like the one in *12 Angry Men* "almost never occur in real life." HANS & VIDMAR, *supra* note 183, at 110. Research has shown that the "[p]ressures to conform to the group are strong," and "[i]t is only when a minority juror has initial support, in the form of other jurors with similar views, that the probability that a juror will sway the majority or hang the jury improves." *Id.*

[311] *See, e.g.*, KALVEN & ZEISEL, *supra* note 59, at 462; Rita J. Simon, *Jury Nullification, or Prejudice and Ignorance in the Marion Barry Trial*, 20 J. CRIM. JUST. 261, 263 (1992) ("There were no in-

vince others in order to produce a hung jury, but studies also have shown that when there are only one or two holdout jurors, they find it difficult to maintain their position and eventually conform to the majority position.[312]

The judge also urges the jurors to come to a verdict should their deliberations reach a stalemate.[313] One effect of the judge's charge may be to pressure holdouts, who are advocating a minority position such as nullification, to relent and to vote with the others. Finally, jurors know that their verdict is one that will be announced in open court,[314] in the presence of the judge, parties, and public, and on which they might be individually polled.[315] Thus, there are pressures on the jurors inside and outside of the jury room to follow the law.

Perhaps the most important institutional constraint is a diverse jury. With diversity, there is a greater likelihood that jurors will bring different perspectives to the jury room, that they will be able to correct each other's mistaken views,[316] and that prejudices will not go unchallenged. If jurors are drawn from different backgrounds, they will contribute different points of view to deliberations. With a diverse jury, jurors will challenge each other's views,[317] including their views of the evidence and of witnesses' credibility. For a diverse jury to agree to nullify means that the case must be so compelling that all of the jurors, in spite of their different backgrounds and perspectives, nevertheless agree that this case is an appropriate one for nullification.

Under the process view of the jury, nullification provides certain benefits in the limited circumstances in which it is likely to occur.[318] Although

---

stances [in data from the University of Chicago Experimental Jury Project] in which one juror or even two held out against the other ten or eleven and then succeeded in persuading them to adopt their position.").

[312] *See supra* notes 234, 307. For anecdotal examples, see *Inside the Jury Room* transcript, *supra* note 16, at 24 ("'I will not hold out to hold up 11 people that are very strong in their feelings. I would—I will change and vote along with you to make a unanimous vote.'") (quoting Juror Karl Buetow); William Finnegan, *Doubt*, NEW YORKER, Jan. 31, 1994, at 48, 53 ("On our second day of deliberations, the school teacher and I quickly caved in. I don't know what her rationale was, but I cobbled together a little theory about reasonable doubt and an alibi defense.").

[313] *See supra* note 240 (describing *Allen* charge).

[314] *See* FED. R. CRIM. P. 31(a) ("The verdict . . . shall be returned by the jury to the judge in open court.").

[315] *See* FED. R. CRIM. P. 31(d) ("When a verdict is returned and before it is recorded the jury shall be polled at the request of any party or upon the court's own motion.").

[316] *See* Ballew v. Georgia, 435 U.S. 223, 233 n.15 (1978) (citing a study indicating that individual prejudice is more easily overcome in group situations); HANS & VIDMAR, *supra* note 183, at 50 ("The jury's heterogeneous makeup may also lessen the power of prejudice. Biases for and against the defendant, if evenly distributed on the jury, may cancel each other out.").

[317] *See* HANS & VIDMAR, *supra* note 183, at 50 ("[A] jury composed of individuals with a wide range of experiences, backgrounds, and knowledge is more likely to perceive the facts from different perspectives and thus engage in a vigorous and thorough debate.").

[318] I assume nullification occurs infrequently. I make this assumption based on the institutional constraints, *see supra* Part V.B.3., that I believe limit juries' opportunities to nullify. In view of these

there are potential harms, they are likely to be constrained by institutional features of the jury. For those who adhere to a conventional view of the jury, however, even these limited instances of nullification are harmful, and they seek to curtail them.

VI. DEBATE OVER FUTURE DIRECTIONS

On one side of the current debate about nullification are those who hold a conventional view of the jury and would limit the jury's opportunities to engage in nullification. Some judges and academics have proposed ways that this might be accomplished. On the other side of the debate, some academics and activists have advocated a call to arms for jurors so that they enter the courtroom and jury room with knowledge of their power to nullify and with an intent to use it. My process view of the jury occupies a middle ground in this debate. It embraces a broad role for the jury, one that recognizes the benefits of nullification, but eschews either extreme of limiting or promoting nullification. My suggestion is that through a modification of current jury instructions, courts could finally treat juries in a manner consistent with a process view of their roles, which includes nullification.

A. Limiting Nullification

1. Judicial Intervention.—The Second Circuit has recently led the way in an effort to limit the jury's opportunities to nullify.[319] The Second Circuit held in *United States v. Thomas*[320] that the trial judge should interview any juror urging nullification to determine if that was the juror's intent, and if so, to remove that juror from the jury, even if the jury were already in the midst of its deliberations.[321] This approach is one way of making practice conform more closely to the conventional view of the jury.

What the Second Circuit hoped to accomplish with this approach was to prevent the jury from engaging in jury nullification if the court became aware of its intent, but not to delve so deeply into the workings of the jury

constraints, nullification is likely to occur only in the most extreme cases. At least one other scholar shares my assumption. *See infra* note 351 and accompanying text. There is a need, however, for empirical work to establish whether this assumption is justified.

[319] *See* United States v. Thomas, 116 F.3d 606 (2d Cir. 1997). In *Thomas*, several of the defendants had been convicted of violations of federal narcotics laws and then appealed on the ground that the district court judge abused his discretion by removing one of the jurors pursuant to Federal Rule of Criminal Procedure 23(b). *See* FED. R. CRIM. P. 23(b) ("[I]f the court finds it necessary to excuse a juror for just cause after the jury has retired to consider its verdict, in the diseretion of the court a valid verdict may be returned by the remaining 11 jurors."). There were two sets of defendants and two separate trials. The appeal decided in *Thomas* involved the set of defendants convicted in the second trial: Grady Thomas, Ramse Thomas, Jason Thomas, Tracey Thomas, and Loray Thomas. *See Thomas*, 116 F.3d at 608-09.

[320] *See id.* at 606.

[321] *See id.* at 608.

that the secrecy of the jury room deliberations would be violated.[322] In short, the Second Circuit hoped to strike a balance. Judges do not have to allow jury nullification to take place if they are alerted to it in some way; however, they do not have to police the jury room searching out jurors who might be urging nullification. This compromise means that some instances of jury nullification will still take place, but not if the court has any notice of them.

The issue of nullification arose in *United States v. Thomas*[323] when the trial judge received a note from one juror with a complaint that Juror No. 5, who had been the subject of earlier juror complaints, had a "'predisposed disposition'"[324] and was preventing the jury from reaching a verdict. The trial judge interviewed all of the jurors *in camera* and on the record in an effort to determine whether Juror No. 5, the only African-American juror, should be permitted to continue. The interviews yielded a range of responses from the jurors, including one juror who claimed that Juror No. 5 was voting for acquittal because the defendants were his "'people'"[325] to several jurors who said that Juror No. 5 was basing his views on the evidence.[326] Juror No. 5 himself gave no indication in his interview that he was basing his vote on anything other than the evidence.[327] The trial judge concluded that Juror No. 5 would not convict regardless of the evidence and dismissed him from the jury.[328] The eleven jurors continued their deliberations and voted to convict all of the defendants except one.[329]

The Second Circuit concluded that it is the task of the trial judge to dismiss for "just cause" a juror who is intent on nullifying, but that a trial judge must make sufficient inquiry to determine if that is really the juror's intent, and that the trial judge in this case had not done so.[330] The Second Circuit reached this decision by attempting to balance the need of jurors to base their decision on the law as it is given to them by the judge with a need

---

[322] *See id.*

[323] *See id.* at 609.

[324] *Id.* at 611.

[325] *Id.*

[326] *See id.*

[327] *See id.*; Reporter's Transcript of Proceedings, Feb. 24, 1995, at 4029, United States v. Thomas (N.D.N.Y. 1995) (No. 94-Cr-181) ("When I make a decision to send someone to prison . . . I want to know that it's clear in my mind beyond a reasonable doubt.") (quoting Juror No. 5).

[328] The trial judge concluded that Juror No. 5 refused to convict based on "'preconceived, fixed, cultural, economic, [or] social . . . reasons that are totally improper and impermissible.'" *Thomas*, 116 F.3d at 612 (quoting trial judge).

[329] The jury found Grady, Ramse, Tracey, and Terrence Thomas guilty on all counts, Jason Thomas guilty on three of the four counts against him, and Carrie and Loray Thomas each guilty on a conspiracy count. The jury deadlocked on the fourth count against Jason Thomas and acquitted Carrie and Loray Thomas of possession with intent to distribute a controlled substance. Stephon Russell was acquitted on the only count with which he was charged, and therefore, was not part of this appeal. *See id.* Terrence Thomas and Carrie Thomas did not appeal their convictions. *See id.* at 609 n.3.

[330] *See id.* at 617-18.

to protect the secrecy of the jury's deliberations if the jury is already in the midst of deliberations.[331] The appellate court reasoned that if a judge makes too searching an inquiry, then he or she will invade the province of the jury, threaten the secrecy of the jury deliberations, and perhaps inhibit the jury from engaging in robust deliberations. If, however, the judge allows a juror with the intent to nullify to remain on the jury then the judge may be permitting nullification even though "trial courts have the duty to forestall or prevent such conduct, whether by firm instruction or admonition or, where it does not interfere with guaranteed rights or the need to protect the secrecy of jury deliberations, . . . by dismissal of an offending juror from the venire or the jury."[332]

Although the Second Circuit hoped that its approach would root out nullification without having the judge play too intrusive a role, its approach is seriously flawed. To begin with, this approach creates the potential for the trial judge to abuse his or her power. It has placed the judge in the position of deciding whether a juror is likely to nullify. The Second Circuit tried to proceed cautiously, explaining that trial judges must respect the secrecy of jury deliberations, and therefore, they can investigate only subject to strict limitations.[333] If there is any indication that the juror is basing his or her view on reasonable doubt, then the juror should not be dismissed. The appellate court believed that only such a high evidentiary standard would protect jurors from unduly intrusive scrutiny and erroneous dismissal.[334] Yet, even a high evidentiary standard requires the judge to interview the juror and to determine the juror's reasons for his or her interim vote even when the jurors are in the midst of deliberations. There is a danger that the judge will be guided by his or her views of what the appropriate outcome of the case should be and may be more likely to dismiss a juror

[331] *See id.* at 618 ("Once a jury retires to the deliberation room, the presiding judge's duty to dismiss jurors for misconduct comes into conflict with a duty that is equally, if not more, important—safeguarding the secrecy of jury deliberations.").

[332] *Id.* at 616.

[333] *See id.* at 621 ("[T]o determine whether a juror is bent on defiant disregard of the applicable law, the court would generally need to intrude into the juror's thought processes. Such an investigation must be subject to strict limitations.").

[334] *See id.* at 622 ("Given the necessary limitations on a court's investigatory authority in cases involving a juror's alleged refusal to follow the law, a lower evidentiary standard could lead to the removal of jurors on the basis of their view of the sufficiency of the prosecution's evidence.").

whose views do not accord with those of the judge.[335] This harkens back to the early days of the jury in England when jurors could be kept in the jury room without food or water until they reached a verdict that was consistent with the one the judge had reached.[336] If the juror says that he or she is leaning toward acquittal based on reasonable doubt, but the judge believes the defendant should really be convicted, then the judge is more likely to be suspicious of the juror's reasoning and to think that the juror is really intending to nullify than if the judge had thought an acquittal was appropriate. Thus, the judge's own view of the correct outcome can color the judge's assessment of the juror's credibility. The trial judge, already in a position of power, has been given even greater power by the Second Circuit. The trial judge's assessment of the juror's intent is likely to be shown great deference by the appellate court because the appellate court will have only the cold record on which to rely, whereas the trial judge will have the actual juror present.[337]

---

[335] An example of this, at least as described by the juror's lawyer Paul Grant, is the case of Laura J. Kriho, a juror in a drug trial. She claimed she was never asked directly during voir dire, and therefore never disclosed, that she had been charged with possession of LSD and had received a deferred judgment and that she believed in jury nullification. Once selected to serve, she did research on the Internet to learn about the penalty in the case. As a result of these actions, she was charged with perjury. Although the drug trial had ended in a hung jury, with Ms. Kriho voting for acquittal, she was later tried before a judge on the perjury charges. One cynical view of this case is that if Ms. Kriho had voted to convict, her transgressions during voir dire and deliberations would have been overlooked. *See* Harvey A. Silverglate, *The Perils of Being a Juror With a Conscience*, NAT'L L.J., Dec. 23, 1996, at A17.

[336] *See* Bushel's Case, 124 Eng. Rep. 1006, 1009 (C.P. 1670) (holding that jurors may not be fined or imprisoned for their verdict). This case arose when Quakers William Penn and William Mead were charged with the common-law crimes of unlawful assembly and disturbance of the peace while addressing a large crowd outside the Friends' Meeting House on Gracechurch Street on August 14, 1670. *See* GREEN, *supra* note 178, at 222. Penn and Mead admitted that they had been preaching and praying but denied that any law of England made it a crime for people to assemble to worship God. Penn urged the jury, "who are my judges," to go behind the indictment and decide what the common law meant by unlawful assembly and disturbance of the peace. *Id.* at 224 (citation omitted). Initially, the jury found Penn "guilty of speaking in Gracechurch Street," *id.* at 225, but the court sent the jury back for further deliberations. It returned after finding Penn guilty of "speaking or preaching to an assembly," and finding Mead not guilty. *Id.* The court ordered the jury "'locked up, without meat, drink, fire, and tobacco'" and said to the jurors: "'[W]e will have a verdict by the help of God, or you shall starve for it.'" Scheflin, *supra* note 36, at 170 (quoting Penn & Meads' Case, 6 Howell's 951, 963 (1670)). Eventually, the jury rendered a verdict of not guilty for both Penn and Mead. The court accepted the verdict, but fined the jury for rendering a verdict contrary to the evidence and instructions. *See* GREEN, *supra* note 178, at 225.

Rather than pay his fine, juror Edward Bushel went to prison and filed a habeas petition challenging his confinement. In the landmark decision of *Bushel's Case*, the Court of Common Pleas, in an opinion authored by Chief Justice Vaughan, ruled that jurors may never be fined or imprisoned for their verdicts, save for ministerial offenses, such as bribes. *See* 124 Eng. Rep. at 1013. Although this case did not officially recognize the right of juries to decide questions of law, it did establish that juries could not be punished for acquitting a defendant, thus establishing the power of the criminal jury to nullify.

[337] This type of decision is similar to Batson v. Kentucky, 476 U.S. 79 (1986), in which the trial judge must decide whether the reason given by the attorney attempting to exercise his or her peremptory challenge is based on an impermissible characteristic like race. The reasons given by attorneys to justify

The Second Circuit's approach also has the potential to wreak havoc with jury deliberations. Although the Second Circuit was careful to say that the judge should only interview a juror who has indicated an inclination to nullify, or about whom others suspect such an inclination,[338] the threat of an interview with the judge could be used by those jurors who seek to convince a holdout to go along with the majority's position. Research has shown that when there are only one or two holdouts, they have a hard time maintaining their position in the face of pressure from other jurors.[339] The position of holdouts, at least in the Second Circuit, has become even more precarious now that the majority can threaten to describe any holdouts as potential nullifiers, even if they are not. Holdouts who base their minority view on reasonable doubt, not nullification, might feel overwhelmed by the threat of exposure to the judge and the possibility of dismissal so that they abandon their position. Moreover, if the one or two holdouts maintained their position, the resnlt would be a hung jury. Thus, the Second Circuit's opinion reduces not only the chances of a nullifying jury, but also, perhaps inadvertently, the chances of a hung jury.

The Second Circuit's approach also runs the risk of chilling jury deliberations. Although the court noted the need to preserve jury secrecy in order to encourage robust deliberations, the threat of an interview with the judge and the embarrassment of dismissal may encourage jurors to be less candid in their deliberations. If they are thinking nullifying thoughts, they might keep them to themselves. Or, even if they would like to take an unpopular point of view based on reasonable doubt, they might think twice knowing that fellow jurors might accuse them of contemplating nullification. If they do take an unpopular position, and other jurors decide that they are impeding deliberations, rather than having to convince them by argument, the other jurors merely have to send a note to the judge suggesting that the obstinate jurors are nullifying jurors. Of course, jurors might be unfamiliar with the Second Circuit's decision and know nothing about the new role of the trial judge and the threat he or she poses to their continued jury service, and so their behavior during deliberations might not be altered in any way. Such ignorance, however, would be short-lived as the practice of dismissing nullifying jurors becomes more prevalent. If jurors do learn

their peremptorics are typically accepted by trial judges, and they no longer need to be relevant to the case, *see* Purkett v. Elem, 514 U.S. 765 (1995) (*per curiam*) (holding that the reason given for exercising a peremptory need not be relevant to the case). Appellate courts typically defer to trial judges' decisions of this kind because they have only the cold record before them, whereas trial judges have the advantage of an attorney's demeanor to help them decide whether the attorney's reason was pretextual.

338 *See Thomas*, 116 F.3d at 622 (applying a high evidentiary standard set forth in this opinion to "*any case* where the juror allegedly refuses to follow the law—whether the juror himself requests to be discharged from duty or, as in the instant ease, fellow jurors raise allegations of this form of misconduct").

339 *See supra* notes 307, 310-12.

about the practice, which has already received extensive press coverage,[340] those who are interviewed can dissemble in their responses to the judge, having learned that it is better to say that they are plagued by reasonable doubt than that they are inclined to nullify.

The Second Circuit's approach also assumes that judges can discern the nullifying juror from the reasonable doubt juror. Unless a juror uses the exact language of reasonable doubt, judges may be inclined to think that the juror intends to nullify. Judges have many pressures on them to dismiss a difficult juror: if they do not dismiss such a juror, then deliberations will be lengthier, court dockets will become further backlogged, and a hung jury might necessitate a re-trial. These are institutional pressures that may lead a judge to err on the side of dismissing a juror, even though the Second Circuit has warned judges to err in the other direction.

Finally, the Second Circuit's approach is likely to run into constitutional problems as well. The Sixth Amendment requires that a defendant be tried by an "impartial jury."[341] If the judge can remove jurors who may prove unpopular among their fellow jurors for any number of reasons, including that they espouse a minority point of view, then in what sense is the defendant receiving a "jury" trial consistent with the Sixth Amendment? It may be a jury in the sense that there is a group, but if the judge can act as supervisor of the group, and remove those who prove difficult, then the jury has lost much of its independence. Also, in what sense is the jury still "impartial" if those with a different point of view have been removed from the jury, leaving only those who share the same view to continue with deliberations?[342]

---

[340] *See, e.g.*, Bruce Fein, *A Commentary: Curbing Verdicts That Defy the Law*, WASH. TIMES, May 28, 1997, at A12 (describing the *Thomas* opinion as "logically and intellectually messy"); Paul Grant, *Nullified Jurors = Nullified Justice*, NAT'L L.J., June 23, 1997, at A15 (describing the *Thomas* decision as "[f]ollowing an ever-increasing hostility of courts toward the doctrine of jury nullification"); Otto G. Obermaier, *Second Circuit Court of Appeals Tries To Nullify Jury Nullification*, N.Y. L.J., July 7, 1997, at 7 (suggesting that *Thomas* may eventually lead to the trial judge becoming "the 13th, and most powerful, juror"); Tracey Tully, *5 Family Members Face Second Narcotics Trial*, TIMES UNION (Albany), Sept. 30, 1997, at B7 (reporting that lawyers considered *Thomas* "groundbreaking not because it called for a new trial, but because it reaffirmed a judge's right to dismiss jurors who seek to nullify the law based on their self-styled notions of justice").

[341] The Sixth Amendment requires in relevant part: "In all criminal prosecutions, the accused shall enjoy the right to a speedy and public trial, by an impartial jury of the State and district wherein the crime shall have been committed . . . ." U.S. CONST. amend. VI.

[342] Admittedly, there is some precedent for this in that jurors who are opposed to the death penalty can be excluded from the jury in a capital case. *See* Witherspoon v. Illinois, 391 U.S. 510, 523 (1968) (excluding for cause jurors who would "automatically vote against the imposition of capital punishment" or whose "attitude toward the death penalty would prevent them from making an impartial decision as to the defendant's guilt."). Thus, the Supreme Court has said that an impartial jury can exclude those with a particular point of view. However, in the capital context, jurors with such fixed views are removed during the voir dire, whereas in this case, a juror who was judged impartial during voir dire is removed during deliberations.

2. *Nullification as An Affirmative Defense.*—Another proposal, suggested by Professor Andrew Leipold, is to make nullification an affirmative defense and, at the same time, allow judges to review acquittals and require special verdicts from juries in criminal cases.[343] His proposal, consistent with a conventional view of the jury, is designed to limit nullification. In Leipold's view, nullification imposes more costs than benefits on the criminal justice system,[344] and while he would not eliminate nullification entirely, he would limit the instances in which it could take place.[345] According to his proposal, a jury should only be able to consider nullification in certain kinds of cases, namely those established by the legislature.[346] In this way, there would be legitimacy because the legislature, rather than the jury, would decide the types of cases in which nullification could even be considered, and there would be consistency because the legislature, rather than the jury, would set policy. If a given case met the statutory criteria—and it would be up to the judge to decide if the threshold had been met[347]—then a criminal defendant could argne nullification as an affirmative defense. The jury, having been informed about nullification in appropriate cases, could then decide whether to nullify.

Once Leipold has limited the jury to nullification in only certain types of cases, he would do away with certain procedural devices that he believes have been in place largely to protect the jury's power to nullify in any criminal case. One procedural change he would make is to allow the government to appeal after the jury has acquitted a criminal defendant.[348] Without this change, Leipold argues, the prosecutor is unduly hampered and must accept a jury verdict that could be based on jury error. Leipold would therefore allow judicial review of jury acquittals. Leipold would also have the judge decide whether to have the jury render a special verdict in a criminal case.[349] Only in this way could the judge have some assurance that the jury had not nullified improperly.

---

343 *See* Andrew D. Leipold, *Rethinking Jury Nullification*, 82 VA. L. REV. 253, 312-24 (1996).

344 *See id.* at 296-311.

345 *See id.* at 312 ("Eliminating all vestiges of the jury's nullification power is probably impossible, and is certainly undesirable.").

346 *See id.* at 313.

347 *See id.* at 312-13 ("To prevent the jury from being distracted, the trial judge requires the defendant to present some threshold showing of the affirmative defense [of nullification] before the court will allow argument on the issue or instruct on its elements.").

348 *See id.* at 318 ("Most significantly, if the government believed that an acquittal was infiuenced by a trial error, it could appeal."). Leipold agrees that his suggestion runs counter to the Double Jeopardy Clause, *see id.* at 267-68, and a line of Supreme Court cases proteeting it. *See id.* at 318 ("The idea of government appeals is radical (and flies in the face of many Supreme Court opinions) . . . .").

349 *See id.* at 321 ("If a judge thought that the jury would be tempted to stray beyond the boundaries of the law, she could require the panel to specify the greunds for its decision.").

What underlies Leipold's proposal is not only a pro prosecution stance, which he readily admits,[350] but also a conventional view of the jury's role. Leipold has a distrust of juries and a great deal of faith in judges. He is willing to substitute the view of a judge for that of a jury. He is willing to have a judge decide when a defendant has met the threshold criteria before the jury can consider nullification. He is willing to have a judge review a jury's verdict of acquittal; and he is willing to have a judge structure the jury's deliberations through the use of a special verdict. Leipold, like the Second Circuit, is shifting jury tasks to the judge so that the judge is supervising the jury more closely. While Leipold, like the Second Circuit, is unwilling to have the judge patrol the jury so as to extirpate all nullification, he is willing to have the judge play a more intrusive role than current practice permits so as to limit nullification.

Leipold would like to reduce jury discretion, which allows for nullification, and is willing to do so even if it means increasing legislative, judicial, and prosecutorial discretion. His concerns about jury nullification loom large, even though most criminal cases end in convictions, and, as he acknowledges, the jury's power to nullify is "rarely exercised."[351] To limit jury discretion and the opportunity it provides for nullification, he would enhance the legislature's role by having it define types of cases that are appropriate for nullification, even though the jury currently performs that function, albeit on a case-by-case basis. One has to wonder why the legislature would be inclined to be generous about defining situations in which juries could decide not to follow the laws passed by the legislature. Similarly, Leipold would add to the judge's power by having the judge decide if a case is appropriate for nullification based on the legislature's criteria and if the jury should proceed by way of a special verdict structured by the judge rather than by general verdict structured by the jury. He would also have the judge, rather than the jury, have the last word about acquittals. Finally, Leipold would add to prosecutorial power, by allowing prosecutors to appeal acquittals. They would have discretion to decide whether to appeal, and would be able to bring to bear the enormous resources of the government to an extended prosecution of the defendant. While Leipold acknowledges that these changes come at the expense of the defendant, he fails to recognize that they also come at the expense of the jury. Leipold considers whether the judge should not be permitted to go further, and to take a criminal case away from a jury if, in the judge's view, the facts were undisputed and the prosecution had proven its case beyond a reasonable doubt, much as the judge can do in a civil trial. In civil cases, under Federal Rule of Civil Procedure 50, the judge can enter a judgment as a matter of law either before the case goes to the jury or after a jury returns a verdict.[352]

---

350 *See id.* at 324 (conceding that "the proposed changes would undeniably favor the prosecution").

351 *Id.* at 259.

352 This rule provides in relevant part:

Leipold decides, however, that although "[t]here is no logical reason" to preclude such a possibility,[353] as a practical matter, the only remedy should be a new trial.[354]

B. Increasing Nullification

Whereas Leipold's proposal to limit nullification takes a prosecutor's perspective, Paul Butler's proposal to increase nullification takes a defendant's perspective. However, what both proposals fail to do, though in quite different ways, is to approach nullification from the jury's perspective.

1. Race-Based Nullification.—As described in Part V,[355] Butler proposes to increase instances of nullification so that nullification becomes an effective vehicle for political change. His proposal is for every African-American juror who is asked to judge an African-American defendant charged with a nonviolent, victimless crime to nullify so as not to send another African-American man to jail. He admits that his concern is with the African-American community, and he is simply using the jury and its nullification power as an instrument to achieve long overdue justice for that community. He views the criminal justice system as racist and therefore feels justified in urging African Americans to use whatever tools the system makes available to them, such as nullification, to subvert the system. In Part V, I analyzed Butler's proposal and the dangers it presents to the jury; here I simply want to make the additional point that he is driven to use the jury and nullification to achieve what he believes will be benefits for the African-American community.

2. Agenda-Based Nullification.—FIJA, like Butler, also wants to promote nullification. Although its goals are more diffuse, including opposition to a wide range of laws from drugs to guns, it, too, would like nullification to become more commonplace. Toward that end, FIJA has been actively educating citizens about the jury's power to nullify. It un-

> If during a trial by jury a party has been fully heard on an issue and there is no legally sufficient evidentiary basis for a reasonable jury to find for that party on that issue, the court may determine the issue against that party and may grant a motion for judgment as a matter of law against that party....

FED. R. CIV. P. 50 (a)(1).

[353] Leipold, *supra* note 343, at 319; *see id.* ("Logic also suggests that a trial judge should be able to overturn an acquittal and enter a judgment of conviction; such a ruling should not interfere with the Sixth Amendment any more than judgments as a matter of law violate the Seventh Amendment."); *id.* at 266 ("Surely accurate and rational decisions are at least as important in criminal cases as in civil proceedings, and thus logic suggests that judges should have the same power to prevent unreasonable verdicts.") (footnote omitted).

[354] *See id.* at 320.

[355] *See supra* text accompanying notes 259-84.

dertakes this activity through a variety of forms of grassroots outreach, including leaflets at the courthouse steps, a newsletter, a web site, bumper stickers, and advertisements. It has also been the catalyst behind a number of bills in state legislatures that would require jurors to be informed of their power to nullify.[356] Underlying FIJA's educational efforts is a desire to use the jury as a vehicle for challenging certain laws that its members oppose. FIJA wants jurors to enter the courtroom and jury room prepared to nullify so as to register their disagreement with those laws. What distinguishes FIJA's approach from a legitimate use of nullification is that FIJA encourages its members and others to begin jury service with their verdicts already decided. They are not moved to nullify after deliberation and consideration of the case before them, but rather, they begin their jury service with their views already formed.

C. Recognizing Nullification

While those who hold a conventional view of the jury are in denial about nullification and those who are activists are devising new ways to use nullification to further their causes, the need for a theory of the jury that encompasses all of its varied roles, including nullification, grows ever more pressing. Toward this end, the process view provides a theory that is consistent with how the jury works in practice. The conventional view creates a chasm between how the jury actually functions and how those functions are described. By ascribing to the jury only one role, the conventional view offers a parsimonious description of the jury, and when the jury plays more than that one role, then the jury is charged with overreaching. By embracing a broad view of the jury, which includes its varied roles, the jury can be appreciated, rather than constrained, when it exercises the full range of its roles, including nullification.

The conventional view of the jury and nullification should be abandoned and replaced with a more expansive view that takes account of the varied roles that the jury actually plays, including the constructive role that nullification can potentially play. Rather than trying to reduce the jury's role to make it conform to the conventional view, which is what the Second Circuit and others would do, a better course would be to recognize the jury's several roles and to revise the theory of the jury so that it adequately describes the workings of the modern-day jury.

One way to begin this process—and it is only a beginning—is to rewrite the instruction that the court gives to the jury about its proper role. Today, in most courtrooms throughout the country, judges instruct jurors to the effect that they "must apply the law as I [the judge] state to you, to the facts, as you determine them."[357] This instruction gives the jurors an un-

[356] *See supra* notes 288-89 (describing FIJA's legislative efforts).

[357] 1 CALIFORNIA JURY INSTRUCTIONS, CRIMINAL (CALJIC), no. 1.00, at 4-5 (1988).

duly limited view of their role; it perpetuates a view of the jury as the conventionalists would like the jury to be, but not as the jury really is. The disjuncture between the instruction and the roles the jury actually performs is significant because when juries perform more than is encompassed by the limited instruction, including nullification, there is an outcry and judges and academics look for new ways to constrain the jury. In addition, an instruction that so circumscribes the jury's role and denies the possibility of nullification leaves jurors open to suggestions made by the activists that they have a power, such as the power to nullify, but that knowledge of it is being kept from them. Indeed, not only are jurors not told of that power, but they are told the exact opposite: They only have the power the judge has described.

Instead of instructing juries that they perform the conventionalists' vision of the jury's role, courts should instruct jurors more accurately on their roles. Admittedly, courts must proceed carefully so as not to foment nullification. Nullification should be reserved for compelling cases. Courts could borrow language from an instruction suggested by John Adams. He would instruct juries, in part, as follows: "It is not only [a juror's] right, but his [or her] duty . . . to find the verdict according to his [or her] own best understanding, judgment and conscience . . . ."[358]

The virtues of such an instruction are that it suggests that the jury performs more than mechanical operations, whether factfinding or applying law, and that the jury engages in interpretive activity that involves jurors' understanding and judgment. Further, in some cases, conscience might compel a verdict that is not suggested by the letter of the law. While the instruction does not elaborate on nullification, and in fact does not even use the word, it hints at nullification. The instruction allows for the possibility of nullification, and does not require jurors to disobey the judge's instruction if they choose to nullify in the end.

The instruction is open to criticism from those on both sides of the nullification debate. Conventionalists would claim the instruction goes too far, suggesting to jurors a role that is too broad, and intrudes upon the roles of the judge and the legislature. Activists would say that the instruction does not go far enough because it fails to inform jurors about nullification explicitly and the ways that it can be used to change the laws or the criminal justice system. Although the proposed instruction is subject to both these criticisms, I think that is inevitable because the process view of the jury, and the potentially beneficial role that nullification can play, occupies a

[358] Howe, *supra* note 154, at 605 (quoting 2 LIFE AND WORKS OF JOHN ADAMS 253-55 (C.F. Adams ed., 1856)). Admittedly, John Adams was writing at a time when only men could serve as jurors, and thus, I have taken the liberty of updating his language to include both men and women. I have also taken the liberty of suggesting an abridged version of John Adams's instruction. The full instruction, which I provide here, goes further than even a process view of nullification and the jury: "It is not only [a juror's] right, but his duty . . . to find the verdict according to his own best understanding, judgment and conscience, though in direct opposition to the direction of the court." *Id.*

middle ground in this debate, and will be subject to criticism from both sides. My point is simply that how courts describe the jury's role to jurors, who might know little else about the jury system and the trial process than what they have gleaned from television and the movies, is important. Courts need to revise the instruction they give to jurors about their roles, whether they use the version I have suggested or a similar one, so that it reflects the breadth of the jury's roles.

The debate about whether courts should instruct juries about nullification is not a new one. It peaked in the 1970s during the Vietnam War and has not been the subject of much attention since. I do not intend to revisit that debate, which was fueled by the Vietnam War, and I do not think that I need to because the instruction I propose does not tell jurors explicitly about nullification. Rather, it outlines the contours of the jury's role in language broad enough to encompass nullification. The important point is that it does not mislead jurors, telling them that their role is quite limited, when in fact, it is not. Although a revised instruction is only a first step,[359] it is an important first step in teaching jurors about the jury and in correcting the view that is officially conveyed by courts, which is that the jury performs a very limited function. Only when the jury's role is understood as broad will courts no longer perpetuate the myth that the nullifying jury is always bad.

VII. CONCLUSION

In much of the literature on nullification, both academic and judicial, nullification is portrayed as a negative act on the part of the jury that threatens to undermine the judicial system. Working from this view, judges and academics have considered ways to constrain the jury so that it does not engage in nullification.

Working from a broader, more complex view of the jury, as I have presented, nullification can be seen as a positive act on balance. In the three situations in which nullification is likely to occur, nullification provides important benefits to the judicial system. When the jury nullifies by refusing to convict a particular defendant, the jury is indicating to the prosecution that it has become overzealous. When the jury nullifies by refusing to convict under a bad law, the jury is alerting the legislature that it needs to fix the law. When the jury nullifies in response to social conditions, the jury may be suggesting to the judiciary that there are problems in the criminal justice system. This last type of nullification is the least effective because the jury's messages may be difficult to discern and because the jury loses its special competence the further it moves from the particular case before it.

The efforts to limit all forms of nullification, as the Second Circuit and others would do, seem likely to harm the jury. But there is no need to limit

---

359 A second step would entail similar revision of the juror's oath. For an example of a typical oath used today, see *supra* note 300.

jury nullification because it is, by and large, beneficial to the judicial system. Nor is there any need to constrain the power of the jury because it is, for the most part, wisely used. The most pressing need, however, is to replace a limited view of the jury and a negative view of nullification with a process view that recognizes the full panoply of the jury's roles, including nullification, and the place to start is by re-examining the lessons that courts teach jurors everyday about their proper roles.

[7]

A DEFENCE OF JURY NULLIFICATION

THOM BROOKS

'Jury lawlessness is the great corrective of law in its actual administration.'
-Roscoe Pound[1]

ABSTRACT. In both Great Britain and the United States there has been a growing debate about the modern acceptability of jury nullification. Properly understood, juries do not have any constitutional right to ignore the law, but they do have the power to do so nevertheless. Juries that nullify may be motivated by a variety of concerns: too harsh sentences, improper government action, racism, etc. In this article, I shall attempt to defend jury nullification on a number of grounds. First, I discuss the use of general verdicts and reject their replacement in criminal trials by special verdicts. Second, I examine verdicts based upon mistakes and racial prejudice, turning my attention to perverse verdicts and the question of whether or not juries are guilty of legislating when nullifying the law. Finally, I look at the problem of the awarding of excessive damages by juries. My goal will be to provide a sound theoretical defence of the practice of jury nullification.

KEY WORDS: bifurcated trials, damages, equity, general verdicts, Hegel, jury, libel, nullification, perverse verdicts, punishment, Rawls, rights, special verdicts, trial

INTRODUCTION

In both Great Britain and the United States there has been a growing debate about the modern acceptability of jury nullification.[2] Jury nullification occurs when the jury acquits defendants it would declare guilty if following the court's legal instruction. Thus, juries are said to 'nullify' the law insofar as they depart from the law when rendering a verdict. Properly understood, juries do not

[1] R. Pound, 'Law in Books and Law in Action', *American Law Review* 44 (1910), 12–34, at 18.

[2] The term 'jury nullification' is synonymous with 'jury equity'. The use of jury nullification has been suspected of playing a role in the infamous trials of O. J. Simpson and Rodney King in the last decade. See *People v Simpson*, No. BA097211 (Cal. Super. Ct. 1995); *People v Powell*, No. BA035498 (Cal. Super. Ct. 1991).

have any constitutional *right* to ignore the law, but they do have the *power* to do so nevertheless.[3] The power to ignore law stems from the jury's ability to return a general verdict of 'guilty' or 'not guilty' without any justification: juries may convict or acquit for any reason acceptable to them. Juries that nullify may be motivated by a variety of concerns: too harsh sentences, improper government action, racism, etc. While there is no evidence that jury nullification happens more than infrequently at best, critics charge that it occurs too often and that its use must be curbed.[4] One critic, Sir Robin Auld, argues:

> I regard the ability of jurors to acquit, and it also follows, convict, in defiance of the law and in disregard of their oaths, as more than illogicality. It is a blatant affront to the legal process and the main purpose of the criminal justice system—the control of crime—of which they are so important a part.[5]

Many who oppose jury nullification highlight its adverse effect on the rule of law and point to instances of racial bias amongst jury members.[6] On the other hand, those who defend jury nullification tend to emphasize examples where juries have reacted nobly against illegitimate state oppression.

In this article, I shall attempt to defend jury nullification on a number of grounds. First, I discuss the use of general verdicts and reject their replacement in criminal trials by special verdicts. Second, I

---

[3] *Sparf v United States*, 156 U.S. 51, 102-3 (1895); *United States v Moylan*, 417 F. 2d 1002, 1006-7 (1969). See *United States v Battiste*, 24 F. Cas. 1042, 1043 (C. C. D. Mass. 1835) (No. 14,545): '[t]he jury have not the right, though they may have the power, in rendering a general verdict, to determine the law in any case, civil or criminal'.

[4] Different studies put the number of 'questionable convictions' from anywhere between two and three percent of all cases: see J. Baldwin and M. McConville, 'Trial by Jury: Some Empirical Evidence on Contested Criminal Cases in England', *Law and Social Review* 13 (1979), 861–90, p. 861; P. Duff and M. Findlay, 'The Politics of Jury Reform', in eds M. Findlay and P. Duff, *The Jury Under Attack* (London: Butterworths 1988), 220; C. Weinberg-Brodt, 'Jury Nullification and Jury-Control Procedures', *New York University Law Review* 65 (1990), 825–70, p. 826; M. Zander and P. Henderson, 'The Crown Court Study' (RCCJ Research Study No. 19, 1993), 170-71; and S. Doran and J. Jackson, 'The Case for Jury Waiver', *Criminal Law Review* (1997), 155–72, p. 158.

[5] Ian Dennis, 'The Auld Review: Part 2', *Criminal Law Review* (2002), 1–2.

[6] For example, Blom-Cooper argues '[t]here can be no room for what the jury perceives to be an oppressive law, and to decline to apply it'. -L. Blom-Cooper, 'Article 6 and Modes of Criminal Trial', *European Human Rights Law Review* 1 (2001), 1–14, p. 6.

examine verdicts based upon mistakes and racial prejudice, turning my attention to perverse verdicts and the question of whether or not juries are guilty of legislating when nullifying the law. Finally, I look at the problem of the awarding of excessive damages by juries. My goal will be to provide a sound theoretical defence of the practice of jury nullification.[7]

A large part of any such defence will rest on the reasonableness of the right to trial by jury in the first place, itself a matter of great debate. Indeed, some have likened the jury trial to the 'apparent foolishness inherent in asking the ignorant to use the incomprehensible to decide the unknowable'.[8] Whilst I have defended the right to trial by jury elsewhere, I will assume here that it is at least minimally justifiable.[9]

General Verdicts

The modern practice of juries returning general verdicts originated only with the famous Bushell's case: the trial of the Quakers William Penn and William Mead for violating the Conventicle Act of 1670,[10] which outlawed religious practices incompatible with those of the Church of England.[11] Both Penn and Mead agreed they had violated the Conventicle Act in court. Nevertheless, the jury refused to convict either Penn or Mead despite being locked up overnight by the judge without food, water or a chamber-pot. Angrily, the judge had the jurors imprisoned until they paid a fine for their failure to apply the law in conformity with his legal opinion. Four of the jurors, including Bushell the foreman, refused to pay the fine and spent several months

[7] I shall look at jury nullification in criminal trials primarily, although the problem of excessive damages in civil trials will also be examined. For an excellent look at jury nullification in civil trials, see L. Noah, 'Civil Jury Nullification', *Iowa Law Review* 86 (2001), 1601–58.

[8] See A. Basdekis, 'Perfection by Nullification', *Yale Law Journal* 105 (1996), 2285–90.

[9] For examples of defences of the right to trial by jury, see my 'The Right to Trial by Jury', *Journal of Applied Philosophy*, 21 (2004), 197–212; S. J. Clark, 'The Courage of Our Convictions', *Michigan Law Review* 97 (1999), 2381–447; and R. N. Jonakait, *The American Jury System* (New Haven: Yale University Press, 2003). On jury nullification and the right to trial by jury, see P. Devlin, 'The Conscience of the Jury', *Law Quarterly Review* 107 (1991), 398–404; M. D. A. Freeman, 'Why Not a Jury Nullification Statute Here Too?' *New Law Journal* 131 (1981), 304–6.

[10] Conventicle Act, 1670, 22 Car. II, ch. 1.

[11] 1 Vaughan 135, 124 Eng. Rep. 1006 (C.P. 1670).

in prison.[12] The jurors appealed their convictions and the case was heard by Lord Vaughan who has traditionally been thought by legal theorists to have argued for the right of juries to determine both the law and facts when rendering a verdict. This long-held interpretation of Vaughan's view is challenged forcefully by Simon Stern, who claims Vaughan did no such thing:

> Vaughan relied in part on the observation that reasonable people may disagree about a witness's credibility or the reliability of the evidence; in such cases, he argued, the jurors should form their own views and should not be punished if these views differed from the judge's.[13]

Nevertheless, Bushell's case certainly did make a fundamental change in the common law by introducing the right of jurors to render verdicts without fear of imprisonment.

This class of verdicts are called 'general verdicts', that is, they are verdicts in which the jury finds defendants either 'guilty' or 'not guilty' without having to provide any justification for its decision. This practice has been accepted in the US at least since *United States v Spock*[14] as a necessary safeguard of the jury's independence, as it has been thought that general verdicts best allow a jury to render verdicts most consistent with its conscience.[15] Through the issuing of general verdicts, juries have been seen to have the *power*, although not the *right*, not to apply the law as the court understands it. For example, in *United States v Moylan,*[16] the court said:

> We recognize, as appellants urge, the undisputed power of the jury to acquit, even if its verdict is contrary to the law as given by the judge and contrary to the evidence. This is a power that must exist as long as we adhere to the general verdict in criminal cases, for the courts cannot search the minds of the jurors to find the basis upon which they judge. If the jury feels that the law under which the defendant is accused is unjust, or that exigent circumstances justified the actions of the accused, or for any

[12] See S. Enright and J. Morton, *Taking Liberties: The Criminal Jury in the 1990s* (London: Weidenfeld & Nicolson, 1990), 15.

[13] S. Stern, 'Note. Between Local Knowledge and National Politics: Debating Rationales for Jury Nullifaction After Bushell's Case', *Yale Law Journal* 111 (2002), 1816.

[14] 416 F. 2d at 181-82 (1st Cir. 1969).

[15] In addition, *Spock* rejects any directions from the judge that might affect the jury's deliberation. Convictions have been overturned where '[t]he special findings' form ... set the tone of the deliberations by directing the jury down a path towards a guilty verdict'. -*State v Surette*, 544 A. 2d 823, 825 (N.H. 1988). See *United States v Palmeri*, 630 F. 2d 192, 202-03 (3rd. Cir. 1980); *State v Hardison*, 492 A. 2d 1009, 1015 (N.J. 1985).

[16] 417 F. 2d 1002 (4th Cir. 1969).

reason which appeals to their logic or passion, the jury has the power to acquit, and the courts must abide by that decision.[17]

However juries may come to a verdict, they still have a duty to apply the law as declared by the court.[18] This is due to the modern division of labour between courts as finders of law and juries as finders of facts.[19] In this view, juries are instructed to obey the law and ought not to base their verdicts on whether or not they approve of the law.[20] Opponents of jury nullification often argue that a nullifying jury is doing just this. Indeed, in *United States v Simpson*[21] the court argued that '[t]he "conscience verdicts" which result from exercise of this power [of nullification] often involves juries in the task of judging both law and facts'.[22]

Admittedly, it is rather difficult to discern accurately whether or not, in fact, a jury *is* judging both law and facts: the jury simply issues its general verdict.[23] Yet, while juries may certainly come to verdicts

[17] Ibid., 1006.

[18] See *Spark v United States*,156 U.S. 51, 106 (1895); *United States v Dellinger*, 472 F. 2d 340, 408 (7th Cir. 1972). In Maryland and Indiana the judge issues directions to the jury informing it of its power to nullify. Perhaps surprisingly, there is no evidence that nullifications have risen as a result: see D. N. Dorfman and C. K. Iijima, 'Fictions, Fault, and Forgiveness: Jury Nullification in a New Context', *University of Michigan Journal of Law Reform* (1995), 908–13.

[19] Some argue the division is useful as it spares judges from bribes: see J. H. Merryman and D. S. Clark, *Comparative Law: Western European and Latin American Legal Systems: Cases and Materials* (Indianapolis: Bobbs-Merrill, 1978), 657.

[20] See *United States v Boardman*, 419 F. 2d 110, 116 (1st Cir. 1969); *United States v Moylan*, 417 F. 2d 1002, 1006 (4th Cir. 1969); *United States v Dellinger*, 472 F. 2d 340, 408 (7th Cir. 1972); *United States v Simpson*, 460 F. 2d 515, 519 (9th Cir. 1972); *United States v Washington*, 705 F. 2d 489, 494 (D.C. Cir. 1983). For a contrary view, see D. C. Brody, 'Sparf & Dougherty Revisited: Why the Court Should Instruct the Jury of its Nullification Right', *American Criminal Law Review* 33 (1995), 89–122; R. E. Korroch and M. J. Davidson, 'Jury Nullification: A Call for Justice or an Invitation to Anarchy?' *Military Law Review* 139 (1993), 131–52.

[21] 460 F. 2d 515 (9th Cir. 1972): see R. F. Schopp, 'Verdicts of Conscience: Nullification and Necessity as Jury Responses to Crimes of Conscience', *Southern California Law Review* 69 (1996), 2039–116.

[22] op. cit., 519.

[23] Justice Antonin Scalia says that 'it is no more possible to demonstrate the inconsistency of two opinions based upon a "totality of the circumstances" test than it is to demonstrate the inconsistency of two jury verdicts': A. Scalia, 'The Rule of Law as a Law of Rules', *University of Chicago Law Review* 56 (1989), 1175–88, p. 1180. In addition, Scalia says that 'I frankly do not know why we treat some of these questions as matters of fact and others as matters of law.' - 1182.

primarily on account of a distaste for a particular issue of law, the courts have generally held a high threshold in favour of the presumption that juries are acting appropriately as a fact finding body. For example, in *Grobbelaar v News Group Newspapers Ltd*,[24] Lord Bingham says: '[I]t should not be lightly assumed that, in failing to be satisfied that a burden of proof had been discharged, a jury had acted perversely'.[25]

However, this ambiguity about general verdicts has led opponents of jury nullification to argue that juries should give reasoned verdicts instead. Thus, some opponents argue that the jury's use of general verdicts rather than reasoned verdicts 'marks jury procedure out from all other forms of procedure, criminal or civil'.[26] Yet this is not even remotely true in either the United States or Britain: in trials of first instance, bench trials do not give reasons for their decisions either. The vast majority of cases – ninety-five percent or higher – are plea bargained, where no reasons are given for the judge's decision.[27] In Britain, this may have to change: the European Court of Human Rights has ruled that convicted defendants should know the reasons behind their conviction.[28] As a result, a growing number of legal theorists have been calling for the return of special verdicts in criminal trials, arguing that it would eliminate jury nullification and make verdicts immune from human rights attacks in the European Court. With special verdicts, judges would present the jury with a set of factual questions they must answer, leading only to a verdict of guilty or not guilty. Even those who believe jury nullification is not always undesirable argue for the return of special verdicts. For example, John Jackson says:

> But there arguably remains a role even in the 21st century for juries to exercise equity in cases where the merits of a particular case demand that the law be stretched in a manner which could not be achieved by a professional judge. Even if this role is conceded juries could still be required to disclose by means of special verdict that they are satisfied that there is a basis in fact for a conviction but be enabled nev-

[24] [2003] E.M.L.R. 1; [2002] U.K.H.L. 40 HL.

[25] Ibid., para. 57.

[26] J. Carruthers, 'Are Juries Safe?' *Scots Law Times* 25 (2001), 217–21, p. 218: see also P. W. Ferguson, 'Unreasonable Jury Verdicts', *Scots Law Times* 16 (1999), 125–28.

[27] See J. Morton, 'Behind Closed Doors', *New Law Journal* (2000), 1843.

[28] See Doran and Jackson, op. cit., 169.

ertheless to record an acquittal. Juries would then be required to expose publicly the fact that they are acting in a nullification capacity.[29]

The growing appeal of special verdicts has also crossed over to American legal theorists, perhaps encouraged by their use in trials for capital offences. In the US, there had been a problem of provoking 'arbitrary' jury nullification in mandatory sentencing: if the jury found a defendant guilty, the defendant received a mandatory death sentence.[30] Juries were thought to believe themselves responsible for executing defendants and began to acquit defendants against professional legal opinion. Since the mid-1970s, whenever the Supreme Court has discussed 'jury nullification', it has done so only in this context.[31] The Court decided to bifurcate trials for capital offences, where juries must specify relevant aggravating or mitigating circumstances that led them to a recommendation of capital punishment if they return a general verdict of 'guilty'. Those who support the use of special verdicts in other kinds of criminal trial in the US and Britain point out its constitutional use in American capital trials, believing the use of special verdicts would play to the jury's strength as determiners of facts.[32]

Notwithstanding reservations some legal theorists have regarding bifurcated trials,[33] critics of special verdicts raise important criticisms. First, the thought that there can be only one clear conclusion in many cases rests on a view that legal rules determine all possible outcomes: they simply do not. Indeed, we may have as many diffi-

[29] J. Jackson, 'Modes of Trial: Shifting the Balance Towards the Professional Judge', *Criminal Law Review* (2002), 249–71, p. 270.

[30] *Graham v Cullins*, 506 U.S. 461, 486 (1993) (Thomas, J., concurring): see *Woodson v North Carolina*, 428 U.S. 280, at 302–03 (1976).

[31] See *Furman v Georgia*, 408 U.S. 238, 247, 298 (1972); *Gregg v Georgia*, 428 U.S 153, 199, 221 (1976); *Roberts v Louisiana*, 428 U.S. 325, 346–48, 360–61 (1976) (White, J., dissenting); *Woodson v North Carolina*, 428 U.S. 280, 293 (1976) (Stewart, J.); *Beck v Alabama*, 447 U.S. 625, 640 (1980) (Stevens, J.); *Enmund v Florida*, 458 U.S. 782, 817, 818 (1982) (O'Connor, J., dissenting); *Caldwell v Mississippi*, 472 U.S. 320, 323 (1985) (Marshall, J.); *Lockhart v McCree*, 476 U.S. 162 (1986) (Rehnquist, J.); *Sumner v Shuman*, 483 U.S. 66, 88n13 (1987) (Blackmun, J.); *Gilmore v Taylor*, 508 U.S. 333, 362 (1993) (Blackmun, J., dissenting); *Johnson v Texas*, 509 U.S. 350, 380 (1993) (O'Connor, J., dissenting). Also see my 'Retributivist Arguments against Capital Punishment', *Journal of Social Philosophy* 35 (2004), 188–97.

[32] K. H. Nepveu, 'Beyond "Guilty" or "Not Guilty": Giving Special Verdicts in Criminal Jury Trials', *Yale Law and Policy Review* 21 (2003), 263–300, p. 268.

[33] See J. M. Granholm and W. J. Richards, 'Bifurcated Justice: How Trial-Splitting Devices Defeat the Jury's Role', *University of Toledo Law Review* 26 (1995), 525–36.

culties accepting the questions put to the jury as the jury's reasons for coming to seemingly perverse general verdicts. Second, it is also thought special verdicts might interfere with jury deliberations. Since Bushell's case, the role of the jury's conscience in acquitting or convicting defendants has been central. Juries may be influenced to return a verdict they believe unwarranted because of excessive pressure exerted by the trial judge, something Bushell's case over three hundred years ago was rightly meant to eradicate. As a result, special verdicts may close out the option of jury nullification at the cost of possibly impugning the jury's conscience. If, in fact, the jury is to play a primary role in the courtroom, then it must be allowed to bring its collective conscience into play: surely, if a scholarly knowledge of legal texts were most important in adjudicating, then there would not be a particular need for juries.[34] Finally, even those who believe the special verdict ought to be employed in criminal trials confess: '[w]hile the jurors who were given special verdicts understood better the legal question of burden of proof, they did no better than the control group in applying that knowledge to fact patterns'.[35] Thus, special verdicts do not seem to improve the jury's legal understanding. If this is the case and we believe that the legal right to trial by jury is a right worth retaining, then it would appear that special verdicts, even if practically feasible, are unnecessary and unwarranted.[36]

'MISTAKEN' VERDICTS

Critics tend to determine how often juries decide cases 'correctly' by assessing how often judges would have decided cases likewise, so

[34] I would argue this is an important objection due to the fact that juries due play an important role in the criminal justice system. Thus, the justness of the right to trial by jury is presupposed. See note 10 above.

[35] Nepveu, op. cit., 263. See E. C. Wiggins and S. J. Breckler, 'Special Verdicts as Guides to Jury Decision Making', *Law and Psychology Review* 14 (1990), 28–29.

[36] There is another issue raised by proponents of special verdicts. They complain that while convictions can be appealed, there cannot be a retrial for the same offence due to the double jeopardy rule if the jury elects to acquit. It is thought that special verdicts might offer grounds for convicting those defendants acquitted by juries which render perverse verdicts. However, this seems unconstitutional as long as the double jeopardy rule remains constitutional: see *Palko v Connecticut*, 302 U.S. 319 (1937); and, in Britain, P. Roberts, 'Double Jeopardy Law Reform: A Criminal Justice Commentary', *Modern Law Review* 65 (2002), 393–424.

implying that judges decide cases correctly – which is not always true. For example, in *Bush v Gore*[37] judges could not agree on the relevant facts of the case nor on applicable legislation and precedents. While far from a proponent of jury trials, Judge Jerome Frank argues that

> the lawyer faces a multitude of variable factors which he cannot definitely ascertain … . The ability to answer unequivocally many so-called legal questions does not, then, signify, by any manner of means, that a lawyer, however experienced, can unequivocally tell his client that which a client wants to know. Only a soothsayer, a prophet, or a person gifted with clairvoyance, can tell a man what are his enforceable rights arising out of any particular transaction, or against any other person, before a lawsuit with respect to that transaction, or that person, has arisen. For only a clairvoyant can foretell what evidence will be introduced and will be believed, and can foresee what will be the reaction of the trial judge *or* the jurors to such testimony as he *or* they may believe.[38]

If Judge Frank is right, we ought not think there is always, or even usually, one correct decision for every case which any competently trained judge may ascertain.

Nevertheless, when held to this standard, juries may be said to make 'correct' decisions–that is, they agree with the decisions of judges–at least seventy five percent of the time.[39] This is not to say that juries incorrectly decide one quarter of all cases, but rather that judges would have decided differently in those cases. In these instances, critics charge juries with making mistakes. That is, verdicts delivered by juries that differ from verdicts judges would have delivered are thought to be not only a disagreement between juries and judges, but a disagreement where the judges are thought to be correct. Of course, the decisions of judges are not always correct and, therefore, their decisions cannot provide us with an absolute measure of what a correct decision would be in any particular case.

In addition, there are a number of simple measures juries might employ to best enable them to render verdicts. For example, defenders of the jury trial propose that jurors should be allowed to

[37] 531 U.S. 98 (2000).

[38] Jerome Frank, *Courts on Trial: Myth and Reality in American Justice* (Princeton: Princeton University Press, 1950), 25 (emphasis added).

[39] See H. Kalven Jr and H. Zeisel, *The American Jury* (Boston: Little, Brown, & Co., 1966), 57; P. C. Ellsworth and A. Reifman, 'Juror Comprehension and Public Policy: Perceived Problems and Proposed Solutions', *Psychology, Public Policy and Law* (2000), 788–821, p. 796. Also see M. J. Saks, 'Judicial Nullification', *Indiana Law Journal* 68 (1993), 1281–95, p. 1295; R. L. Wissler, A. J. Hart, and M. J. Saks, 'Decisionmaking About General Damages: A Comparison of Jurors, Judges, and Lawyers', *Michigan Law Review* 98 (1999), 751–826.

become more actively involved in the trial, through the encouragement of taking notes during the trial for use in verdict deliberation and questioning witnesses, and have access to court transcripts when rendering verdicts.[40] Moreover, others suggest that these 'mistakes' are not a jury's fault and are instead the result of shortcomings in the investigation and trial process.[41]

A full debate on the relative abilities of judges and juries to render correct verdicts is beyond the scope of this article. Suffice it to say that juries (as well as judges) render mistaken verdicts on occasion.[42] One well known mistaken verdict took place in Britain in *R v Young*,[43] where four jurors met in a hotel while deliberating a verdict and attempted to communicate with one of the accused's victims by means of a ouija board.[44] Aside from obvious examples like this, it has been argued that juries are most likely to render mistaken verdicts in cases that are particularly complex, such as in fraud trials.[45]

The decision *In re Japanese Electronic Products Antitrust Litigation*[46] held that the 'Seventh Amendment does not guarantee the right to jury trial when lawsuit is so complex that jury will not be able to perform its task of rational decision making with a

[40] See S. L. Friedland, 'The Competency and Responsibility of Jurors in Deciding Cases', *Northwestern University Law Review* 85 (1990), 190–220. Many of these reforms have been introduced in New Zealand with great success. See W. Young, 'Summing-up to Juries in Criminal Cases—What Jury Research says about Current Rules and Practice', *Criminal Law Review* (2003), 665–89 esp. p. 685.

[41] B. Houlder, 'The Importance of Preserving the Jury System and the Right of Election for Trial', *Criminal Law Review* (1997), 875–81, p. 879. Judge William Young argues: '[t]here is no sure method of assessing the extent to which the substantive results produced by the system of trial by jury are right.'-'Summing-up to Juries', op. cit., 665.

[42] See my 'The Right to Trial by Jury', *Journal of Applied Philosophy*, forthcoming.

[43] [1995] 2 Cr. App. R. 379.

[44] Id. Jurors came to the conclusion that the accused was guilty. The conviction was 'quashed', or overturned, and a retrial ordered. Also see *Vaise v Delaval* (1785) 1 Term Rep. 11; 99 E.R. 944 where the jury decided a case by tossing a coin.

[45] Of course, most cases do not present clear instances of mistakes and may be the result of statements or directions by attorneys or judges. For example, in the British case *R v Leer*, the arresting officers claimed Leer admitted in questioning that he carried a fish knife for self-defence 'in case someone had a go at him'. Defence evidence was not called and the judge directed the jury to convict Leer for possessing an offensive weapon without reasonable excuse. Nevertheless, the conviction was quashed on the grounds that an 'acquittal would not have been perverse': *R v Leer* [1982] WL 220823.

[46] 631 F. 2d 1069 (3rd. Cir. 1980).

reasonable understanding of the evidence and the relevant legal rules'.[47] The court argued that while jury nullification 'may be legitimate when the jury actually modifies the law to conform to community values', this did not apply when the jury could not understand the evidence.[48] Are judges capable of understanding such evidence whether or not they have an ability to nullify? The court thought they were:

> Although we cannot presume that a judge will be more intelligent than a jury or more familiar with technical subject matters, a judge will almost surely have substantial familiarity with the process of civil litigation .... A judge's abilities are, of course, not unbounded. It is conceivable that a case might be so complex that a judge could not decide it rationally and competently. However, the possibility of such a case cannot justify trial by jury. [49]

What the court fails to see is that if judges may not always be able to decide a case 'rationally and competently,' it does not particularly justify bench trials either.

Of course, law is not the only profession that has become increasingly specialized. Scott Brewer argues:

> As scientific theories continue to become more specialized, complex, and relevant to a widening range of cases, this incoherence between normative aspiration and actual doctrinal and institutional procedure will increasingly threaten the legitimacy of nonexperts' legal decisions.[50]

Thus, there is reason for increasing concern that neither judges nor juries are well-equipped for the task of weighing expert testimonies. However, while expert advice is always beneficial, we might endanger judicial transparency – itself a valuable legal virtue – by relying on experts alone to make every decision. Without transparency, defendants may be charged and convicted of crimes in a public hearing, but be unable to understand the legal arguments leading to their conviction. As a result, it is easy to see the possibility of courtroom debate becoming the exclusive domain of legal professionals, where transparency is not achieved despite

[47] Ibid.

[48] Ibid., 1085.

[49] Ibid., 1087.

[50] S. Brewer, 'Scientific Expert Testimony and Intellectual Due Process', *Yale Law Journal* 107 (1998), 1535–1681, p. 1539.

well-publicized proceedings.[51] For this reason, G. W. F. Hegel argued that the use of non-professionals in a jury was crucial to avoid the danger that 'knowledge of right and of the course of court proceedings, as well as the ability to pursue one's rights, may become the *property* of a class which makes itself exclusive ... by the terminology it uses'.[52] Therefore the complexity of a case may not best be handled by experts alone, as if experts always agreed, unless we would be happy to sacrifice judicial transparency—which may carry even more troublesome consequences.[53]

Whatever the ultimately true facts of a case, we may worry about the jury's use of 'fictions' in order to acquit defendants who would otherwise deserve conviction. David Dorfman and Chris Iijima argue that juries often nullify 'by bringing extralegal concerns into their deliberations or by engaging in fictions about the elements of the crime or the credibility of the evidence'.[54] This echoes one of the conclusions of Harry Kalven and Hans Zeisel's well-documented, but now dated, study of American juries:

> The upshot is that when the jury reaches a different conclusion from the judge on the same evidence, it does so not because it is a sloppy or inaccurate finder of facts, but because it gives recognition to values which fall outside the official rules.[55]

The argument appears to presuppose that legal rules may often justify more than one verdict, so that in order to choose which verdict is best, we may be obliged to use extra-legal concerns such as moral

[51] A good example of professional manipulation of the legal system to the detriment of the general public might be the Republic of Ireland under British rule: see D. Johnson, 'Trial by Jury in Ireland 1860–1914', *Journal of Legislative History* 17 (1996), 270–93. In addition, Jackson and Doran argue that'[t]he gradual waning of the jury's influence has led in many common law jurisdictions including England and Wales to substantial numbers of cases being concluded on the basis of professional advice and negotiation which is not subject to any open scrutiny.' -J. Jackson and S. Doran, *Judge Without Jury: Diplock Trials in the Adversary System* (Oxford: Clarendon, 1995), 298.

[52] G. W. F. Hegel, *Elements of the Philosophy of Right*, ed. A. W. Wood, trans. H. B. Nisbet (Cambridge: Cambridge University Press, 1991), 258 [§228 Remark]. Emphasis is given. See also G. W. F. Hegel, *Lectures on Natural Right and Political Science: The First Philosophy of Right, Heidelberg 1817–1818 with Additions from the Lectures of 1818–1819*, trans. J. M. Stewart & P. C. Hodgson (Berkeley: University of California, 1995), 203–5 [§116].

[53] The possibility of losing transparency would hold even if experts were to agree.

[54] See Dorfman and Iijima, op. cit., 883.

[55] Kalven and Zeisel, op. cit., 495: see also Lord Devlin, *Trial by Jury* (London: Methuen, 1956), 153.

values. If legal rules do not lead to one verdict in every case, and yet we must reach a verdict in these cases, there does not appear to be anything particularly unconstitutional about the use of moral principles embedded in law in the absence of clear legal rules. Nor is the use of moral principles the only way in which to decide such cases.

Of course, not all concerns that critics highlight about jury trials can be acceptable, in particular regarding racist juries.[56] For example, and more commonly in the American South,[57] convictions for alleged violations of civil rights legislation were often met by jury nullification. Perhaps the judicial process is not best suited for the task of combating segregation: when rulings began to disallow segregation, many of them were unenforceable. N. W. Barber says: 'desegregation would have been better effected through statutory and executive action, which could have provided a comprehensive and enforceable solution to the problem; such a solution, however, was not immediately forthcoming'.[58] One of the problems, according to Peter Bachrach, was that the purpose of civil rights rulings and legislation 'was to change, by use of the law, ingrained behavior patterns of the community, rather than to reflect – which is the objective of the jury trial – attitudes and mores of the community'.[59] If the jury is to give expression to community standards that are racist, then jury verdicts may well be racially prejudiced, which is clearly unacceptable. Moreover, many have noted the phenomenon of African-American juries voting to acquit defendants in light of damning evidence to the contrary, most notably the acquittal of former Washington DC Mayor Marion Barry, who was caught on FBI videotape smoking cocaine.[60] In these instances, Paul Butler argues, jury nullification is a useful tool to address 'antisocial conduct', in particular racial discrimination. 'for pragmatic and political reasons, the black commu-

[56] See P. Robertshaw, 'Responding to Bias Amongst Jurors', *Journal of Criminal Law* 66 (2002), 84–95.

[57] Of course, I would not want to suggest that racist juries were absent in northern American states.

[58] N. W. Barber, 'Prelude to the Separation of Powers', *Cambridge Law Journal* 59 (2001), 59–88, p. 79.

[59] P. Bachrach, 'The Senate Debate on the Right to Jury Trial versus the Right to Vote Controversy: A Case Study in Liberal Thought', *Ethics* 68 (1958), 210–16, p. 211.

[60] P. Butler, 'Racially Based Jury Nullification: Black Power in the Criminal Justice System', *Yale Law Journal* 105 (1995), 677–725, p. 679–80.

nity is better off when some nonviolent lawbreakers remain in the community rather than go to prison'.[61]

Therefore, racial prejudice and the effects of racial discrimination may cause juries to acquit, as well as to convict, defendants who deserve to be treated otherwise. Indeed, juries can acquit or convict for any reason, as they need not offer reasons in rendering general verdicts. However, there are procedural protections against unsafe convictions for cases where no reasonable grounds for the conviction can be ascertained by an appellate court. If juries mistakenly convict a defendant, the defendant may be set free on appeal. Moreover, great care is taken in *voir dire*, at least in the US, to prevent potential jurors who have prejudicial views from sitting on juries.

These procedural protections against unsafe convictions apply equally to judges. For example, the European Court of Human Rights has argued that judges should remove themselves from cases where 'there is a legitimate reason to fear a lack of impartiality'.[62] The Court ruled that '[w]hat is at stake is the confidence which the courts must inspire in the public in a democratic society'.[63] In the US, Justice Black argued in the anti-communist trial of *Sacher v United States*[64] that 'a jury is all the more necessary to obtain a fair trial when the alleged offense relates to conduct that has personally affronted a judge'.[65]

Yet we still might complain that the guilty may be acquitted, as jury acquittals are final, due largely to long-standing precedent on the double jeopardy rule. Certainly, this is a legitimate concern. However, a judicial system with greater safeguards against unsafe conviction rather than wrongful acquittal may be the necessary product of a larger legal vision that takes seriously the presumption of innocence unless one is found guilty beyond reasonable doubt, and that holds it is better to set the guilty free than imprison the innocent.

---

[61] Ibid. Butler's claim is that sending African-Americans to prison for non-violent crimes they commit is often worse for their community than not sending them to prison: see also L. X. Do, 'Jury Nullification and Race-Conscious Reasonable Doubt: Overlapping Reifications of Commonsense Justice and the Potential Voir Dire Mistake', *UCLA Law Review* 47 (2000), 1843–83.

[62] *Piersack v Belgium*, 1 Oct 1982, Series A No. 53, 14–15, para. 30.

[63] Ibid.

[64] 343 U.S. 1 (1952).

[65] Ibid., 23. Others, such as Judith Resnik, worry that judges might lose judicial legitimacy by 'pursuing a jurisdictional vision on behalf of the federal judiciary': see J. Resnik, 'Trial as Error, Jurisdiction as Injury: Transforming the Meaning of Article III', *Harvard Law Review* 113 (2000), 924–1035, p. 932.

We might have to sacrifice this legal vision in order to address wrongful acquittals, something that we might be ill-advised to do.

Finally, there is one last issue regarding mistaken verdicts: there is an important difference between jury nullification and a jury's rendering a mistaken verdict. For example, Nancy Marder argues that it is by no means clear that juries do nullify:

> Jury nullification requires a subjective intent by the jurors to nullify, even if they do not use that exact word. Mere mistake is not nullification. Thus, if a jury misunderstand the law, misjudged the credibility of a witness, such a mistake, even if unreasonable, is not the same as nullification.[66]

Marder's point is well taken. In order to combat instances of jury nullification, opponents of the practice would have to demonstrate not only that the jury chose mistakenly, but also that it chose knowingly. Thus, if juries render perverse verdicts owing to incompetence in complex trials, we would be wrong to call these verdicts 'jury nullification'. If juries are as poor fact-finders as some critics maintain, those critics have no clear reason to oppose jury nullification as such: for it cannot occur if they are right.[67] Thus we cannot criticize juries for engaging in nullification if they render a mistaken verdict without any intention to nullify.[68]

Perverse Verdicts[69]

One major problem for critics of jury trials is the fact that, on occasion, juries decide cases differently from the way professional judges would have done, rendering so-called 'perverse verdicts'. Critics argue that when this happens, juries are effectively rewriting

[66] N. S. Marder, 'The Myth of the Nullifying Jury', *Northwestern University Law Review* 93 (1999), 877–959, p. 882.

[67] In many cases, apparent instances of jury nullification are attributed to the poor directions of judges: see *Carl Ryan Masters v Chief Constable of Sussex* [2002] E.W.C.A. Civ 1482 CA, Sir Murray Stuart Smith at para. 49.

[68] I am indebted to Peter Jones for making this observation.

[69] This section closely follows my 'The Right to Trial by Jury', *Journal of Applied Philosophy*, 21 (2004), 198–200.

the law, something neither juries nor judges should do.[70] For example, Judge R. J. O'Hanlon says that:

> it is often put forward as one of the merits of the jury system that a jury can bring about changes in the law of the land by refusing to enforce laws which appear to them to be unjust or oppressive in some way ... . What this means in reality is that the jury, having taken an oath that they will 'true verdicts give according to the evidence' have broken their oath by refusing to give effect to the law of the land. They have usurped the role of parliament which is entrusted by the people with the task of making laws which are in conformity with the will of the people. However pardonable such action on the part of the jury may be in defiance of an oppressive and autocratic regime, it is indefensible in a modern democracy where fundamental rights and freedoms are protected by the country's constitution.[71]

O'Hanlon should not suggest that judges never adjudicate in this manner. In fact, as Darbyshire notes, lay justices and judges 'are frequently criticised for their irrational and inconsistent sentencing patterns and gratuitous remarks'.[72] Indeed, in jurisdictions where the judiciary offers reasoned judgements for its decisions – such as the United States' Supreme Court – it has been observed that politics is 'inherent in the judicial process'.[73] Hence, this "problem" of judicial decisions failing to apply relevant laws is not unique to activist juries.

[70] Penny Darbyshire argues: '[w]hat business have the jury to be rewriting the law? ... [t]he jury is an anti-democratic, irrational and haphazard legislator, whose erratic and secret decisions run counter to the rule of law.'-P. Darbyshire, 'The Lamp That Shows That Freedom Lives—Is It Worth the Candle?' *Criminal Law Review* (1991), 740–52, p. 750. See also R. St. John, 'License to Nullify: The Democratic and Constitutional Deficiencies of Authorised Jury Lawmaking', *Yale Law Journal* 106 (1997), 2563–97, p. 2579.

[71] R. J. O'Hanlon, 'The Sacred Cow of Trial by Jury', *Irish Jurist* 25/27 (1990/1992), 57–68, p. 68. See also Blom-Cooper, op. cit., 6: 'There can be no room for what the jury perceives to be an oppressive law, and to decline to apply it'.

[72] Darbyshire, op. cit., 751; Scalia, op. cit., 1178.

[73] See E. Lazarus, *Closed Chambers: The Rise, Fall, and Future of the Modern Supreme Court* (Harmondsworth: Penguin, 1999) and K. O'Connor, 'The Supreme Court and the South', *Journal of Politics* 63 (2001), 701–16, p. 702.

Nevertheless, the idea that the court's function is to apply, not create, the law is popular in both civil and common law jurisdictions.[74] In civil law jurisdictions such as France and Germany, there is not a strict doctrine of precedent: the law can be applied with some variation in identical cases by the courts.[75] The argument is that the creation of judicial precedent effectively creates new laws. For example, abortion was made legal in all fifty American states not by legislative mandate, but by the high court decision *Roe v Wade*.[76] Thus the use of judicial precedent may in effect 'make new laws', although it is important to note the fact that the decisions of juries do not offer any precedent.

What justifies the right of juries to refuse to adjudicate according to laws that might appear unjustified to them? Critics charge that both judges and juries should always apply the relevant case law without reservation. This is a gross misunderstanding of the judiciary's role, which is to determine the applicability of law.[77] For example, consider the relationship between a national legislature and a local government. We might attempt to plot this relationship on a linear scale: on one side is the national legislature, whose laws have universal scope; on the other side is the local government, which can legislate only for a particular locality and at the discretion of the national government. Both legislative bodies have the ability to legislate. The difference is that the scope of one is far wider than that of the other.

Judicial courts might be thought of similarly. On one end of the scale might lie the constitutional courts; on the other, criminal courts such as those that employ juries. Both judicial bodies have the ability to adjudicate. For instance, constitutional courts do not have the

[74] German philosophers such as Fichte and Hegel even questioned whether the judiciary could ever be independently separate from other governmental branches of power: if the executive's duty is to apply universal laws approved by the legislature in particular cases, then the judiciary is best seen as part of the executive. See J. G. Fichte, *Foundations of Natural Right According to the Principles of the Wissenschaftslehre*, ed. F. Neuhouser, trans. M. Bauer (Cambridge: Cambridge University Press, 2000), 142–43 [§16:161–62] and G. W. F. Hegel, *Elements of the Philosophy of Right* op. cit., 308 [§273], 328 [§287], and 330 [§290 Addition].

[75] This is not to say that the system suffers from irrationality, as lower courts do tend to follow decisions of higher courts. Nor would it be true to say that detailed judgements with full statements of statutory and judicial authority for decision are not given: see R. Youngs, *English, French and German Comparative Law* (London: Cavendish 1998), 51–3.

[76] 410 U.S. 113 (1973).

[77] Barber, op. cit., 60.

power to make new laws or even to enforce laws. On the contrary, they have only the power to declare whether or not certain legislation ought to be recognised (i.e., whether it is constitutional). In this manner, the judiciary acts as a check on the executive and legislative branches, by prescribing their scope of power.[78] Constitutional courts have the ability to nullify or uphold universally any law. Jury courts have similar powers with much less scope. As judicial bodies, juries have the right to adjudicate. Similarly to the role of local government in the legislative branch, the jury's power extends to its particular jurisdiction only. For a jury, this jurisdiction is the particular trial which confronts them.

If we were to argue that juries lack a right to determine the applicability of laws limited to their particular cases, this bottom tier of the judiciary would lack the ability to function as a part of the judiciary. Indeed, we have no similar expectations with other branches: we accept the right of local government to make laws limited in scope and local police to enforce law and order in their communities. Thus, juries in no instance can be said to usurp power from the legislature. Juries can do only what all judicial bodies are entitled to do: determine the applicability of the law. The difference between the constitutional court and the jury is that the former determines the law's applicability in *all* cases; while the jury determines applicability in the *particular* case they have been selected for.[79] It is therefore highly significant to recognise the fact that the decisions of juries carry no precedent – as their powers to adjudicate are limited to a single case – whereas higher court decisions do carry precedent – as their powers have wider scope.[80]

[78] One consequence is that juries serve as a popular check on the legislative and executive branches. Of course, democratic citizens have the ability to extend accountability to politicians, but the citizenry may do so only generally, either for or against a candidate. Citizens largely lack a means of having an influence on particular legislation (especially if not high profile). Juries are best suited for democratic citizens having a say on particular laws normally beyond their grasp. In this sense, juries expand democratic checks and balances.

[79] See A. Norrie, 'From Criminal Law to Legal Theory: The Mysterious Case of the Reasonable Glue Sniffer', *Modern Law Review* 65 (2002), 538–55, p. 538.

[80] T. R. S. Allan argues that '[t]here is therefore scope for the jury to take account of justice and morality in reaching its verdict, even if in doing so it departs to some extent from the judge's interpretation of the applicable law'.-*Law, Liberty, and Justice: The Legal Foundations of British Constitutionalism* (Oxford: Clarendon, 1993), 118.

More importantly, opponents of jury nullification are wrong to claim that nullification may undermine both the rule of law[81] and democracy by 'thwarting the will of the legislature'[82] because the decision of how best to apply particular laws in criminal trials is not legislative at all.[83] Indeed, Dorfman and Iijima argue that '[a] jury's decision to allow a lawbreaker to go free does not compromise the integrity of the rule of law any more than the decision of an individual police officer or prosecutor not to arrest or prosecute a lawbreaker prior to trial'.[84] Furthermore, M. B. E. Smith is right to say that '[n]ullification suspends intact some part of the law that applies to a particular case; it leaves that law unchanged'.[85]

The Problem of Damages

While this article has defended the use of general verdicts and the competence of juries to ascertain facts, and argued that nullification does not amount to legislating, a special problem remains: the awarding of excessive damages by juries. Some legal theorists call this phenomenon 'the libel lottery'.[86] Supporting examples are numerous. In England, a jury awarded a well-known football player £85,000 in a libel suit relating to the player's part in match-fixing. On appeal, the award for damages was slashed to just £1.[87] Sonia Sutcliffe, the wife of the Yorkshire Ripper, was awarded £600,000 against *Private Eye*: it was later reduced to on appeal £60,000. Several similar cases exist in the US as well.

---

[81] Ibid., 2564.

[82] Blom-Cooper, op. cit., 6.

[83] See Dorfman and Iijima, op. cit., 895. Enright and Morton claim that 'although every juror is required to swear or affirm to give "a true verdict according to the evidence", this has never been what society has wanted or expected from juries. If this were all that were required, then the professional tribunal, a judge or judges, magistrates both lay and professional would all provide a cheaper, better fact-finding body and, for the authorities, a more reliable forum.'-Enright and Morton, op. cit., 124.

[84] See Dorfman and Iijima, op. cit., 896.

[85] M. B. E. Smith, 'May Judges Ever Nullify the Law?' *Notre Dame Law Review* 74 (1999), 1657–71, pp. 1658–59.

[86] See P. March, 'The End of the Libel Lottery', *Entertainment Law Review* 9 (1998), 222–26.

[87] *Grobbelaar v News Group Newspapers Ltd* [2002] U.K.H.L. 40.

The complaint commonly made of jury monetary rewards is that they are often inconsistent, unpredictable and (on occasion) excessive.[88] However, there may well be good reasons for this well-known problem. For example, the Supreme Court of Missouri has said:

> One of the most difficult decisions facing the jury in a personal injury action is to decide the amount of monetary award, if any, that the plaintiff is entitled to be awarded as compensation for past, present and future pain and suffering. The measure of pain and suffering ... is and has been what is fair and reasonable. There is no fixed measure, table or standard which the jury can use as an accurate index to establish an award of damages. No method is available to the jury by which it can objectively evaluate such damages. From time immemorial, the judicial measure of damages for pain and suffering has been fair and reasonable compensation.[89]

It might seem to follow that judges would be better equipped to assign monetary rewards more consistently and predictably, as they would most likely be involved in several cases. Of course, if there were some guide juries could consider in awarding damages, the problem of 'the libel lottery' might be solved. Juries could choose to ignore these guidelines; but, if they did, their monetary award could be changed by an appellate court, as has in fact happened. Indeed, guidelines could help the jury gain a better understanding of what a 'fair and reasonable compensation' may be. This is not to say that caps on monetary awards are justified: legal theorists have come to see the importance of being able to account for the distinct nuances of each case.[90] Indeed, if someone were to have lost tangible earnings due to libel, it might be uncontroversial to argue these earnings are due to her by the libelling party. In such circumstances, it could be argued that an injustice is done in capping awards if persons are prevented from being awarded the full monies due to them. It may well be strange that juries receive instructional guidelines on relevant considerations for determining whether or not there was a criminal (or civil) violation, but no guidelines on relevant considerations for determining damages. However, there seems no good reason why instruction on compensation cannot be given to juries.

[88] See C. Chejfec, 'Tort Reform in the United States: A State by State Review', *International Insurance Law Review* 4 (1996), 74–85, p. 77.

[89] *Graeff v Baptist Temple of Springfield*, 576 SW 2d 291, 301–302 (Mo. 1978).

[90] W. P. Keeton, 'Introduction to Symposium on Developments in Tort Law and Tort Reform', *St. Mary's Law Journal* 18 (1987), 669–72.

Some legal theorists, such as Paul Mogin, argue that only judges should set any punitive damages.[91] It is true that the jury's determination of punitive, as opposed to purely monetary, damages has been less of a problem.[92] It is a curiosity, though, that juries have been thought to be best suited to the task of determining the most severe penalty, capital punishment. Nevertheless, those who argue that only judges should set punitive damages point to the use of bifurcation in capital trials, but neglect the central role of the jury in determining the 'damages', namely, whether or not there should be an acquittal, a life sentence, or a death sentence. In *Ring v Arizona*,[93] the Court argued that the right to trial by jury was a right of defendants to have their punishment decided by a jury, rather than by the judge, at the original trial.[94] The Court has said: '[w]e cannot believe that it is wise or expedient to place the life or liberty of any person accused of crime, even by his own consent, at the disposal of any one man ... so long as man is a fallible being'.[95] If the Court is justified in holding such a view, it seems rather strange that we should trust only juries to impose the most extreme punishment in American law, yet not trust them with penalties far less severe than the life and death of an individual. This difficulty needs to be addressed before we end the jury's right to determine damages. However, first there should be an attempt to draw up guidelines on compensation for juries to consider when determining monetary damages.

Conclusion

In this article, I have tried to defend jury nullification on several grounds: the preferability of general verdicts to special verdicts; the competence of juries to ascertain facts commensurable, if not

[91] P. Mogin, 'Why Judges, Not Juries, Should Set Punitive Damages', *University of Chicago Law Review* 65 (1998), 179–224, p. 179.

[92] See *Cumber v Chief Constable of Hampshire* [1995] 92(8) L.S.G. 39 Times, January 28, 1995; *Timmerman v Schroeder*, 454 P. 2d 522, 525 (Kan. 1969). Also see E. Buckett, 'Civil Actions Against the Police', *Journal of Personal Injury Law* 3 (2002), 241–45; D. Tausz and D. C. Ormerod, 'Aggravated Trespass: Damage to Crops', *Criminal Law Review* (2002), 128–9.

[93] 2002 WL 1357257.

[94] Ibid. (Ginsburg, J.).

[95] *State v Worden*, 46 Conn. 349, 367 (1878).

preferable, to that of judges; the right of the judiciary to adjudicate; that jury nullification does not amount to legislating; and that the problem of excessive monetary awards can best be addressed by issuing general guidelines rather than by handing this duty over to judges.

One last line of defence remains. No one disputes the fact that juries help to promote the legitimacy of verdicts. Ian Dennis says:

> The jury secures legitimacy of conviction, not only by deciding that the defendant is in fact guilty of the offence charged, but also by certifying, as the constitutional representatives of the community, that he is properly to be blamed and punished for breach of a criminal prohibition that ought to be observed.[96]

The claim is not only that justice must be done, but also that it must be manifestly seen to be done.[97] By and large, juries accomplish this task perfectly well. While it might not be one's favoured defence of jury nullification, a defender may be right to claim that occasional perverse and mistaken verdicts are a price well worth paying if it secures the public's faith in the justice system and, especially, in the punishment of its members.[98]

In *A Theory of Justice*, John Rawls calls the 'judicial virtues' of impartiality and considerateness 'the excellences of intellect and sensibility'.[99] If he is right, we should not try to curtail or eliminate the power of juries to nullify the law. Provided juries continue to be instructed on matters of law by judges, 'intellect' and common

[96] Dennis, op. cit., 2.

[97] *R v Sussex Justices, ex parte McCarthy* [1924] 1 KB 256 *per* Lord Hewart CJ: 'a long line of cases shows that it is not merely of some importance but is of fundamental importance that justice should not only be done, but should manifestly and undoubtedly be seen to be done': see *DeCubber v Belgium* [26 October 1984, Series A, 1986]; N. Blake, 'The Case for the Jury', in eds. M. Findlay and P. Duff, *The Jury Under Attack* (London: Butterworths 1988), 140–60, at 143.

[98] H. L. A. Hart seems to be favourable to this position. He says: 'Bentham thought it most important that punishment should be "unpopular" and, though he did not rest his *rationale* for the admission of excuses on the grounds suggested here, was of the opinion that the satisfaction given by punishment of offenders to the public was an element to be taken into account in assessing its utility.' -*Punishment and Responsibility: Essays in the Philosophy of Law* (Oxford: Oxford University Press, 1968), 240.

[99] John Rawls, *A Theory of Justice* (Cambridge: Harvard University Press, 1971), 517.

'sensibility' may be best brought together by allowing the flourishing of judicial virtue.[100]

Department of Politics
University of Newcastle
Newcastle upon Tyne NE1 7RU
UK
E-mail: t.brooks@newcastle.ac.uk

[100] Previous versions of this article were presented at the Association for Legal and Social Philosophy conference at the University of Newcastle; the European Ethics Summit at the European Union Parliament in Brussels, Belgium; the Ockham Society at the University of Oxford; the Philosophy Society at the University of Sheffield; and the Senior Postgraduate Seminar at the University of Sheffield. I am most grateful to Brenda Almond, Reza Banakar, Chris Bennett, Stephan Blatti, Meagan Brooks, Roger Cotterrell, Fabian Freyenhagen, Andrew Howatt, David Liggins, Matt Matravers, Joe Morrison, James Penner, Jenny Szende, and, especially, Antony Duff, Penny Darbyshire, Peter Jones, and anonymous referees for this journal for their very helpful comments on earlier drafts.

Part IV
Trial Reform

[8]

The Lamp That Shows That Freedom Lives—Is it Worth the Candle?

By Penny Darbyshire

Kingston Law School

Summary: *My aim is to question the traditional justifications used in praise and defence of the jury, suggesting that some of them are conceptually unsound. I argue that jury defenders inflate the jury's importance by portraying the "right" to jury trial as central to the criminal justice system and as a guardian of due process and civil liberties.*

In this paper, I hope to examine some of the commonly held beliefs and assumptions which underlie traditional and oft-repeated adulation of jury trial. I take as my starting point Ashworth's 1979 plea on the criminal justice system that we "should devote some time to reflection on the theory behind it all."[1] Theory, says Ashworth, "is essential, because social and legal arrangements—especially in so sensitive an area as criminal justice—need to be *justified* if they are to be acceptable." Ashworth suggests, and I accept for the purposes of this paper, that the general justifying aim of the administration of criminal justice is that the guilty should be detected, convicted and duly sentenced, which he calls, for convenience, "crime control."

The jury has probably provoked more comment and research than any other component of the criminal justice system. It seems to attract the most praise and least theoretical analysis. There is a wealth of material on the common law jury, predominantly American, English and Australian, and defenders of the jury seem to outnumber its opponents by about a hundred to one. There are few notable works which make a serious attempt to analyse the basis of the jury: Bankowski and Mungham[2]; Freeman[3]; Duff and Findlay[4] and Bankowski.[5]

Everyone seems to have an opinion on the jury and few are indifferent. It is as much the territory of the journalist, the politician, the pressure group and the lay person as it is of the lawyer or the academic. This is as it should be and hardly surprising, considering its very essence as a powerfully symbolic lay element in the criminal justice system. Juries, as Baldwin and McConville observe,[6] provoke comments which are little short of hysterical. The academic owes it to the rest, however, to be a little more analytical and to justify her or his assertions.

---

[1] Ashworth, A.J., "Concepts of Criminal Justice," [1979] Crim.L.R. 412, at p.412.

[2] Bankowski, Z. and Mungham, G., "The Jury as Process," in Carlen, P., ed., *The Sociology of Law*, 1976.

[3] Freeman, M.D.A., "The Jury on Trial," [1981] C.L.P. 65.

[4] Duff, P. and Findlay, M., "The Jury in England: Practice and Ideology," (1982) 10 I.J.L.S. 253.

[5] Bankowski, Z., "The Jury and Reality," in Findlay, M. and Duff, P., *The Jury Under Attack*, 1988.

[6] Baldwin, J. and McConville, M., *Jury Trials*, 1979, at p.1.

The English legal system has traditionally been characterised by smug complacency amongst lawyers, politicians and lay people alike. We seldom feel the need to justify our institutions, in the way required by Ashworth. Knowing that our legal system has been copied by newer anglophone countries, we assume that it must be a sound model. We have heard propaganda, since childhood, that our legal system is the best in the world, the epitome of the due process model.

Such complacency has allowed our legal system to remain virtually static between the Judicature Acts of the 1870s and the sweeping reforms 1980s and 1990s, with minor disturbances such as the introduction of juvenile courts and the C.P.S. When we do examine our legal system, via Royal Commissions, review boards, working parties and the like, we tend to focus on existing institutions and to examine the part and not the whole. Most proposals for change, this century, have been shelved or rejected. The Civil Justice Review was quite revolutionary in its breadth, its depth and it success rate. Moreover, it was shockingly heretical in asking whether we really need two levels of trial court and on what basis we can justify dividing the work between them. One can only hope that this pattern is repeated by the new Royal Commission on Criminal Justice.

The Commission must ask the parallel questions of why we have two levels of criminal trial court and whether we are justified, in the sense Ashworth demands, in retaining three sets of decision makers within them: lay magistrates, advised mostly by non-lawyers; stipendiary magistrates, advised mostly by lawyers; and the judge and jury. There is little legal logic or design in the division of their jurisdictions. They have simply evolved through the last 10 centuries or more.

If the jury is such a "palladium" of English justice (Blackstone[7]), why is it reserved for such a small number of cases, most defendants being treated to the quicker, cheaper, less flamboyant "trivial"[8] justice of the magistrates' court? If the jury is such a guardian of our liberties and of justice, are we implying that magistrates dispense some lesser form of justice? Are we implying, since we invest so much cash and rhetoric in the jury system, that it is more likely to do justice and get the verdict right, whatever that means, than the magistrates? If so, why do we, in this, the fairest of legal systems, allow most of our defendants to be processed by the magistrates' courts? And, this being the case, why have academics invested so much argument and research into the jury?

There is one obvious answer to my questions here. The symbolic function of the jury far outweighs its practical significance. I shall argue in this paper that this sentimental attachment to the symbol of the jury is dangerous. Adulation of the jury is based on no justification or spurious justification. It has fed public complacency with the English legal system and distracted attention from its evils: a systematic lack of due process pre-trial and post-trial and certain deficiencies in the trial process itself. It has distorted the truth. The truth is that for most people who pass through the criminal justice system this palladium is simply not available and for those who can and do submit themselves to its verdict, it will not necessarily safeguard their civil liberties.

[7] Blackstone, W., *Commentaries*, Vol. IV, 1776, at p.349.
[8] McBarnet, D., *Conviction*, 1981.

A "Constitutional Right" to jury trial

This justification for the jury is perhaps the best known and the most often served up without explanation, as a self-evident truth. Three problems arise under this heading:

a. the supposed guarantee of a right to jury trial in Magna Carta;
b. what is meant by a *constitutional* right to jury trial in the English legal system; and
c. what is meant, in jurisprudential terms, by asserting that there is a *right* to jury trial.

a. Magna Carta

Many writers claim that jury trial was enshrined as a constitutional right in Magna Carta, 1215, clause 39, which provided for a "trial by peers."[9] Later authors undoubtedly derived this myth from Devlin, who perpetuated it in 1956, having taken it from Blackstone's *Commentaries*.[10]

Whilst Blackstone's grandiloquent account of the English legal system in the eighteenth century is of great entertainment value, few later legal historians or constitutional lawyers would accept it as historically accurate. Some of his assertions have been used to quite an alarming extent, however, in establishing the constitutional foundations of newer common law jurisdictions.

The famous clause 39 of Magna Carta reads:

> "*Nullus liber homo capiatur vel imprisonetur, aut disseisiatur aut utlagetur, aut exuletur, aut aliquo modo destruatur, nec super eum ibimus nec super eum mittemus, nisi per legale judicium parium vel per legum terrae.*"

which Holdsworth[11] translates as:

> "No freeman shall be taken or/and imprisoned, or disseised, or exiled, or in any way destroyed, nor will we go upon him nor will we send upon him, except by the lawful judgment of his peers or/and by the law of the land."

Legal historians have been at pains to point out that clause 39 has nothing to do with trial by jury and, as Cornish said,[12] "It has always been bad history to trace the system back to Magna Carta." Holdsworth acknowledges that the misinterpretation of clause 39 has had sweeping effects on English constitutional history but explains:

> " . . . it is also clear that the words *judicium parium* do not refer to trial by jury. A trial by a royal judge and a body of recognitors was exactly what the barons did not want. What they did want was firstly a tribunal of the old type in which all the suitors were judges of both law and fact, and secondly a tribunal in which they would not be judged by their inferiors. Some of

---

[9] *e.g.* Devlin, P., *Trial By Jury*, 1956, at p.164 and Blake, N., "The Case For The Jury"; Brown, D. and Neal, D., "Show Trials: The Media and the Gang of Twelve"; Frieberg, A., "Jury Selection in Trials of Commonwealth Offences," all in Findlay and Duff, 1988, *op. cit.*

[10] *loc. cit.*

[11] Holdsworth, W., *A History of English Law*, Vol. 1, 1903, 7th ed., 1956, at p.59.

[12] Cornish, W.R., *The Jury*, 1968, at p.12.

> them did not consider that the royal judge, none of them would have considered that a body of recognitors, were their peers."

Earlier, in his *History of Trial By Jury*,[13] Forsyth had said that it was a common but erroneous opinion that *judicium parium* or trial by one's peers had reference to the jury and had misled many, including Blackstone. He explains that *judicium* implies the decision of a judge, not a jury verdict. I would add that it is crucial to remember that, in 1215, the jury was still a group of oathswearing witnesses, or compurgators. They did not pronounce judgment. The *pares*, suggests Forsyth, were:

> "members of the county and other courts, who discharged the function of judges, and who were the peers or fellows of the parties before them."[14]

As these and other historians have pointed out, by Magna Carta the barons simply sought to secure a deal from King John, within which they safeguarded their right to be judged by judges of no lesser rank then themselves. *Liber homo* has been translated as either "freeman" or "freeholder" and "freeman" did not mean what it does today. As we should remember from school history, freemen were a limited class in the feudal system.

b. A constitutional right?

Even if one were to concede that it has become a constitutional convention, since the fourteenth century, when statute prescribed that jurors be independent, that juries be used in certain criminal trials, I balk at the concept of trial by jury's being "more than one wheel of the constitution."[15] Devlin and others speak as if there were an entrenched right to jury trial, as there is in the United States Constitution or the Canadian Bill or Rights. The concept of a "constitutional right" has, historically, been so alien to British constitutional lawyers, that the phrase seldom appeared in textbooks before the 1980s and now it only appears in the context of the debate over the need for a Bill of Rights. Indeed, the call for a Bill of Rights has arisen for this very reason: the sovereignty of parliament dictates that we do not have any entrenched rights, especially in issues beyond the grasp of EC or international law. This is manifest in relation to jury trial. Parliament has almost rendered the civil jury extinct and has continually eroded the use and availability of the jury in the criminal trial.

c. A right?

There is a also a jurisprudential problem with those who justify the use of jury trial as a right. The term "right," at least to "will" theorists, implies a choice. When we speak of procedural rights in the criminal justice system, we imply a choice. For example, I do not have to exercise my right of silence, Similarly, if I am charged with an offence which is triable either way, I can choose to be tried by judge and jury or magistrates. This choice can properly be called a "right" to jury trial. What of indictable offences? Here, I must appear before the Crown

---

13 1852, at p.108.
14 *op. cit.*, at p.110.
15 Devlin, *op. cit.*, at p.164.

Court, where my only choice is as to plea. My only right is as to trial. I cannot choose to be tried by judge alone, as I could in the United States. Thus, it is correct to speak of a "right to jury trial" in the United States but not to speak of jury trial's being a "right," in general terms, in the English legal system, as so many defenders of the jury are wont to do.[16]

By reasoning thus, I am accepting that the essence of a right must be a power of waiver. MacCormick[17] would take issue with this and argue that restricting my power of waiver does not negate my right. To this, I would repeat Simmonds' reply "It is doubtful if paternalism of this kind is best interpreted as a protection of the party's rights."[18]

Not only does the concept of a right to jury trial in indictable offences fail to accord with "will" theories of rights, it also fails to satisfy classical "interest" theories of rights and I would extend my argument here to include triable either way offences. According to interest theories, as I would apply them here, jury trial can only be described as a "right" if the intended beneficiary of the court's duty to provide that right is the defendant. If the purpose of jury trial is primarily ideological, as I argue here, as a symbol to legitimate the criminal justice system, then the defendant is the unintended beneficiary and thus cannot be said to have real right to jury trial.

"Trial By Peers": random or representative or selected by "Voir Dire"?

My next objection is to the jury protagonists' lack of clarity over what virtues they are celebrating in the composition of "trial by peers." A similar point has been raised before, by Marshall[19] and Duff and Findlay,[20] but bears repeating, since it seems to have been ignored. Frequently, randomness is treated as a synonym for representativeness and some even fail to recognise that any form of *voir dire* is incompatible with the other two concepts. This problem is faced by Enright and Morton[21] and Gobert[22] and touched on but not tackled by Bankowski. While I will accept that a random jury can be said to represent the community in the most abstract sense, many writers assume random selection will, magically, throw up a representative cross section of the population, reflecting the views of the community at large. For example, Frieberg,[23] says:

> "The legitimacy of the jury's role depends upon a strict adherence to some basic tenets of jury selection procedures, principally random selection and impartiality. A key factor in ensuring the jury's impartiality is its representativeness. The aim of jury selection is to create a jury of one's peers."

The conceptual confusion here is quite breathtaking. Indeed, Frieberg cites the Departmental Committee on Jury Service (1965), making the same mistake: "A

---

[16] For example, Enright, S. and Morton, J., *Taking Liberties: The Criminal Jury In The 1990s*, 1990, dust-jacket.
[17] As paraphrased by Simmonds, *infra*.
[18] Simmonds, N.E., *Central Issues In Jurisprudence*, 1986, at p.138.
[19] Marshall, G., "The Judgment of One's Peers," in *The British Jury System*, 1975, at p.5.
[20] 1982, *op. cit.*
[21] 1990, *op. cit.*
[22] Gobert, J.J., "The Peremptory Challenge—An Obituary," [1989] Crim.L.R. 528.
[23] *op. cit.*, at p.133.

jury should represent a cross-section drawn at random from the community . . ."

Random selection from the community is unlikely to produce a cross-section, unless some form of stratified sampling is used, which is not the case in summoning a jury. Random selection may throw up juries which are all male, all Conservative, all white.

As to my second point, many civil libertarians hail the right to a randomly selected jury as part of our constitutional heritage and in this notion ground their objections to vetting by the prosecution.[24] Many of these see nothing incompatible in also arguing for defence rights of challenge to be strengthened.

Apart from these problems, civil libertarian claims to a right to trial by random jury is historically and factually inaccurate. Property qualifications were only abolished in 1972, before which jurors were all householders, mostly male. Many assert that "the law" prescribes random selection. For instance, Thompson[25]: "That is the common understanding of the common law of this land." There is no case authority for this notion. Many rely on the Lord Chief Justice's 1973 Practice Direction, declaring "A jury consists of 12 individuals chosen at random . . . "[26] but Practice Directions are not "the law." Indeed, the key statute on jury composition is the Juries Act 1974, which makes no mention of randomness and provides for its very antithesis, its schedules excluding long lists of the ineligible, the disqualified and the excusable.

Furthermore, different practices of local summoning officers in excusing summoned jurors further distorts jury randomness or representativeness, as Baldwin and McConville found.[27] Moreover, "self-deselection" of unwilling jurors from the panel exacerbates this distortion.[28] The truth is that juries are far from being either a random or a representative section of the population.

An injection of democracy into the legal system

"Each jury is a little parliament," says Devlin[29] and cites Blackstone in support. He celebrates and justifies the jury, along with so many others, as a symbol of participatory democracy. This symbolism has been analysed and defended most carefully by Bankowski and Mungham[30]; Freeman[31] and Bankowski.[32]

One element of this notion is that lay involvement in the legal system gives people confidence in its fairness, especially if they are personally involved. As Cornish said[33]:

---

[24] Thompson, E.P., "The State Versus Its Enemies," 1978, *New Society* 127: Harman, H. and Griffith, J.A.G., *Justice Deserted*, 1979; Lord Denning in *R.* v. *Crown Court at Sheffield, ex parte Brownlow* [1980] 2 All E.R. 444, at p.453; East, R., "Jury Packing: A Thing of the Past?" 48 M.L.R. 520 (1985) and several writers in Findlay and Duff, 1988.

[25] *op. cit.*

[26] (1973) 57 Cr.App.R. 345.

[27] *op. cit.*, Chap. 6.

[28] I explore this point at length in Darbyshire, P., "Notes of A Lawyer Juror," [1990] N.L.J. 1264.

[29] *op. cit.*, at p.164.

[30] *op. cit.*

[31] *op. cit.*

[32] *op. cit.*

[33] *op. cit.*, at p.255.

> " . . . the system has the intrinsic advantage that in drawing upon a steady stream of ordinary citizens it is not only educating them in the work of the courts, but also, since they are generally satisfied with their own performance, sending them back to their ordinary lives with a sense of the fairness and propriety of the judicial process in this country."

and McEldowney goes as far as to claim: "jury service has now become a citizen's right as well as his duty."[34] This kind of romaticism is quite devoid of constitutional or jurisprudential support. The power of the symbolism of participatory democracy is, however, highly significant. It underlies most pro-jury polemic produced by lawyers, academics, civil libertarians, politicians and public alike. As Cornish says:

> "It would certainly be foolish to dismiss too hastily the obvious fact that a great many people simply *believe* in the jury system."[35]

If jurors' personal accounts are to be believed, however, many people strain to avoid jury service and, of those who do not, many are bored, resentful and generally disillusioned by their experience.[36]

Most of the those who justify the jury as the quintessence of lay participation in a lawyers' paradise ignore the massive involvement of lay people in decision making in the English legal system. Devlin and Blackstone argue as if democracy would collapse into tyranny if we were to abolish "this sacred bulwark of our nation" (Blackstone) and "the lamp that shows that freedom lives" (Devlin). Modern repitition of these sentiments either ignores the part played by over 28,000 lay justices in our criminal justice system, or disregards them as part of the legal establishment. Blackstone clearly viewed them as such, in the eighteenth century. While I would concede that the twentieth century lay justices are not representative of the community as a whole,[37] I would point out that neither is the jury, as I have argued above.

I couple these objections with the observation that the jury's symbolic significance is magnified beyond its practical significance by the media, as well as academics, thus unwittingly misleading the public. Of criminal cases, about 5 per cent. are dealt with by the Crown Court. Of those cases, over two thirds are resolved in a guilty plea,[38] leaving just under 2 per cent. to be tried by jury.

Yet, so powerful is the symbol of jury trial that the public image of a criminal trial is surely a Crown Court trial, complete with wigs, gowns, a red judge and Rumpole in defence: a dramatic portrayal repeated on news items which so often focus on the swing doors of the Old Bailey. In contrast, the "trivial" activities of the magistrates' courts seldom make the national news, yet it is to the jus-

---

[34] McEldowney, J.F., " 'Stand By For The Crown': An Historical Analysis," [1979] Crim.L.R. 272.

[35] *op. cit.*, at p.254.

[36] For an exploration of this point, see Darbyshire. *op. cit.*

[37] See Baldwin, J., "The Social Composition of The Magistracy," (1976) 28 Brit. J. Criminol. 171; Burney, E., J.P.: *Magistrate, Court and Community*, 1979; King, M., and May, C., *Black Magistrates*, 1985.

[38] See the Annual Judicial Statistics and Zander, M., "What the Annual Statistics Tell Us About Pleas and Acquittals," [1991] Crim.L.R. 252.

tice of the magistrates that most people will, or must, submit, should they be charged with a criminal offence.

Jury equity: our defence against state power

Justifications for the jury under this heading are so often recited that their sources are too many to mention, but among them are Blackstone, Devlin, Thompson, Harman and Griffith, Bankowski and Mungham and most writers in Findlay and Duff. There are several ideas here:

a. that in "State" trials, the jury will acquit where it sees the defendant has been prosecuted unfairly;
b. that the jury will acquit in ordinary cases, where it considers the prosecution unfair or the law to be unpopular, or sympathises with the defendant;
c. that in doing either of these things, if may disobey the law and apply its own equity, thus acting as a democratic brake on the State.

Much of the pro-jury polemic eulogises the jury for departing from the law. For instance, Kalven and Zeisel said:

> "It represents also an impressive way of building discretion, equity and flexibility into a legal system. Not the least of the advantages is that the jury, relieved of the burdens of creating precedent, can bend the law without breaking it.
> Whether or not one comes to admire the jury system as much as we have, it must rank as a daring effort in human arrangement to work out a solution to the tensions between law and equity and anarchy."[39]

Presented with this image of the plucky little jury battling it out on our behalf against the all powerful State, who can fail to share the civil libertarian outrage when the jury is vetted or statute removes more offences from the ambit of jury trial? This imagery does not, however, bear close scrutiny.

a. "State" trials

This justification has been examined and found waiting by Williams[40] and Cornish,[41] who cited many such trials where the jury convicted. For all those who now cite the acquittal of Clive Ponting, I would remind them of the so called Winchester Three, the Guildford Four, the Maguires and the Birmingham Six. In these last three, the police were clearly over-anxious to secure convictions, to be seen to be satisfying the clamour for crime control from an outraged British public. They appear to have ignored many of the (weak) safeguards of due process provided for the defendants at the pre-trial stage, and to have fabricated evidence and extracted false confessions. The juries were not to be blamed for these wrongful convictions but they failed to remedy the lack of due process at the pre-trial stage and thus did not provide the break on oppress-

[39] Kalven, H. and Zeisel, H., "The American Jury," (1966) *New Society* 290.
[40] Williams, G., *The Proof of Guilt*, 3rd. ed., 1963.
[41] *op. cit.*

ive state activity claimed for the jury by its defenders. Devlin's "lamp that shows that freedom lives" did not offer a glimmer of hope to these defendants.

b. Unfair laws/oppressive prosecutions

Defences of the jury under this heading usually emphasise the examples of juries re-writing the law to suit the defence. Writers conveniently disregard or underrate the fact that jury equity is a double-edged sword which may also convict the innocent. For instance, Freeman[42] and Bankowski[43] cite McCabe and Purves'[44] example of a hot-dog salesman, acquitted of wounding on the illegitimate ground of provocation, presumably by a sympathetic jury. Freeman concludes:

> "What they were saying was that provocation ought to be a defence not merely to charges of murder and in saying this they would have the support of the bulk of the population."

I have two objections to this. First, in the absence of a reasoned decision, how do we know whether juries acquit out of sympathy or for some extraneous reason? Secondly, the argument ignores the potential for wrongful convictions in allowing the jury to re-write the law.

Baldwin and McConville[45] found little evidence of this romantic notion of jury equity. Unexpected verdicts apparently occurred at random. Personal accounts of ex-jurors indicate that they will sometimes acquit or convict, for a variety of extraneous reasons which have nothing to do with replacing the law with their own sense of fairness or equity. They include the pressure of incarceration in the jury room and the replacement of the high standard of proof "beyond reasonable doubt" with a lesser standard of proof "on the balance of probabilities."[46]

Jurors also sometimes base their decisions on sympathy or hostility towards other trial participants, notably counsel and witnesses, as indicated by the accounts in Barber and Gordon's book[47] and elsewhere. To illustrate this, I will counter the story of the hot-dog salesman with a story of my own. I sent my new first year law students out to watch courts of their own choice. They were asked to report back to tutorials but to no set structure. Several groups gave me different accounts of the same case which had taken their fancy because of the dramatic content and the surprising result.

A shop assistant was charged with theft of 20 items of clothing from her employers. She did not deny that she had ripped off the price labels, hidden the clothes in a bag in a cupboard and then taken them home and gone abroad for a fortnight's holiday. Her defence was that she had taken the bag home by accident and had meant to pay for the clothes. When she discovered her error, she had panicked and gone away on holiday. The students thought defence counsel's performance was "brilliant" and they had noted (and some had learned) some

[42] *op. cit.*
[43] *op. cit.*
[44] McCabe, S. and Purves, R., *The Jury At Work*, 1972.
[45] *op. cit.*
[46] See Darbyshire, P., *op. cit.*
[47] Barber, D., and Gordon, G., *Members of the Jury*, 1976.

of his tear-jerking lines. By contrast, prosecuting counsel was portrayed as a "wimp," who was a little disorganised. The defendant was acquitted.

By great good luck, I met one of the jurors, the following week, socially. When I asked her why they had acquitted, the main reason that she gave was that prosecuting counsel had "put the jury's backs up." "The judge even had to send us out to give him a ticking-off," she explained. As my students had already told me, the judge had indeed sent out the jury, in order to conduct a trial within a trial on the admissibility of evidence, which my students had observed from the gallery. The juror then went on to recount the performance of defence counsel, whose impressive lines she had also learned.

Even the most avid jury defenders would find it hard to justify this sort of jury behaviour in terms which are theoretically warrantable. It certainly does not bear out the notion of Bankowski and Mungham[48] and others that the jury helps to "cultivate alternative realities in the courtroom."

What jury defenders must also face is the research finding of Baldwin and McConville of a disturbingly high number of doubtful convictions, showing that odd decisions by the jury may convict the innocent as well as acquit the guilty. This has serious implications for what Ashworth[49] has termed principles of fairness and weighting in the criminal justice system. As Baldwin and McConville said:

> "But the performance of the jury did not always appear to accord with the principle underlying the trial system in England that it is better to acquit those who are probably guilty than to convict any who are possibly innocent. On the contrary, the jury appeared on occasion to be over-ready to acquit those who were probably guilty and insufficiently prepared to protect the possibly innocent."[50]

This finding has important bearings on the principle upon which our criminal justice system seeks to strike a balance between convicting the innocent and acquitting the guilty and the margins of error we are prepared to allow from the unattainable ideal line of convicting all the guilty and acquitting all the innocent.

Ashworth has examined this principle and pointed out that the two margins are not the same:

> "Indeed it has traditionally been said that, far from there being any such equivalence, it is better that 10 guilty men should go free than one innocent man should be convicted. This proposition clearly indicates a weighting of the rules towards protection of the defendant: what are its credentials? Its main strength is said to lie in its valuation of individual rights and individual suffering. Thus it insists that the liberty of an innocent individual should not be sacrificed in order to increase the efficiency of crime control."[51]

Ashworth, Williams[52] and Allen[53] have all examined this 10 to one ratio,

---

[48] 1976, *op. cit.*, at p.222.
[49] 1979, *op. cit.*.
[50] 1979, *op. cit.*, at p.128.
[51] *op. cit.*, at p.416.
[52] *op. cit*, at p.186.
[53] Allen, C.K., *Law in the Making*, 1931, p.286.

acknowledging that it has been variously expressed as 20 to one, five to one and 100 to one. They all point to the great importance of the ratio. As Ashworth says:

> "If the maxim is really meant to say something about the balance of the criminal justice system, the ratio it expresses cannot be a matter of indifference."

This ratio is often discussed in the context of procedural rules designed to protect the defendant, as it is by Ashworth and Williams, but I would suggest that, theoretically, the entire functioning and structure of our criminal justice system should be geared towards satisfying the ratio. Baldwin and McConville's findings that 36 per cent. of their sample of acquittals and 5 per cent. of their convictions were questionable clearly indicates that the 10 to one ratio may not always be fulfilled by jury trial.

Furthermore, wrongful convictions are a double failure of abstract justice in a system aimed at crime control tempered by due process. Not only do the real culprits go free, as in a wrongful acquittal, defeating crime control, but there is an overwhelming loss of due process to the innocents convicted.

c. The jury replacing the law with their own equity

My next objection is to the support given to the jury as a re-drafter of the law in the example of the hot-dog salesman. What business have the jury to be re-writing the law? Arguments along this line are not novel. Weber objected to the misfit of jury equity in an otherwise rational legal system and the point has been well expanded by Frank,[54] Duff and Findlay[55] and McHugh,[56] amongst others. The jury is an anti-democratic, irrational and haphazard legislator, whose erratic and secret decisions run counter to the rule of law. Freeman asserts, on the acquittal of the hot-dog salesman, that the jury were saying that the defence of provocation ought to have been available "and in saying this they would have the support of the bulk of the population."[57] How, I would ask, does the jury, or Freeman, know what the bulk of the population want? We have elected the House of Commons and selected the Law Lords to re-write the law for us. As Duff and Findlay argue, far from being Devlin's "little parliament," the jury is the very antithesis, "unaccountable and its decision is designed to permit no argument." They continue, in a point pertinent to Freeman's hot-dog salesman:

> " . . . The jury, so irrationally selected, would appear to be a crude engine for the job of checking unpopular laws . . . The jury then may be counter-productive in such situations, as the legislature may not feel constrained to intervene if they know that harsh or outdated laws are not being strictly applied."[58]

Finally, I would add, in respect of those instances where the jury base their

---

[54] Frank, J., 1949, as cited by Duff and Findlay, 1982, *infra*.
[55] 1982, *loc. cit.*
[56] McHugh, M., "Jurors' Deliberations, Jury Secrecy, Public Policy and the Law of Contempt," in Findlay and Duff, 1988, *loc. cit.*
[57] *loc. cit.*, at p.93.
[58] *op. cit.*, at p.259.

decision on something extraneous, as in my theft example, that we do have a legitimate expectation, surely, that the jury will at least address the issue before them. There is little point in the Court of Appeal and House of Lords, as well as countless academics, agonising over the definitions of the components of Theft Act, such as appropriation and dishonesty, if the jury are to accord their verdict as a reward for the good looks and charm of the best barrister.

Freeman and Bankowski and Mungham have attempted to defend jury irrationality in an otherwise supposedly rational adversarial system. I would argue that this is anomalous. Lay justices and judges are frequently criticised for their irrational and inconsistent sentencing patterns and gratuitous remarks, as are civil juries criticised for irrational awards of damages. Why, then, is it theoretically warrantable and praiseworthy behaviour in this tiny element of decision-making in our criminal justice system that they act irrationally?

The sacrosanctity of the verdict

One more undesirable aspect of the sacrosanctity of the jury is the sheer impenetrability of its verdict. The consequences of this have been discussed by Williams[59]; Baldwin and McConville[60]; Duff and Findlay[61]; McHugh[62] and others. There are two important results: first, the reluctance of the Court of Appeal to overturn a jury's verdict, which has been criticised repeatedly, especially by Justice and the Home Affairs Select Committee (1981–1982) as being almost a brick wall in the path of access to justice at the post-trial stage. This point has been explored at length before, so I would only add that Lord Lane L.C.J. used the excuse of non-interference with the jury's verdict, for disallowing the 1987 appeal of the Birmingham Six.

The second major result of jury sacrosanctity is section 8 of the Contempt of Court Act 1981, which precludes discussion and observation of a real jury verdict and thus renders much of the debate on the jury's function purely speculative.[63]

Conclusion

Too often, eulogies are heaped upon the jury by its defenders who blindly follow their predecessors' mistakes (on Magna Carta) or atheoretical assertions (on jury trial as a constitutional right). They confuse randomness with representativeness and justify the jury as a democractic guardian of civil liberties re-writing the law on our behalf.

In heaping unquestioning praise on the jury, the commentators deceive themselves and the public into thinking jury trial is the "centrepiece" (Blake),[64] of the criminal justice system. A mass of research on pre-trial decision-making and

---

[59] *op. cit.*
[60] 1979, *op. cit.*
[61] 1982, *op. cit.*
[62] *op. cit.*
[63] Note the failure of the recent Courts (Research) Bill, which would have repealed this section, in relation to genuine research.
[64] *op. cit.*

plea-bargaining[65] has taught us that this is simply not the case. As Ashworth reminded us in 1988: "There are few who would now propound the view that the centrepiece of the English criminal process is the trial,"[66] but the jury defenders are still doing just this.

In reality, only a tiny fraction of cases find their way to the Crown Court, with many defendants "opting" for summary trial simply because they do not know or understand or care about their "right" to jury trial or because they want to "get it over with" in the magistrates' court. Most people pass through the court simply to be sentenced for a guilty plea, which may be the result of a bargain struck by a calculating and persuasive lawyer, who may leave his client protesting his innocence years later.

Of the minority of cases where a trial does take place, its usual forum is the unromantic and unseen magistrates' court, where McBarnet's[67] "ideology of triviality" is daily acted out and upon which the majority of defendants must rely for the benefit of "participatory democracy" and the safeguarding of their civil liberties.

There is not space in this article to explore alternative decision-makers. Existing ones, such as magistrates and judge-only courts are fraught with problems of their own,[68] but it should be remembered that existing models are not the only ones. In an atmosphere of reform and argument surrounding the Royal Commission on Criminal Justice, there has never been a better time to question the status quo and the traditional justifications which have underpinned it and to see if there is not some better, new, alternative.

---

[65] For instance, Dell, S, *Silent in Court*, 1971; Bottomley, A.K., *Decisions in the Penal Process*, 1973; Bottoms, A.E. and McClean, J.D., *Defendants in the Criminal Process*, 1976; Baldwin, J., and McConville, M., *Negotiated Justice*, 1977.

[66] Ashworth, A.J., "Criminal Justice and the Criminal Process," 28 Brit. J. Criminol. 111 (1988).

[67] McBarnet, D., *op. cit.*

[68] On magistrates' courts, see Hood, R., *Sentencing in Magistrates' Courts*, 1962; Burney, *op. cit.*; McBarnet, *op. cit.*; Darbyshire, P., *The Magistrates' Clerk*, 1984; Carlen, P., *Magistrates' Justice*, 1976; King and May, *op. cit.*; Parker, H., Sumner, M., and Jarvis, G., *Unmasking the Magistrates*, 1989 and many Home Office Studies. The judge-only courts in Northern Ireland are not unproblematic, in principle and practice.

[9]

The Case for Jury Waiver

By Sean Doran and John Jackson

Respectively Reader in Law and Professor of Public Law, The Queen's University of Belfast

Summary: *The article proposes the adoption of an idea which has been notably absent from debates in the criminal justice field in the United Kingdom, despite its acceptance in other jurisdictions which employ jury trial for serious criminal cases. This is jury waiver, not in the sense that the accused may opt for summary trial in place of jury trial, but that the accused may instead choose to be tried in the Crown Court by a judge sitting without a jury.*

The description of jury trial as a "right" enjoyed by defendants in the criminal process has properly been challenged on the ground that it is misleading. An accused person intending to contest charges of the most serious variety, such as homicide or wounding with intent, has no choice in the matter: the language of compulsion is more appropriate than that of rights.[1] At the other end of the scale, most crimes are triable only summarily and no one would seriously contend that the availability of jury trial should be extended to them.[2]

Those cases in which there *is* a "right" to jury trial in the sense that the accused may choose jury trial over another alternative are confined to that intermediate category of offences which are triable either way.[3] Granted, this category is a large one which includes some of the most common offences such as burglary and theft. Even in this context, however, talk of a "right" to jury trial is somewhat misplaced, as the desire of an accused person to be tried summarily in respect of these offences will be overridden if the magistrates determine that the accused would be more suitably committed for trial in the Crown Court.[4] Further, research has indicated a high rate of correspondence between prosecution representations on mode of trial

[1] See P. Darbyshire, "The Lamp That Shows That Freedom Lives: Is it Worth the Candle?" [1991] Crim.L.R. 740 at 743–744.

[2] See A. Ashworth, *The Criminal Process* (1994), p.247 (and see generally pp.246–252).

[3] The governing legislation is the Criminal Law Act 1977. The mechanics of election of mode of trial will not be discussed in the present article.

[4] The considerations to be taken into account by the court in making the decision are set out in the Magistrates' Courts Act 1980, s.19. In addition to the respective views of prosecution and defence, these include the nature of the case, the seriousness of the circumstances and the adequacy of the punishment which could be inflicted by the court of summary trial. Guidance on the magistrates' decision is provided in *Mode of Trial Guidelines*, issued with the indorsement of the Lord Chief Justice: see *Blackstone's Criminal Practice* (6th ed., 1996), pp.997–999. See also S. White, "The Antecedents of the Mode of Trial Guidelines" [1996] Crim.L.R. 471.

and magistrates' decisions.[5] The result is that the right to jury trial is only truly asserted in situations where the magistrates regard an offence triable either way as suitable for summary trial, but the defence wishes to elect Crown Court trial.

The purpose of these observations is not to challenge the significance of jury trial within the criminal process. The debate on the merits of jury trial has never been short of contributors and this article does not seek to add a further voice.[6] Rather, echoing Professor Ashworth's recent call for greater care to be taken in the delineation of rights in the criminal process,[7] the article proposes that the option of jury trial should be matched by the alternative option of trial by a judge sitting alone in the Crown Court. In all cases where the accused is committed for trial in the Crown Court, the availability of jury trial would therefore constitute a right properly so-called in that it would be subject to waiver by the accused. Defendants would continue to have only a limited right to choose their trial venue (in favour of Crown Court trial in either way offences), but when committed to the Crown Court they would also have a right to choose between jury trial and trial by judge alone.

It should be noted at the outset that, while the notion of jury waiver has received little attention in debates on the criminal process in the United Kingdom, it has become a generally accepted practice in other criminal justice systems modelled on the English system of trial by jury. In the United States, for example, the practice of waiver had a long history in many of the states even before its indorsement by the Supreme Court in 1930.[8] Jurisdictions such as Canada,[9] New Zealand[10] and a

[5] D. Riley and J. Vennard, *Triable Either-Way Cases: Crown Court or Magistrates' Court?* (Home Office Research Study, 1988), p.11. For commentary on the relationship between prosecutors' representations and magistrates' committal decisions, see Ashworth, *op. cit.*, n.2 above, pp.234–236.

[6] For notable contributions to the debate in recent years, see Darbyshire, *op. cit.*, n.1 above and the collection of essays in M. Findlay and P. Duff (eds), *The Jury Under Attack* (1988).

[7] A. Ashworth, "Crime, Community and Creeping Consequentialism" [1996] Crim.L.R. 220.

[8] *Patton v. United States*, 281 U.S. 276 (1930). The basic right to jury trial is enshrined in the Sixth Amendment of the U.S. Constitution. A brief historical account of waiver in the U.S. is contained in H. Kalven and H. Zeisel, *The American Jury* (1966), pp.22–24. All states have come to accept the practice, albeit with different procedural rules attached.

[9] The criminal court system which operates across the provinces in Canada is a varied and rather complex one: for discussion, see The Law Reform Commission of Canada, *Toward a Unified Criminal Court* (Working Paper 59, 1989). The following is a very basic outline of the relevant provisions governing the operation of waiver. The Canadian Charter of Rights and Freedoms, s.11(f), provides a right to jury trial for offences carrying a maximum of at least five years' imprisonment. The Canadian Criminal code, s.471, states that, except where otherwise provided, indictable offences shall be tried by a court composed of judge and jury. For most indictable offences, the Code provides that the accused may elect trial by judge and jury, trial by a superior court judge alone or trial by a lower court judge (s.536). The most serious offences, such as murder, are listed in s.469 and can only be tried by a superior court of criminal jurisdiction, with s.473 making provision for waiver of jury trial with the Attorney-General's consent (prior to 1985, waiver was not permitted in respect of such offences except in Alberta, but the Code was amended to allow waiver generally in such cases: Criminal Law Amendment Act 1985, c.19, s.64). For discussion of the provisions, see *Turpin* (1989) 48 C.C.C. (3d) 8 (Supreme Court of Canada); *Bryant* (1984) 16 C.C.C. (3d) 408 (Ontario Court of Appeal); *Cardinal* (1996) 105 C.C.C. (3d) 163 (Alberta Court of Queen's Bench).

[10] The right to trial by jury is one of the minimum standards of criminal procedure set out in s.25 of the New Zealand Bill of Rights Act 1990 (s. 25(e)). Provisions were introduced in

number of Australian states[11] have also given effect in different ways to the proposal at the centre of the present article.

In the first section, we assess the arguments in favour of the introduction of the waiver option in this jurisdiction. The following section addresses the possible objections to such a scheme. A third section deals with the mechanics of waiver and the article concludes by considering the implications of non-jury trial for the future of the criminal process.

Why waiver?

This is an appropriate time to present jury waiver as a feasible option for reform for at least two reasons. The first is that against the background of growing calls for judges to adopt a more active role in the trial process, it would seem appropriate to consider the possibility of devolving to judges ultimate responsibility for the decision on guilt or innocence. Yet when the Royal Commission called for greater judicial activism in, for example, the halting of weak cases,[12] the questioning of witnesses, the control of improper tactics by barristers[13] and the calling of witnesses,[14] it gave no consideration to this possibility.

Instead it recommended that the defence lose the right to elect jury trial for either way offences,[15] provoking such controversy that the proposal was ultimately shelved.[16] Implicit in this recommendation was the assumption that Crown Court trial by jury or summary trial before magistrates were the only available mechanisms for trying criminal cases. The proposal was criticised for its unqualified acceptance that summary trial is adequately equipped to deal with a broader range of serious contested cases.[17] The Commission's reasoning could also be questioned, however, on the basis of its complete failure to address the feasibility of a mode of trial

1979 enabling trial by judge alone in the case of persons committed to the High Court for trial (other than where the maximum term of imprisonment is life or 14 years or more): see the Crimes Act 1961, ss.361B and 361C (as amended).

[11] South Australia was the first Australian state to permit waiver in trials on indictment, by amendment in 1984 of the Juries Act 1927, s.7. Waiver is also now permitted in the Australian Capital Territory (Supreme Court Act 1933, s.68B), New South Wales (Criminal Procedure Act 1986, s.32) and Western Australia (Criminal Code, s.651A). See *Halsbury's Laws of Australia* (LEXIS Service), Vol. 9, Title 130. The Commonwealth Constitution, s.80, states: "The trial on indictment of any offence against any law of the Commonwealth shall be by jury . . ." In *Brown* (1986) 160 C.L.R. 171, the High Court of Australia held (by a three to two majority) that the clear words of s.80 precluded a person from electing trial by judge alone for an offence against the law of the Commonwealth, despite the existence within a State (in this case South Australia) of a statutory provision permitting waiver in trials on indictment. The judgments in *Brown* are replete with illuminating historical and comparative discussion of the status of jury trial as a privilege or a right within the constitutional framework of Australia, the USA and beyond.

[12] *Report of the Royal Commission on Criminal Justice* (Cm. 2263, 1993), Chap. 4, paras. 41–42.

[13] *ibid.* Chap. 8, paras. 12–14.

[14] *ibid.* Chap. 8, para. 18.

[15] *ibid.* Chap. 6, paras. 4–19.

[16] For comment on the immediate reaction to this proposal, see G. Maher, "Reforming the Criminal Process: A Scottish Perspective" in M. McConville and L. Bridges (eds), *Criminal Justice in Crisis* (1994).

[17] The Commission's comment that "[m]agistrates' courts conduct over 93% of all criminal cases and should be trusted to try cases fairly" (Chap. 6, para. 18 of the Report) was described elsewhere by one of the authors as a "classic *non sequitur*": see J. Jackson, "Trial by Jury and

involving neither the jury nor magistrates, namely the bench trial (as it is known in North America) whereby the trial judge assumes the jury's fact-finding mantle. It is not intended to argue that the bench trial be adopted as a replacement for summary trial in the case of either way offences. Rather, the proposal which we consider is that in cases where jury trial is available to the accused, the defence ought to be permitted to opt for a Crown Court trial but without a jury.

This leads to the second reason for the contemporary attractiveness of waiver, namely that the portrayal of the jury as "defence-friendly" has become increasingly outdated. It is true that jury acquittal rates are consistently higher than acquittal rates in magistrates' courts.[18] It is also true that juries may acquit against the weight of the evidence, either out of sympathy for the accused or as an expression of dissatisfaction at the application of the law in an individual case.[19] On the other hand, the more worrying phenomenon of doubtful jury convictions has caused concern for researchers in the past and resurfaced recently in a well publicised case in which the trial judge took the unusual step of expressing doubt about the jury's finding of guilt.[20]

In Kalven and Zeisel's seminal work on the American jury system in 1966, which was broadly welcomed as affirming the strength of jury trial, juries were reckoned to have been less lenient than the judge in a small but significant proportion (3 per cent) of the cases analysed.[21] Baldwin and McConville's study of jury trials in England also found evidence of strong disagreement between professionals and juries over certain convictions. More than 5 per cent of those found guilty by a jury were considered by professionals to have been convicted in questionable circumstances, a statistic which the authors regarded as the most disturbing to arise from their study.[22] Although studies of this nature were criticised on the ground that juries were being judged by the standards of professional lawyers, thus ignoring the fact that part of the jury's very rationale is its non-legal perspective,[23] their effect was at least to dispel the myth that juries are universally more favourably disposed than professional judges towards defence lines of argument. More recently, in the Crown Court study conducted for the Royal Commission, judges and prosecution barristers thought that jury convictions ran contrary to the evidence or the law in 2 per cent of cases.[24]

Judicial protectiveness towards the accused was manifested in extreme form in the aftermath of a trial in May 1995 when the presiding judge, Rougier J., wrote to the Lord Chancellor's Department expressing concern over the safety of the conviction

Alternative Modes of Trial" in McConville and Bridges (eds), *op. cit.*, n.16 above. See also Ashworth, *op. cit.*, n.2 above, pp.244–245.

[18] See discussion by Ashworth, *op. cit.*, n.2 above, p. 231.

[19] For a discussion of the concept of "jury equity", see P. Devlin, "The Conscience of the Jury" (1991) 107 L.Q.R. 388. For a more sceptical view, see Darbyshire, *op. cit.*, n.1 above, pp.747–751. For the argument that the jury's right to determine the law and the facts should be enshrined in statute, see M. D. A. Freeman, "Why Not a Jury Nullification Statute Here Too?" (1981) 131 N.L.J. 304.

[20] See nn.25 and 26 below and accompanying text.

[21] Kalven and Zeisel, *op. cit.*, n.8 above, pp.58–59.

[22] J. Baldwin and M. McConville, *Jury Trials*, (1979), Chap. 5.

[23] See, for example, M. Freeman, "The Social Construction of Truth: Some Thoughts on Jury Trials and Current Research into Juries" (1978) 1 *Preston Polytechnic Law Review* 3.

[24] M. Zander and P. Henderson, *The Crown Court Study* (RCCJ Research Study No. 19, 1993), pp.170–171.

of the accused for the murder of his girlfriend's parents.[25] The letter was in turn appended by defence counsel to the appeal papers and the Court of Appeal overturned the conviction.[26] Recent research has also identified a tendency of judges to withdraw cases from the jury in cases arguably falling outside the criteria laid down in *Galbraith*,[27] which sanctions withdrawal only in cases where the judge is of the opinion that no reasonable jury could properly convict on the evidence.[28] One might add to this the increasing willingness of judges to pre-empt possible jury prejudice towards the accused in cases where adverse media publicity has affected the chances of a fair trial.[29] Such developments indicate at the very least that judges are aware of their responsibility for the prevention of miscarriages of justice, a responsibility which has arguably been more keenly felt in the climate following the crisis of confidence in the system which gave rise to the Royal Commission's report.[30]

While this provides one general reason why defendants might be willing to place their fate in the hands of a professional judge rather than a jury, a more compelling argument for allowing jury waiver is that judges may actually be better equipped to analyse certain kinds of evidence or handle certain types of issue than juries. A notable feature of the case mentioned above in which Rougier J. expressed reservations about the jury's verdict was that the strongest item of evidence in the prosecution case was that of a partial thumbprint on a piece of crockery connecting the accused to the scene of the killing. The jury evidently did not accept the defence contention that he could have left the print on one of a number of other occasions when he had visited the victims' house. There is an interesting parallel here with some of the reactions to the recent revelation that equipment used by a laboratory, which had been responsible for forensic evidence used by the prosecution in a number of explosives cases since 1989, had been contaminated.[31] Apart from concerns about the safety of convictions in certain specific cases, a recurring general opinion in the ensuing outcry was that juries tend to be in awe of scientific evidence of this kind and are neither willing nor qualified to scrutinise such evidence in critical fashion.[32]

Some support for this view emerged from a study which the authors conducted into the operation of the Diplock court system in Northern Ireland.[33] Since 1973, cases connected with Northern Ireland's troubles have been tried by a Crown Court judge sitting alone without a jury.[34] The main purpose of our study was to compare and contrast the approaches to fact-finding adopted by juries and professional

[25] L. Donegan, "Trial and error?", *The Guardian*, May 10, 1995.

[26] At the time of writing, the Court of Appeal had not issued its reasons for allowing the appeal: see *The Times*, April 26, 1996.

[27] [1981] 2 All E.R. 1060.

[28] See B. Block, C. Corbett and J. Peay, *Ordered and directed acquittals in the Crown Court* (RCCJ Research Study No. 15). For a summary of the research, see "Ordered and Directed Acquittals in the Crown Court: A Time of Change?" [1993] Crim.L.R. 95.

[29] For discussion of this issue following the halting of the prosecution of Geoff Knights for assault last year, see R. Greenslade, "Press and Prejudice", *The Guardian*, October 9, 1995.

[30] For discussion of this theme, see S. Doran (forthcoming article in *The Times*).

[31] See R. Ford, "Lab tests cast doubt on IRA convictions", *The Times*, May 15, 1996.

[32] See F. Bawden, "Who checks forensics?", *The Times*, May 28, 1996.

[33] J. Jackson and S. Doran, *Judge Without Jury: Diplock Trials in the Adversary System* (1995).

[34] *ibid.* Chap. 2 (dealing with the introduction, history and operation of the system).

judges and the research involved both observation of trials and interviews with judges and counsel.[35] Within the Diplock scheme for allocating cases to jury and non-jury trial, the defence obviously has no say in the matter. Significantly, however, some defence counsel said that they would actually prefer non-jury trials in cases turning on forensic evidence. One expressed the view that judges had a better grasp of forensic matters: "Where one is dealing with a forensic exercise which is purely an intellectual, logical, rational exercise in forensics I am much happier having a Diplock judge dealing with that than a jury who may not really listen and not attach a great deal of significance to that and attach significance to something more emotive."[36] Other counsel argued to the contrary, but significant in itself is the finding that some defence counsel would on certain occasions prefer the professional forum to that of jury trial.[37]

In respect of identification evidence, this preference was even more prevalent. Almost without exception counsel in our survey believed that judges were more aware of the inherent dangers of identification evidence than juries and most said that they would prefer such cases to be tried by judge alone.[38] Judges, it was felt, were keenly alert to the message of the *Turnbull*[39] principles and would lean towards acquittal in cases where "legal" weaknesses in the prosecution case might not have caused juries to hesitate in finding factual guilt. The attraction of non-jury trial was noted by counsel not only in respect of types of evidence, but also in respect of certain types of case. A common view, for example, was that sexual cases were often difficult to defend before a jury. One counsel observed that in a case he was due to defend, "it would suit me nearly as well not to have a jury at all because I would rather the case was dealt with in a colder, unemotional fashion because there's enough emotion to start with."[40]

On the other hand, defence counsel did stress that, if it was a matter of choice, they would opt for a jury in most cases. A central reason was that on matters of credibility, which are at the heart of many trials, it was easier to persuade a jury to entertain doubt as to the defendant's guilt. While it is clear then that the jury retains a strong attraction, in particular from a defence perspective, there are occasions on which defendants might opt for the professional alternative. In the next section, we address the objections which might be raised to making this option available.

Arguments against the non-jury option

Opposition to the jury waiver proposal is likely to be founded on four central arguments. First, jury waiver would further undermine the institution of jury trial. Secondly, the proposal runs against the grain of the culture and tradition of our trial system. Thirdly, judges would not welcome the added responsibility of deciding on

[35] *ibid.* Chap. 4 (methodology).

[36] *ibid.* p.231.

[37] For an interesting recent example from Canada of this line of argument having a direct influence on the defence decision to waive jury trial, see *Cardinal* (1996) 105 C.C.C. (3d) 163 (Alberta Court of Appeal), a murder case involving a serious causation issue which the defence thought more suitable for a judge to deal with than a jury.

[38] Jackson and Doran, *op. cit.*, n.33 above, pp.229–230.

[39] [1977] 2 Q.B. 224.

[40] Jackson and Doran, *op. cit.*, n.33 above, p.229.

guilt or innocence. Finally, the defence should not have full control over the decision on mode of trial.

The most obvious result of the conferment on the defence of an option to have a case tried in the Crown Court without a jury would be a reduction in the number of jury trials. While recognising the central part which the jury continues to play in cases of serious crime, it is trite to remark that reliance on the jury in our legal system generally has declined through the years: juries are now used only in limited circumstances in civil cases[41] and a growing number of criminal cases have been diverted to summary trial.[42] Defenders of the institution of jury trial may naturally seek to resist any measure which leads to a further diminution in the number of jury trials. Indeed such resistance has contributed to the shelving of some prominent reform proposals in recent times. We have already mentioned the fate of the Royal Commission's proposal to remove the defendant's right to opt for jury trial in cases triable either way.[43] More significantly, the Roskill Committee's proposal that serious fraud trials be tried by a judge and professional assessors rather than a jury[44] met with stern opposition and was not implemented.[45]

The jury waiver proposal is, however, of an altogether different variety. This enlargement of defence options would only pose a threat to the institution of jury trial if it brought about a widespread defection from jury trial by defendants seeking a more sympathetic hearing before a judge. This is of course highly unlikely, but even if such a vote of no confidence in the jury were to be registered, it would be a matter of defence choice and could hardly be met with the objection that a vital protective mechanism for the accused had forcibly been removed. Indeed it might be argued that the proposal would actually *strengthen* the institution of the jury. If it is accepted that judges are better equipped to assess certain forms of evidence and argument, then the chances of juries making erroneous decisions would be reduced by the exercise of waiver in such cases.

The second argument to be confronted is that trial by professional judges goes against the grain of tradition in the United Kingdom. An immediate reply would be that judges have adapted readily to the handling of both factual and legal matters in the majority of civil trials. The obvious riposte is that there is a world of difference between the resolution of civil disputes and the trial of serious criminal cases, in particular as regards the potential seriousness of the consequences for one of the parties, namely the accused. It should be recalled, however, that a significant number of summary cases are handled by legally qualified stipendiary magistrates[46]

[41] For discussion, see J. R. Spencer, *Jackson's Machinery of Justice* (1989), pp.394–396.

[42] The range of offences in respect of which the accused could opt for trial by jury has been reduced since the recommendation of the James Committee in 1975 that a number of offences be transferred to the sole jurisdiction of magistrates: *The Distribution of Criminal Business Between the Crown Court and Magistrates' Courts: Report of the Interdepartmental Committee* (Cmnd. 6323, 1975). See the Criminal Law Act 1977, s.15, and the Criminal Justice Act 1988, ss.37–39.

[43] See nn.15 and 16 above and accompanying text.

[44] See *Report of the Fraud Trials Committee* (1986), paras. 1.6 and 8.52–8.74.

[45] For a useful critique, see R. Harding, "Jury Performance in Complex Cases" in Findlay and Duff (eds), *op. cit.*, n.6 above, pp.75–79.

[46] For discussion, see C. Walker and K. Starmer (eds), *Justice in Error* (1993), p.148. The Royal Commission recommended the use of stipendiary magistrates on a wider scale: see Chap. 8, para. 103. Note that in Northern Ireland, the courts of summary jurisdiction are presided over by legally qualified resident magistrates ("R.M.s"): see B. Dickson, *The Legal System of Northern Ireland* (3rd ed., 1993), pp.23–24.

and in Scotland a sizeable proportion of cases are tried by a sheriff without a jury.[47]

Reference has also been made above to the Diplock court system in Northern Ireland. Although the system was born of political expediency and although it has proved controversial throughout its existence,[48] the system has at least demonstrated that trial without jury is not wholly unfeasible within a jurisdiction close in heritage to that of England and Wales. Since 1973 around one-third of all serious criminal cases in Northern Ireland have been tried without a jury and it is worth noting that these have not all been connected with paramilitary activity: due to the way in which the system of allocating cases works, some "ordinary" cases with no paramilitary background have to be tried without a jury.[49] This is not to say that the Diplock system should be put forward as a model for reform. As will be suggested in the following section, careful thought ought to be given to remodelling the structure of the trial in the jury's absence. This did not occur prior to the introduction of Diplock courts, which have operated on the arguably misguided premise that the removal of the jury does not necessitate any fundamental changes in the rules and conventions attaching to jury trial.

An even more pertinent response to the cultural objection is that, as we have seen, jury waiver is a well established feature of other jurisdictions with which we share a common legal heritage, most notably perhaps the United States.[50] Although it is difficult to glean an accurate impression of the prevalence of "bench trials" in the United States, statistics indicate that they comprise around 14 per cent of all federal trials, with the numbers for individual states varying considerably.[51] No jurisdiction is perceived as more inseparably wedded to the ideal of jury trial than the United States: the right is constitutionally enshrined for all offences for which the maximum term of imprisonment is more than six months.[52] If waiver is accepted in that jurisdiction, then why does our tradition militate so strongly against it?

One answer to this question might be located in the next source of objection to waiver: that English judges would be reluctant to accept the change in function which the bench trial would entail. Speculating on the feasibility of importing joint decision-making arrangements between judges and jurors, as favoured in certain Continental jurisdictions, to the English setting, Munday has commented: "one senses that English judges, who have a long tradition of umpiring trials rather than sitting in judgment . . . would be resistant to a procedure that compelled them to

[47] For further details, see G. Maher, *op. cit.*, n.16 above, p.63.

[48] For a review of the Diplock controversy, see Jackson and Doran, *op. cit.*, n.33 above, pp.29–52. See also S. Greer and A. White, *Abolishing the Diplock Courts: The Case for Restoring Jury Trial to Scheduled Offences in Northern Ireland* (1986).

[49] For a critique of the system of allocation and proposals for reform, see Jackson and Doran, "Diplock and the Presumption Against Jury Trial: a critique" [1992] Crim.L.R. 755. Prior to the enactment of the latest version of the emergency legislation (Northern Ireland (Emergency Provisions) Act 1996), the major difficulty was that cases of robbery and aggravated burglary in which a firearm was alleged to have been used could not be diverted to jury trial by the Attorney-General, unlike most of the other offences listed in Schedule 1 to the Act as being triable by judge alone.

[50] One could also point to other common law jurisdictions such as Israel, Singapore and now Malaysia, in which trial by judge alone is the norm for serious criminal cases.

[51] See generally S. Doran, J. Jackson and M. L. Seigel, "Rethinking Adversariness in Nonjury Criminal Trials" (1995) 23 *American Journal of Criminal Law* 1 at 8–11.

[52] U.S. Constitution, Sixth Amendment; see *Blanton v. City of North Las Vegas*, 489 U.S. 538 (1989).

share in the jury's task."[53] Arguably a procedure that would involve the *assumption* of the jury's task might be even less palatable.

This argument tends, however, to underplay the already broad responsibilities of trial judges which impinge directly on the decision on the accused's guilt or innocence and which often draw judges into the arena of fact.[54] We have already referred to the judge's power to withdraw weak cases from the jury.[55] Decisions which judges make on the admissibility of evidence, in particular regarding confessions and the accused's bad character, are not necessarily determinative of guilt but often have a profound impact on the trial's outcome. Judges in the United Kingdom also enjoy a broad latitude to comment on the evidence in summing up to the jury, a power which implicitly recognises a judicial responsibility to assist the jury in its fact-finding task.[56] Judicial duties at this stage of the trial even extend to the salvaging of possible defences which may be available to the accused on the evidence, but which have not specifically been raised.[57] It may nonetheless be objected that the burden of responsibility for the ultimate decision on guilt would be too onerous. The fact, however, that the accused has *chosen* to entrust this responsibility to the judge tends to weaken this argument and, as we shall note in the next section, the judge's decision should have to be a fully reasoned one, with the normal avenues of appeal remaining open.

The final objection to be confronted is that the defence ought not to have a full measure of control over the mode of trial. The suggestion, however, is not that defendants should always as a matter of principle be entitled to absolute control in this matter. The argument rather rests very precisely on the "right" to jury trial. If it is considered that defendants should have a right to jury trial in cases deemed suitably serious, then it logically follows that they should also have a right to waive it. If, on the other hand, it is considered that jury trial should be defended without the need to see it as a "right", there is no case for considering waiver. Without entering into a full-scale debate on the reasons for jury trial, it is our argument that jury trial should be seen not merely as a means of providing confidence in verdicts, but also as a strong enough protection for defendants to warrant it being regarded as a "right". It follows that defendants should then be entitled to waive such a "right" when they believe, for whatever reason, that it may not in an individual case enure to their benefit. Whether there are circumstances in which the prosecution or the court should be able to block the defence option is one of the matters to be addressed when considering how a system of waiver might operate in practice.

The mechanics of waiver

The aim of the present article until this point has been to offer a principled argument in favour of waiver and to present the issue for debate. If the general idea

[53] R. Munday, "Jury trial, continental style" (1993) 13 *Legal Studies* 204 at 223.

[54] See generally J. Jackson, "Judicial Responsibility in Criminal Proceedings" (1996) 49 *Current Legal Problems* 59.

[55] See nn.27 and 28 above and accompanying text.

[56] For an incisive critique of this power, see D. Wolchover, "Should Judges Sum Up on the Facts?" [1989] Crim.L.R. 781. For an American perspective, see S. Saltzburg,"The Unnecessarily Expanding Role of the American Trial Judge" (1978) 63 *Virginia Law Review* 1.

[57] See S. Doran, "Alternative Defences: the 'invisible burden' on the trial judge" [1991] Crim.L.R. 878.

were to meet with acceptance, thought would have to be given to the specifics of its practical operation. In this context a number of issues would need to be resolved, including the method of implementing the scheme; the range of offences in respect of which the waiver option would be available; the rights and responsibilities of the judge and the prosecution *vis-à-vis* the accused's choice of procedure; the timing of the decision to waive jury trial; the position of accused persons who are jointly tried; and other important matters such as the possibility of requiring judges to give reasons for decisions in non-jury trials and rights of appeal. More generally, a question would arise as to whether the formal structure of the criminal trial should be altered significantly in the jury's absence. It is these issues to which we now turn.

Implementation

Implementation of the basic procedure could presumably be accomplished by a straightforward statutory provision to the effect that in cases where the accused has a right to jury trial, he or she may elect to be tried by a Crown Court judge sitting alone. There are numerous precedents for this in other jurisdictions. In New Zealand, for example, the relevant provision expressly provides that the defence may give notice to the Registrar of the court of committal, within a specified period from the date of committal, of the accused's wish to be tried by a High Court judge sitting without a jury.[58] A related but more difficult issue is whether the right to waive jury trial should apply to all offences for which there is provision for jury trial or be confined to a class of cases which would exclude the most serious. The latter approach appears to have been favoured by certain jurisdictions in which waiver is permitted. In Canada until 1985, for example, the general rule was that serious offences such as murder *had* to be tried by a superior court judge sitting with a jury.[59] The right of waiver is curtailed to an even greater extent in New Zealand, where the legislation prevents election of judge-only trials by defendants charged with offences carrying a maximum sentence of at least 14 years' imprisonment or a mandatory life term.[60] Inherent in the approach adopted in these jurisdictions would appear to be a conception of jury trial as a matter of public interest, divorced from the interests of the accused, in respect of the most serious offences in the criminal calendar.[61]

From one angle, such a conception is understandable, given the strength of the tradition of jury trial in the jurisdictions which we have mentioned. On the other

[58] Crimes Act 1961, s.361B.

[59] See n.9 above.

[60] Crimes Act 1961, s.361B. But note the view expressed by Hammond J. in *Perks* [1993] N.Z.L.R. 572 (involving a charge of sexual violation, which carries a maximum term of 14 years' imprisonment and therefore falls outside the remit of the waiver provision): "It may be that the right of an accused to select the mode of trial ought to be wider in relation to this (and perhaps other) offences. And there is much to be said for the notion that an accused should have the fundamental right to be tried in that forum which fits her sense of where justice to her will be done" (at 575).

[61] For an expression of this view, see the landmark decision in *Brown v. R.* (1986) 160 C.L.R. 171, in which the High Court of Australia ruled that the effect of a constitutional provision stating that the trial on indictment of an offence against a law of the Commonwealth "shall" be by jury (s.80) was to prevent waiver by the accused in respect of such an offence; Deane J. opined: "That constitutional guarantee [of trial by jury] is . . . for the benefit of the community as a whole as well as for the benefit of the individual accused" (at 201).

hand, it may be argued that the option ought not to be restricted in this way. Certainly the logic of the argument which we have developed in the present article, stemming from a belief that the right to jury trial should be mirrored by a corresponding right to forgo it, would point against any prohibition on waiver in respect of any offence for which jury trial is available to the accused. In short, the argument of principle for waiver stands independent of the nature of offences, but obviously the matter is one which would be open to further debate were the argument of principle to be accepted.

Role of prosecution and judge

The next issue of practical significance, which is also affected by the characterisation of jury trial as either a matter of defence right or of public interest, is whether the defence option should be capable of being overridden by the prosecution or by the trial judge. One consequence of adherence to the notion of jury trial as a right to be either exercised or waived by the defence would be to deny the prosecution a say in the matter. This is not the position, however, in Canada, where the Attorney-General's consent is required to waiver in respect of the most serious offences,[62] and in most American jurisdictions, including the federal courts, where waiver is operative only by consent of both parties and the judge.[63] In New Zealand, on the other hand, the prosecution have no power to override the defendant's wishes, although the judge may do so if he or she considers that it is in the interests of justice that the case should be tried by a jury.[64]

In our view, even if it were conceded that there are classes of serious offence in which the public interest in securing a jury verdict should always outweigh the defendant's wish to be tried without a jury, a strong argument of principle could still be made against allowing the prosecution to override the defendant's decision in cases where waiver was to be permitted. The role of the prosecution in mode of trial decisions has been the subject of considerable discussion. In Scotland, the prosecution has control over the mode and venue of trial.[65] The James Committee's report in 1975 on distribution of business between Crown Courts and magistrates' courts predated the establishment of the Crown Prosecution Service and it was not surprising therefore that it argued against the investigating authority being given

[62] See the Criminal Code, ss.473 and 568. Interestingly, in a number of recent decisions, Canadian courts have insisted that the Crown should have a reason of substance to justify a refusal of consent: see, for example, *Cardinal* (1996) 105 C.C.C. (3d) 163; *Bird* (1996) 107 C.C.C. (3d) 186 (Alberta Court of Queen's Bench).

[63] See C. H. Whitbread and C. Slobogin, *Criminal Procedure* (3rd ed., 1983), p.670. In *Singer v. United States*, 380 U.S. 24 (1965), the Supreme Court upheld the constitutionality of Fed.R. Crim. P. 23a, permitting prosecution vetoes of jury waivers. In *Patton*, U.S. 276 (1930), the landmark decision sanctioning the practice of waiver from which R. 23a was derived, the Supreme Court noted: "[T]he maintenance of the jury as a fact-finding body in criminal cases is of such importance and has such a place in our traditions, that, before any waiver can become effective, the consent of government counsel and the sanction of the court must be had . . ." (at 312).

[64] Crimes Act 1961, ss.361B and 361C. But see *Narain* [1988] 1 N.Z.L.R. 580: court will generally assume that the defence is the best judge of the interests of justice as far as the accused is concerned.

[65] For a description of the system of allocation of cases to different levels of trial in Scotland, see the Royal Commission's Report, Chap. 6, para. 12. See also Maher, *op. cit.*, n.16 above.

control over mode of trial decisions.[66] The Royal Commission too, however, argued that "the different history and context in England and Wales" militated against importing the Scottish system.[67] Prosecutors do in fact have considerable influence over the mode of trial decision. The high rate of correspondence between the views of prosecutors and magistrates' decisions was noted above,[68] and it has been observed that prosecutors may adapt charges to ensure summary trial in particular cases.[69]

Significantly, however, the abiding principle in English criminal procedure is that the choice of level of trial is outside the province of the prosecutor. In the context of jury waiver, this principle ought to apply with even greater force. The waiver proposal presupposes equivalence between jury trial and trial by judge alone: put simply, they are two methods of conducting a trial on indictment, with the same sentencing powers available to the court in the event of a conviction in either forum. The prosecution's duty is to prosecute cases in the public interest before a publicly accepted independent and impartial tribunal,[70] not to choose the forum in which it believes there is a stronger chance of conviction.[71] On a more practical level, it has been indicated in the American context where the prosecution does have the power of veto over the defendant's waiver that the prosecutor may be under an indirect pressure not to "insult" the judge by insisting on jury trial, as the judge may be less favourably disposed towards the prosecutor in future cases because of the vote of no confidence which the veto might be seen to entail.[72] Arguably, if the prosecution's decision might come to depend on considerations such as this, then it is preferable that the matter should be left out of its hands altogether.

One added factor which this article has so far omitted from the equation is that of the efficient use of resources. Trial by judge alone involves considerably less expense than jury trial (at least in terms of the hearing itself as opposed to the preparation) and there would be a certain irony in the notion of a public prosecution service seeking to place greater demands on the public purse by insisting on a jury trial in circumstances where the defence has freely agreed to waiver. Arguments of a similar nature may be levelled against the idea of permitting the trial judge to override the defence option, although some provision might have to be made to permit the judge to stand down from the case if there were particular reasons why he or she would be unsuitable to try the case, such as an awareness of the accused's prior acquaintance with the criminal courts.

Before moving on from the role of prosecution and judge in the mechanics of waiver, it is worth considering a related avenue of possible procedural reform which is rooted in a rather different philosophy from the defence rights perspective which

[66] The James Committee, *op. cit.*, n.42 above, Chap. 1, paras. 60–61.

[67] Chap. 6, para. 12.

[68] See n.5 above and accompanying text.

[69] For discussion of this issue, see Ashworth, *op. cit.*, n.2 above, pp.236–242 (but note the observation at p.255 that there is an internal Crown Prosecution Service memorandum instructing prosecutors not to alter charges after mode of trial has been determined by defence election or magistrates' decision).

[70] There is certainly no doubt that trial by judge alone would meet the standard of a fair trial prescribed in Article 6 of the European Convention on Human Rights.

[71] The *Code for Crown Prosecutors* (1994) in fact stipulates that prosecutors operate on the basis of the *Mode of Trial Guidelines* (see n.4 above) and should recommend Crown Court trial when the guidelines require them to do so: para. 8.1.

[72] See G. Fletcher, *With Justice for Some: Victims' Rights in Criminal Trials* (1995), p.168.

underpins the present article. If waiver of jury trial by the defence were to be given serious consideration, the question would doubtless arise as to whether the prosecution or trial judge should ever be enabled to initiate the procedure which would lead to a case being tried without a jury. It is difficult to imagine the trial judge being empowered to deprive the accused of jury trial in this way and to assume for himself or herself the task of determining the accused's criminal liability. As for the prosecution, however, such an idea may have some contemporary resonance in the context of fraud trials. Although, as mentioned before, the Roskill Committee's proposal to remove the jury from serious fraud trials was shelved,[73] the problematic aspects of jury trial in such cases have not abated. Most notably, the acquittal of the Maxwell brothers in January 1996 and the subsequent halting of the second trial of Kevin Maxwell in September refuelled scepticism in some quarters of the jury's capacity in this field.[74]

An argument might also be advanced that there ought to be a special provision enabling the prosecution to divert from jury trial cases involving a high security risk or where actual or potential jurors might be exposed to personal danger. In the Republic of Ireland, for example, the Director of Public Prosecutions has a general power to request trial in Dublin's Special Criminal Court, which is composed of three judges, if he or she considers that the ordinary courts are not adequate to deal with a particular case.[75] Admittedly, the analogy is not a direct one in that the Special Court is, as its name suggests, a tribunal specially devised to deal with particular classes of offence, namely those connected with political violence, but the power could be classified as a form of prosecution waiver of jury trial. In the present article, it is not our purpose to consider the general appropriateness of jury trial for cases of complexity or cases involving a security risk. It is worth noting, however, that if the issue of defence waiver were to be placed on the reform agenda, then the issue of prosecution waiver would in all probability arise for discussion also. A proposal for *general* prosecution waiver would clearly run against the grain of the argument in the present article, based as it is on fortification of the defence "right" to jury trial, but the case for enhanced prosecution rights in specific classes of case could not be dismissed out of hand without further debate.

Timing of the decision

A further practical issue which would have to be resolved is the timing of the defence decision to waive jury trial. There are a number of possibilities here. First, the election might be made at the magistrates' court hearing to determine mode of trial in cases which are triable either summarily or on indictment. Once the accused had elected trial on indictment or the court had determined that trial on indictment was more appropriate,[76] then the accused might be required to state a preference for either trial by jury or trial by a judge sitting without a jury. The second possibility—and a more attractive one in that it would ensure consistency between offences triable either way and offences triable only on indictment—would be to

[73] See nn.44 and 45 above and accompanying text.

[74] See M. McConville, "Putting Juries on Trial", *The Times*, January 30, 1996; P. Binning, "Are Juries Essential?", *The Times*, September 24, 1996.

[75] Offences Against the State Act 1939, ss.46–47.

[76] The provisions which govern the matter are contained in the Magistrates' Courts Act 1981, ss.18–21.

require the option to waive to be exercised at the committal stage. The third possibility would be to require notice of an intention to waive before a certain point in time between committal and trial. In New Zealand, for example, the defence must give notice within 28 days of the committal proceedings.[77] Finally, the matter could be left open right up until the arraignment, although one danger of such an approach is that defendants might be encouraged to "shop" for a particular judge who might, for example, be disposed to deal more leniently with the particular class of offence involved.[78]

A closely related question is whether the defence decision would be reversible. This matter caused some difficulty in Canada in the 1970s, when it was suggested that defendants were using the process of election as a tactic to delay trial, most frequently by electing jury trial on their initial appearance in court and then re-electing judge only trial at a late stage. The Law Reform Commission of Canada proposed that re-election should only be permissible as of right within a limited period of committal, after which the defence would have to show valid cause for re-election and obtain the consent of the Crown and the court.[79] The law was changed accordingly to allow re-election as of right only up until 14 days after committal.[80] Arguably, a similar approach could be taken to this issue as is currently adopted in this jurisdiction in respect of a defendant's desire to change election of mode of trial; in such circumstances, the court has a discretion to allow withdrawal of the original election, taking into account such matters as the accused's degree of understanding of his or her original choice.[81] This raises a further important procedural point which would have to be addressed, namely the steps to be taken to ensure that the accused was made as fully aware as possible of the nature and significance of the decision involved in opting to waive trial by jury, responsibility for which would presumably fall on both the accused's legal advisers and the court.[82]

A final difficulty relating to the decision on waiver would be how to proceed in the event of co-defendants opting for different modes of trial. In New Zealand, each

[77] Crimes Act 1961, s.361B.

[78] See Binning, *op. cit.*, n.74 above. Note that in Western Australia, the election must be made before the identity of the judge is known: Criminal Code, s.651A. Interestingly, in a recent Canadian case, the Alberta Court of Queen's Bench disapproved of the Crown's decision to withhold consent to waiver, on the ground that the Crown had been motivated in whole or in part by a consideration of the identity of the assigned judge: *Bird* (1996) 107 C.C.C. (ed) 186.

[79] Law Reform Commission of Canada, *Criminal Procedure—Part I: Miscellaneous Amendments* (Report 9, 1978).

[80] The relevant provision is now Criminal Code, s.561 (the change was initially effected by the Criminal Law Amendment Act 1985, s.110). For discussion, see *Ruston* (1991) 63 C.C.C. (3d) 419.

[81] See *R. v. Birmingham Justices, ex p. Hodgson* [1985] Q.B. 1131.

[82] Note that the provision permitting waiver in South Australia requires that the judge be "satisfied that the accused, before making the election, sought and received legal advice in relation to the election from a legal practitioner" (Juries Act 1927, s.7). An analogy might also be drawn with the provision in the Criminal Justice and Public Order Act 1994 governing inferences from the accused's failure to testify at trial; the court has to satisfy itself that the accused has been made aware of the potential consequences of not testifying (s.35): see *Cowan, Gayle and Ricciardi* [1995] 4 All E.R. 939.

co-accused must apply for trial by judge alone for waiver to become operative.[83] It is, however, difficult as a matter of principle to argue that a decision by one co-accused to opt for jury trial should thereby tie the other to that mode of proceeding if we are to adhere to the notion of jury trial as a right which may be waived. It may be, therefore, that the decision to waive jury trial by one of a number of co-accused would necessitate separate trials. From an economic perspective, such a solution may not be attractive, but the cost incurred would arguably be well offset by the general savings in court time which would accrue from implementation of the waiver option.

The trial process

Once the procedural aspects of the decision on waiver were settled, it would then be important to consider whether any adaptations would have to be made to the conventional jury trial structure. One advantage of trial by a professional judge over its lay counterpart is that the giving of reasons for decisions is facilitated. In Diplock courts in Northern Ireland, judges are required to deliver a reasoned judgment in the event of a conviction[84] and in practice they also give reasons for acquittal.[85] By contrast, reasoned judgments are not common in bench trials in the United States.[86] We would favour a requirement that judges give reasons in support of conviction: not only would this ensure proper accountability for decisions, but it might also reinforce the attractiveness of the waiver option in preference to the inscrutable nature of the jury's verdict. A related question is whether, given the absence of the jury at trial, the accused ought to be given enhanced rights of appeal. The Diplock system affords an automatic right of appeal,[87] but the compulsory nature of the denial of jury trial called for some compensation for the accused and the right of appeal was an obvious choice. In the context of voluntary jury waiver, it can be argued that the accused's opportunity to appeal ought to be no different from that in jury cases, a view which would accord with the theory of the professional trial as an alternative as opposed to a lesser form of adjudication.

On a broader level, it may be argued that the transition to non-jury trial as an option in respect of indictable offences ought to be accompanied by a more radical upheaval of evidential and procedural rules, in recognition of the different context in which the process of proving facts would be set.[88] What our research into Diplock trials in Northern Ireland revealed was that the general nature of the "contest" at trial tended to be transformed, from a full-scale forensic battle between defence and

[83] Crimes Act 1961, ss.361B(4) and 361C(5). In the context of a consideration of alternative approaches to the trial of serious fraud, Levi has suggested that waiver might be permitted if all accused agreed, enabling "severed components of one 'case' to undergo different modes of trial if the defendants wished it": M. Levi, *The Investigation, Prosecution and Trial of Serious Fraud* (RCCJ Research Study No. 14, 1993), p.193.

[84] Northern Ireland (Emergency Provisions) Act 1996, s.11(5). For observations on the judge's role in giving judgment, see *Thompson* [1977] N.I. 74 at 83. In New Zealand, it has been held that the judge's decision is intended to be a verdict and need not be supported by elaborate reasons: *Connell* [1985] 2 N.Z.L.R. 233; *Walters* [1993] 1 N.Z.L.R. 533 (Court of Appeal).

[85] This is not necessarily a desirable practice: for discussion, see Jackson and Doran, *op. cit.*, n.33 above, pp.272–274.

[86] See Doran, Jackson and Seigel, *op. cit.*, n.51 above, p.45.

[87] Northern Ireland (Emergency Provisions) Act 1996, s.11(6).

[88] This theme is considered in detail in Doran, Jackson and Seigel, *op. cit.*, n.51 above.

prosecution on the whole gamut of issues arising on the facts to a more focused dispute between the parties (and at times the judge) on key issues. In the absence of the jury, the usual inhibitions on judicial intervention do not exist and, indeed, intervention by the trial judge can on occasions be of positive benefit to the parties in that it offers an insight into how the mind of the fact-finder is working which would rarely be afforded in the context of jury trial. As for the operation of the rules of evidence in the jury's absence, it may be argued on the one hand that the purpose of certain rules is less easily accomplished in that the fact-finder may gain "professional" insights into the background of a case which would not be as accessible to a jury. A judge may, for example, more readily suspect that if good character evidence is not adduced on behalf of a defendant in the course of the trial, then the likelihood is that the defendant wishes to avoid revelation of a criminal record.[89] On the other hand, it may be argued that rigid adherence to certain rules is less desirable in the non-jury context. We might, for example, more readily entrust a judge to deal with hearsay evidence than a jury and the requirement of a judgment would ensure that any reliance on such evidence would be accompanied by a fully reasoned assessment of its relevance and weight.[90]

With such considerations in mind, attention could be devoted to devising an entirely new approach to the presentation of evidence in non-jury trials in keeping with the realities of proof in the changed environment. First, the limits of the judge's role at trial could be redrawn to allow greater freedom in the questioning of witnesses and in engagement in argument with counsel. Secondly, a review of the rules of evidence could be conducted with a view to their redefinition as appropriate in the non-jury setting. And thirdly, thought could be given to methods of ensuring that the judge's position of strength would not operate to the prejudice of the accused. We have argued elsewhere, for example, that the judge should be required to deliver a "provisional" judgment at the close of the evidence, which (if in favour of conviction) would then be subject to argumentation by both parties before the delivery of the ultimate judicial findings. In this way, the danger of judicial reliance on prejudicial information might be countered at trial by a process of adversarial debate.[91]

Detailed consideration of such ideas would, however, be impossible within the confines of the present article. The upshot is that trial by judge alone need not take the form of a trial whose rules of evidence and procedure are predicated on the presence of the jury, yet from which the jury is absent. Indeed, when put in these terms, the adherence to jury trial norms in non-jury trials appears somewhat illogical. In brief, acceptance of the waiver principle would not only necessitate procedural change, it would also invite a reassessment of our conventional understanding of the adversarial trial.

[89] See Jackson and Doran, *op. cit.*, n.33 above, p.244.

[90] For a detailed scrutiny of the desirability of enforcing rules of evidence in the non-jury criminal context, see A. L. Levin and H. K. Cohen, "The Exclusionary Rules in Nonjury Criminal Cases" (1971) 119 *University of Pennsylvania Law Review* 905. For a comparison of the effect of prejudicial information on judges and juries, see S. Landsman and R. F. Rakos, "A Preliminary Inquiry into the Effect of Potentially Biasing Information on Judges and Jurors in Civil Litigation" (1994) 12 *Behavioral Sciences and the Law* 113.

[91] For development of this idea, see Jackson and Doran, *op. cit.*, n.33 above, pp.274–276; Doran, Jackson and Seigel, *op. cit.*, n.51 above, pp.54–57.

Conclusion

This article has presented the case for a procedural reform that has already found favour in legal systems which have evolved from the same adversarial tradition as our own. One general criticism sometimes directed at the adversarial approach to the resolution of criminal matters is that the philosophy of party control over the contours of a dispute results in a largely unquestioning acceptance by the court of trial of a plea of guilty which has on the face of it been entered voluntarily by an accused, but it is in reality often the product of a bargain over charge and sentencing discount.[92] A contrast is drawn with inquisitorial systems in which the court is under a duty to satisfy itself that the prosecution evidence is of sufficient strength to warrant conviction.[93] Rather than putting forward the case for a system of jury waiver in isolation, one could present the measure as part of a more ambitious reform package designed to ensure greater judicial supervision over the defendant's plea.

It is fair to say that judges have in recent years been drawn into a more directorial role in pre-trial criminal proceedings. In particular, the philosophy behind the development of plea and directions hearings has been to enable judges to ensure that the issues to be determined at trial are clarified in advance and to avoid unnecessarily wasted effort in the preparation for trial.[94] In the event of a guilty plea, however, the judge's responsibility does not extend to an inquiry into whether a finding of guilt in the case is justified on the basis of the prosecution evidence. Even if a "*Newton* hearing" is held in advance of sentence, such a hearing proceeds on an assumption of the accused's guilt and is directed only at resolving a substantial divergence between the defence and prosecution version of the facts.[95] It could be argued that in *all* cases an open hearing before a judge, with proper safeguards for accused persons, would be a more acceptable way of disposing of cases than a plea negotiated by lawyers outside court, the basis of which is not subject to court scrutiny, a process accounting for the vast majority of criminal cases which pass through our system at present.[96] Perhaps the true choice facing the accused should not be whether to plead guilty or not guilty, but to choose to have the case heard by a judge or a jury. Thus, even where the accused is not contesting the charges, the evidence would at least be subjected to scrutiny by a judge—a "slow plea" as such hearings are known in the United States[97]—even if in many cases the assessment of the evidence would be a matter of formality.

[92] For a critique of the excessive dependence on the guilty plea and of the "plea bargaining" to which this gives rise, see A. W. Alschuler, "Implementing the Criminal Defendant's Rights to Trial: Alternatives to the Plea Bargaining System" (1983) 50 *University of Chicago Law Review* 931.

[93] See Ashworth, *op. cit.*, n.2 above, pp.257–258.

[94] See now the provisions in Part III of the Criminal Procedure and Investigations Act 1996.

[95] The practice of conducting such hearings derives from *Newton* (1982) 77 Cr.App.R. 13. For explanation and discussion of *Newton* hearings, see *Blackstone's Criminal Practice* (1996), paras. D16.2–D16.13.

[96] For a useful discussion of the guilty plea rate, see Ashworth, *op. cit.*, n.2 above, pp.258–260.

[97] See L. M. Mather, *Plea Bargaining or Trial?* (1979), p.2 and pp.149–150. For further discussion of this theme, see Jackson and Doran, *op. cit.*, n.33 above, pp.300–301.

These wider issues merit closer attention, but a full investigation of them would be beyond the scope of the present article. If the principle of waiver were accepted, other debates on the role of judges and juries in the criminal process would doubtless be reopened. This article has argued for jury trial to be reconstituted as a "right" properly so-called. Arguably, the future of the institution of the jury itself will depend on the development of the judicial role at trial. As we have indicated, the portrayal of judges and juries as masters of law and fact respectively is attractively simple but is in practice misleading. Even in jury trials, the scope of judicial responsibility is frequently underestimated. The time is right to look beyond the traditional bounds of our trial process and to carry this responsibility a significant step further. The aims of maximising efficiency and invigorating defence rights are often set in conflict. Waiver, however, would contribute to the achievement of both.

[10]

Modes of Trial: Shifting the Balance towards the Professional Judge

By John Jackson
School of Law, Queen's University Belfast

Summary: *This article discusses the approach of the Auld Review of the Criminal Courts of England and Wales towards modes of trial with particular emphasis on the following: first, the recommendation for a third tier of jurisdiction; secondly, the changes recommended for serious offences; and, thirdly, the proposals for making juries more accountable for their actions and decisions. It is argued that the proposals extend the influence of the professional judge in criminal trial decision making at the expense of lay participation.*

Introduction

One of the refreshing aspects of Lord Justice Auld's *Review of the Criminal Courts of England and Wales* has been the extent to which it has been prepared to raise the level of debate in England and Wales over modes of trial beyond the choice between trial by jury and trial by magistrates.[1] Throughout England, Wales, Scotland and Ireland, north and south, there is a large variety of modes of trial to deal with summary and more serious cases.[2] Even within the jurisdiction of England and Wales itself, there are a number of modes of trial that fall outside the norm, including professional judges sitting alone as district judges in the magistrates' court, district judges sitting with lay magistrates in family and youth courts and judges sitting with two or more magistrates in the Crown Court as a court of appeal by way of rehearing from magistrates' courts. Yet these 'mixed' tribunals have received little attention,[3] and the debate over modes of trial in recent years has been dominated by the issue of whether defendants who are charged with offences triable "either-way" in the magistrates' court or the Crown Court should no longer have the right to elect for jury trial. This was the central recommendation of the Royal Commission on Criminal Justice in 1993 and it has dominated the mode of trial

[1] (2001) London: H.M.S.O. The report will hereafter usually be referred to as "the Review".

[2] For a useful catalogue of the variety of structures employed to deal with summary cases, see S. Doran and R. Glenn, *Lay Involvement in Adjudication* (2000) London: H.M.S.O., Research Report No. 11 of the Criminal Justice Review Group.

[3] Glanville Williams was, however, an advocate of this form of tribunal for serious offences over many years. See G. Williams, *The Proof of Guilt* (1963, 3rd ed. London: Stevens) 298–300 and his letter to *The Times*, November 5, 1988.

debate ever since with two Bills introduced by the Government on the subject in 1999 and 2000.[4] The recommendation led to inflated claims on both sides, with those on the Government side who favour abolition of the right of election claiming that abolition would result in major savings in terms of cost and a reduction in delay and those favouring retention arguing that abolition represents a fundamental assault on the ancient "right" to jury trial.[5] Although the Review was established primarily to increase efficiency in the workings of the criminal courts,[6] the terms of reference given to it were so wide,[7] including a "review into the practices and procedures of the criminal courts at every level", that there was no way that it was going to be able to avoid the right of election debate.

The Review has raised the level of the debate by looking more searchingly at modes of trial throughout the jurisdiction than the Royal Commission of Criminal Justice was prepared to do in its report in 1993. Although the Royal Commission sparked off the right of election debate, it was content to consign more cases to the magistrates' courts without considering how justice is dispensed there. By contrast, the Review, admittedly with much more research on magistrates' courts at its disposal,[8] examined magistrates' justice as well as trial by jury and the result of its examination of the criminal courts as a whole is a proposal to shake up criminal courts more radically than at any time since the Beeching Commission's report in 1971.[9] The cornerstone of the structural reforms it proposes is a unified criminal court which would consist of three Divisions: a Crown Division constituting the present Crown Court with jurisdiction over all indictable matters and such "either-way" cases as are allocated to it, a new District Division consisting of a judge—usually a district judge—sitting with at least two experienced magistrates to exercise jurisdiction over those "either-way" cases allocated to it and a Magistrates' Division to exercise jurisdiction over summary cases and those "either-way cases" allocated to it.

These proposals will prove no less controversial than the recommendation that the Review also endorses that defendants should lose the right of election in "either-way" cases. Indeed it has been estimated that the effect of introducing a middle tier of jurisdiction is that fewer cases are likely to end up before the jury than under the Government's own proposals under the Mode of Trial Bills.[10] Apart from "either-way" cases the Review also makes several controversial recommendations which will restrict jury trial even in respect of indictable cases. It is proposed that as an

[4] See Royal Commission on Criminal Justice, *Report* (1993, London: H.M.S.O.) 85–89 and the Criminal Justice (Mode of Trial) (No. 1) Bill (1999) and No. 2 (Bill) (2000).

[5] The debate is summarised at pp.186–192 of the Review. See also S. Lloyd-Bostock and C. Thomas, "Juries and Reform in England and Wales" in N. Vidmar (ed.), *World Jury Systems* (2000, Oxford: Oxford University Press) 62–66, A. Sanders and R. Young, *Criminal Justice* (2000, 2nd ed. London: Butterworths) 540–548.

[6] For discussion of the background to the establishment of the Review, see M. Zander, "What on Earth is Lord Justice Auld Supposed To Do?" [2000] Crim.L.R. 419.

[7] See p.1 of the Review.

[8] Recent studies discussed by the Review include P. Seago, C. Walker and D. Wall, "The Development of the Professional Magistracy in England and Wales" [2000] Crim.L.R. 631, R. Morgan and N. Russell, *The judiciary in the magistrates' court* (2000, London: Home Office) R.D.S. Occasional Paper No. 66, A. Sanders, *Community Justice: Modernising the Magistracy in England and Wales* (2001, London: Institute of Public Policy Research).

[9] *Royal Commission on Assizes and Quarter Sessions* (1969, London: H.M.S.O.).

[10] M. Zander, "Lord Justice Auld's Review of the Criminal Courts: A Response" (2001), available at www.lse.ac.uk/Depts/law, 32.

alternative to trial by judge and jury in serious and complex fraud cases, the trial judge should be able to direct trial by himself sitting with lay members. All cases involving young defendants who are presently committed to the Crown Court for trial should in future be tried in the youth court consisting of a judge sitting with at least two experienced magistrates. Finally, defendants should themselves be able to opt for trial by judge alone with the consent of the court in all cases tried on indictment. If implemented, these proposals would be tantamount to a considerable erosion of trial by jury. But the Review is not merely content to restrict the scope of jury trial. It also proposes that much greater control should be placed over the jury in those remaining cases that are assigned to it by recommending that section 8 of the Contempt of Court Act 1981 should be amended to permit judges to inquire into alleged improprieties by a jury and that trial judges should be permitted to require a jury to answer publicly each of a series of questions put to it and to declare a verdict in accordance with those answers. These proposals, together with the recommendation that the prosecution should have a right of appeal against a special verdict which reveals on its terms that it is "perverse", would effectively make juries much more accountable in their decision making to judges.

It would be impossible in the space of this article to consider all of these radical proposals in detail. In the sections that follow we will first consider the general approach adopted by the Review which led it to recommend such a radical mode of trial agenda. The article will then focus on the proposed "hybrid" tribunal for the middle tier of jurisdiction, the new modes of trial proposed for serious offences and the recommendations that are designed to make juries more accountable for how they behave and for the decisions which they reach.

The general approach

It is sometimes the experience of recent independent reviews established by government that they come to unpredictable conclusions. The Royal Commission on Criminal Justice was appointed over 10 years ago in the wake of what was commonly considered to be a crisis in criminal justice arising out of a number of miscarriages of justice and out of this crisis an expectation arose that radical reforms would be recommended to deal with this problem.[11] In the event a number of important recommendations for change were made but many commented on the institutional conservatism of the report and on its failure to assert or reinforce basic fundamental values and human rights.[12] By contrast, the Auld Review was established against the background of government concerns about the efficiency of the workings of the courts and was designed, as Michael Zander has put it, to "do a Woolf" on the criminal courts.[13] In the event, as already pointed out,[14] the Review

[11] This expectation was built up to some extent by the Government itself. The terms of reference given to the Commission required it to consider the possibility of the courts having an investigative role both before and during the trial and the Home Secretary at the time said that the Commission must judge between the present adversarial system and the inquisitorial system in France. See *Sunday Times*, September 29, 1991. For media reporting of the crisis at the time, see R. Nobles and D. Schiff, *Understanding Miscarriages of Justice* (2000, Oxford: Clarendon) 117–149.

[12] See generally M. McConville and L. Bridges (eds.), *Criminal Justice in Crisis* (1994, Aldershot: Elgar).

[13] *op. cit.*, n.6 above, 421.

[14] [2001] Crim.L.R. 928.

is not an overtly managerialist report. Within its terms of reference, the Review obviously had to be concerned with efficiency but the report shows an awareness of the need for fairness and human rights, although it eschews any attempt to identify the overarching aims of the criminal justice system and explicitly does not consider that it was within its terms of reference to consider whether the present balance of the criminal trial should be tipped so as to favour one party more than the other.[15] Unlike the Royal Commission which was complacent in places abut the degree of public confidence in the conduct of criminal trials,[16] the Review refers to the fact that the public appears to have little confidence in the daily working of the courts, despite efforts made to make improvements, although it is wary of using public opinion as a measure of court performance and what needs to be done to improve it.[17] Above all, the Review was prepared to consider radical solutions. Sir Robin Auld reports that he rapidly concluded that he could not conduct the review in a structured way by examining each part of the system in isolation from the whole and he prepared at an early stage to consider questions of structure, jurisdiction and management in the context of the system as a whole.[18] This was no doubt helped by his willingness to engage in extensive consultation and unlike the Royal Commission to visit a range of jurisdictions outside England and Wales and to convene conferences specifically to learn about other systems.[19]

This is not the place to consider why the approaches of the two Reviews have been so different. Some might put the differences down to the way the terms of reference were framed. It has been noted that despite the context in which the Royal Commission was established, the terms of reference reflected "a centre of gravity" that was more concerned with efficient resource management than miscarriages of justice.[20] Conversely, although the terms of reference of the Auld Review emphasised efficiency in terms of the working of the courts they also referred to the need to deliver justice fairly and to promote public confidence and, unlike the Royal Commission's terms of reference, the Review was not required explicitly to have regard to the efficient use of resources in the recommendations which it made. Others might point to the different composition of the reviews. Unlike the Royal Commission which consisted of a large body of members, the Review was dominated by one individual, although it was assisted by experts. In order to reach unanimity a committee is required to search for compromise solutions whereas a single person is freer to put forward his or her own radical solutions. All this is not to denigrate the work of the Royal Commission which, in addition to its report, and unlike the Review, was able to commission a large number of very informed pieces of research.[21] It does highlight, however, how the manner in which reviews are

[15] Review, 11.

[16] J. Jackson, "The Royal Commission on Criminal Justice: The Evidence Recommendations" [1993] Crim.L.R. 817.

[17] Review, 2, 18.

[18] *ibid.*, 3.

[19] The Royal Commission visited Scotland while Sir Robin Auld visited court centres in Scotland, Northern Ireland, the United States and Canada.

[20] N. Lacey, "Missing the Wood . . . Pragmatism versus Theory in the Royal Commission" in McConville and Bridges, *op. cit.*, n.12 above, 12, 31.

[21] By contrast the Review only commissioned a "few limited projects of research" (p.5), which are listed at the end of Appendix 3.

established can influence both the way they are conducted and the conclusions that are reached.[22]

The Review's willingness to accept the need for radical changes in order to promote justice, efficiency and public confidence and to look beyond traditional practices within the jurisdiction is characterised by its approach towards modes of trial and trial procedures. It is true that Chapter 1 of the Review makes clear that it accepts some longstanding features of criminal trials in England and Wales. It accepts that the resolution of questions of fact going to the issue of guilt should continue in the main to be the responsibility of lay magistrates and juries and therefore accepts this traditional feature of the English system. It accepts that there is no persuasive case for a general move away from the adversarial system which has long been a hallmark of common law systems and it also accepts the traditional categorisation of offences into summary, indictable and triable "either-way". Beyond these traditional features, however, the Review approaches these issues more by way of principle than by way of tradition and at the beginning of Chapter 7 it sets out a number of principles or "propositions",[23] as it prefers to call them, to guide the way criminal courts should be structured. First of all, although different cases may call for different tribunals, practices and procedures, each should be capable of providing for a fair hearing and of securing a just outcome. Secondly, the nature of the tribunal to which a case is allocated and its procedures should be proportionate in form, time and cost to the seriousness and/or complexity of the alleged offence and the severity of the potential sentence. Thirdly, the allocation decision should be taken by the court.

Although the Review describes these as "blinding glimpses of the obvious",[24] the third is particularly controversial within the English context. It is hard to disagree with the principle that the decision where a defendant should be tried should not be one for the defendant alone to decide. As the Review points out, the public have an interest in this decision as well as the accused as only finite resources can be allocated to the criminal justice system. But to establish the principle that there should be different modes of trial according to the seriousness of the offence and potential seriousness of the sentence and that decisions on mode of trial be taken in the public interest rather than by defendants says nothing about what the different modes of trial should be and how exactly the lines should be drawn. The Review could have taken the opportunity to recommend that it is in the public interest for defendants to be accorded a right to jury trial for a certain level of offence and in so far as there should remain a category of "either-way" offences recommended that defendants should continue to exercise a right of election. But the Review does not proceed in this manner. It points out that England and Wales is possibly the only jurisdiction to accord defendants this privilege and even within the English tradition it is difficult to defend this right on the basis of some constitutional entitlement to jury trial. The elective right to jury trial in "either-way" cases only developed over

[22] For further reflections on the role of reviews in the process of criminal justice law reform with reference to the Criminal Justice Review in Northern Ireland, see J. Jackson, "Shaping the Future of Criminal Justice" in C. J. Harvey (ed.), *Human Rights, Equality and Democratic Renewal in Northern Ireland* (2001), 163.

[23] Review, 269.

[24] *ibid.*

the last 150 years and Parliament has modified or removed the right in respect of a number of offences in recent years.[25]

The Review accepts, of course, that individuals have a right to a fair trial at every level of jurisdiction and this requires conformity with the European jurisprudence that "there are sufficient guarantees to exclude any objectively justified or legitimate doubts as to the impartiality of the tribunal".[26] It also accepts that some cases justify more "searching pre-trial and trial procedures" than other cases.[27] But it appears to reject the idea that there should be some inherent right to a particular mode of trial even in the most serious circumstances. In particular, although it endorses lay justice as "useful citizenship" and as a powerful contributor to public confidence,[28] it is not inclined to consider that defendants have any right to jury trial or to any lay form of justice. It rejects the proposition that trial by jury is a constitutional entitlement rooted in English history and the idea that there is any right to lay justice under the European Convention on Human Rights or under the jurisprudence of the European Court.

At the summary level of jurisdiction, it points out that the debate over lay and professional judging has largely consisted of the "deployment of ideologies to support unsound or out-dated comparisons and rival caricatures" and goes on to observe that "the reality is that District Judges and magistrates today are closer in their social and legal culture than many give them credit for".[29] Magistrates are not "surrogate jurors" and it is simplistic to equate trained and largely experienced lay judges sitting as judges of law and fact up to about once a week for on average between 10 and 20 years with those who know little or nothing of the system and probably only serve as finders of fact for a fortnight or so once or twice in a lifetime. Since the boundaries between lay and professional judging are so decidedly blurred at the magistrates' court level, the Review does not recommend that there should always be a lay magistrate in a summary trial and it also rejects Andrew Sanders's proposal that there should be a mixed tribunal at this level.[30]

Even in jury trials where there is clearly a world of difference between the professional judge and the lay juror, the Review sees the two acting in "partnership" rather than independently, making "separate and overlapping contributions to the final outcome".[31] The Review recognises that many are still attached to the idea that there is still a role for juries to dispense with the law in defiance of the judge in particular cases. But it is strongly against any such role, regarding it as a blatant affront to the legal process and the main purpose of the criminal justice system which is to control crime and goes so far as to recommend that there should be a legal declaration, by statute if necessary, that juries have no right to acquit defendants in defiance of the law or in disregard of the evidence. Even accepting that juries should be confined to deciding issues of fact, however, their position within the trial can serve as a valuable protection to accused persons. The Review appears to take the view that if it can be shown that another form of tribunal might perform the fact-finding role better than juries, then the rationale for jury trial

[25] *ibid.*, 138.
[26] *ibid.*, 158.
[27] *ibid.*, 197.
[28] *ibid.*, 14.
[29] *ibid.*, 103.
[30] *op. cit.*, n.8 above.
[31] *ibid.*, 136.

largely falls away. This explains the readiness with which it is able to contemplate the withdrawal of the jury in middle range and even serious cases, even though it states that any change to the system of trial by jury requires a compelling case. But as we shall see below it can be argued that juries perform a valuable function in reinforcing adversarial protections for the accused and this raises issues which go beyond the question of their competence as a fact-finding tribunal.

The Review also declines to give much weight in determining modes of trial to considerations of public confidence. It accepts that trial by lay magistrates and trial by jury have widespread support but regards public confidence as an elusive concept on which to determine how well a criminal justice system is performing and what needs to be done to improve it. This appears to have been borne out by some of the research into the attitudes towards lay magistrates and district judges which demonstrated that there was considerable public ignorance of the criminal justice system.[32] Views often depend upon the context in which questions are put. The Review reports the view of one contributor, for example, that attitudes towards the lay magistracy depend much on whether people are considering the elective right to jury trial (when they are often portrayed as part of the establishment) or the merits of lay and professional judges (when they are depicted as the near equivalent of the jury). This is not to deny the importance of public confidence as a factor to be considered in any review of procedures but public confidence is not an end in itself: "it is or should be an outcome of a fair and efficient system".[33]

An example of how the Review believes public confidence issues should be tackled is to be found in its treatment of magistrates' justice. Although the Review reports that "the overwhelming evidence in the Review is that lay and district judges do a good job in their separate ways",[34] it accepts that there are confidence issues to be addressed in relation to magistrates' justice. In particular it accepts that defendants and particularly ethnic and other minorities perceive themselves to have a better chance of acquittal in the Crown Court than in the magistrates' court. But at this point another proposition or principle comes into play, namely that concerns about the quality of justice in one level of court should not be a basis for allocation of cases to another higher level. In a sentence which encapsulates its general philosophy, the Review goes on to state: "No system of justice should be structured or operated on the basis that part of it is not working properly: it should be made to work properly at all levels."[35] To make magistrates' justice "work properly" in the interests of fairness and efficiency, the Review makes a number of welcome recommendations. It endorses the current levels of summary work assigned to district judges and magistrates, with district judges being assigned cases of factual and legal complexity. But it accepts that more needs to be done to ensure that benches of magistrates reflect more broadly than at present the communities they serve and makes a number of recommendations to broaden the range of persons who are appointed to the magistracy. The Review also believes there is scope for improved training of magistrates and calls for more consistent training and a more effective appraisal system. To deal with the growing concern that members of ethnic minority communities experience discrimination within the criminal justice system,

[32] See the findings of the reports by Morgan and Russell and by Sanders, *op. cit.*, n.8 above, discussed by the Review at 105.
[33] Review, 106.
[34] *ibid.*, 109.
[35] *ibid.*, 269.

the Review also considers that there is an urgent need to establish a system for comprehensive and accurate collation of data about minority ethnic representation in the system and relative outcomes of each stage of the process.

Having rejected the idea that modes of trial should be dictated by any notion of individual rights or of public confidence, the Review prefers then a philosophy of seeing what works. The general approach adopted is that a combination of lay and professional approaches should be brought to bear at each level of justice commensurate with the particular issues being tried, with everything done to maximise efficiency and fairness at each level. This pragmatic approach of seeing "what works" on an issue by issue basis has the attraction of flexibility but as we shall see it enabled the Review to recommend a number of changes in modes of trial which would have the effect of marking a decisive shift away from jury trial.

A further question is how and where lines should be drawn between levels of justice. The Review considers that all decisions as to where "either-way" offences should be allocated should be taken after plea in the Magistrates' Division of the new unified court structure and where there is dispute over venue a district judge should be entrusted with the decision. The court should allocate "either-way" offences according to the seriousness of the alleged offence and the circumstances of the defendant in accordance with statutory and broadly drawn criteria looking at the case at its worst from the point of view of the defendant and bearing in mind the jurisdiction of each Division. The recommendation to bear in mind the sentencing jurisdiction of each Division is given teeth by a further recommendation which would abolish the procedure whereby magistrates may commit cases tried in the magistrates' court for sentence to the Crown Court. The effect of this is that where a decision is made that an "either-way" offence should be tried summarily and it turns out in the course of the trial that the facts and circumstances justify a higher sentence than the court can impose, there is no procedure for committing the case to a higher court for sentence. District judges are as a consequence likely to lean, as the Review recommends them to do, on the side of allocating cases on the basis of the worst case scenario for defendants and consequently to err on the side of referring cases to the higher level.

The recommendation that magistrates should lose the power to commit for sentence stems from another simple proposition which the Review found applies in other jurisdictions, namely that after allocation all cases should start and finish at the same level subject to an appeal. If the Review had not gone on to recommend a third tier of jurisdiction and had simply recommended the continuation of two modes of trial, this might well have taken the sting out of the tail of much of the right of election debate. Much of the debate has centred on the proposition that defendants should have a right to jury trial in cases where defendants are at risk of losing their liberty beyond the summary jurisdiction of six months.[36] The Review considers that there should be no change in the level of summary jurisdiction presently defined as a general limit of six months custody or £5,000. If magistrates no longer had the power to commit for sentence to the Crown Court, defendants

[36] Although defendants have no right of election in "either way" cases in Scotland, it has been pointed out that this principle presently underpins the different procedures for determining modes of trial in both Scotland and England and Wales: see the letter by Professor Lee Bridges in [2000] Crim.L.R. 512.

would no longer be sent for trial in summary cases where a more severe sentence than six months would be warranted on conviction.

Of course, there remains the kind of cases where the consequences of conviction would be very severe for defendants because of loss of reputation even if the sentence were a light one. Although this is an issue that loomed large in debates on the Government's Mode of Trial Bills, the Review is unclear as to how such cases should be treated. It makes it clear that even where a sentence in an individual case would not exceed the relevant limit, it *could* still be allocated to a higher level of court by means of its seriousness, whatever the likely sentence, but it may be argued that the Review should have been clearer about the criteria it wanted to see applied. Even if this had been done, of course, questions would still be raised about the principle that the courts should decide where cases should be allocated in cases of choice rather than the defendant. Concerns have been raised about the ability of magistrates to apply the Mode of Trial Guidelines fairly and consistently.[37] To ensure consistency the Review recommends that both sides should have a right of appeal to the Crown Court but questions remain about whether courts can be trusted to give enough weight to questions of seriousness from a defendant's point of view given the pressures of speed and costs on them.[38] Opponents of the proposal to abolish the right of election have been concerned that this would mean a diminution in jury trial. As we have said, a number of other proposals made by the Review will have this effect as well and it is time to turn to these: first, to the proposed third tier of jurisdiction and then to the proposals for new modes of trial in serious cases.

A Third Tier of Justice?

The proposal that would do most to undermine jury trial is the recommendation that there should be a third tier of jurisdiction exercised within a new District Division consisting of a judge and two experienced magistrates to bridge the gap between summary trial and trial on indictment. A third tier would cater for the middle range of cases that do not warrant the cumbersome and expensive fact finding procedures of judge and jury but which are sufficiently serious or difficult or which have such potentially serious consequences for the public and the defendant to merit a combination of professional and lay judges working together in a simpler way than is manifested in judge and jury trials. The new Division would have jurisdiction over "either-way" offences but the Review is not very definitive about what the limits of its jurisdiction should be, suggesting cases where "the defendant could face a sentence of imprisonment of up to, say, two years or a substantial financial or other punishment of an amount or severity to be determined".[39]

It is difficult to be precise about how many "either-way" cases would be heard by this new District Division. The suggestion is that if there is a real possibility that the appropriate sentence on conviction would exceed six months custody but not, say, two years, the matters should be allocated to the Division. This means that the District Division would take in those "either-way" cases within these limits which are presently tried summarily because magistrates decide this is suitable and no

[37] See Sanders and Young, *op. cit.*, n.5 above, 530–548.

[38] See A. Ashworth, *The Criminal Process: An Evaluative Study* (2000, 2nd ed., Oxford: Oxford University Press) 258–259.

[39] Review, 277.

election is made by the defendant for jury trial. In addition the Division would take in a range of cases within these limits which are presently committed for Crown Court trial. Michael Zander has estimated that the total number of jury trials in 1999 that would under these proposals have been allocated on the basis of sentence to non-jury trial would have been of the order of 16,000.[40] The Review does not consider that all cases which do not exceed the two year limit should be diverted from jury trial to the new District Division or the Magistrates' Division, as it would be open for a case which is not likely to exceed this limit to still be allocated to the Crown Division on the basis of "seriousness" criteria which the Review leaves unclear. But there is little doubt that there are large numbers of persons who would on these proposals have their cases allocated to the new District Division rather than to jury trial and one commentator has estimated that the right to jury trial would be lost in approximately 90 per cent of cases.[41]

This raises questions about what is lost and what is gained by these proposals. Consistent with the pragmatic approach it adopts, the Review considers that it is time to break the current inflexibility of sending middle range cases either to summary trial where defendants are not guaranteed to be heard by a sufficiently experienced tribunal to deal with their case or to the Crown Court where the mode of trial is too cumbersome and expensive for what is needed. As the Review puts it, the main rationale for mixed tribunals is that "they combine the advantages of the legal knowledge and experience of the professional judge with community representation in the form of lay magistrates".[42] The flexibility in matching cases around the borderline with a more suitable tribunal is therefore the main advantage put forward for the proposal.

There is little doubt that the proposal would bring a number of efficiency savings in terms of delay and cost but the question remains whether the new tribunal would be a more suitable mode of trial for these cases. The defendants in those cases which come within the limits of the new District Division but which would presently be sent for summary trial would receive a higher level of justice than they would presently obtain in the magistrates' court. If their case would now be tried by a district judge sitting alone, they would obtain in the new mixed tribunal the additional advantages that may be claimed for a collective decision and some form of lay representation—one judge and two lay magistrates. If, on the other hand, they would now be tried by lay magistrates, they would obtain the advantage of a legally trained judge to hear their case in addition to community representation. But it may be questioned how necessary these additional advantages are in cases where magistrates have made a decision under the existing criteria that the case is not of such a serious character as to merit Crown Court trial and under the Mode of Trial Guidelines that the case does not involve a degree of complexity in terms of difficult questions of fact or law to be sent to Crown Court trial.[43] In addition the defendant will not have exercised his or her right to elect Crown Court trial. In these circumstances is a higher standard of justice necessary?

If a third tier of justice is *unnecessary* for cases which are presently heard summarily, a further question is whether it is *sufficient* for those cases which come

[40] *op. cit.*, n.10 above, 35.

[41] R. Amlot, (2001) 151 N.L.J. 1461.

[42] Review, 276.

[43] See s.19 of the Magistrates' Court Act 1980 and the revised National Mode of Trial Guidelines reported in *Blackstone's Criminal Practice* (2001), para. D3.7.

within the jurisdiction of the proposed new District Division but which are presently committed for Crown Court trial either because magistrates decide under the existing criteria that the case is more suitable for Crown Court trial or because the defendant has exercised his or her right of election. Where the committal decision is made by magistrates on grounds of legal or factual complexity, the Review appears to consider that there should be enough flexibility within the new Division to obtain the necessary expertise to try such a case. It recommends that while the judge in the District Division would normally be a district judge, depending on the case and circumstances it could be a judge of any level from High Court to Recorder so that a case involving young children or complex issues, or a grave case against a young defendant presently beyond the jurisdiction of the youth court could be assigned to a court presided over by a High Court judge or a Circuit Judge. The Review even retains the flexibility of a case being tried in the District Division by a judge alone where the defendant wants this option for any of the reasons that defendants would opt for trial by judge alone in the Crown Court.

But legal or factual complexity is not, of course, the only reason why a jury trial might be considered more suitable than trial by magistrates. The cases that come within the jurisdiction of the proposed District Division include those where there is a "real possibility" that the sentence on conviction will exceed six months and in most jurisdictions that have retained the jury system such cases would normally be tried by a jury. Numerous justifications have been claimed for jury trial but at their heart, as the Review itself accepts,[44] is the jury's valued role in serious cases of bringing a considerable community input into trial decision making. This raises a crucial question whether the new tribunal would encompass enough community representation to satisfy this middle range of serious cases. Michael Zander has made the point that whatever the merits of the mixed tribunal it cannot be suggested that it is an improvement in terms of community representation over trial by jury.[45] The suggestion seems to be that the kind of community representation which there will be in such cases is *sufficient* to meet the bulk of middle range cases. We have seen that the Review itself makes the argument that the boundaries between trained lay magistrates and district judges are not that great and that it is misleading to characterise lay magistrates as "surrogate jurors". Partly to offset the need to ensure that the decisions of the mixed tribunal are truly collective and not the result of a dominant presiding judge, the Review recommends that the lay magistrates who would sit on it would need to be experienced so as to hold their own with the judge. In shifting the balance of community representation on the mixed tribunal away from younger, less experienced magistrates towards presumably older, more experienced ones, however, the Review is proposing to skew community representation in a very particular direction with the result that the tribunal is likely to achieve even *less* community representation than is presently evidenced in many summary trials.

Of course, we have seen that the Review places little direct weight on any right to lay representation and is more concerned with whether any new procedure will achieve the necessary balance between fairness and efficiency. But this raises the further question whether the diminished community representation on the mixed tribunal is sufficiently fair for the middle range of cases for which it is proposed. In

[44] See, *e.g.*, Review, 140.
[45] *op. cit.*, n.10 above, 28.

our study of Diplock trials in Northern Ireland which made comparisons between trials by judge alone and trials by jury we found that the defendant suffers an adversarial deficit in non-jury trials in at least two respects.[46] First, there is the fact that lay triers of fact can afford to take a more wide-ranging view of the merits of the prosecution case than any professional tribunal. We have seen that the Review expresses strong views about the notion of jury "equity" but one of the advantages of a lay approach is that even when trying to work within the parameters of the criminal law it is able to take a fresh perspective towards the case which professional judges sitting over a period of time hearing case after case may lose. The Review rejects the view that magistrates are necessarily any more case-hardened than jurors but we found that a professional approach necessitates a certain case-hardening in the sense that it demands that a colder, unemotional attitude is taken towards the evidence.[47] If this is accepted it is likely that experienced magistrates sitting with a professional judge are more likely to adopt a considerably more professional approach towards the evidence than a lay jury.

The second respect in which the accused suffers an adversarial deficit in a professional single judge trial is derived not so much from the different approach which the professional takes towards the evidence as from the different position which professionals occupy in the proceedings. One of the advantages in strictly separating questions of fact from questions of law is that the lay tribunal charged with deciding questions of fact can be kept ignorant of aspects of inadmissible and prejudicial evidence. One way in which it might be possible to keep such evidence from triers of fact in a mixed tribunal is by allocating questions of law to the professional judge and allocating questions of fact to the lay magistrates. The Review does not go this far. Instead it suggests that the professional judge should deal with all questions of law, procedure and evidence, hearing arguments and making rulings where necessary in the absence of the magistrates when it would be potentially unfairly prejudicial to the defendant to make such rulings in their presence. This would seem to permit a judge to rule a confession inadmissible or to make rulings on the admissibility of character evidence in the absence of magistrates with the result that magistrates need never hear of any evidence ruled inadmissible. But the Review goes on to consider that for all other purposes the tribunal would constitute a single tribunal hearing all the evidence together. At the close of the trial the judge and magistrates would retire together to consider the question of guilt or innocence, although the task of passing sentence would be reserved to the judge. There is a danger here that the judge may form a strong view of the evidence from inadmissible evidence which inevitably colours the discussion of guilt or innocence. A further danger is that the presiding judge may taint the tribunal with inadmissible evidence to which he or she has been privy, albeit inadvertently. The problem of triers of fact becoming privy to such evidence has, of course, long been a feature of trial by magistrates and it is not unknown for inadmissible evidence even to come to the attention of jurors.[48] The Review's answer to the problem lies in reform of the law of evidence where it recommends a move away from orality and rules of inadmissibility to "trusting" fact finders to assess the weight of evidence for

[46] J. Jackson and S. Doran, *Judge without Jury: Diplock Trials in the Adversary System* (1995, Oxford: Clarendon Press) 293.

[47] *ibid.*, 232.

[48] See M. Wasik, "Magistrates: Knowledge of Previous Convictions" [1996] Crim.L.R. 851, R. Munday, "Irregular Disclosure of Evidence of Bad Character" [1990] Crim.L.R. 92.

themselves.[49] But this assumes that fact finders can be trusted with such evidence. Recent research on the effect of admitting previous convictions before tribunals of fact is not altogether encouraging in this respect and does not offer any confidence for believing that magistrates can be trusted with such evidence any more than juries.[50]

A further problem with the professional trial was found to lie in the degree of dominance which professional judges were able to take over the conduct of the case thereby discouraging the defence from mounting a full contest to the prosecution case. Jurors by contrast traditionally assume a passive role throughout the trial allowing the parties to develop their case relatively uninhibited by the intrusion of an active trier of fact. One of the advantages of a mixed tribunal may be that a collegiate bench would be unable quite so easily to communicate its views about a case at an early stage of the proceedings as a single judge. The Review's recommendation that the tribunal should consist of experienced magistrates who can offset any inclination on the part of a presiding judge to dominate proceedings may in this respect work to the advantage of an accused. The truth is, however, that very little is known about how the collegiate benches operate whether they be composed of professionals, lay triers of fact or are mixed. Mixed tribunals operate in a number of civil law jurisdictions but while there has been research into the degree of participation observed by lay judges in mixed tribunals,[51] little research has been undertaken into the way in which mixed tribunals interact with the parties in the case. One way to offset any adversarial deficit resulting from a more intrusive tribunal might be to insist that the tribunal must be unanimous before a guilty verdict may be returned. But in common with other mixed tribunals around the world, the Review considers that decisions of guilt may be reached by a majority only, with the judge giving the reasoned decision of the court, even presumably where he or she is outvoted by the two lay members. Another mechanism to ensure that the tribunal responds fully to the submissions of the parties on guilt or innocence of the defendant would be for the tribunal to deliver a fully reasoned provisional decision which either party could respond to before final judgment.

The lack of information as to how a mixed tribunal along the lines recommended by the Review would operate is likely to lead to reservations as to whether any adversarial deficit which the defendant suffers by dint of the absence of the jury can be sufficiently addressed by such a tribunal. Given the relative seriousness of the cases which it is proposed that such a tribunal would deal with, it may be thought that it is too great a risk to subject defendants to it against their will. The Review itself starts from the position that any change to the system of trial by jury requires a compelling case and it is submitted that the lack of evidence about the operation of a mixed tribunal is a fatal weakness in the case for such a far reaching shift from jury trial to mixed tribunal as that recommended by the Review. It may be, however,

[49] Review, 541.

[50] See S. Lloyd-Bostock, "The Effects on Juries of Hearing About the Defendant's Previous Convictions: A Simulation Study" [2000] Crim.L.R. 734 and S. Lloyd-Bostock, *The Effects on Magistrates of Learning that the Defendant has a Previous Conviction* (2000), London: Lord Chancellor's Department, Research Series No. 3/00.

[51] For a good overview of this research see K. S. Ivkovic, "Lay Participation in Decision-making: A Croatian Perspective on Mixed Tribunals" (1997) 36 *Howard Journal of Criminal Justice* 406, 406–408. See also J. Seekings and C. Murray, *Lay Assessors in South Africa's Magistrates' Courts* (1998), University of Capetown.

that thought should nevertheless be given to rolling out this mode of trial in a greater variety of cases than hitherto, especially with the consent of the accused. If we were to hold to the line that defendants should not lose their right to choose trial by jury in any case where they are liable to be sentenced to six months or more, it would still be possible to roll out a mixed tribunal with a jurisdiction similar to that recommended by the Review in middle range cases where the defendant elected to be tried in this manner. If the Review's recommendation that appeals against conviction and sentence from the magistrates' court to the Crown Court by way of a rehearing should be abolished were not accepted, it would also be possible to extend the jurisdiction of the mixed tribunal to these appeals. An evaluation of the operation of the mixed tribunal could then be made and decisions to extend its jurisdiction with more far reaching consequences for defendants could be made on the basis of more informed knowledge.

New modes of trial for serious offences

Although the Review considers that the trial of the most serious offences is best conducted by means of a judge and jury in the majority of cases, it believes that a number of improvements are needed to improve jury trial and that some cases are not suited to jury trial at all. While acknowledging that trial by jury is a hallowed institution which commands much public confidence, it states that support for it is not universal, not least among those who have been jurors, and considers that one of the problems is that juries do not reflect the broad range of skills and experience or ethnic diversity of the communities from which they are drawn. Although there has been little empirical support in England and Wales for the view that jurors themselves have a negative view of jury service or that they are unrepresentative of the population as a whole,[52] there is evidence which the Review points to for the view that large numbers of people are able to avoid jury service through being ineligible, disqualified or excused,[53] and the Review believes that if the pool from which jurors are drawn were increased this should improve the quality of juries and reduce the general burden of jury service. To this end it makes a number of recommendations drawn from U.S. jurisdictions such as enlarging the sources for jury qualification and removing the main categories of ineligibility and excusal as of right.

These proposals would all have the effect of strengthening the operation of the principle of random selection but, in a recommendation which harks back to an earlier recommendation of the Royal Commission on Criminal Justice, it controversially proposes to modify the principle in trials where race is likely to be a relevant issue by enabling up to three people from any ethnic minority group to sit on a jury. This is recommended not on the basis that persons have a right to have represented on the jury someone from their background but on the basis of studies suggesting that white juries are or are perceived to be less fair to black than to white

[52] Michael Zander has pointed out that the only major survey of jurors in England and Wales shows an overwhelmingly positive view of jury service and that as regards age and ethnic balance the jury is broadly representative of the general population: *op. cit.*, n.10 above, 7–8. See M. Zander and P. Henderson, *The Crown Court Study* (1993, London: H.M.S.O.) Royal Commission on Criminal Justice, Research Study No. 19, 231–236.

[53] See J. Airs and A. Shaw, *Jury Excusal and Deferral* (1999) London: Home Office Research and Statistics, Research Findings No. 102.

people.[54] Such studies as there are, however, do not indicate that concerns about racial bias are limited to cases where race becomes an issue in the trial.[55] Despite the difficulties associated with a proposal which permits a judge to engineer the composition of the jury in certain cases but not otherwise, the Review preferred this solution to a procedure enabling parties to challenge jurors by way of North American jury examination or by means of peremptory challenge. It has been pointed out that one serious consequences of the abolition of the peremptory challenge was that a potential means of ensuring a racial mix on juries was lost.[56] In this context it is interesting to observe the experience of Northern Ireland where the right of peremptory challenge has been deliberately retained as a "safety valve" enabling defendants to correct any perceived religious imbalance.[57]

Another possible "safety valve" for defendants who have little confidence in the ability of a jury to try their case fairly is that they should be able to opt for trial by judge alone. Although this is not a reform that figured prominently in its consultation process, the Review reports that it is a mode of trial which is in widespread use in other common law jurisdictions in a variety of circumstances where defendants do not trust juries to try their cases competently and fairly. These include cases where defendants are concerned about whether juries will understand their case, cases where there are technical defences and where it is desirable to have a reasoned decision, cases where they face offences which have considerable emotional overtones or which have attracted adverse publicity and cases involving types of evidence such as confession or identification evidence which judges may subject to greater scrutiny than juries. Although this mode of trial runs against the grain of tradition in England and Wales, the Review believes that there is a strong case for its introduction. In cases where there are potentially serious consequences for defendants there are good reasons for making defendants as comfortable as possible with their mode of trial and it has been argued in an article in this *Review* that there is a case for jury waiver.[58] We put forward the case earlier on the footing that if it is considered that defendants should have a right to jury trial in cases deemed suitably serious, then there is a logic in saying that they should be able to waive it. But this would seem to run against the Review's principle that defendants should not be able to choose their mode of trial and, in keeping with its general approach, the Review makes its recommendation that defendants should be able to opt for trial by judge alone subject to the consent of the court.

The proposal that the consent of the court is necessary may need further thought as it raises the question as to when a judge should withhold consent and whether there should be an appeal against the judge's decision in order to ensure consistency of practice between judges. The Review rather tentatively considers that the public

[54] See the discussion of research findings by P. Darbyshire, "What can the English Legal System Learn From Jury Research Published up to 2000?", a paper commissioned by the Review and accessible online via the Criminal Court Review website: www.criminal-courts-review.org.uk. See also the concerns expressed in Zander and Henderson, *op. cit.*, n.52 above, 241.

[55] See Sanders and Young, *op. cit.*, n.5 above, 565–566.

[56] Lloyd-Bostock and Thomas, *op. cit.*, n.5 above, 74.

[57] J. Jackson, K. Quinn and T. O'Malley, "The Jury System in Contemporary Ireland: In the Shadow of a Troubled Past" in Vidmar, *op. cit.*, n.5 above, 310.

[58] S. Doran and J. Jackson, "The Case for Jury Waiver" [1997] Crim.L.R. 155. See also the view of the Northern Ireland Human Rights Commission, *Making a Bill of Rights for Northern Ireland* (2001), 13.

interest may require a jury in cases of certain offences against the State or public order but puts forward no justification for this view. Ironically, it is these very kinds of offences in respect of which it has been considered necessary to abolish jury trials in Northern Ireland.[59] To the extent that this argument rests on a belief that there would be greater public confidence in a jury decision in such cases, this would seem to run counter to the Review's view that public confidence should not dictate a particular mode of trial and that the key question is whether the mode of trial is fair and efficient. There are strong grounds for presuming that the defendant is the best judge of fairness in such cases,[60] and as regards efficiency it may be argued that this mode of trial is considerably more efficient in terms of use of resources than jury trial.[61] The Review acknowledges that there are other practical questions which would require attention. One of these relates to the time at which the defendant should exercise the option so as to prevent "judge-shopping". It is proposed that defendants should opt early in the preparation for trial but this would prevent defendants electing for this mode of trial after a particular jury had been chosen which they were unhappy with and would thereby inhibit the attraction of the proposal in so far as it is designed to offer a "safety-valve" for defendants.

Apart from the need to permit defendants to argue for trial by judge alone, the Review considers that there are certain kinds of cases which are unsuitable for jury trial whatever the defendant's attitude. It makes a number of recommendations designed to make it easier for jurors who come fresh to the forensic process to understand the trial process and the issues in the case at hand. Despite these recommendations the Review considers that there are certain kinds of cases of such complexity that are too difficult for juries to deal with. The obvious candidate which has been the subject of considerable debate in England and Wales are cases of serious and complex fraud. The Review recommends that in these cases the trial judge should have the power to direct in the interests of justice trial by the judge sitting with lay members drawn from a panel of experts in various specialities maintained by the Lord Chancellor, although defendants would retain their power to opt for trial by judge alone.

The Review accepts that there are other cases of considerable complexity involving medical or scientific issues and accepts the logic that there is a strong case for extending this reform to other cases of complexity as well. But in keeping with its pragmatic approach it considers that there is something to be said for establishing these new procedures in a limited category of cases first of all before rolling out the reform to other kinds of cases. Of course, it is exactly this kind of logic which has so alarmed defenders of the jury about the proposal to withdraw the jury in serious and complex fraud trials.[62] Although the Review claims that the preponderance of research evidence supports the obvious proposition that the more complicated the

[59] *op. cit.*, n.46 above, chapter 2.

[60] This seems to be the attitude taken by the New Zealand courts where the court may override the defendant's wishes "in the interests of justice": see s.361B of the Crimes Act 1961 and *Narain* [1988] 1 N.Z.L.R. 580. For recent discussion, see New Zealand Law Commission, *Juries in Criminal Trials* (2001), Law Commission report No. 69, 21–25.

[61] In our comparison of jury trials and trials by judge alone in the Northern Ireland Diplock system we found that there was a marked tendency for Diplock trials to be shorter than jury trials, see J. Jackson and S. Doran, *op. cit.*, n.46 above, 198.

[62] See S. Doran, "Trial by Jury" in M. McConville and G. Wilson, *The English Criminal Process* (2002, Oxford: Oxford University Press) (forthcoming). For further discussion of the proposal to try fraud cases without juries, see the article by David Corker in this issue.

issue the more difficult it is for juries, the research commissioned by the Review on what can be learned from jury research made no attempt to examine jury research into complex and lengthy serious fraud trials.[63] Despite the wealth of research work on juries highlighted in Appendix 2 of the Report, little work has been done, certainly in this country, into the performance of juries in fraud and other complex cases and it would seem that there is an insecure basis for justifying the Review's proposals on grounds of complexity alone. There remains, however, another factor which the Review found compelling which is that many serious fraud trials in particular can impose considerable burdens on the jurors who have to hear them. Michael Zander has considered with some reluctance that the difficulty in finding juries for these cases that are a true cross-section of society justifies the Review recommendation.[64] If this were the only ground for justifying trials without a jury in these cases the criteria to be applied by judges in deciding whether to order a trial without a jury would have to be narrowed quite considerably. The Review makes a number of recommendations to ensure that juries are not deprived of a range of professional skills and it appears to endorse the Royal Commission's view that only literate persons should serve as jurors in fraud cases by suggesting that judges should have the power to act as a filter to ensure that illiterate persons do not sit as jurors in fraud trials or other cases involving critical documentary evidence. The case for a non-jury trial would only then be made out where it proves impossible to empanel a jury with sufficient professional and literacy skills.

Another kind of case which the Review considers unsuited for jury trial is one involving young defendants. It refers to the decision of the European Court in *T and V v. United Kingdom* as raising a number of issues about the appropriateness of the public, formal and otherwise intimidating procedure of a Crown Court trial for young children charged with grave offences.[65] The Practice Direction issued in response to this decision contained valuable guidance for minimising many of these features but the Review still questions whether Crown Court trial is the appropriate forum. This points more to the unsuitability of Crown Court trial procedures for hearing these cases than to the inappropriateness of the jury as a tribunal for hearing them. Admittedly, the presence of the jury itself can instil a greater formality into trial procedure but it would not seem to be impossible to provide for trial by jury in the less formal and private atmosphere of a special youth court. Two other factors are mentioned by the Review for justifying the absence of the jury in these cases. First, the Review points to the need to deal with youth cases speedily and compares the performance of the Crown Court in this respect unfavourably with that of the youth court. Again, however, this factor points to the need to try all youth cases under the same roof rather than to exclude juries from the most serious cases. Of more direct relevance to juries is the second factor that judges receive training to handle cases involving young defendants whereas juries, of course, do not. But trained judges should be able to advise jurors on any expertise they have gained through training on matters of fact in the course of their summing up and in any event it has been questioned whether largely white middle class males in their late 40s are better equipped, even with the benefit of training, to try these cases than

[63] See P. Darbyshire, "What Can We Learn from Published Jury Research? Findings for the Criminal Courts Review 2001" [2001] Crim.L.R. 970, 979.

[64] *op. cit.*, n.8 above, 24.

[65] (1999) 30 E.H.R.R. 121.

jurors.[66] If there was an acceptance that trained judges were better equipped to handle young defendant cases, this raises the further question whether there may not be other cases involving child witnesses but not child defendants which may be better dealt with by judges than by juries. The logic would point to excluding juries in these cases as well and indeed the Review questions the appropriateness of juries trying child abuse cases without making any specific recommendation on this. Again, it would seem that the proper response to these concerns is to evaluate the performance of juries in these cases before considering any recommendations for change.

All these proposals for non-jury trial would clearly have the effect of restricting jury trial. In the case of the proposals for jury waiver and serious fraud it is uncertain how great the restrictions would be as it is uncertain how often defendants would wish to opt for a trial by judge alone and how often judges would agree to the ordering of a non-jury trial in serious fraud cases. In the case of young defendants, however, who for this purpose include all defendants under 18, the number of cases could be quite considerable. The Review states that in 1999, 4,718 young defendants were committed for trial to the Crown Court. What is so sweeping about the proposal is that unlike the others the defendant is not even given an opportunity to argue for jury trial in a particular case. To those who are already concerned at the large number of near adults who are tried in the youth court in the absence of a jury,[67] the proposal will surely be unacceptable and it is unlikely to find favour in this form even with those who are more inclined to agree with the Review that decisions involving the mode of trial for young persons should be left to the courts.[68]

Shifting the balance between judge and jury

The Review's radical agenda for change does not stop at the point where it is content for cases to be tried by jury. We have already mentioned the changes which are recommended to the composition of the jury in order to improve the quality of jury decision making. The Review, however, considers that it is necessary to take steps to control the jury once it has been empanelled. One of these is the recommendation that section 8 of the Contempt of Court Act 1981 should be amended to permit where appropriate inquiry by the trial judge and/or the Court of Appeal into alleged impropriety by a jury whether in the course of its deliberations or otherwise. The Review suggests that section 8 needs to be changed for two reasons, first that the bar on an appellate court inquiring into and remedying bias or other impropriety is indefensible and capable of causing injustice and secondly that it is also highly vulnerable to challenge under Article 6 of the European Convention on Human Rights.

The injustice that may arise by the provision was illustrated in *Young*, the famous ouija board case referred to by the Review where the Court of Appeal indicated that it had jurisdiction to inquire into whether jurors had conducted a ouija board session in a hotel room but not into what had taken place in the jury room.[69] The human rights argument would seem to stem from *Sander v. United Kingdom*, where

[66] See *The Times*, December 7, 2001.
[67] See, *e.g.*, Sanders and Young, *op. cit.*, n.5 above, 540.
[68] See, *e.g.*, Zander, *op. cit.*, n.10 above, 24–25.
[69] [1995] 2 Cr.App.R. 379.

the European Court of Human Rights held that the applicant did not receive a fair trial when during the trial of two Asian defendants a juror had sent a note to the trial judge alleging that two of his fellow jurors had been making openly racist remarks and jokes.[70] The next morning the judge received two further notes, one from a juror admitting he had made racist jokes and that he was sorry he had given offence and another signed by all the jurors, including the juror who had sent the complaint stating that they utterly refuted any allegation of bias. The European Court held that there was sufficient evidence to give rise to legitimate doubts as to the impartiality of the jury.

It has been argued that section 8 cannot be read compatibly with Article 6 when the section frustrates the investigation of a genuine complaint which if true would mean that the defendant had not received a fair trial.[71] Whatever the strength of the arguments about enabling the Court of Appeal to investigate complaints after a conviction,[72] there would seem to be a strong case for at least allowing trial judges in the course of the trial to investigate complaints of impropriety. The difficulty is how far judges should be permitted to go in this direction. When jurors swear an oath to give a true verdict according to the evidence it may be argued that they agree to engage in a process of deliberation on the evidence and the drawing of lots or the use of ouija boards would seem to be well outside these limits. More difficulty arises when judges are asked to intervene over allegations concerning the content of what was said in a jury room. It is easy to condemn statements of racial bias against the accused but what about complaints of bias against victims and witnesses? The European Court has held that under Article 2 of the European Convention states must take steps to protect individuals whose lives are known to be at risk from the criminal acts of others.[73] To take an extreme example, what should a judge do when a complaint is made that a jury is about to acquit a defendant who is charged with the attempted murder of a victim and there is strong evidence against him and evidence also that he is likely to remain a serious risk to the victim's life? A further question is what a judge should do when a complaint is made that jurors are engaging in jury nullification. We have seen that the Review would seem to have no difficulty in regarding statements of nullification as improper. The Californian Supreme Court has gone so far as to consider that jurors who express their intent to engage in nullification should be discharged during deliberation.[74] But it is unlikely there will be a consensus that judicial inquiries should be as intrusive as this. A distinction has traditionally been made between allegations of improper influences extrinsic to the deliberation process which may be investigated and statements made in the course of the deliberation process which are inadmissible in a number of jurisdictions.[75] This would not necessarily prevent inquiries being made about what happened in the jury room, where say, it is alleged that one juror

[70] [2000] 8 B.H.R.C. 279.

[71] K. Starmer, M. Strange and Q. Whitaker, *Criminal Justice, Police Powers and Human Rights* (2001, London: Blackstone) 160–161. See also J. R. Spencer, "Inscrutable Verdicts, the Duty to Give Reasons and Article 6 of the European Convention on Human Rights" (2001) 1 Archbold News, 5–6.

[72] See Michael Zander's comments on this, *op. cit.*, n.10 above, 17–18.

[73] *Osman v. United Kingdom* [1999] E.H.R.L.R. 228.

[74] *People v. Williams*, Cal., No. S066106, *People v. Cleveland*, Cal., No. S078537 (2001).

[75] Archbold, *Criminal Pleading, Evidence and Practice* (2001), 4–254. See *Blackwell* [1995] 2 Cr.App.R. 625, *Pan; Sawyer* (2001) 200 D.L.R. (4th) 577, r.606(b) of the Federal Rules of Evidence.

was assaulting another and may even cover the ouija board example. But it would seem that pressure is mounting for some relaxation of this rule in cases where irregularities are alleged in the conduct of jury deliberations.

Although a change to section 8 allowing judges to make inquiries into the deliberation process may prove controversial, it would be likely to affect only a minority of cases as such inquiries would be dependent on allegations of impropriety being made by jurors against their fellow jurors. What is arguably much more intrusive is the Review's further recommendation that in appropriate cases judges should be permitted to require a jury to answer publicly a series of questions which lead logically to a verdict of guilty or not guilty and to declare a verdict in accordance with those answers. It is important to take this recommendation in two stages. The first stage relates to putting a series of questions to jurors to help structure their decision making. The Review makes the point that the manner in which directions are issued to juries with often many and complex alternatives being put to them must be very difficult for them, untrained as they are in such close analysis. Instead of directing jurors on the law the Review adopts the suggestions made by the late Professor Griew that judges should pose questions of fact which reflect the state of the law.[76] Although there is little evidence in England and Wales to suggest that jurors have much difficulty following judges' present directions on the facts and the law,[77] there is an abundance of social science evidence elsewhere to suggest that in "study after study jurors do not understand the law they are given, often performing at no better than chance levels on objective tests of comprehension".[78] Field experiments have shown that in trials where juries were asked to answer questions in a special verdict form, jurors reported feeling better informed, more satisfied and more confident that their verdict was correct and reflected a proper understanding of the judge's instruction.[79] A number of jurisdictions are now regarding it as sensible to give jurors a series of questions for them to consider in the course of their deliberations at least in complex cases.[80] One danger is that jurors may be tempted to answer "yes" or "no" to the questions put in perfunctory fashion, with little discussion of the evidence. To combat this, however, juries could be asked to begin their deliberation with a discussion of the questions put rather than by a vote, so that an "evidence-driven" rather than a "vote-driven" approach is taken.

A further question is whether juries should be *required* to answer these questions in certain cases. Here the emphasis shifts away from what can be done to help aid jury decision making towards what can be required of juries to make them more accountable for the decisions they reach. The Review again appears to consider that there are both human rights reasons and reasons of justice for requiring special verdicts. The Review makes the point that the jury is unique among decision makers

[76] E. Griew, "Summing Up the Law" [1989] Crim.L.R. 768.

[77] Zander, *op. cit.*, n.10 above, 72.

[78] P. Ellsworth and A. Reifman, "Juror Comprehension and Public Policy: Perceived Problems and Proposed Solutions" (2001) *Psychology, Public Policy and the Law.*

[79] L. Heuer and S. D. Penrod, "Trial Complexity: A field investigation of its meaning and effects" (1994) 18 *Law and Human Behaviour* 29. See also E. C. Wiggins and S. J. Breckler, "Special Verdicts as Guides to Jury Decision Making" (1990) 14 *Law & Psychology Review* 1.

[80] See *e.g.* New Zealand Law Reform Commission, *op. cit.*, n.60 above, para. 318.

in the English criminal trial process in not having to explain its decision.[81] It accepts that the European Court would not consider the unreasoned verdict to breach Article 6 but considers that the English courts may be more determinative than the European Court in this respect. The notion that English courts will be prepared to challenge the traditional general verdict has been questioned.[82] In any event to move towards special verdicts purely to conform to what future human rights jurisprudence *may* require seems a rather thin basis for reform. The question remains whether there are sound reasons in principle for such a reform. The Review considers that there are a number of advantages in the proposal: it would reduce the ability of juries to return a perverse verdict of guilty or not guilty, it would lead to a more honest and open system of justice, it should induce a more structured debate in the jury room, it could identify the impact of controversially admitted evidence on the verdict and could lead to more informed appellate decisions.

Whatever the merits of the proposal, however, there are a number of practical difficulties with it as it stands. The Review envisages the judge requiring public answers to questions "where he considers it appropriate" but gives no indication as to what these cases may be.[83] To avoid inconsistent judicial practices there would need at the least to be some guidance given as to when special verdicts are appropriate. Then there may be a difficulty in the formulation of questions, particularly in complex cases where there are a number of defendants who are facing multiple charges. The Review acknowledges that there might also be an increase in non-unanimous verdicts as jurors will have to agree on each ingredient of the offence charged before they may convict. Strictly speaking, this is no different from the existing position.[84] But the fact that juries must explicitly answer questions to this effect may increase the scope for disagreement.

The Review accepts that the proposal will encounter strong opposition from those who cherish the jury's ability to enter a perverse verdict. It is suggested that a distinction may be made here between making juries accountable for convictions and making them accountable for acquittals. While we have traditionally permitted juries a nullification role in respect of acquittals,[85] we do not permit them to ignore the law in order to convict on the basis of some extra-legal standard. Convictions must be based on the declared law and this is why we permit the defence to appeal against wrongful convictions and permit appellate courts to quash convictions which are not based on the law and the evidence. It would seem therefore that there is nothing in principle wrong in requiring juries to provide answers to questions on elements of the criminal charge as a means of arriving at a guilty verdict. It is different in the case of acquittals. There is not the space here to revisit the long-standing debate over jury nullification. It can be plausibly argued that in a modern democracy where citizens are given human rights protections and remedies against abuse of process, it is anachronistic to consider that there remains a role for juries

[81] See also L. Blom-Cooper, "Article 6 and Modes of Criminal Trial" (2001) E.H.R.L.R. 1.

[82] [2002] Crim.L.R. 2.

[83] Review, 538.

[84] See *Brown* (1983) 79 Cr.App.R. 15, *Giannetto* [1997] 1 Cr.App.R. 1. See R. Taylor, "Jury Unanimity in Homicide" [2001] Crim.L.R. 283.

[85] See M. D. A. Freeman, "The Jury on Trial" [1981] C.L.P. 65.

to act as a "stop gap" against state oppression.[86] But there arguably remains a role even in the 21st century for juries to exercise equity in cases where the merits of a particular case demand that the law be stretched in a manner which could not be achieved by a professional judge.[87] Even if this role is conceded juries could still be required to disclose by means of a special verdict that they are satisfied that there is a basis in fact for a conviction but be enabled nevertheless to record an acquittal. Juries would then be required to expose publicly the fact that they are acting in a nullification capacity. This might make juries think very carefully about acting in such a role but it might also inhibit them from making a decision genuinely on the merits. Alternatively, the prospect of publicly acting in this role might encourage juries to exercise their nullification role *more* frequently and bring them in consequence into more open confrontation with the law than would be desirable. The jury's exercise of nullification is best viewed as a private act of dissent from legal norms and for this reason it would arguably be inconsistent for the legal system to require a public explanation for it, just as it is considered by some inconsistent for the legal system to allow instructions permitting jury nullification.[88]

Conclusion

The shift that the Review recommends away from lay judging both at the intermediate level of middle range offences and at the most serious end of the offence spectrum is likely to encounter strong opposition as the Review's conception of the lay role in criminal proceedings, and in particular the limited role it conceives for juries, is controversial. There are signs that the Government has already rejected the proposal for a third tier of jurisdiction before the consultation period has ended.[89] It would be unfortunate, however, if this were to overshadow many of the pragmatic and sensible reforms which the Review recommends on modes of trial and trial procedures. While there will be opposition to the idea of a third tier of jurisdiction as it is presently proposed on the ground that it eats too far into the jury's jurisdiction, the concept of a third tier which can combine a measure of lay participation with appropriate legal expertise for middle range offences should not be ruled out. Similarly, the idea that defendants should be able to opt for trial by judge alone and the ideas for encouraging more structured decision making on the part of juries make a lot of sense. All these ideas would need to be carefully evaluated on a limited basis. It has been suggested that a third tier could be evaluated on the basis of a more limited jurisdiction than the Review proposes. Similarly, the idea of jury waiver could be extended to a category of middle range offences and evaluated in the first place on this basis. The idea of structured questions for juries together with other suggested reforms on jury trials such as providing juries with a more substantial opening statement from the judges, copies of the indictment and a case and issues summary could similarly be rolled out on an experimental basis.

[86] The Review points out (at p.139) that over the last two centuries judges have been more instrumental than juries in declaring and protecting the rights of citizens.

[87] See P. Devlin, *Trial by Jury* (1956, London: Stevens) 154.

[88] See, *e.g.*, R. F. Schopp, "Verdicts of Conscience: Nullification and Necessity as Jury Responses to Crimes of Conscience" (1996) 69 So.Cal.L.R. 2039 (1996).

[89] See *The Times*, January 21, 2002.

Other reforms, arguably, need more careful evaluation before they are implemented. It is suggested that more work needs to be done on the competence of jury decision making in serious fraud and other complex cases and in children's cases. A programme of jury research is also needed to evaluate evidence reforms which depend on trusting the jury and other triers of fact with inadmissible prejudicial evidence before they are implemented. For these reasons it is disappointing that the Review felt unable to recommend amending section 8 of the Contempt of Court Act to enable research on real juries to be undertaken. There is, of course, a considerable body of existing research on juries but valuable as it is, much of it has been conducted in other jurisdictions such as the United States where trial conditions are different. There are also limitations in the methods used in the existing research. Much can be learned from using mock juries or laboratory conditions, or asking real jurors and other participants for their impressions of jury performance but there would also be merit in observing the performance of real juries to see how the system and the rules of procedure and evidence might be improved.[90] Of course, as the Royal Commission on Criminal Justice recommended, such research would have to be carefully controlled but it is rather out of keeping with the general approach of the Review which urges policy makers to inform themselves in a more thorough and measured way than they do now of what changes are required, for it to rule out any amendment of section 8 to permit some authorised jury research to take place.

Policy makers unfortunately have a habit of ignoring the Review's advice to proceed on the basis of informed choice. At the beginning of its report the Review refers to the fact that too often in recent years insufficiently considered legislative reforms have been hurried through in response to political pressures or for quick political advantage. The Review has been a useful exercise in focusing lenses on the longer term and if some of the longer term suggestions such as the need for a statutory-based Criminal Justice Consultative Council, a unified criminal court system and a comprehensive code of criminal law were carried forward this would be a welcome move. Unfortunately, there is a long history of independent reviews being ignored and the alternative scenario is that the Government will focus on the short term reforms it wishes to push through and that the rest of the report will be largely ignored. It would be most unfortunate if a Review which has focused on the longer term were to be used by government in the kind of short term manner which the Review criticises. All those who contributed so helpfully to the Review now have an obligation to see that this does not happen.

[90] Zander, *op. cit.*, n.10 above, 15–16.

Part V
The Civil Trial

[11]

Why Judges, Not Juries, Should Set Punitive Damages

Paul Mogin†

In March 1989, the *Exxon Valdez* ran aground and spilled millions of gallons of oil into Prince William Sound. The trial court phase of the private civil suit concerning that accident culminated in 1996 in a $5.057 billion judgment against Exxon.[1] Almost the entire judgment was based on a jury's award of $5 billion in punitive damages[2]—the largest monetary penalty ever imposed in an American court.

If Exxon had been convicted of a crime, a judge would have determined its sentence.[3] If Exxon had been found liable for a civil penalty under the Clean Water Act, a judge would have set the amount of its penalty.[4] Punitive damages "share key characteristics of criminal sanctions"[5] and are also similar to civil statutory penalties.[6] But because Exxon's penalty was in the form of

---

† Partner, Williams & Connolly, Washington, D.C.

[1] *In re Exxon Valdez*, No A-89-0095-CV (D Alaska, Sept 24, 1996), appeal pending.

[2] *In re Exxon Valdez*, No A-89-0095-CV, 1995 US Dist LEXIS 12952, *12 (D Alaska).

[3] In criminal cases (other than capital cases) sentences are determined by judges in both federal court and the courts of all but eight states. By statute, defendants in six states have a right, in cases triable to a jury, to have a jury fix their punishment, within the limits establisbed by statute. Ark Code Ann § 5-4-103 (Michie 1993); Ky Rev Stat Ann § 532.055(2) (Baldwin 1990 & Supp 1997); Miss Code §§ 97-3-67, 97-3-71 (1994) (granting this right only for crimes of rape and statutory rape); 57 Okla Stat Ann § 353 (West 1991); Tex Crim Proc Code Ann Art 37.07 § 2(b)(2) (Vernon 1981 & Supp 1997) (giving defendant right to choose judge or jury); Va Code § 19.2-295 (1995 & Supp 1997). In Tennessee, defendants have sucb a rigbt in misdemeanor cases. Tenn Code Ann § 40-20-104 (Michie 1990). In Missouri, a trial judge can impose a sentence less than or equal to the sentence chosen by the jury. Mo Ann Stat § 557.036(3) (Vernon 1979 & Supp 1997).

Pursuant to a court-approved settlement with the stato and federal governments, Exxon had pled guilty in 1991 to four misdemeanors, paid a $25 million fine (remitted from $150 million because Exxon had spent $2.5 billion in cleanup costs), and agreed to pay $900 million in additional cleanup costs. *Judge Endorses $1 Billion Exxon Valdez Settlement*, Wash Post A4 (Oct 9, 1991); Tom Kenworthy and Hal Bernton, *$1 Billion-Plus Accord Reached in Exxon Spill*, Wash Post A6 (Oct 1, 1991).

[4] See 33 USC § 1319(d) (1994); *Tull v United States*, 481 US 412, 426-27 (1987).

[5] *Landgraf v USI Film Products*, 511 US 244, 281 (1994) (holding that the punitive damages provision of Section 102(b)(1) of the Civil Rights Act of 1991 cannot be applied to conduct that occurred bofore the law was enacted).

[6] *Tull*, 481 US at 422 n 7.

punitive damages, a jury determined how much Exxon should pay.

The *Exxon Valdez* litigation epitomizes a disparity in the allocation of penalty-setting power that exists both in federal court and in nearly all state courts.[7] Noting this disparity, the Fourth Circuit recently adopted a new and more stringent standard for post-trial review of jury awards of punitive damages.[8] It concluded that, to the extent that a punitive damages award rests on a policy judgment (as opposed to a determination of the facts), a trial judge deciding a motion for remittitur may independently assess how much the defendant should be punished.[9]

Similarly, bills concerning product liability cases introduced in Congress in recent years would have given both federal and state trial judges a greater role in awarding punitive damages. In general, the bills would cap punitive damages at the greater of $250,000 or two times compensatory damages, and a jury's award exceeding the cap could stand only if the trial judge determined in a separate proceeding that the jury's award was warranted.[10]

This Article considers whether, as to cases brought in federal court, the courts can and should go further than either the Fourth Circuit or the recent bills, and squarely place all of the

---

[7] Juries set punitive damages in the first instance in federal court and in the courts of nearly every state that permits the recovery of such damages. The exceptions are the Kansas courts and, in certain actions, the Connecticut courts. Kan Stat Ann § 60-3701(a) (Supp 1992); Gen Stat Conn §§ 31-290a(b), 35-53(b), 36a-618, 42-110g(a), 46a-98(d), 52-240b (1997).

[8] *Atlas Food Systems & Services v Crane National Vendors*, 99 F3d 587, 594-95 (4th Cir 1996).

[9] The Fourth Circuit acknowledged that juries are well suited to determine facts relevant to the amount of punitive damages, but stressed that "other policy-related elements—e.g., the likelihood that an award will deter the defendant or others from engaging in similar conduct—are not factual questions and, therefore, are more appropriately decided by the trial judge." Id at 594. The Fourth Circuit concluded that "when reviewing the *amount* of a jury's punitive award under Federal Rule of Civil Procedure 59, the district court has a participatory decisionmaking role that it does not have when reviewing a jury's findings based solely on facts." Id. "While a district court must give due respect to a jury's comparative advantages in initially deciding upon the amount of punitive damages to award, the court may depart from that award to the extent that it concludes that its own comparative advantages warrant such a departure. . . . The court's review of the amount of a punitive damage award should involve comparison of the court's independent judgment on the appropriate amount with the jury's award to determine whether the jury's award is so excessive as to work an injustice." Id at 595.

[10] See S 5, 105th Cong, 1st Sess § 108 (Jan 21, 1997); S 648, 105th Cong, 1st Sess § 108 (Jan 21, 1997). In March 1996, Congress passed a bill containing similar provisions, but President Clinton veteed it. Common Sense Product Liability Reform Act of 1996, introduced as Common Sense Product Liability Reform Act of 1995, HR 956, 104th Cong, 2d Sess (Feb 15, 1995), in 141 Cong Rec H 1849 (Feb 15 1995). On May 6, 1996, the House failed to override the veto.

power to decide the amount of punitive damages with trial judges.[11] The Supreme Court has never decided whether the Seventh Amendment, which preserves the right to a jury trial in civil cases brought in federal court,[12] confers a right to have punitive damages set by a jury.[13] Three Justices recently implied that the Amendment confers no such right, observing, in *Gasperini v Center for Humanities, Inc*,[14] that "the level of punitive damages is not really a 'fact' 'tried' by the jury."

---

[11] In 1991, President Bush's Council on Competitiveness advocated shifting the power to assess punitive damages from juries to judges. See A Report from the President's Council on Competitiveness, *Agenda for Civil Justice Reform in America* 22 (1991). A Senate committee has done likewise. See S 44, 98th Cong, 2d Sess § 12(c) (1984) (proposed law providing for judicial assessment of punitive damages in product liability cases in federal court), discussed in Preduct Liability Act, S Rep No 476, 98th Cong, 2d Sess 59 (1984) (committee report accompanying S 44). See also S 100, 99th Cong, 1st Sess § 12(c) (1985) (bill containing similar provision); HR 5214, 98th Cong, 2d Sess § 11(b), (c) (1984) (providing for judicial determination of both liability for, and amount of, punitive damages); S 2631, 97th Cong, 2d Sess §13(c) (1982) (same). Many commentators agree. See, for example, Lisa M. Sharkey, Comment, *Judge or Jury: Who Should Assess Punitive Damages?*, 64 U Cin L Rev 1089, 1128-29 (1996); David G. Owen, Comment, *Civil Punishment and the Public Good*, 56 S Cal L Rev 103, 120 (1992); Dorsey H. Ellis, Jr., *Punitive Damages, Due Process, and the Jury*, 40 Ala L Rev 975, 1005-07 (1989); Richard C. Ausness, *Retribution and Deterrence: The Role of Punitive Damages in Products Liability Litigation*, 74 Ky L J 1, 124 (1985); James B. Sales and Kenneth B. Cole, Jr., *Punitive Damages: A Relic That Has Outlived Its Origins*, 37 Vand L Rev 1117, 1167-68 (1984); Jane Mallor and Barry Reberts, *Punitive Damages: Toward a Principled Approach*, 31 Hastinge L J 639, 664 (1980). Judge Kozinski also has questioned the assignment to juries of the power to set punitive damages. See Alex Kozinski, *The Case of Punitive Damages vs. Democracy*, Ind Law 12 (Oct 30-Nov 12, 1996).

[12] "In Suits at common law, where the value in controversy shall exceed twenty dollars, the right of trial by jury shall be preserved, and no fact tried by a jury, shall be otherwise re-examined in any Court of the United States, than according to the rules of the common law." US Const, Amend VII.

[13] Unlike nearly all of the other protections of the Bill of Rights, the guarantees of the Seventh Amendment have not been held to apply te the states through the Fourteenth Amendment. "The Seventh Amendment . . . governs proceedings in federal court, but not in state court." *Gasperini v Center for Humanities, Inc*, 116 S Ct 2211, 2222 (1996) (footnote omitted). See *Walker v Sauvinet*, 92 US 90, 92 (1875) (Seventh Amendment is not a "privilege or immunity . . . which the states are forbidden by the Fourteenth Amendment to abridge."). The Seventh Amendment governs the right to jury trial in diversity as well as federal question cases. *Simler v Conner*, 372 US 221, 222 (1963).

[14] 116 S Ct 2211, 2235 (1996) (Scalia, joined by Rehnquist and Thomas, dissenting). Justice Scalia was quoting the Re-examination Clause of the Seventh Amendment, which provides that "no fact tried by a jury, shall bo otherwise re-examined in any Court of the United States, than according te the rules of the common law." US Const, Amend VII. The issue in *Gasperini*, which involved an award of compensatory damages, was whether the Re-examination Clause precludes appellate review when a trial court denies a motion seeking a new trial because the jury's verdict was excessive. The Court held that the Re-examination Clanse does not preclude such review. 116 S Ct at 2223-24. Justice Scalia, joined by Chief Justice Rehnquist and Justice Thomas, would have held that the Re-examination Clause prohibits appellate review of awards of compensatory damages, but apparently would have reached a different conclusion as to punitive damages because the

The Supreme Court's 1987 decision in *Tull v United States*[15] also indicates that the Seventh Amendment may not require jury assessment of the amount of punitive damages. *Tull* held that a citizen sued by the United States for a penalty under the Clean Water Act had a right to have a jury determine his liability for a penalty, but *not* its amount. The Court broadly stated that "[n]othing in the Amendment's language suggests that the right to a jury trial extends to the remedy phase of a civil trial,"[16] and that it had seen "no evidence that the Framers meant to extend the right to a jury to the remedy phase of a civil trial."[17]

It is time to recognize that, at least in federal court, asking juries to set punitive damages is neither constitutionally required nor sound policy. The responsibility to decide the amount of punitive damages, if the jury finds the defendant liable for such damages, should rest with the trial judge.

Part I of this Article discusses the origins of the Seventh Amendment and the basic principles reflected in the Supreme Court decisions interpreting it. Special attention is given to the Supreme Court decisions establishing that the Seventh Amend-

---

amount of punitive damages is not a "fact" tried by a jury. Id at 2231-36.

Whether state jury-trial guarantees entitle a party to have a jury set punitive damages is similarly an open question in most states. Forty-seven state constitutions protect the right to jury trial in civil cases in state court. See Ala Const, Art I, § 11; Alaska Const, Art I, § 16; Ariz Const, Art II, § 23; Ark Const, Art II, § 7; Cal Const, Art I, § 16; Conn Const, Art I, § 19; Del Const, Art 1, § 4; Fla Const, Art I, § 22; Ga Const, Art I, § 1, ¶ 11; Hawaii Const, Art I, § 13; Idaho Const, Art I, § 7; Ill Const, Art I, § 13; Ind Const, Art I, § 20; Iowa Const, Art I, § 9; Kan Const, Bill of Rights § 5; Ky Const, Bill of Rights § 7; Me Const, Art I, § 20; Md Const, Declaration of Rights, Art 23; Mass Const, pt I, Art 15; Mich Const, Art I, § 14; Minn Const, Art I, § 4; Miss Const, Art III, § 31; Mo Const, Art 1, § 22(a); Mont Const, Art II, § 26; Neb Const, Art I, § 6; Nev Const, Art I, § 3; NH Const, pt I, Art 20; NJ Const, Art I, ¶ 9; NM Const, Art II, § 12; NY Const, Art I, § 2; NC Const, Art I, § 25 (limiting preservation of civil jury trial to "all controversies at law respecting property"); ND Const, Art I, § 13; Ohio Const, Art I, § 5; Okla Const, Art II, § 19; Or Const, Art VII, § 3; Pa Const, Art I, § 6; RI Const, Art I, § 15; SC Const, Art I, § 14; SD Const, Art VI, § 6; Tenn Const, Art I, § 6; Tex Const, Art I, § 15; Utah Const, Art I, § 10 (held to protect civil jury right in *International Harvester Credit Corp v Pioneer Tractor and Implement, Inc*, 626 P2d 418, 421 (Utah 1981)); Vt Const, ch I, Art 12; Va Const, Art I, § 11; Wash Const, Art I, § 21; W Va Const, Art III, § 13; Wis Const, Art I, § 5. Compare *Smith v Printup*, 254 Kan 315, 866 P2d 985, 994 (1993) (holding that there is no right to have a jury set punitive damages), with *Zoppo v Homestead Insurance Co*, 71 Ohio St 3d 552, 644 NE2d 397, 401 (Ohio 1994), cert denied, 116 S Ct 56 (1995) (voiding statute that permitted court to set punitive damages), and *Henderson By Hartsfield v Alabama Power Co*, 627 S2d 878, 885-86, 893-94 (Ala 1993) (striking down legislative cap on punitive damages as violating the right to trial by jury).

[15] 481 US 412, 426-27 (1987).

[16] Id at 426 n 9.

[17] Id. The Fourth Circuit relied upon *Tull* in its recent decision endorsing more stringent review of jury awards of punitive damages. *Atlas*, 99 F3d at 595.

ment preserves only the substance of the right of trial by jury that was recognized by the English common law in the eighteenth century.

Part II examines certain Supreme Court decisions that some courts and commentators have read as establishing a Seventh Amendment right to a jury determination of the amount of punitive damages. This Part concludes that the decisions do not establish the existence of such a right.

Part III analyzes the Supreme Court's decision in *Tull*.

Part IV demonstrates that having juries fix punitive damages is not necessary to preserve the substance of the common-law right to trial by jury. Under the English common law, there was no right to a trial by jury on the issue of damages. In some cases damages were determined in a trial by jury before a judge, but often they were set by an inquest jury in a proceeding before a sheriff pursuant to a writ of inquiry. Such an inquest was intended to inform the conscience of the court, which could instead assess damages itself. Moreover, the common law developed for centuries before 1791, but punitive damages were not recognized until 1763.[18] In one of the early cases allowing damages in excess of the plaintiff's injury, damages were decided by a jury pursuant to a writ of inquiry.[19] Punitive damages today also differ significantly from punitive damages in eighteenth century England.

Part V argues that, as a matter of policy, the power to set punitive damages in federal court should rest with trial judges, subject to appellate review, rather than with juries. Judges are less susceptible to emotional factors, less likely to be unduly influenced by a defendant's wealth, more experienced in imposing punishment, and more knowledgeable of the punishment imposed in other cases.

Finally, Part VI shows that neither a new statute nor an amendment to the Federal Rules of Civil Procedure is necessary to permit federal trial judges to determine the amount of punitive damages.

I. History of the Seventh Amendment and Its Interpretation

The Constitution approved in September 1787 by the Constitutional Convention in Philadelphia guaranteed the right to a

---

[18] See *Wilkes v Wood*, Lofft 1, 98 Eng Rep 489, 498-99 (CP 1763); *Huckle v Money*, 2 Wils KB 205, 95 Eng Rep 768, 769 (KB 1763).

[19] See *Benson v Frederick*, 3 Burr 1845, 97 Eng Rep 1130, 1130 (KB 1766).

jury trial in criminal cases,[20] but it said nothing of the right to a jury trial in civil cases. It also lacked a bill of rights. The proposed Constitution became the focus of a vigorous debate throughout the country, with the Anti-Federalists vociferously attacking it and the Federalists defending it. The Anti-Federalists objected most strongly to the lack of a bill of rights, the Supreme Court's appellate jurisdiction as to law and fact, and the absence of a civil jury-trial guarantee.[21]

In several states, the Anti-Federalists succeeded in obtaining support for proposed amendments protecting the right to jury trial in civil cases. The Virginia Ratifying Convention urged the adoption of an amendment providing that, "in controversies respecting property, and in suits between man and man, the ancient trial by jury is one of the greatest securities to the rights of the people, and [is] to remain sacred and inviolable."[22] New York's convention proposed essentially the same amendment.[23] The Massachusetts and New Hampshire conventions proposed an amendment stating that "[i]n civil actions between Citizens of different States every issue of fact arising in Actions at common law shall be tried by a Jury, if the parties, or either of them, request it."[24]

In response, the Federalists denied that the Constitution was intended to limit jury trials in civil cases,[25] and they promised to enact legislation to protect the right to a jury trial in such cases.[26] The Anti-Federalists insisted, however, on a constitutional guarantee.[27] Their efforts led to the inclusion in the Bill of Rights of what became the Seventh Amendment, guaranteeing a jury trial in suits at common law and restricting re-examination of jury verdicts:

> In Suits at common law, where the value in controversy shall exceed twenty dollars, the right of trial by jury shall be pre-

---

[20] US Const, Art IV, § 2, cl 3.

[21] See Edith Guild Henderson, *The Background of the Seventh Amendment*, 80 Harv L Rev 289, 295 (1966).

[22] Jonathan Elliot, 3 *The Debates in the Several State Conventions, on the Adoption of the Federal Constitution* 658 (2d ed 1836) ("*Elliot's Debates*").

[23] 1 *Elliot's Debates* at 328-29.

[24] Ralph Ketcham, ed, *The Anti-Federalist Papers and the Constitutional Convention Debates* 219 (Mentor 1986); 1 *Elliot's Debates* at 326.

[25] See, for example, Federalist 83 (Hamilton), in Clinton Rossiter, ed, *The Federalist Papers* 495, 498-99 (Mentor 1961).

[26] See Charles W. Wolfram, *The Constitutional History of the Seventh Amendment*, 57 Minn L Rev 639, 666 (1973).

[27] See, for example, 3 *Elliot's Debates* at 579, 651-52.

> served, and no fact tried by a jury, shall be otherwise re-examined in any Court of the United States, than according to the rules of the common law.[28]

The Bill of Rights was approved by Congress in September 1789,[29] and obtained the required approval of three-fourths of the states in late 1791.[30]

Although the general words of the Seventh Amendment were sufficient to secure agreement in 1791, their meaning has been sharply disputod many times in the two centuries since.[31] The Supreme Court has interpreted the Seventh Amendment in dozens of decisions, not all of them consistent with each other.[32]

Despite the controversy and uncertainty that have surrounded the Seventh Amendment, several pertinent principles concerning its scope are reasonably well established. The Supreme Court has held that the "common law" referred to in the Seventh Amendment is the common law of England,[33] though not all aspects of the English jury-trial system that existed in 1791

---

[28] US Const, Amend VII.

[29] 1 Stat 98 (1789).

[30] See Wolfram, 57 Minn L Rev at 730 (cited in note 26) (reviewing the constitutional history of the Seventh Amendment).

[31] The Seventh Amendment has generated extensive scholarly commentary. Some of the leading articles are Wolfram, 57 Minn L Rev 639 (cited in note 26); Martin H. Redish, *Seventh Amendment Right to Jury Trial: A Study in the Irrationality of Rational Decision Making*, 70 Nw U L Rev 486 (1975) (arguing that the Supreme Court should take account of social conditions when interpreting the Seventh Amendment); Harold Chesnin and Geoffrey C. Hazard, Jr., *Chancery Procedure and the Seventh Amendment: Jury Trial of Issues in Equity Cases Before 1791*, 83 Yale L J 999 (1974) (showing that jury practice was in transition in England during the 1790s, and suggesting that Seventh Amendment interpretation is more complex than previously thought); Henderson, 80 Harv L Rev 289 (cited in note 21) (arguing that the Seventh Amendment was not intended to codify existing jury practice because there was no consistont practice in 1791); and Austin Wakeman Scott, *Trial by Jury and the Reform of Civil Procedure*, 31 Harv L Rev 669 (1918) (discussing historical features of trial by jury and examining methods for controlling jury power).

[32] Compare, for example, *Dimick v Schiedt*, 293 US 474, 487 (1935) ("[H]ere, we are dealing with a constitutional provision which has in effect adopted the rules of the common law, in respect of trial by jury, as these rules existed in 1791."), with *Gasperini v Center for Humanities, Inc*, 116 S Ct 2211, 2224 n 20 (1996) (noting that the meaning of the Seventh Amendment was not fixed as of 1791). See also notes 60, 75-76, and accompanying text.

[33] *Markman v Westview Instruments, Inc*, 116 S Ct 1384, 1389 (1996); *Baltimore & Carolina Line, Inc v Redman*, 295 US 654, 657 (1935); *Dimick*, 293 US at 476-77; *Thompson v Utah*, 170 US 343, 350 (1898), overruled on other grounds by *Collins v Youngblood*, 497 US 37 (1989). See *United States v Wonson*, 28 F Cases 745, 750 (Cir Ct D Mass 1812) (opinion by Stery). Compare *Markman*, 116 S Ct at 1389 n 3 ("Our formulations of the historical test do not deal with the possibility of conflict between actual English common law practice and American assumptions about what that practice was, or between English and American practices at the relevant time.").

are preserved against change.[34] As a result, opinions interpreting the Amendment have often included attempts to delve into the law of eighteenth century England.[35] The Court has also held that the Jury Trial Clause and the Re-examination Clause are independent.[36] Thus, even if a matter is not triable of right to a jury under the Jury Trial Clause, if it is so tried the Re-examination Clause limits post-trial and appellate review of the jury's verdict.

Although the Jury Trial Clause refers to "Suits at common law," it has been interpreted to guarantee a jury trial not only on causes of action that existed under the English common law, but also on many causes of action not recognized until long after 1791. In several cases, the Supreme Court has applied a two-pronged test in deciding whether a party is entitled to a jury trial on a cause of action unknown to the English common law: the first prong compares the new cause of action with actions brought in eighteenth century England and asks whether similar causes of action were tried to a jury; the second prong examines the nature of the remedy sought.[37]

It is well-settled that, even if a given cause of action triggers a right to a jury trial, that right does not necessarily encompass all issues relating to that cause of action.[38] In its most recent discussion of this aspect of Seventh Amendment doctrine, the Supreme Court explained in *Markman v Westview Instruments,*

---

[34] See notes 45-68, 76-77, and accompanying text.

[35] See, for example, *Markman*, 116 S Ct at 1389-93.

[36] *Parsons v Bedford*, 28 US (3 Pet) 433, 447 (1830).

[37] See *Wooddell v International Brotherhood of Electrical Workers*, 502 US 93, 97-98 (1991); *Chauffeurs, Teamsters and Helpers Local 391 v Terry*, 494 US 558, 565 (1990) (plurality opinion); *Granfinanciera, SA v Nordberg*, 492 US 33, 42 (1989); *Tull*, 481 US at 417-18. In its recent decision in *Markman*, where it was undisputed that the cause of action at issue triggered a right to jury trial on some issues, the Court applied the first prong of this test but not the second. 116 S Ct at 1389-92. Earlier cases had treated the second prong as more important. See *Terry*, 494 US at 565 (plurality opinion); *Granfinanciera*, 492 US at 42; *Tull*, 481 US at 421. See also *Curtis v Loether*, 415 US 189, 194 (1974) (implying that "the relief sought here" prong is "more important" than analogous common law actions).

At least two cases applying the two-pronged test treated the presence of a claim for money damages as a factor strongly indicating that a particular cause of action triggered a right to a jury trial. See *Terry*, 494 US at 570; *Curtis*, 415 US at 196-97.

In dicta in a 1970 decision, the Court identified a third facter bearing on whether an issue is triable as of right to a jury: "the practical abilities and limitations of juries." *Ross v Bernhard*, 396 US 531, 538 n 10 (1970). Most of the Court's Seventh Amendment decisions since *Ross* have ignored this factor. See, for example, *Terry*, 494 US at 565 (using two-prong test); *Granfinanciera*, 492 US at 42 (same). Part of the *Markman* opinion can be read as reviving it as a significant consideration when history does not supply a clear answer. 116 S Ct at 1395.

[38] *Markman*, 116 S Ct at 1389-90; *Tull*, 481 US at 427.

Inc[39] that, "[i]f the action in question belongs in the law category, we then ask whether the particular trial decision must fall to the jury in order to preserve the substance of the common law right as it existed in 1791."[40] For example, even if a statutory cause of action triggers the right to a jury trial under the Seventh Amendment, a discretionary award of attorney's fees under the statute may be determined by the trial court, not by a jury.[41]

The statement from *Markman* just quoted also embodies another established—but far from precise—principle of Seventh Amendment jurisprudence: the principle that the Amendment preserves only "the substance of the common law right" of trial by jury.[42] The Supreme Court has declared that "the Amendment was designed to preserve the basic institution of jury trial in only its most fundamental elements,"[43] and that "[o]nly those incidents which are regarded as fundamental, as inherent in and of the essence of the system of trial by jury, are placed beyond the reach of the legislature."[44]

A series of nineteenth century Supreme Court decisions applying this fundamental-elements principle approved the directed verdict without pointing to any clear precedent for it in eighteenth century English law.[45] Similarly, early in this century the Court held that the Seventh Amendment does not prohibit summary judgment, a procedural device that was unknown in England in 1791.[46]

The fundamental-elements principle also was reflected in the Court's 1897 decision in *Walker v New Mexico & Pacific Railroad Co*,[47] where a jury's answers to special interrogatories were inconsistent with its general verdict. The issue was whether the trial court could enter judgment based on the answers to the special

---

[39] 116 S Ct 1384 (1996).

[40] Id at 1389.

[41] See, for example, *Columbus Mills, Inc v Freeland*, 918 F2d 1575, 1578 (11th Cir 1990); *Pan Am World Airways, Inc v Ramos*, 357 F2d 341, 342 (1st Cir 1966); *Swofford v B & W, Inc*, 336 F2d 406, 413 (5th Cir 1964).

[42] *Markman*, 116 S Ct at 1389; *Colgrove v Battin*, 413 US 149, 156-57 (1973); *Baltimore & Carolina Line, Inc v Redman*, 295 US 654, 657 (1935). See *Capital Traction Co v Hof*, 174 US 1, 23 (1899) ("It is not 'trial by jury,' but 'the right of trial by jury,' which the Amendment declares 'shall be preserved.'").

[43] *Galloway v United States*, 319 US 372, 392 (1943).

[44] *Tull*, 481 US at 426, quoting *Colgrove*, 413 US at 156 n 11 (quoting Scott, 31 Harv L Rev at 671 (cited in note 31)); *Markman*, 116 S Ct at 1389.

[45] See *Baylis v Travellers' Insurance Co*, 113 US 316, 320-21 (1885); *Oscanyan v Arms Co*, 103 US 261, 266-67 (1880); *Pleasants v Fant*, 89 US (22 Wall) 116, 120-21 (1874); *Parks v Ross*, 52 US (11 How) 362, 372-73 (1850).

[46] *Fidelity & Deposit Co v United States*, 187 US 315, 319-21 (1902).

[47] 165 US 593, 594-95 (1897).

interrogatories or could only grant a new trial. The Supreme Court did not cite any precedent in the English common law for entering a judgment contrary to the jury's general verdict.[48] But it held that the Seventh Amendment posed no obstacle to entry of such a judgment, because the purpose of the Amendment "is not to preserve mere matters of form and procedure but substance of right."[49]

Numerous decisions in this century reflect the continuing importance of the fundamental-elements principle. In 1920, the Supreme Court held in *Ex parte Peterson*[50] that the Seventh Amendment was not violated by the appointment of an auditor to make a preliminary investigation, hear witnesses, examine financial records, and prepare a report to be admitted at trial as prima facie evidence. The Court acknowledged that "there did not exist in England, or so far as appears in any of the colonies, any officer, permanent or temporary, who, in connection with trials by jury, exercised the powers of an auditor above described."[51] The Court nonetheless found no constitutional violation, because "[n]ew devices may be used to adapt the ancient institution [of jury trial] to present needs and to make of it an efficient instrument in the administration of justice."[52]

In 1931, the Court held in *Gasoline Products Co v Champlin Refining Co*[53] that when a new trial is granted because of an error relating to one issue, the retrial may be limited to that issue, provided that "the issue to be retried is so distinct and separable from the others that a trial of it alone may be had without injustice." The Court so held despite the settled rule of the English common law that a retrial had to be of the entire case.[54]

In the 1943 case *Galloway v United States*,[55] Justice Black, joined in dissent by Justices Douglas and Murphy, attacked as violative of the Seventh Amendment the expanded use of the directed verdict that had been approved in a series of Supreme Court decisions between 1871 and 1929. In response, a six-Justice majority emphasized that the Constitution preserved only the most fundamental elements of the English jury-trial system:

---

[48] Id at 596-97.
[49] Id at 596.
[50] 253 US 300, 310 (1920).
[51] Id at 307-08.
[52] Id at 309-10.
[53] 283 US 494, 500 (1931).
[54] See id at 497.
[55] 319 US 372, 404-05 (1943).

> The Amendment did not bind the federal courts to the exact procedural incidents or details of jury trial according to the common law in 1791, any more than it tied them to the common law system of pleading or the specific rules of evidence then prevailing. Nor were "the rules of the common law" then prevalent, including those relating to the procedure by which the judge regulated the jury's role on questions of fact, crystallized in a fixed and immutable system. On the contrary, they were constantly changing and developing during the late eighteenth and early nineteenth centuries. In 1791 this process already had resulted in widely divergent common-law rules on procedural matters among the states, and between them and England. And none of the contemporaneous rules regarding judicial control of the evidence going to juries or its sufficiency to support a verdict had reached any precise, much less final, form. In addition, the passage of time has obscured much of the procedure which then may have had more or less definite form, even for historical purposes.
>
> . . .
>
> [T]he Amendment was designed to preserve the basic institution of jury trial in only its most fundamental elements, not the great mass of procedural forms and details, varying even then so widely among common-law jurisdictions.[56]

In its 1973 decision in *Colgrove v Battin*,[57] a sharply divided Court relied upon the fundamental-elements doctrine in holding that the "jury trial," as guaranteed by the Seventh Amendment, may be a trial before a jury of only six persons.[58] The Court so held despite the tradition of twelve-person juries dating back at least to the fourteenth century,[59] and despite the fact that many of the Court's own decisions had assumed that the Seventh Amendment requires a twelve-person jury.[60] In an opinion by

---

[56] Id at 390-92 (footnotes omitted).

[57] 413 US 149, 157, 160 (1973).

[58] Compare Richard Arnold, *Trial by Jury: The Constitutional Right to a Jury of Twelve in Civil Trials*, 22 Hofstra L Rev 1 (1993) (criticizing *Colgrove*).

[59] See *Colgrove*, 413 US at 176-77 (Marshall dissenting); Arnold, 22 Hofstra L Rev at 8.

[60] See *Slocum v New York Life Insurance Co*, 228 US 364, 397 (1913); *Maxwell v Dow*, 176 US 581, 586 (1900) (criminal case noting that Seventh Amendment right "implies that there shall be an unanimous verdict of twelve jurors"); *Capital Traction Co*, 174 US at 13. Several other cases assume twelve-person juries, without discussing the Seventh Amendment. See *Crowell v Benson*, 285 US 22, 61 (1932); *Herron v Southern Pacific Co*, 283 US 91, 95 (1931); *Railroad Co v Stout*, 84 US (17 Wall) 657, 664 (1873).

Justice Brennan, the Court explained that the divergence of state practices in 1791 had meant that the civil jury-trial provision of the Bill of Rights "would necessarily have to be general," and that in fact "the right was limited in general words to 'suits at common law.'"[61] The Court could "only conclude . . . that by referring to the 'common law,' the Framers of the Seventh Amendment were concerned with preserving the *right* of trial by jury in civil cases where it existed at common law, rather than the various incidents of trial by jury."[62] The Court framed the question as "whether a jury of 12 is of the substance of the common-law right of trial by jury,"[63] and concluded that it was not.[64]

In its 1979 decision in *Parklane Hosiery Co v Shore*,[65] the Court again relied upon the fundamental-elements principle. The Securities and Exchange Commission ("SEC") had brought an equitable action in which it had secured a declaratory judgment against a corporation for issuing a false and misleading proxy statement.[66] The Court held that the Seventh Amendment posed no obstacle to applying the doctrine of collateral estoppel against the corporation in a subsequent legal action by a class of stockholders, thus precluding the corporation from denying that the proxy statement was false and misleading.[67] The Court so ruled even though at common law mutuality of parties was required before a party could be bound by a prior judgment, and the stockholders had not been parties to the SEC action.[68]

In its 1996 decision in *Markman*, the Court held that the Seventh Amendment right to a jury trial, though applicable to patent-infringement actions, does not confer a right to have a patent construed by a jury.[69] The critical question, the Court said, was "whether the particular trial decision must fall to the jury in order to preserve the substance of the common-law right as it existed in 1791."[70] To answer the question, the Court explained, "the sounder course, when available, is to classify a mongrel practice . . . by using the historical method, much as we do in charac-

[61] *Colgrove*, 413 US at 155.
[62] Id at 155-56 (footnotes omitted).
[63] Id at 157.
[64] Id.
[65] 439 US 322 (1979).
[66] Id at 324-25.
[67] Id at 337.
[68] See id at 335-37.
[69] 116 S Ct at 1389, 1396.
[70] Id at 1389.

terizing the suits and actions within which they arise."[71] If an "exact antecedent" is lacking, "the best hope lies in comparing the modern practice to earlier ones whose allocation to court or jury we do know, . . . seeking the best analogy we can between an old and the new."[72]

Gasperini, the Court's most recent Seventh Amendment decision, is also instructive, although it involved the Reexamination Clause rather than the Jury Trial Clause.[73] At issue was the permissibility of appellate review of the denial of a motion te set aside a jury verdict as excessive.[74] In several opinions from the late nineteenth and early twentieth centuries, the Court had interpreted the Seventh Amendment to bar such review.[75] In *Gasperini*, however, the Court held such review to be "reconcilable with the Seventh Amendment as a control necessary and proper to the fair administration of justice."[76] The Court cited no precedent for the practice in eighteenth century English law. Instead, the Court indicated that the meaning of the Seventh Amendment was not frozen in 1791:

> If the meaning of the Seventh Amendment were fixed at 1791, our civil juries would remain, as they unquestionably were at common law, 'twelve good men and true' . . . . But see *Colgrove v. Battin* (six-member jury for civil trial satisfies Seventh Amendment's guarantee). Procedures we have regarded as compatible with the Seventh Amendment, although not in conformity with practice at common law when the Amendment was adopted, include new trials restricted to the determination of damages, and Federal Rule of Civil Procedure 50(b)'s motion for judgment as a matter of law.[77]

---

[71] Id at 1390.

[72] Id (citations omitted).

[73] See 116 S Ct at 2222.

[74] Id at 2216-17. The verdict in *Gasperini* was for compensatory damages only.

[75] See, for example, *Lincoln v Power*, 151 US 436, 437-38 (1894); *Railroad Co v Fraloff*, 100 US 24, 31-32 (1879).

[76] 116 S Ct at 2223.

[77] Id at 2224 n 20 (citations omitted). See also id at 2225-30 (Stovens dissenting) (disagreeing with the majority on another issue, but agreeing that the Seventh Amendment did not bar appellate review and stating that "[t]here is nothing in its history or language to suggest that the Amendment had any purpose but to preserve the essentials of the jury trial as it was known to the common law before the adoption of the Constitution," quoting *Dimick*, 293 US at 490 (Stone dissenting)). "Judgment as a matter of law" is the term added to FRCP 50 in 1991, replacing the torms "directed verdict" and "judgment notwithstanding the verdict" in federal practice. 28 USCA Rule 50 (1992 & Supp 1997) (Advisory Committee notes).

The principle that the Seventh Amendment preserves only the most fundamental incidents of the English jury-trial system has greatly restricted the reach of the Amendment. The impact of the fundamental-elements principle can be seen today in matters as basic as the number of jurors in the jury box; motions made before, during, and after trial; and the scope of appellate review.

II. Supreme Court Cases Purportedly Establishing the Right to Have a Jury Set Punitive Damages

Some courts and commentators have suggested that certain decisions of the Supreme Court involving awards of damages establish that the Seventh Amendment right to jury trial extends to determining the amount of punitive damages. This Part shows why those cases do not resolve this issue.

A. *Barry v Edmunds*

The Supreme Court's 1886 decision in *Barry v Edmunds*[78] has been cited as authority that the Seventh Amendment confers a right to have a jury set punitive damages.[79] The Court held that an action for trespass should not have been dismissed by the trial court for failure to satisfy the federal amount-in-controversy requirement, which at that time was $500.[80] The trial court had explained that "if the jury should render a verdict for ($500) five hundred dollars damages such verdict would be excessive, and the court would feel compelled to set it aside."[81] The Supreme Court concluded that, to the contrary, a jury could award more than $500, because the value of the horse forcibly taken from the plaintiff by the defendant ($100) "would not necessarily cover [the plaintiff's] actual, direct, and immediate pecuniary loss,"[82] and because the jury could award punitive damages.[83]

Of particular pertinence is the following passage in the Supreme Court's opinion:

> There was clear error in the Circuit Court in its ruling, as matter of law, that there could be no lawful recovery . . . of an amount equal to that which is necessary to support the

[78] 116 US 550 (1886).

[79] See, for example, *Henderson By Hartsfield v Alabama Power Co*, 627 S2d 878, 888-91 (Ala 1993).

[80] See *Barry*, 116 US at 565.

[81] Id at 558.

[82] Id at 562.

[83] Id.

> jurisdiction of the court. The same error was repeated in acting upon the statement, that a verdict, if rendered for that amount, would be excessive and set aside for that reason—a statement which could not, at any rate, be judicially made before such a verdict was in fact rendered. It adds, indeed, to the principal error, if any distinction can be made, that which consists in encroaching upon the province of the jury. . . . [I]n such cases as the present, and other actions for torts where no precise rule of law fixes the recoverable damages, it is the peculiar function of the jury to determine the amount by their verdict. . . . [A] verdict will not be set aside in a case of *tort* for excessive damages "unless the court can clearly see that the jury have committed some very gross and palpable error, or have acted under some improper bias, influence or prejudice, or have totally mistaken the rules of law by which the damages are to be regulated"—that is, "unless the verdict is so excessive or outrageous," with reference to all the circumstances of the case, "as to demonstrate that the jury have acted against the rules of law, or have suffered their passions, their prejudices, or their perverse disregard of justice to mislead them." In no case is it permissible for the court to substitute itself for the jury, and compel a compliance on the part of the latter with its own view of the facts in evidence, as the standard and measure of that justice, *which the jury itself is the appointed constitutional tribunal to award.*[84]

It is clear from the parts of the opinion immediately preceding[85] and following this passage[86] that the "damages" referred to included punitive as well as compensatory damages. Therefore, the Court's statement that "the jury itself is the appointed constitutional tribunal to award" damages[87] could be read to mean that the Jury Trial Clause entitles a party to have a jury determine the amount of punitive damages.

---

[84] Id at 565 (latter emphasis added), quoting *Whipple v Cumberland Manufacturing Co*, 29 F Cases 934, 937-38, 2 Story 661, 670 (Cir Ct D Me 1843).

[85] *Barry*, 116 US at 562 ("It is equally clear . . . that the plaintiff is not limited in his recovery to the mere value of the property taken," and may "be entitled to exemplary damages.").

[86] Id at 566 ("The dignity and value of the rights assailed, and the power and authority of the source from which the assault proceeds, are elements to be considered in the computation of damages, not only compensation for the direct loss inflictod, but a remedy and prevention for the greator wrong and injury involved in the apprehension of its repetition.").

[87] Id at 565.

But, considered in its entirety, *Barry* does not so hold. Whether compensatory damages or punitive damages were to be determined by a jury if the case proceeded to trial was not at issue; the trial court had explicitly assumed that damages would be for the jury to assess if the case were tried.[88] The trial court had nevertheless dismissed the action because it had concluded that any jury verdict of more than $500 would have been excessive.[89] The Court's statement that "the jury itself is the appointed constitutional tribunal to award" damages followed a discussion that focused on the limitations of a court's power to set aside as excessive a jury's verdict in a tort action.[90] The statement thus appears to have been made with reference to the Re-examination Clause rather than the Jury Trial Clause. The Court also spoke generally of damages in tort, and did not specifically address punitive damages.[91]

B. *Curtis v Loether*

Eighty-eight years after *Barry*, the Court addressed the right to a jury trial in another case involving a prayer for punitive damages. But, again, it did not hold that there was a right to have the jury set those damages.

In *Curtis v Loether*,[92] an African-American woman alleged that two white men had refused to rent her an apartment because of her race, in violation of Title VIII of the Civil Rights Act of 1968.[93] Her complaint sought injunctive relief and punitive

---

[88] See id at 558.

[89] See id.

[90] Id at 565.

[91] In *Defender Industries, Inc v Northwestern Mutual Life Insurance Co*, 938 F2d 502 (4th Cir 1991) (en banc), the Fourth Circuit cited *Kennon v Gilmer*, 131 US 22 (1889), to support its conclusion that the Seventh Amendment right to jury trial extends to the amount of punitive damages. 938 F2d at 506. In *Kennon*, a jury awarded compensatory damages of $20,750. On appeal, the territorial supreme court held that the damages were excessive and reduced the judgment to $10,750, without allowing the plaintiff to choose a new trial instead. 131 US at 24. The United States Supreme Court held that this reduction violated the Seventh Amendment. 131 US at 27-30. For two reasons, *Kennon* does not indicate that the Seventh Amendment entitles a party to a jury determination of the amount of punitive damages. First, there is no indication that the case involved an award of punitive damages. Second, what issues were triable to a jury was not in question; the issue of damages had been submitted to the jury. The Supreme Court's decision was based on the appellate court's action in substituting its estimate of the damages for the jury's and not affording the plaintiff the opportunity for a new trial if he found unacceptable whatever remittitur the court ordered. See 131 US at 29-30. *Kennon* is properly understood as a decision based on the Re-examination Clause rather than the Jury Trial Clause.

[92] 415 US 189, 189-90 (1974).

[93] 42 USC § 3604(a) (1994).

damages (which the statute permitted in the amount of $1,000 or less). The prayer for injunctive relief was decided before trial, and at trial the plaintiff sought to recover compensatory as well as punitive damages.[94] The trial court refused the defendants' request for a jury trial.[95] After a bench trial, it found no actual damages but awarded $250 in punitive damages.[96]

The Supreme Court held that the defendants should have been afforded a jury trial. "The Seventh Amendment does apply," the Court declared, "to actions enforcing statutory rights, and requires a jury trial upon demand, if the statute creates legal rights and remedies, enforceable in an action for damages in the ordinary courts of law."[97]

The Court concluded that the action was one to enforce "legal rights."[98] First, "[a] damages action under the statute sounds basically in tort—the statute merely defines a new legal duty," and the cause of action is "analogous to a number of tort actions recognized at common law."[99] Second, and according to the Court more important, "the relief sought here—actual and punitive damages—is the traditional form of relief offered in the courts of law."[100] The Court also commented that, whatever might be the merit of circuit court decisions that had characterized backpay awarded in Title VII employment discrimination cases as "equitable," "there is surely no basis for characterizing the award of compensatory and punitive damages here as equitable relief."[101]

Like *Barry*, *Curtis* does not establish that the Seventh Amendment entitles a party to have a jury set punitive damages. In *Curtis* the trial court had decided *all* issues without a jury—including whether the defendants had discriminated against the plaintiff because of her race, whether she had suffered actual damages, whether punitive damages were warranted, and if so what the amount of punitive damages should be.[102] In holding that the defendants had been improperly denied a jury trial, the Supreme Court did not specify whether a judge or a jury should determine the amount of punitive damages.[103]

---

[94] 415 US at 190 & n 1.
[95] Id at 190-91.
[96] Id at 191.
[97] Id at 194.
[98] Id at 195.
[99] Id.
[100] Id at 196 (footnote omitted).
[101] Id at 197 (footnote omitted).
[102] See id at 191.
[103] See id at 198.

In defending the denial of a jury trial, the plaintiff had stressed in the Supreme Court that the only damages she sought in her complaint were punitive damages.[104] Significantly, the Court did not state that it made no difference whether only punitive damages were sought, but instead noted that the plaintiff "later sought to recover actual damages as well," that the pretrial order listed actual damages as an issue to be tried, and that at trial the plaintiff unsuccessfully attempted to prove such damages.[105]

In distinguishing fair housing actions under Title VIII from employment actions for reinstatement and backpay under Title VII (which several courts of appeals had held did not trigger the right te a jury trial),[106] the *Curtis* Court stressed that "the decision whether to award backpay is committed to the discretion of the trial judge," whereas "[t]here is no comparable discretion [under Title VIII]: if a plaintiff proves unlawful discrimination and actual damages, he is entitled to judgment for that amount."[107] The Court's distinction depended on the presence of a claim for actual damages. Furthermore, in this respect punitive damages are similar to backpay under Title VII, not to actual damages under Title VIII. Punitive damages are awarded as a matter of discretion; there is no entitlement to them.[108]

The Court also stated that "[w]e need not, and do not, go so far as to say that any award of monetary relief must necessarily be 'legal' relief."[109] Immediately following that statement, the Court cited two of its prior decisions and, in a footnote, page 414 of the Fifth Circuit's decision in *Swofford v B & W, Inc.*[110] The Fifth Circuit stated there that the Supreme Court's decisions in *Beacon Theatres, Inc v Westover*[111] and *Dairy Queen, Inc v Wood*[112]

[104] See id at 190 n 1.

[105] Id.

[106] See id at 196 & n 13. In 1991, Title VII was amended to permit recovery of compensatory and punitive damages, and to afford a right to a jury trial when damages are sought. Civil Rights Act of 1991, Pub L No 102-166, § 102, 105 Stat 1071 (1991), codified at 42 USC § 1981a (1994).

[107] *Curtis*, 415 US at 197.

[108] See, for example, Restatement (Second) of Torts § 908 comment d (1979); *Shepherd Components, Ine v Brice Petrides-Donohue & Associates, Inc*, 473 NW2d 612, 619 (Iowa 1991) ("We have stated that punitive damages are not allowed as a matter of right and are discretionary."); *Alabama Power Co v Rembert*, 282 Ala 5, 208 S2d 205, 206 (1968) ("Punitive damages are not recoverable as a matter of right except as provided by statute.").

[109] *Curtis*, 415 US at 196.

[110] 336 F2d 406, 414 (5th Cir 1964). The other cases cited were *Mitchell v De Mario Jewelry, Inc*, 361 US 288 (1960), and *Porter v Warner Holding Co*, 328 US 395 (1946).

[111] 359 US 500 (1959).

[112] 369 US 469 (1962).

had not "converted typical non-jury claims, or remedies, into jury ones" and had not "suddenly converted *any* money request into a money claim triable by jury."[113] Moreover, the *Swofford* court had made those statements in support of its conclusion that "*exemplary damages* and attorneys' fees are not money claims triable by jury, although they are awarded in a 'legal' action."[114]

The Supreme Court's citation of *Swofford*, together with the care the Court took to point out that the issue of actual damages had been tried,[115] suggests that the Court did not intend to decide whether there is a right to have a jury set punitive damages.

III. *TULL V UNITED STATES*

Not only has the Supreme Court never held that the Seventh Amendment guarantees a right to a jury trial on the amount of punitive damages, but in its 1987 decision in *Tull v United States*, the Court ruled that the Seventh Amendment does not entitle a defendant to have a jury determine the amount of a civil penalty.[116]

Tull involved an action by the federal government against a real estate developer, Edward Tull, for a civil penalty under the Clean Water Act ("CWA").[117] The government sought a penalty of nearly $23 million.[118] The trial court denied Tull's demand for a jury trial and, after a bench trial, held him liable and assessed a penalty of $325,000.[119]

In an opinion by Justice Brennan, the Supreme Court held that Tull had a right to a jury trial on his liability for a penalty,[120] but not on the amount of the penalty.[121] It was permissible, the Court ruled, for Congress to vest trial judges with the power to set the amount of penalties under the CWA.[122] The Court explained that having the jury "determine the remedy in a trial in

---

[113] *Swofford*, 336 F2d at 414.

[114] Id at 413 (emphasis added). *Swofford* involved a claim of patent infringement, but the court's holding that there was no right to a jury trial on exemplary damages was based on the nature of that remedy, not on the nature of the claim; the court specifically noted that "[a] claim for damages based upon a charge of infringement of patent is plainly a 'legal' claim." Id at 410 n 5. The opinion in *Swofford* was written by Judge Rives and joined by Chief Judge Tuttle and Judge Wisdom.

[115] See *Curtis*, 415 US at 190 n 1.

[116] 481 US at 426-27.

[117] 33 USC § 1319(d) (1994). See *Tull*, 481 US at 414.

[118] *Tull*, 481 US at 415.

[119] Id.

[120] Id at 424-25.

[121] Id at 425-27.

[122] Id at 426-27.

which it must determine liability" is not "necessary" "to preserve the 'substance of the common law right of trial by jury.'"[123] In a footnote, the Court added the very broad statement that "[n]othing in the Amendment's language suggests that the right to a jury trial extends to the remedy phase of a civil trial."[124] The Court said it had been "presented with no evidence that the Framers meant to extend the right to a jury to the remedy phase of a civil trial."[125]

The Court went on to explain:

> The assessment of a civil penalty is not one of the "most fundamental elements." Congress' authority to fix the penalty by statute has not been questioned, and it was also the British practice. In the United States, the action to recover civil penalties usually seeks the amount fixed by Congress. The assessment of civil penalties thus cannot be said to involve the "substance of a common-law right to a trial by jury," nor a "fundamental element of a jury trial."[126]

The Court added two other justifications for its conclusion that Tull had no right to have a jury determine his penalty. First, "[s]ince Congress itself may fix the civil penalties, it may delegate that determination to trial judges."[127] Second, "[i]n this case, highly discretionary calculations that take into account multiple factors are necessary in order to set civil penalties under the Clean Water Act. These are the kinds of calculations traditionally performed by judges."[128]

Although *Tull* involved a statutory civil penalty rather than punitive damages, the Court's opinion specifically notes that "the remedy of civil penalties is similar to the remedy of punitive damages, another legal remedy that is not a fixed fine."[129] More-

---

[123] Id at 425-26 (footnotes omitted), quoting *Colgrove*, 413 US at 157.

[124] 481 US at 426 n 9.

[125] Id.

[126] Id at 426 (citations omitted).

[127] Id at 427.

[128] Id, citing *Albemarle Paper Co v Moody*, 422 US 405, 442-43 (1975) (Rehnquist concurring). In his concurring opinion in *Albemarle*, Justice Rehnquist suggested that if backpay were routinely awarded under Title VII upon a finding of discrimination, rather than on a case-by-case basis in the discretion of the court, the right te a jury trial would be triggered. 422 US at 443. (In 1991, Congress amended Title VII to provide a right to a jury trial whenever damages are sought. See note 106.)

[129] 481 US at 422 n 7. See also id at 422 (describing punitive damages as an example of a remedy "intonded to punish culpable individuals" that was "issued by courts of law, not courts of equity"); *Minneapolis and St Louis Railway Co v Beckwith*, 129 US 26, 36 (1889) (describing punitive damages as "one mode of imposing a penalty for the violation of duty"). The statements in *Tull* about punitive damages appear in the part of the opinion

over, while two dissenting Justices argued that the decision was inconsistent with the traditional treatment of punitive damages,[130] the majority did not distinguish punitive damages or indicate that its decision would have no impact on claims for punitive damages. When *Tull* was decided, the Supreme Court had begun to devote increasing attention to cases involving large awards of punitive damages.[131] The Court surely would have been aware of the potential implications of its decision for punitive damages; indeed, its broad language questioning whether the right to jury trial extends to the determination of remedies at all[132] may well have been included for the very purpose of inviting a rethinking of the treatment of punitive damages. In light of *Tull*, as well as the recent statement of three Justices that "the level of punitive damages is not really a 'fact' 'tried' by the jury,"[133] whether a party has a right under the Seventh Amendment to have a jury set punitive damages is very much an open question.[134]

---

holding that the defendant had a right to have a jury decide his liability for a penalty. 481 US at 422-25.

[130] See 481 US at 428 (Scalia, joined by Stevens, concurring in part and dissenting in part) ("I can recall no precedent for judgment of civil liability by jury but assessment of amount by the court. Even punitive damages are assessed by the jury when liability is determined in that fashion.").

[131] Three weeks before *Tull* was decided, the Court decided a case involving what was then the largest punitive damages award ever, a $3 billion award against Texaco. See *Pennzoil Co v Texaco, Inc*, 481 US 1, 4 (1987). See also *Bankers Life & Casualty Co v Crenshaw*, 480 US 915 (1987) (noting probable jurisdiction in case involving constitutional challenges to $1.6 million punitive award), decided on other grounds, 486 US 71, 80 (1988); *Aetna Life Insurance Co v Lavoie*, 475 US 813, 816 (1986) (involving a $3.5 million punitive award).

[132] See *Tull*, 481 US at 425-26.

[133] *Gasperini*, 116 S Ct at 2235 (Scalia, joined by Rehnquist and Thomas, dissenting).

[134] See Colleen P. Murphy, *Integrating the Constitutional Authority of Civil and Criminal Juries*, 61 Geo Wash L Rev 723, 803 (1993) (arguing that the Seventh Amendment does not require that a jury determine the amount of punitive damages). In 1989, two years after *Tull*, a panel of the Fourth Circuit held, in *Shamblin's Ready Mix, Inc v Eaton Corp*, 873 F2d 736, 742 (4th Cir 1989) (opinion by Butzner), that there is no right to a jury trial on the amount of punitive damages. In 1991, the Fourth Circuit, sitting en banc, overruled *Shamblin's*. *Defender Industries, Inc v Northwestern Mutual Life Insurance Co*, 938 F2d 502, 507 (4th Cir 1991). In *Defender Industries*, the trial court, upon finding the jury's punitive damages award te be grossly excessive, had not followed the familiar procedure of ordering a new trial unless the plaintiff accepted a remittitur, but instead had ordered that judgment be entered in a reduced amount. Id at 505. Because the jury had been asked te return a verdict assessing punitive damages, with no suggestion that the verdict would be simply advisory, the Fourth Circuit could have overturned the trial court's ruling solely on the basis of the Re-examination Clause. Compare *Browning-Ferris Industries of Vermont, Inc v Kelco Disposal, Inc*, 492 US 257, 280 & n 26 (1989) (relying in part on Seventh Amendment in according considerable deference to trial court's denial of new trial motion in case involving large punitive damages award). But the Fourth Circuit went further, concluding that "assessment by a jury of the amount of punitive damages is

IV. PUNITIVE DAMAGES IN EIGHTEENTH CENTURY ENGLAND

Since the existence of a right to have a jury set punitive damages is an open question under Supreme Court precedent, the critical questions are whether jury determination of the amount of punitive damages was within "the 'substance of the common law right of trial by jury,'"[135] and was one of the "most fundamental elements"[136] of the jury-trial system in eighteenth century England. While the vagueness of these formulations means that their application to specific issues will almost always be debatable, they would appear to indicate that there is no right under the Seventh Amendment to have a jury set punitive damages.

A. Absence of Right to Have a Jury Determine Damages

In his opinion for the Court in *Tull*, Justice Breunan strongly questioned whether the Seventh Amendment was intended to guarantee a right to a jury in "the remedy phase of a civil trial,"[137] but failed to cite any authority suggesting that the Jury Trial Clause was not intended to apply to determinations of remedy. Perhaps because of the terseness of the Court's discussion, this part of *Tull* has not been accorded much significance in subsequent cases in the lower federal courts or in state courts concerning the existence of a right to have a jury set punitive damages.[138]

The distinction suggested in *Tull* does in fact find support in the English common law. The common-law allocation of responsibility to determine damages calls into question whether the Seventh Amendment even guarantees the right to have a jury set compensatory damages, let alone punitive damages.

---

an inherent and fundamental element of the common-law rigbt to trial by jury." 938 F2d at 507. See also *Johnson v Hugo's Skateway*, 974 F2d 1408, 1416 (4th Cir 1992) (en banc); *Mattison v Dallas Carrier Corp*, 947 F2d 95, 107-08 (4th Cir 1991).

More recently, a Fourth Circuit panel has relied upon *Tull*, notwithstanding *Defender Industries*, in adopting a novel and more demanding standard to govern post-trial review of punitive damages awards. *Atlas Food Systems and Services v Crane National Vendors*, 99 F3d 587, 594-95 (4th Cir 1996) (discussed in noto 9).

[135] *Tull*, 481 US at 426, quoting *Colgrove*, 413 US at 157.

[136] *Galloway*, 319 US at 392.

[137] 481 US at 426 n 9.

[138] See, for example, *Defender Industries*, 938 F2d at 506 (noting that "*Tull* does contain some rather broad language," but concluding that *Tull* "cannot stand for the proposition that a plaintiff bringing a stato common-law cause of action does not have a right to a jury determination of the amount of punitive damages").

In jury trials at common law, the jury could award damages.[139] When it did so, the amount of its award was subject to only limited review.[140] But there was no *right* to have damages determined in a trial by jury.

Damages were frequently assessed in a separate proceeding conducted by a sheriff rather than in a trial by jury. This separate proceeding was held when a plaintiff obtained an interlocutory judgment by confession, default, or the overruling of a demurrer.[141] Following the interlocutory judgment, damages were determined pursuant te a writ of inquiry.[142] A writ of inquiry was issued by the court in which the action was pending and was executed by the sheriff. It stated that "the plaintiff ought to recover his damages . . . . But because it is unknown what damages he hath sustained . . . , the sheriff is commanded, that by the oath of twelve honest and lawful men of his county, he diligently inquire the same; and return the inquisition into court."[143] The inquest jury sometimes had more than twelve members.[144]

When a writ of inquiry was executed, the inquiry into damages was conducted before the sheriff or an undersheriff.[145] According to one estimate, in the seventeenth century there were five times as many inquiries into damages before sheriffs as there were trials involving damages before *nisi prius* judges.[146]

The English courts recognized that there was "a difference between a principal verdict of a jury, and a writ of inquiry of

---

[139] See, for example, *Grey v Grant*, 2 Wils KB 251, 95 Eng Rep 794, 795 (KB 1764).

[140] See *Sharpe v Brice*, 2 Black W 942, 96 Eng Rep 557, 557 (CP 1774); *Beardmore v Carrington*, 2 Wils KB 244, 95 Eng Rep 790, 793 (KB 1764).

[141] See Clinton W. Francis, *The Structure of Judicial Administration and the Development of Contract Law in Seventeenth Century Englaud*, 83 Colum L Rev 35, 64 & n 139 (1983); Thomas Chitty, 2 *Archibold's Practice of the Courts of Queen's Bench in Personal Actions and Ejectment* 930, 982-86 (H. Sweet 11th ed 1862). If, however, issues of fact were tried to a jury before the argument on a demurrer and resolved in the plaintiff's favor, the jury trying such issues would also assess damages. James Stephen, *Lush's Practice of the Superior Courts of Common Law at Westminster* 596 (C. Reader 2d ed 1856).

[142] See William Blackstone, 3 *Commentaries on the Laws of England* 397-98 (Chicago 1979); Francis, 83 Colum L Rev at 64. An exception developed in the eighteenth century for actions in which the damages could be calculated with certainty. Damages in such cases were calculated hy a court officer. See Clinton W. Francis, *Practice, Strategy, and Institution: Debt Collection in the English Common-Law Courts, 1740-1840*, 80 Nw U L Rev 807, 815 n 20 (1986); Chitty, 2 *Archibold's Practice* at 983-84.

[143] William Tidd, 1 *The Practice of the Courts of King's Bench and Common Pleas* 573 (Rohert E. Small 4th ed 1856).

[144] See, for example, *Proceedings on a Writ of Inquiry of Damages between His Royal Highness James Duke of York, in an Action upon the Statute de Scandalis Magnatum, and Titus Oates*, 3 St Trials 987, 987 (KB 1684) (inquest jury comprised of fifteen men).

[145] See Francis, 83 Colum L Rev at 64; Chitty, 2 *Archibold's Practice* at 987.

[146] See Francis, 83 Colum L Rev at 64.

damages; the latter being only an inquest of office to inform the conscience of the Court, and which they might have assessed themselves without any inquest at all."[147] It was recognized that courts, "if they please, may themselves assess the damages."[148] Although courts seldom set aside a verdict returned pursuant to a writ of inquiry,[149] their power to assess damages themselves without an inquest was not questioned.[150]

At common law, when a defendant contested liability but did not file a demurrer, damages as well as liability were decided in a jury trial.[151] But the practice following default, confession of judgment, and overruling of a demurrer suggests that in other cases damages were decided by a jury as a matter of convenience, rather than because a party was deemed to have a right to have a jury assess them.[152]

The case law in this country concerning defaults supports this interpretation. In 1797, in a case in which a federal trial

---

[147] *Beardmore*, 95 Eng Rep at 792. See also *Bruce v Rawlins*, 3 Wils KB 61, 95 Eng Rep 934, 934 (KB 1770); *Hewit v Mantel*, 2 Wils KB 372, 95 Eng Rep 868, 870 (KB 1768).

[148] *Bruce*, 95 Eng Rep at 934. See *Hewit*, 95 Eng Rep at 870; *Beardmore*, 95 Eng Rep at 792; Chitty, 2 *Archibold's Practice* at 992-93 (cited in note 141). See also *Welch v Tennessee Valley Authority*, 108 F2d 95, 99 (6th Cir 1939) ("Courts of England, at the time of the adoption of the Constitution, did not lack the power to fix damages in many cases at common law. They frequently fixed the amount on judgment by default and on demurrer."); Editorial, *Assessment of Damages Upon Default*, 7 Yale L J 311, 311 (1898) ("At common law, upon a default, the assessment of damages, whether liquidated or unliquidated, was never referable of right to a jury.").

[149] See Francis, 83 Colum L Rev at 90-91 (cited in note 141). See also *Burges v Nightingale*, Barnes 230, 94 Eng Rep 890, 890 (CP 1736) ("Where the jury find any damages, the inquisition must stand.").

[150] In *Dimick v Schiedt*, 293 US 474 (1935), Justice Sutherland's opinion for the Court discussed writs of inquiry as follows:

> The power of the court to increase or diminish damages assessed upon a writ of inquiry was likewise upheld; but this upon the ground that the justices might themselves have awarded damages without the writ, and the inquisition, therefore, was nothing more than an inquest for their information. But even this rule seems long since to have fallen into disuse, the more modern practice being to award a new writ of inquiry in all cases in which the court would award a new trial.

Id at 478-79 (citations omitted). The Court did not suggest that as of 1791 any question had been raised as to the power of English judges to assess damages themselves without a writ of inquiry, or that the English courts had recognized a right to have damages assessed in a jury trial rather than pursuant to a writ of inquiry.

[151] See *Tullidge v Wade*, 3 Wils KB 18, 95 Eng Rep 909, 909 (KB 1769).

[152] See *Raymond v Danbury & NR Co*, 20 F Cases 332, 333 (Cir Ct D Conn 1877) ("The assessment of damages by a jury, in actions, of tort, was . . . a matter of practice, and not of right."); *Pierre v Eastern Air Lines, Inc*, 152 F Supp 486, 488 (D NJ 1957) ("At common law the assessment of damages in a default, in tort and in contract, was not considered a function of the jury and stood upon a different footing from the trial of issues of fact. The measuring of damages by a jury, therefore, would seem to be a matter of practice rather than of right.").

court assessed damages itself after a default, the Supreme Court affirmed the judgment,[153] necessarily rejecting the defendant's claim that damages should have been assessed by the jury.[154] The defendant had relied upon the provision of the Judiciary Act of 1789 requiring that all issues of fact be decided by a jury.[155]

Similarly, the lower federal courts have almost uniformly held that the Seventh Amendment does not confer a right to have a jury determine damages after a default.[156] The rule that there is no right to a jury trial after a default has been applied not just against defaulting defendants, but against plaintiffs seeking a jury trial on damages after a defendant's default.[157] These decisions thus cannot be attributed to an unstated doctrine of waiver or forfeiture; they instead are a latter-day reflection of the absence at common law of a right to a jury trial on damages.

B. Considerations Peculiar to Punitive Damages

The absence at common law of a right to have the amount of damages decided by a jury suggests that it might even be consistent with the Seventh Amendment for federal judges to determine the amount of compensatory damages.[158] But whether or not

---

[153] See *Brown v Van Braam*, 3 US (3 Dall) 344, 356 (1797).

[154] See id at 347-48 (stating defendant's claim).

[155] See id at 352, citing An Act to regulate Processes in the Courts of the United States, § 34, 1 Stat 92 (1789).

[156] See *Goldman, Antonetti, Ferraiuoli, Axtmayer & Hertell v Medfit International, Inc*, 982 F2d 686, 692 n 15 (1st Cir 1993); *Adriana International Corp v Thoeren*, 913 F2d 1406, 1414 (9th Cir 1990); *Eisler v Strizler*, 535 F2d 148, 153 (1st Cir 1976); *Henry v Sneiders*, 490 F2d 315, 318 (9th Cir 1974); *Midland Contracting Co v Toledo Foundry & Machine Co*, 154 F 797, 799-800 (7th Cir 1907) (discussing Seventh Amendment rights, although deciding case on state-law grounds); *Frankart Distributors, Inc v Levitz*, 796 F Supp 75, 76 (E D NY 1992); *Kormes v Weis, Voisin & Co, Inc*, 61 FRD 608, 609 (E D Pa 1974); *Gill v Stolow*, 18 FRD 508, 510 (S D NY 1955), revd on other grounds, 240 F2d 669, 670 (2d Cir 1957). See FRCP 55(b)(2) (providing for jury trial on the issue of damages after a default only when required by a federal statute). But see *Byrd v Keene Corp*, 104 FRD 10, 12 (E D Pa 1984) (noting that although the decision whether to enter a default judgment is left to the court's discretion, the "parties may exercise their statutory and constitutional right to jury trial at that hearing").

[157] See *Benz v Skiba, Skiba & Glomski*, 164 FRD 115, 116 (D Me 1995); *Johnson v Bridgeport Deoxidized Bronze & Metal Co*, 125 F 631, 632 (Cir Ct D Conn 1903); *Raymond*, 20 F Cases at 333-34. See *In re Dierschke*, 975 F2d 181, 185 (5th Cir 1992) ("It is also 'clear . . . that in a default case neither the plaintiff nor the defendant has a constitutional right to jury trial on the issue of damages,'" quoting James W. Moore, 5 *Moore's Federal Practice* § 38.19[3] (Matthew Bender 1996)).

[158] In *Dimick v Schiedt*, 293 US 474 (1935), however, which held that additur violates the Re-examination Clause, the five-Justice majority stated that, when a verdict is excessive or inadequate, "both parties remain entitled *as they were entitled in the first instance*, to have a jury properly determine the question of liability and the extent of the injury by an assessment of damages." Id at 486 (emphasis added). (*Dimick* did not involve an award

such a practice would be permissible, there are considerations peculiar to punitive damages that confirm that the Seventh Amendment should not be interpreted to require that punitive damages be set by juries.

First, the English cases prior to 1791 that endorsed punitive damages (which were then referred to as exemplary damages) spoke of the *power* of the jury to award such damages, not of any *right* of a party to have a jury set them. For example, in *Wilkes v Wood*,[159] the Court of King's Bench stated that "a jury have it in their power to give damages for more than the injury received." Moreover, punitive damages were not restricted to jury trials. In *Benson v Frederick*,[160] one of the early decisions upholding a damage award in excess of the plaintiff's loss, the damages had been determined not in a trial by jury but in an inquest before a jury pursuant to a writ of inquiry.

The absence of English authority recognizing a right to have a jury determine the amount of punitive damages is not surprising in light of the English practice in criminal cases. Judges, not juries, determined sentences (though juries sometimes refused to find the defendant guilty because of concern about the harsh punishment he could face if convicted).[161] Since there was no right to have a jury determine the degree of punishment in criminal cases—where a defendant's life or liberty was at stake—it would have been anomalous to recognize a right to have a monetary punishment fixed by a jury.

Second, although the common law had developed over several centuries, punitive damages were first recognized in 1763.[162] The awards of punitive damages returned in jury trials in a number of cases between 1763 and 1791 hardly made jury determination of such damages one of the most fundamental elements of the jury-trial system.[163]

---

of punitive damages.) In 1791, compensation was also a basic and long-established purpose of common law causes of action. See, for example, *Anonymous*, YB 6 Edw 4, fol 7, pl 18 (KB 1466). A powerful argument can be made that the jury's role would be impermissibly trivialized if even compensatory damages were determined by the judge.

[159] Lofft 1, 98 Eng Rep 489, 498 (CP 1763).

[160] 3 Burr 1845, 97 Eng Rep 1130, 1130 (KB 1766).

[161] See Leon Radzinowicz, 1 *A History of English Criminal Law and its Administration from 1750* 93-95 (Stevens 1948) (discussing acquittals in cases involving small offenses punishable by death).

[162] See *Wilkes*, 98 Eng Rep at 498; *Huckle v Money*, 2 Wils KB 205, 95 Eng Rep 768, 769 (KB 1763).

[163] In *Defender Industries, Inc v Northwestern Mutual Life Insurance Co*, 938 F2d 502, 507 (4th Cir 1991) (en banc), the Fourth Circuit cited, as support for its conclusion that the Seventh Amendment confers a right to have a jury set punitive damages, the Supreme

As the Supreme Court stressed in *Galloway v United States*, the rules of the common law "were constantly changing and developing during the late eighteenth and early nineteenth centuries."[164] Because capacity for change was an inherent part of the common law, the common law of England in 1791 possessed the capacity to adopt changes in the procedures for resolving particular issues, including punitive damages. Since punitive damages were ouly a recent arrival on the legal scene, had not been awarded exclusively in jury trials, and had not been declared to be triable to a jury as of right,[165] it is not reasonable to interpret a constitutional amendment preserving the right of trial by jury in suits "at common law" as forever requiring that juries set such damages.

Third, there are important differences between punitive damages under modern American law and punitive damages under eighteenth century English law. As Professor Charles McCormick noted, "[i]t is only in America that the cases clearly have separated exemplary from compensatory damages."[166] In this country punitive damages are the subject of separate instructions, and in nearly all states the jury, if it chooses to award such damages, identifies in its verdict separate sums for compensatory and punitive damages. In contrast, in eighteenth century England, punitive damages typically were not a separate element of recovery. In *Huckle v Money*,[167] one of the first cases to recognize such damages, the jury returned an undifferentiated verdict of £300. Lord Camden had instructed the jurors that "they were not bound to any certain damages";[168] there was no instruction to consider separately what damages the jurors might deem appropri-

---

Court's statement in *Pacific Mutual Life Insurance Co v Haslip*, 499 US 1, 15 (1991), that "[u]nder the traditional common-law approach, the amount of the punitive award is initially determined by a jury." In context, however, it is apparent that the Court's statement in *Haslip*—which involved a challenge under the Due Process Clause of the Fourteenth Amendment to a punitive damages award in a trial in state court not subject to the Seventh Amendment—was not directed to the English common law, but to the common law in the United States prior to the adoption of the Fourteenth Amendment in 1868. The Court had no reason to consider, and there is no indication that it did consider, whether jury determination of the amount of punitive damages was a significant part (if it was any part at all) of the right to jury trial in eighteenth century England.

[164] 319 US at 391 (footnote omitted). See also *Gasperini*, 116 S Ct at 2224 n 20 (meaning of the Seventh Amendment not fixed as of 1791); Wolfram, 57 Minn L Rev at 736-37 (cited in note 26) (arguing that the understanding in 1791 of "common law" involved "flexibility and capacity for growth in order to respond to changing social pressures").

[165] See text accompanying notes 139-53 and 159-64.

[166] Charles T. McCormick, *Handbook on the Law of Damages* 278 (West 1935).

[167] 2 Wils KB 205, 95 Eng Rep 768 (KB 1763).

[168] Id at 769.

ate as punishment. Similarly, the report of *Wilkes v Wood*, a related case in which the jury awarded £1000, indicates that Lord Pratt gave instructions to the jury to the effect that

> a jury have it in their power to give damages for more than the injury received. Damages are designed not only as a satisfaction to the injured person, but likewise as punishment to the guilty, to deter from any such proceeding for the future, and as a proof of the detestation of the jury to the action itself.[169]

This instruction identified punishment as an additional purpose of damages, but did not ask the jury to return a separate award of punitive damages.

In several of the pre-1791 English cases that endorsed punitive damages, not only were such damages not a distinct element of recovery, but the rationale of punishment or setting an example was blended with the compensatory rationale of remedying an insult to the plaintiff. For example, in *Tullidge v Wade*,[170] the court upheld a jury's verdict of £50 against a defendant who "got [the plaintiff's daughtor] with child." Again there is no indication that the jury was instructed to consider what sum should be awarded as punitive damages or as punishment. And two of the three judges stressed the insult to the plaintiff in concluding that the verdict should stand.[171]

C. Criminal Cases

A comparison to criminal cases is also instructive. Just as the Seventh Amendment preserves the right to jury trial in civil cases, both the Sixth Amendment and Article III, Section 2, guarantee the right to jury trial in criminal cases. Indeed, the Supreme Court has called the Sixth Amendment right to jury

---

[169] 98 Eng Rep at 498-99.

[170] 3 Wils KB 18, 95 Eng Rep 909, 909 (KB 1769).

[171] See id at 909 (opinion by Wilmot) ("the plaintiff having received this insult in his own house"), 910 (opinion by Bathurst) ("In actions of this nature, and of assaults, the circumstances of time and place, when and where the insult is given, require different damages."). See also *Benson*, 97 Eng Rep at 1130 (opinion by Lord Mansfield) (arguing that the plaintiff, "though not much hurt indeed, was scandalized and disgraced"); *Grey*, 95 Eng Rep at 795 ("[T]be plaintiff has been used unlike a gentleman by the defendant."). In 1935, Professor McCormick wrote that "[i]n England . . . it is still not entirely clear whether the accepted theory [of punitive damages] is that they are a distinct and strictly punitive element of the recovery, or they are merely a swollen or 'aggravated' allowance of compensatory damages permitted in cases of outrage." McCormick, *Handbook* at 278 (cited in note 166) (footnote omitted).

trial "fundamental to the American scheme of justice" and has held that that right—unlike the Seventh Amendment right to jury trial—must be honored in state as well as federal court.[172]

But the Court also has held that the Sixth Amendment does not give a criminal defendant a right to have a jury determine his sentence.[173] Even in a capital case, it is permissible to assign full responsibility for deciding the defendant's sentence to the judge.[174] If a citizen whose life or liberty is at stake does not have a right to have a jury determine his punishment, it is difficult to fathom why a citizen seeking punitive damages or seeking to avoid their imposition should have a right to have a jury determine the amount.

V. The Reasons Why Judges Rather than Juries Should Set Punitive Damages

If the Seventh Amendment does not dictate that juries set punitive damages, then the allocation of power to set such damages, in cases brought in federal court, is a matter of policy. This Part first will examine several considerations supporting allocation of this power to trial judges, and then show that the general justifications for jury trials in civil cases do not outweigh those considerations.

A. Policies Supporting Assessment of Punitive Damages by Judges

More than a century ago, the Supreme Court of Texas observed:

> A power such as may be exercised by juries in awarding exemplary damages is liable to great abuse,—may often lead to great oppression. . . . In cases based on facts which merit condemnation, or even punishment, though not by law constituting crime, juries, under commendable impulses, but with judgment warped by passion, no doubt often render excessive verdicts.[175]

---

[172] *Duncan v Louisiana*, 391 US 145, 149 (1968).

[173] See *Walton v Arizona*, 497 US 639, 647-49 (1990); *Hildwin v Florida*, 490 US 638, 640-41 (1989) (per curiam); *McMillan v Pennsylvania*, 477 US 79, 93 (1986); *Spaziano v Florida*, 468 US 447, 459 (1984).

[174] *Walton*, 497 US at 647-49; *Hildwin*, 490 US at 640-41.

[175] *Tynberg v Cohen*, 76 Tex 409, 13 SW 315, 317 (1890).

This observation was made in support of the need to exercise, "firmly and fearlessly," the power to grant a new trial when a jury's punitive damages award is excessive,[176] but it also points to a reason that judges are better equipped than juries to set punitive damages in the first place. Just as the Supreme Court has held that judges are better suited than juries to construe patents,[177] judges are also better suited to mete out punishment. They are more likely to be able to base the severity of the penalty on a rational assessment of the facts, rather than an emotional reaction to the defendant's misconduct. As was said in an analysis of the allocation of power to determine sentences in criminal cases, "juries are more easily influenced by emotional factors than judges, who, due to their experience, are better able to make an objective determination of the penalty to be inflicted."[178]

It might be objected that the argument proves too much, for emotional factors also may influence jury awards of compensatory damages, yet juries are nevertheless asked to set compensatory damages. But assigning the determination of punitive damages to an emotion-prone decisionmaker is much more troubling than assigning the determination of compensatory damages to such a decisionmaker. In the words of the Supreme Court, punitive damages are "private fines."[179] But unlike criminal fines and civil statutory penalties, they are generally not subject to any cap.[180] The criteria that govern the determination of the amount of punitive damages confer enormous discretion.[181] Yet punitive damages

---

[176] Id ("[T]here is no class of cases in which the conservatism of the judge should more frequently find field for action.").

[177] See *Markman*, 116 S Ct at 1395 (holding that judges rather than juries should construe patents in part because "a jury's capability to evaluate demeanor, to sense the 'mainsprings of human conduct,' or te reflect community standards, are much less significant than a trained ability to evaluate the testimony in relation to the overall structure of the patent") (citations omitted).

[178] Comment, *Consideration of Punishment by Juries*, 17 U Chi L Rev 400, 406 (1950). See also *Moreno v Consolidated Rail Corp*, 99 F3d 782, 792 (6th Cir 1996) (en banc) (declining to hold that punitive damages are available under the Rehabilitation Act of 1973, 29 USC § 794 (1985 & Supp 1997), in part because "[t]he whole issue of punitive damages is becoming an increasingly problematic one, of course, as a sort of game-show mentality leads some contemporary juries to award punitive damages in amounts that seem utterly capricious").

[179] *Gertz v Robert Welch, Inc*, 418 US 323, 350 (1974).

[180] A minority of jurisdictious have statutery caps on punitive damages in some or all actions. See, for example, Fla Stat Ann § 768.73 (West 1997); Tex Civ Pract & Rem Code Ann § 41.008 (Vernon 1997).

[181] See, for example, *Guzman v Western State Bank of Devils Lake*, 540 F2d 948, 954 (8th Cir 1976) ("In reviewing an award of punitive damages there is no basis from which an appellate court may measure damage."); *Rowlett v Anheuser-Busch, Inc*, 832 F2d 194, 207 (1st Cir 1987) (same).

are awarded without the necessity for proof beyond a reasonable doubt and without many of the other protections afforded in criminal cases to minimize the risk of punishing the innocent. It is extremely problematic to give a broad power to punish to a decisionmaker that is particularly susceptible to passion and emotion, in a proceeding that lacks many of the safeguards that usually precede the meting out of punishment.[182]

A related consideration that favors having judges set punitive damages derives from the role that the defendant's wealth plays in setting punitive damages. In most civil cases, evidence of a party's wealth is inadmissible.[183] "The underlying reason for the rule is that such evidence tends to inject into the case a foreigu, diverting, and distracting issue which may effectuate prejudicial results."[184] But when the amount of punitive damages is at issue, a plaintiff is allowed to introduce evidence of the defendant's finances,[185] on the theory that "the degree of punishment or deterrence resulting from a judgment is to some extent in proportion to

---

[182] The National Law Journal's annual surveys of large jury verdicts, while perhaps not complete, suggest the frequency with which juries return enormous awards of punitive damages. The 1993 survey reported four punitive damages awards of $250 million or more, three awards of approximately $100 million, ten awards of between $20 million and $100 million, and ten awards of between $5 million and $20 million. *Despite Tort Reform, Huge Verdicts Continue Climbing*, Natl L J S2-S12, S14, S16-S17 (Jan 17, 1994). The 1994 survey reported the $5 billion award in the *Exxon Valdez* case, a $1.2 billion award in a suit for human rights abuses brought against the estate of Ferdinand Marcos, an award of $173 million, sixteen awards of between $20 million and $100 million, and thirteen more awards of between $5 million and $20 million. *Verdicts: The Big Numbers of 1994*, Natl L J C2-C16 (Feb 6, 1995). The 1995 survey reperted a $400 million award, two $300 million awards, a $175 million award, six awards of between $50 million and $70 million, seven awards of between $20 million and $25 million, and seven awards of between $7 million and $19 million. *Verdicts: The Big Numbers of 1995,* Natl L J C2-C15 (Feb 5, 1996). The 1996 survey reperted a $386 million award, a $210 million award, a $200 million award, six awards of between $100 million and $150 million, seven awards of between $23 million and $60 million, seven awards of between $12 million and $18 million, and three awards of approximately $10 million. *Verdicts: The Big Numbers of 1996,* Natl L J C2-C10, C12, C14 (Feb 10, 1997).

A study of jury awards in state courts of general jurisdiction in the seventy-five largest counties in cases involving tort, contract, and real property claims, for the year ended June 30, 1992, identified 364 awards of punitive damages; the mean award was $735,000 and the median award $50,000. *Bureau of Justice Statistics Special Report: Civil Jury Cases and Verdicts in Large Counties* 1, 8 (DOJ 1995).

[183] See, for example, *Geddes, PMC v United Financial Group*, 559 F2d 557, 560 (9th Cir 1977); *Eisenhauer v Burger*, 431 F2d 833, 837 (6th Cir 1970); *Blankenship v Rowntree*, 219 F2d 597, 598 (10th Cir 1955). See also *Parkins v Brown*, 241 F2d 367, 368 n 2 (5th Cir 1957) (allowing evidence of wealth "only if the evidence develops a case warranting the jury in awarding punitive or exemplary damages").

[184] *Blankenship*, 219 F2d at 598.

[185] See Gerald W. Boston, *Punitive Damages in Tort Law* § 32:1 at 2-3 (Clark, Boardman 1993).

the means of the guilty person."[186] Whatever the merits of the theory,[187] evidence that a defendant has a huge net worth often contributes to a staggering verdict.

The Supreme Court recognized this problem in *Honda Motor Co v Oberg*,[188] in which it held that a state violates due process by letting juries set punitive damages but not permitting review by a trial or appellate court for excessiveness. The Court stressed that "the presentation of evidence of a defendant's net worth creates the potential that juries will use their verdicts to express biases against big businesses, particularly those without strong local presences."[189] Unless the amount of punitive damages is determined in a separate phase of the trial, it seems clear that admission of evidence of wealth also may skew the jury's assessment of liability for compensatory and punitive damages and of the amount of compensatory damages. The significant increase in income inequality among Americans since the 1960s[190] has likely exacerbated the risk created by admission of evidence of wealth.

Judges are better suited than juries to give appropriate weight to a defendant's finances. They are less likely to be swayed by arguments that seek to base the calculation of punitive damages on a percentage of the defendant's net wealth or income.

Because of their responsibility for sentencing in criminal cases and for imposing civil statutory penalties, judges ordinarily have much more experience than jurors in determining punishments and far more familiarity with the sanctions imposed for

[186] Restatement (Second) of Torts § 908 comment e (1977).

[187] In the case of organizational defendants, the theory has been sharply criticized on the ground that profit-maximizing organizations are interested in the *marginal* (not the total) costs of activities relative to the marginal benefits. The tetal wealth of the organization generally bas little to do with the expected marginal costs or benefits of actions. It has been argued that, by linking punitive damages to wealth, the law creates too much deterrence for large corporations and teo little for small ones. See Robert D. Cooter, *Punitive Damages for Deterrence: When and How Much?*, 40 Ala L Rev 1143, 1176-77 (1989); Malcolm E. Wheeler, *A Proposal for Further Common Law Development of the Use of Punitive Damages in Modern Product Liability Litigation*, 40 Ala L Rev 919, 950-51 (1989); Dorsey D. Ellis, Jr., *Fairness and Efficiency in the Law of Punitive Damages*, 56 S Cal L Rev 1, 62 (1982). See also *Zazú Designs v L'Oréal, SA*, 979 F2d 499, 508 (7th Cir 1992); *Thomas v E.J. Korvette, Inc*, 329 F Supp 1163, 1170 (E D Pa 1971), revd on other grounds, 476 F2d 471 (3d Cir 1973) ("[I]t is probably safe to assume that any substantial amount of punitive damages would have deterrent effect, irrespective of the size of the corporation.").

[188] 512 US 415, 432 (1994).

[189] Id.

[190] See Daniel A. Weinberg, *A Brief Look at Postwar U.S. Income Inequality*, Current Population Reports P60-191 (Census Bureau June 1996) (finding 22.4 percent increase in income inequality from 1968 to 1994, using the Gini index of income concentration).

various types of misconduct.[191] Referring to Alabama's procedures for setting punitive damages, Justice Powell once observed in a draft opinion that "[t]he jurors who pass sentence on tort defendants according to these procedures probably have never decided a punitive damages case before. Thus, they have no basis for de-

---

[191] See *Atlas Food Systems and Services, Inc v Crane National Vendors, Inc*, 99 F3d 587, 594 (4th Cir 1996):

> [P]olicy-related elements—e.g., the likelihood that an award will deter the defendant or others from engaging in similar conduct—are not factual questions and, therefore, are more appropriately decided by the trial judge. The judge's unique vantage point and day-to-day experience with such matters lend expertise and consistency. . . . [T]he district courts . . . themselves are required frequently to impose penalties for punishment and deterrence in a wide array of circumstances, both in civil and in criminal contexts. Indeed, in criminal cases, our system gives juries virtually no input, except in capital cases, to determine the amount of ponalties.

See also *Gilbert v St. Louis-San Francisco Railroad Co*, 514 F2d 1277, 1280-81 (5th Cir 1975) (stressing that compensatory and punitive damages "are not administrable in the same fashion," and upholding remittitur of award from $225,000 to $60,000 because trial judge "could not justify, on principles of legal policy, a jury award in this case which so vastly exceeded an earlier award in a stronger case"); Owen, Comment, 56 S Cal L Rev at 120 (cited in note 11) ("Judges have more familiarity than do juries with distinguishing 'wrong' from 'very wrong' behavior (and fixing the appropriate level of punishment therefor) upon a formal social scale . . . ."); *Zoppo v Homestead Insurance Co*, 71 Ohio St 3d 552, 644 NE2d 397, 404 (1994) (Wright, joined by Moyer, dissenting):

> In order to reach a fair punishment, the decision-maker must be able to compare the wrongful conduct in this case against similar conduct in other cases. Additionally, such a broad perspoctive is essential in order to set a level of damages which, while fair, will adequately deter such wrongful conduct in the future. This broad perspective, which is necessary to give effect to the purposes of punitive damages, makes the judge and not the jury the appropriate decision-maker. The knowledge and experience necessary to set punitive damages effectively are unique to the judge alone.

The *Zoppo* majority held that a statute ordering judicial assessment of punitive damages violated the right to jury trial protected by the Ohio Constitution, id at 401, and did not address whether, as a matter of policy, judges or juries are better suited to assess punitive damages. Compare *Torres v North American Van Lines, Inc*, 135 Ariz 35, 658 P2d 835, 841 (Ariz App 1982) (relying in part on trial judge's experience in personal injury lawsuits in affirming remittitur that cut punitive damages award by 75 percent). Since they took effect in 1987, the Federal Sentencing Guidelines have been interpreted by many courts to limit significantly the ability of federal judges te tailor sentences to the facts of the case. In *Koon v United States*, 116 S Ct 2035 (1996), however, the Supreme Court emphasized the importance of taking into account individual circumstances in sentencing under the Guidelines. Id at 2053 ("It has been uniform and coustant in the federal judicial tradition for the sentencing judge to consider every convicted porson as an individual and every case as a unique study in the human failings that sometimes mitigate, sometimes magnify, the crime and punishment to ensue."); see also id at 2044 (noting that Congress "[a]cknowledged the wisdom, even the necessity, of sentencing procedures that take into account individual circumstances"). Even when a court does not depart from the Guidelines range deemed to be applicable, it must exercise discretion in choosing a sentence within the range.

termining what penalties are common in particular kinds of cases."[192]

Because judges are in a better position to impose a punishment that is in line with the punishments imposed for similar misconduct, determination of the amount of punitive damages by judges would promote the interest in treating like cases alike.[193] As Professor Colleen Murphy has written, "[w]ith professional and ongoing experience in matters of public policy, the judge presumably effectuates public policy goals with greater consistency than the one-time jury."[194]

Whereas jury verdicts awarding punitive damages simply indicate a dollar amount, a judge could be required to state the reasons for the amount of punitive damages awarded.[195] This would greatly facilitate appellate review.[196] Under the current procedure, one can only speculate as to what led the jury to award punitive damages in the amount it chose. It may have relied upon an improper premise or one unsupported by the record, but the error may never be known. A requirement that a judge state the reasons for a punitive damages award would reduce the risk of undisclosed error.

Although trial judges' statements of reasons would reveal some errors that might go uncorrected on appeal if made by a jury, in general shifting to judges the responsibility to set punitive damages would have the salutary effect of reducing the role of appellate courts in setting punitive damages.[197] Under the ex-

---

[192] *Aetna Life Insurance Co v Lavoie*, 475 US 813 (1986) (draft opinion of Powell), excerpted in Lewis Powell, *The 'Bizarre Results' of Punitive Damages*, Wall St J A21 (Mar 8, 1995).

[193] Compare *Markman*, 116 S Ct at 1396 (holding that judges rather than juries should construe patents in part because of "the importance of uniformity in the treatment of a given patent").

[194] Murphy, 61 Geo Wash L Rev at 739-40 (cited in note 134) (footnotes omitted).

[195] Some state appellate courts have imposed similar requirements with respect to trial court rulings on post-trial motions challenging a jury's punitive damages award as excessive. See, for example, *VF Corp v Wrexham Aviation Corp*, 112 Md App 703, 686 A2d 647, 660 (1996), cert granted, 346 Md 28, 686 A2d 647 (1997); *Hodges v S.C. Toof & Co*, 833 SW2d 896, 902 (Tenn 1992).

[196] See Redish, 70 Nw U L Rev at 504 n 75 (cited in note 31) (noting that factual findings by district judges "must be made explicitly, and are subject to appellate review," but "[f]act findings by juries . . . usually come in the form of an enigmatic general verdict, and are less susceptible to appellate review"). See also Charles E. Wyzanski, Jr., *A Trial Judge's Freedom and Responsibility*, 65 Harv L Rev 1281, 1292-93 (1952) (arguing that judges should stato the reasons for sentences in criminal cases, as a safeguard against "emotion or other transient factors").

[197] See generally Charles Alan Wright, *The Doubtful Omniscience of Appellate Courts*, 41 Minn L Rev 751, 752-58 (1957).

isting system of jury awards of punitive damages, the real determination of punitive damages often takes place on appeal.[198] In countless cases, appellate courts have drastically reduced awards of punitive damages.[199] Appellate courts have taken such action despite the vagueness of the criteria governing the determination of the amount of punitive damages.[200]

---

[198] A study of punitive damage awards returned in product liability cases between 1965 and 1990 found that roughly 55 percent were affirmed; the remainder were reversed or reduced. Michael Rustadt, *Demystifying Punitive Damages in Product Liability Cases: A Survey of a Quarter Century of Trial Verdicts* 31-32 (Roscoe Pound Foundation 1991).

[199] See, for example, *Lee v Edwards*, 101 F3d 805, 812-13 (2d Cir 1996) (reducing jury's $200,000 punitive damages award to $75,000); *Continental Trend Resources, Inc v OXY USA, Inc*, 101 F3d 634, 643 (10th Cir 1996), cert denied, 117 S Ct 1846 (1997) (reducing $30 million punitive damages award to $6 million); *Vasbinder v Scott*, 976 F2d 118, 121-22 (2d Cir 1992) (reducing two $150,000 punitive damages awards to $20,000 and $30,000); *Mason v Texaco, Inc*, 948 F2d 1546, 1561 (10th Cir 1991) (halving $25 million punitive damages award); *Rowlett v Anheuser-Busch, Inc*, 832 F2d 194, 206-07 (1st Cir 1987) (reducing punitive damages award from $3 million to $300,000); *Hollins v Powell*, 773 F2d 191, 194, 198 (8th Cir 1985) (reducing $500,000 punitive damages award to $2,000); *Ramsey v American Air Filter Co*, 772 F2d 1303, 1314 (7th Cir 1985) (reducing $150,000 punitive damages award to $20,000); *Morrill v Becton, Dickinson and Co*, 747 F2d 1217, 1225 (8th Cir 1984) (reducing $20 million punitive damages award to $3 million); *Bell v City of Milwaukee*, 746 F2d 1205, 1267 (7th Cir 1984) (reducing $350,000 punitive damages award to $50,000). See generally Eric Sehnapper, *Judges Against Juries—Appellate Review of Federal Civil Jury Verdicts*, 1989 Wis L Rev 237, 334-36. For similar state decisions, see, for example, *Texaco, Inc v Pennzoil Co*, 729 SW2d 768, 784, 865-66 (Tex App 1987) (reducing $3 billion punitive damages award to $1 billion); *Faulk v Aware, Inc*, 244 NYS2d 259, 266 (NY App Div 1963) (reducing two $1.25 million punitive damages awards to $50,000 and $100,000), affd, 14 NY2d 899, 200 NE2d 778 (1964); *Miller v Schnitzer*, 78 Nev 301, 371 P2d 824, 829, 831 n 3 (1962) (reducing $50,000 punitive damages award to $5,000).

[200] Judge Lee Sarokin described judicial intervention with respect to punitive damages as follows:

> With the vague guidance given to juries as to the means for calculating [punitive] damages, it is difficult to justify judicial intercession on the basis that the amount of the award is invalid as a matter of law. What occurs in reality is an independent factual finding by the court simply that the penalty is too great.

Juzwin v Amtorg Trading Corp, 705 F Supp 1053, 1057 (D NJ 1989), modified on other grounds, 718 F Supp 1233 (D NJ 1989). Although it is submitted that Judge Sarokin was incorrect in using the term "factual finding" to describe the determination of the proper amount of punitive damages, he shrewdly looked behind the rhetoric of deference that often obscures a de novo judicial assessment of how severe the penalty should be. See also *Miller*, 371 P2d at 829 (citations omitted):

> One cannot avoid thinking that the general rules offered to explain the reviewing court's decision are tailored to fit its feeling about the particular case before it. If that court does not approve the verdict it will state that the jury was motivated by passion or prejudice or that a "reasonable relationship" between the punitive and compensatory awards does not exist; or that the amount of the award is "enormous." On the other hand, the reviewing court in affirming the award may rely upen the converse of the reasons just mentioned, or upen a strong presumption in favor of the verdict as confirmed by the trial judge in refusing a new trial, or some other equally plausible statement.

If trial judges were responsible for awarding punitive damages, there would likely be fewer enormous awards. The occasions for appellate intervention would be fewer, and appellate courts could be expected to heed more closely precedents that ostensibly limit appellate review of the amount of damages awarded.[201] The result of having trial judges set punitive damages would be to reduce the frequency with which punitive damages are effectively set on a cold record by judges who heard none of the testimony presented at trial.[202]

Judges are also better equipped than juries to give proper weight to other sanctions that have been imposed on the defendant for the same conduct. Under the law of many states, prior fines, civil penalties, or awards of punitive damages militate in favor of a lower punitive award.[203] As a practical matter, however, to require a defendant to present such proof to a jury is virtually to eliminate prior punishment as a mitigating factor. As Judge Sarokin observed with respect to evidence of prior punitive awards, "[t]o require a defendant to present such prejudicial evidence to a jury as its only alternative is to place it between Scylla and Charybdis."[204] Evidence that another jury, court, or agency

Under traditional doctrine, a plaintiff may decline a remittitur and insist upon a new trial. See, for example, *Vasbinder*, 976 F2d at 122-23. With respect to punitive awards, some appellate decisions have departed from this principle, remanding with instructions to enter judgment in a reduced amount, rather than affording the plaintiff the option of a new trial. See, for example, *Rowlett*, 832 F2d at 207; *Guzman*, 540 F2d at 954.

[201] See, for example, *Browning-Ferris Industries of Vermont, Inc v Kelco Disposal, Inc*, 492 US 257, 279 (1989) (holding that trial court's ruling on motion for remittitur is reviewable "under an abuse-of-discretion standard") (footnote omitted). In *BMW of North America, Inc v Gore*, 116 S Ct 1589, 1598-1604 (1996), the Supreme Court identified three "guideposts" that led it to conclude that an award of punitive damages was so excessive as to violate the Due Process Clause of the Fourteenth Amendment. The application of the due process limitation established in *BMW* may not be subject to the abuse-of-discretion standard.

[202] On a related point, see Patrick E. Higginbotham, *Juries and the Death Penalty*, 41 Case W Res L Rev 1047, 1065 (1991) ("[W]e should submit the capital sentencing decision either to the judge or to the jury but not to both, and we should not permit it to be made independently by an appellate court.").

[203] See, for example, *Green Oil Co v Hornsby*, 539 S2d 218, 224 (Ala 1989). See generally Restatement (Second) of Torts § 908 comment e (1977) ("Another factor that may affect the amount of punitive damages is the existence of multiple claims by numerous persons affected by the wrongdoer's conduct.").

[204] *Juzwin*, 705 F Supp at 1056, modified on other grounds, 718 F Supp 1233 (D NJ 1989). See also *Garnes v Fleming Landfill, Inc*, 186 W Va 656, 413 SE2d 897, 909 (1991) (Judge rather than jury should consider prior criminal sanctions or civil awards.); Model Punitive Damages Act § 10(a), 14 ULA 63 (Cum Ann Pkt Pt 1997) (Court may reduce punitive damages award if defendant was previously found liable for punitive damages under a final judgment arising from the same course of conduct, and the second award would be unfairly duplicative.).

has sanctioned the defendant is at least as likely to lead a jury to increase its award as it is to lead it to reduce the award.

If judges set punitive damages, cases in which such damages were found to be warranted also could be resolved more quickly and with less expense. Today it is not unusual for a jury's punitive damages award to be followed by further proceedings at the trial court level that may stretch out over several months. In addition to memoranda of law supporting and opposing a remittitur, evidence not before the jury is often tendered and considered.[205] If the trial judge grants a remittitur which the plaintiff accepts, the defendant may still appeal. Vesting in judges the authority to set punitive damages would significantly shorten the process.

B. The Insufficient Advantages of Assessment by Juries

The foregoing considerations strongly support shifting to judges the responsibility to decide the amount of punitive damages. They are not outweighed by the interests that might be served by leaving that responsibility with juries.

The Supreme Court has said that the purpose of jury trials in civil cases is "to assure a fair and equitable resolution of factual issues."[206] Although other interests are served by civil jury trials, the notion that a jury has a superior ability to decide issues of credibility and other factual issues is plainly one of the principal justifications for civil jury trials.

This justification provides little support for asking juries to set punitive damages. No doubt the parties may dispute some facts relevant to the amount of punitive damages. In general, however, fact resolution is likely to be less significant than the exercise of judgment as to how large an award is warranted to serve the purposes of punitive damages.[207] When the amount of punitive damages is considered, ordinarily the jury already will have found that the defendant committed a wrong that caused injury to the plaintiff, determined the extent of the plaintiff's injuries (economic and noneconomic), and determined that the defendant acted with the degree of culpability necessary to permit an award of punitive damages. Factual disputes certainly can remain, just as in a criminal case there can be factual disputes relating to sentencing. But in most cases the determination of the

---

[205] See, for example, *Dunn v HOVIC*, 1 F3d 1371, 1389-91 (3d Cir 1993) (en banc).

[206] *Colgrove*, 413 US at 157, citing *Gasoline Products Co v Champlin Co*, 283 US 494, 498 (1931).

[207] Compare *Markman*, 116 S Ct at 1395.

amount of punitive damages is driven not by factual questions but by a subjective judgment as to the amount that will serve the purposes of punitive damages (typically, punishing the defendant and deterring both the defendant and others from similar conduct in the future[208]). As Professor Ellis has observed, determining the amount of punitive damages "does not require answering a 'what happened' question. Rather, it embodies the question, 'what ought to happen' to the defendant."[209]

Jury detormination of the amount of punitive damages also might be deemed preferable because a jury's verdict reflects the judgment of all the jurors, whereas a judge's determination is the judgment of one man or woman.[210]

A nineteenth century Supreme Court decision, *Railroad Co v Stout*,[211] though not involving punitive damages, endorsed the wisdom-of-many justification for jury trials. Stout, a six-year old, seriously injured a foot while playing on an unguarded railroad turntable located near a public road. The facts were not in dispute. The jury returned a verdict of $7,500 against the railroad.

---

[208] See Boston, *Punitive Damages* at §§ 2:6-2:7 (cited in note 185).

[209] Ellis, 40 Ala L Rev at 1004 (cited in note 11). See Murphy, 61 Geo Wash L Rev at 802 (cited in note 134) ("Even if some factors are questions of pure fact—for example, the profitability of defendant's misconduct—the calculation of punitive damages cannot be said to be fact-dependent . . . .") (footnote omitted). See also *Gasperini*, 116 S Ct at 2235 (Scalia dissenting) ("[T]he level of punitive damages is not really a 'fact' 'tried' by the jury."). The distinctive character of punitive damages determinations was aptly described by a Justice of the Supreme Court of Oregon:

> In the trial of a criminal case the jury finds the facts and two days thereafter the judge imposes sentence. I have never heard it suggested that the judge in so doing is finding the facts. He is exercising a purely discretionary power to impose punishment, a power which is limited by the statutory maximum sentence which may be imposed. In the same manner the jury, in determining whether to assess punitive damages and in what amonnt, exercises a purely discretionary power based upon the facts which it has already found, a power which resembles that of the trial judge, except for the fact that his discretion is limited by statute whereas theirs is without limit unless the court imposes one.

Van Lom v Schneiderman, 17 Or 89, 210 P2d 461, 475-76 (1949) (Brand concurring in part and dissenting in part). See also *Prince v Peterson*, 538 P2d 1325, 1329 (Utah 1975) (noting that in awarding punitive damages "the jury exercises a quasi-judicial function") (footnote omitted).

That setting punitive damages may involve some factual questions does not suggest that judges are incapable of setting such damages. "Courts pass upon a vast number of questions of fact. . . . [T]here is not, and never was, any such thing in jury trials as an allotment of all questions of fact to the jury. The jury sinply decides some questions of fact." James Thayer, *A Preliminary Treatise on Evidence at the Common Law* 185 (Kelley 1969) (originally published 1898).

[210] See Charles Jared Knight, Note, *State-Law Punitive Damage Schemes and the Seventh Amendment Right to Jury Trial in the Federal Courts*, 14 Rev Litig 657, 683 (1995).

[211] 84 US (17 Wall) 657, 663-64 (1873).

In the Supreme Court the railroad argued that, since the facts were undisputed, the issue of its negligence should have been decided by the judge as a matter of law.[212] The Court rejected the argument, explaining that in most cases of alleged negligence,

> [u]pon the facts proven in such cases, it is a matter of judgment and discretion, of sound inference, what is the deduction to be drawn from the undisputed facts. . . . Twelve men of the average of the community, comprising men of education and men of little education, men of learning and men whose learning consists only in what they have themselves seen and heard, the merchant, the mechanic, the farmer, the laborer; these sit together, consult, apply their separate experience of the affairs of life to the facts proven, and draw a unanimous conclusion. This average judgment thus given it is the great effort of the law to obtain. It is assumed that twelve men know more of the common affairs of life than does one man, that they can draw wiser and safer conclusions from admitted facts thus occurring than can a single judge.[213]

Today civil juries in federal court generally have only six or eight members rather than twelve. More importantly, however, the nature of the decision involved in awarding punitive damages suggests that the wisdom of a judge is preferable in this instance to the collective wisdom of a jury. Choosing an amount of punitive damages differs fundamentally from the determination of whether a party was negligent and from other applications of law to fact that are submitted to the jury even when the facts are undisputed (if reasonable persons could disagree about the outcome). The determination of whether a party was negligent, though certainly subjective in part, is guided by consideration of what a reasonable person in the defendant's shoes would have done. For most other issues decided by a jury there are similar objective criteria. The choice of the amount of punitive damages is not guided in any comparable way that makes the jury's knowledge of "the common affairs of life"[214] particularly useful.

---

[212] Id at 659.

[213] Id at 663-64. See *Bailey v Central Vermont Railway, Inc*, 319 US 350, 353 (1943) ("[T]he fact that fair-minded men might reach different conclusions, emphasize[s] the appropriateuess of leaving the question to the jury."); *Orkin Exterminating Co v Truly Nolen, Inc*, 117 S2d 419, 423 (Fla Dist Ct App 1960).

[214] *Stout*, 84 US at 664.

Another justification often advanced for jury trials in civil cases is the risk of judicial bias. This justification was advanced by the Anti-Federalists,[215] who in urging a jury-trial guarantee for civil cases quoted the following statement by Blackstone:

> The impartial administration of justice, which secures both our persons and our properties, is the great end of civil society. But if that be entirely entrusted to the magistracy, a select body of men, and those generally selected by the prince or such as enjoy the highest offices in the state, their decisions, in spite of their own natural integrity, will have frequently an involuntary bias towards those of their own rank and dignity; it is not to be expected from human nature that *the few* should be always attentive to the interests and good of *the many*.[216]

In Pennsylvania, the Anti-Federalists cited an outrageous search by a constable that had resulted in an award of damages by a jury, and predicted that a "lordly court of justice" sitting without a jury would be "ready to protect the officers of government against the weak and helpless citizens."[217]

It cannot be denied that in some instances bias could infect determinations of punitive damages by federal judges. But this possibility does not provide a good reason for continuing to leave those determinations in the hands of juries in all cases. First, a check against the operation of judicial bias would be provided by the fact that the amount of punitive damages would not be decided by the judge unless the jury first determined that the defendant was liable for punitive damages. Second, the strong tradition of independence and professionalism that has developed in the federal judiciary reduces the risk of judicial bias.[218] Third, the

---

[215] See Centinel, in Herbert J. Storing, ed, 2 *The Complete Anti-Federalist* 143, 149 (Chicago 1981).

[216] Blackstone, 3 *Commentaries on the Laws of England* at 379 (cited in note 142) (emphasis added).

[217] *Pennsylvania Packet* (Oct 23, 1787), in John Bach McMaster and Frederick D. Stone, eds, *Pennsylvania and the Federal Constitution* 154 (Hist Soc Penn 1888). The author went on to say that if federal officers "commit similar or greater indignities, in such cases a trial by jury would be our safest resource, heavy damages would at once punish the offender and deter others from committing the same." Id. See also *Essays by a Farmer*, Maryland Gaz (Feb 15, 1788), in Stering, ed, 5 *The Complete Anti-Federalist* at 14.

[218] See Redish, 70 Nw U L Rev at 504 n 75 (cited in note 31) ("[B]ecause of the generally careful selection process, federal judges are likely to be highly experienced, intelligent individuals steeped in traditious of the law. Thus, it is probable that at least in most cases judges will be better able to control their prejudices than will jurors.").

risk of judicial bias could be further reduced by having juries continue to set punitive damages in cases involving alleged abuses of government power, in which a judge's status as part of the government might be a source of bias.[219]

It has been suggested that juries should set punitive damages because juries better represent the values of the community.[220] One of the functions of the jury system undoubtedly is to permit the ideals and beliefs of ordinary citizens to influence the administration of the law.[221] This function of jury trials provides little justification, however, for having juries set punitive damages.

Any allocation of decisionmaking authority to judges could be said to reduce the influence that community values exert through jury verdicts, but the law entrusts many important decisions to

---

[219] Punitive damages were first recognized by English courts in cases in which official power had been abused and juries returned awards far in excess of the plaintiffs' actual loss. See *Wilkes*, 98 Eng Rep at 498-99; *Huckle*, 95 Eng Rep at 768-69.

If further protection against judicial bias in the award of punitive damages were deemed important, a proposal made years ago by the late Judge Edward J. Devitt could be adopted in part. Although Judge Devitt advocated amending the Constitution te eliminate the right to a jury trial in civil cases, he also suggested that, short of such an amendment, the statute permitting a party to seek disqualification of a judge based on bias or prejudice, 28 USC § 144, be amended "to provide a peremptory challenge when counsel questioned the fairness of the assigned judge," so that more litigants would be willing to waive a jury trial. Edward J. Devitt, *Federal Civil Jury Trials Should Be Abolished*, 60 ABA J 570, 572 (1974). Such a peremptery challenge could be provided in cases in which punitive damages are sought. In 1997, bills were introduced in Congress that would have given each side in a case in federal court one opportunity to request reassignment of the case te a different judge. HR 520, 105th Cong, 1st Sess § 2 (1997) (civil and criminal cases); HR 1252, 105th Cong, 1st Sess § 6 (1997) (civil cases only).

The Anti-Federalists also touted jury trials in civil cases as a safeguard against corruption, on the ground that it is more difficult to bribe jurors than judges because "it is not, generally, known till the hour the cause comes on for trial, what persons are to form the jury." Federal Farmer 15 (Jan 18, 1788), in Storing, ed, 2 *The Complete Anti-Federalist* at 321 (cited in note 215). See also Federalist 83 (Hamilton), in Rossiter, ed, *The Federalist Papers* at 500 (cited in note 25) ("there is always more time and better opportunity to tampor with a standing bedy of magistrates than with a jury summoned for the occasion"). The extended length of many modern jury trials would seem to make the lack of pretrial knowledge of the jurors' identity a poor safeguard against bribery. Moreover, bribery of judges has been an extremely rare occurrence in the federal judicial system.

[220] See Alan Howard Scheiner, Note, *Judicial Assessment of Punitive Damages, the Seventh Amendment, aud the Politics of Jury Power*, 91 Colum L Rov 142, 188-89, 196-97 (1991). See also *Knecht v Radiac Abrasives, Inc*, 219 Ill App 3d 379, 579 NE2d 1248, 1251 (1991) ("The jury, with its unique ability to articulate community values, should decide whether punitive damages should be imposed.").

[221] See, for example, *Markman*, 116 S Ct at 1395 (referring to jury's ability "to reflect community standards"); Oliver Wendell Holmes, *Law in Science and Science in Law*, 12 Harv L Rov 443, 459-60 (1899) (citing the jury's role in keeping the law in accord with community values as a function served by entrusting determinations of negligence to the jury).

judges, such as sentencing, imposition of civil penalties, and grant or denial of injunctions and declaratory judgments. Moreover, as Judge Kozinski has noted recently, whereas "[l]egislators are popularly elected and represent a variety of geographic and other interests . . . [,] any group of six or 12 individuals may have views wholly unrepresentative of the community at large."[222] The reduction in the size of civil juries in federal cases makes particularly suspect the notion that a jury is a reliable barometer of community values. When the issue of the proper amount of punitive damages arises, the defendant already has been found, ordinarily by a jury, to have engaged in culpable conduct. Particularly given the other considerations suggesting that judges are better equipped than jurors to set punitive damages, it seems better to bypass this one opportunity for the expression of community values through juries, and to rely on judges to be guided by established norms of which they will be well aware (such as the need to respect persons and property).

Jury trials also afford citizens an opportunity to participate in government. As one Anti-Federalist tract argued,

> The trial by jury in the judicial department, and the collection of the people by their representatives in the legislature, are those fortunate inventions which have procured for them, in this country, their true proportion of influence, and the wisest and most fit means of protecting themselves in the community. Their situation, as jurors and representatives, enables them to acquire information and knowledge in the affairs and government of the society; and to come forward, in turn, as the centinels and guardians of each other.[223]

The participatory function of jury trials is important, but it does not deserve great weight with respect to the allocation of power under consideration here. To assign judges the power to set punitive damages would merely confer on judges the power to decide one aspect (the determination of amount) of one remedy (punitive damages). It would not substantially reduce the opportunity for public participation in government through jury service.[224]

---

[222] Kozinski, Ind Law at 12 (cited in note 11). See also Martin A. Kotler, *Reappraising the Jury's Role as Finder of Fact*, 20 Ga L Rev 123, 171-72 (1985) (arguing that juries are not "representative of the same group of persons as the legislature").

[223] Federal Farmer 4 (Oct 12, 1787), in Stering, ed, 2 *The Complete Anti-Federalist* at 249-50 (cited in note 215). See Scheiner, Note, 91 Colum L Rev at 195 (cited in note 220) ("[J]ury participation in the assessment of damages is a living form of direct democracy.").

[224] See, for example, Comment, *Criminal Safeguards and the Punitive Damages Defendant*, 34 U Chi L Rev 408, 421 (1967) ("[D]emocracy will not falter if a jury does not par-

It has been argued that juries should set punitive damages because "the right to trial by jury lends credence to the decisions of our courts and engenders public confidence in the legal system," and "any efforts on behalf of the judiciary to substantially detract from that right . . . will weaken the confidence of the people in the courts."[225] Although it is true that jury trials traditionally have been thought to be important in maintaining confidence in the legal system, the reality is that awards of punitive damages returned by juries are set aside altogether or reduced in an extraordinarily high percentage of cases.[226] If anything, taking determinations of the amount of punitive damages away from juries might well increase public confidence in the judicial system, because it would end a type of jury verdict that is partially or entirely overturned with exceptional frequency—perhaps more often than any other type of jury verdict. Moreover, the suggested change would merely take from the jury one part of one issue; juries would still determine liability for compensatory damages, amount of compensatory damages, and liability for punitive damages.

C. Summary

In cases brought in federal court, the responsibility to set punitive damages should rest with the trial judge (except in cases involving alleged abuses of governmental power).[227] The jury could be asked to return an advisory verdict on the amount of punitive damages; Federal Rule of Civil Procedure 39(c) expressly authorizes the use of advisory juries.[228] Ultimately, however, the power to determine the proper amount of punitive damages should rest with the trial judge, subject to appellate review.[229]

VI. IMPLEMENTING THE CHANGE

It might be questioned whether federal courts, even if disposed to do so, can implement the change recommended here on their own, or whether they must await a statute or an amend-

ticipate in *every* proceeding.").

[225] Knight, Note, 14 Rev Litig at 683-84 (cited in note 210).

[226] See notes 198-99.

[227] See text accompanying notes 218-20.

[228] See generally Note, *Practice and Potential of the Advisory Jury*, 100 Harv L Rev 1363, 1364-67 (1987).

[229] Where not precluded by a jury-trial guarantee of the applicable state constitution, the proposal advanced here may also merit consideration in state court systems with a strong tradition of a professional and independent judiciary.

ment to the Federal Rules of Civil Procedure. No statute or amendment to the Rules is necessary.

In *Colgrove*,[230] the Supreme Court upheld a local federal court rule providing that juries in civil cases would consist of six persons. Not only was there no statute or Federal Rule of Civil Procedure authorizing six-person juries, but at that time Rule 48 provided that "[t]he parties may stipulate that the jury shall consist of any number less than twelve"[231] and thus contemplated a twelve-person jury absent such a stipulation. The Court held that Rule 48 was no obstacle to the local rule, because it was drafted in light of the assumption, held in *Colgrove* to be incorrect, that a trial by jury meant a trial by a jury of twelve persons.[232] Since no provision of the Federal Rules of Civil Procedure even reflects the assumption that juries are to set punitive damages, under *Colgrove* federal courts are free to adopt local rules providing for judicial determination of the amount of punitive damages. Even absent a local rule, an individual judge presumably may consider providing in a pretrial order that the amount of punitive damages will be set by the court if liability for such damages is found by the jury.[233]

CONCLUSION

An award of punitive damages is a "windfall" to the plaintiff.[234] As one court put it, the plaintiff "is the fortuitous beneficiary of such an award simply because there is no one else to receive it."[235] It would be anomalous if the fortuitous beneficiary of a windfall had a constitutional right to choose the decisionmaker who determines the amount of the windfall. It would also be anomalous if defendants in civil cases had a constitutional right

---

[230] 413 US at 163-64.

[231] See id at 185 (Marshall dissenting).

[232] See id at 163-64. Rule 48 was amended in 1991 to direct trial courts to seat juries of not fewer than six and not more than twelve members. 28 USCA Rule 48 (1992).

[233] In diversity cases, a state practice of asking juries to fix punitive damages need not be followed unless it is bound up with state-created rights and obligations. The allocation of power between judges and juries is ordinarily a matter of federal procedural law, not an issue on which state law must be followed under the *Erie* doctrine. See *Byrd v Blue Ridge Rural Electric Cooperative*, 356 US 525, 535-40 (1958); *Meyers v Selznick Co*, 373 F2d 218, 222 n 1 (2d Cir 1966). Compare *Tingley Systems, Inc v Norse Systems, Inc*, 49 F3d 93, 96 (2d Cir 1994) (provision of Connecticut Unfair Trade Practices Act assigning determination of punitive damages to judge would have justified a new trial in case brought in federal court, where the district court has submitted the issue of punitive damages te the jury).

[234] *City of Newport v Fact Concerts, Inc*, 453 US 247, 267 (1981).

[235] *Katko v Briney*, 183 NW2d 657, 662 (Iowa 1971).

to have punitive damages set by a jury, whereas in criminal cases judges determine sentences of imprisonment (and in some cases even death[236]). Because the Seventh Amendment need not and should not be interpreted to entitle either plaintiffs or defendants to have a jury fix punitive damages, judicial assessment of punitive damages merits much more consideration than it has received, as an alternative to caps and other reforms designed to curb excessive awards.

[236] See Ala Code § 13A-5-47(e) (Michie 1994); Fla Stat Ann § 921.141(3) (West 1996).

[12]

DECISIONMAKING ABOUT GENERAL DAMAGES: A COMPARISON OF JURORS, JUDGES, AND LAWYERS

*Roselle L. Wissler**
*Allen J. Hart***
*Michael J. Saks****

---

* Independent Research Consultant. Formerly, Co-Principal Investigator of the Non-Economic Damages Decisionmaking Project at the University of Iowa College of Law and Department of Psychology. Ph.D. 1986, Boston College. — Ed. This research was supported by grant No. SBR-9422789 from the Law and Social Sciences Program of the National Science Foundation. The points of view expressed here are those of the authors and do not necessarily represent the position of the National Science Foundation. The authors thank George Woodworth, David Baldus, David Evans, Will Guild, Beth Bing, Justice James Heiple, and Dean Harry Wellington for assistance with various phases of this study. Address correspondence to Michael J. Saks, College of Law, University of Iowa, Iowa City, IA 52242; michael-saks@uiowa.edu.

** Assistant Professor of Psychology, Amherst College. Ph.D. 1991, Harvard University. — Ed.

*** Edward F. Howrey Professor of Law and Professor of Psychology, the University of Iowa. Ph.D. 1975, Ohio State University; M.S.L. 1985, Yale Law School. — Ed.

I. THE DEBATE OVER JURY PERFORMANCE

Placing important decisions in the hands of the civil jury — made up of ordinary citizens untrained in the law — has long been criticized. For example, Erwin Griswold, law school dean and Solicitor General of the United States, asked, "Why should anyone think that 12 persons brought in from the street, selected in various ways, for their lack of general ability, should have any special capacity for deciding controversies between persons?"[1] And Jerome Frank, law professor, aggressive legal realist, and judge, argued that juries are uncertain, capricious, and unpredictable, ignorant and prejudiced, poor factfinders, gullible, and incapable of following complex legal rules,[2] thus making "the orderly administration of justice virtually impossible."[3] The great weakness of even the most thoughtful of these criticisms is that they are based on little more than anecdote[4] and assertion, rather than anything resembling systematic empirical evidence.

The first major study of jury decisionmaking was designed with the awareness that any assessment of the jury ultimately had to be made in comparison with judges, the decisionmakers who would replace the jury in any cases juries would not be permitted to decide.[5] Accordingly, Harry Kalven and Hans Zeisel asked judges in 8,000 civil and criminal cases sampled from around the United States how they would have decided each case if it were a bench trial instead of a jury trial.[6] By comparing these responses to the actual jury verdicts, Kalven and Zeisel found that judges and juries agreed on the verdict in personal injury cases 79% of the time.[7] They also found that when jurors and judges disagreed, the jury was no more inclined than the judge to favor plaintiffs over defendants,[8] that the agreement-disagreement ratios remained the same for both easy and difficult cases (suggesting no lack

1. 1962-1963 HARVARD LAW SCHOOL DEAN'S REPORT 5-6, *quoted in* HARRY KALVEN, JR. & HANS ZEISEL, THE AMERICAN JURY 5 (1966).

2. *See* JEROME FRANK, LAW AND THE MODERN MIND 183-99 (6th ed., Anchor Books 1963).

3. *Id.* at 195; *see also* JEROME FRANK, COURTS ON TRIAL 111-25 (1949).

4. *See* Michael J. Saks, *Do We Really Know Anything About the Behavior of the Tort Litigation System — And Why Not?*, 140 U. PA. L. REV. 1147, 1161 (1992) ("The trouble with legislation by anecdote is not just that some of them are false or misleading. Even if true and accurate, anecdotes contribute little to developing a meaningful picture of the situation about which we are concerned.... The proportion of cases that results in one or the other error, and the ratio of one kind of error to the other, ought to be of greater interest to serious policy-makers than a handful of anecdotes on either side of the issue."); Marc Galanter et al., *How to Improve Civil Justice Policy*, 77 JUDICATURE 185, 185 (1994) ("Improving the civil justice system requires thoughtful, objective analysis based on sound empirical data. The lack of systematic, cumulative data in this area makes it possible for far-reaching policy proposals to be advanced on the basis of tendentious anecdotes and numbers. A bias in which solutions to perceived problems are developed by reference to unusual and atypical cases goes unchallenged. Not surprisingly, the effects of the resulting policies are often unanticipated."), *quoted in* Brian J. Ostrom et al., *A Step Above Anecdote: A Profile of the Civil Jury in the 1990s*, 79 JUDICATURE 233, 234 (1996).

5. *See generally* Harry Kalven, Jr., *The Dignity of the Civil Jury*, 50 VA. L. REV. 1055, 1055-56, 1056 n.3 (1964).

6. *See id.* at 1063.

7. *See id.* at 1065.

8. *See id.*

of comprehension by the juries),[9] and that the judges rarely thought the juries' verdicts were unreasonable in light of the available evidence and applicable law.[10] In fact, the only noteworthy difference was that when juries did find liability, they awarded on average 20% more than judges said they would have awarded.[11] Even that, however, was a more modest difference than critics of the jury would have had us believe. Perhaps because Kalven and Zeisel's research findings provided so little support to the usual criticisms, the critics fell silent for a generation.

But by the mid-1980s, criticism of the civil jury returned with vigor, part of a more wide-ranging attack on the civil justice system (in particular, the tort system).[12] "One of the most criticized aspects of jury behavior" has been juries' awards of general damages, also known as noneconomic damages or by the synecdoche "pain and suffering" awards.[13] Unlike special or "economic" damages, the jury receives little guidance regarding what a correct general damages award might be. And, unlike punitive damages, which are similarly lacking in guidance but which are rarely awarded in accident cases, general damages are proper in every personal injury case in which awards are made.

---

9. *See id.* at 1066.

10. *See id.* at 1067.

11. *See id.* at 1065.

12. In general these attacks were no more grounded in empirical research than earlier assaults. Where data were mentioned, their interpretation often was rather careless. For extensive discussions and evaluations of that body of "evidence," see STEPHEN DANIELS & JOANNE MARTIN, CIVIL JURIES AND THE POLITICS OF REFORM (1995); Marc Galanter, *Jury Shadows: Reflections on the Civil Jury and the "Litigation Explosion," in* THE AMERICAN CIVIL JURY: FINAL REPORT OF THE 1986 CHIEF JUSTICE EARL WARREN CONFERENCE ON ADVOCACY IN THE UNITED STATES 15 (1987); Robert E. Litan, *Introduction, in* VERDICT: ASSESSING THE CIVIL JURY SYSTEM (Robert E. Litan ed., 1993); Robert J. MacCoun, *Inside the Black Box: What Empirical Research Tells Us About Decisionmaking by Civil Juries, in* VERDICT: ASSESSING THE CIVIL JURY SYSTEM 137 (Robert E. Litan ed., 1993); Peter H. Schuck, *Mapping the Debate on Jury Reform, in* VERDICT: ASSESSING THE CIVIL JURY SYSTEM 306 (Robert E. Litan ed., 1993); NEIL VIDMAR, MEDICAL MALPRACTICE AND THE AMERICAN JURY: CONFRONTING THE MYTHS ABOUT JURY INCOMPETENCE, DEEP POCKETS AND OUTRAGEOUS DAMAGE AWARDS (1995); Stephen Daniels, *The Question of Jury Competence and the Politics of Civil Justice Reform: Symbols, Rhetoric, and Agenda Building*, LAW & CONTEMP. PROBS., Autumn 1989, at 269, 292-308; Marc Galanter, *The Day After the Litigation Explosion*, 46 MD. L. REV. 3 (1986); Marc Galanter, *News from Nowhere: The Debased Debate on Civil Justice*, 71 DENV. U. L. REV. 77 (1993); Marc Galanter, *Real World Torts: An Antidote to Anecdote*, 55 MD. L. REV. 1093 (1996); Saks, *supra* note 4; and Neil Vidmar, *The Performance of the American Civil Jury: An Empirical Perspective*, 40 ARIZ. L. REV. 849 (1998).

13. Neil Vidmar, *Pap and Circumstance: What Jury Verdict Statistics Can Tell Us About Jury Behavior and the Tort System*, 28 SUFFOLK U. L. REV. 1205, 1224 (1994); *see also* Oscar G. Chase, *Helping Jurors Determine Pain and Suffering Awards*, 23 HOFSTRA L. REV. 763, 768-69 (1995) (asserting unexplainable variation among awards of pain and suffering in wrongful death cases); Kirk B. Johnson et al., *A Fault-Based Administrative Alternative for Resolving Medical Malpractice Claims*, 42 VAND. L. REV. 1365, 1369-70 (1989) (asserting unjustified variation in awards for comparable injuries caused by medical malpractice and other tortious acts).

Moreover, general damages constitute about fifty-five to sixty percent of personal injury damages awards.[14] It is no surprise, then, that general damages have been at the center of contemporary debates on juries and the civil justice system.

The critics of the civil jury assert that awards generally are unreliable, capricious, and "out of control."[15] More specifically, general damages are alleged to be both excessive and influenced by inappropriate considerations, such as sympathy for the victims and the defendant's apparent ability to pay.[16] By implication then, jury decisions about general damages are thought to be insufficiently responsive to proper considerations, namely, the nature of the injury and its impact on the plaintiff's life. Moreover, implicit in these allegations is a problem that Jerome Frank had made explicit: that jurors do not think about cases the same way judges and lawyers do.

Although research has begun to focus on damages, these studies have thus far left the basic issues underlying the criticisms of jury awards largely unanswered.[17] These basic issues are how jurors perceive injuries and translate those perceptions into dollar awards, and whether jurors' decisionmaking processes differ fundamentally from those of judges (and lawyers).[18] The research reported in this Article investigates jurors' perceptions of injury seriousness and awards of general damages, and, like Kalven and Zeisel, compares them to judges' and lawyers' responses to the same injuries. The results of this most basic comparison have significant implications for criticisms of jury awards and for legal policy concerning jury trials.[19]

---

14. *See* Neil Vidmar et al., *Jury Awards for Medical Malpractice and Post-Verdict Adjustments of Those Awards*, 48 DEPAUL L. REV. 265, 296 (1998).

15. See criticisms reviewed in works at *supra* note 12.

16. Documentation of the various allegations can be found in the works cited *supra* note 12.

17. Much of the empirical research literature on compensatory damages is discussed in our review of the relevant literature, *infra*, Section II.B.

18. Despite the well known research strategy of Kalven & Zeisel, only a few studies have directly compared the performance of jurors to judges. *See* Edmund S. Howe & Thomas C. Loftus, *Integration of Intention and Outcome Information by Students and Circuit Court Judges: Design Economy and Individual Differences*, 22 J. APPLIED SOC. PSYCHOL. 102 (1992); Stephen Landsman & Richard Rakos, *A Preliminary Inquiry into the Effect of Potentially Biasing Information on Judges and Jurors in Civil Litigation*, 12 BEHAV. SCI. & L. 113 (1994); Gary L. Wells, *Naked Statistical Evidence of Liability: Is Subjective Probability Enough?*, 62 J. PERS. SOC. PSYCHOL. 739 (1992). None of these addressed, however, the question of damages. Another study contains a partial comparison (6 judges in a group composed mostly of lawyers). *See* Neil Vidmar & Jeffrey J. Rice, *Assessments of Noneconomic Damage Awards in Medical Negligence: A Comparison of Jurors with Legal Professionals*, 78 IOWA L. REV. 883 (1993). All of these studies found no differences in decisionmaking between judges and jurors.

19. A more detailed explication of the research questions is presented *infra* Section III.A, and a more detailed discussion of the policy implications of the findings appears *infra* Section V.D.

To provide the context for our research, Part II of this Article briefly summarizes relevant aspects of the law and the empirical research literature. The law governing general damages offers no real guidance to jurors or anyone else called upon to award damages at trial. Empirical research shows that jurors display a substantial amount of sensitivity to the relative seriousness of injuries (vertical equity) in awarding general damages, but also a considerable amount of variation within levels of severity (horizontal inequity). This body of research, however, has some conceptual and methodological weaknesses; thus, important empirical questions remain.

Part III describes the research methods and design of our study. In brief, we sampled hundreds of jurors, judges, plaintiffs' lawyers, and defense lawyers from urban and rural regions of two different states. Through telephone interviews, we presented dozens of different injuries (two per interviewee) to the respondents and had them evaluate the seriousness of the injuries and specify what general damages award seemed appropriate for the injury suffered.

We used the survey responses to develop predictive (and arguably, explanatory) models of the decisionmaking of each group. We then used these statistical models to determine for each group which attributes of the injuries had what degree of impact on severity judgments and on awards, as well as how differences in the decisionmakers' geography, demography, and experiences affected their decisions. Part IV presents the results of these analyses. In short, the models evidence a remarkable degree of similarity among all groups of decisionmakers, plus a high degree of predictability, in regard to their judgments of injury severity. As to the translation of injury perceptions into monetary awards, however, more differences among the groups appeared, and the predictive power of the models declined.

Part V presents our conclusions with respect to both the empirical findings and their policy implications. Taken together, the findings suggest that the differences between jurors' awards and those of the other groups do not reflect fundamental differences in decisionmaking, but rather a loss of consistency in translating perceptions of severity into damages awards. That loss of consistency likely can be attributed to the fact that in assessing the value of a single case, jurors lack the frame of reference created by other cases that is readily available to judges and lawyers. If that diagnosis is correct, it suggests that some rather modest changes in procedure are likely to be sufficient to enable jurors' general damages awards to closely approximate those of judges in stability and predictability.

II. General Damages: The Law and the Empirical Research

A. *The Law of General Damages*

In tort cases, general damages are awarded to compensate plaintiffs for physical pain, mental suffering, disability, disfigurement, loss of enjoyment of life, and other similar harms.[20] While these "noneconomic" damages may not be inherently different from "economic" damages such as lost earnings and medical expenses, markets exist to supply the values of the latter but not the former.[21] If art can acquire a market value, in principle, so can the loss of sight. The problem is that people do not normally buy and sell the sorts of sensory, motor, cognitive, and other capacities that are injured in accidents. The result is that to compensate for noneconomic losses, the law must turn to an alternative source of values, namely, the social judgment of the community, typically supplied by juries. A task that involves assigning a value to the virtually undefinable is, by definition, challenging to perform and at least as challenging to evaluate. "One of the most difficult decisions facing the jury in a personal injury case is the size of the monetary award for pain and suffering, since there is no objective method of evaluating such damages."[22]

The law itself provides essentially no guidance to jurors in reaching a "correct" general damages award. For instance, the Restatement (Second) of Torts notes that "[t]he discretion of the judge or jury determines the amount of recovery, the only standard being such an amount as a reasonable person would estimate as fair compensation."[23] In addition, the law requires that damages be particularized to both the details of the objective injury and its subjective effect on the

20. *See generally* RESTATEMENT (SECOND) OF TORTS § 905 (1979); 22 AM. JUR. 2D *Damages* § 28 (1988).

21. *See* Ted R. Miller, *Willingness to Pay Comes of Age: Will the System Survive?*, 83 NW. U. L. REV. 876, 896-900 (1989); W. Kip Viscusi, *Pain and Suffering in Product Liability Cases: Systematic Compensation or Capricious Awards?*, 8 INT'L REV. L. & ECON. 203 (1988).

22. AM. JUR. 2D *Damages* § 260 (1988); *see also* R. Perry Sentell, Jr., *The Georgia Jury and Negligence: The View from the Trenches*, 28 GA. L. REV. 1, 97-98 (1993) (summarizing a survey of Georgia plaintiffs' and defense lawyers which found that they thought the most troublesome issue for the jury is a lack of guidance on how to assess damages, especially for pain and suffering); Neil Vidmar, *Empirical Evidence on the Deep Pockets Hypothesis: Jury Awards for Pain and Suffering in Medical Malpractice Cases*, 43 DUKE L.J. 217 (1993).

23. RESTATEMENT (SECOND) OF TORTS § 912 cmt. b (1979).

individual victim.[24] By implication, then, the law expects awards to reflect considerable variability.[25]

Of course, the law has as little guidance to offer judges and lawyers in this pursuit as it does to juries. Nonetheless, critics of juries seem to believe that judges and lawyers somehow acquire judgmental capabilities that juries lack, producing judgments which are somehow more "accurate," or at least more consistent, than those provided by jurors.

B. *Empirical Research on Damages Awards*

Researchers have sought to identify the determinants of damages awards. In archival studies, researchers have found that from half to almost three-fourths of the variation in awards actually made by juries (and sometimes by judges) can be accounted for by various measures of injury severity, such as medical expenses or ratings of severity and duration, as well as by other predictors.[26] The measures of injury type, severity, and permanence are consistently the strongest predictors of awards, with injuries of greater severity and duration tending to receive more compensation than less severe and more temporary injuries. Similarly, simulation studies, which examine mock jurors' awards in response to experimentally manipulated cases, also find the size of the award to correspond to the severity of the injury.[27]

Despite these substantial predictive relationships, the findings suggest there are both random and systematic errors in awards. The same

24. *See generally* David W. Leebron, *Final Moments: Damages for Pain and Suffering Prior to Death*, 64 N.Y.U. L. REV. 256, 265 (1989).

25. Nevertheless, many trial participants and commentators wish for less variability and more predictability than the law thus far has been able to design.

26. *See* AUDREY CHIN & MARK A. PETERSON, DEEP POCKETS, EMPTY POCKETS: WHO WINS IN COOK COUNTY JURY TRIALS (1985); MARK A. PETERSON, COMPENSATION FOR INJURIES: CIVIL JURY VERDICTS IN COOK COUNTY (1984); David Baldus et al., *Improving Judicial Oversight of Jury Damage Assessments: A Proposal for the Comparative Additur/Remittitur Review of Awards for Nonpecuniary Harms and Punitive Damages*, 80 IOWA L. REV. 1109 (1995); Randall Bovbjerg et al., *Juries and Justice: Are Malpractice and Other Injuries Created Equal?*, LAW & CONTEMP. PROBS., Winter 1991, at 5 [hereinafter Bovbjerg et al., *Juries and Justice*]; Randall R. Bovbjerg et al., *Valuing Life and Limb in Tort: Scheduling "Pain and Suffering,"* 83 NW. U. L. REV. 908 (1989) [hereinafter Bovbjerg et al., *Valuing Life and Limb*]; Frank A. Sloan & Chee Ruey Hsieh, *Variability in Medical Malpractice Payments: Is the Compensation Fair?*, 24 LAW & SOC'Y REV. 997 (1990); Viscusi, *supra* note 21.

27. *See* Jane Goodman et al., *Runaway Verdicts or Reasoned Determinations: Mock Juror Strategies in Awarding Damages*, 29 JURIMETRICS 285, 289 (1989); Valerie Hans & M. David Ermann, *Responses to Corporate Versus Individual Wrongdoing*, 13 LAW & HUM. BEHAV. 151 (1989); Michael J. Saks et al., *Reducing Variability in Civil Jury Awards*, 21 LAW & HUM. BEHAV. 243 (1997); Vidmar & Rice, *supra* note 18; Roselle L. Wissler et al., *Explaining "Pain and Suffering" Awards: the Role of Injury Characteristics and Fault Attributions*, 21 LAW & HUM. BEHAV. 181 (1997). *But see* Corinne Cather et al., *Plaintiff Injury and Defendant Reprehensibility: Implications for Compensatory and Punitive Damage Awards*, 20 LAW & HUM. BEHAV. 189 (1996) (finding no difference in awards as a function of injury severity).

studies that find high correlations between injury severity and awards (termed "vertical equity") also report considerable variation in the amounts awarded for injuries at the same level of severity (referred to as "horizontal inequity"),[28] which suggests the presence of a good deal of random error.[29]

Systematic error in awards is seen in a number of studies which have found that, despite general vertical equity, plaintiffs with small losses tend to be overcompensated and those with large losses tend to be undercompensated.[30] Moreover, several factors which should not have an effect on general damages awards, such as type of defendant (e.g., individual versus corporation) or type of case (e.g., auto crash versus medical malpractice)[31] nevertheless seem to systematically influence the size of awards.[32] In addition, some evidence suggests that where jurors reside influences their awards — that jurors in urban areas generally make larger awards than those in rural areas,[33] and that

---

28. *See* CHIN & PETERSON, *supra* note 26; Sloan & Hsieh, *supra* note 26; Viscusi, *supra* note 21.

29. In simulation studies, for instance, mock jurors are presented with identical case facts, yet the jurors produce an array of different awards, not one single award. *See* sources cited *supra* note 27. Of course, a complete absence of variability among a group of decisionmakers seldom occurs. For a glimpse of the variability of other decisionmakers, see *infra* Table 5. Accordingly, commentators who lament "horizontal inequity" cannot be suggesting that its existence demonstrates a defect in the system of damages. What they really ought to be arguing is that the amount of horizontal variability is greater than they believe it should be.

30. *See* ALFRED F. CONARD ET AL., AUTOMOBILE ACCIDENT COSTS AND PAYMENTS: STUDIES IN THE ECONOMICS OF INJURY REPARATION at 248-52 (1964); ELIZABETH M. KING & JAMES P. SMITH, ECONOMIC LOSS AND COMPENSATION IN AVIATION ACCIDENTS at 74-76 (1988).

31. *See* CHIN & PETERSON, *supra* note 26; PETERSON, *supra* note 26; Baldus et al., *supra* note 26; Bovbjerg et al., *Juries and Justice*, *supra* note 26; Bovbjerg et al., *Valuing Life and Limb*, *supra* note 26; James K. Hammitt et al., *Tort Standards and Jury Decisions*, 14 J. LEGAL STUD. 751 (1985); Viscusi, *supra* note 21; David C. Baldus et al., Children's Models for Compensatory Damages (1992) (unpublished manuscript, on file with the authors).

32. Simulation studies, however, have added important qualifications and refinements to conclusions about the way in which these factors affect awards. Most importantly, they have found that differences in compensatory awards previously attributed to a "deep pocket" effect are not the result of differences in the defendants' wealth. *See* Robert J. MacCoun, *Differential Treatment of Corporate Defendants by Juries: An Examination of the "Deep-Pockets" Hypothesis*, 30 LAW & SOC'Y REV. 121 (1996); Neil Vidmar, et al., *Damage Awards and Jurors' Responsibility Ascriptions in Medical Versus Automobile Negligence Cases*, 12 BEHAV. SCI. & L. 149 (1994); Vidmar, *supra* note 22; William D. Woody et al., Compensating Plaintiffs and Punishing Defendants: Is Bifurcation Necessary? (1998) (unpublished manuscript, on file with the authors) (presented at the biennial meeting of the American Psychology-Law Society, Redondo Beach, Cal., 1998). Instead, the differences in awards are due to differences in perceptions of the defendants' intentionality, responsibility, recklessness, or competence to avoid the injury. *See* Valerie P. Hans, *The Jury's Response to Business and Corporate Wrongdoing*, 52 LAW & CONTEMP. PROBS., Autumn 1989, at 177; Hans & Ermann, *supra* note 27; *see also* Goodman, et al., *supra* note 27; MacCoun, *supra* note 12; Vidmar et al., *supra* note 14.

33. *See* PATRICIA M. DANZON, MEDICAL MALPRACTICE: THEORY, EVIDENCE, AND PUBLIC POLICY 74-75 (1985).

jurors in some states characteristically make smaller or larger awards than those in other states.[34] Thus, awards may depend on more than the characteristics of injuries and their sequelae.

For answering questions of how jurors respond to the attributes of the injuries in making their general damages awards, the archival studies are insufficient in one or more ways. Typically, most jury awards are reported as single aggregate awards, instead of being separated into their component parts. Thus, researchers generally use the total, undifferentiated award, not the specific general damages component.[35] And efforts by some researchers to disaggregate the awards after the fact[36] tend to produce erroneous estimates of the general component.[37]

Additionally, the degree of horizontal inequity suggested by many of the studies may reflect the limitations of the measurements used as much as any random error in jurors' decisions. For example, the severity of injuries usually has been measured by grading a vast array of injuries on a scale of no more than eight or nine points.[38] Each point on such a scale necessarily captures a range of injuries having different degrees of severity.[39] That jurors would rate the injuries more finely, and award different amounts to injuries that researchers have treated as identical, is hardly a failing of juror decisionmaking.

Further, these scales are unidimensional measures, though injuries, like most social objects and events, occupy a multidimensional space. For example, on the National Association of Insurance Commissioners' ("NAIC") Severity of Injury Scale, burns, surgical material left in a patient, drug side effects, and brain damage all are scored as Level 4 injuries. The Procrustean compression by researchers into a single dimension of what the decisionmakers almost certainly saw as a multidimensional injury squanders explanatory potential.[40] Evidence of this

---

34. *See* DANIELS & MARTIN, *supra* note 12.

35. *See* CHIN & PETERSON, *supra* note 26; PETERSON, *supra* note 26; Bovbjerg et al., *Juries and Justice*, *supra* note 26; Sloan & Hsieh, *supra* note 26.

36. *See* Bovbjerg et al., *Valuing Life and Limb*, *supra* note 26; Viscusi, *supra* note 21.

37. *See* Neil Vidmar, *Making Inferences About Jury Behavior from Jury Verdict Statistics: Cautions About the Lorelei's Lied*, 18 LAW & HUM. BEHAV. 599 (1994); Vidmar et al., *supra* note 14.

38. Some researchers use the Severity of Injury Scale developed by the National Association of Insurance Commissioners, *see* NAIC MALPRACTICE CLAIMS: FINAL COMPILATION (1980), which ranges from one (emotional injury only) to nine (death). *See* DANZON, *supra* note 33; Bovbjerg et al., *Juries and Justice*, *supra* note 26.

39. *See* Oscar G. Chase, *Helping Jurors Determine Pain and Suffering Awards*, *in* REFORMING THE CIVIL JUSTICE SYSTEM 339, 354 (Larry Kramer ed., 1996); Gary T. Schwartz, *Proposals for Reforming Pain and Suffering Awards*, *in* REFORMING THE CIVIL JUSTICE SYSTEM 416, 419 (Larry Kramer ed., 1996)

40. *See* Allen J. Hart et al., *Multidimensional Perceptions of Illness and Injury*, 2 CURRENT RES. SOC. PSYCHOL. 30 (Sept. 11, 1997) <http://www.uiowa.edu/~grpproc/crisp/crisp.html>; Andrew J. Slain et al., Multidimensional Perceptions of Injury: Implications for

problem is provided by data from simulation jurors, whose assessments of injuries on four dimensions (disability, mental suffering, disfigurement, pain) better predicted their general damages awards (accounting for 74% of the variance) than did a single predictor based on the same jurors' assessments of the overall severity of injury (61% of the variance in awards), which in turn was a better predictor than the NAIC scale (44%).[41]

In addition to poor measurement of injuries, the studies finding substantial horizontal inequity also fail to take into account legally relevant differences among injury victims.[42] For example, the exact same permanent loss of hearing *should* produce a larger general damages award for a musician than for a novelist. Moreover, a permanent injury should result in a larger award to compensate a 20-year-old plaintiff for 60 years of future pain and suffering than to compensate a 60-year-old plaintiff for 20 years.[43] All of these are examples of vertical equity mistaken for horizontal inequity.

Of course, to demonstrate that horizontal inequity has been overestimated in the literature is not to say that real sources of horizontal inequity, both random and systematic, do not exist. But we should not mistake one problem for another. And we certainly should not mistake the limitations of the studies for the limitations of juror decisionmaking.

In all of these studies, it is impossible to know how well or poorly the jurors have done because there are almost no data for answering the inescapable question of "compared to what?" As Kalven and Zeisel noted long ago, in the study of juries, the usual answer to that question is: compared to the decision a judge would make in the same case, because judges are the most likely alternative to jurors.[44] More recently, the answer might include alternative dispute resolution forums in which the decisionmakers might be lawyers (in the role of arbitrators) or other professionals (as members of compensation boards). Studies using a straightforward comparison of damages awarded by judges and by juries suffer from case selection confounds because, owing to the strategic choices of lawyers, different mixes of cases go to juries than go to judges.[45] Two recent studies overcame

the "Adversary Culture" (1998) (unpublished manuscript, on file with the authors) (presented at the Biennial Meeting of the American Psychology-Law Society, Redondo Beach, Cal., 1998).

41. *See* Wissler et al., *supra* note 27, at 195-202 (Experiment 2).

42. Jurors evaluating general damages may and should take into account such things as pre-injury health, post-injury recovery, lifestyle, occupation, and social circumstances. *See* RESTATEMENT (SECOND) OF TORTS § 905 cmt. i (1979).

43. *See* RESTATEMENT (SECOND) OF TORTS § 905 (1979).

44. *See* HARRY KALVEN, JR. & HANS ZEISEL, THE AMERICAN JURY (1966).

45. *See* Kevin M. Clermont & Theodore Eisenberg, *Trial by Jury or Judge: Transcending Empiricism*, 77 CORNELL L. REV. 1124 (1992).

this problem by presenting the same case facts to arbitrators[46] and to senior lawyers,[47] as well as to jurors. Both studies found no significant differences in the general damages awards given by the different types of decisionmakers.[48]

Significantly, prior studies tell researchers and reformers little about how jurors decide awards. As Goodman notes, "[l]ittle is known about the strategies or cognitive processes used by jurors in determining damages."[49] Such research is needed because "although critics tend to focus on the *outcomes* of jury decisionmaking — liability verdicts and damages awards — effective evaluation and implementation of policy also require an understanding of the *process* of jury decisionmaking."[50]

Thus, fundamental questions about jurors' decisionmaking about general damages remain unanswered. What is the content and organization of people's perceptions of injuries? Given that most people have little systematic experience evaluating injuries, but generally respond with intuitive, "gut" reactions, we might expect considerable random variation across individuals. How much random variation is there? By contrast, are systematic variations to be found between social groups? Are major differences to be found in perceptions of injuries or in the special challenge of translating those perceptions into dollar awards?[51] Does this translation step reveal its own systematic differences among groups? Most importantly, do judges and lawyers see or value injuries differently, or show less variability, than the ordinary citizens who serve on juries?

III. The Present Research

A. *Overview*

The present study asks how the core attributes of injuries affect decisionmakers' perceptions of the injuries, how those perceptions are translated into dollar awards, and whether (and if so, how) these patterns of response differ among jurors, judges, and lawyers. This re-

46. *See* Vidmar & Rice, *supra* note 18.

47. *See* Vidmar, *supra* note 12, at 229-234.

48. *See* Vidmar & Rice, *supra* note 18.

49. *See* Goodman et al., *supra* note 27; *see also* Jane Goodman et al., *Money, Sex, and Death: Gender Bias in Wrongful Death Damage Awards*, 25 L. & SOC'Y REV. 263, 264 (1991) ("Little is known about factors that influence jury damage awards in civil cases.").

50. MacCoun, *supra* note 12, at 137 (emphasis in original).

51. *See* Cass R. Sunstein et al., *Assessing Punitive Damages (With Notes on Cognition and Valuation in Law)*, 107 YALE L.J. 2071 (1998); Daniel Kahneman et al., *Shared Outrage and Erratic Awards: The Psychology of Punitive Damages*, 16 J. RISK & UNCERTAINTY 49 (1998) (a somewhat more technical presentation of the same study as Sunstein et al.); Wissler et al., *supra* note 27.

search took the form of a fractional factorial survey,[52] in which numerous and diverse injury scenarios were presented to judges, lawyers, and jurors. The respondents were asked to evaluate the injuries on several dimensions, to indicate their judgment of the injury's overall severity, and to provide an appropriate award. Respondents were selected from two different states, which were chosen on the basis of previous research suggesting that the damages awards in one were characteristically high and the other characteristically low relative to other states.[53] Respondents also were stratified within each state by their urban or rural location, another factor previous research suggested was related to award size.[54]

The present design avoids the confounding inherent in purely observational research. By presenting an identical set of injuries to jurors in both states, and in both urban and rural areas, the factorial survey permits a test of whether awards are a function of where the jurors reside (that is, economic and cultural differences between states or between rural and urban dwellers within states) or of the mix of cases to which they are responding. Similarly, by having jurors, judges, and lawyers respond to exactly the same group of injuries, the present study eliminates the confounding of the decisionmaker with the case mix. Thus, unlike passive observational studies, the present design can distinguish the attributes of the decisionmakers from the attributes of the cases they are deciding. The comparative nature of the present research allows us to see how similar or different the decisionmaking groups are in their decision processes and responses. Asking respondents to evaluate injuries on a separate set of scales and to make general damages awards allows us to build decision models of both the injury-evaluation phase of their thinking and the award-making phase, and to compare these decision processes.

The pattern of findings obtained will imply different diagnoses and different policy solutions to improving the process of awarding general damages. For example, if jurors' injury severity evaluations or damages awards were not highly predictable, but no less predictable than those of judges and lawyers, that would suggest that the problem is not properly ascribed to *jurors*, but is attributable to the nature of the decisionmaking task, and replacing jurors with judges offers no solution. Alternatively, if all groups were equally predictable, but jurors relied exclusively on one dimension of injury, such as mental suffering, while judges and lawyers relied on a definable mix of all injury attributes, then differences between decisionmaker groups would imply system-

52. *See* PETER H. ROSSI & STEVEN L. NOCK, MEASURING SOCIAL JUDGMENTS: THE FACTORIAL SURVEY APPROACH (1982).

53. *See* DANIELS & MARTIN, *supra* note 12.

54. *See generally* DANZON, *supra* note 33.

atic differences in decisions and outcomes. Similarly, if jurors showed a high degree of unpredictability in both injury evaluations and awards, but judges and lawyers showed a high degree of predictability in both, then it becomes plausible to think that replacing jurors with judges would produce more stable patterns of awards.

B. *Design*

This study is a fractional factorial survey — that is, a fractional experimental design conducted in the manner of a survey.[55] The study utilized 62 injury case summaries, grouped into 31 pairs. Each pair was heard by a subset of the respondents; each respondent heard one injury pair. Thus, injury was both a between- and within-subjects factor. The respondents were drawn from three populations — jury-eligible citizens, judges, and lawyers — stratified by rural and urban counties in the states of Illinois and New York. Respondents rated each injury on several dimensions and provided damages awards.

1. *Case Summaries*

The 62 case summaries were adapted from actual personal injury cases[56] and represented a broad spectrum of injuries. The injuries encompassed different types: nerve damage and paralysis (e.g., quadriplegia, temporary paralysis of two fingers); head injuries and brain damage (e.g., epilepsy, permanent vegetative state); sensory loss (e.g., vision, smell); cuts (e.g., on face, legs); harm to internal organs (e.g., loss of kidney, spleen); illnesses (e.g., leukemia, lung cancer); burns (e.g., second degree on lower body, third degree over 80% of body); and orthopedic injuries (e.g., fracture, sprain, amputation). We did not include cases in which the plaintiff had died or in which the plaintiff suffered only emotional distress unaccompanied by physical injury.

The case summaries included a description of the nature, severity, and location of the injury; the nature, painfulness, duration, and restrictions associated with the treatment and healing process; any anxiety, fear, embarrassment, or depression about the injury, its impact, treatment, or prognosis; the current status of the plaintiff's pain, disfigurement, mental state, and physical impairment; and the likelihood and extent of future improvement or deterioration and treatment or care needs.[57] These injury characteristics were suggested by the legal

55. *See generally* ROSSI & NOCK, *supra* note 52.

56. The cases were selected from those identified in a study by Baldus et al., *supra* note 26.

57. See Appendix A for several examples of case summaries.

literature,[58] workers' compensation schedules,[59] British compensation schedules for personal injury cases,[60] and empirical research in this area.[61]

The case summaries noted the age of the plaintiff, who was said to be 37 years old in one case in each pair and 33 years old in the other case. The plaintiff's age was specified in order to reduce the variability in awards that would result if compensation for future pain and suffering for permanent injuries were based on different life expectancies (e.g., if some respondents thought they were compensating a 20-year-old for 60 years of pain and suffering while others thought they were compensating a 60-year-old for 20 years).[62] The mid-thirties were chosen as representative of a fairly large range of ages and unlikely to involve special considerations that might arise for young or elderly plaintiffs. In order to discover the dimensions along which people view injuries and determine awards, independent of other contextual factors, no details were supplied about the plaintiff (other than age),[63] about the defendant, or about the circumstances that caused the injuries.[64]

58. *See* RESTATEMENT (SECOND) OF TORTS §§ 905, 912 cmt. b (1979); 22 AM. JUR. 2D *Damages* §§ 240-241, 252-256, 269, 271, 275, 293-387 (1988); 1 MARILYN MINZER ET AL., DAMAGES IN TORT ACTIONS (1993); JEROME MIRZA, ILLINOIS TORT LAW & PRACTICE (2d ed. 1989); 36 NY JUR. 2D *Damages* §§ 56-66, 96-99 (1984); MICHAEL J. POLELLE & BRUCE L. OTTLEY, ILLINOIS TORT LAW (1985); Robert W. Phillpott, Jr., ed., *Quantum Study*, 42 LOY. L. REV. 817 (1997); Carl T. Drechsler, Annotation, *Excessiveness or Adequacy of Damages Awarded for Injuries to Arms and Hands*, 12 A.L.R. 4th 96 (1981); Carl T. Drechsler, Annotation, *Excessiveness or Adequacy of Damages Awarded for Injuries to Legs and Feet*, 13 A.L.R. 4th 212 (1981).

59. *See* ALBERT J. MILLUS & WILLARD J. GENTILE, WORKERS' COMPENSATION LAW AND INSURANCE 93-194 (2d ed. 1980); JEFFREY V. NACKLEY, PRIMER ON WORKERS' COMPENSATION (2d ed. 1989).

60. *See* PETER CANE, ATIYAH'S ACCIDENTS, COMPENSATION AND THE LAW (4th ed. 1987); JUDICIAL STUDIES BOARD, GUIDELINES FOR THE ASSESSMENT OF GENERAL DAMAGES IN PERSONAL INJURY CASES (1992); DAVID A. KEMP & MARGARET S. KEMP, QUANTUM OF DAMAGES (1992); JOHN MUNKMAN, DAMAGES FOR PERSONAL INJURY AND DEATH (8th ed. 1989); David A. Kemp, *Damages for Non-Pecuniary Loss*, *in* DAMAGES FOR PERSONAL INJURY AND DEATH (David Kemp ed., 1993).

61. *See* CHIN & PETERSON, *supra* note 26; Baldus et al., *supra* note 26; Hart et al., *supra* note 40; Viscusi, *supra* note 21; Wissler et al., *supra* note 27.

62. *See* Baldus et al., *supra* note 26; Bovbjerg et al., *Valuing Life and Limb*, *supra* note 26.

63. Respondents who requested more information about the plaintiff were told to assume that the person was of average good health and had an average lifestyle before the injury.

64. A potential criticism of our methodology is that our findings, based on relatively brief injury descriptions, might not be consistent with those that would be obtained with a fuller presentation of information, such as at trial. *See* Vladimir J. Konecni & Ebbe B. Ebbesen, *External Validity of Research in Legal Psychology*, 3 LAW & HUM. BEHAV. 39 (1979); Wayne Weiten & Shari S. Diamond, *A Critical Review of the Jury Simulation Paradigm: The Case of Defendant Characteristics*, 3 LAW & HUM. BEHAV. 71 (1979). Few respondents commented that they did not have enough information about the injuries themselves; those who requested additional information sought contextual information that we had deliber-

2. *Sampling Locations*

Our sample was stratified by state and, within state, by rural and urban counties. Illinois was selected to represent a characteristically low-award state and New York a high-award state.[65] For sampling purposes, population density figures were used to designate counties as rural or urban.[66] In Illinois, Cook County (population density of about 5,000 people per square mile) was designated urban and counties with fewer than 115 people per square mile were designated rural; counties with an intermediate population density were not included. In New York state, Queens, Bronx, Kings, and New York Counties (population densities ranging between 17,000 and 53,000 people per square mile) were designated urban. For the jury-eligible sample, New York counties with fewer than 200 people per square mile were designated rural, and respondents were not drawn from counties with an intermediate population density. In order to obtain an adequate sample of judges and personal injury lawyers, however, New York counties with an intermediate population density were included among the rural counties.[67]

C. *Respondents*

We drew representative samples from three populations: jury-eligible citizens, judges, and lawyers.

1. *Jurors*

Random-digit dialing was used to obtain the sample of jury-eligible (i.e., 18 years or older) citizens (hereafter referred to as "jurors").

ately withheld in order to eliminate its potential confounding effects. As discussed in Wissler et al., *supra* note 27, short as opposed to longer injury descriptions did not produce differences in injury ratings, awards, or the relationship between the two.

65. The median 1988-90 jury award in Cook County (Chicago), Illinois, was $32,550, compared to from $242,500 to $417,200 in several urban New York counties. *See* DANIELS & MARTIN, *supra* note 12, at 70-71. When the awards were adjusted for differences in the amount in controversy subject to the jurisdiction of courts in the two states, Cook County's median award increased to $162,316, but was still well below that of New York urban counties. Median awards in rural counties ranged from $24,868 to $39,180 in Illinois and from $66,000 to $192,500 in New York. *See id.*

66. The population density figures were obtained from the U.S. Bureau of the Census at its internet site at <www.census.gov/population/censusdata/90den_stco.txt>. These designations were used for sampling purposes only; the rural/urban variable used in the analyses relied on the respondents' self-report of where they live (jurors), where jurors in their courts live (judges), or where personal injury plaintiffs in their cases live (lawyers).

67. The population density (number of people per square mile) of these intermediate counties was as follows: twelve counties between 200 and 1000, four counties between 1000 and about 2000, and two counties between approximately 4,500 and 6,500.

Five hundred fifty-eight jurors completed an interview.[68] Accordingly, each injury pair was heard by 18 jurors. Half of the jurors (279) were from each state; within each state, two-thirds (186) were from urban counties and one-third (93) were from rural counties.[69]

The jurors who completed the survey comprised a variety of education, income, and age groups. Five percent of jurors had not completed high school, 24% were high school graduates, 32% had attended college, 24% were college graduates, and 15% had done some post-college study or held an advanced degree. Eleven percent of jurors had a household income less than $15,000; 23% from $15,000 to $30,000; 31% from $31,000 to $50,000; 20% from $51,000 to $75,000; and 15% over $75,000. The jurors ranged in age from 18 to 92 (mean = 41, median = 39). We over-sampled male respondents in order to obtain relatively equal numbers of male (49%) and female (51%) respondents. Only 12% of the jurors knew someone who suffered from the condition in one of the scenarios they heard.

2. *Judges*

We obtained the names of state general jurisdiction civil trial judges from directories and from the court system's administrative office in each state. Two hundred forty-four judges completed an interview.[70] Accordingly, most injury pairs were heard by eight judges, but four pairs were heard by only seven judges.[71] Approximately half of the judges were from each state (124 from Illinois, 120 from New York). In Illinois, approximately half of the respondents (52%) were

68. The response rate for each area was as follows: Illinois urban, 19%; Illinois rural, 28%; New York urban, 20%; New York rural, 26%. These are conservatively estimated response rates. Because the computer-assisted telephone interviewing system used to conduct the interviews counted calls, not people, we are unable to obtain more exact response rates than these.

The essential question, however, is whether the respondents are representative of the populations from which they are drawn. We found the age, income, and education distributions of our respondents to approximate fairly closely the distributions of those demographic characteristics in each state, as shown by census data. Census data were obtained through the United State Census Bureau's world wide web pages: venus.census.gov/cdrom/lookup/cmd=tables/db=C90STF3A/lev=state/FO=FIPS.state/Fl=stab.geo/sel=36,new [for New York] and venus.census.gov/cdrom/lookup/cmd=tables/db=C90STF3A/lev=state/FO=FIPS.state/Fl=stab.geo/sel=17,new [for Illinois]. The exception is that the lowest income and education groups are somewhat underrepresented among our respondents, a pattern typical of telephone survey research.

69. When asked where they live, 48% of jurors said a large city, 19% said the suburbs of a large city, 7% said a medium-sized city, and 26% said a small town or rural area. For purposes of analysis, the first two categories were designated "urban" and the latter two were designated "rural."

70. The response rate for each area was as follows: Illinois urban, 68%; Illinois rural, 91%; New York urban, 54%; New York rural, 62%.

71. We were unable to get an eighth judge for each of these four pairs due to the relatively small number of civil trial judges in New York courts and their limited availability.

from urban and half (48%) from rural counties. In New York, due to the limited number of judges in rural counties, 71% of the respondents were from urban counties and 29% were from rural counties.[72]

Personal injury cases composed from 1% to 100% of the judges' caseload (mean = 52%, median = 50%). The judges had been hearing personal injury cases from 1 to 34 years (mean = 9, median = 7). Most of the judges (87%) were male. Fifty-seven percent of the judges either personally knew someone with the condition or had heard a case involving the injury presented in one of the scenarios they were given.

3. *Lawyers*

We obtained the names of lawyers from several different directories.[73] Two hundred forty-eight lawyers completed an interview.[74] Thus, each injury pair was heard by eight lawyers. Half of the lawyers (124) were from each state and, within each state, half primarily represented plaintiffs and half primarily represented defendants. In each state, over half of the respondents (56%) were from urban counties and almost half (44%) were from rural counties.

Personal injury cases composed from 1% to 100% of the lawyers' caseload (mean = 69%, median = 80%). The lawyers had been handling personal injury cases from 2 to 61 years (mean = 22, median = 20). Sixty percent of the lawyers had never served as an arbitrator in a personal injury case, 14% had done so rarely, 20% occasionally, and 6% often. Although we over-sampled women lawyers, 90% of those interviewed were men. Seventy percent of the lawyers either personally knew someone with the condition or had been involved in a case in which the plaintiff had the injury presented in one of the scenarios they were given.

D. *Procedures*

Prior to calling the judges and lawyers, we sent each a letter explaining the purpose of the study, the time involvement, and the confidentiality of their responses, and advising them of the upcoming phone call. The mailing included a letter from a prominent member of

72. When asked where most of the jurors in their courts live, 45% of all judges said a large city, 17% said the suburbs of a large city, 9% said a medium-sized city, and 29% said a small town or rural area. Thus, across both states, 62% of judges were from urban courts and 38% were from rural courts.

73. These were the Membership Directory of the Defense Research Institute, the Desk Reference of the Association of Trial Lawyers of America, the Martindale-Hubbell Law Directory, and West's Legal Directories.

74. The response rate for each area was as follows: Illinois urban, 83%; Illinois rural, 86%; New York urban, 70%; New York rural, 74%.

their state's legal community urging their participation in our research. Jurors did not receive a letter in advance.

All respondents were contacted by telephone and were asked to participate in a study of people's decisions about how much monetary compensation an injured person should receive for general damages. Respondents were told that they would hear summaries of two cases and would be asked to give their reactions to each. Respondents also were told that, in an earlier trial, a jury had found the defendant to be responsible for the plaintiff's injury and had compensated the plaintiff for medical expenses and lost earnings. We emphasized that the respondent was to focus on how much pain and suffering the injury has caused the plaintiff and how much money would provide fair compensation for those general damages.

The interviewer read the respondent the first case summary, followed by jury instructions that were adapted from standard instructions used in each state.[75] Although instructions for the two states differed somewhat and therefore created a slight confounding of instructions and population, using instructions that correctly reflected the law in each state was necessary to have credible instructions for the judges and lawyers.

Respondents then were asked to indicate how much money they would award the plaintiff for general damages, how much they thought the average juror would award the plaintiff, and to rate the plaintiff's injury on five dimensions. This entire procedure was then repeated for the second case. Finally, the respondents were asked sociodemographic questions.[76]

E. *Measures*

1. *Awards for General Damages*

A review of the awards for general damages for each injury revealed that the highest award for some injuries was more than five times as large as the second highest award.[77] Of the 62 injuries, these

75. *See* Appendix B. The instructions used for Illinois respondents were adapted from ILLINOIS PATTERN JURY INSTRUCTIONS — CIVIL, §§ 30.00-30.05 (3d ed. 1994). The instructions used for New York respondents were adapted from NEW YORK PATTERN JURY INSTRUCTIONS - CIVIL § 2:280 (2d ed. 1994).

76. Appendix B contains the interview protocol used.

77. Respondents who gave an award of zero were dropped from the study if the reason for their award was (a) they felt the defendant was not responsible (despite the fact that the stimulus materials had stated that a prior jury already had established the defendant's liability), or (b) they did not believe in the concept of compensation for general damages. If a potential juror in an actual trial expressed the latter attitude during jury selection, the person would be excluded from the jury. During the trial, the judge would admonish a juror expressing this attitude that the law had established the plaintiff's right to compensation for general damages and that one's duty as a juror was to determine a fair amount. Respondents who gave a zero dollar award were retained if they gave reasons such as: the pain was

outliers were found in 23 injuries for jurors, 5 for judges, and 6 for lawyers. Each outlier was recoded to the value at three standard deviations above the mean of the distribution (calculated without the outlier). If that recoded value would have altered the rank order of the awards, however, the outlier was recoded instead to the value at the next quarter-standard-deviation increment above the second highest award. The recoding of outliers to 3 or 4 standard deviations above the mean reduced their undue influence on the distribution without the loss of data.[78]

After this adjustment, the lawyers' and judges' awards for each injury showed no serious departures from normality. The jurors' awards for some injuries, however, were moderately positively skewed. Accordingly, we applied a square root transformation to the awards of all three groups.[79] The square root transformation adequately reduced the skewness of the jurors' awards without overcorrecting the judges' and lawyers' awards, providing a comparable award measure for the three groups.[80]

2. *Injury Perceptions*

Respondents were asked to give their impressions of the plaintiff's injuries on several dimensions, each rated on a five-point, Likert-type scale. Specifically, respondents were asked to indicate how much physical pain, mental suffering, disability, and disfigurement the given injury will have caused the plaintiff. For each of these dimensions, respondents were asked to consider both its amount and duration. Respondents also were asked to indicate how severe the injury was overall.

only temporary; the injury was not disabling, not serious, or caused no permanent damage; or the plaintiff was unconscious and, thus, did not experience pain and suffering.

78. *See generally* BARBARA G. TABACHNICK & LINDA S. FIDELL, USING MULTIVARIATE STATISTICS (1983).

79. The purpose of transforming non-normal distributions is to make them more nearly normal in order to use statistical procedures that require normality; to use highly skewed distributions could lead to misleading results. It is important to realize that correlations among variables depend most heavily on the rank order of cases along each measure and much less on the relative distances between the cases. The transformations do not alter the rank order. When looking for *relationships* among variables, the use of such transformations advances the effectiveness and validity of the search. Nonetheless some authors have criticized the use of such data transformations on the grounds that "defendants and plaintiffs live in a world of real dollars, not of log dollars." Sunstein et al., *supra* note 51, at 2077 n.21.

80. A log transformation was not used because it somewhat overcorrected the skewness in jurors' awards and substantially overcorrected the judges' and lawyers' awards.

3. *Sociodemographic Characteristics*

For all members of the three respondent groups, we recorded their gender, state, and the rural/urban status of their locale (for jurors, where they lived; for judges, where their court's jurors lived; and for lawyers, where plaintiffs in their cases lived). In addition, all groups were asked whether they knew of someone who had the condition presented in either of the scenarios they were given. Jurors also were asked their age as well as their education and income level. Judges and lawyers were asked what percentage of their caseload was comprised of personal injury cases and for how many years they had been hearing or handling personal injury cases. The lawyers also were asked whether and how frequently they had served as an arbitrator in personal injury cases.

F. *Analyses*

1. *Overview*

Two sets of analyses were conducted to examine the factors that predict respondents' (a) perceptions of the overall *severity* of the injury, and (b) *awards* for general damages. For each set of analyses, two sets of factors were used as predictors: the respondents' subjective assessments of the injuries on the dimensions of pain, disability, disfigurement, and mental suffering; and the respondents' sociodemographic characteristics. All measures were standardized in order to provide coefficient estimates that could be used to interpret the relative contribution of the predictors within each model and to facilitate the screening of interactions. The analyses were conducted separately for jurors, judges, plaintiffs' lawyers, and defense lawyers.

Each set of analyses consisted of the following. To accommodate both the within- and between-subjects aspects of the design, a series of mixed linear model analyses was conducted to assess the unique contribution of each predictor. First, all predictors were entered simultaneously in a single analysis. Next, interactions among the predictors were tested. Finally, nonsignificant terms were sequentially eliminated from the model until a final model was obtained that consisted of significant interactions and main effects that either were significant or were a component of a significant interaction. To assess the collective predictive strength of the items, multiple regression analyses were conducted on the full and final models. In addition, the zero-order correlation of each predictor with awards and overall severity was examined to assess each predictor's total contribution (i.e., both unique and shared variance).[81] Comparisons of the structure and relative

81. See Appendix C for a brief summary of some concepts of regression analysis.

strength of the models were made across the four respondent groups and between the award and severity models.

2. *Order Effects*

The order in which the injuries in each pair were presented was counterbalanced. Nonetheless, we examined whether the order of presentation affected respondents' awards and ratings. The principal effect of order was that jurors' awards were higher for the second injury they heard than for the first one.[82] Jurors' ratings of the overall severity of the injury were somewhat higher for the first injury they heard than for the second one.[83] For judges, plaintiffs' lawyers, and defense lawyers, the order in which the injuries were heard did not affect awards or overall severity ratings.[84] Finding an order effect for jurors but not for judges or lawyers is not surprising, given the jurors' lack of experience with determining personal injury awards.

Ideally, we would have included order as a predictor in the mixed models, but we did not so that the sets of analyses across the four respondent groups would be parallel. Order could not be included in the models for lawyers because the order in which the injuries were heard was confounded with their rural/urban location. The effect of excluding order from the jurors' analyses is to increase the error variance and, thus, to produce a more conservative estimate of the predictive strength of the models.

IV. RESULTS

The results will be presented in four Sections. The first presents the empirically derived models of the factors that account for judgments of injury severity. Separate models were developed for each group of decisionmakers: jurors, judges, plaintiffs' lawyers, and defense lawyers. Each model consists of respondents' ratings of four core attributes of injuries — physical pain, mental suffering, disability, and disfigurement — plus various demographic factors as predictors. The second Section presents models, using the same factors as predictors, to account for respondents' awards of general damages. The third Section compares the various decisionmakers' severity assessments, awards, and predictions of how much the "average juror" would award for the same injuries. The final Section demonstrates the

82. $F(2,556) = 4.44, p < .05$.

83. $F(2,554) = 2.54, p = .08$.

84. For each respondent group, order interacted significantly with several of the predictors when predicting overall severity. When predicting awards, order interacted with pain ratings for the jurors, but did not interact with any predictors for the judge or lawyer groups.

variability-reducing power of combining individual decisionmakers into groups, such as juries.

A. *Assessments of Overall Injury Severity: The Role of Injury Attributes and Sociodemographic Characteristics*

1. *Jurors' Assessments*

First, we examined the extent to which jurors' ratings of the injuries on four core attributes and jurors' sociodemographic characteristics predicted their assessments of the overall severity of the injuries. Combined in a multiple regression analysis, these factors together accounted for 72% of the variance in jurors' assessments of the injuries' overall severity. The four injury attribute ratings combined accounted for 71% of the variance. The sociodemographic characteristics together accounted for only 3% of the variance in judgments of overall severity.[85]

To examine which particular factors were related to jurors' assessments of the overall severity of the injuries, jurors' injury ratings and sociodemographic characteristics were entered in a mixed linear model analysis. Both the full model and the final model are shown in Table 1A. In the full model, all items were entered simultaneously. The final model, which resulted from testing the interactions among the predictors and sequentially eliminating nonsignificant terms, included only those items that had a significant influence on judgments of overall severity or that were a component of a significant interaction.

The final model also accounted for 72% of the variance. The ratings of each of the four core injury attributes were significantly related to assessments of overall injury severity. Perceptions of disability and mental suffering had the largest effect on overall severity judgments, almost twice as large as the influence of perceptions of pain and disfigurement. Higher ratings of the injuries on each of these attributes were associated with greater perceived overall injury severity. Comparing the relative magnitude of the Betas with the relative magnitude of the bivariate correlation coefficients,[86] we see that the contributions of pain and disfigurement in the multivariate analysis were reduced

85. The variance accounted for by individual predictors, or groups of predictors, does not simply add together to equal the amount of variance accounted for by all of them combined because the components often are somewhat redundant. As here, the total variance accounted for seems to be less than the sum of its component parts. Other times, *see infra* Section IV.B.1, the combined variables can account for more than the sum of their parts.

86. *See* Table 1A. The Betas reflect only the unique contribution of each item, whereas the *r*'s reflect both unique and shared contributions combined. For an explanation of the statistical terms used in this Section, see Appendix C.

because of the variance in severity they shared with disability and mental suffering ratings.[87]

None of the sociodemographic characteristics had a significant effect on perceptions of overall injury severity.[88] The main effects of state, income, and age were included in the final model because each was a component of a significant interaction, not because they themselves were significant predictors.

Several of the injury ratings interacted with other predictors to affect judgments of overall severity: pain and state of residence, pain and disability, pain and income, and disfigurement and age. For each of the interactions, higher ratings of the injury attribute led to significantly higher overall severity ratings at all levels of the other injury rating or sociodemographic characteristic, but the size of the effect varied depending on the level of the other factor. Specifically, perceptions of pain had a larger influence on the overall severity judgments for jurors in New York than for jurors in Illinois. In addition, pain ratings' contribution to overall severity tended to decrease as the level of disability increased and as the jurors' household income increased. Disfigurement ratings made a smaller contribution to the severity judgments of younger jurors than of other jurors. Although statistically significant, the contribution of each interaction was small relative to that of each of the four injury ratings and did not change the interpretation of the injury ratings' contribution to judgments of overall severity.

87. The inter-item correlations among the four injury ratings ranged from .49 to .67; the correlations among the sociodemographic characteristics ranged from .01 to .18, with the exception of $r = .45$ for income and education; and the correlations between the two sets of factors ranged from .01 to .13.

88. Familiarity with the injury might not have been significantly related to overall severity ratings for several reasons. First, only a relatively small portion (12%) of the jurors knew someone with the particular injury they were asked to judge, making it more difficult to detect an effect. Second, it is plausible that knowing someone who had a serious injury has the opposite effect on severity ratings as does knowing someone who had a minor injury. That is, familiarity with a minor injury might confirm its minimal impact and produce lower severity ratings than if one were not familiar with that injury. Conversely, an understanding of the truly devastating impact of major injuries may produce higher severity ratings than if one were not familiar with the injury. These countervailing responses might cancel each other out.

TABLE 1: OVERALL INJURY SEVERITY ASSESSMENTS

A. *Jurors' Assessments*

Variable	Bivariate	All items entered simulataneously		Final model			
	r	Beta	*F*	Beta	*F*	df	Interactions
mental suffering	.74	.34	195.76***	.34	193.65***	(1,478)	
pain	.59	.16	57.27***	.19	53.86***	(1,478)	
disability	.75	.37	221.73***	.35	209.17***	(1,478)	
disfigurement	.61	.15	47.06***	.17	57.58***	(1,478)	
state	-.01	.05	2.27	.05	2.29		
rural/urban	.09	-.06	2.29	--	--		
gender	.03	.04	1.23	--	--		
income	-.10	.03	2.10	.03	2.21	(1,504)	
education	-.12	-.03	1.89	--	--		
age	-.03	-.02	1.83	-.03	2.96$^+$	(1,504)	
familiar with injury	-.02	.01	.22	--	--		
			(R^2 = .72)	-.08	5.68*	(1,478)	pain x state
				-.05	7.48**	(1,478)	pain x disability
				-.04	5.24*	(1,478)	pain x income
				.04	5.01*	(1,478)	disfigurement x age
					(R^2 = .72)		

Note: In the final model, the standard error of the Betas ranged from .02 to .03.
*** p < .001
** p < .01
* p < .05
+ p < .10

2. *Judges' Assessments*

The same approach was used to model and account for judges' assessments of overall injury severity. Ratings of injuries on the four core attributes, together with the judges' sociodemographic characteristics, accounted for 70% of the variance in their assessments of the injuries' severity. The four injury attribute ratings accounted for 69% of the variance; the sociodemographic characteristics combined accounted for only 2% of the variance in judgments of overall severity.

In the final model, which accounted for 69% of the variance, ratings of each of the four core injury attributes were significantly related to assessments of overall injury severity (*see* Table 1B). Ratings of the extent of disability made the largest contribution to overall severity judgments, followed by ratings of mental suffering. Ratings of disfigurement and pain also made significant, although substantially smaller, contributions to perceptions of severity. Higher ratings of the injuries on each of these attributes were associated with greater perceived overall injury severity. Comparing the relative magnitude of the Betas with that of the bivariate correlation coefficients, we can see that the contributions of mental suffering, disfigurement, and pain ratings were reduced because of the variance in overall severity that they shared with disability ratings.[89]

None of the sociodemographic characteristics made a significant contribution to perceptions of overall injury severity. However, the state in which the judges presided interacted with disability ratings to affect overall severity judgments. Specifically, disability made a larger contribution to overall severity ratings for New York judges than for Illinois judges. Because higher disability ratings led to significantly higher overall severity ratings for both New York and Illinois judges, the interaction did not alter the interpretation of disability's influence on severity judgments. The contribution of the interaction was similar in magnitude to the contribution of disfigurement and pain ratings.

89. The inter-item correlations among the four injury ratings ranged from .39 to .60; the correlations among the sociodemographic characteristics ranged from .02 to .33, with the exception of $r = .55$ for the percentage of personal injury cases in the judges' caseload and rural/urban location; and the correlations between the two sets of factors ranged from .01 to .14.

TABLE 1: OVERALL INJURY SEVERITY ASSESSMENTS (CONTINUED)

B. *Judges' Assessments*

Variable	Bivariate	All items entered simulataneously		Final model			
	r	Beta	*F*	Beta	*F*	df	Interactions
mental suffering	.71	.34	88.56***	.33	87.21***	(1,206)	
pain	.46	.10	8.78**	.09	9.07**	(1,206)	
disability	.76	.48	176.33***	.53	177.71***	(1,206)	
disfigurement	.49	.08	6.52*	.10	10.16**	(1,206)	
state	.07	-.03	.33	-.01	.05	(1,235)	
rural/urban	.05	.08	1.53	--	--		
gender	.04	.05	.33	--	--		
familiar with injury	-.06	-.01	.13	--	--		
% caseload that is personal injury	.11	.02	.37	--	--		
# years hearing pi cases	.03	-.02	.63	--	--		
			(R^2 = .70)	-.13	5.72*	(1,206)	disability x state
					(R^2 = .69)		

Note: In the final model, the standard error of the Betas ranged from .03 to .05.
*** $p < .001$
** $p < .01$
* $p < .05$

3. *Plaintiffs' Lawyers' Assessments*

Together, the plaintiffs' lawyers' injury ratings and their sociodemographic characteristics accounted for 78% of the variance in their judgments of the injuries' overall severity. The four injury attribute ratings accounted for 78% of the variance; the sociodemographic variables together accounted for only 3% of the variance in judgments of overall severity.

In the final model, which also accounted for 78% of the variance, ratings on each of the four core injury attributes made a significant contribution to assessments of overall severity. Ratings of the extent of disability made the largest contribution to judgments of overall severity, followed by mental suffering (*see* Table 1C). Ratings of pain and disfigurement made significant but considerably smaller contributions. Higher ratings of the injury on each of these dimensions contributed to greater perceived overall injury severity. The contribution of mental suffering, pain, and disfigurement ratings in the multivariate analysis was reduced because of the variance in overall severity ratings shared with disability.[90]

None of the sociodemographic characteristics made a significant contribution to perceptions of overall severity.[91] Rural/urban setting interacted with ratings of mental suffering to influence judgments of overall injury severity, although it did not alter the interpretation of the relationship of mental suffering and severity. Mental suffering made a slightly greater contribution to severity ratings for plaintiffs' lawyers whose clients came mostly from rural settings than for those whose clients came mostly from urban settings. The contribution of this interaction was comparable to that of the pain and disfigurement ratings.

90. The inter-item correlations among the four injury ratings ranged from .40 to .53; the correlations among the sociodemographic characteristics ranged from .01 to .33; and the correlations between the two sets of factors ranged from .01 to .16.

91. The number of years that the plaintiffs' lawyers had been handling personal injury cases was not included in the multivariate analyses because of missing data. But it appears from the very small bivariate correlation between number of years in personal injury practice and overall severity ratings, $r(147) = -.01$, that no relationship exists between these variables.

TABLE 1: OVERALL INJURY SEVERITY ASSESSMENTS (CONTINUED)

C. *Plaintiffs' Lawyers' Assessments*

Variable	Bivariate	All items entered simulataneously		Final model			
	r	Beta	*F*	Beta	*F*	df	Interactions
mental suffering	.80	.40	67.74***	.32	70.15***	(1,106)	
pain	.57	.11	7.28**	.12	8.85**	(1,106)	
disability	.80	.44	86.45***	.45	99.72***	(1,106)	
disfigurement	.52	.10	6.47*	.11	7.74**	(1,106)	
state	-.04	-.03	.23	--	--		
rural/urban	.08	.01	.02	.01	.01	(1,121)	
gender	.07	-.07	.46	--	--		
familiar with injury	-.07	.05	1.88	--	--		
% caseload that is personal injury	.05	-.01	.11	--	--		
how often serve as pi arbitrator	-.02	-.01	.01	--	--		
			(R^2 = .78)	.13	4.07*	(1,106)	mental suffering x rural/urban
					(R^2 = .78)		

Note: In the final model, the standard error of the Betas ranged from .04 to .06.
*** $p < .001$
** $p < .01$
* $p < .05$

4. *Defense Lawyers' Assessments*

Defense lawyers' injury attribute ratings and their sociodemographic characteristics together accounted for 75% of the variance in their assessments of the injuries' overall severity. The four injury ratings accounted for 75% of the variance; the sociodemographic characteristics together accounted for only 1% of the variance.

The final model accounted for 75% of the variance. Perceptions of mental suffering made the largest contribution to assessments of overall severity in the final model (*see* Table 1D), followed by disability ratings. Ratings of disfigurement made a significant though substantially smaller contribution to overall severity. Pain ratings made no significant independent contribution to overall severity judgments, but instead influenced overall severity indirectly through pain's relationship with the other injury attributes. Comparing the relative magnitude of the Betas with the relative magnitude of the bivariate correlation coefficients, we see that the effect of pain, and to a lesser extent disfigurement, in the multivariate analysis was reduced because of shared variance.[92]

None of the sociodemographic variables made a significant contribution to perceptions of overall injury severity,[93] and none of the predictors interacted significantly to influence severity ratings.

92. The inter-item correlations among the four injury ratings ranged from .31 to .46, with the exception of $r = .72$ for disability and mental suffering; the correlations among the sociodemographic characteristics ranged from .01 to .21; and the correlations between the two sets of factors ranged from .01 to .13.

93. The number of years that the defense lawyers had been handling personal injury cases was not included in the multivariate analyses because of missing data. But it appears from the very small bivariate correlation between number of years in personal injury practice and overall severity ratings, $r(165) = .04$, that no relationship exists between these variables.

TABLE 1: OVERALL INJURY SEVERITY ASSESSMENTS (CONTINUED)

D. *Defense Lawyers' Assessments*

Variable	Bivariate	All items entered simulataneously		Final model			
	r	Beta	*F*	Beta	*F*	df	Interactions
mental suffering	.79	.48	101.66***	.47	105.19***	(1,110)	
pain	.46	.05	1.77	--	--		
disability	.79	.37	56.01***	.39	69.54***	(1,110)	
disfigurement	.47	.10	8.04**	.11	10.36**	(1,110)	
state	.02	-.05	.57	--	--		
rural/urban	.03	.05	.42	--	--		
gender	-.06	.08	.31	--	--		
familiar with injury	-.07	.01	.01	--	--		
% caseload that is personal injury	-.01	-.04	.88	--	--		
how often serve as pi arbitrator	-.09	.04	1.13	--	--		
			(R^2 = .75)		(R^2 = .75)		

Note: In the final model, the standard error of the Betas ranged from .03 to .05.
*** $p < .001$
** $p < .01$

5. *Comparison of Injury Severity Models Across the Four Groups*

By comparing the final models for each group of decisionmakers, we can learn about the factors, the weights of those factors, and the predictability of the judgments of overall severity made by jurors, judges, and lawyers. The similarities among these diverse decisionmakers are far more striking than their differences. The judgments of all four groups were highly predictable, and the factors that had great influence — as well as those that had little or no influence — were very similar among all groups.

The predictability of severity judgments, as measured by the total proportion of variance accounted for by each of the final models, was large and similar for each of the groups: 72% for jurors, 69% for judges, 78% for plaintiffs' lawyers, and 75% for defense lawyers. For all groups, variation in severity ratings was to a far greater extent the product of differences in the injuries being responded to than it was the product of individual differences among the respondents. The variation of responses of different people to the *same* injury was small and similar across the four groups.[94] That is, members of each group responded similarly in assessing the severity of the injuries involved in a given case. And, as one should expect, the variation in responses of the same person to *different* injuries was many times larger than that of different people to the same injury.[95]

For all four groups, the only main effects that remained in the final models as significant predictors of overall severity were the core injury attributes — none of the socio-demographic characteristics made a significant contribution. For jurors, judges, and plaintiffs' lawyers, disability made the largest contribution, followed by mental suffering; pain and disfigurement made significant but smaller contributions. The model for defense lawyers differed from the other three in that mental suffering was the most powerful influence while disability was second,[96] and pain did not make a significant unique contribution to overall severity. Interactions involving sociodemographic characteristics played only a small role in the models: the magnitude of their influence was fairly small, and none changed the interpretation of the injury ratings' influence on overall severity assessments.

94. The between-subjects covariance parameter estimate was .006 for jurors, -.008 for judges, -.003 for plaintiffs' lawyers, and .06 for defense lawyers.

95. The within-subjects covariance parameter estimate was .27 for jurors, .31 for judges, .23 for plaintiffs' lawyers, and .17 for defense lawyers.

96. Shared variance could explain the reduced impact of disability for defense lawyers compared to the other groups. For them, the correlation between disability and mental suffering was $r = .72$, while it was smaller for the other groups.

B. *Predicting General Damages Awards: Translating Injury Judgments into Dollars*

The same predictive data and the same modeling techniques as above were used to account for the general damages awards. In contrast to the high degree of predictability of perceptions of injury severity, models for general damages awards show less predictability and greater decisionmaking complexity. Even so, across the groups of decisionmakers, a considerable degree of similarity remains in the patterns of variables that influence the damages awards.

1. *Jurors' Awards*

We examined the extent to which jurors' perceptions of the injuries on the four core attributes[97] and their sociodemographic characteristics predicted awards (which had been square-root transformed). Combined in a multiple regression analysis, these factors accounted for 21% of the variance in awards. Ratings of the four core injury attributes accounted for 17% of the variance; the sociodemographic characteristics accounted for only 2% of the variance in awards.

The final model accounted for 23% of the variance in awards for general damages. Of the four injury ratings, perceptions of disability had the greatest impact on awards, more than twice as large as ratings of either mental suffering or disfigurement (*see* Table 2A). Higher ratings of the injury on each of these three attributes were associated with larger awards. Pain ratings did not have a significant unique effect on awards when combined with the other predictors. Given the bivariate correlation between pain ratings and awards, pain apparently affected awards through its relationship with the other injury ratings. The influence of pain ratings, and to a lesser extent disfigurement and mental suffering, was reduced in the multivariate analysis due to the variance in awards shared with disability.

Of the sociodemographic characteristics, gender was the most strongly related to awards. In fact, the magnitude of gender's influence on awards was second only to that of disability. Income also had a significant but smaller influence on awards. Male jurors gave larger awards than female jurors, and jurors with higher household incomes gave larger awards than those with lower incomes.

Several of the predictors interacted to affect awards in a manner that altered the interpretation of the injury attributes' influence on awards. Examining the interaction of disfigurement ratings with rural/urban residence showed that as perceptions of disfigurement in-

97. Because the four specific injury ratings were highly correlated with overall severity ratings, overall injury severity was not included as a predictor of awards in order to avoid multicollinearity.

creased, awards increased for urban jurors but not for rural jurors. The nature of the interaction of pain ratings and education was such that as pain ratings increased, awards increased for those jurors who were college graduates but not for jurors with other levels of education. Finally, the interaction of disfigurement and disability ratings showed that as the perception of disfigurement increased, awards increased only at the higher levels of disability, while higher disability ratings were related to larger awards at all levels of disfigurement. The influence of each of these interactions was similar in magnitude to the impact of mental suffering and disfigurement ratings and household income.

In sum, jurors gave larger awards when they saw the injuries as involving a greater degree of disability and mental suffering and when the jurors were male or had a higher household income. Greater perceived disfigurement led to giving larger awards only when it was associated with higher levels of disability and only for urban jurors. Greater perceived pain led to giving larger awards only for college graduates.

TABLE 2: PAIN AND SUFFERING AWARDS (SQUARE-ROOT TRANSFORMED)

A. *Jurors' Awards*

Variable	Bivariate	All items entered simulataneously		Final model			
	r	Beta	*F*	Beta	*F*	df	Interactions
mental suffering	.34	.13	10.61**	.13	10.69**	(1,481)	
pain	.24	.02	.24	.02	.38	(1,481)	
disability	.38	.28	46.54***	.31	57.06***	(1,481)	
disfigurement	.32	.12	10.86**	.15	4.59*	(1,481)	
state	.05	-.05	.61	--	--		
rural/urban	.08	-.05	.47	-.05	.45	(1,505)	
gender	-.12	.26	15.79***	.26	15.74***	(1,505)	
income	.07	.11	8.25**	.11	8.41**	(1,505)	
education	.07	.05	2.21*	.06	2.63	(1,505)	
age	.02	.02	.40	--	--		
familiar with injury	-.01	.02	.44	--	--		
			(R^2 = .21)	-.13	5.28*	(1,481)	disfigurement x rural/urban
				.10	12.88***	(1,481)	pain x education
				.08	7.23***	(1,481)	disfigurement x disability
					(R^2 = .23)		

Note: In the final model, the standard error of the Betas ranged from .03 to .07.
*** $p < .001$
** $p < .01$
* $p < .05$

2. *Judges' Awards*

Judges' perceptions of the injuries and their sociodemographic characteristics accounted for 44% of the variance in square-root awards. The four injury attributes accounted for 40% of the variance; the sociodemographic variables accounted for only 4% of the variance in awards.

The final model accounted for 42% of the variance in judges' awards for general damages. Of the four injury ratings, disability had the greatest influence on awards, almost twice as large as that of mental suffering (*see* Table 2B). Disfigurement ratings had a smaller, but significant, impact on awards. Higher ratings of the injury on each of these three dimensions were associated with larger awards. Perceptions of pain did not have a significant unique influence on awards when combined with the other predictors, although its bivariate correlation with awards was moderate. Pain apparently does not affect awards independently but does so through its relationship with the other ratings. The effect of perceptions of pain, and to a lesser extent perceptions of mental suffering and disfigurement, was reduced because of shared variance.

Of the sociodemographic characteristics, only the state in which the judges presided affected their awards. New York judges gave larger general damages awards than did Illinois judges. Additionally, the state in which the judges presided interacted with disability ratings to affect awards. Specifically, disability had a greater impact on awards for New York judges than for Illinois judges, although higher disability ratings led to significantly larger awards in both states. The influences of the state and of the interaction were similar in magnitude to the effect of perceptions of mental suffering.

In sum, judges gave larger awards when they saw the injuries as involving a greater degree of disability, mental suffering, and disfigurement, and when the judges presided in New York courts rather than in Illinois courts. Perceived disability had a greater effect on awards for New York judges than for Illinois judges.

TABLE 2: PAIN AND SUFFERING AWARDS (CONTINUED)

B. *Judges' Awards*

Variable	Bivariate	All items entered simulataneously		Final model			
	r	Beta	*F*	Beta	*F*	df	Interactions
mental suffering	.53	.24	26.41***	.25	27.85***	(1,212)	
pain	.36	.04	.75	--	--		
disability	.58	.34	51.95***	.49	68.06***	(1,212)	
disfigurement	.38	.13	8.66**	.12	8.02**	(1,212)	
state	.14	-.22	8.42**	-.23	10.40**	(1,236)	
rural/urban	.12	-.12	1.69	--	--		
gender	.02	.14	1.41	--	--		
familiar with injury	-.04	-.03	.49	--	--		
% caseload that is personal injury	.11	.01	.07	--	--		
# years hearing pi cases	-.01	-.04	1.30	--	--		
			(R^2 = .44)	-.21	9.56**	(1,212)	disability x state
					(R^2 = .42)		

Note: In the final model, the standard error of the Betas ranged from .04 to .07.
*** $p < .001$
** $p < .01$

3. *Plaintiffs' Lawyers' Awards*

Plaintiffs' lawyers' perceptions of the injuries and their sociodemographic characteristics accounted for 37% of the variance in their square-root awards. The four injury attributes accounted for 34% of the variance; the set of sociodemographic characteristics accounted for only 1% of the variance in awards.

The final model accounted for 48% of the variance in awards for general damages. Of the four injury attributes, disability had the greatest impact on awards in the final model, followed by mental suffering (*see* Table 2C). Higher ratings of the injury along these dimensions were associated with larger awards. Perceptions of pain and disfigurement did not have a significant effect on awards in the multivariate analysis, despite their moderate bivariate correlations with awards. Thus, pain and disfigurement did not affect awards independently but through their relationship with the other ratings.

Of the sociodemographic characteristics, only the state in which plaintiffs' lawyers practiced had even a marginally significant influence on awards. Specifically, New York plaintiffs' lawyers tended to award more than did Illinois plaintiffs' lawyers. None of the other demographic characteristics were associated with awards.[98]

Several of the predictors interacted, having a substantial effect on awards and altering the interpretation of the effect of injury attributes and demographic characteristics on awards. First, the state in which the lawyers practiced interacted with how often they had served as an arbitrator in personal injury cases. New York plaintiffs' lawyers who had frequently served as arbitrators gave larger awards than those who had served less often, while the pattern was reversed for Illinois plaintiffs' lawyers. Second, the interaction of familiarity with the type of injury presented and rural/urban practice indicated that familiarity with the injury led to significantly larger awards for urban plaintiffs' lawyers but had no effect on rural lawyers' awards. Third, the interaction of disfigurement and disability ratings showed that perceptions of greater disfigurement were significantly related to larger awards only at the highest level of disability, while higher disability ratings were related to larger awards at all levels of disfigurement. Fourth, disability perceptions and state interacted such that although higher disability ratings were related to larger awards for plaintiffs' lawyers in both states, the magnitude of the relationship between disability ratings and awards was almost twice as large in New York as in Illinois. Finally,

98. The number of years that the plaintiffs' lawyers had been handling personal injury cases was not included in the multivariate analyses because of missing data, but it appears from the very small bivariate correlation between number of years in personal injury practice and awards, $r(148) = .05$, that no relationship exists between these variables.

perceived disability interacted with the frequency with which the lawyers had served as arbitrators, but no systematic, interpretable pattern appeared.

In sum, plaintiffs' lawyers gave larger awards when they saw the injuries as involving a greater degree of disability and mental suffering. If they practiced in New York rather than in Illinois, they were marginally more likely to give larger awards. Moreover, five different interaction effects emerged, consisting of complex relationships involving either the perception of disability or the location (state as well as urban/rural) of their law practice.

TABLE 2: PAIN AND SUFFERING AWARDS (CONTINUED)

C. *Plaintiffs' Lawyers' Awards*

Variable	Bivariate *r*	All items entered simulataneously Beta	All items entered simulataneously *F*	Final model Beta	Final model *F*	Final model df	Interactions
mental suffering	.50	.26	10.94**	.28	17.16***	(1,106)	
pain	.35	-.03	.18	--	--		
disability	.53	.28	13.93***	.46	27.28***	(1,106)	
disfigurement	.40	.11	2.81+	.05	.63	(1,106)	
state	.02	-.18	3.18+	-.19	3.89+	(1,118)	
rural/urban	.05	.05	.17	.06	.42	(1,118)	
gender	-.05	.20	1.73	--	--		
familiar with injury	-.01	.09	2.8+	.20	2.46	(1,118)	
% caseload that is personal injury	.02	-.02	.17	--	--		
how often serve as pi arbitrator	.06	.06	1.23	.30	1.97	(1,118)	
			(R^2 = .37)	-.44	17.03***	(1,118)	how often pi arbitrator x state
				-.25	6.88*	(1,106)	familiar with injury x rural/urban
				.23	17.05***	(1,106)	disability x disfigurement
				-.21	4.97*	(1,106)	disability x state
				.14	8.60**	(1,106)	disability x how often pi arbitrator
					(R^2 =.48)		

Note: In the final model, the standard error of the Betas ranged from .05 to .11.
*** $p < .001$
** $p < .01$
* $p < .05$
+ $p < .10$

4. *Defense Lawyers' Awards*

Defense lawyers' perceptions of the injuries and their sociodemographic characteristics accounted for 52% of the variance in their square-root awards. The four specific injury ratings combined accounted for 50% of the variance in awards; the sociodemographic characteristics together accounted for 4% of the variance in awards.

The final model accounted for 58% of the variance in general damages awards. Perceptions of mental suffering had the greatest impact on awards (*see* Table 2D). Disability and disfigurement ratings also had a significant effect on awards. Higher ratings of the injury on each of these dimensions were associated with larger awards. Pain ratings had no significant independent effect on awards, despite a moderate bivariate correlation. Thus, pain influenced awards indirectly through its relationship with the other injury ratings. The influences of disfigurement and disability also were somewhat reduced because of the variance in awards they shared with the other injury ratings.

The state in which the defense lawyers practiced was the only sociodemographic characteristic to have a significant effect on awards.[99] Defense lawyers practicing in New York awarded more than those in Illinois. The magnitude of the impact of state on awards was comparable to that of disability ratings.

Several of the predictors interacted to affect awards. The significant interaction of mental suffering and perceived disability had an effect on awards comparable in magnitude to that of disability ratings and the state in which the lawyers practiced. The nature of this interaction was such that greater perceived disability resulted in larger awards only at the highest level of mental suffering, while greater perceived mental suffering led to larger awards at each level of disability, with an increasing impact as the level of disability increased. The interaction of pain and disfigurement ratings showed that greater perceived pain led to larger awards only at the highest level of disfigurement, and greater perceived disfigurement led to larger awards only at moderate and severe levels of pain. Finally, the interaction of perceived disfigurement with the proportion of the defense lawyers' caseload that was personal injury work showed that higher disfigurement ratings were significantly related to larger awards only for those defense lawyers for whom personal injury cases comprised half or less

99. The number of years that the defense lawyers had been handling personal injury cases was not included in the multivariate analyses because of missing data, but it appears from the very small bivariate correlation between number of years in personal injury practice and awards, $r(166) = -.08$, that no relationship exists between these variables.

of their caseload. The influence of these latter two interactions on awards was comparable in magnitude to that of disfigurement ratings.

In sum, defense lawyers gave larger awards when they saw the injuries as involving a greater degree of mental suffering, disability, and disfigurement and if they practiced in New York rather than in Illinois. The influence of disability, disfigurement, and pain was qualified by three significant interactions with other predictors.

TABLE 2: PAIN AND SUFFERING AWARDS (CONTINUED)

D. *Defense Lawyers' Awards*

Variable	Bivariate	All items entered simulataneously		Final model			
	r	Beta	*F*	Beta	*F*	df	Interactions
mental suffering	.66	.38	31.21***	.40	39.32***	(1,104)	
pain	.37	.03	.23	.03	.46	(1,104)	
disability	.60	.23	10.26**	.23	11.77***	(1,104)	
disfigurement	.47	.18	11.85***	.14	8.53**	(1,104)	
state	.10	-.24	7.54**	-.24	8.28**	(1,120)	
rural/urban	.03	-.02	.04	--	--		
gender	-.01	-.15	.59	--	--		
familiar with injury	-.10	-.01	.01	--	--		
% caseload that is personal injury	-.06	-.05	1.00	-.06	1.82	(1,120)	
how often serve as pi arbitrator	-.14	-.03	.40	--	--		
			(R^2 = .52)	.20	15.19***	(1,104)	mental suffering x disability
				.13	8.58**	(1,104)	pain x disfigurement
				-.12	8.18**	(1,104)	disfigurement x % caseload pi
					(R^2 = .58)		

Note: In the final model, the standard error of the Betas ranged from .04 to .08.
*** $p < .001$
** $p < .01$

5. *Comparison of Award Models Across the Four Groups*

Earlier, we had seen that the regression models predicting overall injury severity ratings for all four groups of decisionmakers showed the groups to be remarkably similar in nearly every respect. The regression models in this Section aim to account for variation in the general damages awards. With these models, we see a decline in predictability for all four groups and greater divergence among them. At the same time, important parallels continue to exist.

The final models for each group accounted for a moderate proportion of the variance in awards: 23% for jurors, 42% for judges, 48% for plaintiffs' lawyers, and 58% for defense lawyers. Although it is more difficult to predict the awards made by all of these decisionmakers, the translation from perceptions of injury severity to damages awards has led to the greatest decline in predictability for the model of jurors' decisions. Of course, this may be as much a statement about the limitations of the predictive model to capture what jurors are doing as it is a statement about the jurors' decisions.

Nonetheless, confirming the preceding impressions, the variation of responses of different people to the *same* injury was greater for jurors than for the other groups.[100] These patterns of predictability and intra-injury variability in awards are not surprising, given that jurors have essentially no experience assigning a dollar value to injuries while the other groups do. In addition, had we been able to include an order term in the jurors' model to reflect the fact that there was a significant order effect for jurors (which was not found for the other groups), the error variance for jurors likely would have been reduced.[101]

For all groups, the variation in responses of the same person to *different* injuries was much larger than that of different decisionmakers to the same injury.[102] The somewhat lower variability in awards for defense lawyers when the same person was reacting to different injuries suggests they may be less responsive to case details. Thus, the greater predictability of awards for defense lawyers does not necessarily mean they are "better" at this task, but instead that their responses might be less nuanced or more mechanical.

For all groups, some of the variability in awards might be due to the fact that, in order to avoid potentially confounding contextual factors, the case summaries did not describe the plaintiffs or their pre-

100. The between-subjects covariance parameter estimate was .21 for jurors, compared to .06 for judges, .01 for plaintiffs' lawyers, and .02 for defense lawyers

101. *See supra* note 82 and accompanying text.

102. The within-subjects covariance parameter estimate was .56 for jurors, .47 for judges, .48 for plaintiffs' lawyers, and .35 for defense lawyers.

injury lifestyles. Depending on the extent of changes in a plaintiff's work, family, and recreational life, the same injury could be seen to have a different impact on different plaintiffs and, thus, merit different awards. Numerous judges and lawyers requested information about the plaintiff's gender, occupation, lifestyle, family, and other background details.[103] For instance, some wanted to know the plaintiff's gender because they felt a scar on a female plaintiff's face would warrant more compensation than the same injury for a male plaintiff. Thus, award variability might be greater because respondents brought different assumptions about the plaintiff to bear on the task.[104]

The respondent groups showed important similarities in the role that injury attributes played in their awards, but also some differences. For all four groups, pain ratings had no significant unique influence on awards. For jurors, judges, and plaintiffs' lawyers, perceptions of disability had the greatest impact on awards — about twice as large as the impact of the second strongest predictor — while for defense lawyers, perceptions of mental suffering had the largest effect on awards. Mental suffering had a significant effect on awards for all four groups. Perceived disfigurement had a significant impact on awards for all groups except plaintiffs' lawyers. For all groups except judges, the interpretation of the effect of some of the injury attributes was qualified by significant interactions with the sociodemographic characteristics.

In all instances, higher ratings on the injury attributes were associated with larger awards. This suggests considerable vertical equity in awards — that all groups gave larger awards to plaintiffs with injuries involving a greater degree of disability, mental suffering, and (except for plaintiffs' lawyers) disfigurement. Additional data provide evidence of considerable vertical equity for all groups. For each injury, the mean award and mean assessment of overall injury severity were calculated within each respondent group. These items then were correlated, using the injury scenario as the unit of analysis ($n = 62$). The correlation between overall severity and awards was .83 for jurors, .88

103. Recall that, if they inquired, respondents were told that the plaintiff was of average good health and had an average lifestyle before the injury, which seemed to be sufficient information for most of the respondents.

104. It is interesting to note that, during the interviews, lawyers and judges requested information that, legally, should have no relevance for awards for general damages, but which revealed their own search for shortcuts to estimating general damages. For instance, they wanted to know the amount of the plaintiff's medical expenses and lost wages so that they could use a formula to calculate awards for general damages. That judges and lawyers sometimes grasped at such shortcuts suggests that they did not have much better bearings than jurors in the chartless seas of determining general damages awards. They also wanted to know the effect of the injury on employment status. Relatedly, Vidmar & Rice, *supra* note 18, at 896-97, found that experienced lawyers serving as arbitrators tended to make more improper use of information than lay jurors had, such as using evidence of liability to fix damages and increasing the size of awards to cover attorneys' fees.

for judges, .77 for plaintiffs' lawyers, and .88 for defense lawyers.[105] Thus, all groups gave larger awards to plaintiffs with injuries seen as more severe and smaller awards to plaintiffs with injuries viewed as less severe.

One or more demographic variables had a significant and large effect on the awards for each of the four groups. Judges and lawyers in New York gave larger awards than did their counterparts in Illinois.[106] Comparing the moderate multivariate influence of state on awards with its smaller bivariate relationship in each of these groups suggests that state suppressed irrelevant variance in the other variables in the equation. This may suggest that a constellation of subtle differences exists between New York and Illinois judges and lawyers, which in the multivariate analysis is captured by the single variable of state. For jurors, the state in which they lived was not related to awards, but gender and household income were, with male jurors and jurors with higher incomes giving larger awards.[107]

C. *Comparing Jurors', Judges', and Lawyers' Injury Severity Assessments, Awards, and Predictions of the "Average Juror's" Awards*

Next, we compare the general tendencies of jurors, judges, plaintiffs' lawyers, and defense lawyers, as groups, to perceive injuries as more or less serious and to give awards that are relatively higher or lower. In addition, we report a number of analyses relating to respondents' estimates of what the "average juror" would award.

105. Calculating these correlations without first averaging across people, that is, using the respondent instead of the injury as the unit of analysis, produces these relationships: .38 for jurors, .65 for judges, .61 for plaintiffs' lawyers, and .71 for defense lawyers. The lower correlation for jurors no doubt reflects the greater variability noted above.

106. Larger awards by New York judges and lawyers may reflect the fact that New York instructions explicitly include compensation for "loss of enjoyment of life," while the Illinois instructions do not specify that this component should be considered in determining general damages. *Compare* NEW YORK PATTERN JURY INSTRUCTIONS - CIVIL § 2:280.1 (2d ed. 1994) *with* ILLINOIS PATTERN JURY INSTRUCTIONS - CIVIL, §§ 30.00 - 30.05 (3d ed. 1994). Cutting the other way, New York instructions direct that compensation be given only for *conscious* pain and suffering, while Illinois instructions do not address this issue. *Compare* NEW YORK PATTERN JURY INSTRUCTIONS - CIVIL § 2:280 cmt. (2d ed. 1994) *with* ILLINOIS PATTERN JURY INSTRUCTIONS - CIVIL, § 30.05 (3d ed. 1994). Although this difference would tend to produce smaller awards in New York, it was unlikely to have much effect in the present study because the plaintiff was not conscious of her or his condition in only two of our 62 injuries.

107. Gender might not have been related to awards for judges or lawyers because only a relatively small portion of each group was female (13% of judges, 13% of plaintiffs' lawyers, and 7% of defense lawyers), making it more difficult to detect an effect. Or perhaps because they have learned to see damages in similar ways regardless of their gender.

1. *Comparison of Overall Severity Assessments*

Do the four different groups of decisionmakers, in the two different states, vary in their perceptions of the severity of the injuries, so that some see the same injury as more severe and others see it as less severe? To answer this question, for each respondent group, the mean overall severity rating was calculated for each injury, separately within each state. Table 3 presents these data, averaged across the 62 injuries. A repeated-measures analysis of variance ("ANOVA") was then conducted to compare the severity judgments across the groups, using injury as the unit of analysis.

TABLE 3: RATINGS OF OVERALL INJURY SEVERITY

	Illinois	*New York*
Jurors	3.64	3.63
Judges	3.31	3.46
Plaintiffs' Lawyers	3.52	3.42
Defense Lawyers	3.12	3.17

Note: Each cell represents a mean taken over all 62 injuries.
Ratings were made on a five-point scale, with 5 designated as "extremely severe."

In each state, the four respondent groups differed in their assessments of overall injury severity.[108] For Illinois respondents, follow-up analyses showed that jurors rated the injuries as more severe than did judges[109] and defense lawyers,[110] but did not differ from plaintiffs' lawyers. Plaintiffs' lawyers rated the injuries as more severe than did judges.[111] Defense lawyers rated the injuries as less severe than did all other groups.[112] For New York respondents, follow-up analyses showed that jurors rated the injuries as more severe than all other groups,[113] and defense lawyers rated the injuries as less severe than all other groups.[114] Plaintiffs' lawyers' severity ratings did not differ significantly from judges' ratings. Thus, jurors tended to rate the injuries as more severe than the other groups, and defense lawyers rated them as less severe than the other groups.

108. Illinois: $F(3,183) = 14.78, p < .001$; New York: $F(3,183) = 11.70, p < .001$.

109. $F(1,61) = 27.75, p < .001$.

110. $F(1,61) = 34.02, p < .001$.

111. $F(1,61) = 6.33, p < .05$.

112. Versus jurors: $F(1,61) = 34.02, p < .001$. Versus judges: $F(1,61) = 5.12, p < .05$. Versus plaintiffs' lawyers: $F(1,61) = 16.66, p < .001$.

113. Versus judges: $F(1,61) = 7.47, p < .01$. Versus plaintiffs' lawyers: $F(1,61) = 7.13, p < .05$. Versus defense lawyers: $F(1,61) = 30.88, p < .001$.

114. Versus judges: $F(1,61) = 15.63, p < .001$. Versus plaintiffs' lawyers: $F(1,61) = 6.88, p < .05$. Versus jurors: $F(1,61) = 30.88, p < .001$.

To what extent did the different groups agree on which injuries were more severe and which less? Correlations were computed using the mean overall severity ratings calculated for each group, separately for each injury. Jurors' overall severity assessments were highly correlated with those of the other groups. In Illinois, the correlation of jurors' severity ratings with those of judges was $r = .84$; with those of plaintiffs' lawyers, $r = .72$; and with those of defense lawyers, $r = .74$.[115] In New York, the correlation of jurors' severity ratings with those of judges was $r = .90$; with those of plaintiffs' lawyers, $r = .82$; and with those of defense lawyers, $r = .81$.[116] The intercorrelations of overall severity ratings among judges, plaintiffs' lawyers, and defense lawyers ranged from .69 to .78 in Illinois and from .76 to .85 in New York. Thus, injuries seen as more severe by one group tended strongly to be seen as more severe by the other groups.

2. *Comparison of Awards*

Do the four different groups of decisionmakers, in the two different states, vary in the damages awards they offer, such that some award more and others less for the same injury? To answer this question, for each respondent group, the mean square-root award was calculated for each injury, separately within each state. Table 4 presents these data, averaged across the 62 injuries. A repeated-measures ANOVA was conducted to compare the awards across the groups, with injury as the unit of analysis.

TABLE 4: GENERAL DAMAGES AWARDS

	Illinois	*New York*
Jurors	665	746
Judges	567	716
Plaintiffs' Lawyers	780	817
Defense Lawyers	561	659

Note: Each cell represents a mean taken over all 62 injuries.
The damage awards are square-root transformations of dollar distributions.

In Illinois, awards differed by respondent group.[117] Follow-up analyses showed that jurors' awards did not differ from those of plaintiffs' lawyers, but both gave awards that were larger than those of

115. For each of the preceding correlations, $n = 62$ injuries and the significance level was $p < .001$.

116. For each of the immediately preceding correlations, $n = 62$ injuries and the significance level was $p < .001$.

117. $F(3,183) = 7.55, p < .001$.

judges[118] and defense lawyers.[119] Defense lawyers' awards did not differ significantly from judges' awards. In New York, awards differed marginally by respondent group.[120] Follow-up analyses showed that jurors' awards were marginally larger than those of defense lawyers[121] and did not differ from those of judges and plaintiffs' lawyers. Plaintiffs' lawyers' awards were significantly larger than those of defense lawyers[122] and marginally larger than those of judges.[123] Defense lawyers' awards were marginally smaller than judges' awards.[124] Thus, in both states, plaintiffs' lawyers and jurors tended to give the largest awards, while defense lawyers tended to give the smallest awards. Given that jurors tended to rate the injuries as more severe than the other groups (and the defense lawyers rated them as least severe), and that the relationship between severity assessments and awards is strong, it would not be unreasonable for jurors' awards to be commensurately larger (and defense lawyers' awards smaller).

To what extent did the different groups agree on which injuries deserved higher general damages awards and which were entitled to lower awards? Correlations were computed using the mean square-root award for each injury within each group, using injury as the unit of analysis. Jurors' awards were highly correlated with those of the other groups. In Illinois, the correlation of jurors' awards with judges' awards was $r = .73$; with plaintiffs' lawyers' awards, $r = .63$; and with defense lawyers' awards, $r = .71$.[125] In New York, the correlation of jurors' awards with judges' awards was $r = .69$; with plaintiffs' lawyers' awards, $r = .60$; and with defense lawyers' awards, $r = .66$.[126] The intercorrelations among the judges' and lawyers' awards ranged from .73 to .83 in Illinois and from .66 to .83 in New York. Thus, injuries that were given larger awards by one group also tended to be given larger awards by the other groups.

118. Versus jurors: $F(1,61) = 6.59, p < .05$. Versus plaintiffs' lawyers: $F(1,61) = 11.01, p < .01$.

119. Versus jurors: $F(1,61) = 6.64, p < .05$. Versus plaintiffs' lawyers, $F(1,61) = 12.69, p < .01$.

120. $F(3,183) = 2.56, p = .06$.

121. $F(1,61) = 2.88, p = .095$.

122. $F(1,61) = 5.14, p < .05$.

123. $F(1,61) = 2.97, p = .09$.

124. $F(1,61) = 2.88, p = .095$.

125. For each of the preceding correlations, $n = 62$ injuries and the significance level was $p < .001$.

126. For each of the immediately preceding correlations, $n = 62$ injuries and the significance level was $p < .001$.

3. *Comparison of Each Group's Award with Its Prediction of the "Average Juror's" Award*

Do the four different groups of decisionmakers, in the two different states, vary in their estimates of how much the "average juror" would award in general damages? Do some groups expect jurors to give awards that are more different from their own awards than other groups do? Are some groups' estimates of jurors' awards closer to the awards actually given by jurors in this study than other groups' estimates? Respondents in each of the four groups were asked, after indicating their own award, what they thought the "average juror" would award for the same injury. Each group's median award and median predicted "average juror" award were calculated for each injury, separately within each state.[127] Dependent-group t-tests then were conducted.

The estimated jurors' awards given by New York judges were larger than the awards they themselves gave,[128] while those estimated by Illinois judges did not differ from their own awards. Defense lawyers in Illinois[129] and New York[130] both gave estimated jurors' awards that were larger than the awards they themselves gave. Plaintiffs' lawyers' awards did not differ from their predicted jurors' awards in either state. And jurors themselves gave estimated "average juror" awards that were larger than the awards they themselves gave.[131]

Despite differences in the award amount predicted, all groups gave larger predicted jurors' awards to the injuries for which they themselves gave larger awards, and gave smaller predicted awards to the injuries for which they themselves gave smaller awards. In Illinois, the correlations between each group's own awards and their predicted "average juror" awards were $r = .91$ for jurors, $r = .49$ for judges, $r = .82$ for plaintiffs' lawyers, and $r = .93$ for defense lawyers.[132] In New York, the correlations between each group's own awards and their predicted "average juror" awards were $r = .88$ for jurors, $r = .95$ for judges, $r = .96$ for plaintiffs' lawyers, and $r = .89$ for defense lawyers.[133] Thus, all groups expect jurors' vertical equity to be quite similar to their own.

127. Because the data for this group of analyses consisted of raw damages estimates, medians were used to reduce the influence of outliers.

128. $t(61) = 3.60, p < .01$.

129. $t(61) = 3.32, p < .01$.

130. $t(61) = 2.67, p < .05$.

131. Illinois jurors: $t(61) = 3.17, p < .01$. New York jurors: $t(61) = 3.60, p < .01$.

132. For each of the preceding correlations, $n = 62$ injuries and the significance level was $p < .001$.

133. For each of the immediately preceding correlations, $n = 62$ injuries and the significance level was $p < .001$.

How well could judges and lawyers predict what awards jurors would give? Within each state, we compared judges' and lawyers' "average juror" awards with the actual awards given by the jurors in our study. In Illinois, the awards actually given by jurors were smaller than what plaintiffs' lawyers[134] and defense lawyers[135] predicted they would be, but did not differ from the judges' predictions. In New York, the awards given by jurors were smaller than what judges[136] and defense lawyers[137] predicted they would be, but did not differ from the plaintiffs' lawyers' predictions. Generally, then, the awards jurors actually gave tended to be smaller than the awards judges and lawyers predicted they would give.

Correlations between jurors' actual awards and the awards predicted for them by judges and lawyers tell us how well those legal professionals could anticipate which injuries would evoke larger and which would evoke smaller awards from jurors; that is, the extent to which judges and lawyers could predict the vertical variation in jurors' responses to injuries. These correlations varied considerably. In Illinois, the correlations between jurors' actual awards and the awards predicted for them by both plaintiffs' lawyers[138] and defense lawyers[139] were significant, while the correlation with the awards predicted by judges was only marginally significant.[140] In New York, the correlations between jurors' actual awards and the awards predicted by judges[141] and defense lawyers[142] were significant, but the correlation with plaintiffs' lawyers' predicted awards was not.[143] The range in these correlations (from .21 to .78) is striking, especially considering that it is plaintiffs' lawyers who do both best (in Illinois) and worst (in New York) at anticipating the vertical variation in jurors' reactions to the injuries.

D. *The Stabilizing Power of Aggregation into Groups*

Thus far, we have been speaking as though jurors made decisions individually, as judges do in bench trials, rather than in groups, as juries. The greater observed variability in the awards of jurors, as com-

134. $t(61) = 2.19, p < .05$.

135. $t(61) = 2.45, p < .05$.

136. $t(61) = 2.10, p < .05$.

137. $t(61) = 2.49, p < .05$.

138. $r(60) = .78, p < .001$.

139. $r(60) = .37, p < .01$.

140. $r(60) = .24, p = .06$.

141. $r(60) = .46, p < .001$.

142. $r(60) = .47, p < .001$.

143. $r(60) = .21, p = .10$.

pared to those of judges and lawyers, would decrease if the individuals were combined into juries, as they are in actual trials. That group decisions decrease in variability (and increase in predictability) compared to the decisions of the individuals who compose the groups, is to be expected both from basic statistical[144] and social psychological[145] properties of groups. In addition, studies that have tested this question directly using mock jurors and juries have found that, for the same case, awards of deliberating juries are less variable than awards of jurors deciding damages as individuals.[146] Thus, the data we have presented to this point, on individuals, overstates the variability.[147]

Our final set of analyses is essentially (and merely) a demonstration of the phenomenon that when individuals decide as groups their

144. Larger samples produce distributions with smaller standard errors than smaller samples. For example, a set of samples of size 6 or 12 as compared to samples of size 1.

145. People in decisionmaking groups tend to coalesce toward a consensus; their shifts tend to be toward, rather than away from, each other. This is a basic aspect of group behavior, which has long been observed. *See, e.g.*, A. PAUL HARE, HANDBOOK OF SMALL GROUP RESEARCH 19 (1976) (groups tend to establish norms which are viewed as legitimate by group members); MUZAFIR SHERIF, THE PSYCHOLOGY OF SOCIAL NORMS 104 (1936) (people in social interaction gravitate toward sharing the perceptions and judgments of those with whom they interact).

146. *See* Shari Seidman Diamond et al., *Juror Judgments About Liability and Damages: Sources of Variability and Ways to Increase Consistency*, 48 DEPAUL L. REV. 301, 316 tbl. IV (1998) (finding the standard deviation of their individual jurors' general damages awards to be $4,255,056 compared to $714,556 for decisions on the same case facts by deliberating juries); Shari S. Diamond & Jonathan D. Casper, UNDERSTANDING JURIES (forthcoming) (using data from a completely different set of jurors and a completely different case and finding the standard deviation of jurors' awards to be $175,988 and of juries' awards to be $122,749).

147. The only suggestion to the contrary of which we are aware appears in Sunstein et al., *supra* note 51. They allude to the familiar notion that larger groups (such as juries) show less variability than smaller groups or individuals. But they also argue that there exists an "amplification of bias" by which group deliberation would produce greater variance than was found in their study of individual mock jurors. *See id.* at 2101 n.128. This argument confuses several principles upon which it relies. Sunstein et al. are correct that group deliberation produces group polarization, a post-deliberation shift toward positions more extreme than the prediscussion central tendency of the individuals. *See, e.g.*, Martin F. Kaplan, *Discussion Polarization Effects in a Modified Jury Decision Paradigm: Informational Influences*, 40 SOCIOMETRY 262 (1977); Serge Moscovici & Marisa Zavalloni, *The Group as a Polarizer of Attitudes*, 12 J. PERSONALITY & SOC. PSYCHOL. 125 (1969); David G. Myers & Helmut Lamm, *The Group Polarization Phenomenon*, 83 PSYCHOL. BULL. 602 (1976). But they overlook the fact that groups tend to coalesce around that more extreme position. Thus, in a given case, groups will be more consistent than individuals at the same time that they will be more extreme (in whichever direction). When Sunstein et al. jump from the phenomenon of deliberation-induced shifts to the conclusion of "even greater variance," Sunstein et al., *supra* note 51, at 2101 n.128, they have jumped from thinking about the variance for a given case to the variance of the mass of cases. That is, some *types of cases* will shift one way and some the other way, resulting in greater variance across a set of *different* cases. But that phenomenon is irrelevant to the policy issue of variability among *like* cases. The unwanted variability in cases is not that different cases receive different awards (vertical equity requires that they do), but that any given case would receive different awards from different decisionmakers (that would be horizontal inequity). The available evidence supports the conclusion that variance declines when we move from jurors to juries. *See supra* note 146.

decisions are more consistent and predictable than when they decide the same question as individuals. These analyses were conducted on only the first of the two injuries evaluated by each of our respondents; that is, all 62 injuries were included, but only the data of those that were the first of the pair a respondent heard.

Treating each decision by a judge as if it were a decision in a bench trial, we calculated the standard deviation of those raw general damages awards. This is analogous to calculating the standard deviation for a set of awards from a sample of bench trials in a jurisdiction. When considering the same set of injuries, the standard deviation of awards made by Illinois judges was approximately 2.3 million and by New York judges about 1.5 million. Doing the same analysis for individual jurors, as if they decided cases individually as judges do, we find much greater variability in response to the same set of injuries. The standard deviation for Illinois jurors was about 10.0 million, and for New York jurors about 16.6 million.

To estimate the awards that would be made if individual jurors had been grouped into juries and asked to decide awards as a group, we created statistical groups by taking the median[148] of the raw awards of all jurors who evaluated the same injury, for each of the 62 injuries, separately within each state. In this way we made "juries" of 4 or 5 persons each. Although the mix of injuries is as varied as in either of the preceding analyses, the standard deviation shrinks considerably: to about 755,000 for Illinois "juries" and about 543,000 for New York "juries." Thus, the awards of *juries* were less varied than those of judges.[149]

These analyses do not purport to give the actual standard deviation that would be obtained by combining the actual individuals into groups and having them reach consensus in group deliberation. These analyses merely illustrate the phenomenon and its general tendencies, namely, that groups produce more stable and more predictable estimates than individuals.[150] Considering that there were few extreme

148. The median of individual judgments provides a very good estimate of the group judgment. *See* Shari Seidman Diamond & Jonathan D. Casper, *Blindfolding the Jury to Verdict Consequences: Damages, Experts, and the Civil Jury*, 26 L. & SOC'Y REV. 513, 545 tbl. 4 (1992), which found that using medians of individual pre-deliberation judgments to estimate group decisions correlated .62 with the decisions of deliberating juries composed of those same individuals. By contrast, other plausible methods of statistically estimating the group decision had lower, sometimes much lower, correlations.

149. A better test of this, but a far more expensive one, would have jurors deliberate as groups, and would treat those group judgments as the ones to be modeled and compared to those of judges and lawyers.

150. Moreover, larger groups do so to a greater extent than smaller groups. *See* Michael J. Saks, *The Smaller the Jury, the Greater the Unpredictability*, 79 JUDICATURE 263 (1996); *see also* Michael J. Saks & Mollie Weighner Marti, *A Meta-Analysis of the Effects of Jury Size*, 21 LAW & HUM. BEHAV. 451, 463-64 (1997).

outliers to begin with,[151] it is easy to see how a juror recommending an extreme award could be outnumbered and reined in by the majority of jurors preferring more moderate awards.

V. Conclusions

This concluding Part will begin by summarizing the study's findings (Sections A through C). Section D will consider the implications of the findings for legal policy concerning the determination of general damages by juries. Section E will raise further empirical research questions that remain to be asked and answered.

A. *Perceptions of Injury Severity*

Several important conclusions can be drawn from the analyses examining the different decisionmakers' judgments of the overall severity of the injuries.

First, the regression models suggest that different decisionmakers — people with different roles in the legal system, different experience with personal injury cases, and different demographic backgrounds — relied on the same injury attributes in similar ways and gave them similar relative weight when evaluating the severity of injuries.[152] For all groups, the extent of perceived disability and mental suffering were the strongest predictors of overall severity judgments, with disfigurement and pain making smaller contributions.[153] The only notable departure from the pattern was the model for defense lawyers, for whom mental suffering had the most powerful influence (whereas for the other three groups it was disability) and pain did not have a significant unique influence. Nevertheless, all of the regression models accounted for a large, and similar, proportion of variance in the decisionmakers' judgments of overall severity: 69% for judges, 72% for jurors,[154] 75% for defense lawyers, and 78% for plaintiff's lawyers.

Second, all four groups of decisionmakers had generally similar perceptions of what injuries are of relatively greater or lesser severity. Shared vertical equity is evident from the finding that jurors' overall severity assessments were highly correlated with those of the other groups, ranging from .72 to .84 in Illinois and from .81 to .90 in New

151. See the Measures section, *supra* Section III.E.1, for a discussion of how we identified extreme outliers. They constituted 2.32% of the jurors' awards. For comparison, extreme outliers constituted 1.03% of judges' and 1.21% of lawyers' awards.

152. *See* Table 1.

153. A similar pattern was seen in the two studies in Wissler et al., *supra* note 27.

154. Similarly, in the two studies in Wissler et al., *supra* note 27, at 189, 200, undergraduates' injury perceptions accounted for 75% and 89%, respectively, of the variance in their overall severity assessments.

York. Jurors tended to assess injuries as being more severe than the other groups did, while defense lawyers tended, even more strongly, to see injuries as less severe than the other groups did. Nonetheless, injuries seen as more severe by one group tended strongly to be seen as more severe by the other groups.

The remarkable similarity across the varied decisionmakers' response patterns when judging the severity of injuries has important implications. The findings suggest that jurors approach the task of evaluating injuries no differently than judges and lawyers do. Thus, assertions that jurors cannot intelligently evaluate injuries or have idiosyncratic reactions to injuries are simply incorrect, or at least ill-focused. Indeed, if any one group emerges as being out of step with all of the others, it is defense lawyers. This has somewhat paradoxical implications. When members of the defense bar evaluate the performance of jurors, and gauge them to be off the mark,[155] these lawyers no doubt reach that assessment by comparing the jurors' conclusions to their own. But their own impressions of injuries are the ones that depart most from the pattern shared by the other decisionmaking groups, at least in regard to judgments of injury severity.

Third, for all groups, while the core attributes of injuries accounted for the lion's share of variance in severity judgments, the sociodemographic variables played essentially no role. Because a finding that the background characteristics of the decisionmakers have little or no impact on their decisions may surprise readers unacquainted with the relevant literature, it may be worth mentioning that this merely extends a finding now well established elsewhere in the jury decision-making literature. Though most of that research has been on criminal trials, juror sociodemographic characteristics also have been found to play only a modest role in their civil liability verdicts,[156] certainly compared to the dominant impact of evidence and arguments presented in the cases. The present study, along with other recent research, suggests that what had been learned about liability verdicts can be extended to damages-relevant responses: individual differences make little difference.[157]

155. For example, James Griffith, an attorney specializing in medical malpractice defense, wrote, "There's no limit on what jurors can award for pain and suffering, so too often they act like Santa Claus, handing out millions of dollars in cases involving comparatively minor injuries." James Griffith, *What it Will Take to Solve the Malpractice Crisis,* MED. ECON. Sept. 27, 1982, at 195.

156. *See* Shari Seidman Diamond, *Scientific Jury Selection: What Social Scientists Know and Do Not Know*, 73 JUDICATURE 178, 180 (1990); Steven D. Penrod, *Predictors of Jury Decision-making in Criminal and Civil Cases: A Field Experiment*, 3 FORENSIC REP. 261 (1990); Michael J. Saks, *What Do Jury Experiments Tell Us About How Juries (Should) Make Decisions?*, 6 S. CAL. INTERDISC. L.J. 1, 9-13 (1998).

157. *See* Diamond et al., *supra* note 146, at 314 (finding, in a study that used a videotaped presentation of a highly realistic simulated trial to 1042 mock jurors from Cook County, Illinois, that "[o]ur attempt to trace the sources of this variation [in damages

B. *General Damages Awards*

The picture becomes somewhat blurred when the transition is made from perceptions of the overall severity of injuries to placing dollar values on them. First, for awards, the regression models for the different groups of decisionmakers differed more from each other in terms of the factors that account for awards as well as the relative influence of the core injury attributes and the sociodemographic characteristics.[158] Second, the model for each group of decisionmakers accounted for a smaller proportion of the variance in awards than in severity assessments.

While similarities were found, different respondent groups gave differing weight to the various injury attributes when awarding damages. Defense lawyers differed from all other groups in that for them mental suffering weighed more heavily than disability. And plaintiffs' lawyers differed from all other groups in that for them disfigurement did not have a significant impact on awards. Thus, the impact of the injury attributes on jurors' awards more closely resembled their impact on judges' awards, and their impact on the lawyers' awards diverged from both judges and jurors. Nonetheless, there were important similarities among the decisionmakers regarding which injury attributes were predictive of their general damages awards. For all respondent groups, perceived pain was related to awards only indirectly through its association with the other injury attributes, while greater perceived disability and mental suffering were strongly associated with larger awards.[159]

Compared to the models of severity assessments, sociodemographic characteristics played a larger role in awards, both directly and through their interaction with other factors. For jurors, gender and income were predictive in both states. Men and wealthier jurors awarded more than women and poorer jurors. One explanation for these findings might be that in a task as undefined as awarding general damages, people rely on the only reference scale with which they are familiar, namely their own. Those who are accustomed to dealing in larger amounts fit the cases onto a mental reference scale that runs into higher numbers. This would explain not only the finding that wealthier individuals give higher awards, but also that on average men give higher awards than women. Another explanation might be more cultural: that something in their value system leads people of higher

awards] to individual differences in the background and attitude of jurors met with little success"); *see also id.* at 307 tbl. I.

158. *See* Table 2.

159. For jurors and lawyers, some of the main effects of the injury attributes are qualified by interactions. See the Results Section, *supra* Section IV.B, for the details.

socioeconomic status to place a higher monetary value on personal injuries and their sequella.

In contrast to jurors, the significant demographic variable for judges and lawyers in this study was state. Generally, judges and lawyers in New York gave larger awards than those in Illinois. Several explanations are possible. For the same reasons that wealthier jurors gave larger awards, it may be that wealthier lawyers and judges (i.e., the ones in New York) give larger awards. Another possible explanation is the differences between the two states in the laws regarding damages awards. In New York, loss of enjoyment of life is considered a distinct element of damages, but in Illinois it is subsumed as part of mental suffering. This would be expected to lead to higher awards by New York judges and lawyers. Though all respondents were read the instructions based on those in their state, the same effect might not have arisen for jurors because they are less likely to be attuned to the finer details in the instructions than are lawyers and judges (indeed, most of the lawyers and judges presumably already know their respective state's rules).[160] Yet another explanation might be that the judges and lawyers in each state know that theirs is thought to be a relatively low or high award jurisdiction and act in accord with those expectations, while jurors do not know that they are "supposed" to give higher awards if they are in New York and lower awards if they are in Illinois.

Nonetheless, the paucity of relationships between most of the demographic variables and awards (collectively accounting for only 1% to 4% of the variance in awards) is the more important part of the story.[161] Several of these non-differences are especially worthy of note. Illinois jurors did not give awards that differed from those of New York jurors. And the awards of jurors living in rural areas did not differ from those of jurors living in urban areas.[162] These non-differences contrast with findings of archival studies, which suggested that, on a national spectrum, New York jurors give relatively high awards while Illinois jurors give relatively low awards,[163] and that ur-

160. Instructions are often difficult for jurors to understand. *See* Michael J. Saks, *Judicial Nullification*, 68 IND. L.J. 1281, 1282-83 (1993).

161. As noted previously, research has found little relationship between jurors' sociodemographic attributes and the verdicts of the jurors or the juries on which they sit. *See supra* notes 156-157 and accompanying text.

162. Although rural or urban locale did not affect the size of awards, it did interact with perceived disfigurement such that disfigurement had a significant impact on the awards of urban jurors but not rural jurors.

163. *See* DANIELS & MARTIN, *supra* note 12, at 69-90. A possible explanation for the differences observed by Daniels and Martin is that their data were based on total awards, and interstate differences in medical expenses, earnings, and the cost of living could account for differences in awards.

ban jurors award more than rural jurors.[164] Those archival studies could not control for the kinds of cases that jurors in the different locales were deciding because they had no data on the nature of the cases themselves, so they could not determine whether observed differences were due to differences in the tendencies of the jurors or to differences in the cases being presented to those jurors. Because the current study presented an identical set of cases to jurors in the two regions of the two states, our findings suggest that the differences observed in those other studies were due not to differences in the jurors but to differences in the mix of cases that came to trial in the different locales.[165]

In addition to differences in the components of the models, awards were less predictable than were severity assessments. The regression model for each group, especially for jurors, accounted for a smaller proportion of the variance in awards: 23% for jurors, 42% for judges, 48% for plaintiffs' lawyers, and 58% for defense lawyers.[166] The lack of information about the plaintiff's gender and pre-injury lifestyle might have contributed to the variability in awards for all groups. The jurors' lack of experience in assigning a dollar value seems an obvious explanation for the greater variability and lower predictability of jurors' awards.

164. *See* DANZON, *supra* note 33, at 63, 74-75. A possible explanation for the differences observed by Danzon is that her data could reflect differences in medical expenses, earnings, and the cost of living in urban versus rural areas.

165. Another difference is that Danzon's research used *states* as the unit of analysis, rather than individuals or juries. Inferences drawn about relationships at the state level may or may not hold at smaller levels of aggregation. This problem is known as the "ecological fallacy." Thus, while Danzon found that urban areas (actually, relatively more urban states) experienced larger awards than more rural areas (actually, relatively more rural states), there is no reason to expect her findings to apply to urban versus rural areas within states, or to people from urban versus rural areas.

166. It is worth noting that the proportions of variance in awards accounted for by the present data are lower than those of other studies cited in our Introduction. This difference may suggest an important cognitive insight. Our study had respondents rating each injury without comparison to others, or in comparison with one other injury (when rating the second in the pair). Most of the other studies had respondents or coders rating larger numbers of injuries. No doubt if we had people rank order our 62 cases and then used that as a predictor of awards, the correlation would rise considerably. In our own studies of damages, all using similar procedures, when each respondent evaluated 12 or 13 cases, the $R^2 = .74$. *See* Wissler et al., *supra* note 27, at 201. When each respondent evaluated 5 cases, the $R^2 = .54$. *See id.* at 195. And in the present study, where each juror evaluated 2 cases (so half the time were evaluating the first of the pair), the $R^2 = .23$. If this insight is correct, the higher proportions of variance accounted for in the models of judges and lawyers reflect their having (in their heads, from the numerous other cases they have known) a more complete cognitive reference scale of injuries to provide a context for thinking about the case now under consideration. That, in turn, suggests a relatively simple and yet potentially powerful reform — providing jurors with a frame of reference for determining the appropriate general damages award — that should produce considerable improvement in the predictability and stability of jurors' awards of general damages. The issue of providing jurors with such guidance is discussed below.

The decreased predictability of jurors' awards might also be explained by the difference in education, income, and gender between jurors (as a group) compared to judges and lawyers.[167] When looking only at those subgroups of jurors who most closely approximate judges and lawyers on these dimensions, we find the greatest predictability of awards compared to those jurors who are least similar. For jurors with post-college study or an advanced degree, the full regression model accounted for 29% of the variance in awards, with progressively lesser amounts of variance accounted for as the level of education declined, culminating in a model that accounted for 14% of the variance in awards for jurors who had not graduated from high school. For jurors with household incomes over $75,000, the model accounted for 32% of the variance in awards, with progressively lesser amounts of variance accounted for as the level of income declined, culminating in a model that accounted for 20% of the variance in awards for jurors with incomes below $15,000. And for male jurors, the model accounted for 27% of the variance in awards, compared to 15% for women jurors. Thus, to some extent, the differences in the predictability of jurors' awards, compared to those of judges and lawyers, is a product of social differences and not simply differences in the extent of experience in awarding general damages for injuries.

Given the small variability in assessments of injury severity within each respondent group and the strong relationship between overall severity assessments and awards, the variability in awards would seem to be due largely to differences in the metrics people use to convert perceptions of injury severity into awards.[168] Why didn't we find more variability in the severity ratings instead of only in the dollar awards? Perhaps the five-point severity rating scale limits the expression of one's evaluation of injuries or consideration of subtle distinctions among them, compared to the more fine-grained and unbounded nature of dollar scales. Thus, the lack of variability in severity ratings might be due to the insufficiency of the rating scale producing an apparent consistency in judgments rather than to a truly better quality of decisionmaking.

Despite the lesser predictability of awards, the correlations between severity ratings and awards (using the injury scenarios as the unit of analysis) showed a strong association between the degree of perceived injury severity and the size of the awards given. These correlations were .83 for jurors, .88 for judges, .77 for plaintiffs' lawyers, and .88 for defense lawyers. This finding replicates the high degree of vertical equity in awards found in other studies.[169] In addition, shared

167. *See supra* Section III.C.

168. See related discussions in Sunstein et al., *supra* note 51, at 2106-07, and Wissler et al., *supra* note 27, at 193.

169. See studies cited *supra* notes 26-27.

vertical equity is evident from the finding that jurors' damages awards were well correlated with those of the other groups, ranging from .63 to .73 in Illinois and from .60 to .69 in New York.[170] These findings indicate that all groups tended to agree on which injuries deserved higher general damages awards and which deserved smaller ones.

Even an examination of the absolute level of awards, however, does not find jurors to be out of line. Averaged over all cases, jurors and plaintiffs' lawyers tended to give the highest awards, defense lawyers the lowest, and judges gave an intermediate amount.[171] What might account for the higher awards given by jurors? One obvious "statistical" explanation is that the greater variability of individual jurors' awards allows the average to shift upward more readily than downward. A second, "vertical equity," explanation is that it is appropriate that the jurors' awards would be larger than those of other groups because jurors rated the injuries as more severe. A third possible explanation is an artifact of the media's reporting of jury awards, which tends to cover higher award amounts.[172] While lawyers and judges would be aware that there are many small awards that are not reported for every large verdict that is reported, jurors are less likely to know that, and their frames of reference would be affected accordingly. A final possible explanation is an artifact of our interview procedures. By asking judges and lawyers, but not jurors, in both states to make what they regarded as appropriate awards, regardless of any caps in effect in their states, we were unavoidably reminding them of caps, which might have artificially pushed down their awards.

In sum, the way in which the damages decisionmaking models of jurors differ most from those of judges and lawyers is in their variability, not in the patterns of the factors that affect their awards. And this variability among *jurors* is almost certain to decline when the decisionmakers consist of *juries*.[173] This study was not able to do more than demonstrate that general effect: the awards of (statistically created) *juries* were less varied than those of judges, while the awards of *jurors* were far more varied than those of judges.

170. The findings of Vidmar & Rice, *supra* note 18 — that jurors and arbitrators have similar patterns of correlations of perceptions of disfigurement, etc., with awards — parallel our own. In both states, our findings showed the lowest correlation was between jurors and plaintiffs' lawyers, suggesting an interesting area of further study.

171. *See* Table 4.

172. *See* Daniel S. Bailis & Robert J. MacCoun, *Estimating Liability Risks with the Media as Your Guide: A Content Analysis of Media Coverage of Tort Litigation*, 20 LAW & HUM. BEHAV. 419, 421, 426 (1996) ("It is a small step to assert that reading about million-dollar verdicts might lead people to overestimate the frequency of large jury awards."); *see also* Michael J. Saks, *Public Opinion About the Civil Jury: Can Reality be Found in the Illusions?*, 48 DEPAUL L. REV. 221, 231-34 (1998).

173. *See* discussion *supra* notes 144-151 and accompanying text.

C. *Judges' and Lawyers' Predictions of the Awards of the "Average Juror"*

When asked to predict the awards that would be made by the "average juror," judges in New York, defense lawyers in both states, and the jurors themselves, predicted that the average juror would give awards that were larger than they themselves would give in the same case. Apparently, the members of most groups, with plaintiffs' lawyers being the unsurprising exception, think that the awards they personally would give are lower than those given by jurors. Despite these differences in the predicted awards, judges and lawyers expected jurors to share their relative assessments of damages — giving larger awards in the cases where they themselves gave larger awards, and smaller awards in the cases where they themselves gave smaller awards.[174] Thus, all groups expected the average juror's awards to have vertical equity that strongly paralleled their own, but to be shifted upward.

The awards our jurors actually gave tended to be smaller than the awards the judges and lawyers predicted they would give. One might expect the expertise of judges and lawyers to include accurate predictions of what jurors will do. We would be hesitant to make too much of this systematic bias (overprediction), except that it is consistent with findings where lawyers have been asked to estimate the size of jury awards in their states.[175] Systematic errors call for explanations; we can only speculate on one. A generations-old legal folklore about the excesses of civil jurors, compounded by the public rhetoric of more recent years, may prevent lawyers from recognizing what jurors actually do. Even without such folklore, or perhaps at the root of it, the "availability heuristic" might be operating[176] — a cognitive bias which suggests that judges and lawyers will have a tendency to more easily recall surprisingly large awards, and then to estimate the overall behavior of juries from those more "available," but less representative, instances.[177]

174. The correlations between the lawyers' and judges' own awards and the awards they predicted the "average juror" would give ranged from .49 to .93 in Illinois and from .89 to .96 in New York.

175. *See, e.g.*, Donald R. Songer, *Tort Reform in South Carolina: The Effect of Empirical Research on Elite Perceptions Concerning Jury Verdicts*, 39 S.C. L. REV. 585 (1988).

176. *See* Amos Tversky & Daniel Kahneman, *Availability: A Heuristic for Judging Frequency and Probability*, 5 COGNITIVE PSYCHOL. 207 (1973); Amos Tversky & Daniel Kahneman, *Judgment under Uncertainty: Heuristics and Biases*, 185 SCIENCE 1124 (1974).

177. The correlations between what judges and lawyers predicted the average juror would award and what our jurors in fact awarded present an odd pattern, with some of the most wide-ranging correlations found in the entire study. Plaintiffs' lawyers do both the best (in Illinois, $r = .78$) and the worst (in New York, $r = .21$) job of predicting our jurors' awards in the cases. Perhaps the lack of a real pattern is the most one can say about these correlations.

D. *Policy Implications*

The dominant theme of these findings is one of considerable similarity across the various groups of decisionmakers in the structure of thinking about injury severity and awards. Most importantly, an impressive similarity exists in the injury attributes that drive their decisions, the weight given to those attributes, and the shared sense of vertical equity held by jurors, judges, plaintiffs' lawyers, and defense lawyers alike. These findings suggest that commonly voiced speculations about the inability or irrationality of jurors in evaluating injuries are misconceived, because on that task jurors were nearly indistinguishable from judges and lawyers. These data also reveal, contrary to some discussions in the literature, no differences between jurors in two different states and in different regions of the same state when they are asked to respond to the same set of injuries.

If there is any basis for concern, it is the translation from perceptions of injuries into dollar valuations. But that is a problem not with jurors alone, but with the task — judges and lawyers similarly display decreased predictability, albeit a smaller decrease, as they move from severity assessment to damages valuation, and reveal more between-group differences in the models that predict their decisions. Thus, improvements, if justified as desirable policy, should be concerned less with who is to make the decisions about general damages and more with making the task more achievable.

1. *Whether the Role of the Jury Should Be Reduced*

Should the role of the jury in making general damages awards be reduced or eliminated? Should the determination of those awards, as others have suggested in the context of punitive damages, be transferred from jurors to judges?[178] The main argument for doing this is that judges would produce more predictable awards than juries.[179]

178. *See* Sunstein et al., *supra* note 51, at 2112-13 ("It would be reasonable to react to our study by suggesting a simple reform: Juries should decide questions of civil liability, just as they do questions of criminal liability. But judges should decide on the appropriate level of punitive damages, just as they do criminal punishment, subject, in both cases, to guidelines laid down in advance."). Sunstein et al. presented 28 variations of 10 case vignettes to 899 randomly selected registered voters in Travis County, Texas, and asked them to (a) evaluate the cases, and (b) recommend punitive damages awards to assess against the defendants in those cases. *Id.* at 2095. Sunstein et al. found that jurors were breathtakingly consistent in their judgments of the defendant's outrageousness ($r = .99$), but that variability increased (reliability and predictability decreased) in the second step, namely translating those judgments into punitive awards ($r = .42$). *Id.* at 2098, 2103. Sunstein et al. conclude that "individual differences in dollar awards produce severe unpredictability and highly erratic outcomes," *id.* at 2103, and implicitly assume, without any data, that judges would make very different decisions than jurors do, *id.* at 2113.

179. Perhaps it goes without saying that predictability and consistency might be purchased at the cost of more important values. For example, the rule of thumb some lawyers use to come up with a figure for general damages for purposes of settlement negotiation —

First of all, it is not clear from the empirical evidence that transferring the task from juries to judges would increase predictability at all, much less to the satisfaction of those calling for such a reform. Our findings show a fairly high correlation between awards given by judges and those given by individual jurors (r's = .73 and .69 in the two states respectively).[180] Based on the decision models we developed, the predictability of jurors' general damages awards, expressed as a correlation, is $r = .48$, while that of judges is .65.[181] That suggests that judges also are far from perfect. And jurors, as well as judges, perform this task at a level of reliability that compares favorably to that of other important societal decisionmaking. As Table 5 indicates, juror evaluations of injury severity and damages are of comparable consistency and predictability to the decisions of a considerable array of other decisionmakers who are thought to be far more expert and who are performing tasks thought to be much better defined than that of assessing general damages.

multiplying medical specials by three — would, if adopted as a legal rule for assigning damages, produce highly predictable outcomes, but at the expense of injury- and victim-specific considerations. Sometimes the amount awarded would be too great and sometimes it would be too small.

It may be worth noting that some level of variability is beneficial to the legal process. The proper level of uncertainty helps to promote settlements, while not promoting so many that courts do not receive the cases necessary to monitor society's disputes, and thereby to continually refine and announce the law. For more detailed discussion of this point, see Michael J. Saks, *Enhancing and Restraining Accuracy in Adjudication*, 51 LAW & CONTEMP. PROBS. 243 (1988). A rational goal would be to aim to calibrate the level of uncertainty to seek its optimal level, rather than to aim to eliminate uncertainty from the litigation system.

180. Thus, we found higher reliability in awards (in terms of agreement between judges and jurors) than Sunstein et al. did (in terms of agreement among jurors). Perhaps this reflects differences in the challenge of assigning dollar values for general damages versus for punitive damages. If so, it implies that Sunstein et al.'s speculation that their findings would generalize to other juror decision tasks about damages is unwarranted. Sunstein et al., *supra* note 51, at 2131-38.

181. Taking the square root of the R-squareds in Tables 2A and 2B, for jurors and judges, respectively.

TABLE 5: RELIABILITY OF VARIOUS DECISIONMAKERS MAKING VARIOUS DECISIONS

Decisionmakers and Tasks	*Strength of Association*
Jurors evaluating outrageousness of tortious conduct (reliability)[a]	**.99**
Jurors and Judges evaluating injury severity (reliability) (in IL & NY, respectively)[b]	**.84, .90**
Jurors evaluating injury severity (predictive validity)[b]	**.85**
Judges evaluating injury severity (predictive validity)[b]	**.83**
Jurors and Judges deciding amount of general damages (reliability) (in IL & NY, respectively)[b]	**.73, .69**
Judges deciding general damages (predictive validity)[b]	**.65**
Juries and Judges deciding on personal injury liability (reliability)[c]	**.58**
Federal judges deciding criminal sentences (reliability)[d]	**.58**
Four different kinds of business experts rating strategic attributes associated with competitive moves in 15 different companies (reliability)[e]	**.55, .55, .50, .47**
Scientists deciding merits of research proposals (reliability)[f]	**.50**
Jurors deciding general damages (predictive validity)[b]	**.48**
Doctors diagnosing skin diseases (reliability) (three different diseases)[g]	.36, .48, .48
Jurors deciding punitive damages (reliability)[a]	**.42**
Employment interviewers deciding on qualifications for hiring (reliability)[h]	**.40**
Navy pilots rating technical effectiveness of aircraft (reliability) (three different sets of measures)[i]	**.28, .12, .16**
Psychiatric diagnoses (reliability)[j]	.13, .22

Note: Pearson correlations or multiple correlations are in bold; Cohen kappas are in regular font. In a few instances, the tabled correlation values had to be calculated from rates of agreement given in the original sources.

The data in the table are taken from the following studies:

a. Cass R. Sunstein et al., *Assessing Punitive Damages (with Notes on Cognition and Valuation in Law)*, 107 YALE L.J. 2071 (1998).

b. The study reported in this Article.

c. Henry Kalven, Jr., *The Dignity of the Civil Jury*, 50 VA. L. REV. 1055 (1964).

d. Shari S. Diamond & Hans Zeisel, *Sentencing Councils: A Study of Sentence Disparity and Its Reduction*, 43 U. CHI. L. REV. 109 (1975).

e. Ming-Jer Chen et al., *An Exploration of the Expertness of Outside Informants*, 36 ACADEMY OF MANAGEMENT J. 1614 (1993).

f. S. Cole et al., *Chance and Consensus in Peer Review,* 214 SCIENCE 881 (1981).

g. John D. Whited et al., *Primary Care Clinicians' Performance for Detecting Actinic Keratoses and Skin Cancer,* 157 ARCHIVES OF INTERNAL MEDICINE 985 (1997).

h. R.S. Uhrbrock, *The Personnel Interview,* 1 PERSONNEL PSYCHOLOGY 273 (1948).

i. Leonard Adelman & Michael L. Donnell, *An Empirical Study Comparing Pilots' Interrater Reliability Ratings for Workload and Effectiveness,* 18 IEEE TRANSACTIONS ON SYSTEMS, MAN, AND CYBERNETICS 978 (1988).

j. Pierre Leichner et al., *A Study of the Reliability of the Clinical Oral Examination in Psychiatry,* 29 CANADIAN J. PSYCHIATRY 394 (1984).

Moreover, there is good reason to believe that juries (groups) produce considerably more stable and predictable outcomes compared to jurors (individuals).[182] Consequently, decisions of *juries* may approach, or even exceed, the stability and predictability of decisions of individual judges. Without persuasive data to the contrary, entertaining a reform that would reduce or eliminate the role of juries in making damages awards seems premature.

But assuming that, at the end of the day, it is concluded that a marginal advantage in the predictability of general damages awards favoring judges does exist, is the transfer of responsibility from juries to judges wise policy? The answer lies in weighing this small gain in predictability against what would be lost.

A core benefit of juries is the sampling function they provide. The law apparently has discovered that the best substitute for a market to generate the values of the sorts of losses subsumed under general damages is to sample the judgment of the community. Moreover, if it is to tailor damages to the actual losses incurred, it must do its sampling on a case-by-case basis. To accomplish these functions, juries not only are quite an efficient method, they are the only available method. Without juries, the ability to estimate the community's sense of the value of the ability to see or to hear or to walk or to have children or to be a whole human being is forfeited. That juries consist of groups, drawn more or less at random from the community, is essential to the sampling function. Imperfect sampling though it may be, it is less imperfect than having no sampling at all.

In addition, juries offer several collateral benefits. One is that they reduce bias by dividing decisionmaking functions between judge and jury. The judge is free to know everything, and can act to screen out biasing, speculative, or otherwise inadmissible evidence and arguments about what the damages should be. The jury then is able to consider only proper evidence and arguments in reaching its decisions. Even when this is imperfect, it is a considerable improvement on re-

182. *See supra* Section IV.D.

quiring judges to know what a factfinder should not know, and then to try to decide in spite of that knowledge.[183]

Another collateral benefit is the "lightning rod" function of juries. That is, by being the primary decisionmakers, juries become the targets of criticism, thereby drawing the fire away from judges. Moreover, juries can dissipate the attacks better than judges could. A jury that attracts the ire of the public fades back into the community and is replaced by another jury for the next trial. In contrast, as judges render one verdict after another, they risk accumulating criticism for successive unpopular decisions. Further, the unpopular decisions of judges, unlike those of juries, might be viewed as the edicts of an unelected elite rather than as the sentiments of the general community. The very criticism directed at some juries may illustrate their performance of a lightning rod function.[184] To say the least, it is not obvious that the marginal benefit of increased predictability of judges' decisions (if such a benefit were to materialize) outweighs the various benefits provided by the use of juries — especially considering that most of the time juries reach decisions that judges regard as reasonable.[185]

2. *Reforms Consistent with the Available Data*

Sensible and moderate reforms to reduce unpredictability, focusing on procedural adjustments, could improve on an essentially sound system.

One approach would be to increase the size of juries (from the six or eight civil jurors now found in many federal and state jurisdictions to the traditional twelve of the common law) in order to reduce unwanted variability and increase stability and predictability.[186]

A second method, which emphasizes the diversity among injuries, would be to provide jurors with descriptions of a range of injuries as a basis for forming a reference scale with which to compare the case at bar.[187] By seeing the injury under consideration in the context of other

183. Of course, many judges believe that they can perform this cognitive feat, but what little hard data exist on the subject indicates that judges are no better than jurors at disregarding evidence they are not supposed to know. *See* Landsman & Rakos, *supra* note 18.

184. Especially in cases where jurors have made unpopular decisions with which judges have not manifested disagreement.

185. *See* Valerie P. Hans, *Attitudes Toward the Civil Jury: A Crisis of Confidence?*, *in* VERDICT: ASSESSING THE CIVIL JURY SYSTEM 248, 262-65 (Robert E. Litan ed., 1993). It is also worth noting that the law has mechanisms for reining in the rare runaway jury, namely additur/remittitur review and appeals.

186. *See* Diamond et al., *supra* note 146; Saks, *supra* note 150; Saks & Marti, *supra* note 150.

187. *See supra* note 166 and accompanying text; *see also* Sunstein et al., *supra* note 51, at 2104.

injuries, jurors would gain the advantage possessed by judges and lawyers and insurance claims representatives — an appreciation of the diverse universe of injuries.

Another powerful yet modest reform would be to pool jury awards made for similar injuries, and to present these cases and their award distributions to juries for guidance in reaching their general damages awards[188] and to judges for conducting their additur/remittitur reviews.[189] New decisions would continuously be added to update the data pool.[190] In either use, they could be offered as true "guidelines" — suggestions which could be departed from to the extent that the instant case differed from those guideline cases.[191] Pooling verdicts in similar cases, and funneling those back to juries (or judges), magnifies the benefit of sampling community judgments. Thus, rather than reducing the role of the jury, we can reduce a possible disadvantage (unpredictability) by making more use of one of its principal advantages (sampling). As the data of this study suggest, the problem with general damages is not who makes the decision; rather, the problem is the inherent difficulty of the decision being made.

E. *Postscript*

The present study leaves open several important questions. Although there is a strong underlying similarity of judgments among groups, especially concerning the nature of injuries, how might the models of award decisions be improved? Relatedly, what accounts for any differences that do exist among the models of the groups studied? Why, exactly, do defense lawyers' decision models depart from those of the other groups? Why, exactly, are jurors more variable than the others, even though their decision models are so similar?[192]

The research described in this Article presented jurors, judges, and lawyers with bare-bones cases, consisting almost exclusively of facts about the injuries and their sequella. Understanding how decision-

188. *See* Saks et al., *supra* note 27 (reporting a jury simulation experiment showing that giving mock jurors guidance tended to reduce the variability of general damages awards for medium- and high-severity injuries).

189. *See* Baldus et al., *supra* note 26.

190. For details of a methodology for gathering and using such data in courts, see Baldus et al., *supra* note 26. *See also* Bovbjerg et al., *Valuing Life and Limb*, *supra* note 26.

191. Others have discussed these and additional techniques for dealing with this problem. *See* ABA REPORT OF THE ACTION COMMISSION TO IMPROVE THE TORT LIABILITY SYSTEM 10-15 (1987); ALI REPORTERS' STUDY ON ENTERPRISE LIABILITY FOR PERSONAL INJURY, 199-230 (1991); Bovbjerg et al., *Valuing Life and Limb*, *supra* note 26; Diamond et al., *supra* note 146; Mark Geistfeld, *Placing a Price on Pain and Suffering: A Method for Helping Juries Determine Tort Damages for Nonmonetary Injuries*, 83 CAL. L. REV. 775 (1995); Sunstein et al., *supra* note 51.

192. The obvious hypothesis that the latter finding is due to a lack of experience with the task is only that, a hypothesis.

makers respond to the core attributes of injuries is only a first step. The models we have obtained can be built upon, layer by layer, systematically adding legally permissible contextual factors that should influence perceptions of the impact of injuries and the consequent damages. Then extra-legal contextual factors, including characteristics of cases, plaintiffs, and defendants, can be added. Although these ought not to affect damages awards, some of them are likely to, and identifying them can add to the predictive accuracy of the model. Finally, we can experiment with procedural and evidentiary variations that may affect the uses jurors (and judges and lawyers) make of the information they receive, and which may increase the predictability and decrease the variability of awards. Thus, the models developed in the present study, which already embody a considerable amount of predictive power, seem likely to be amenable to improvement through additional stages of model development.

APPENDIX A:
EXAMPLES OF INJURY DESCRIPTIONS

The two bones in the plaintiff's lower right leg were badly broken in several places. The 33-year-old plaintiff's leg was so disrupted that repair of the blood vessels was impossible and surgical amputation of the leg just below the knee was necessary. Over parts of three years, the plaintiff was hospitalized on many occasions and underwent several painful operations. The plaintiff was fitted with an artificial leg. Because the artificial leg causes the leg stump to become raw and inflamed, the plaintiff can walk for only brief periods.

The 33-year-old plaintiff suffered numerous cuts on the left forearm. The cuts required 40 stitches. The injury left several small scars that are permanent.

The 37-year-old plaintiff suffered scarring of the lungs, which affects their ability to absorb oxygen. Also, the lining of the lungs has hardened, making it difficult for them to move air in and out. These conditions make the plaintiff short of breath, more susceptible to flu and pneumonia, and more likely to develop lung cancer. The plaintiff cannot walk very far without getting winded and becoming exhausted. The plaintiff will continue to get worse and has a 50-50 chance of dying within five years.

The 33-year-old plaintiff suffered burns that caused blistering and destroyed tissue on the face and over 80% of the body. The plaintiff's wounds and their treatment were extremely painful. During the first two months in the hospital, the plaintiff underwent massive infusions of blood plasma and a procedure of salves, bandaging, chlorine baths, and cutting away the dead tissue from the burned areas. Over several years, the plaintiff had extensive skin graft surgery and received further treatment. The plaintiff suffered from painful tightening of the scar tissue, which impaired the mobility of joints and required constant surgical repairs. All of this required 70 operations, and at least ten more operations will be necessary over the next ten years. The plaintiff's skin resembles a patchwork quilt, and extremes of heat and cold will always be painful.

The 33-year-old plaintiff suffered a broken right wrist. The plaintiff, who is right-handed, had to wear a cast for one month. For a few months, the plaintiff's wrist was somewhat weak and less flexible. Thereafter, the wrist healed completely.

The 33-year-old plaintiff suffered a broken pelvis, such that the bone was splintered into fragments. In addition, the fragments on the left side were out of position and surgery was required to set them. The plaintiff spent one month in the hospital, followed by another month of bed rest at home. Over the next several months, the plaintiff gradually was able to walk and to resume normal activities.

APPENDIX B: INTERVIEW PROTOCOL FOR JURY-ELIGIBLE CITIZENS[193]

Introduction to the interview:

We are studying people's decisions about how much monetary compensation an injured person should receive in a lawsuit. We want to talk to people like you who could end up serving as jurors and making these kinds of decisions.

The interview will last about ten minutes. I will read you brief summaries of two real cases and then ask you for your reactions to them. The cases may contain some graphic details about the injuries.

These cases involve an injured person, called the plaintiff, and the party responsible for the injury, called the defendant. According to the law, when the defendant is found to be responsible, plaintiffs are entitled to receive compensation for their medical expenses, lost wages, and the pain and suffering they have experienced.

In each case that I'm going to read you, a jury in an earlier trial found the defendant to be legally responsible for the plaintiff's injury. Also at that trial, the jury compensated the plaintiff for medical expenses and lost wages. So all you have to focus on here is how much pain and suffering this injury has caused the plaintiff and how much money would provide fair compensation for that pain and suffering.

So for each case, I am going to ask you to come up with a dollar amount for the plaintiff's pain and suffering and to give me your impressions of the injury. For example, to rate how much physical pain the injury has caused. If I ask any question that you do not wish to answer, let me know and we'll move on to the next question. All your answers will be kept confidential and will be seen only by the researchers directly involved with this project.

The first case was then read, followed by these instructions and questions:

To remind you, a jury in an earlier trial found the defendant in this case to be legally responsible for the plaintiff's injury or illness. Also in that trial, the jury compensated the plaintiff for medical expenses and lost wages. So leave those out of your calculation.

193. The introduction to the interview for lawyers and judges varied somewhat from the introduction for jurors. The jurors' introduction had more information about the study (since they had not received a letter about the study in advance of the phone call) and more explanation of personal injury cases. The same instructions for determining an award were read to all respondent groups within each state. The questions about the awards and the injuries were asked of all participants in the same order. The particular socio-demographic items varied with the respondent group; the questions asked of each group are included here.

New York:

You should focus only on compensating the plaintiff for the injury and for any conscious pain and suffering that the plaintiff experienced in the past, or will experience in the future with reasonable certainty. In deciding the amount to be awarded for the injury and for conscious pain and suffering, you may take into consideration any physical pain, mental suffering, disability, disfigurement, or loss of the ability to enjoy life. There is no exact standard for fixing the compensation to be awarded. Any award that you make should be fair and reasonable in light of the facts you have heard. Disregard any caps on pain and suffering in your state and give the award you think the injury should receive without regard to any cap.

Illinois:

You should focus only on compensating the plaintiff for any physical pain, mental suffering, disability, or disfigurement that the plaintiff experienced in the past, or will experience in the future with reasonable certainty, as a result of the injury. In deciding the amount to be awarded, you may consider the nature, extent, and duration of the injury. There is no exact standard for fixing the compensation to be awarded. Any award that you make should be fair and reasonable in light of the facts you have heard. Disregard any caps on pain and suffering in your state and give the award you think the injury should receive without regard to any cap.[194]

With all this in mind, how much money would you award to the plaintiff?

[If the respondent answered zero]

Why do you think the plaintiff should receive no compensation?

If the respondent said, in effect, the defendant was "not guilty" or "not liable," the interviewer replied: Let me remind you that a jury in an earlier trial found the defendant in this case to be legally responsible for the plaintiff's injury or illness.

With this in mind, how much money would you award to the plaintiff?

How much money do you think the average juror would award this plaintiff?

Now I'm going to ask you five questions about your impressions of the injuries the plaintiff suffered. For each question, I'd like you to indicate your judgment on a five-point scale.

194. The last sentence in the instructions in both states was included for only the judges and lawyers, who would tend to be aware of existing caps while the jurors would not.

1. Considering both the amount of physical pain and how long it will last, how much physical pain will this injury have caused the plaintiff? From one, no pain at all, to five extreme pain?
2. Considering both the amount of mental suffering (that is, worry, fear, depression, and so forth) and how long it will last, how much mental suffering will this injury have caused the plaintiff? From one, no mental suffering at all, to five, extreme mental suffering?
3. Considering both the amount of disability and how long it will last, how much disability will this injury have caused the plaintiff? From one, no disability at all, to five, extreme disability?
4. Considering both the amount of disfigurement and how long it will last, how much disfigurement will this injury have caused the plaintiff? From one, no disfigurement at all, to five, extreme disfigurement?
5. Overall, considering all aspects, how severe is the injury to the plaintiff? From one, not at all severe, to five, extremely severe?

The second case was then read, followed again by the award instructions. The same award and injury questions as above were asked for the second case.

After the awards and injury ratings were made for the second case, the following socio-demographic information was obtained.

JURORS

In order to be sure that we have a fair representation of all kinds of people, we'd like to ask you the following questions.

Do you personally know anyone who has had either of the conditions I have read to you about? IF YES: which one?

How would you describe where you live? Would you say it is: a large city; the suburbs of a large city; a medium-sized city; or a small town or rural area?

What is your age?

What is the highest level of education you have completed?

0 - 8th grade
9 - 11th grade
high school graduate
some college
college graduate
post-college study or degree

Please tell me which of the following ranges best describes your total annual household income.

less than $15,000
$15,000 - $30,000
$31,000 - $50,000
$51,000 - $75,000
over $75,000

Thank you for your participation in this interview. The answers you have provided will assist the researchers in their study of legal decision making. Thank you very much for your time.

The following information also was recorded but was not asked of the participants:

gender: male, female
state: Illinois, New York
from urban or rural county group: urban, rural

JUDGES

About what percentage of the cases that come before you are personal injury cases?

Do the people who serve as jurors in your court come mostly: from a large city; from the suburbs of a large city; from a medium-sized city; or from a small town or rural area?

Do you personally know anyone who has had either of the conditions I have read to you about, or have you heard a case involving either of these conditions? IF YES: which one?

For approximately how many years have you been hearing personal injury cases as a judge?

That concludes the interview. Would you like to receive a summary of the results of the study when it is completed?

Thank you for your participation in this interview. The answers you have provided will assist the researchers in their study of damages decision-making. Thank you very much for your time.

The following information also was recorded but was not asked of the participants:

gender: male, female
state: Illinois, New York
from urban or rural county group: urban, rural

LAWYERS

What percentage of your work involves representing clients in personal injury cases?

In personal injury cases, do you represent: mostly plaintiffs, mostly defendants, or both about equally?

In the personal injury cases that you have worked on, do the plaintiffs come mostly: from a large city; from the suburbs of a large city; from a medium-sized city; or from a small town or rural area?

Do you personally know anyone who has had either of the conditions I have read to you about, or have you been involved in a case in which the plaintiff had either of these conditions? IF YES: which one?

Have you served as an arbitrator in a personal injury case?

IF YES: Have you done that: rarely, occasionally, or often?

For approximately how many years have you been handling personal injury cases?

That concludes the interview. Would you like to receive a summary of the results of the study when it is completed?

Thank you for your participation in this interview. The answers you have provided will assist the researchers in their study of damages decision-making. Thank you very much for your time.

The following information also was recorded but was not asked of the participants:

gender: male, female

state: Illinois, New York

from urban or rural county group: urban, rural

from plaintiff or defense group: plaintiff, defense

APPENDIX C: SUMMARY OF REGRESSION ANALYSIS CONCEPTS

Percentage of variance. The percentage of variance accounted for tells us how well a group of variables included in a predictive model accounts for what one seeks to predict, such as awards. Zero percent of the variance in awards accounted for by injury ratings and demographics would reflect a complete absence of predictive power; 100% of the variance accounted for would reflect perfect predictive power.

Statistical significance of the predictor variables in the model. Only those variables that have a statistically significant relationship to the variable being predicted make a contribution to the predictive model. Thus, variables that are not statistically significant are omitted from the model.

Interactions. Sometimes the relationship of a predictor variable to the variable being predicted is affected by another predictor variable. In such circumstances one can add to the predictive power of a model by including these statistically significant "interactions" between predictor variables in the model. For example, we found that disability interacted with state, such that disability had a greater impact on awards for New York judges than for Illinois judges.

Direction of effect. The main effects (variables acting individually) and interaction effects (variables acting jointly) can predict either increases or decreases in the variable being predicted.

Magnitude of effect. Some predictors are more powerful than others. The magnitude of an effect is typically reflected in a "regression coefficient" (such as a Beta weight), and these are presented in a table of the regression results. One of the most intuitively meaningful ways to understand the magnitude of effect of a predictor is simply to compare it to other predictors.

Shared variance and unique variance. Sometimes different predictors are correlated with each other (that is, they "share variance"), so that there is redundancy in their predictive power. The amount of variance attributable to a given predictor and that predictor alone ("unique variance") is determined statistically by regression analysis by removing the redundancy. In order to compare the extent to which a given predictor's predictive power is a result of its shared versus unique influence, we compare the magnitude of its uncontrolled effect on the variable being predicted (given by a simple zero-order correlation, bivariate r, in which no other variables are controlled) with the magnitude of its effect on the variable being predicted in the regression model (given by Beta, in which the effect of other variables has been removed).

The reader who wishes to understand these statistical techniques even more deeply might consult one of the many textbooks on the topic, or, for a treatment designed for judges and lawyers, read Daniel L. Rubinfeld, *Guide to Multiple Regression,* § 4, *in* MODERN SCIENTIFIC EVIDENCE: THE LAW AND SCIENCE OF EXPERT TESTIMONY (David L. Faigman, David H. Kaye, Michael J. Saks & Joseph Sanders eds., 1997).

Part VI
Trials and Terrorism

[13]

TERRORISM ON TRIAL: THE PRESIDENT'S CONSTITUTIONAL AUTHORITY TO ORDER THE PROSECUTION OF SUSPECTED TERRORISTS BY MILITARY COMMISSION

CHRISTOPHER M. EVANS

INTRODUCTION

On November 13, 2001, President George W. Bush, in his capacity as commander in chief, promulgated a Military Order authorizing the trial of noncitizens suspected of complicity in the brutal attacks on September 11, 2001, before specially convened military commissions.[1] The Military Order of November 13 establishes that, unlike trials in federal district courts, judicial review of the commission proceedings will be strictly prohibited.[2] The commissions also differ considerably from the courts-martial provided under the Uniform Code of Military Justice (UCMJ).[3] Courts-martial are appealable on all issues of fact

---

1. Military Order of November 13, 2001: Detention, Treatment, and Trial of Certain Non-Citizens in the War Against Terrorism, 66 Fed. Reg. 57,833 (Nov. 13, 2001) [hereinafter *Military Order*]. "Military commissions," as discussed here, are a type of military tribunal, which is a blanket term that also includes courts-martial and courts of inquiry. This distinction is indicated in the Uniform Code of Military Justice:

> The provisions of this chapter conferring jurisdiction upon courts-martial do not deprive military commissions, provost courts, *or other military tribunals* of concurrent jurisdiction with respect to offenders or offenses that by statute or by the law of war may be tried by military commissions, provost courts, or other military tribunals.

10 U.S.C. § 821 (2000) (emphasis added).

2. *Military Order* § 7(b)(2), *supra* note 1, at 57,835–36. So long as the military commissions are not convened within the territorial jurisdiction of the United States, denial of judicial review will likely pass constitutional muster. *See* Johnson v. Eisentrager, 339 U.S. 763, 786 (1950) (declining to extend constitutional protections to enemy aliens tried before military commission outside the sovereign territory of the United States for violations of the laws of war). The Supreme Court has "characterized as 'well-established' the 'power of the military to exercise jurisdiction over... enemy belligerents, prisoners of war, or others charged with violating the laws of war.'" *Id.* at 786 (quoting Duncan v. Kahanamoku, 327 U.S. 304, 313–14 (1946)).

3. 10 U.S.C. §§ 801–946 (2000).

and law[4] and, furthermore, adhere to strict rules of evidence.[5] The commissions, on the other hand, only follow evidentiary guidelines established by the Secretary of Defense in his discretion.[6]

The Military Order creating these commissions reflects the Bush administration's trepidation about prosecuting suspected terrorists through the ordinary criminal justice system, which, it is feared, could lead to substantial delays and even acquittals based on legal technicalities.[7] President Bush's decision to convene military commissions is also predicated upon the belief that terrorist acts amount to acts of war, and that, accordingly, suspected terrorists should be treated as war criminals.[8] However, despite the president's repeated pronouncements that the September 11 attacks constituted violations of the law of war, thus empowering him to convene military commissions,[9] the November 13 Order has been heavily criticized as an unconstitutional expansion of executive authority with the potential for significant abuse.[10] By contrast, supporters of the commissions maintain that the Military Order is a valid exercise of the president's commander in chief power, and that the president's broad latitude to

---

4. 10 U.S.C. § 866(c).

5. *See* 10 U.S.C. § 836(a) (explaining that rules and procedures for courts-martial shall apply principles of law and rules of evidence generally recognized in federal district courts).

6. *See Military Order* § 4(c)(3), *supra* note 1, at 57,835 (stating that evidence will be admitted "as would, in the opinion of the presiding officer of the military commission . . . have probative value to a reasonable person"); *see also id.* § 6(a) (requiring the Secretary of Defense to "issue such orders and regulations as may be necessary to carry out provisions of the order"); *see also* Department of Defense Military Commission Order No. 1, March 21, 2002, *at* http://www.defenselink.mil/news/Mar2002/d20020321ord.pdf (on file with the *Duke Law Journal*) (detailing procedures for trials by military commission of suspected terrorists, including the rights to a presumption of innocence, to choose counsel, to see the prosecution's evidence, to a public trial, and to remain silent).

7. *See* Anthony Lewis, *Dust in Our Eyes*, N.Y. TIMES, Dec. 4, 2001, at A21 (attacking President Bush's order as "extraordinarily ill-drafted").

8. *See Military Order* § 1(e), *supra* note 1, at 57,833 ("International terrorists, including members of al Qaeda, have carried out attacks on the United States . . . on a scale that has created a state of armed conflict.").

9. *See, e.g.*, William Glaberson, *Support for Bush's Antiterror Plan*, N.Y. TIMES, Dec. 5, 2001, at B6 (detailing legal grounds for the president's exceedingly broad powers); David E. Sanger, *President Defends Military Tribunals*, N.Y. TIMES, Nov. 30, 2001, at A1 (quoting the president's statement that "[t]he enemy has declared war on us").

10. *See, e.g.*, Louis Fisher, *Bush Can't Rely On FDR Precedent*, L.A. TIMES, Dec. 2, 2001, at M3 (arguing that the commissions offer the potential for abuse); Katharine Q. Seelye, *In Letter, 300 Law Professors Oppose Tribunals Plan*, N.Y. TIMES, Dec. 8, 2001, at A1 (citing a letter that originated at Yale Law School that asserts that the commissions are legally deficient).

protect national security permits the Bush administration to proclaim war against terrorism.[11]

This Note analyzes the president's legal predicate for authorizing military commissions in response to the attacks on September 11. It concludes that, under *Ex parte Quirin*,[12] the president's Order is constitutional. The attacks of September 11 were so catastrophic in their purpose and effect as to constitute "hostile acts" in violation of the laws of war.[13] Because the attacks commenced an imperfect or "quasi war," the *jus in bello* was triggered, thus giving the president valid authority to convene the commissions to punish these acts as war crimes under *Ex parte Quirin*.[14] This Note maintains, however, that the Military Order is nevertheless an extralegal action because it is inconsistent with existing international law. The laws of war, a subset of the law of nations, apply only to state actors, not to independent terrorist organizations such as those believed to be responsible for the September 11 atrocities.[15] Despite the administration's attempt to effect a rapid change in customary international law so as to apply the laws of war to nonstate actors,[16] such a change, even if possible, cannot be made retroactive to the events of September 11. Thus, these commissions lack legal justification under international law.

Part I of this Note briefly summarizes the events of September 11 and then discusses the November 13 Military Order. Part II examines the historical precedent for convening military commissions to prosecute war crimes, and it also considers the various arguments supporting the president's Military Order. Part III describes the unique factual background and holding of *Ex parte Quirin*, and then analyzes

11. *See, e.g.*, Glaberson, *supra* note 9, at B6 ("The precedents are overwhelmingly in favor of what the president is doing.").

12. 317 U.S. 1, 48 (1942) (upholding President Roosevelt's power to establish military commissions for violations of the law of war by enemy saboteurs during World War II).

13. *See infra* Part III.B.

14. *See infra* notes 105–113 and accompanying text.

15. *See, e.g.*, MICHAEL BYERS, CUSTOM, POWER AND THE POWER OF RULES 75 (1999) (discussing the principle of full legal personality in international law and the procedural protections it can invoke).

16. *On DOJ Oversight: Preserving Our Freedoms While Defending Against Terrorism: Hearing On Review of Military Terrorism Tribunals Before the Senate Comm. on the Judiciary*, 107th Cong. (2001) [hereinafter *Hearings*] 2001 WL 26187921 (testimony of Scott L. Silliman, Executive Director for the Center on Law, Ethics and National Security, Duke University School of Law).

the applicability of this opinion to the acts of September 11. Despite the clear differences between the Bush administration's military campaign and the World War II context in which *Ex parte Quirin* was decided, this Note concludes that this opinion provides a valid constitutional basis for the November 13 Military Order. Part IV discusses the inapplicability of the laws of war to terrorist organizations and the Bush administration's attempt to bring about a sudden change in existing customary international law. Finally, this Note considers the policy implications of using military commissions, as well as the administration's desired change in customary international law. It is argued here that, despite its constitutionality, the Military Order is both unwise and inconsistent with existing law.

I. THE SEPTEMBER 11 ATTACKS AND THE PRESIDENT'S MILITARY ORDER ESTABLISHING MILITARY COMMISSIONS

The brutal acts of September 11, 2001, closely resembled a surprise enemy attack both in their planning and in their devastating consequences. The destruction of the World Trade Center in New York City and portions of the Pentagon in Washington, D.C., killed approximately three thousand people.[17] Although parallels have been drawn between these events and Japan's attack on Pearl Harbor in 1941, which left 2,403 people dead,[18] the attacks of September 11 were worse in terms of the number of casualties suffered, and also marked the largest killing of civilians on the U.S. mainland in the history of the United States.[19] So grave were these attacks that on September 14, 2001, President Bush proclaimed a national emergency.[20] The events of September 11 also resulted in a novel and complex political situation. The attack on Pearl Harbor was attributable to a hostile nation then at war with U.S. allies. The suicide missions of September 11, however, were not linked to an identifiable state but, rather, to the loosely knit al Qaeda terrorist network allegedly directed by suspected terrorist Osama bin Laden, and actively supported by the

17. Yochi J. Dreazen, *Power-Plant Operators Are Alerted to Threat of Potential Terrorist Plot*, WALL ST. J., Feb. 1, 2002, at A4.

18. THE ECONOMIST, *The New Enemy*, Sept. 15, 2001, at 15.

19. THE ECONOMIST, *The Day the World Changed*, Sept. 15, 2001, at 13.

20. Proclamation No. 7463, 66 Fed. Reg. 48,199 (Sept. 14, 2001) *reprinted in* 50 U.S.C. § 1621 (2000).

Taliban government in Afghanistan,[21] a rogue regime never officially recognized by the United States.[22]

President Bush made clear in the aftermath of the attacks that the United States would treat these acts as *casus belli*, calling them "not acts of terrorism but acts of war."[23] The Military Order of November 13 reiterated the belief that the terrorist attacks were so severe as to have created a state of armed conflict, thus enabling President Bush to establish military commissions to prosecute those responsible.[24] Specifically, the Order provides:

> To protect the United States and its citizens, and for the effective conduct of military operations and prevention of terrorist attacks, it is necessary for individuals subject to this order pursuant to section 2 hereof to be detained, and, when tried, to be tried for violations of the laws of war and other applicable laws by military tribunals.[25]

The Order cites as its legal basis the president's power as commander in chief vested in him by the Constitution and laws of the United States, including the Authorization for Use of Military Force Joint Resolution passed on September 18, 2001,[26] and sections 821 and 836 of the UCMJ.[27] The Order also cites President Bush's declaration of a national emergency, and states that "this emergency constitutes an urgent and compelling government interest, and that issuance of this order is necessary to meet the emergency."[28]

21. *See* Elizabeth Bumiller, *Bush Pledges Attack on Afghanistan Unless It Surrenders Bin Laden Now*, N.Y. TIMES, Sept. 21, 2001, at A1 (discussing President Bush's address to Congress on September 20, 2001, in which he demanded that the Taliban hand over members of the al Qaeda network to the United States).

22. *See* Press Release, Office of the White House Press Secretary, Status of Detainees *at* Guantanamo (Feb. 7, 2002), http://www.whitehouse.gov/news/releases/2002/02/20020207-13.html (on file with the *Duke Law Journal*) [hereinafter Press Release] (explaining that al Qaeda is a foreign terrorist group, and thus its members are not entitled to POW status); Katharine Q. Seelye, *In Shift, Bush Says Geneva Rules Fit Taliban Captives*, N.Y. TIMES, Feb. 7, 2002, at A1 (explaining President Bush's application of the Geneva convention to Taliban captives but not to al Qaeda detainees).

23. *The New Enemy*, *supra* note 18, at 16.

24. *See Military Order* §§ 1(a)–(g), *supra* note 1, at 57,833 (detailing findings in support of military commissions).

25. *Id.* § 1(e).

26. S.J. Res. 23, 107th Cong., 115 Stat. 224 (2001).

27. 10 U.S.C. §§ 821, 836 (2000) (stating that the jurisdiction of courts-martial is nonexclusive, and giving the president the authority to prescribe rules for use in courts-martial and other military tribunals).

28. *Military Order* § 1(g), *supra* note 1, at 57,834.

During the operations in Afghanistan, which commenced several weeks after September 11, when the Taliban refused to hand bin Laden over to the United States,[29] U.S. forces captured various members of al Qaeda and the Taliban regime.[30] Beginning in January, 2002, these captives were transferred to the United States Naval Base at Guantanamo Bay, Cuba, where they remain confined, presumably awaiting trial before military commissions.[31]

II. ASSERTED SOURCES OF THE PRESIDENT'S AUTHORITY TO CONVENE MILITARY COMMISSIONS

A. *Historical Practice*

The November 13 Military Order was an extraordinary measure. No president had authorized the use of such commissions within the United States in over half a century. The Bush administration's decision to do so, however, is not without precedent. The laws of war have long recognized that military commissions can be convened to prosecute war crimes during an armed conflict.[32] "The [military] commission," as one authority notes, "is simply an instrumentality for the more efficient execution of the laws of war."[33] There is, moreover, a long-established history of using military commissions to try those accused of "[v]iolations of the laws and usages of war" dating back to the early years of the Republic.[34] Throughout the Revolutionary War, a number of enemy spies were tried and convicted before military

29. *See* Peter Baker, *Taliban Preparing Capital for War; Trenches Are Dug, Men Conscripted*, WASH. POST, Oct. 2, 2001, at A1 (describing militia fortification of Kabul in anticipation of American forces after the failure of the Taliban to hand over Osama bin Laden to the United States).

30. *See* John Mintz, *Extended Detention in Cuba Mulled*, WASH. POST, Feb. 13, 2002, at A16 (envisioning the United States Naval Base at Guantanamo Bay, Cuba, to which al Qaeda captives were sent, as a "terrorist penal colony for years to come").

31. *Id.*

32. WILLIAM WINTHROP, MILITARY LAW AND PRECEDENTS 330 (2d ed. 1920); *see also Ex parte* Quirin, 317 U.S. 1, 38–43 (1942) (explaining that the Constitution does not require offenses against the law of war to be tried before a jury). The "laws of war," part of the law of nations, are comprised of both treaties and general, or customary, international law. *See* Alfred P. Rubin, Remarks at the Annual Meeting of the American Society of International Law (Apr. 25, 1985), *in* 79 AM. SOC'Y INT'L L. PROC. 109, 111 (1985) (discussing the sources and principles underlying the laws of war in the context of terrorism).

33. WINTHROP, *supra* note 32, at 330.

34. *Id.* at 332.

commissions.[35] George Washington personally ordered the executions of several of those convicted.[36]

Military commissions were also used extensively during the Civil War to try offenses against the laws of war.[37] One notable trial before a military commission during the Civil War involved Confederate saboteurs who attempted to disrupt the Union war effort by burning down various buildings in New York City.[38] A Confederate army captain, Robert Kennedy, was found to have attempted, while in disguise, to set fire to several of the city's buildings.[39] Tried before a military commission in 1865, Kennedy was sentenced to hang for acting as a spy and "undertaking to carry on irregular and unlawful warfare."[40] Another Confederate saboteur, John Y. Beall, was tried before a military commission for his role in the hijacking of a Union vessel and for his unsuccessful attempt to derail a train in New York State—also while in disguise.[41] Adjudged a spy and a guerilla, Beall was also sentenced to be hanged.[42] The history of the Civil War is replete with similar cases in which Confederate spies and saboteurs were tried, sentenced and put to death by military commissions.[43]

Constitutionally speaking, presidential authority to establish such commissions, derived from the president's commander in chief powers, is limited.[44] The Constitution vests the president, as commander in chief, with the power to wage wars that Congress has declared, and to execute all laws passed by Congress defining and punishing offenses committed against the law of nations, including those govern-

35. *Ex parte* Quirin, 317 U.S. 1, 42 n.14 (1942) (describing numerous cases tried before commissions during the American Revolution); *see also* WINTHROP, *supra* note 32, at 832–33 (describing similar trials conducted during the Mexican War).

36. *Quirin*, 317 U.S. at 42 n.14.

37. *See* Spencer J. Crona & Neal A. Richardson, *Justice For War Criminals of Invisible Armies: A New Legal and Military Approach to Terrorism*, 21 OKLA. CITY U. L. REV. 349, 368 (1996) (describing various instances in which military commissions were used to prosecute Confederate soldiers during the Civil War).

38. *Quirin*, 317 U.S. at 32 n.10.

39. *Id.*

40. *Id.*

41. *Id.*

42. *Id.*

43. *See id.* (discussing several examples of Confederate spies tried before military commissions).

44. *See* U.S. CONST. art. II, § 2 (stating that "[t]he President shall be Commander in Chief of the Army and Navy of the United States, and of the Militia of the several States, when called into the actual Service of the United States").

ing the conduct of war, the *jus in bello*.[45] Article 21 of the UCMJ provides that military commissions have "concurrent jurisdiction with respect to offenders or offenses that by statute or by the law of war may be tried by military commissions . . . or other military tribunals."[46] Thus, assuming there is an underlying statute defining certain acts as violations of the law of war (or if recognized war crimes were committed during the course of an armed conflict), the president may, in his capacity as commander in chief, constitutionally establish military commissions to punish those acts.

B. The President's Power Over Foreign Affairs

Congress never formally declared war with regard to the Bush administration's military action in Afghanistan; and because the September 11 attacks are believed to have been committed by terrorist organizations without state sponsorship, it is unclear whether the attacks constitute war crimes.[47] Thus, the current scenario does not fit easily alongside the historical precedents for the establishment of military commissions to punish war crimes. Officials within the Bush administration have employed a range of arguments with which they seek to justify the November 13 Military Order. The administration has argued, for example, that the United States is in a state of armed conflict,[48] and that the president has very broad powers to protect national security in wartime.[49] In making this argument, supporters of the Military Order have cited *United States v. Curtiss-Wright Export Corp.*[50] as a plausible basis for President Bush's Order to establish the military commissions.[51] At issue in *Curtiss-Wright* was a congressional joint resolution that prohibited arms sales to Paraguay and Bolivia, which were at war, and conditioned its continuance on President Roosevelt's issuance of a proclamation as to its effect in helping to restore peace to that region.[52] The Curtiss-Wright Corporation, charged

45. *Quirin*, 317 U.S. at 26.

46. 10 U.S.C. § 821 (2000).

47. Rubin, *supra* note 32, at 111.

48. *See, e.g.*, *Military Order* § 1(a), *supra* note 1, at 57,833 (stating that the terrorist attacks have "created a state of armed conflict").

49. Glaberson, *supra* note 9, at B6 (describing lawyers' efforts to assemble a "talking-points brief in defense of the administration's actions").

50. 299 U.S. 304 (1936).

51. Glaberson, *supra* note 9, at B6 (citing a recent brief written by former Deputy Attorney General George Terwilliger in support of the Order).

52. 299 U.S. at 314–15.

with violating the arms embargo, argued that because the joint resolution was conditioned on a discretionary presidential proclamation regarding a foreign conflict, it constituted an unconstitutional delegation of legislative authority to the executive.[53]

The Court drew a dichotomy between the powers of the federal government over foreign relations on the one hand, and domestic affairs on the other. "The broad statement that the federal government can exercise no powers except those specifically enumerated in the Constitution," Justice Sutherland wrote, "is categorically true only in respect of our internal affairs."[54] *Curtiss-Wright* thus established the president as the "sole organ of the nation in its external relations, and its sole representative with foreign nations."[55] Thus, according to *Curtiss-Wright*, the president's power to act as the federal government's sole organ in external affairs does not, unlike the domestic sphere, require congressional authorization.[56] Bush administration lawyers contend that this plenary and exclusive power over foreigu affairs is a valid basis upon which the president can convene military commissions.[57]

This argument, however, is not easily applied to the present situation. First, whether or not the United States is "at war," as some have maintained, is debatable. It thus cannot be assumed automatically that the president was acting in the realm of "external affairs" when he issued the November 13 Order, as the "sole organ" theory would require.[58] Justice Sutherland emphasized that the president's "sole organ" power is limited to foreign affairs whereas in domestic affairs the president is constrained by the need for congressional authorization.[59] It is beyond this Note's scope to categorize precisely where the November 13 Military Order falls on the spectrum between domestic and foreign affairs, but it does seem to have some implications for the domestic sphere. For example, the Order has a law en-

53. *Id.* at 315.

54. *Id.* at 315–16.

55. *Id.* at 319.

56. *Id.* at 320; *see also* LAURENCE H. TRIBE, AMERICAN CONSTITUTIONAL LAW § 402, at 213 (2d ed. 1988) (stating that, in the domestic sphere, the president's constitutional role "is thus largely ancillary to that of Congress").

57. *See* Glaberson, *supra* note 9, at B6 ("[S]upporters of the measures have begun to outline a legal defense of the actions, saying that the president has broad powers to protect national security in wartime . . . .").

58. *Curtiss-Wright*, 299 U.S. at 319.

59. *See id.* at 315–16 (distinguishing the scope of the exercise of general executive power over internal affairs from the exercise of power over foreign affairs).

forcement component, as it provides for the prosecution by military commissions of violations of the laws of war and "other applicable laws."[60] Furthermore, other departments and agencies such as the FBI are obliged, to the maximum extent permitted by law, to assist the Secretary of Defense "as he may request to implement this order."[61] This provision, which pertains not only to external relations but also to domestic security, may serve as a basis for the detention of suspected terrorists who may be turned over to the Department of Defense for trial before a commission. Therefore, in contrast to the presidential proclamation at issue in *Curtiss-Wright*, which fit clearly into the realm of external relations, President Bush's Order has significant implications for domestic affairs. *Curtiss-Wright*'s "sole organ" theory is, accordingly, inapplicable here.

C. *"Crisis Government" and Prerogative Power*

Proponents of the Military Order have, similarly, invoked the concept of crisis government[62] and the need for undefined power in the national government during certain crises.[63] This theory is based on the notion of prerogative power applied to presidential actions of an extraconstitutional nature. The concept was first articulated by Alexander Hamilton in *The Federalist No. 23*, in which he asserted:

> The circumstances that endanger the safety of nations are infinite, and for this reason no constitutional shackles can wisely be imposed on the power to which the care of it is committed. This power ought to be co-extensive with all the possible combinations of such circumstances; and ought to be under the direction of the same councils which are appointed to preside over the common defense.[64]

60. *Military Order* § 1(e), *supra* note 1, at 57,833.

61. *Id.* at 57,385.

62. For a discussion of crisis government, see Martin S. Sheffer, *Does Absolute Power Corrupt Absolutely?*, 24 OKLA. CITY U. L. REV. 233, 233–34 (1999):

> ... [R]eality ... demonstrates that war and peace are not the same thing, cannot coexist in the same place at the same time, and constitutional provisions applicable in time of peace may not be equally applicable in time of war. In other words, the Constitution does not function normally in abnormal times.

See also EDWARD S. CORWIN, THE PRESIDENT: OFFICE AND POWERS, 1787–1957, at 3 (4th ed. 1957) (discussing how the indefiniteness of executive power makes it particularly responsive to national emergencies).

63. *See* Glaberson, *supra* note 9, at B6 (explaining the legal justifications offered by supporters of the "[second] Bush Administration's antiterrorism crackdown").

64. THE FEDERALIST NO. 23, at 153 (Alexander Hamilton) (Clinton Rossiter ed., 1961).

The theory of crisis government as a basis for the Military Order is, however, palpably inapposite here. Although President Bush proclaimed a national emergency in the wake of the attacks,[65] such actions or statements cannot serve as a valid legal predicate for the November 13 Order. "The Constitution," as one scholar has explained, "recognizes no 'emergency powers,' whether for the President, or for other branches of the federal government."[66] Even in declared emergencies, the president's powers are limited to those either conferred by the Constitution or authorized by Congress.[67] In *Ex parte Milligan*,[68] the Supreme Court rejected the idea that emergency powers, even during times of armed conflict, could be a basis for the president's authority to establish military commissions to prosecute war crimes.[69] "No doctrine," wrote Justice Davis, "involving more pernicious consequences, was ever invented . . . than that any of [the Constitution's] provisions can be suspended during any of the great exigencies of government."[70] *Milligan* involved the issue of trying a U.S. citizen before a commission during the Civil War when courts of law were open and available, and is therefore more significant here because of the politically charged context in which it was decided than for its actual holding.[71] Nevertheless, *Milligan*'s rejection of emergency powers as a basis for the president's authority to establish military commissions remains binding.

III. THE CONSTITUTIONALITY OF THE NOVEMBER 13 MILITARY ORDER UNDER *EX PARTE QUIRIN*

A. *The Legal Precedent*

Both proponents and critics of the Bush administration's plan to use military commissions have invoked the Supreme Court's decision

65. Proclamation No. 7463, 66 Fed. Reg. 48,199 (Sept. 14, 2001), *reprinted in* 50 U.S.C. § 1621 (West, WESTLAW through P.L. 107-89).

66. LOUIS HENKIN, FOREIGN AFFAIRS AND THE U.S. CONSTITUTION 53 (2d ed. 1996).

67. *Id.*

68. 71 U.S. (4 Wall.) 2 (1866).

69. *Id.* at 118–27.

70. *Id.* at 121.

71. The November 13 Military Order applies only to noncitizens. *Military Order* §2, *supra* note 1, at 57,833–34. The current situation is also distinguishable from the Civil War context in which *Milligan* was decided because it is unclear whether the United States is technically at war. *See infra* notes 96–98 and accompanying text.

in *Ex parte Quirin*,[72] upholding President Roosevelt's authority to establish military commissions in the United States for the prosecution of war crimes during the Second World War. Proponents cite *Quirin* as a clear affirmation of the president's power to convene such commissions for violations of the laws of war.[73] Skeptics of the November 13 Order, on the other hand, are careful to distinguish the specific factual context in which *Quirin* was decided from the present setting.[74] A careful aualysis of *Quirin* is therefore necessary, as the constitutionality of President Bush's Military Order, if challenged in court, will likely hinge in large part ou how this decision is interpreted.

Quirin involved a petition for habeas corpus, filed by suspected German saboteurs captured within the United States during the Second World War, to challenge the constitutionality of their trial by military commission when the federal district courts were open and available. The saboteurs landed in two teams on July 12 and 17, 1942, off the shores of Long Island aud Florida, respectively.[75] All were agents of Nazi Germany.[76] They arrived armed with various explosive devices intending to disrupt America's war effort by destroying transportation and industrial facilities throughout the United States.[77] The saboteurs were, however, apprehended and taken into custody by the FBI.[78] Based on concerns similar to those of the Bush administration about proceeding through the criminal justice system, Attorney General Fraucis Biddle prepared a memorandum for the president recommending that, as commander in chief, he appoint a special military commission to prosecute the suspects for violations of the law of war.[79] Thus, on July 2, 1942, President Roosevelt issued an order es-

72. 317 U.S. 1, 36–37 (1942) (upholding a trial of alleged unlawful combatants ["enemy belligerents"] before a military commission for violations of the laws of war upon entry into the United States in a time of war for the purpose of executing hostile acts).

73. Glaberson, *supra* note 9, at B6.

74. *See, e.g.*, Fisher, *supra* note 10, at M3 (contrasting the World War II setting in which President Roosevelt established commissions to prosecute the saboteurs with the present circumstances).

75. *Ex parte* Quirin, 317 U.S. 1, 21 (1942).

76. *Id.* at 20–21.

77. Michal R. Belknap, *The Supreme Court Goes to War: The Meaning and Implications of the Nazi Saboteur Case*, 89 MIL. L. REV. 59, 62 (1980).

78. *Id.*

79. FRANCIS BIDDLE, IN BRIEF AUTHORITY 328–30 (1962); *see also* Belknap, *supra* note 77, at 75 ("'The time may now have come,' the government's brief observed, 'when the exigencies of . . . war must force a recognition that every foot of this country is within the theatre of operations.' The test of whether or not the civil courts were open to punish crimes, it was argued, was now 'unrealistic.'" (citing Brief for Respondent, Burger v. Cox, 317 U.S. 1 (1942))).

tablishing a military commission for the trial of the saboteurs "for offenses against the law of war and the Articles of War" adopted by Congress.[80] Roosevelt then issued a Proclamation declaring that "all persons who are . . . citizens . . . of any nation at war with the United States . . . and who during time of war . . . are charged with . . . violations of the law of war, shall be subject to the law of war and to the jurisdiction of military tribunals."[81] The military commission convened on July 8, 1942, and proceeded to try the eight saboteurs,[82] six of whom were eventually sentenced to death.[83]

Chief Justice Stone's opinion in *Quirin* dismissed the petitioners' argument, based on *Ex parte Milligan*, that as long as civil courts were available, the president was without authority to establish military commissions.[84] The Court stated that the Constitution does not require that offenses against the law of war be tried before a jury.[85] The opinion also established at the outset the presumption that presidential actions taken pursuant to the commander in chief power during wartime are valid, unless those actions are clearly in conflict with the Constitution.[86] Chief Justice Stone wrote, "[T]he detention and trial of petitioners—ordered by the President in the declared exercise of his powers as Commander in Chief of the Army in time of war and of grave public danger—*are not to be set aside by the courts without the clear conviction*" that they are in violation of the Constitution or laws of the United States.[87]

The Court found no such conflict with regard to President Roosevelt's Military Order, as it was promulgated during wartime pursuant to Articles of War adopted by Congress.[88] The Court then went on to determine *who* may be tried before military commissions for violations of the law of war. The Court distinguished carefully between "lawful combatants," who are subject to capture and detention as

80. 7 Fed. Reg. 5,103, 5,103 (1942); *see also Quirin*, 317 U.S. at 22 (summarizing the president's actions in appointing a military commission).

81. Proclamation No. 2561, 7 Fed. Reg. 5,101, 5,101 (1942); *see also Quirin*, 317 U.S. at 22–23 (discussing the Proclamation).

82. *Quirin*, 317 U.S. at 23–24.

83. BIDDLE, *supra* note 79, at 339.

84. *Quirin*, 317 U.S. at 24–25.

85. *Id.* at 40.

86. *Id.* at 25.

87. *Id.* (emphasis added).

88. *Id.* at 28.

prisoners of war by opposing military forces, and "unlawful combatants" who may be brought before military commissions:

> The spy who secretly and without uniform passes the military lines of a belligerent in time of war, seeking to gather military information and communicate it to the enemy, or an enemy combatant who without uniform comes secretly through the lines for the purpose of waging war by destruction of life or property, are familiar examples of belligerents who are generally deemed . . . offenders against the law of war subject to trial and punishment by military tribunals.[89]

The eight German saboteurs had been apprehended wearing civilian clothes rather than their military uniforms "during time of war,"[90] with the intent to commit "hostile acts involving destruction of life or property,"[91] and were acting as agents of an enemy nation at war with the United States—the Third Reich.[92] The saboteurs were accordingly found to be unlawful combatants, triable before a military commission for violations of the law of war.[93]

Thus, under *Quirin*, the requirements for a suspect to be an unlawful combatant subject to trial by military commission for violations of the law of war may be summarized as follows: There must be entry into the United States in a time of war for the purpose of committing hostile acts by "enemy belligerents" disguised in civilian clothing instead of their military uniforms.[94] It should be observed that "hostile acts," as defined in *Quirin*, are not limited to assaults on military targets.[95]

B. *The Applicability of* Ex parte Quirin *to the Attacks of September 11*

It is clear from the preceding discussion of *Quirin* that the situation in which President Roosevelt authorized military commissions to be established was entirely different from the context in which President Bush promulgated his Military Order on November 13. President Roosevelt authorized commissions in the midst of a war declared by Congress, and the eight German saboteurs were acting as agents of

89. *Id.* at 31.
90. *Id.* at 35
91. *Id.*
92. *Id.* at 21–22.
93. *Id.* at 46.
94. *Id.* at 37.
95. *Id.*

a declared enemy state. Here, by contrast, the United States was not in a state of armed conflict on the morning of September 11, prior to the attacks. Moreover, it is unclear whether the suspected terrorists were sponsored by any recognized state.[96] Critics of the Bush administration's Military Order thus contend that because the United States was not at war *as of* the morning of September 11, the attacks cannot be considered violations of the law of war.[97] It is maintained, therefore, that *Quirin* is inapposite because of the unique factual situation in which it was decided.[98] This argument is predicated on the idea that a declared war, or at least a state of armed conflict, must already exist for there to be a violation of the law of war.[99] "The notion of war crimes," one scholar has explained, "presupposes a war . . . ."[100]

Critics of the November 13 Order also distinguish *Quirin* because President Roosevelt, unlike President Bush, acted pursuant to an express congressional declaration of war.[101] Thus, under Justice Jackson's typology of presidential power in his oft-cited concurrence in *Youngstown Sheet & Tube Co. v. Sawyer*,[102] President Roosevelt's authority was at its zenith, as he was acting pursuant to an express congressional authorization.[103] It is argued, therefore, that even if one were to accept the assertion that the United States was engaged in some sort of armed conflict with such groups as al Qaeda prior to the September 11 attacks, President Bush lacks the clear authority that was available to President Roosevelt.[104]

Despite these obvious differences, a close reading of *Quirin* reveals that it may nevertheless serve as a valid predicate for the Bush

96. The issue of state sponsorship is addressed in Part IV, *infra*.

97. *See Hearings*, *supra* note 16 (testimony of Scott L. Silliman).

98. *See id.*; Fisher, *supra* note 10, at M3 (drawing attention to the unique wartime situation in which *Quirin* was decided).

99. *Hearings*, *supra* note 16 (testimony of Scott L. Silliman).

100. DONALD A. WELLS, WAR CRIMES AND LAWS OF WAR 41 (2d ed. 1991).

101. *See Hearings*, *supra* note 16 (testimony of Scott L. Silliman).

102. 343 U.S. 579 (1952).

103. *See id.* at 635 (Jackson, J., concurring) (stating that presidential power is at its greatest when exercised in conjunction with Congressional authority). According to Justice Jackson's typology, when the president acts pursuant to either an explicit or implied congressional authorization, his authority is at its maximum. *Id.* at 635. When the president acts without either a congressional grant or denial of authority, his power falls within a "zone of twilight in which he and Congress may have concurrent authority, or in which its distribution is uncertain." *Id.* at 637. However, when the president acts incompatibly with the express or implied will of Congress, his authority is at its "lowest ebb, for then he can rely only upon his own constitutional powers minus any constitutional powers of Congress over the matter." *Id.*

104. *See Hearings*, *supra* note 16 (testimony of Scott L. Silliman).

administration's Military Order of November 13. The attacks of September 11 constituted hostile acts so severe in both their purpose and their effect as to be war crimes; these acts therefore commenced a state of armed conflict, thus giving the president the authority to establish military commissions to punish the acts as violations of the law of war. While there has not been a congressional declaration of war as there was in *Quirin*, the United States was, as of the attacks, engaged—and has remained engaged—in a state of "quasi war."[105]

The text of the November 13 Military Order indicates that it was promulgated partly on the notion that the attacks of September 11 were so severe that they rose to the level of "hostile acts" under the law of war, thus giving rise to an armed conflict. Section 1(a) of the Order states that "[i]nternational terrorists, including members of al Qaeda, have carried out attacks on United States diplomatic and military personnel . . . within the United States *on a scale that has created a state of armed conflict* that requires the use of the United States Armed Forces."[106] This idea is based upon the argument that catastrophic terrorist acts can be so grave as to rise to the level of war crimes. The theory is, essentially, that terrorist attacks constitute acts of aggression, target innocent civilians for indiscriminate assault, and are carried out by irregular saboteur forces that neither identify themselves nor openly bear arms.[107] Terrorist acts, thus defined, are not functionally different from the crimes for which, for example, the eight saboteurs in *Quirin* were charged and prosecuted. Such acts, it is maintained, should be regarded as war crimes or crimes against humanity.[108] President Bush has both implicitly and explicitly made this argument in various public pronouncements since September 11. "Non-U.S. citizens who plan and/or commit mass murder," the president has asserted, "are more than criminal suspects. They are unlawful combatants who seek to destroy our country and our way of life."[109] It is highly significant, moreover, that the United States' NATO allies appear to have recognized the September 11 attacks as the inception of an armed conflict. In response to the September 11

105. *See generally* Fisher, *supra* note 10 (criticizing analogies between the Bush and Roosevelt decisions to authorize military commissions).

106. *Military Order* § 1(a), *supra* note 1, at 833 (emphasis added).

107. *See* Crona & Richardson, *supra* note 37, at 359 (citing YOSSEF BODANSKY, TARGET AMERICAN & THE WEST 2–3 (1993)).

108. *See id.* at 351 (citing the U.S. government's opening statement, during the second World Trade Center bombing trial, that "[t]his is a case involving a war").

109. Sanger, *supra* note 9, at A1.

attacks, NATO invoked Article 5 of its Charter on mutual defense for the first time in its history, which binds the signatories to regard an attack on one member as an attack on all.[110]

The assertion that the terrorist acts of September 11 could rise to the level of war crimes or crimes against humanity finds support in accepted principles of the law of war. In his famous treatise on military law and the law of war, William Winthrop explained, "[i]t is forbidden by the usages of civilized nations to take the lives of, or commit violence against, non-combatants and private individuals not in arms, including women and children . . . ."[111] Such acts, the treatise explains, constitute illegal warfare.[112] This well-established principle is based on the writings of early war theoreticians who had proposed bans on the use of incendiaries, as well as the strategy of making deliberate attacks on civilian populations.[113]

There can be little doubt, therefore, that according to accepted principles of the laws of war,[114] the attacks of September 11 were severe enough in terms of their purpose and effect to constitute war crimes. However, under *Quirin*, for the perpetrators of these assaults to have the status of unlawful belligerents, and thus be subject to trial by military commissions, the acts must have been committed "in time of war."[115] As the Court in *Quirin* explained, "those who during time of war pass surreptitiously from enemy territory into our own . . . for the commission of hostile acts involving destruction of life or property, have the status of unlawful combatants punishable as such by military commission."[116]

It is widely accepted that the assailants of September 11 and their accomplices entered the United States for the purpose of committing "hostile acts involving destruction of life or property" on a horrendous scale, and tragically were successful. Under *Quirin*, therefore, these attacks would seem to constitute "hostile and war-like act[s]"[117]

---

110. *The Day the World Changed*, *supra* note 19, at 14.

111. WINTHROP, *supra* note 32, at 315.

112. *Id.*

113. *See* WELLS, *supra* note 100, at 73 (noting, for example, that "[e]arly Roman Catholic Church Councils had proposed bans on the use of incendiaries, poisons, and the crossbow, as well as against the strategy of making deliberate war on civilians").

114. *See id.* at 73–85 (explaining general tenets of the laws of war); WINTHROP, *supra* note 32, at 315–21 (same).

115. *Ex parte* Quirin, 317 U.S. 1, 37 (1942).

116. *Id.* at 35.

117. *Id.* at 37.

capable of subjecting those responsible to punishment by military commissions. The real issue, then, is whether the attacks can be considered to have been executed "in time of war" (thus giving those responsible the status of "unlawful combatants") as *Quirin* would seem to require.

In describing the German saboteurs' unlawful warlike acts, the *Quirin* Court held that, "[b]y passing our boundaries for such [unlawful] purposes without uniform or other emblem signifying their belligerent status . . . such enemies *become unlawful belligerents* subject to trial and punishment [by military commission]."[118] This statement, as applied to the facts in *Quirin*, meant that once the saboteurs had passed surreptitiously and in civilian clothing into the United States with the intent to commit hostile and warlike acts, they acquired the status of unlawful belligerents, even though they were apprehended before they could execute their scheme. Applying this framework to the events of September 11, it would appear that once the terrorists boarded their respective planes with the intent to commit hostile, warlike acts, they similarly acquired the status of unlawful belligerents.

In *Quirin*, of course, the existence of a declared war meant that the saboteurs' unlawful acts were necessarily committed in wartime. However, as one international law scholar has argued, "as soon as the activities of any armed group reach the level at which the laws of war should apply, those laws must apply even if the enemy army is called 'terrorist' or engages in acts which violate the laws of war."[119] As discussed previously, there can be little doubt that the September 11 attacks were severe enough to constitute war crimes or crimes against humanity.[120] These acts of aggression, as the November 13 Order states, created a state of armed conflict.[121] Therefore, according to the analytical framework of *Quirin*, upon the event of the plane hijackings, the terrorists and their accomplices became unlawful belligerents, punishable by military commissions for offenses against the law of war. The Court in *Quirin* stated that "[t]he offense was complete when with that purpose [the saboteurs] entered . . . our territory in time of war . . . ."[122] On September 11, the attacks gave rise to a state

118. *Id.* (emphasis added).

119. Rubin, *supra* note 32, at 110.

120. *See supra* notes 105–116 and accompanying text.

121. *Military Order* § 1(a), *supra* note 1, at 57,833.

122. *Quirin*, 317 U.S. at 38.

of armed conflict and thus, technically, mark the inception of this resulting state of conflict. Therefore, the attacks, properly considered, are violations of the law of war. The ensuing state of armed conflict cannot be considered separately from the events that began the conflict.

Still, there are significant differences between the state of armed conflict in which the United States is presently engaged and the official wartime situation in which President Roosevelt authorized the use of military commissions. Despite the president's proclaimed "war on terrorism,"[123] the United States is not officially at war, as critics of the Military Order have been quick to observe. Thus, while President Roosevelt was acting pursuant to express congressional authority and, therefore, according to Justice Jackson's concurring opinion in *Youngstown*, was at the apogee of his power, President Bush's authority to convene commissions is less certain.[124] *Quirin* nevertheless provides a valid constitutional basis for the president's Order. While President Bush lacks a congressional declaration of war, Congress did pass, and President Bush signed, the Authorization for Use of Military Force Joint Resolution, which enables the president to use "all necessary and appropriate force against those nations, organizations, or persons" that he determines planned or aided the terrorist attacks of September 11.[125]

Presidents have been able to rely on such congressional statements as the basis for their authority in armed conflicts even without an official declaration of war, as demonstrated in Vietnam with the Gulf of Tonkin Resolution.[126] The power of Congress to declare war has long been recognized as the power to define war. In *Talbot v. Seeman*,[127] for example, the Supreme Court recognized Congress's power to declare a "partial war" targeted at a specific form of enemy aggression, even while the United States was not "at war" with the enemy nation in the traditional sense.[128] In *Talbot*, the Court ruled on

123. For a discussion of President Bush's objectives, see Bumiller, *supra* note 21, at A1.

124. *See supra* notes 101–105 and accompanying text.

125. S.J. Res. 23, 107th Cong., 115 Stat. 224 (2001).

126. HENKIN, *supra* note 66, at 47; *see also* Sheffer, *supra* note 62, at 281 (arguing that the Tonkin Gulf Resolution was the "functional equivalent" of a declaration of war).

127. 5 U.S. (1 Cranch) 1 (1801).

128. *Id.* at 15; *see also* Crona & Richardson, *supra* note 37, at 361 ("A reasonable inference from Chief Justice Marshall's analysis [in *Talbot*] is that the War Powers Clause enabled Congress to authorize hostilities against a particular kind of predatory military activity *without* declaring a full-scale war against a nation in the traditional sense.").

certain measures Congress had adopted to deal with French privateers who were preying on American commercial vessels. Chief Justice Marshall held that "[C]ongress may authorize general hostilities . . . or partial hostilities, in which case the laws of war, so far as they actually apply to our situation, must be noticed."[129] Therefore, according to *Talbot*, the Constitution seems to recognize imperfect, or "quasi," war. The War Powers Clause[130] allows Congress to authorize the use of force against specific types of predatory military activities without declaring a full-scale war.[131]

It is established, moreover, that in response to an attack upon the United States, such as that which occurred on September 11, the president has unquestioned constitutional authority as commander in chief to defend the nation.[132] Without a congressional declaration of war, or even other authorization from Congress, the power of the president to engage the armed forces in conflict to "repel invasion" is clearly established.[133] Congressional authorization to respond to an attack on the United States is simply assumed.[134] Thus, in such circumstances, the president has the authority not only to repel the attack, but also to wage to whatever extent necessary the war imposed on the United States.[135]

Justice Stone's opinion in *Quirin* seems to contemplate the president's authority to punish violations of the law of war through military commissions, even in the absence of an express declaration of war by Congress. Nowhere in the opinion is there any mention of the need for a congressional declaration of war. It would be strange, furthermore, if in light of the Supreme Court's recognition of imperfect war, *Quirin* was confined only to expressly declared wars. That the Court in *Quirin* may have contemplated the president's power to establish military commissions in situations other than in an officially

129. *Talbot*, 5 U.S. (1 Cranch) at 28.

130. U.S. CONST. art. I, § 8, cl. 11 ("The Congress shall have Power . . . . [t]o declare War, grant Letters of Marque and Reprisal, and make Rules concerning Captures on Land and Water.").

131. *Talbot*, 5 U.S. (1 Cranch) at 28.

132. *See* HENKIN, *supra* note 66, at 47–48 ("Without awaiting a Congressional declaration of war, or other authorization from Congress, the power of the President to use the troops and do anything else necessary to repel invasion is beyond question.").

133. The Prize Cases, 67 U.S. (2 Black) 635, 668 (1862) ("If a war be made by invasion of a foreign nation, the President is not only authorized but bound to resist by force.").

134. HENKIN, *supra* note 66, at 48.

135. *See The Prize Cases*, 67 U.S. (2 Black) at 668 ("He does not initiate the war, but is bound to accept the challenge without waiting for any special legislative authority.").

declared war also seems plausible because of an ambiguous statement toward the end of the opinion, which leaves room for a broad reading of the case. "We have no occasion now," said the Court, "to define with meticulous care the ultimate boundaries of the jurisdiction of military tribunals to try persons according to the law of war."[136] It is important to note that because the customary laws of war apply to cases of international armed conflict as well as to officially declared war, an actual declaration of war is not an essential condition for the application of this body of law.[137]

Thus, the broadly worded Joint Resolution of September 14 seems to have put the president in a very strong position by giving him the authority to conduct a constitutionally recognized "quasi war." President Bush therefore has the constitutional power under *Quirin* to establish military commissions to punish offenses against the law of war, even without an official declaration by Congress.

IV. Remaining Obstacles to the Use of Commissions: Extralegality Under Customary International Law and Policy Ramifications

A. *Inconsistency With International Law*

While the Bush administration's Military Order technically meets the constitutional requirements set forth in *Ex parte Quirin*, it is inconsistent with international law, of which the laws of war are a subset. Under existing international law, only states are recognized as having legal "personality"—that is, the capacity to hold rights and to be subject to obligations within the international legal system.[138] The laws of war, therefore, apply only to state actors, not to individuals.[139] Despite the increase in incidents of international terrorism over the past several decades, the laws of war do not make special provision

136. *Ex parte* Quirin, 317 U.S. 1, 45–46 (1942) ("We hold only that *those particular acts* constitute an offense against the law of war which the Constitution authorizes to be tried by military commission.") (emphasis added).

137. U.S. DEP'T OF THE ARMY, FIELD MANUAL NO. 27-10: THE LAW OF LAND WARFARE 8 (1956).

138. BYERS, *supra* note 15, at 75.

139. *See* W.J. Fenrick, Remarks at the Annual Meeting of the American Society of International Law (Apr. 25, 1985), *in* 79 AM. SOC'Y INT'L L. PROC. 112, 114 (1985) ("Except in the near nonexistent case of the *leveé on mass*, individuals have no legal right to assume combatant status on their own initiative. Individuals may perform the most monstrous acts for what they consider to be the purest of motives.").

for terrorists or terrorist activities.[140] Thus, for individuals to be tried and punished for offenses against the laws of war, they must be acting as agents of a recognized state.[141] In *Quirin*, for example, the eight saboteurs were agents of Nazi Germany and could thus be tried for offenses in violation of the law of war.[142] Those supposedly responsible for the attacks on September 11, by contrast, were acting not as agents of any recognized state but, rather, as members of an independent terrorist organization.[143] These suspects therefore cannot, consistent with *existing* international law, be tried before military commissions for violating the laws of war.

Recognizing this obstacle, the Bush administration is seeking to effect a rapid change in customary international law so that the laws of war can be made applicable to such nonstate actors as the members of al Qaeda.[144] The United States cannot, however, effectuate such a change unilaterally. Customary international law results from a consensual process of consistent and general practice among states, which they follow out of a sense of legal obligation, or *opinio juris*.[145] New customary rules (e.g., the recognition that the law of war applies to individual nonstate actors) must derive from the state practice of a large number of states.[146] States creating new customary rules must intend for those rules to exist and must adjust their practices accordingly.[147]

While a new rule recognizing that the laws of war may be applied to independent terrorist organizations may be evolving, no consistent

140. Frits Kalshoven, Remarks at the Annual Meeting of the American Society of International Law (Apr. 25, 1985), *in* 79 AM. SOC'Y INT'L L. PROC. 114, 115 (1985).

141. *See, e.g.*, *Quirin*, 317 U.S. at 35–36 (holding that saboteurs acting as agents for the Third Reich could be prosecuted for violations of the laws of war).

142. *Id.*

143. *See* Bumiller, *supra* note 21, at A1 (stating that President Bush declared that al Qaeda was a "terrorist network that . . . involved thousands of people in more than 60 countries"). While al Qaeda is believed to have been supported by the Taliban regime in Afghanistan, *id.*, the Taliban was considered a rogue regime and was never officially recognized by the United States. *See* AHMED RASHID, TALIBAN 118 (2000) ("Mullah Omar . . . periodically offer[ed] the U.S. and U.N. an end to poppy cultivation, if the Taliban were given international recognition – the first time a movement controlling 90 percent of a country had offered the international community such an option.").

144. *Hearings*, *supra* note 16 (testimony of Scott L. Silliman).

145. RESTATEMENT (THIRD) OF FOREIGN RELATIONS LAW § 102(2) (1986); BYERS, *supra* note 15, at 130.

146. BYERS, *supra* note 15, at 193.

147. *Id.*

and general state practice has yet emerged.[148] To apply the laws of war to nonstate terrorist groups is to recognize implicitly that such entities have international legal personality.[149] The Bush administration has announced, however, that the prisoners held at the U.S. Naval Base in Guantanamo are not legally entitled to Prisoner of War (POW) status under the Third Geneva Convention of 1949, although the detainees will be treated "in a manner *consistent with the principles*" of the Convention.[150] As a justification for the denial of POW status for the al Qaeda suspects, the Bush administration has announced that "Al-Qaeda is not a state party to the Geneva Convention; it is a foreign terrorist group. As such, its members are not entitled to POW status."[151] Not only is this decision lacking in precedent,[152] it applies existing rules of international law, which recognize only states as having legal personality, to what the Bush administration is seeking to establish as a new customary rule. No consistent and general state

148. A declared practice by one state alone could, if acquiesced to by other states, constitute a modification of customary international law. *Id.* at 133 (citing *Case Concerning Military and Paramilitary Activities In and Against Nicaragua*, 1986 I.C.J. 109 (para. 207)). The United States, however, is the only nation currently following this practice, and has been criticized for it. *See, e.g.*, Thalif Deen, *Rights: Int'l Bodies Oppose U.S., Western Curbs on Freedom*, INTER PRESS SERV., Nov. 29, 2001 (detailing the concerns of Mary Robinson, U.N. High Commissioner for Human Rights, over planned trials before military commissions); Betsy Pisik, *U.S. Ambassador Brushes Off Rights Concerns*, WASH. TIMES, Nov. 30, 2001, at A17 (describing sharp criticism abroad of the November 13 Military Order establishing commissions); Sebastian Rotella, *Saudi-Backed Web Supports Terrorism, Book Asserts France: "Forbidden Truth" Details Kingdom's Role in Funding Bin Laden and Contends Geopolitical Concerns Have Influenced U.S. Policy*, L.A. TIMES, Jan. 13, 2002, at A11 (noting the French government's criticism of the U.S. plan to prosecute suspected terrorists before military commissions).

149. *See* BYERS, *supra* note 15, at 75:

> In the international legal system the principle of personality has the consequence that only those individuals or entities which have international legal personality are entitled to participate in the process of customary international law, and only those individuals or entities which have full international legal personality are entitled to participate fully in that process.

150. Press Release, *supra* note 22 (emphasis added). The Bush administration is presumably seeking to avoid classifying the Taliban and al Qaeda suspects as POWs because such status would, under Article 102 of the Third Geneva Convention of 1949, prevent them from being tried by military commissions. Article 102 states "A prisoner of war can be validly sentenced only if the sentence has been pronounced by the same courts according to the same procedure as in the case of members of the armed forces of the Detaining Power." Geneva Convention Relative to the Treatment of Prisoners of War, Aug. 12, 1949, art. 102, 75 U.N.T.S. 135. Therefore, POW status in this case would entitle the Guantanamo suspects to trial by courts-martial, pursuant to the UCMJ and entailing the full protections afforded to American military personnel. *Id.*

151. Press Release, *supra* note 22.

152. *See* Seelye, *supra* note 22, at A1 (discussing the Pentagon's decision in Vietnam to grant the Vietcong POW status).

practice recognizing the legal personality of independent terrorist groups can thus be determined to have evolved.

Even if such a custom does take shape, however, it cannot be applied retroactively through the November 13 Military Order to the acts of September 11 without violating the *Ex Post Facto* Clause of the Constitution.[153] Customary international law is incorporated into the federal common law.[154] To apply a customary rule retroactively, therefore, would quite clearly constitute an *ex post facto* law, as the laws of war at the time of the September 11 attacks did not apply to nonstate entities. The Order, as currently written, will thus remain an extralegal action under existing international law.

B. Policy Implications Concerning the Use of Military Commissions

Assuming the possibility that the United States could bring about a rapid change in existing customary international law so that the law of war could be applied to nonstate terrorist groups, there are serious policy considerations that mitigate against doing so. As one scholar has noted, "One man's terrorist is another's freedom fighter."[155] Such a rule would open nongovernmental organizations, including relief agencies, to politically motivated prosecutions throughout the developing world.[156]

Furthermore, to characterize members in terrorist organizations as unlawful combatants and recognize them as subject to the laws of war could mean that, in certain instances, members of terrorist groups might be entitled to combatant and POW status.[157] Such recognition would thus confer a degree of political legitimacy and respectability upon such groups that is neither warranted nor prudent.

153. U.S. CONST. art. I, § 9, cl. 3.

154. The Nereide, 13 U.S. (9 Cranch) 388, 423 (1815) ("[T]he Court is bound by the law of nations which is part of the law of the land."); Harold Hongju Koh, *Is International Law Really State Law?*, 111 HARV. L. REV. 1824, 1824 (1998).

155. Fenrick, *supra* note 139, at 112.

156. *Id.*

157. *See id.* at 113 ("[I]f the [terrorist] organizations and their members accept and apply the laws of armed conflict, they cannot be referred to as 'terrorist organizations' in any legal sense. Compliance with the law brings respectability in its train."). The Bush administration's decision not to classify officially the Guantanamo detainees as POWs has come under serious criticism as inconsistent with the Geneva Convention. *See* Katherine Q. Seelye, *A P.O.W. Tangle: What the Law Says*, N.Y. TIMES, Jan. 29, 2002, at A14 (quoting one critic of the decision as saying "since the United States government engaged in armed conflict in Afghanistan—by bombing and undertaking other military operations—the Geneva Conventions clearly do apply to that conflict").

It has been suggested that the problems facing the president's Military Order could be remedied through legislation if Congress were to amend 10 U.S.C. § 821 by authorizing commissions to prosecute not just violations of the laws of war but, also, violations of the broader laws of nations, which includes terrorism.[158] Such a change would give the president a clear statutory basis to establish commissions for the prosecution of terrorists.[159] As with the proposed change in customary international law, however, there are policy concerns that the use of military commissions might hinder the international campaign against terrorism. Spain, for example, has refused to extradite several suspected accomplices in the September 11 attacks to the United States because of fears that the suspected accomplices will face the death penalty.[160] Proceeding with military commissions in which defendants can be sentenced by two-thirds of the appointed members[161] is not likely to induce needed cooperation.

Trials in federal district courts or international war crimes tribunals would provide the most effective opportunities to convince the international community that the United States is proceeding fairly. With many Arab nations highly skeptical of the United States' military campaign,[162] trials before military commissions are not the best means by which to make the case against terrorism, and those responsible for it, to the world community. In a period during which the international campaign against terrorism has achieved significant success, it would be a mistake to give the terrorists any such benefit.

CONCLUSION

The November 13 Military Order authorizing noncitizens suspected of complicity in the attacks of September 11, 2001 to be tried by specially convened military commissions was an extraordinary measure designed to deal with an extraordinary problem—a surprise attack by an independent enemy force that does not fit easily into existing legal categories of lawful or unlawful combatants.

---

158. *Hearings*, *supra* note 16 (testimony of Scott L. Silliman).

159. *See id.* (stating that such a change "would empower military commissions . . . to prosecute acts of terrorism outside the context of a recognized state of armed conflict").

160. Frank Rich, *Confessions of a Traitor*, N.Y. TIMES, Dec. 8, 2001, at A23.

161. Department of Defense Military Commission Order, *supra* note 6, § 6(f).

162. *Poll: Muslims Call U.S. 'Ruthless, Arrogant'*, CNN.com, *at* http://www.cnn.com/2002/US/02/26/gallup.muslims/index.html (Feb. 26, 2002) (on file with the *Duke Law Journal*) (describing a poll in which a majority of people interviewed in nine Muslim countries were found to have unfavorable opinions of the United States and President Bush).

Although, under Supreme Court precedent, the Order technically meets constitutional muster, it is inconsistent with existing international law, which holds that only state actors have legal personality that subjects them to the laws of war. While this inconsistency may change over time if new rules of customary international law develop, the Military Order, as currently written, retroactively applies what may be a developing customary rule in violation of the *Ex Post Facto* Clause of the Constitution. A new rule of international law, which recognizes that the *jus belli* can be applied to such entities as al Qaeda, may be applied to terrorists in the future if such a rule develops. There are, however, a host of serious policy considerations that must be considered aside from the expediency of applying such a rule as a means of prosecuting the war on terrorism.

[14]

JUDICIAL REVIEW OF COUNTER-TERRORISM MEASURES: THE ISRAELI MODEL FOR THE ROLE OF THE JUDICIARY DURING THE TERROR ERA*

YIGAL MERSEL**

Terrorism has become a global phenomenon. It no longer affects just conflict-torn regions and fragile, hyper-cleavaged societies. Democracies, old and new, face a real challenge in the twenty-first century: how to maintain their democratic structure and principles, on the one hand, while decisively and effectively responding to the terror threat, on the other. As such, democracies have a constant need to balance democratic values and security. The main responsibility for confronting the danger of terrorism falls to the executive branch, and, to a lesser extent, the legislative branch.[1] Both are accountable to voters and directly responsible for guaran-

---

* This paper was written during my stay at NYU Law School 2003-2004, as Hauser Global Researcher, Fulbright Scholar and Emile Noel Fellow at the Jean Monnet Center. It was presented at a lecture given at NYU Center on Law and Security on February 2004, as well as at a lecture given at NYU Law School in the 9th Annual Herbert Rubin and Judge Rose Luttan Rubin International Law Symposium—"Foreign Relations Jurisprudence in the Post 9/11 Era" (February 2005).

Please note that this paper was completed and processed for printing before the Supreme Court of Israel decided the case regarding the eligibility of West Bank inhabitants to citizenship (see HCJ 7052/03 [2006] Adalha v. Minister of Interior (Unpublished, available at http://elyon1.court.gov.il/files/03/520/070/a47/03070520.a47.HTM)(Isr.)). For this reason, the paper will not refer to that important decision. That recent decision is worth by itself a separate analysis.

I wish to thank Joseph Weiler, Stephan Schulhofer, Eyal Benvenisti, Richard Pildes, Roger Zakheim, Roy Sheindorf, Yaron Gotleib, Karen Greenberg, Elizabeth Oliner Justin Florence, and Yoni Rosenzweig, as well as the editors of NEW YORK UNIVERSITY JOURNAL OF INTERNATIONAL LAW AND POLITICS, for their most helpful comments and assistance.

** Registrar of the Supreme Court, Israel. The arguments in this paper reflect the opinions of the author only and do not constitute an official statement of the Israeli Supreme court.

1. For an elaboration on the special role of the legislature via the executive in times of crises, and the role of the judiciary as enforcer of the legislature sovereignty, see Samuel Issacharoff & Richard H. Pildes, *Between Civil*

teeing both public safety and democracy. These branches are in charge of identifying the country's needs and hazards, framing a clear policy in response to these threats, and enforcing that policy. At the end of the day, counter-terrorism activity is mostly a combined effort of the executive and the legislature.

The role of the judiciary in the challenge of fighting terrorism, however, is not so obvious, as manifested recently in a number of dramatic decisions of the U.S. Supreme Court.[2] Indeed, judicial review of the measures and means used by other branches—be it counter-terrorism legislation like the Patriot Act[3] or executive counter-terrorism actions and policies like detentions and interrogations—raises many questions: Are these state actions subject to judicial review at all? Are they within the law or should they be considered as an extra-legal domain?[4] Can the courts decide the proper way to fight terrorism, and even if they can, should they? Do courts have the tools to adjudicate such delicate issues? Will judicial interference burden the fight against terrorism? Should these issues be left to the expert and accountable entities of the state, namely the legislature and the executive? If, after considering these questions, one concludes that courts should adjudicate counter-terrorism activities just as they adjudicate any other state action, there still nevertheless remain questions specific to the war against terror: Which law is applicable to these counter-terrorist activities? Is it the law of war? Or perhaps criminal law? And finally, what is the plausible balance between human rights and public safety in the era of terrorism?

This Article focuses on one case study to address most of these questions—the adjudication of counter-terrorism activities by the Israeli Supreme Court in recent years. It proposes a

---

Libertarianism and Executive Unilateralism: An Institutional Process Approach to Rights During Wartime, 5 THEORETICAL INQUIRIES L. 1 (2004).

2. *See* Rasul v. Bush, 542 U.S. 466 (2004); Hamdi v. Rumsfeld, 542 U.S. 507 (2004); Rumsfeld v. Padilla, 542 U.S. 426 (2004).

3. Uniting and Strengthening America by Providing Appropriate Tools Required to Intercept and Obstruct Terrorism (USA PATRIOT Act) Act of 2001, Pub. L. No. 107-56, 115 Stat. 272.

4. *See* Oren Gross, *Chaos and Rules: Should Responses to Violent Crises Always Be Constitutional?*, 112 YALE L.J. 1011, 1023 (2003) (arguing that war against terrorism can be conducted outside the law and that the executive's actions will be analyzed after the emergency ends); Diane P. Wood, *The Rule of Law in Times of Stress*, 70 U. CHI. L. REV. 455, 459 (2003) (arguing that the war against terror must be within the rule of law).

model for counter-terrorism adjudication, taking into account the special features of the terror problem within the legal context. This Article will show what possible role a Supreme Court can have in times of terror and what theoretical and practical developments in both substantive and procedural law may be adopted in order to preserve the rule of law and national security. I primarily argue that despite the unique characteristics of the "Terror Era," courts are still a crucial element in maintaining democracy and a proper separation of powers within government. The judiciary must not be left aside, for it has an important role in these matters, especially in times of crises. Using the right judicial doctrines and understanding the nature of crisis periods, as well as the limits of the courts, can result in a model of judicial review which, at the end of the day, will reinforce democracy and strengthen its ability to combat its enemies. A possible model of this kind is the jurisprudence of the Israeli Supreme Court in recent years.

The Supreme Court of Israel has dealt many times with questions regarding the role of the Court in the era of terrorism. The State of Israel, since its establishment, has been involved in wars and constant threats to domestic security. Counter-terrorism has become a part of daily reality in Israel. The last years, however, have been particularly severe, even in the abnormal context of Israeli reality.[5] Since September 2000, Israel has experienced frequent terror attacks, involving suicide bombings of buses, malls, and other public facilities, and deadly ambushes on cars.[6] Many Israeli citizens have been murdered in these attacks. Thousands more have been wounded.[7] Israel's economy and the rhythms of daily life have been severely damaged. Without opening discussion on the many dimensions of the Israeli-Palestinian conflict, it seems widely accepted that activities aimed solely at killing innocent

---

5. *See* Yuval Shany, *Israeli Counter-terrorism Measures: Are They "Kosher" Under International Law?*, *in* TERRORISM AND INTERNATIONAL LAW: CHALLENGES AND RESPONSES 96, 101-02 (Michael N. Schmitt & Gian Luca Beruto eds., 2003), *available at* http://web.iihl.org/iihl/Album/terrorism-law.pdf.

6. For a detailed description of this background, see Shany, *supra* note 5, at 100-02.

7. See the description given by the court itself in HCJ 2056/04 [2004], Beit Sourik Village Council v. Gov't of Israel, 58(5) P.D. 807, ¶ 1 (Isr.), *available at* http://elyon1.court.gov.il/eng/verdict/framesetSrch.html.

civilians should be considered terrorism.[8] This is the kind of frequent exposure to terrorism that other Western countries dread.

Under this terrorist assault, Israeli security forces—the Israeli Defense Force and other agencies—have taken numerous steps, ranging from border closings to "targeted killings." Many of these counter-terrorism measures were challenged before the Israeli Supreme Court.[9] Some of them were declared unlawful; others were ruled permissible.[10] Some decisions were heavily criticized by public officials and public opinion. Others were accepted calmly. All of these cases involved the basic question raised above: what is the proper role of the court in counter-terrorism adjudication? This Article analyzes the answer of the Israeli Supreme Court to this question. I argue that there is a distinct model for the role of the judiciary in a democracy during times of national crisis and the Terror Era. The approach of the Israeli judiciary is unique in comparison with the judges and courts in other democracies[11] and is especially remarkable when taking into account the context of the troubling reality in Israel. The Article analyzes this Is-

8. *See* Emanuel Gross, *Democracy in the War Against Terrorism–The Israeli Experience*, 35 LOY. L.A. L. REV. 1161, 1164-66 (2002) [hereinafter Gross, *Democracy in War*]; Emanuel Gross, *Democracy's Struggle Against Terrorism: The Powers of Military Commanders to Decide Upon the Demolition of Houses, the Imposition of Curfews, Blockades, Encirclements and the Declaration of an Area as a Closed Military Area*, 30 GA. J. INT'L & COMP. L. 165, 179 (2002) [hereinafter Gross, *Democracy's Struggle*] ("There is no doubt that the activities carried out in Israel at present are violent activities carried out by terrorist organizations."); Desmond K. Derrington, *The Terrorist Threat: Australia's Response*, 13 IND. INT'L & COMP. L. REV. 699, 699 (2003) ("Terrorism . . . may be described as an attack on innocent civilian targets for the propose of furthering a political cause"); Shany, *supra* note 5, at 102. For a wider definition—and its critics—see Kent Roach, *The New Terrorism Offences and the Criminal Law*, *in* THE SECURITY OF FREEDOM—ESSAYS ON CANADIAN ANTI-TERRORISM BILL 151, 154-160 (Ronald J. Daniels et al. eds., 2001).

9. *See infra* Part I.

10. *See infra* Part I.

11. I do not analyze the broader comparison between the powers and jurisprudence of the Israeli Supreme Court to other courts in various democracies. For an example of such an analysis comparing the Israeli Supreme Court with the United States Supreme Court, see Marcia Gelpe, *Constraints on Supreme Court Authority in Israel and the United States: Phenomenal Cosmic Powers; Itty Bitty Living Space*, 13 EMORY INT'L L. REV. 493 (1999); John T. Parry, *Judicial Restraints on Illegal State Violence: Israel and the United States*, 35 VAND. J. TRANSANT'L L. 73 (2002).

raeli jurisprudence as a possible model for the role of courts in times of terrorism and heightened counter-terrorism activity. I will not seek to justify these specific decisions or to comment on the larger and more complex aspects of the Israeli-Palestinian conflict;[12] rather, the Article highlights the philosophy of the judicial review in these cases. One might question the relevance of the Israeli experience due to the special Israeli circumstances. Indeed, the Israeli reality is a special one. Other countries might have different views regarding the role of courts in counter-terrorism matters.[13] These varying stances arise from the constitutional traditions and democratic legacies of those nations and are linked to national histories and previous experiences in times of war or crisis. As a result of these diverging legacies, comparing different countries in this context is not always easy, but it is still essential. As terrorism has become a global phenomenon, the problems it raises are similar from one country to another. All democracies seek the proper balance between human rights and security, all democracies seek a clear definition of the role of courts in times of national emergency, and all democracies can learn from one another. Despite historical differences between countries, comparative law might provide new insights regarding the role courts can play in times of national crisis.[14] In this context, the Israeli model regarding the role of the courts in adjudicating counter-terrorism can offer an interesting and useful comparison, despite the obvious differences between nations.

Part I outlines some of the major cases where the Israeli Supreme Court has reviewed counter-terrorism measures. This

---

12. For more elaborated research on the different opinions of the Israeli Supreme Court and the administrated territories, see generally DAVID KRETZMER, THE OCCUPATION OF JUSTICE (2002). I rely heavily on this seminal work, as many of the cases of counter-terrorism were also connected to the administrated territories. There are, however, cases and counter-terrorism activities that are not connected to the administrated territories; these justify a distinct overview. For a further analysis of the legal aspects of Israeli-Palestinian conflict, see also Shany, *supra* note 5, at 97-103.

13. *See, e.g.*, Stephan J. Schulhofer, *Checks and Balances in Wartime: American, British and Israeli Experiences*, 102 MICH. L. REV. 1906 (2004); Mary Arden, *Human Rights in the Age of Terrorism*, 121 L. Q. REV. 604, 619 (2005).

14. For a discussion on the importance and relevance of comparative law, see Aharon Barak, *Foreword: A Judge on Judging: The Role of a Supreme Court in a Democracy*, 116 HARV. L. REV. 16, 110-14 (2002) [hereinafter Barak, *A Judge on Judging*].

outline will provide a basic knowledge about the different issues brought before the Court and the wide range of cases it has handled, revealing the willingness of the Court to consider almost any case on its merits, regardless of its "operational" or "wartime" character. Part II connects the legal dots among the cases to reveal underlying theories of counter-terrorism adjudication that the Court is advancing. I argue that the Court is willing to review a broad range of counter-terrorism activities and has special legal mechanisms for balancing human rights and public safety. Part III argues that the Israeli Supreme Court's practice is a model for other democracies. I also present parameters for evaluating the Israeli practice and suggest that other democracies might consider the adoption of that model in equivalent circumstances.

I. Legal Challenges to Counter-Terrorism Measures

Analysis of cases is the most effective way to examine the Israeli Supreme Court's perspective in regard to its role in counter-terrorism. Since judges seldom opine on these issues ex-officio,[15] they mostly do so either explicitly in their written opinions or, more subtly, through the outcome of their judgments. Thus, I refer mostly to the cases themselves.[16] I outline some of the main counter-terrorism decisions, especially those since 2000, and I refer to categories of cases based on the specific counter-terrorism measure challenged before the Court. This presentation will enable us not only to get a fair impression of the variety of cases that the Court was willing to address but also of the difficult reality that Israeli society and courts face. It will also show how far-ranging the adjudication of counter-terrorism measures has become. It is important to note that the following discussion does not comprehensively cover all of the hundreds of opinions that constitute the Israeli

15. *See id.* at 148-60; Dorit Beinisch, *The Role of the Supreme Court in the Fight Against Terrorism*, 37 Isr. L. Rev. 281, 298 (2004); Aharon Barak, *The Role of a Supreme Court in a Democracy and the Fight Against Terrorism*, 58 U. Miami. L. Rev. 125 (2003).

16. For historical reasons, the Israeli Supreme Court traditionally has been the only court that heard cases against the state in constitutional and administrative matters. Today, some of these cases are heard before District courts, but the more important ones, including most of the counter-terrorism-cases, are still heard by the Supreme Court in the first and last instance. For a further description, see Kretzmer, *supra* note 12, at 10-11.

court's jurisprudence on these issues. My aim is not to report on all of these cases and the specific developments of the case law, but rather to use some of the cases to highlight the main philosophy of the Court in adjudicating counter-terrorism.

This section is divided according to the different forms of counter-terrorism measures reviewed by the Court: preventive measures such as detention and arrest, assigned residence of inhabitants, house demolitions, and the "separation fence;" interrogation methods; the course of actual combatant activity; provisions for civil liability of the armed forces; and electoral laws banning candidates who support terror activities.

A. *Preventative Measures*

Perhaps the most obvious counter-terrorism tactic is prevention. Thus, Israeli security forces have exerted a great deal of effort tracing potential terrorists and thwarting their activities. Most of these counter-terrorism methods have been challenged in the Israeli Supreme Court, examples of which I discuss below.[17]

1. *Detention and Arrest*

One of the basic counter-terrorism measures often used by the security services is detention and arrest, mostly in order to prevent future terrorist acts. Israeli legislation provides a specific framework for this activity: administrative detention, which differs from regular criminal detention.[18] Administrative detention is exercised by the executive branch, does not require a prior judicial order, and can be used only for preventing danger rather than as a sanction.[19] Its legality has

---

17. I do not address all of the practices challenged in the Supreme Court—such as curfews, blockades or deportations—as it is my goal only to create a baseline for the characteristics of the court's jurisprudence. For other challenges to the court, see Gross, *Democracy in War, supra* note 8, at 1209-14; Gross, *Democracy's Struggle, supra* note 8, at 212-28. For a discussion on deportations, see Kretzmer, *supra* note 12, at 165-86.

18. *See* Emergency Powers (Detention) Law, 5739-1979, 33 L.S.I. 89-92 (Isr.) (outlining procedure for detention).

19. *See, e.g.*, ADA 10/80 [1980], Kahana v. Minister of Defense, 35(2) P.D. 253, 257-60 (Isr); ADA 4/94 [1994], Ben-Horin v. State of Israel, 48(5) P.D. 329, 333-37 (Isr).

subsequently been reviewed by the courts.[20] In the early 1990s, a group of Lebanese, including some suspected terrorists, were arrested through this administrative detention procedure.[21] After some time, however, it became clear that the sole justification for their arrest was the fact that terror organizations were allegedly holding Israeli soldiers as hostages; the Lebanese were detained as "bargaining chips" to use in future negotiations for the release of the Israeli hostages.[22] A panel for the Court first held in a 2-1 decision that the administrative detention law authorized detention for reasons of state security and that the possible release of Israeli soldiers satisfied this requirement.[23] This decision was, however, overturned by a 6-3 decision in 2000.[24] The Court held that the scope of the term "state security" should be interpreted by balancing human dignity and state security.[25] After applying this balancing test, the court ruled that a person cannot be held in detention solely to be employed as a "bargaining chip," nor can he be held responsible for the wrongs of others despite the fact that his detention might be crucial to state security and the return of the Israeli soldiers.[26] As a result of this decision, most of the Lebanese detainees were released, although two were kept in administrative detention after it was proven that their release might endanger state security.[27]

In an ancillary case, the court considered the legality of the state's refusal to allow these Lebanese prisoners visits from the Red Cross.[28] Israel refused this access for security reasons,

20. The Emergency Powers (Detention) Law sets a mechanism according to which a detainee must be brought in front of the president of a district court within 48 hours of his arrest, for a judicial review of the detention. A further review of the detention is done every three months by the court. *Id.* art. 4-5.

21. ADA 10/94 [1997], Anonymous Persons v. Minister of Defense, 53(1) P.D. 97 (Isr.).

22. *See id.* at 111 (Dorner, J., dissenting).

23. *See id.* at 109-10.

24. *See* CrimA 7048/97 [2000], Anonymous Persons v. Minister of Defense, 54(1) P.D. 721 (Isr.).

25. *Id.* at 740-41.

26. *Id.* at 741-42.

27. *See* CrimA 5652/00 [2000], Ubeid v. Minister of Defense, 55(4) P.D. 913 (Isr.).

28. HCJ 794/98 [2001], Ubeid. v. Minister of Defense, 55(5) P.D. 769 (Isr.).

namely because Israel was not given any information about the condition of the Israeli POWs.[29] The Lebanese detainees petitioned the court, arguing that they were entitled to these visits.[30] The court ruled that the petitioners were indeed entitled to Red Cross visits by balancing state security on the one hand and humanitarian consideration on the other.[31] As time goes on, the court noted, the weight of the humanitarian interest increases while the weight of the security concern decreases.[32] Since the detainees were held for many years, and in light of the humanitarian concern, the Court decided that they were entitled to Red Cross visits despite the lack of reciprocity.[33]

In a more recent decision, the court dealt with detentions exercised during the military operation known as "Protective Wall" (or "Defensive Shield").[34] This operation, undertaken by the Israel Defense Force (IDF) as a reaction to the bombing of a Passover dinner in an Israeli hotel that killed dozens,[35] included searches and arrests of terrorists in the West Bank.[36] Throughout the course of the operation, thousands of people were arrested. The prevailing law on which these arrests were based enabled the military to hold detainees without judicial review of their arrest for twelve days.[37] Due to the massive numbers of detainees, the law also allowed the military to postpone the initial questioning of the detainees for up to four days after their arrest.[38] The court struck down these two pro-

---

29. *Id.* at 772-73.
30. *Id.* at 771-72.
31. *Id.* at 773-75.
32. *Id.* at 774.
33. *Id.*
34. *See* HCJ 3278/02 [2002], Ctr. for the Def. of the Individual v. IDF Commander, 57(1) P.D. ¶¶ 1-2 (Isr.), *available at* http://elyon1.court.gov.il/eng/verdict/framesetSrch.html.
35. For a more detailed description of the operation and its legal aspects, see Shany, *supra* note 5, at 110-13.
36. The legal basis for these detentions is not the Israeli law, which is not directly applicable to the administrated territories, but rather local law dating back to the British Mandate. *See* Defense (Emergency) Regulations, 1945, Palestine Gazette 1083, art. 111 (Isr.); s*ee also* KRETZMER, *supra* note 12, at 129-30.
37. Israel Defense Force, Order Number 1505: Detentions in Time of Warfare (Temporary Order), Amend. 2 (June 4, 2002).
38. *See* HCJ 3239/02 [2002], Marab v. IDF Commander in the West Bank, 57(2) P.D. 349, ¶ 6 (Isr.), *available at* http://elyon1.court.gov.il/eng/verdict/framesetSrch.html.

visions. It ruled that prompt judicial review of detention is an inherent part of the legality of the detention measures, especially while the detainee is still presumed innocent, as is the case in most administrative detentions.[39] On this basis, the practice of allowing twelve days before judicial review of the detention was declared illegal under international law and Israeli administrative law principles.[40] The court also found the practice of holding detainees for four days with no actual questioning to be illegal on the same grounds, finding this period to be too long a delay for a simple questioning that might show immediately whether there was justification for the detention.[41]

Following these massive arrests, the detainees were placed in detention camps in the West Bank and in Israeli territory.[42] Petitions were brought to the court by detainees in both camps arguing that the detention conditions were inhumane and in violation of international law.[43] They claimed they were held in overcrowded tents, and were exposed to harsh weather conditions with inadequate bedding, a shortage of food, a deprivation of personal belongings, and insufficient medical treatment.[44] The court reviewed the factual and legal issues behind each of their claims and found that, although most of the claims were eventually satisfactorily resolved by the detaining authorities, some specific improvement had to be made in order to respect the detainees' human dignity and to meet the standards of international law.[45] The Court declared that

39. *Id.* ¶¶ 26-27, 36.

40. *See id.* ¶¶ 32-36.

41. *See id.* ¶¶ 48-49.

42. For the facts of the cases, see HCJ 5591/02 [2002], Yassin v. Commander of Kziot Military Camp, 57(1) P.D. 403, ¶¶ 1-2 (Isr.), *available at* http://elyon1.court.gov.il/eng/verdict/framesetSrch.html; HCJ 3278/02 [2002]; Ctr. for the Def. of the Individual v. IDF Commander, 57(1) P.D. 385, ¶ 2 (Isr.), *available at* http://elyon1.court.gov.il/eng/verdict/frameset Srch.html.

43. *See Yassin,* 57(1) P.D. ¶¶ 3, 6; HCJ 3278/02 [2002], Ctr. for the Def. of the Individual v. IDF Commander, 57(1) P.D. ¶¶ 3-5 (Isr.), *available at* http://elyon1.court.gov.il/eng/verdict/framesetSrch.html.

44. *See* HCJ 5591/02, Yassin v. Commander of Kziot Military Camp, 57(1) P.D. 403, ¶¶ 3, 6 (Isr.), *available at* http://elyon1.court.gov.il/eng/verdict/framesetSrch.html; *Ctr. for the Def. of the Individual,* 57(1) P.D. ¶¶ 3-5.

45. *See Yassin,* 57(1) P.D. ¶¶ 14-20; *Ctr. for the Def. of the Individual,* 57(1) P.D. ¶ 28.

some aspects of the detention conditions in the early stages of the camps' operation were therefore illegal.[46]

2. *Assigned Residence*

One of the means used by the IDF in order to prevent suicide bombings was an order of assigned residence. This order, issued under the authority of Article 78 of the Fourth Geneva Convention,[47] authorized the transfer of an individual from one area within the administrated territories to another.[48] It was used against family members of suicide bombers, who had allegedly cooperated with and assisted the bombers.[49] Three petitions were submitted to the Supreme Court, challenging the legality and the factual basis of the orders.[50]

---

46. *See Yassin*, 57(1) P.D. ¶ 14; *Ctr. for the Def. of the Individual*, 57(1) P.D. ¶ 26.

47. The article states:

> If the Occupying Power considers it necessary, for imperative reasons of security, to take safety measures concerning protected persons, it may, at the most, subject them to assigned residence or to internment. Decisions regarding such assigned residence or internment shall be made according to a regular procedure to be prescribed by the Occupying Power in accordance with the provisions of the present Convention. This procedure shall include the right of appeal for the parties concerned. Appeals shall be decided with the least possible delay. In the event of the decision being upheld, it shall be subject to periodical review, if possible every six months, by a competent body set up by the said Power. Protected persons made subject to assigned residence and thus required to leave their homes shall enjoy the full benefit of Article 39 of the present Convention.

Geneva Convention Relative to the Protection of Civilian Persons in Time of War art. 78, Aug. 12, 1949, 6 U.S.T. 3516, 75 U.N.T.S. 287.

48. The assignment was from the West Bank to the Gaza Strip. One of the points the Court had to address was whether these two territories could be perceived as one territorial unit, rather than as two distinct ones. The later possibility would face the argument that the assignment was actually a deportation and legally problematic under Article 49 of the Geneva Convention. For a critical review of the Court's decision in this aspect, see Eyal Benvenisti, Case Review: Ajuri et al. v. IDF Commander in the West Bank et al. (unpublished manuscript), *available at* http://www.tau.ac.il/law/members/benvenisti/articals/Ajuri%20et%20al-1.pdf; Shany, *supra* note 5, at 110.

49. *See* HCJ 7015/02 [2002], Ajuri v. IDF Commander in the West Bank, 56(6) P.D. 352, ¶¶ 5, 9, 31-39 (Isr.), *available at* http://elyon1.court.gov.il/eng/verdict/framesetSrch.html.

50. *See id.*

The Court ruled that Article 78 does enable the military commander to assign the residence of an inhabitant for security reasons. However, this power cannot be used against an innocent person only in order to deter others. It can only be used against a person who himself poses a danger.[51] It is a preventative measure and not a sanction. Furthermore, this action should be used proportionally to the present danger, and only after pursuing less rights-infringing means such as normal criminal proceedings.[52] Finally, the Court emphasized that the authority needed to have a firm evidentiary basis before moving an individual, and needed to show at least a reasonable possibility that the assignee presented a real threat of danger.[53] Following this reasoning, the Court upheld two of the decisions to assign residence.[54] The Court cancelled another order, finding insufficient evidence of the person's direct involvement in aiding terrorist activity.[55]

3. *House Demolitions*

In many cases following a terrorist attack, the IDF demolishes the house of the terrorist.[56] It does this mainly to deter

---

51. *See id.* ¶ 24. A different question was whether the decision could take into consideration whether the outcome would deter others in addition to the individual in question. The court answered this question in the affirmative, holding that the deterrence of other terrorists could be considered along with the deterrence of the individual assignee. *See id.* ¶ 27.

52. *See id.* ¶¶ 24-26. In a later case, for example, the Court noted that the principle of proportionality was properly respected as the length of the assigned residence was proportional to the specific danger of each individual. Furthermore, it held that the assigned residence is less of an infringement upon human liberty than detention and thus its usage is preferred if it achieves the required goal of deterrence. *See* HCJ 9586/03 [2003], Sulama v. IDF Commander in the West Bank, 58(2) P.D. 342, 346-47 (Isr.).

53. *See Ajuri*, 56(6) P.D. ¶ 25.

54. *Id.* ¶¶ 32, 36.

55. *Id.* ¶ 39. For further consideration of this decision, see Detlev F. Vagts, *Ajuri v. Idf Commander in West Bank. Case No. HCJ 7015/02. [2002] Isr.L.Rep 1. Supreme Court of Israel, September 3, 2002*, 97 AM. J. INT'L L. 173 (2003). The author notes that "[o]ne wonders whether, if security problems in the United States were to reach the same level of intensity, American courts would do as well." *Id.* at 175.

56. For the origins of this power in Israeli domestic law and in the administrated territories, see Gross, *Democracy in War, supra* note 8, at 1204-06.

terrorists.[57] This measure is administrative rather than part of any criminal procedure, and is considered severe because it often results in the loss of housing for an entire family, even though the family was not involved in the terrorist activity.[58] As a matter of practice, the IDF has also used this tactic in cases where the terrorist died or escaped from the country.[59] In numerous cases, petitioners have requested that the Court cancel these demolition orders.[60] Upon review, the Court ruled that this counter-terrorism method can be used to deter terrorists but not to punish them, and that no international or domestic law renders the practice illegal.[61] The fact that other people, namely the families of the terrorists, were affected by this action was not found to make the action itself illegal under international law.[62] However, there are some restraints on the use of this power. For instance, the Court decided that generally there should be a hearing before the execution of the order.[63] Furthermore, this action should be carried out according to principles of proportionality. If it is possible to accomplish the same goal by demolishing only a part of the house or one room, or by sealing the house, then it should not be destroyed.[64]

4. *The "Separation Fence"*

The most recent decisions handed down by the Court regarding counter-terrorism measures ruled on the legality of

---

57. For a general overview of the house demolition practice, including the policy arguments underlying it, and statistical data on its usage, see Brian Farrell, *Israeli Demolition of Palestinian Houses as a Punitive Measure: Application of International Law to Regulation 119*, 28 BROOK. J. INT'L L. 871, 884-99 (2003).

58. *See, e.g.*, HCJ 4772 [1992], Hizran v. IDF Commander in Judea and Samaria, 46(2) P.D. 150, 154 (Isr.).

59. *See* KRETZMER, *supra* note 12, at 152.

60. *See, e.g.*, HCJ 8575/03 [2004], Azazdin v. IDF Commander in the West Bank, 58(1) P.D. 210 (Isr.); HCJ 8262/03 [2003] Ab-Salim v. IDF Commander in the West Bank, 57(6) P.D. 569 (Isr.); HCJ 8084/02 [2003], Abasi v. Commander of the Homefront, 57(2) P.D. 55 (Isr.).

61. HCJ 6288/03 [2003], Saada v. Commander of the Homefront, 58(2) P.D. 289 (Isr.).

62. HCJ 2977/91 [1992], Muhammed v. Minister of Def., 46(5) P.D. 467, 473 (Isr.).

63. *See* KRETZMER, *supra* note 12, at 155-157.

64. *See* HCJ 5510/92 [1993], Turkeman v. Minister of Def., 48(1) P.D. 217, 219 (Isr.); *see also* Gross, *Democracy in War*, *supra* note 8, at 1206-07.

the "Separation Fence."[65] The Israeli government had decided to build an obstacle to improve and strengthen operational capability in the framework of fighting terror and to prevent the penetration of terrorists from the West Bank, Judea, and Samaria, into Israel.[66] The purpose of the fence was to prevent the uncontrolled passage of residents of the area into Israel and into Israeli towns located nearby.[67] The separation fence was also intended to prevent the smuggling of arms, the infiltration of terror cells into Israel, and new recruits from joining existing cells.[68] In order to build the fence, the Israeli authorities seized large areas of land, mostly Palestinian.[69]

Petitioners argued before the Israeli Supreme Court that the fence was illegal, primarily because it would infringe upon the petitioners' most basic liberties and make access to these agricultural lands difficult if not impossible.[70] Petitioners' ability to go from place to place would depend on a complex and burdensome bureaucratic permit regime. Use of local water wells would not be possible. Shepherding, which depends on access to these wells, would be made difficult. Tens of thousands of olive and fruit trees would be uprooted. The livelihood of many hundreds of Palestinian families, based on agriculture, would be critically injured.[71] Moreover, the petitioners argued that the separation fence would injure not only landowners to whom the orders of seizure apply but also the lives of 35,000 village residents which would be disrupted.[72] Access to medical and other services in East Jerusalem and in other places would become impossible.[73] Children's access to schools in the urban centers and students' access to universi-

65. HCJ 2056/04 [2004], Beit Sourik Village Council v. Gov't of Israel, 58(5) P.D. 807, ¶ 12 (Isr.), *available at* http://elyon1.court.gov.il/eng/verdict/framesetSrch.html; HCJ 7957/04 [2005], Mara'abe et al. v. The Prime Minister, ¶¶ 73-74 (unpublished decision) (Isr.), *available at* http://elyon1.court.gov.il/eng/verdict/framesetSrch.html.

66. *Beit Sourik Village Council*, 58(5) P.D. ¶ 12.

67. *Id.* ¶ 12.

68. *Id.*

69. *Id.* ¶ 8.

70. *Id.* ¶ 9.

71. *Id.*

72. *Id.*

73. *Id.*

ties would be impaired.[74] The petitioners argued, thus, that these injuries could not be justified.[75]

In a detailed decision the court ruled per curium that the petitions should be partly accepted.[76] The Court pointed out that the commander in charge cannot take into account any political considerations but must ground his decision solely on the balance between the needs of the army on the one hand and the needs of the local inhabitants on the other.[77] This balance should be done according to the principle of proportionality.[78] The military decision can be justified therefore only if it meets three conditions. First, the means used must rationally lead to the realization of the objective. Second, the means used must injure the individual to the least extent. Third, the damage caused to the individual by the means used by the army must be of proper proportion to the gain brought about by that means.[79] In applying this three-part test, the court reached the conclusion that some of the seizure actions were unjustified. The Court rationalized that even if it can be assumed that building the fence would achieve and promote national security, and even if there is no alternative means that is less restrictive, some of the seizure actions were illegal under principals of international law and Israeli administrative law because the damage they caused to the individual was not proportional to the gain brought about.[80]

The legality of the separation fence was brought again to the Israeli Supreme Court, following the publication of the advisory opinion of the International Court of Justice which declared the fence to be a violation of international law.[81] The Israeli Supreme Court, in a very detailed decision, did not decide to declare the mere building of the fence a violation of

74. *Id.*
75. *Id.*
76. *Id.* ¶ 86.
77. *Id.* ¶ 27.
78. *See Id.* ¶¶ 36-39.
79. *See Id.* ¶¶ 41-42.
80. *See Id.* ¶¶ 57-59. For a detailed review of the usage of the proportionality test in this case and its analytical critique, see Moshe Cohen-Eliya, *The Formal and the Substantive Meanings of Proportionality in the Supreme Court's Decision Regarding the Security Fence*, 38 Isr. L. Rev. 262 (2005).
81. Legal Consequences of the Construction of a Wall in the Occupied Palestinian Territory, Advisory Opinion, 43 I.L.M. 1009 (July 9, 2004), *available at* http://www.icj-cij.org/icjwww/idocket/imwp/imwpframe.htm.

international law, mainly due to some crucial deficiencies it had found in the advisory opinion of the ICJ.[82] However, while reviewing the legality of specific segments of the fence, the Court ruled that one specific segment violated the principle of proportionality and was therefore illegal. The Court opined that the executive could place the fence in a different location that would achieve the same goal of protecting security while infringing upon the Palestinian inhabitants in a less intrusive manner.[83]

B. *Methods of Interrogation*

Often, the most effective way to prevent and fight terrorism is through information from human resources, generally those held in custody. As important as this source of information may be, it also raises questions about the limits on interrogation techniques and methods.

In 1994, a group of petitioners challenged specific methods of interrogation employed by the Israeli General Security Services (GSS).[84] These methods included, among others, sleep deprivation and handcuffing for long periods of time. The petitioners argued that these practices constituted torture and were thus impermissible.[85] In 1999, in an 8-1 decision, the

82. Though the Israeli Supreme Court did recognize the normative value of the advisory opinion in terms of the current interpretation of international law, it did not follow the ICJ conclusion that the fence was illegal since it found that the ICJ opinion was not based on the same factual basis as the Israeli Court had seen it, both in terms of the necessity of building the fence as well as the amount of harm caused to the Palestinians inhabitants as a result of its construction. *See* HCJ 7957/04, Mara'abe et al. v. The Prime Minister, ¶¶ 73-74 (unpublished decision) (Isr.), *available at* http://elyon1.court.gov.il/eng/verdict/framesetSrch.html. For a further critique of the ICJ decision, both in terms of fact finding as well as its legal reasoning, see Emanuel Gross, *Combating Terrorism: Does Self Defence Include the Security Barrier? The Answer Depends on Who You Ask*, 38 CORNELL INT'L L.J. 569 (2005).

83. *See id.* ¶¶ 112-114.

84. *See* HCJ 5100/94 [1999], Pub. Comm. Against Torture in Israel v. State of Israel, 53(4) P.D. 817, ¶ 33 (Isr.), *available at* http://elyon1.court.gov.il/eng/verdict/framesetSrch.html.

85. As a matter of fact, there were also other petitions of this kind, but in adjudicating those, the Court did not address the core question of the legality of interrogation methods. *See* KRETZMER, *supra* note 12, at 135-140. For a general background to the Israeli practice and the legal efforts to challenge it, see TORTURE—HUMAN RIGHTS, MEDICAL ETHICS AND THE CASE OF ISRAEL 73-95 (Neve Gordon & Ruchama Marton eds., 1995).

court declared these practices to be unlawful.[86] Without explicitly stating whether these practices amounted to torture,[87] the Court held that any infringement of human dignity, and especially of the physical integrity of a detainee, must be proscribed by law. The GSS had failed to point to any legal provision authorizing the use of such methods, and they were therefore declared illegal according to Israeli constitutional and criminal law.[88] The Court added, however, that there might be circumstances where an interrogator would act illegally using such methods but would nevertheless have the opportunity to employ a "necessity" defense which, if successful, would excuse his or her actions and avoid the imposition of criminal liability.[89]

In another case, the Court considered whether the right to a hearing applied during war.[90] The IDF sometimes demolishes houses of terrorists for immediate security reasons, commonly granting a hearing immediately before the execution of the decree.[91] The Court heard the question of whether this right should also be protected during warfare.[92] The Court answered that the right to be heard is elementary and basic and therefore also applicable during times of war.[93] However, this right is not absolute and might be overcome by operational needs if the hearing might jeopardize the mission or risk the lives of soldiers.[94] If there is an operational possibility

86. *See Pub. Comm. Against Torture in Israel*, 53(4) P.D. ¶ 33.

87. The official Israeli position was that these techniques did not amount to torture. For a critique of this position see Barak Cohen, *Democracy and the Mis-Rule of Law: The Israeli Legal System's Failure to Prevent Torture in the Occupied Territories*, 12 IND. INT'L & COMP. L. REV. 75 (2001).

88. *See Pub. Comm. Against Torture in Israel*, 53(4) P.D. ¶ 33. An open question is whether the court would uphold or strike down a law which specifically enables the usage of such interrogation techniques. For different opinions in this regard, see Amnon Reichman & Zvi Kahana, *Israel and the Recognition of Torture: Domestic and International Aspects*, *in* TORTURE AS TORT: COMPARATIVE PERSPECTIVES ON THE DEVELOPMENT OF TRANSNATIONAL HUMAN RIGHTS LITIGATION 631, 633-43 (C. Scott ed., 2001).

89. *See Pub. Comm. Against Torture in Israel*, 53(4) P.D. ¶¶ 33-38.

90. *See* HCJ 6696/02 [2002], Amar v. IDF Commander in the West Bank, 56(6) P.D. 110 (Isr.).

91. *See supra* note 57 and accompanying text.

92. *See Amar*, 56(6) P.D. at 114.

93. *Id.* at 114-16.

94. *Id.*

to provide a hearing, however, the commander in the field must grant it.[95]

C. *Combatant Activity*

Perhaps the most significant cases of counter-terrorism adjudication by the Israeli Supreme Court are those that deal with direct combat activity. In a few decisions, the Supreme Court was asked to rule on the legality of certain fighting strategies and troop movements in real time. These cases demonstrate, again, the intensive involvement of the Court in adjudicating counter-terrorism measures.

In one case, petitioners challenged the usage of flechette shells by the IDF.[96] These shells contain a cluster of steel darts that are dispersed over an area of several hundred square meters upon detonation at a certain altitude.[97] The petitioners argued that the usage of these shells was forbidden under international law since this kind of weapon does not differentiate between combatants and non-combatants.[98] The Court rejected the petition, ruling that this weapon was not banned by any of the conventions that Israel had signed and was not forbidden under international law.[99]

Another challenged provision was a military order that gave the commanding officer the authority to prevent a detainee from meeting with a lawyer for up to thirty-four days.[100] The officer could exercise this authority if he believed that such a meeting would hamper the effectiveness of the interrogation.[101] The Israeli Supreme Court upheld this provision, finding that despite the importance of the basic right to an attorney, it is not an absolute one and could be abridged by a significant security consideration, including the risk of damage

---

95. *Id.*

96. HCJ 8990/02 [2003], Physicians for Human Rights v. O.C Southern Command, 57(4) P.D. 193, ¶ 1 (Isr.), *available at* http://elyon1.court.gov.il/eng/verdict/framesetSrch.html [hereinafter *Physicians III*].

97. *Id.*

98. *See Physicians III*, 57(4) P.D. ¶ 2.

99. *Physicians III*, 57(4) P.D. 193.

100. *See* HCJ 3239/02, Marab v. IDF Commander in the West Bank, 57(2) P.D. 349, ¶¶ 39, 45 (Isr.), *available at* http://elyon1.court.gov.il/eng/verdict/framesetSrch.html.

101. *See id.* ¶ 39.

to an investigation.[102] In the specific circumstances, the Court found the length of the detention to be reasonable.[103]

In another case, the petitioners challenged the practice of the IDF to ask local Palestinian inhabitants to warn a suspect that he is about to be arrested and that there is a potential harm to him and people surrounding him.[104] The Court decided that this practice was forbidden under international law, noting that there is a rule against the compulsory involvement of civilians in combatant activity of the occupying power.[105] This rule also applies in circumstances where the inhabitant agrees to warn the suspect person.[106] The Court pointed out that there is clear tendency of international law to distinguish civilians from combatants.[107] Furthermore, there is an inherent inequality between the occupying force and the local residents and therefore there is a real risk that the inhabitant's consent will not be real.[108] Finally, the risk imposed upon an inhabitant who will be asked to cooperate is greater than one could expect.[109] For these reasons, the Court declared the IDF policy in this regard as unlawful.[110]

---

102. *See id.* ¶ 45.

103. *See id.* ¶ 46.

104. *See* HCJ 3799/02 [2005], Adalah v. GOC Cent. Commander IDF (unpublished decision) (Isr.), *available at* http://elyon1.court.gov.il/eng/verdict/framesetSrch.html (search by case number).

105. *See id.* ¶¶ 21-22.

106. *See id.* ¶¶ 23-24.

107. *See id.* ¶ 24.

108. *See id.*

109. *See id.*

110. *See id.* It is interesting to note that the Justices presiding in this case had seen it as a very hard case. Justice M. Chesin had opined in this context that "The subject is a difficult one. Most difficult. So difficult that a judge might ask himself why he chose the calling of the judiciary, and not of another profession, to fill his time." *Id.* (remarks of Vice President M. Cheshin). For a discussion of the moral and practical problems in the treatment of civilians during counter- terrorism activities, see generally Emanuel Gross, *Use of Civilians as Human Shields: What Legal and Moral Restrictions Pertain to a War Waged by a Democratic State Against Terrorism?*, 16 EMORY INT'L L.REV. 445 (2002) (concluding that inflicting injuries upon innocents is prohibited, however the duty to avoid such harm is not absolute). The author specifically notes that if civilians were forced to march in front of soldiers during military operations in the area, "[s]uch a phenomenon should be condemned and cannot be justified." *Id.* at 506-07.

It should be also mentioned that, at the present, there is a pending petition at the Supreme Court questioning the Israeli practice of targeted killing of terrorists.[111] The petitioners argue that this practice is no different from an administrative assassination or an extra-judicial execution and is thus impermissible under international law.[112]

Other cases challenged before the Court involved not tactics and techniques, but rather specific actions taken by the IDF. In one case, for instance, petitioners argued that IDF soldiers opened fire on ambulances which were evacuating injured Palestinians.[113] The Court did not reach a conclusive result on this matter due to factual deficiencies.[114] It ruled,

111. In a short decision on this matter, given by a three judge panel, the court decided not to intervene in this policy since the decision about which method should be used for counter-terrorism is a matter for the other branches. *See* HCJ 5872/01 [2002], Barakeh v. Prime Minister, 56(3) P.D. 1 (Isr.). However, the issue of targeted killing is again being reviewed by the Court, in an enlarged panel of judges. This time, the Court had explicitly asked the parties to submit written arguments on the applicable law and the legality of this method. *See* HCJ 769/02 [2002], Pub. Comm. Against Torture v. Gov't of Israel (unreported decision) (Isr.), *available at* http://elyon1.court.gov.il/files/02/690/007/a04/02007690.a04.htm.

112. Much had been written on this issue, both for and against. *See, e.g.*, Gross, *Democracy in War*, *supra* note 8, at 1194-1204; Emanuel Gross, *Thwarting Terrorist Acts by Attacking the Perpetrators or their Commanders as an Act of Self-Defense: Human Rights Versus the States Duty to Protect its Citizens*, 15 TEMP. INT'L. & COMP. L. J. 195 (2001) (arguing that the Israeli practice can be seen under certain condition as self defense); J. Nicholas Kendall, *Israeli Counter-Terrorism: "Targeted Killings" Under International Law*, 80 N.C. L. REV. 1069, 1070 (2002) (Israeli practice should not be considered as impermissible assassinations but rather as legitimate self-defense); Orna Ben-Naftali & Keren R. Michaeli, *'We Must Not Make a Scarecrow of the Law': A Legal Analysis of the Israeli Policy of Targeted Killings*, 36 CORNELL INT'L L.J. 233, 290-91 (2003) (concluding that targeted killings of combatants is permissible under exceptional circumstances, while targeted killings of non-combatants is impermissible); George Nolte, *Preventive Use of Force and Preventive Killings: Moves into a Different Legal Order*, 5 THEORETICAL INQUIRIES L. 111 (2004) (discussing whether modern law should define differently the concept of "immediacy," and hence the legality of preventive attacks or targeted killings).

113. *See* HCJ 2117/02 [2002], Physicians for Human Rights v. Commander of the IDF Forces in the West Bank, 56(3) P.D. 26, ¶ 1 (Isr.), *available at* http://elyon1.court.gov.il/eng/verdict/framesetSrch.html [hereinafter *Physicians I*]; *see also* HCJ 8990/02 [2003], Physicians for Human Rights v. O.C. Southern Command, 57(4) P.D. 193 (Isr.), *available at* http://elyon1.court.gov.il/eng/verdict/framesetSrch.html.

114. *See id.* ¶ 4.

however, that this kind of practice, if it existed, would be impermissible under international law unless it were shown that the ambulances were a camouflage for terrorist activity.[115]

A few cases were brought before the court about the curfew around the Church of Nativity in Bethlehem. During fights in that city, a group of Palestinian terrorists had entered the Church of Nativity, which was populated by many church clergy and Palestinian civilians.[116] In the first case, the petitioners argued that there was a shortage of water and food in the church.[117] The Court ruled that there was no shortage.[118] In the second case, the petitioners argued that the curfew was illegal since innocent people were being held in the church as well.[119] The court rejected the petition because there was no evidence that any civilian in the church was not allowed to leave the area on his free will.[120] The Court noted again that there was no shortage of food or water in the church.[121] Eventually, an international compromise brought the curfew to an end, and the civilians were released and the terrorists were deported to European countries.[122] At that point, an additional petition was submitted to the court, this time by an Israeli civilian whose relatives were killed and injured by one of the terrorists who was released from the church, asking the Court to order the Israeli Minister of Justice to request the extradition of these terrorists from the European countries that hosted them.[123] The Court rejected the request because the interna-

115. *See id.* ¶ 9. In a previous case on the same matter, the court noted the duty of the IDF to issue sufficient guidelines for its soldiers regarding the special international law status of medical units. *See* HCJ 2936/02 [2002], Ass'n of Physicians for Human Rights v. Commander of IDF Forces in the West Bank, 56(3) P.D. 3, 5 (Isr.) [hereinafter *Physicians II*].

116. *See* HCJ 3436/02 [2002], La Custodia Internazionale di Terra Santa v. Gov't of Israel, 56(3) P.D. 22, 24 (Isr.); HCJ 3451/02 [2002], Almandi v. Minister of Def., 56(3) P.D. 30, ¶ 11 (Isr.), *available at* http://elyon1.court.gov.il/eng/verdict/framesetSrch.html.

117. *La Custodia Internazionale di Terra Santa*, 56(3) P.D. at 23.

118. *Id.* at 24.

119. *See Almandi*, 56(3) P.D. ¶ 11.

120. *See id.* ¶ 11.

121. *See id.*

122. HCJ 10223/02 [2003], Fish-Lifschitz v. Attorney-General, 57(3) P.D. 517, ¶ 52 (Isr.), *available at* http://elyon1.court.gov.il/eng/verdict/frameset Srch.html.

123. *See id.* ¶ 3.

tional agreement was a matter of Israeli foreign policy in which the Court had no basis for intervening.[124]

D. *Civil Liability*

It is important to note that the legal influence on counter-terrorism activities does not always concern cases of actual fighting or combating.

For instance, a different set of cases confronted by the Supreme Court involved the civil liability of the state for counter-terrorism measures taken by Israeli security forces. Many Palestinians were killed and injured by the activities of Israeli forces in the West Bank between 1987 and 1993. In some cases, it was argued that the shootings were not justified and were, in fact, negligent because the victims were innocent civilians.[125] The state claimed sovereign immunity from some of these suits and others arising from "actions of war."[126] The Court first ruled that the term "war" can include counter-terrorism activities with the exact scope of the term to be decided on a case-by-case basis.[127] However, counter-terrorism actions are not inherently immune from civil liability, the Court decided.[128] In that specific case the Court held that the shooting of a Palestinian was not done in a battle situation presenting actual danger to the Israeli force.[129] Therefore the Court found no justification to grant the state immunity.[130]

In other important decisions, the Court ruled on the required burden of proof for tort litigation of counter-terrorism activity.[131] The Court declined to adopt a rule holding that

124. *See id.* ¶ 5.

125. *See, e.g.*, CA 1071/96 [2004] El-Abed v. State of Israel (unpublished decision) (Isr), *available at* http://elyon1.court.gov.il/files/96/710/010/p04/96010710.p04.pdf; CA 6521/98 [2000] Buatna v. State of Israel (unpublished decision) (Isr), *available at* http://elyon1.court.gov.il/files/98/210/065/a11/98065210.a11.pdf.

126. *See, e.g.*, *El-Abed* ¶ 11; CA 1354/97 [1997] Mahmud v. State of Israel (unpublished decision) (Isr.), *available at* http://elyon1.court.gov.il/files/97/540/013/a07/97013540.a07.pdf; CA 5964/92 [2002], Uda v. State of Israel, 56(4) P.D. 1, 9 (Isr.).

127. *Uda*, 56(4) P.D. at 8-9.

128. *Id.*

129. *Id.* at 9.

130. *Id.*

131. CA 2176/94 [2003], State of Israel v. Tabanja, 57(3) P.D. 693 (Isr.); *El-Abed*.

the state always bears the burden to prove that the shooting was justified.[132] In a more recent case the Court ruled on the relevant standard of care that must be taken in a negligence case during counter-terror and war activity.[133] The main question was whether the standard of care varies between wartime and peacetime.[134] The Court ruled that the mere existence of an emergency does not necessarily change the standard of care.[135] Nevertheless, circumstances of stress, danger, and risk are relevant in assessing liability.[136] In that specific case, the Court ruled that injuries sustained while security forces were breaking apart a violent demonstration constituted negligence. The soldiers were not in danger, and they were firing harmful ammunition in the dark without sufficient warning even though more proportional and less hazardous ammunition and methods were available.[137]

E. *Electoral Laws*

A more remote issue involving counter-terrorism adjudication in the courts was the decision of the Elections Committee to ban the participation of a list of candidates as well as a few individual candidates from the 2003 Knesset elections.[138] The Elections Committee took this action based on a finding that these candidates supported the combat activities of terrorist organizations.[139] The Court ruled that although the Israeli Basic Law allows such a ban,[140] it should be exercised only in

---

132. CA 2176/94 [2003], State of Israel v. Tabanja, 57(3) P.D. 693, 700 (Isr.); *El-Abed* § 17.

133. CA 5604/94 [2004], Hamed v. State of Israel, 58(2) P.D. 498 (Isr).

134. *Id.* at 508.

135. *Id.* at 508-09.

136. *Id.* at 508.

137. *Id.* at 513-14.

138. The Elections Committee held three days of hearings regarding this issue in December 2002. *See Protokolim shel Diyune Vaadat HaB'chirot* [*Minutes of the Deliberations of the Central Elections Committee*] (Dec. 29-31, 2003), *available at* http://www.knesset.gov.il/elections16/heb/protocols/menu.htm.

139. *See id.*; *see also* CA 11280/02 [2003], Cent. Election Comm. v. Tibi, 57(4) P.D. 1, 32-33, 43-46 (Isr.).

140. Basic Law: The Knesset, art. 7A, amend. 35, 5762-2002, 1845 S.H. 440 (Isr.), *available at* http://www.mfa.gov.il/mfa/go.asp?MFAH00h80 (Isr.) ("A candidates list shall not participate in elections to the Knesset, and a person shall not be a candidate for election to the Knesset, if the goals or actions of the list or the actions of the person, expressly or by implication, include one

extreme situations where the candidates' support for terrorists was decisively proven.[141] The Court found insufficient evidence in all cases and hence allowed these candidates to participate in the elections.[142]

II. The Underlying Theory: War Within the Law

What do these cases, collectively, reveal? They show a clear tendency by the Court to adjudicate almost any aspect of counter-terrorism, as well as a willingness to nullify important executive actions. The Israeli court not only hears cases concerning ex post activities, but also considers policies on an ex

of the following: (1) negation of the existence of the State of Israel as a Jewish and democratic state; (2) incitement to racism; (3) support for armed struggle by a hostile state or a terrorist organization against the State of Israel."). For previous usages of this constitutional provision, in cases where the political party was considered as an-democratic or racial, see Raphael Cohen-Almagor, *Disqualification of Lists in 1988 and 1992: A Comparative Analysis, in* Law Justice and the State II 88, 88-103 (Michel Troper & Mikael M. Karlsson eds., 1995); Raphael Cohen-Almagor, *Disqualification of Political Parties in Israel: 1988-1996*, 11 Emory Int'l. L. R. 67 (1997).

141. *See Tibi*, 57(4) P.D. at 27. It should be noted that the possibility to disqualify a list of electoral candidates within a democracy is not an obvious one. *See generally* Yigal Mersel, *The Dissolution of Political Parties: The Problem of Internal Democracy*, 4 Int'l. J. Const. L. 84, 84-87 (2006). Some countries – Germany for instance – grant the Constitutional Court the power to dissolve a non-democratic political party. *See* Donald P. Kommers, The Constitutional Jurisprudence of the Federal Republic of Germany 217-24 (2d ed. 1997). A similar authority exists in Spain. *See* Katherine A. Sawyer, *Rejection of Weimarian Politics or Betrayal of Democracy?: Spain's Proscription of Batasuna Under the European Convention on Human Rights*, 52 Am. U. L. Rev. 1531, 1534-35 (2003); *see also* Leslie Turano, *Spain: Banning Political Parties as a Response to Basque Terrorism*, 1 Int'l. J. Con. L. 730, 730-31 (2003). However, England and the United States are examples of countries which lack this authority. For a comparative analysis of this phenomenon, see Dan Gordon, *Limits on Extremist Political Parties: A Comparison of Israeli Jurisprudence with That of the United States and Germany*, 10 Hastings Int. & Comp. L. Rev. 347 (1987).

142. *See Tibi*, 57(4) P.D. at 43-45, 50-51. It should be noted that the decision in that case was not unanimous, and some Justices joined a minority opinion finding that there was sufficient evidence to ban Azmi Bishara and the Balad Party due to their support of terror activity or the negation of the Jewish-democratic character of the state of Israel. *See id.* at 69-73 (Sternberg-Cohen, J., dissenting with respect to Bishara and Balad Party), 81-82 (Levine, J., dissenting with respect to Bishara and Balad Party), 100-04 (Terkel, J., dissenting with respect to Bishara and Balad Party), 109-13 (Levy, J., dissenting with respect to Bishara and Balad Party).

ante basis.[143] It does not limit the scope of its review to procedural aspects; instead, it rules on delicate issues of combatant activities and interrogation conditions. These decisions and this spectrum of cases, however, do not by themselves make this Israeli jurisprudence a coherent model. Further analysis is needed in order to better understand these rulings and their reasoning. Hence this Part focuses on the main features of Israel's model of counter-terrorism adjudication.

A. *The Starting Point: Rule of Law*

Perhaps the most basic question that the Israeli Court has addressed is the normative framework of counter-terrorism. On numerous occasions the court has ruled, and clearly so, that the war against terror must be fought within the rule of law and not outside of it:

> This combat is not taking place in a normative void. It is being carried out according to the rules of international law, which provide principles and rules for combat activity. The saying, "when the cannons roar, the muses are silent," is incorrect. Cicero's aphorism that laws are silent during war does not reflect modern reality.[144]

The Court used this language despite the fact that the terrorists aim to destabilize the democratic social order of freedom, liberty, and human rights. The idea behind the concept of "war within the law" is that since terrorism is an attempt to break the law and disrupt the public order, the fight against terrorism must be a war fought by the law itself against the forces threatening it.[145] Furthermore, this fight can be conducted only according to the rule of law because "[t]he power of society to stand against its enemies is based on its recognition that it is fighting for values that deserve protection. The

143. *See* H.C.J. 4764/04 [2004], *Physicians for Human Rights et al. v. Commander of the IDF Forces in the Gaza Strip*, 58(5) P.D. 385, ¶ 15 (Isr.), *available at* http://elyon1.court.gov.il/eng/verdict/framesetSrch.html [hereinafter *Physicians IV*] (Barak, J.).

144. H.C.J. 3451/02 [2002], Almandi v. The Minister of Def., 56(3) P.D. 30, ¶ 9 (Isr.), *available at* http://elyon1.court.gov.il/eng/verdict/framesetSrch.html.

145. *Id.* ¶ 9.

rule of law is one of these values."[146] The Court maintains that its proper role in a democracy is to protect the formal and substantive rule of law. It should enforce the law against all state actors, be they legislative or executive, and it should maintain the proper protection of human rights.[147] The Court should, at the same time, balance these principles, rights, and values with the interests of state security and public safety. Judges have a duty to balance national security and human rights, in times of peace and of war.[148] Terrorist actions and counter-terrorism activity are not exceptions to the rule, but rather a more difficult case, as the terrorists do not respects the laws of war. Difficult as it is, the essence of the Court's role may be greater in dire times, when long-term values and principles tend to be pushed aside, not always justifiably, for short-term measures supported by public opinion. The Court is aware that its decisions might not be popular, but this concern does not dilute its duty to protect democratic values and the rule of law. In the court's words:

> [E]ven when the cannons speak, the military must uphold the law. The power of society to stand against its enemies is based on its recognition that it is fighting for values that deserve protection. The rule of law is one of these values . . . [T]he position of the State of Israel is a difficult one. Our role as judges is also not easy. We are doing all we can to balance properly between human rights and the security of the area. In this balance, human rights cannot receive complete protection, as if there were no terror, and State security cannot receive complete protection, as if there were no human rights. A delicate and sensitive balance is required. This is the price of democracy. It is expensive, but worthwhile. It strengthens the State. It provides a reason for its struggle. Our work, as

146. *See* HCJ 7015/02 [2002], Ajuri v. IDF Commander in the West Bank, 56(6) P.D. 352, ¶ 41 (Isr.), *available at* http://elyon1.court.gov.il/eng/verdict/framesetSrch.html (quoting HCJ 168/91, Morcos v. Minister of Def., 45(1) P.D. 467, 470).

147. *See, e.g., Ajuri*, 56(6) P.D. ¶ 41; *Almandi*, 56(3) P.D. ¶ 9.

148. HCJ 3239/02 [2002], Marab v. IDF Commander in the West Bank, 57(2) P.D. 349, ¶ 19 (Isr.), *available at* http://elyon1.court.gov.il/eng/verdict/framesetSrch.html.

judges, is hard. But we cannot escape this difficulty, nor do we wish to do so.[149]

B. *Terrorism and Counter-terrorism: A Holistic Approach*

Another feature of Israeli jurisprudence in these matters is the understanding that terrorism is a complex phenomenon that involves more than just an actual physical threat. Similarly, counter-terrorism involves not only the detention or interrogation of a potential terrorist. It also includes dealing with political support for terror activities, such as that by a political party;[150] it includes issues of free speech, such as the ability to restrict or ban the broadcasting of a movie that describes counter-terrorism activity as war crimes;[151] and further, it includes problems of civil liability in cases of "collateral damage" or injuries to innocent civilians during counter-terrorism operations.[152]

All of these cases, and others, confront the same questions: how should a democracy fight terrorism, and what is the proper balance between human rights and national security? The Court's answer in one case will influence how it decides others. If the Court decides, for instance, that soldiers have a duty of care in torts for injuries to bystanders during operational counter-terrorism activity, that ruling may directly affect how the army functions in future operations. As a result, the Court must adopt a coherent jurisprudence regarding the dif-

---

149. *See Ajuri*, 56(6) P.D. ¶ 41.

150. *See* CA 11280/02 [2003], Cent. Election Comm. v. Tibi, 57(4) P.D. 1 Isr.).

151. In a recent case, the court reversed a decision of the film review board to ban the projection of a film named "Jenin-Jenin." This movie depicted in details the Palestinian argument that the activities of the IDF in the Jenin refugee camp on April 2002, were crimes of war and a massacre. The court held that this decision to ban the movie cannot stand. Despite the fact that the allegations in the movie were proven to be false and despite the emotional stress it caused to Israeli society and to the families of soldiers who died during the activities, a free and democratic society must tolerate this kind of speech and not ban it, especially as there is a more proportional means to cope with it. This is true, said the court, also in times of national crisis although it might be that public safety will be given more importance during these times than in times of peace. *See* HCJ 316/03, Mohamad Bakri v. Israel Film council, 58(1) P.D. 249, ¶¶ 17 (Isr.), *available at* http://elyon1.court.gov.il/eng/verdict/framesetSrch.html.

152. *See supra* notes 126-36132 and accompanying text.

ferent aspects of counter-terrorism. Following the assumption that terrorism and counter-terrorism have many different ramifications, the Court must develop a holistic approach to all of these problems.

C. *Adjudicating Counter terrorism—Procedural Aspects*

One of the immediate questions that arises from the wide perspective adopted by the Court is as follows: what *procedures* are used by the court to implement its basic view regarding the adjudication of counter-terrorism?

1. *The Jurisdiction and Standing Requirement: The Open Court*

An almost directly derivative conclusion of the court's starting viewpoint, according to which counter-terrorism must be within the law and not outside it, is the wide interpretation of its jurisdiction. It has been decided that the Court has jurisdiction over these matters because they involve actions of the executive branch, which are as a matter of principle under the jurisdiction if the Court.[153] Israeli security forces, the army, and other agencies all operate as part of the executive branch and are thus subject to judicial review.[154] Under this approach, there is no activity conducted by the executive that is precluded from the Court's jurisdiction, despite the fact that it might be manifested even during war.[155] Such an approach literally opens the doors of the court to many cases.

A further openness can be found in the standing requirement as adopted—or neglected—by the Court. As the Court sees itself as an essential part of the "democratic triangle" (Legislature-Executive-Judiciary), and as it understands its role as the main guardian of the rule of law, there is almost no standing requirement for the Israeli Supreme Court—not in

153. KRETZMER, *supra* note 12, at 21. *See also* ISRAEL, THE "INTIFADA" AND THE RULE OF LAW 61-70 (David Yahav et al. eds., 1993).

154. *See, e.g.*, HCJ 2056/04 [2004], Beit Sourik Village Council v. Gov't of Israel, 58(5) P.D. 807, ¶ 45 (Isr.), *available at* http://elyon1.court.gov.il/eng/verdict/framesetSrch.html; HCJ 393/82 [1983], Iscan v. Commander of the IDF, 37(4) P.D. 785, 810 (Isr.).

155. *See* HCJ 4764/04 [2004], Physicians for Human Rights v. Commander of the IDF Forces in the Gaza Strip, 58(5) P.D. 385, ¶ 15 (Isr.), *available at* http://elyon1.court.gov.il/eng/verdict/framesetSrch.html; *see also* HCJ 910/86 [1988], Ressler v. Minister of Def., 42(2) P.D. 441, 478.

times of peace and certainly not in time of war.[156] Almost any person directly affected by a state action can come to Court claiming that the action was unlawful.[157] Thus, detainees in Israeli territory were able to challenge their own interrogation methods. The Court is willing to hear cases from inhabitants of the West Bank, despite the fact that Israeli law as such is not directly applicable to these territories.[158] If a petitioner argues that the Israeli military is acting unlawfully, the petition will normally not be rejected on the grounds that the petitioner is not an Israeli citizen or inhabitant.[159] The Court heard, for instance, cases on conditions in detention camps in the West Bank[160] and a petition brought by the family of a person killed in the West Bank in a target killing operation.[161] Furthermore, the Court usually does not require a petitioner to show that a direct interest or right of his was infringed. It is sufficient that a public interest in lawful governance was allegedly at play. Thus, many of the Israeli counter-terrorist activities are challenged in the court by NGO's like the Civil Rights Association, the Public Committee Against Torture,[162] the Center for the Defense of the Individual,[163] and Physicians for Human Rights.[164]

2. *Justiciability*

Traditionally, since the mid-1980s, the Israeli Supreme Court has rarely rejected a case on the basis of nonjusticiabil-

---

156. *See* KRETZMER, *supra* note 12, at 24-25.

157. *See* Barak, *supra* note 14, at 106-09.

158. *See, e.g.*, HCJ 3278/02 [2002], Ctr. for the Def. of the Individual v. IDF Commander, 57(1) P.D. 385, ¶¶ 1-2 (Isr.), *available at* http://elyon1.court.gov.il/eng/verdict/framesetSrch.html.

159. *See* Kretzmer, *supra* note 12, at 19-21.

160. *See supra* notes 38, 44.

161. *See* HCJ 5872/01 [2002], Barakeh v. Prime Minister, 56(3) P.D. 1 (Isr.).

162. *See* HCJ 5100/94 [1999], Pub. Comm. Against Torture in Israel v. The State of Israel, 53(4) P.D. 817, ¶ 2 (Isr.), *available at* http://elyon1.court.gov.il/eng/verdict/framesetSrch.html.

163. HCJ 3239/02 [2002], Marab v. IDF Commander in the West Bank, 57(2) P.D. 349, ¶ 19 (Isr.), *available at* http://elyon1.court.gov.il/eng/verdict/framesetSrch.html. .

164. *See supra* note 99. For an analysis of the role of NGO's and transnational organizations in times of national crises, especially as enforcers of international law, see Catherine Powell, *The Role of Transnational Norm Entrepreneurs in the U.S. "War on Terrorism"*, 5 THEORETICAL INQUIRIES L. 47 (2004).

ity.[165] Institutionally, it usually does not find that another institution—either the Legislature or the Executive—is better equipped to rule on the issue at hand. This idea also applies to counter-terrorism—the Court does not see itself as institutionally unfit to adjudicate issues of counter-terrorism. Furthermore, it almost always finds a normative framework on which it can base its adjudication. Thus, rarely does it reject a case because there is no normative standard for evaluating the legality of the state action.[166] The decision to go to war is thus an administrative decision that can be adjudicated on the basis of the reasonableness doctrine of administrative law;[167] the usage of a certain weapon could be legal or not according to international law,[168] or the legality of interrogation methods can be analyzed according to Israeli constitutional law.[169] There are areas in which the court is more modest than others about intervening in the executive's discretion, but these are mostly cases of foreign relations and international negotiations.[170] Even then, the Court will usually not rule that the issue is nonjusticiable per se, but rather that there is no basis for the Court's interference in the executive's discretion.[171] The number of cases decided on the merits, reported earlier in this Article, shows that almost all counter-terrorism activities have been held, up to this point, justiciable.[172] The reason for rejecting a petition that challenges counter-terrorism activity will result from a declaration that the activity was legal, or reasonable, or that the petition lacked factual basis, but the Court usually does not reject a case on the basis of nonjusticiability.

---

165. *See* KRETZMER, *supra* note 12, at 21-24.

166. *See* Barak, *A Judge on Judging*, *supra* note 14, at 97-101.

167. *See id.* at 98.

168. *Physicians III*, *supra* note 99.

169. HCJ 5100/94 [1999], Pub. Comm. Against Torture in Israel v. The State of Israel, 53(4) P.D. 817, ¶ 18 (Isr.), *available at* http://elyon1.court.gov.il/eng/verdict/framesetSrch.html.

170. HCJ 10223/02 [2003], Fish-Lifschitz v. The Attorney General, 57(3) P.D. 517, ¶ 5 (Isr.), *available at* http://elyon1.court.gov.il/eng/verdict/framesetSrch.html.

171. *See* Barak, *A Judge on Judging*, *supra* note 14, at 97-101.

172. There are, however, rare exceptions. *See* HCJ 5872/01 [2002], Barakeh v. Prime Minister, 56(3) P.D. 1, 16 (Isr.).

3. *Remedies*

Lastly, even when a counter-terrorism case is adjudicated by the Court, there is often a problem with the remedy that might be granted. In many of the cases, the Court is asked to issue an injunction until the hearing itself. For instance, the Court might order officials to refrain from interrogating a person or employing a certain method of counter-terrorism until its legality is analyzed. The decision to issue such an order is a very sensitive one, since issuing an injunction might make the counter-terrorism action ineffective, but refraining from doing so might make the hearing itself ineffective. The Court's practice in this regard is not definitive. In some cases—like some of the interrogation cases[173]—an injunction was issued; in others—like the targeted killings—it was denied.[174]

The problem of remedies becomes even more significant in the final judgment. Even if the Court concludes that a certain administrative activity is illegal, it might not necessarily issue an immediate remedy. For instance, the court might find that the detention of a suspected terrorist was illegal since a certain procedure was omitted. In such a case, the immediate release of the individual might cause a significant risk to public safety. Hence, the court might postpone or suspend the execution of its own judgment for some time, thereby enabling the administration to use an alternative means that is legal. For example, when the Court decided that the detention of a person for twelve days with no judicial review of the arrest was illegal and that the detention of a person for four days without even preliminary questioning of him was also illegal, it did not order the immediate execution of the judgment.[175] Doing so could have had direct consequences on the detention of many suspected terrorists.[176] Hence, the Court ruled

173. KRETZMER, *supra* note 12, at 138-140.

174. *See Pub. Comm. Against Torture*, 53(4) P.D. 817.

175. HCJ 3239/02 [2002], Marab v. IDF Commander in the West Bank, 57(2) P.D. 349, ¶ 49 (Isr.), *available at* http://elyon1.court.gov.il/eng/verdict/framesetSrch.html.

176. This is due to the fact that most of the detainees were detained on the basis of these decrees, which were found eventually as illegal. The immediate execution of the judgment could have raised the argument that all detainees should be released immediately. According to the court in *Marab*, 7,000 people were detained on the basis of these decrees, and during the hearing at the court, 1,600 of them were still in custody. *Id.* ¶ 1.

that its judgment would come into force six months later.[177] This suspension period enables the executive to devise and implement a legal regime of detention and arrest. Thus, by suspending and postponing the execution of its judgment, the Court balances preserving the rule of law on the one hand and promoting public safety on the other. It had also recognized, by this suspension, the primary role of the other branches in effectively combating terror.[178]

D. *Adjudicating Counter-Terrorism – Substantive Aspects*

1. *Which Law? A Three-Step Doctrine*

The most critical question to ask is which standards and legal criteria the court employs in its counter-terrorism jurisprudence. Indeed, the Israeli counter-terrorism adjudication model is characterized not only by procedural features, such as standing and justiciability, but also by substantive ones. In most of the counter-terrorism cases, the Court applies a three-step analysis reviewing the challenged state activity under three different normative frameworks.

The first is international law. In cases involving the administrated territories the court will almost always review the

177. HCJ 3239/02 [2002], Marab v. IDF Commander in the West Bank, 57(2) P.D. 349, ¶ 49 (Isr.), *available at* http://elyon1.court.gov.il/eng/verdict/framesetSrch.html.

178. The Israeli remedial doctrine of suspending the declaration of invalidity – originally formed in Canadian law – has been deployed in different other cases, not necessarily of counter-terrorism. It had been used, for instance, in two cases in which the court stroked-down unconstitutional provisions of laws and as a matter of fact, the court uses this remedy more and more often, sometimes in order to avoid a massive public hazard and normative vacuum; sometimes in order to protect the reliance of third parties; and sometimes in order to enable the other agencies to come up with their own solution to the problem. Yet, it is obviously not a simple remedy and it has its deficiencies, mainly in terms of civil liberties effective protection as well as the rule of law. For an overview of this remedial doctrine in Israeli law and criticisms of it, see generally Yigal Mersel, *Suspending the Declaration of Invalidity*, 9 MISHPAT U'MIMSHAL 39 (2006) (Isr.). For some examples of the usage of the same doctrine in Canadian law, see KENT ROACH, CONSTITUTIONAL REMEDIES IN CANADA ¶¶ 14.1480-14.1790 (1994); PETER. W. HOGG, CONSTITUTIONAL LAW OF CANADA 922-26 (4th ed. 1997); Kent Roach, *Remedial Consensus and Dialogue Under the* Charter*: General Declarations and Delayed Declarations of Invalidity*, 35 U. B.C. L. REV. 211 (2002).

action under the Fourth Geneva Convention,[179] as well as customary and conventional international law.[180] For instance, when the court established the proper timing for judicial review of detentions, it referred to the European Court of Human Rights' jurisprudence on Article 5 of the European Convention on Human Rights.[181] The Court's perspective is that "Israel is not an isolated island. She is a member of an international system," and, therefore, international standards are applicable to counter-terrorism adjudication.[182]

---

179. *See, e.g.*, H.C.J. 3451/02 [2002], Almandi v. The Minister of Def., 56(3) P.D. 30, ¶ 11 (Isr.), *available at* http://elyon1.court.gov.il/eng/verdict/framesetSrch.html. It should be noted that Israel's official position is that the Fourth Geneva convention does not apply to the administrative territories. However, the Israeli government has traditionally accorded its activities with the humanitarian provisions of that convention. *See* Farrell, *supra* note 57, at 913-15. The court, therefore, usually does not rule on the direct applicability of the Fourth Geneva Convention but rather relies on the state's declaration of its acceptance of judicial review of its activities under the humanitarian provisions. *See, e.g.*, HCJ 7015/02 [2002], Ajuri v. IDF Commander in the West Bank, 56(6) P.D. 352, ¶ 13 (Isr.), *available at* http://elyon1.court.gov.il/eng/verdict/framesetSrch.html; HCJ 3278/02 [2002], Ctr. for the Def. of the Individual v. IDF Commander, 57(1) P.D. 385, ¶ 23 (Isr.), *available at* http://elyon1.court.gov.il/eng/verdict/framesetSrch.html; HCJ 2056/04 [2004], Beit Sourik Village Council v. Gov't of Israel, 58(5) P.D. 807, ¶ 23 (Isr.), *available at* http://elyon1.court.gov.il/eng/verdict/framesetSrch.html; *see also* KRETZMER, *supra* note 12, at 31-42. For a critical view of the Israeli position regarding the applicability if the Fourth Geneva Convention, see Shany, *supra* note 5, at 98-99. A different question—which will not be discussed here—is whether terrorists are entitled at all to the protection of the Geneva Convention, an issue which the Israeli Court did not yet profoundly address. *See generally* Marco Sassoli, *"Unlawful Combatants": The Law and Whether It Needs To Be Revised*, 97 AM. SOC'Y INT'L PROC. 196 (2003).

180. See Justice Englard's opinion in *Almandi*, 56(3) P.D. 30.

181. *See Marab*, 57(2) P.D. ¶ 27. For further examples, see, e.g., HCJ 8990/02 [2003], Physicians for Human Rights v. O.C Southern Command, 57(4) P.D. 193, ¶ 1 (Isr.), *available at* http://elyon1.court.gov.il/eng/verdict/framesetSrch.html (referring to the 1980 United Nations Convention on Prohibitions or Restrictions on the Use of Certain Conventional Weapons Which May Be Deemed to be Excessively Injurious or to Have Indiscriminate Effects).

182. *See* HCJ 5591/02 [2002], Yassin v. Commander of Kziot Military Camp, 57(1) P.D. 403, ¶ 11 (Isr.), *available at* http://elyon1.court.gov.il/eng/verdict/framesetSrch.html; *see also Physicians IV*, *supra* note 143, ¶¶ 19-22. It should be noted that this international law analysis has special resonance. Even though Israel is a dualistic state, in which conventional international law only applies if incorporated into Israeli legislation, the Israeli

Second, the Court looks to Israeli administrative common law. The court conceives of any Israeli military action—both within state boundaries or outside them—as an administrative action of Israeli officials.[183] In other words, the Israeli soldier carries with him in his backpack, wherever he goes, not only international law but also the Israeli law.[184] Any counter-terrorism action should therefore be analyzed not only under international law but also under Israeli administrative common law. This body of law may include procedural rights like the right to be heard and also substantive rights like human dignity and liberty, which are codified in Israel's Basic Law.[185] Israeli soldiers have the statutorily-imposed duty to "act with integrity (both [in] substan[ce] and procedur[e]), with reasonableness and proportionality, and [to] appropriately balance individual liberty and the public interest."[186]

Third, the Court enforces military laws and domestic Israeli laws that are applicable to the specific dispute.[187] For example, the Court analyzes the specific provisions of the Israeli detention laws[188] or the laws issued by the military commander, in cases that involve the administrated territories.[189]

Indeed, examining the different bodies of laws applied by the Israeli Supreme Court suggests a few interesting character-

---

Supreme Court does refer occasionally to international law that is not enforceable in that court. *See, e.g.*, *Physicians III*, *supra* note 99.

183. *See, e.g.*, *Beit Sourik Village Council*, 58(5) P.D. ¶ 24; HCJ 393/82 [1983], Iscan v. Commander of the IDF, 37(4) P.D. 785, 810 (Isr.).

184. *Ajuri*, 56(6) P.D. ¶ 13 ("Alongside the rules of international law that apply in our case, the fundamental principles of Israeli administrative law, such as the rules of natural justice, also apply. Indeed, every Israeli soldier carries in his pack both the rules of international law and also the basic principles of Israeli administrative law that are relevant to the issue."); KRETZMER, *supra* note 12, at 25-27.

185. Basic Law: Human Dignity and Liberty, 5752-1992, 1391 S.H. 150 (Isr.), *available at* http://www.knesset.gov.il/laws/special/eng/basic3_eng.htm. *See, e.g.*, *Marab*, 57(2) P.D. ¶¶ 20-21; *Yassin*, 57(1) P.D. ¶ 8.

186. *See Physicians IV*, *supra* note 143, ¶ 19. Sometimes the Court treats cases of administrated territories according to Israeli Constitutional law and balancing between competing rights. *See, e.g.*, H.C.J. 1890/03 [2005], Bethlehem Municipality v. The State of Israel, ¶¶ 11-16 (unpublished decision) (Isr.), *available at* http://elyon1.court.gov.il/eng/verdict/framesetSrch.html.

187. *See* KRETZMER, *supra* note 12, at 27-29.

188. *See Yassin*, 57(1) P.D. ¶¶ 7-10.

189. *Ajuri*, 56(6) P.D. ¶ 6; *Marab*, 57(2) P.D. ¶ 21.

istics of Israeli counter-terrorism adjudication.[190] First, the Court envisions the terrorist threat as an international—rather than a solely domestic—problem. Accordingly, the standards for adjudicating counter-terrorism cases, as well those involving human rights and national security, are international standards.[191] Second, the war against terrorism is an exceptional circumstance but has not been treated with exceptional law. The Court usually refers to existing international law of war and human rights conventions.[192] It has not ruled that terror presents a unique situation outside the force of international law. Third, this three-tiered analysis actually reinforces human rights. In order to justify certain counter-terrorism measures, the state must prove that the operation or action taken is in accordance not only with the relevant direct law (be it detention law, military order or other regulation) but also with the Israeli common law and international law. Legality under one set of laws does not imply per se legality under another set of laws.

2. *Interpreting the Law: Terrorism as New Circumstances*

As noted earlier, the Court has not ruled that counter-terrorism measures are outside the law. It does not assert that international law is inapplicable because it does not fit the reality of terrorism. In a few cases, however, the Court has noted that current international law should be interpreted as taking

190. For further examples of this three-step analysis, see *Yassin,* 57(1) P.D. ¶¶ 7-13.

191. Some argue that this Court's trend is influenced by the importance of international jurisdiction and the risk of criminal and civil liability being imposed upon Israeli officials, including the court itself. *See* Amnon Reichman, *"When We Sit To Judge We Are Being Judged" The Israeli* GSS *Case,* Ex Parte Pinochet *and Domestic/Global Deliberation,* 9 CARDOZO J. INT'L & COMP. L. 41, 46-47 (2001); *see also* Shany, *supra* note 5, at 102-03.

192. These sources include usually the Convention Respecting the Laws and Customs of War on Land, Annex to the Convention: Regulations respecting the laws and customs of war on land, Oct. 18, 1907, 36 Stat. 2277, T.S. No. 539; Geneva Convention Relative to the Protection of Civilian Persons in Time of War, Aug. 12, 1949 6 U.S.T. 3516, 75 U.N.T.S. 287; International Covenant on Civil and Political Rights, Dec. 16, 1966, 999 U.N.T.S. 171 (entered into force Mar. 23, 1976).

into account the modern reality of terror.[193] In a case about the legality of assigned residence, the court opined:

> We have interpreted to the best of our ability the provisions of Art. 78 of the Fourth Geneva Convention. According to all the accepted interpretive approaches, we have sought to give them a meaning that can contend with the new reality that the State of Israel is facing. We doubt whether the drafters of the provisions of Art. 78 of the Fourth Geneva Convention anticipated protected persons who collaborated with terrorists and "living bombs." This new reality requires a dynamic interpretive approach to the provisions of Art. 78 of the Fourth Geneva Convention, so that it can deal with the new reality.[194]

The Court's recent decisions provide further examples. In a case challenging detention conditions, detainees were lodged in tents that did not provide sufficient protection from the weather.[195] Accordingly, the Court referred to Article 85 of the Fourth Geneva Convention, which specifies that detainees should "[b]e accommodated in buildings or quarters which afford every possible safeguard as regards hygiene and health, and provide efficient protection against the rigors of the climate and the effects of war." Citing the official commentator of the convention,[196] the Court suggested that civilian detainees should, in certain circumstances, depending on the length of the detention, be detained in structures of a permanent character.[197] However, the Court noted that this interpretation is contestable under certain circumstances:[198]

> It depends upon the nature of the tents on the one hand, and the conditions of the location on the other. Additionally, a significant factor is whether

193. Kretzmer argues that, at least in the context of the Fourth Geneva Convention, the interpretation adopted would usually be the one that least restricts the sovereignty of the state parties, rather than the one that promotes human rights. KRETZMER, *supra* note 12, at 55-56.

194. *Ajuri*, 56(6) P.D. ¶ 40.

195. *See Yassin*, 57(1) P.D. ¶ 17.

196. INT'L COMM. OF THE RED CROSS, COMMENTARY: IV GENEVA CONVENTION RELATIVE TO THE PROTECTION OF CIVILIAN PERSONS IN TIME OF WAR 386 (Jean S. Pictet ed., Ronald Griffn & C.W. Dumbleton trans., 1958).

197. *See Yassin*, 57(1) P.D. ¶ 17.

198. *See id.*

> the detention is short-term or long-term, whether it lasts months or even years. Ultimately, the test is one of reasonableness and proportionality.[199]

Perhaps the Court's conclusion is better understood in light of the fact that, in this case, the IDF had administratively detained a large number of detainees, all arrested in one major counter-terrorism operation in response to a terror attack.

A similar approach, adapting standard rules to the new circumstances of warfare and counterterrorism, all the while balancing security and human rights, is evidenced in the Court's analysis of the legality of the IDF practice of detention without judicial review for twelve days. In that case, the Court noted:

> The special circumstances of the detention must be taken into account. 'Regular' police detention is not the same as detention carried out 'during warfare in the area' . . . or 'during anti-terrorism operations' . . . . It should not be demanded that the initial investigation be performed under conditions of warfare, nor should it be demanded that a judge accompany the fighting forces. We accept that there is room to postpone the beginning of the investigation, and naturally also the judicial intervention. These may be postponed until after detainees are taken out of the battlefield to a place where the initial investigation and judicial intervention can be carried out properly.[200]

3. *Democratic Struggle Against the Non-Democratic Terrorists*

In numerous decisions, the Court has taken note of the challenge terrorism poses to democracy.[201] Terrorism is characterized not only by its cruelty and damage to innocent civil-

---

199. *See id.*

200. HCJ 3239/02 [2002], Marab v. IDF Commander in the West Bank, 57(2) P.D. 349, ¶ 30 (Isr.), *available at* http://elyon1.court.gov.il/eng/verdict/framesetSrch.html.

201. *See, e.g.*, HCJ 7015/02 [2002], Ajuri v. IDF Commander in the West Bank, 56(6) P.D. 352, ¶ 41 (Isr.), *available at* http://elyon1.court.gov.il/eng/verdict/framesetSrch.html; HCJ 5100/94 [2002], Pub. Comm. Against Torture in Israel v. State of Israel, 53(4) P.D. 817, ¶ 39 (Isr.), *available at* http://elyon1.court.gov.il/eng/verdict/framesetSrch.html.

ians, but also by the way it threatens the democratic order. Indeed, "[i]t is difficult to fight against persons who are prepared to turn themselves into living bombs."[202] The Court has ruled that democracy must tackle terrorism in democratic ways, i.e., in manners respecting human rights. It is an unfair game, notes the Court, but this is the only game a true democracy can play. In the case where the Court banned the use of certain interrogation techniques, it noted:

> This decision opened with a description of the difficult reality in which Israel finds herself. We conclude this judgment by revisiting that harsh reality. We are aware that this decision does make it easier to deal with that reality. This is the destiny of a democracy—it does not see all means as acceptable, and the ways of its enemies are not always open before it. A democracy must sometimes fight with one hand tied behind its back. Even so, a democracy has the upper hand. The rule of law and the liberty of an individual constitute important components in its understanding of security. At the end of the day, they strengthen its spirit and this strength allows it to overcome its difficulties.[203]

Clearly, the Court is aware of the effect its rulings might have on the effectiveness of counter-terrorism measures. Nevertheless, it prefers to pay this price in order to achieve and preserve more important values—the rule of law and democracy.

4. *Terrorists and the Presumption of Innocence*

Some of the Court's cases raise the question of whether the presumption of innocence should apply under the special circumstances of counter- terrorism efforts.[204] In a way, most of the Israeli counter-terrorism activities, as well as the activities challenged in court, were aimed at minimizing the risks of

---

202. *Ajuri*, 56(6) P.D. ¶ 41.

203. *Pub. Comm. Against Torture*, 53(4) P.D. ¶ 39.

204. A more general, theoretical question remains whether there should be a difference in procedural rules and court jurisdiction between cases of terrorism and ordinary criminal offenses. *See, e.g.*, Emanuel Gross, *Trying Terrorists—Justification for Differing Trial Rules: The Balance Between Security Considerations and Human Rights*, 13 IND. INT'L & COMP. L. REV. 1, 3, 96-97 (2002) (finding that terrorist acts should be tried according to the same procedural and evidence rules as any other criminal offence).

terrorism, not at punishing the terrorists themselves. They included mostly preventative measures.[205] These measures, almost by definition, concern people who had not yet been convicted in criminal proceedings. When presented with the question of whether these detainees should be treated as innocent, the Court's answer was clear: as long as they are not convicted, they should enjoy the presumption of innocence.[206] When analyzing the proper standard for conditions in the detention camps, the Court noted that:

> [There is a] possible claim that since the detainees being held in Kziot Camp are terrorists who have harmed innocent people, their detention conditions should not be looked after. This argument is fundamentally incorrect. Those being detained in the Kziot Camp have not been tried; needless to say, they have not been convicted. They still enjoy the presumption of innocence.[207]

Therefore, the Court reasoned, "Not only should we not allow the detention conditions of administrative detainees to fall short of those of convicted prisoners, we should also strive to ensure that the conditions of detainees surpass those provided to prisoners."[208] This standard applies despite horrific terrorist activities allegedly attributed to some of the detainees:

> Prisoners should not be crammed like animals into inadequate spaces. Even those suspected of terrorist activity of the worst kind are entitled to conditions of detention which satisfy minimal standards of humane treatment and ensure basic human necessities. How could we consider ourselves civilized if we did not guarantee civilized standards to those in our custody? Such is the duty of the commander of the area under international law, and such is his duty under our administrative law. Such is the duty of the Israeli gov-

---

205. *See* cases cited *supra* Part I.A.

206. *See* HCJ 5591/02 [2002], Yassin v. Commander of Kziot Military Camp, 57(1) P.D. 403, ¶ 7 (Isr.), *available at* http://elyon1.court.gov.il/eng/verdict/framesetSrch.html.

207. *See id.*

208. *See id.*

> ernment, in accord with its fundamental character: Jewish, democratic and humane.[209]

The Court adopted the same rationale when evaluating the legality of detention itself. When it ruled on detaining a person for twelve days without judicial review of the detention order, the Court held that the right of judicial review becomes even more crucial in cases of preventive detention of people who still enjoy the presumption of innocence.[210] Arbitrary detention must be avoided, the Court reasoned, in order to preserve the individual's right of liberty:

> Thus, a person should not be detained merely because he has been detained during warfare; a person should not be detained merely because he is located in a house or village wherein other detainees are located. The circumstances of his detention must be such that they raise the suspicion that he—he individually and no one else—presents a danger to security. "Such a suspicion may be raised because he was detained in an area of warfare while he was actively fighting or carrying out terrorist activities, or because he is suspect of being involved in warfare or terrorism.[211]

5. *Operational Margin of Deference*

Although there are not procedural hurdles, like standing or justiciability, to its adjudicating terrorism cases, the Court will rarely intervene in actual, operational decisions made by the executive. The Court has noted repeatedly that it will not substitute its own discretion for the executive's decisions about the way to conduct counter-terrorism activities. It intervenes only in cases of extreme unreasonableness or clear illegality.[212] In most of these cases, the court has left a wide margin of deference (what is called the margin of appreciation) to the exec-

209. *See* HCJ 3278/02 [2002], Ctr. for the Def. of the Individual v. IDF Commander, 57(1) P.D. 385, ¶ 24 (Isr.), *available at* http://elyon1.court.gov.il/eng/verdict/framesetSrch.html.

210. HCJ 3239/02 [2002], Marab v. IDF Commander in the West Bank, 57(2) P.D. 349, ¶ 19 (Isr.), *available at* http://elyon1.court.gov.il/eng/verdict/framesetSrch.html.

211. *See id.* ¶ 23.

212. *See* Barak, *A Judge on Judging*, *supra* note 14, at 157-60.

utive to decide which counter-terrorism measures to employ, when to use them, and to what extent.[213] The underlying rationale for deference is the basic notion that the executive and legislative branches—not the Court—must deal with the terrorism problem. Furthermore, especially in cases involving politics and intelligence analysis, the other branches have the expertise regarding the most efficient way to guarantee public safety. The Court's role is, therefore, not to decide how to combat terrorism but rather to review the legality of the method chosen by other powers.[214] The Court focuses, therefore, on the legal and humanitarian aspects of the executive's activities and does not concern itself with operational field decisions.[215] Thus, the Court's jurisprudence sets the borderlines of legality, while leaving broad discretion to the executive within those lines. In short, the Court does not consider itself to be the appropriate decisionmaker in the counter-terrorism effort. :

> In exercising this judicial review, we do not appoint ourselves as experts in security matters. We do not replace the security considerations of the military commander with our own security considerations. We do not adopt any position with regard to the manner in which security matters are conducted . . . our role is to ensure that boundaries are not crossed and that the conditions that restrict the discretion of the military commander are upheld.[216]

Overall, the court hears almost every case concerning counter-terrorism but defiantly refuses to grant remedies in

---

213. In Ajuri v. IDF Commander in the West Bank, the court referred to this idea as the "zone of reasonabless." HCJ 7015/02 [2002], Ajuri v. IDF Commander in the West Bank, 56(6) P.D. 352, ¶ 29 (Isr.), *available at* http://elyon1.court.gov.il/eng/verdict/framesetSrch.html ("The discretion of the military commander to order assigned residence is broad. But it is not absolute discretion. The military commander must exercise his discretion within the framework of the conditions that we have established in this judgment and as prescribed in Art. 78 of the Fourth Geneva Convention and the Amending Order. . . . These parameters create a 'zone' of situations – a kind of 'zone of reasonableness' – within which the military commander may act. He may not deviate from them."); *see also* Barak, *A Judge on Judging, supra* note 14, at 157-60.

214. *Id.* at 159-60.

215. *See Physicians IV, supra* note 143, ¶ 16.

216. *Ajuri,* 56(6) P.D. ¶ 30.

many of these matters.[217] If the executive's method, by itself, is legal, the court will usually not intervene in the decision to use this specific method for counter-terrorism needs.[218] Most of the petitions fall within this margin of deference to the executive and are thereby rejected.[219] Furthermore, most of the cases are heard ex post and not ex ante; the counter-terrorist activity has already occurred. This characteristic narrows, by definition, the actual scope of judicial review.[220]

---

217. *See, e.g.*, the rejections of petitions in HCJ 10467/03 [2004], Sharabati v. Commander of the IDF, 58(1) P.D. 810 (Isr.); HCJ 893/04 [2004], Faraj v. Commander of the IDF, 58(4) P.D. 1 (Isr.); HCJ 4694/04 [2004] Abu-Atara v. IDF Commander in Gaza (unpublished decision) (Isr), *available at* http://elyon1.court.gov.il/files/04/940/046/f02/04046940.f02.pdf; HCJ 8124/04 [2004] Al-Jabari v. IDF Commander in the West Bank (unpublished decision) (Isr.), *available at* http://elyon1.court.gov.il/files/04/240/081/n04/04081240.n04.pdf; HCJ 9586/03 [2004], Salach v. Commander of the IDF, 58(2) P.D. 342 (Isr); HCJ 9535/03 [2004], Dayuk v. Commander of the IDF, 58(2) P.D. 102 (Isr.).

218. In the case of Physicians for Human Rights v. O.C Southern Command, after ruling that the use of flechette shells, by itself, is not forbidden under international law, the court noted that "[p]etitioners request that we prohibit the military from using flechette shells. As the use of such artillery is not prohibited by international conventions, we cannot grant their petition. Our decisions have stated that 'this Court will not intervene in the choice of military weapons, which the respondents use in order to prevent vicious terrorist attacks.'" HCJ 8990/02 [2003], Physicians for Human Rights v. O.C Southern Command, 57(4) P.D. 193 (Isr.), *available at* http://elyon1.court.gov.il/eng/verdict/framesetSrch.html. It should be recalled that this international law analysis has special resonance, even though Israel is a dualistic state, in which conventional international law only applies if incorporated into Israeli legislation. The Israeli Court does refer occasionally to international law that is not enforceable in that court. *Id.*

219. The statistics of the court might not show the whole picture in this context. Hence, it had been found that in many of the rejected cases, the petitioners actually succeeded in their petition. This had happened due to a high rate of out-of-court settlements in these matters. The court's rulings have thus an important effect on out-of-court settlements. *See* Yoav Dotan, *Judicial Rhetoric, Government Lawyers, and Human Rights: The Case of the Israeli High Court of Justice During the Intifada*, 33 LAW & SOC'Y REV. 319 (1999).

220. One example of an ex ante petition concerned methods of interrogations, in which the court ruled on the legality of certain practices without a specific case. *See* HCJ 5100/94 [2002], Pub. Comm. Against Torture in Israel v. The State of Israel, 53(4) P.D. 817, ¶¶ 8-14 (Isr.), *available at* http://elyon1.court.gov.il/eng/verdict/framesetSrch.html. Another example is Physicians for Human Rights et al. v. Commander of the IDF Forces in the Gaza Strip, in which the court had ruled on the legality of the future actions of the IDF in Gaza Strip. *Physicians IV, supra* note 143, ¶ 15.

6. *The Cost of Human Rights: Planning the War Properly*

In more than one case, the Israeli government has argued that the infringement upon human rights occurred, not on account of security concerns, but rather as a result of inadequate resources or unexpected circumstances. For instance, the government argued that it held detainees for eight days (most of the twelve-day period) without even a preliminary questioning because the army did not have enough professional interrogators.[221] Moreover, the executive has argued that it did not have the ability to meet the minimum detention conditions, since the number of detainees arrested during the counter-terrorism activity was overwhelming.[222] The Court has rejected these arguments. It pointed out that almost any counter-terrorism activity is pre-meditated and often with a significant amount of time before execution. Planning for counter-terrorism should include, said the Court, not only operational provisions but also humanitarian ones.[223] The executive branch must take into account humanitarian considerations as well as cost.[224] In rejecting the state's argument about its lack of interrogators:

---

221. HCJ 3239/02 [2002], Marab v. IDF Commander in the West Bank, 57(2) P.D. 349, ¶ 48 (Isr.), *available at* http://elyon1.court.gov.il/eng/verdict/framesetSrch.html.

222. *See* HCJ 3278/02 [2002], Ctr. for the Def. of the Individual v. IDF Commander, 57(1) P.D. 385, ¶ 6 (Isr.), *available at* http://elyon1.court.gov.il/eng/verdict/framesetSrch.html.

223. *See Yassin,* 57(1) P.D. ¶ 14 ("Soon after the reopening of Kziot Camp, conditions of detention there underwent changes. This reopening was done hastily and without preparation. The detention conditions encountered by the first detainees, whose affidavits are attached to this petition, did not meet the necessary minimum standards. There was no justification for this. Operation Defensive Wall was planned in advance. Its main goal was 'to prevail over the Palestinian terror infrastructure, and to prevent the recurrence of the terror attacks which have plagued Israel.' . . . It was obvious to all – or at least should have been obvious—that one of the consequences of the operation would be a large number of detainees. As such, it was necessary to prepare detention facilities in advance, which would satisfy minimum standards. This was not done."); *see also Ctr. for the Def. of the Individual,* 57(1) P.D. ¶ 26.

224. See, for instance, *Marab,* where the court noted that its ruling according to which there has to be a prompt judicial review of the detention will result in a need of more judges. *See Marab,* 57(2) P.D. ¶ 35. In Physicians for Human Rights et al. v. Commander of the IDF Forces in the Gaza Strip, the court held that it is the duty of the commander to ensure that there is

> A society which desires both security and individual liberty must pay the price. The mere lack of investigators cannot justify neglecting to investigate. Everything possible should be done to increase the number of investigators. This will guarantee both security and individual liberty.[225]

III. A Model of Counter-terrorism Adjudication?

Now that the main characteristics of the Israeli jurisprudence have been discerned, there remains a question: can this jurisprudence and its features be described as a model? I argue that the answer is yes.

The basic philosophy of the Court in these counter-terrorism cases is consistent both in terms of its procedural and substantive holdings and the rhetoric it uses to explain them. Because these features are coherent, repetitive, and based on the same foundation, they are a model. The Court's rulings demonstrate a clear stance regarding the rule of law in times of terror and the applicability of legal analysis to counter-terrorism efforts. This legal analysis is based on the recognition of national security as a crucial interest, but not a paramount one. Human rights must be balanced against the nation's security. Despite the fact that terrorists do not respect the law and try to destroy democratic liberties, democracies must apply a different standard by fighting back in a democratic manner. For instance, suspected terrorists must still be presumed innocent. The approach of the Court is to balance human rights and national security on a case-by-case basis; this approach manifests itself in an almost total willingness to hear any case challenging any counter-terrorism activity, without reservations about justiciability or standing. Yet the margin of deference affords a substantial area in which the executive and legislature can employ their unique functional and institutional capabilities. The specific procedures and remedies the Court employs support a general position that counter-terrorism should be adjudicated in a manner that preserves the role and respects the capabilities of the political branches on one

enough medical equipment in the combat zone. This issue must be an integral part of the preparation framework of any military operation. *Physicians IV*, *supra* note 143, ¶ 35; *see Marab*, 57(2) P.D. ¶ 35.

225. *Id.* ¶ 48.

hand, and creates a coherent framework to protect human rights on the other hand. The Court's use of substantive standards—applying international law, common law, and military law to almost any counter-terrorism activity—is the centerpiece of the framework to protect human rights. In striking this balance, when the government's only claim invokes a non-security interest such as a financial burden or poor planning, the Court is more rigorous in its intervention.

Without judging the value of this jurisprudence, one can still conclude that the Israeli court's approach towards the issue of counter-terrorism is distinctive. This distinctiveness also provides a ground for Israeli jurisprudence to be considered as a model.

The last question to be asked, then, is whether the Israeli model of counter-terrorism adjudication should be followed by other courts in different democracies facing the same problems? Since this paper takes a mostly descriptive viewpoint, I will not attempt to answer this complicated question, which has many dimensions and possible answers. I do, however, suggest some guidelines which might serve as criteria for evaluating the Israeli practices and comparing them against the practices of other courts. My suggestion is to evaluate counter-terrorism adjudication on the basis of three parameters:

First, evaluate the potential harm of judicial review to the effectiveness of the counter-terrorism activity at stake. An over-active court in times of crises, one might argue, places national security in danger and breaches the core idea of separation of powers. Any model of counter-terrorism adjudication must be evaluated therefore by taking into account this possible critique.

Second, note the influence of public confidence in the judiciary. It is important to consider not only what courts do, but also what they are seen to be doing.

Third and finally, the effectiveness of any model of counter-terrorism adjudication should be measured not only in terms of national security but also in terms of civil liberties protection. If it is accepted that courts must balance national security with the protection of civil liberties, then any model of counter-terrorism adjudication should be evaluated also in terms of the balance it achieves, not only in terms of effective counter-terrorism, but also in terms of an effective protection of civil liberties.

A. *The Effectiveness of the Counter-Terrorism Activity at Stake*

We all agree that terrorism must be handled rigorously and definitively. It is therefore important to ask whether the Israeli Supreme Court has adjudicated counter-terrorism cases in a way that hinders the war on terror. There is arguably a danger that the Court will get in the way of effective counter-terrorism because it is under-qualified in assessing risks and methods. It might possibly lack the experience or the knowledge to prescribe how to achieve the desired outcome. These shortcomings, as an argument might run, become crucial in times of crisis. The court may have good intentions in balancing this right with another interest, but the risk of mistake is arguably too high, especially given the horrors that might result. Similarly, even if the Court rules correctly, the procedure of judicial review might impede counter-terrorism efforts. Lengthy proceedings might delay important preventative steps. Classified information might be revealed. Furthermore, officials might become hesitant—too hesitant—to act because they foresee possible review by the Court.

Are these doubts justified? If they are, should we narrow the scope of judicial review in these terrorism cases? I say no. Indeed, the Court cannot see the big picture in any case it adjudicates. It also lacks the experience that the executive has in managing security matters. This division of expertise does not mean, however, that the Court should always step out of these conflicts. As mentioned earlier, under the Israeli model, the Court usually does not uproot the executive's discretion. It does not set the goals. It does not choose the means. The only thing it does, in only some cases at that, is set the borders of illegality. In the vast majority of cases, activities are never questioned before the Court at all or are upheld by it.

What about the hard cases: when the Court sets the barrier of illegality, do those rulings actually obstruct counter-terrorism? My answer is again negative. There is always a possibility of a wrong decision or a faulty balancing determination. Courts might have miscalculated the danger of certain circumstances or their probability. But this threat is not unique to the Court. Legislatures and executives are not immune to this risk. Really, which danger is more ominous—an executive power without check in a time of crisis or a potentially erroneous court ruling in one of the rare cases that reaches a court?

Furthermore, courts and judges are asked on a daily basis to balance interests and rights, and to assess dangers and probabilities. If they can do so in criminal law, environmental law, malpractice, or in cases of financial wrongdoing, why should they avoid such practices in times of national crisis?[226] Two factors make this argument even more poignant. First, we should keep in mind that the government tends to overreact in times of crisis and overestimates the danger at hand.[227] Executive overreaching often goes beyond a matter of "being on the safe side" and results in a needless deprivation of human rights, as well as a needless use of resources. We have no reason to say that the Court's rulings—even with many mistakes and opportunities for mistakes—will not lead to a more efficient result. Second, the war against terrorism is indeed a war, but it is a different kind of war. It is a long war, and its end is not easily defined, neither analytically nor practically.[228] The executive's counter-terrorism measures will be in effect for very long periods. Most of these decisions do not involve "ticking bomb" circumstances. Not all of the arrests, deportations and interrogations of individuals are cases involving immediate threats to national security.[229] Accordingly,

226. For an elaboration of this argument, and its application to the post September 11 cases in the U.S., see Peter Margulies, *Judging Terror in the "Zone of Twilight": Exigency, Institutional Equity, and Procedure After September 11*, 84 B.U.L. REV. 383 (2004).

227. *See* Ronald Dworkin, Rights and Terror (Oct. 1, 2003) (unpublished manuscript), *available at* http://www.law.nyu.edu/clppt/program2003/readings/dworkin.pdf. For a detailed analysis of the reasons for executive overreaction in times of national crisis, see Gross, *supra* note 4, at 1022-42. *But see* Eric A. Posner & Adrian Vermeule, Accommodating Emergencies (Chi. Pub. Law & Legal Theory, Working Paper No. 48, 2003), *available at* http://ssrn.comqabstract_id=441343 (presenting opposite approach, arguing that there is no basis to assumption that people and officials tend to overreact and exaggerate in times of crises).

228. Terrorists are not a defined territorial unit or group that can be abolished or can lose de jure. It is also doubtful if the war against terror can even be won de facto, and what would such a win mean exactly.

229. For instance, house demolition practice is conducted in order to deter terrorist. However, the cases show that the deterrence is not of an actual and immediate "ticking bomb" situation but rather a general one. *See, e.g.*, HCJ 10467/03 [2004], Sharabati v. Commander of the IDF, 58(1) P.D. 810

most of the cases heard in the Israeli Court did not involve the "ticking bomb" either. The Court's decisions might have affected counter-terrorism efforts, but these effects are barely a ripple in the ocean of counter-terrorist activities. Especially in this time of the war against terrorism, the fear of an incorrect judicial decision should not be as substantial as in other, more dire circumstances. Even if it occasionally gets in the way, judicial review might be preferable over an uncontrolled executive.

That being said, the Court needs to make sure that its efforts minimize the risk of obstructing essential counter-terrorist measures. Its decisions must be based on firm evidence and a clear understanding of the matter at stake. It may ask the parties—especially the state—to provide the Court with information regarding the importance of the challenged counter-terrorist method and the scope of its usage. It may also ask the state to justify how it selected the specific method it employed. The Israeli case briefings, by both parties, tend to contain this kind of information. For instance, in the assigned residence case, the Court had to rule on the legality of assigned residence of terrorists' relatives who were involved in terror activity.[230] The state specifically argued that this method was perceived by the Palestinian population as an extreme deterrent and was necessary at that time to stop the phenomenon of suicide bombers.[231] Along the same lines, the petitioners in the interrogation techniques case submitted several affidavits of people who were interrogated while being allegedly tortured and were later released with no indictment of any kind.[232] The petitioners argued that these interrogation techniques were used not only in cases of ticking bombs but as a regular method of "fishing" for information.[233] Detailed evidence of

(Isr.); HCJ 893/04 [2004], Faraj v. Commander of the IDF, 58(4) P.D. 1 (Isr.).

230. HCJ 7015/02 [2002], Ajuri v. IDF Commander in the West Bank, 56(6) P.D. 352, ¶ 5 (Isr.), *available at* http://elyon1.court.gov.il/eng/verdict/framesetSrch.html.

231. *Id.* ¶ 5.

232. HCJ 5100/94 [2002], Pub. Comm. Against Torture in Israel v. The State of Israel, 53(4) P.D. 817, ¶ 3 (Isr.), *available at* http://elyon1.court.gov.il/eng/verdict/framesetSrch.html.

233. *See id.* ¶ 14.

this kind is crucial for an effective judicial review of counter-terrorism.

Procedural rules and trial management can also possibly hinder counter-terrorism efforts. Cases involving counter-terrorism measures should be heard as soon as possible. Immediate action is necessary in certain cases for security reasons, and in others, to prevent severe human right violations. Courts should also be sensitive to confidential information and the need for some cases to be closed to the public. Even in terms of remedies, courts should make sure that the ruling will not pose an obstacle to counter-terrorist initiatives. With this concern in mind, the Israeli Supreme Court has more than once suspended enforcement of its judgments in order to enable the legislature or the executive to tailor their activities to make them legal.[234] Even when suspected terrorists were found to be held in illegal detention conditions, the result was not their immediate release but a six-month period to adapt these conditions to the requirements of international and domestic law.[235]

Effectiveness is quite clearly an important parameter in any evaluation of counter-terrorism adjudication. However, any argument accusing the Court of hampering the counter-terrorism effort must be analyzed carefully, taking into account the nature of cases heard by the Court, its specific rulings and remedies, and the benefits of an effective judicial review.

B. *Public Confidence and Court's Legitimacy*

A second factor in counter-terrorism adjudication is public confidence in the Court. The public sentiment can be quite sensitive and volatile in times of national crisis,[236] and it is usually the case that the public cares primarily about its own personal safety. Long-range implications for democratic val-

---

234. HCJ 3239/02 [2002], Marab v. IDF Commander in the West Bank, 57(2) P.D. 349, ¶ 49 (Isr.), *available at* http://elyon1.court.gov.il/eng/verdict/framesetSrch.html. For a further example, not within the counter-terrorism context, see HCJ 6055/95 Sagi Tzemach v. Minister of Defense et al., P.D. 53(5) 241, ¶ 44 (Isr.), *available at* http://elyon1.court.gov.il/eng/verdict/framesetSrch.html.

235. *Marab*, 57(2) P.D. ¶ 49.

236. *See* Lee Epstein et al., *The Supreme Court During Crisis: How War Effects Only Non-War Cases*, 80 N.Y.U. L. Rev. 1 (2005).

ues seem less important. One might argue that adjudicating counter-terrorism might decrease public confidence in courts, as they are not politically accountable. This is especially foreseeable in cases where the Court actually intervenes in the executive's enforcement actions, the way the Israeli court has done in several cases, discussed above. Furthermore, even if the Court does not actually impede counter-terrorist programs, the public might expect that only the accountable branches—the legislature and the executive—will handle counter-terrorism effectively. Indeed, adjudicating counter-terrorism has a possible price-tag: people might blame the Court for handling nonjusticiable issues and interfering with issues that should be handled by other branches. In Israel, this rhetoric had even found its way to a private bill by some Knesset members, who wanted to restrict by law the power of the Supreme Court to adjudicate certain matters, including issues of state security.[237] The Court itself is aware of the problem with public opinion:

> Part of the public will be happy with our decision; another part will oppose it. It is possible that neither the former nor the latter will read the reasoning. But we shall do our work. 'This is our duty and this is our obligation as judges.'[238]

In another case, the author of the opinion wrote:

> I am forced to rule in accordance with the law, in complete awareness that the public at large will not be interested in the legal reasoning behind our decision, but rather in the final result. Conceivably, the status of the Court as an institution that stands above the arguments that divide the public will be damaged. But what can we do, for this is our role and our obligation as judges?[239]

---

237. *See* Draft bill amending Basic Law: The Judiciary (no. 3726), 5762-2002 H.H. 5581 (Isr.), *available at* http://www.knesset.gov.il/privatelaw/data/15/3726.rtf.

238. HCJ 7015/02 [2002], Ajuri v. IDF Commander in the West Bank, 56(6) P.D. 352, ¶ 41 (Isr.), *available at* http://elyon1.court.gov.il/eng/verdict/framesetSrch.html.

239. HCJ 5100/94 [2002], Pub. Comm. Against Torture in Israel v. The State of Israel, 53(4) P.D. 817, ¶ 40 (Isr.), *available at* http://elyon1.court.gov.il/eng/verdict/framesetSrch.html (citing HCJ 390/79, Dawikat v. Gov't of Israel, 34(1) P.D. 1, 4).

The Court acknowledges that it is not disconnected from the Israeli reality, both in terms of public opinion and the daily concerns of average citizens:

> Deciding these petitions weighed heavily on this Court. True, from the legal perspective, the road before us is smooth. We are, however, part of Israeli society. Its problems are known to us and we live its history. We are not isolated in an ivory tower. We live the life of this country. We are aware of the harsh reality of terrorism in which we are, at times, immersed. The possibility that this decision will hamper the ability to properly deal with terrorists and terrorism disturbs us. We are, however, judges. We must decide according to the law.[240]

Indeed, the Court is aware that, in the short term, its broad scope of judicial review might result in sinking public confidence in the Court.[241] Yet it is willing to accept this partial disapproval because it believes its democratic duty is to rule for certain outcomes.[242] Displeasing some people is a natural result of adjudicating any conflict. It seems as if the court assumes that, in the long term, these rulings will reinforce the public confidence in the Court as a stabilizing institution in times of crisis.[243]

Is the Court right to take this approach? The Israeli experience shows that throughout the years, the Supreme Court enjoys almost the highest confidence rate among Israeli institutions.[244] Even taking into account the general tendency of distrust towards Israeli institutions in recent years, the Court has maintained its relatively high degree of public confi-

240. *Pub. Comm. Against Torture in Israel*, 53(4) P.D. ¶ 40; *see also* HCJ 2056/04 [2004], Beit Sourik Village Council v. Gov't of Israel, 58(5) P.D. 807, ¶ 86 (Isr.), *available at* http://elyon1.court.gov.il/eng/verdict/framesetSrch.html.

241. *Id.*

242. *Id.*

243. *Id.*

244. For recent surveys of the Israeli public opinion trust in the Supreme Court, see Asher Arian, Shlomit Barnea & Pazit Ben-Nun, The 2004 Israeli Democracy Index 32-34, 41-42 (2004), *available at* http://www.idi.org.il/english/catalog.asp?pdid=340&tmp=1&did=50; Asher Arian, David Nachmias, Doron Navot & Danielle Shani, The 2003 Democracy Index 21-22 (2003), *available at* http://www.idi.org.il/hebrew/article.asp?id=1461.

dence.[245] It should be mentioned, also, that the public's confidence in the Israeli court is often influenced by other factors, mostly the Court's rulings on the religious-secular divide. To this point, it seems as if the court's counter-terrorism jurisprudence has not resulted in a deepening distrust among Israelis.[246] Furthermore, the proposal to restrict the Court's powers in these matters by law has not garnered substantial support.

The Israeli Court is aware of the immediate reputational cost of its rulings, as well as its long-term gain. It is willing to adjudicate almost any counter-terrorism case by defining legal boundaries. The Court is not acting in a vacuum, however, by trying to conduct the war against terror by itself or by upending the executive's strategy. Most of the cases it hears on these matters are dismissed.[247] Those orders it does grant are not always immediately executed but are sometimes suspended or delayed. Thus, public confidence is a factor taken into account, but it does not completely bar the Court from ruling on these delicate issues. The court certainly, as discussed above, is not reluctant to adjudicate hard cases and even rule against the state in delicate situations.

Public confidence in the Court is an important criterion to use in evaluating counter-terrorism adjudication. Courts can not ignore it totally, but it should not be the sole or even prevailing factor in determining the Court's approach.

C. *Protection of Human Rights*

Third, a court's practice in counter-terrorism cases should take into account human rights. Is the Israeli model granting

245. KRETZMER, *supra* note 12, at 12-13.

246. A similar result was indicated during the first uprising in the West Bank territories of Judea and Samaria, during the late 1980's where most Israelis were willing to give heavy weight to considerations of democracy and civil rights, and not only to national security. *See generally* Asher Arian, *Vox Populi: Public Opinion and National Security*, *in* NATIONAL SECURITY AND DEMOCRACY IN ISRAEL 129, 134-37 (Avner Yaniv ed., 1993).

247. *See* Dotan, *supra* note 219, at 332. It should also be noted that the general statistics of the Israeli Supreme Court show a clear tendency to reject petitions and appeals. In 2004, for instance, the total rate of success in Supreme Court proceedings was 16.5%. THE JUDICIAL AUTHORITY OF THE STATE OF ISRAEL, THE JUDICIAL AUTHORITY OF THE STATE OF ISRAEL, DIN V'HESHBON 'SHNATI 2004 [THE 2004 ANNUAL REPORT ON THE JUDICIARY] 11.

sufficient weight to civil liberties? My view is that the Israeli practice takes rights seriously. The willingness to review almost any governmental action, as well as various cases in which the court had found violations of human rights, prove the adequacy of the Israeli model in terms of human rights protection.

It is true that some of the court rulings were criticized over the years. Some have pointed out that most of the cases are rejected, especially the important ones dealing with basic human rights.[248] The court was blamed, sometimes, for being too loyal to the state.[249] However, these critics focus on the ways in which the Court balances human rights and state security.[250] Usually, they do not argue that the Court should avoid these issues as nonjusticiable or leave them to be shaped through political discourse and public debate.[251]

The Israeli Supreme Court's model of counter-terrorism adjudication should therefore be seen, in my view, as one of the major guarantees for human rights. It is a useful and pow-

---

248. *See, e.g.*, Ralph Ruebner, *Judicial Review and the Rule of Law in the Age of Terrorism: the Experience of Israel – a Comparative Perspective*, 31 GA. J. INT'L. & COMP. L. 493, 506-11 (2003) (describing the court's practice as avoiding the hard cases and as silent in times of war); *see also* Dotan, *supra* note 219. As mentioned earlier, Dotan shows that as a result of the court's activist reputation, many cases are resolved outside the court for the benefit of the petitioners. Hence, the rejection rate in the court does not paint the whole picture. Kretzmer seems to accept this image of the court as a restraint and even argues that this "shadow" of the court is the most effective consequence of its activism, rather than the decisions themselves, which generally tend to legitimate governmental activities. KRETZMER, *supra* note 12, at 190-198.

249. *See* Cohen, *supra* note 87, at 105 ("[t]he Israeli legal regime is largely subject to the powerful grip of the country's national security narrative and the influence of the Israeli government's occupation policies").

250. *See, e.g.*, Yoram Dinstein, *The Israel Supreme Court and the Law of Belligerent Occupation: Demolitions and Sealing Off of Houses*, 29 ISR. Y.B. HUM. RTS. 285, 295-96, 304 (1999); Orna Ben-Naftali & Keren Michaeli, *Ajuri 'The Call of Abraham: Between Man and Makom (Place, God)*, 9 HAMISHPAT 107 (2004) (Isr.) (discussing HCJ 7105/02 Ajuri v. IDF Commander in the West Bank); David Kretzmer, *The Supreme Court and the Fourth Geneva Convention Domestic Enforcement and Interpretation*, 26 MISHPATIM 49 (1995) (Isr.).

251. Kretzmer raises, in his survey, a contrasting argument. He argues, that perhaps the final outcome would have been better if the Supreme Court did not impose it's jurisdiction over the administrated territories. In such circumstances, the Elites would have been better aware of the gap between the mother-country and the administrated territories, and perhaps changing the reality of occupation. *See* Kretzmer, *supra* note 12, at 198.

erful tool for properly balancing state security and human rights. The fine tuning of the model might be criticized like any other ruling; it is only natural that not everyone is in accordance with every judgment. Nevertheless, it can generally be argued that taken as a whole, this model provides a firm framework for human right protection.

Thus, evaluating a given model of counter-terrorism adjudication should involve considering the protection it grants to human rights. This evaluation may include the ability to access the Court and the Court's willingness to hear cases on the merits; the length of proceeding and the procedure used; the applicable norms—domestic, comparative and international law; the remedies granted; and the margin of appreciation given to the government. The Israeli model, as elaborated above, displays a pattern of adjudication in each of these areas. Evaluating its performance in protecting human rights can be part of the comparison between the Israel Court and other courts in various democracies.

IV. Conclusion

The modern threat of terror poses new challenges to democracies. These challenges are not only operational but also legal. We ask how to fight terrorism while preserving democracy and more specifically, what is the role of the judiciary in this regard. This Article presents the Israeli Supreme Court as a model for courts during states of emergency and counter-terrorism activity. The balance between the three major considerations—maintaining effective counter-terrorism policies, upholding public confidence in the courts, and protecting human rights—can lead to different models of judicial review; however, one must compare the different models and consider their advantages and disadvantages in the short and long term. Terror is becoming a global problem. It should be therefore faced—legally and from a global perspective. The Israeli model—built upon many cases, over many years, in the context of an unfortunate and tragic reality—is a worthwhile starting point for such analysis.

Name Index

www.ingramcontent.com/pod-product-compliance
Lightning Source LLC
LaVergne TN
LVHW080802011026
849160LV00015B/1507
9781138378520